Clinical Practice and the Law

For Sorcha, for Grace
and
for my parents

Thank you

Clinical Practice and the Law

SIMON MILLS
MB, BCh, BAO (Dubl), BCL (NUI), MICGP,
Barrister-at-law

Consultant:
PROFESSOR R A J SPENCE
OBE, MA, MD, FRCS
Honorary Professor, University of Ulster
Honorary Professor, The Queens University of Belfast

Tottel
publishing

Published by
Tottel Publishing Ltd
Maxwelton House
41-43 Boltro Road
Haywards Heath
West Sussex
RH16 1BJ

Tottel Publishing Ltd
Fitzwarren Business Centre
26 Upper Pembroke Street
Dublin 2
Ireland

ISBN 13: 978-1-84592-371-6
ISBN 10: 1-84592-371-5

First published 2002
Formerly published by LexisNexis Butterworths

This edition reprinted by Tottel Publishing Ltd 2006

British Library Cataloguing-in-Publication Data
A catalogue record for this book is available from the British Library

Typeset by Marlex Editorial Services Ltd., Dublin, Ireland
Printed and bound in Great Britain by
Hobbs the Printers Ltd., Totton, Hampshire

Foreword

The relationship between medicine and the law is like a long-standing yet stormy marriage. It is at one and the same time a partnership and a battlefield. Each party regards the other with a mixture of respect, admiration, impatience and contempt.

Yet as Simon Mills, himself a barrister and a doctor, demonstrates in this lucid and compassionate book, it is impossible to practise law or medicine effectively and efficiently without an informed understanding of the issues and challenges of the extensive terrain wherein both meet.

He deals with issues such as the definition of death, the decision not to resuscitate, consent to treatment, medical evidence, confidentiality, the insanity defence, issues that are legal as well as medical minefields and does so with an impressive grasp of and respect for the facts.

The result is a book that is mandatory reading for all doctors and lawyers, trained and in training.

Professor Anthony Clare

3 October 2002

Preface

Surgeons must be very careful
When they take the knife!
Underneath their fine incisions
Stirs the culprit, - Life!

Emily Dickinson

The evolution and provision of health services are among the hallmarks of a modern civilised society. Similarly any civilised society will find it nearly impossible to function without laws or other similar rules of conduct. It is true that laws – being engines of an essentially human desire to regulate social living – will be human and imperfect, but their necessity is doubted by few. One of the accusations levied with mutual recrimination – although perhaps with diminishing frequency – by the professions at which this book is directed, namely clinical practitioners and lawyers, is that to each the other's profession and professional standards are somewhat opaque.

I hope that this text will give the clinical practitioner an insight into the mind of the law and help her to see that she is not being forced to conduct her practice on shifting sands, but rather on a largely certain footing, where few enough areas of legal uncertainty exist. The idea of the law as a threat to the practitioner is in part a product of fear and misunderstanding. The converse hope is that that those approaching law and clinical practice from a legal perspective will gain something of an insight into the way that medicine and the allied clinical arts are practised within a legal framework.

But while this book is in some measure about the relationship between health care practitioner and lawyer, it is more particularly about the relationship between practitioner and patient. The bulk of the ways in which law affects clinical practice do not involve lawyers at all: instead the law simply lays out ground rules for contact between practitioner and patient in the common scenarios in which they find themselves. It is true that some situations, such as the question of 'informed consent', may be complex, but others, such as prescribing or the notification of deaths to the coroner, are largely straightforward and essentially administrative and all are in some measure legally regulated. In his wonderful book, *The Doctor, Father Figure or Plumber,*[1] written at a time when "litigation [was] still uncommon", James McCormick presciently drew on a quotation that identifies a source of litigation not in the clash between clinician and lawyer, but in the shortcomings of the therapeutic relationship:

> "Let's start with…your relationship (or lack of one) with your patient. Isn't it strange that the person who first comes to you in complete confidence, fully prepared to refer to you fondly as "my doctor" is the very same person who sues the heck out of you? Quite obviously, somewhere along the line, something went wrong to cause such a wonderful start in a mutually beneficial relationship to end up fraught with suspicion, frustration and anger…

[1] London, 1979

> "You can blame anyone or anything you want – the law, lawyers, courts, juries, insurance companies or the changing times, But if you don't examine yourself, your patient and how the two of you are doing in your human relationship, you will be putting the blame in the wrong place."[2]

This may be overstating the matter somewhat (the quote above is, after all, that of a lawyer) but there is a kernel of truth to it. A successful practitioner-patient relationship is all about communication and a misapprehension of the law can be another stumbling block to good communication. This book then should be regarded as a handbook for good practice – in a legal rather than clinical sense – of the relationship between practitioner and patient. It will not teach the clinical student or practitioner how to be a lawyer, nor will it coach the law student in the intricacies of medico-legal courtroom work but it is hoped that clinician, lawyer and perhaps more importantly, patients will benefit in some measure from the information contained herein.

How to use this book.

If you want to, you can simply ignore the footnotes. This book is not of necessity an academic work, although it can – and hopefully will – be read as one, but is intended to be something of 'user's handbook', albeit a detailed one. I have attempted as far as possible to consign to the footnotes everything that is not essential for a non-legal, non-academic understanding of the subject matter or that would otherwise distract from the explanation of broad principles. For similar reasons, the footnotes can be found at the end of each chapter, rather than at the bottom of each page It is there that the legal reader, or the person with an interest in reading more widely, will find case names, details of statutes and references for articles. The clinically minded reader should hopefully find in the main body of the text alone a thorough review of law as it affects clinical practice written in neither medical nor legal jargon. Hopefully, the legal reader will find the absence of esoteric language – in either medical or legal dialects – an advantage as well.

The non-legal reader who wishes to know more about the law should consider reading Appendix A. References to legal reports are deciphered in the list of common abbreviations found at the back of the book. Each legal case generally comprises the year of the case in brackets, together with the law report text in which the case is found, followed by the page of the report on which the account of the case begins. So [1997] 3 IR 456 refers to a case in volume three of the 1997 Irish Reports, page 456. All the important law reports are to be found on the shelves of the law section in the University libraries. Many other recent or significant judgments are recorded on the excellent UCC-based website http://www.irlii.org (The Irish Legal Information Initiative).

The reader who is more pressed for time can consult the quick reference guides that pepper each chapter. At the end of many sections of the text, important material is summarised in a digestible form. The interested – or confused – reader may then refer back to the text for clarification or elucidation of any topic that whets the appetite or requires greater detail for a more thorough understanding. Whether there is enough

---

2 E Blake Moore, 'Anaesthesia and Analgesia – Current researches', *Lancet,* (1976), no 5, 756. Cited at p 37 of *The Doctor, Father Figure or Plumber.*

material in the quick reference tables alone to get the undergraduate through his or her exams, only time – and students brave enough to rely on the tables alone – will tell. The Tables have their own specific and separate list of their whereabouts at the beginning of the book.

A note on gender

The he *vs* she dilemma foxed the author for quite some time. I was not happy to simply rely on the old shibboleth that "where used in the text, the word 'he' also connotes the female." Instead, I have opted to recognise the reality of 21st century clinical practice in Ireland, namely that the majority of the student and practising body in most fields of clinical endeavour is – or, if present trends continue soon will be – female. Accordingly I have opted to use the female pronoun in the text to denote the clinical practitioner and the male pronoun to denote the patient. It is hoped that no one will be offended or perhaps – more pessimistically – that all will be offended equally. This convention is only departed from where it would make a nonsense of the text to adhere to it slavishly, for example by referring to a pregnant patient as 'he'.

I have attempted to ensure that the law and facts contained in this book are up to date as of the 16th September 2002, although it has been possible to involve a few developments occurring after this date.

Simon Mills

Christchurch

16 September 2002

Acknowledgements

There are number of people who have contributed invaluably to the existence of this book and I would like to name them, so that they can take their share of the credit or blame. Professor Roy Spence was an indefatigable Consultant Editor who was endlessly constructive and perceptive and responded always with courtesy and promptness to the demands of this book in spite of his pressing clinical, academic and other duties. His experience in medicine, textbook-writing and law came to the rescue of nearly every chapter and my only wish is that now the book is finished we might actually get to meet rather than interminably communicating by e-mail. Professor Anthony Clare similarly took time from a busy schedule to contribute a foreword, a gesture that I enormously appreciate from a doctor whom I greatly admire.

In Butterworths, Ciarán Toland shepherded this confused and sometimes addled novice through the whole process, starting with a most auspicious conversation over dinner in the King's Inns and finishing with his calm in the face of my certainty that the book would never be finished. Marian Sullivan, who typeset the book, Michael Murray who indexed it and Ciara Fitzpatrick who edited the text have my most profound gratitude. The production schedule was pushed back a month due to the author having overstretched himself somewhat, but they – together with Ciarán – responded with aplomb.

My work colleagues in my various jobs have been tolerant of my need to concentrate on this work over the last few months, especially my two editors, Aindreas McEntee in the *Irish Medical Times* and Irene Feighan in *The Examiner*. In general practice, Drs. Michael Kearney, Tony Clarke and Dessie Maguire were all forbearance as my distraction levels grew.

Those who read the book and offered suggestions all helped enormously: Grace, Aidan and Sarah O'Regan, Michael Mills, Caroline Philp and most particularly John Guerin. To those who offered to read the book, but never quite got round to it, my thanks too. Needless to say, any errors or idiosyncrasies that remain are mine and mine alone.

The seeds for this book were sown during my time lecturing and researching in the Division of Legal Medicine in University College Dublin. I would like to thank the staff there, Asim Sheikh, Cliodhna McGovern, Bríd McCormack and Denis Cusack for an enjoyable and thought-provoking year. The students who listened to some of the ideas that are now contained in this book and who challenged them with perceptive questions helped to shake my conviction that writing this book would be an easy task. Others provided help with specific requests, furnished me with material for other purposes that ultimately came in handy for this text or responded enthusiastically with offers of help that I did not in the end take up: Anne Drummond of the UCD Programme for Health and Safety at Work; John Kinahan of the Dublin Cemeteries Committee; Tom Joyce, Registrar's Office, Dept of Health and Children; The Medical Council (especially Dr. John Hillery); the Dental Council; An Bord Altranais (especially Thomas St. Ledger); the Dental Council; Paul Ward and Dermot Cahill of the UCD Law Faculty.

The biggest 'without whom…' thanks must go to Grace O'Regan and Sorcha Ní Dhubhghaill. For both of them, I suspect, this book was even more of an endurance test than it was for the author. I have to do a lot of making up to both of them and to both I give not only this book and my thanks, but also my love.

Erratum

Butterworths Ireland draws the reader's attention to the following errors occurring in the endnote system in Chapters 6, 8 and 10. Butterworths Ireland accepts full responsibility for these errors. The following guide should simplify navigation in any affected chapters.

Chapter 6

The following endnote numerals were omitted from the text in error: 6, 8, 14, 57 & 93.
Accordingly:
Endnote numeral 7 in the text corresponds to chapter endnote 6;
Endnote numerals 9 to 13 in the text correspond to chapter endnotes 7 to 11 *(ie* subtract two from endnote numeral);
Endnote numerals 15 to 56 in the text correspond to chapter endnotes 12 to 53 *(ie* subtract three from endnote numeral);
Endnote numerals 58 to 92 in the text correspond to chapter endnotes 54 to 88 *(ie* subtract four from endnote numeral);
Endnote numerals 94 to 101 in the text correspond to chapter endnotes 89 to 96 *(ie* subtract five from endnote numeral).

Chapter 8

Endnote numeral 23 in the text does not correspond with any chapter endnote and there are two endnote numerals denoted with the number 44.
Accordingly:
Endnote numerals 24 to 44 ('Barring Orders') in the text correspond to chapter endnotes 23 to 43 *(ie* subtract one from endnote numeral);
From endnote numeral 44 ('Safety Orders') in the text, the endnotes in the text correspond accurately with the chapter endnotes once more.

Chapter 10

Endnote numeral 21 was omitted from the text.
Accordingly:
Endnote numerals 22 to 35 in the text correspond with chapter endnotes 21 to 34.

Butterworths Ireland apologises to the reader for any difficulty caused by these errors.

Contents

Quick Reference Guides

Table of Statutes

Ireland

Constitution of Ireland

United Kingdom

EU and Council of Europe

Statutory Instruments

Table of Cases

D

E

F

P

Q

R

S

T

U

V

W

X

Z

Chapter 1

Introduction and History

SOME DEFINITIONS

[1.01]

This book examines the subject of 'legal medicine' although somewhat counter-intuitively the phrase 'legal medicine' itself is rarely used in the text. The reasons for this paradox are twofold. The first is simple: this book is not intended solely for doctors, but for those, from whatever discipline, who are interested in how the law interacts with clinical practice. The second reason is that the term is not always understood to mean the same thing by all those who hear it. Some feel the term is unnecessarily restrictive or prefer to call the subject 'forensic medicine' or 'medical jurisprudence'.

One definition of legal medicine might be the professional and academic discipline which concerns itself with legal aspects of medical science, medical practice and other health care delivery problems. 'Forensic medicine' on the other hand is an altogether narrower field, concerned with using medical and other clinical means to achieve the ends of the legal process, such as a successful criminal prosecution or the resolution of a paternity dispute. 'Medical jurisprudence' is, in its technical sense, a more legalistic study of the principles of law that underpin clinical practice, professional ethics and the practitioner-patient relationship. 'Medical law' finally is the study by lawyers of the way the law applies to medicine.

One reason why the term 'legal medicine', rather than the more general 'legal clinical practice', remains relevant to the aim of this book is that it is the medical arena that has most commonly provided the testing ground for many of the legal principles set out in this book. The Irish Medical Council's *Guide to Ethical Conduct and Behaviour*[1] is the most thorough Irish expression of clinical ethical and legal practice. Similarly, it is the doctor-patient relationship that has tended to give rise to the bulk of the case law mentioned in this book as background to the explanation of legal principles. Finally, the author comes from a medical background. For the foregoing reasons, no apologies can be made for the fact that, at times, this text may appear to have something of a medical bias: the bias simply reflects the fact that much of healthcare and clinical litigation has itself, for good or for ill, a medical bias. The important point is this for any who feel alienated by any perceived misplacing of emphasis: the lessons learned from medicine's encounters with the law are generally applicable to all clinical professions.

While this book contains elements of forensics, of jurisprudence, of legal medicine and of medical law, those elements are subsumed by the desire to show a broader picture of the interaction of law, and legal frameworks, with the clinical disciplines in everyday practice. Hence, if any term is accurate to describe the area reviewed it is most probably the broad canvas described by the title of this book, *Clinical Practice and the Law.*

A NEED FOR CLINICAL LEGAL TRAINING?

[1.02]

The Irish universities have a positive approach to law and medicine. Most, if not all, of the law schools offer optional courses in medical law and all of the medical schools teach a compulsory course in forensic or legal medicine, while many non-medical clinical curricula include a module on legal matters. However, the value placed on such courses in the curriculum is of crucial importance to how the lessons will be valued and absorbed by students. Many have bemoaned the lack of emphasis given to medico-legal training for doctors in particular in the modern university. Some have suggested that legal medicine is losing out in an 'overcrowded curriculum'[2] and insofar as this is true, it is regrettable. In the United Kingdom it is increasingly common for the legal aspects of medicine to be taught as an optional rather than compulsory course.

Legal aspects of clinical practice confront doctors, nurses and all other clinical practitioners in almost every aspect of their working lives. It may be a matter of apparently routine conduct, such as completing a driver's licence application for a patient, or it may be a knottier question, such as the decision whether to respect a patient's decision to refuse treatment even where that refusal means the patient will die. In either event, and in many more situations, a grasp of the law can help to ease the doubts that may arise in the mind of the conscientious practitioner who is aware of the legal ramifications of her practice. Other clinical processes that have more than a whiff of law about them include examining assault or accident victims, the certification of death, reporting deaths to a coroner, writing medico-legal reports, and giving evidence. Research has suggested that standards in areas of practice such as recording the cause of death[3] or describing wounds[4] are falling far short of the ideal. Some authors have tried to set out the minimum medico-legal knowledge with which medical undergraduates should be familiar[5] and many of the elements on such a list are applicable to the non-medical clinician in practice.

Figure 1.1 – Important medico-legal and forensic skills

- What to do with a dead body (and what not to do) when suspicions have been aroused of an unnatural death.
- Certification and disposal of the dead.
- The role of the coroner and deaths that must be reported to the coroner.
- The preparation of medico-legal reports and the giving of evidence.
- Litigation and compensation.
- The interpretation of injuries.
- Sexual assault victim examination.
- Principles of medical ethics.

To the somewhat forensic-biased list in Figure 1.1. should be added questions of consent and of negligence, as well the role of the clinician with respect to the driver, the mentally incompetent and the family, all of which obligations are among the areas covered in this text.

Deficiencies in medico-legal training at university are hardly a way in which to deal with the increasing prevalence and potentially bank-breaking costs of clinical litigation in this country. The more informed a practitioner is about the legal framework within which she practises, the better she can be expected to avoid the rare, yet potential, legal pitfalls of her everyday work. Ignorance of the law is one of the clinical practitioner's worst enemies: ignorance may beget fear, errors and taciturnity in the face of any questions about the legal propriety of any course of action. Knowledge and comprehension of even the barest rudiments of the legal facets of patient care can provide certainty and reassurance for practitioner and patient, together with guidelines for best clinical-legal practice and greater confidence in clinicians' communication with patients.

HISTORY OF LEGAL MEDICINE

[1.03]

There are few countries in possession of ancient historical records that cannot lay some form of claim to having played host to the genesis of legal or forensic medicine. The truth, however, is that legal medicine as an independent subject is a comparative latecomer, dating from no earlier than the 18th century. Since then, academia's historical quest has been for what the playwright Arthur Miller has called 'echoes down the corridor':[6] the process of teasing out elements of ancient medicine that bear the primitive hallmarks of what we call 'legal medicine', even though the ancient world would have called it no such thing. Such an historical tour can be a relatively enlightening one however, insofar as it shows the side-by-side evolution of clinical skills and law and an early recognition that the relationship between the two could and should be a symbiotic rather than an antagonistic one.

The dawn of legal medicine

India

[1.04]

One suggested cradle for the legal aspects of medical knowledge – although in reality parallel evolution in a number of different locations and cultures seems most likely, as social living emerged and became the human norm – can be found in the Indian text of *Manu-Smriti*. Hindu tradition dates this teaching to thousands of years BC, although it was not formally assembled in written form until between 200BC and 200AD. Other religious documents, such as the *Vedas* (Sanskrit for 'knowledge'), which date from some time between 1500 and 500BC, were ritual hymns that also contained legal precepts that could be applicable to clinical practice. The ancient Indian testaments include prohibitions on marriage between close relatives and pronouncements on issues of illegitimacy (contained in the *Rig-Veda*). Other *Vedas* mention crimes and their punishments as well as the diagnosis and management of various forms of poisoning.

Egypt

[1.05]

Imhotep, who lived from c 2686BC to 2613BC, was the Grand Vizier, Chief Justice and physician to Pharaoh Djoser of Egypt and is considered by some to have been one of the first 'medico-legal' experts. In truth though, there was little in which he was *not* expert:

he excelled as an administrator, architect, sage and physician and had the decided advantage, at that time, of living a comparatively long life. He was later[7] deified, becoming one of the few Egyptian commoners (and probably the only doctor ever) to achieve such a distinction – the Ancient Greeks and Romans identified him with Aesculapius, the god of healing. He was thought to have been a mythological figure until the 19th century, when archaeological evidence rooted his existence firmly in history rather than legend. Imhotep may have authored the *Edwin Smith Papyrus*, in which more than 90 anatomical terms and 48 injuries are described. He may also have also founded a school of medicine in Memphis, some two millennia before the 'father of medicine' Hippocrates was even born.

China

[1.06]

As long ago as the 5th Century BC,[8] there was an official in China with responsibility for the investigation of suspicious death. A text from that time, known as *The Lu's Spring and Autumn Annals* described how the body decomposed and how wounds such as bruises and fractures could be detected. Around 221 BC, the Qin Dynasty emerged from a period of turmoil and established the first centralised imperial administration in China,[9] including in its bureaucracy one of the first coroner-type roles: the 'lingshi', who was required to examine corpses and to produce reports on certain deaths. A prevailing attitude in the administration of contemporary Chinese justice was that punishment should be proportional to injuries inflicted on the corpse, so evidence disclosed by examination could be extremely important in the ultimate determination of the nature of the sanction to be imposed on a wrongdoer.

In one recorded case,[10] an official by the name of Zhang Ju performed an experiment to try and prove a murder. A man had died but his wife, who was suspected of having murdered him before burning his body, claimed that he had been burnt to death in a fire. Zhang Ju burned two pigs, one living, the other dead: subsequent examination of the corpses showed that the pig that had been dead before the fire had no ashes in its mouth, in marked contrast to the one that had been immolated alive, which had inhaled evidence of the fire. No ashes had been found in the mouth of the deceased and the inference was drawn that he was dead before the fire, a conclusion which lead to the wife admitting her guilt.

By the 7th Century AD, the Chinese had recognised that fingerprints could be of use in identification, although the process of fingerprint classification and the use of fingerprints in crime detection was still many hundreds of years away.[11] By the time of the Song Dynasty (c 1000AD), the law required the appointment of an officer who was obliged in cases of murder to visit the scene as soon as possible and was legally subject to penalties for failing to do so. The officer, who was not necessarily a doctor, was also required to examine the body, certify the death and prepare a post-mortem report, including both a front and rear sketch of the corpse, although oriental modesty provided that the sketch should not include the genitalia. A key early medico-legal text dates from the second century of Song rule (c 1250): *Xi Yuan Ji Lu*, which is generally translated as 'The Washing Away of Wrongs', remained the authoritative text on forensic medicine in China until 1911, when the last emperor was overthrown. Among the guidance given by this book was how to distinguish a drowning victim from a strangulation victim and the various wounds caused by different weapons. Other Chinese texts demonstrate the long lineage of forensic medicine in China: a text from 1694 described subcutaneous haemorrhages for the first time, while another from 1777 described the fracture of the hyoid bone as evidence of hanging or strangulation.[12]

Progress at the interface of law and medicine slowed in China as years went by and as the empire waned and atrophied. Several elements contributed to this. The first was the institutional reluctance of the imperial rulers to open their doors to outside influences. Secondly, the process of post-mortem examination in China tended to be confined to external examination, limiting the degree to which advances in physiological and anatomical understanding could be made. Finally, the humanist revolution that swept Europe during the Renaissance meant that huge strides were being taken in European knowledge of the sciences (including anatomy and physiology) and humanities in which the isolated Chinese could not share and by which they were left behind.

The 'western' world

The ancients

[1.07]

One of the earliest legal codes, dating from approximately 1750BC, is the *Code of Hammurabi*, King of Babylonia, which was found engraved on a diorite column at Susa in Iran. The code consists of 282 provisions and its system of justice, although broadly fair, was informed by the 'eye for an eye' school of thought. The code specifically mentions the question of medical and surgical accidents:

> 'If a physician makes a large incision with the operating knife, and kills his patient, or opens a tumour with the operating knife and cuts out the eye, his hands shall be cut off.'[13]

In the Mediterranean and Aegean regions, both the progenitor of the medical profession, Hippocrates, and the Graeco-Roman physician, Galen, considered medico-legal problems: in particular, concerns about confidentiality, ethics and abortion feature prominently in the *Hippocratic oath*. The philosopher Aristotle fixed the time of the animation of the foetus, or the date on which its soul was conferred,[14] at 40 days.

In Rome, the legislature passed some laws of a medico-legal nature, including portions of the *Lex Duodecim Tabularum*[15] of 449BC, while the *Lex Aquila* of 572BC dealt with the lethality and criminal gravity of certain wounds. The murdered body of Julius Caesar was examined by Antistius, who offered the opinion that of the 23 wounds inflicted by the conspirators, only one, a stab wound to the chest, was fatal.[16] *The Code of Justinian*, a mammoth compendium of all Roman law, drew a distinction between medical witnesses and other witnesses, a distinction that lives on in modern times in the form of the expert witness.[17]

The dark ages

[1.08]

When Germanic peoples began from the late 4th century AD onwards to overrun, conquer and then re-conquer at will the increasingly disjointed Roman empire, included in the laws they laid down – the *Leges Barbarorum*[18] – were rules that compelled courts to rely on medical expertise when evaluating wounds. Born in turn out of these laws were exhaustive compilations of the different injuries and the respective compensation payable for such wounds (the 'Wergeld'[19]) by the perpetrator of the injuries. It has been suggested by some that the role of the physician or surgeon was not only in the assessment of injuries but also in the drafting of the laws themselves. Similar laws were still being passed half a thousand years later: the *Sachsenspiegel* ('Saxon mirror') of 1225 provided for medical experts who had sworn an oath to assist the courts. Laws such as these helped to codify society's response to violent death and to avoid or at least modify the idiosyncrasies and excesses of personal vendettas and blood feuds.

German law was a significant factor in the development of legal thought, including the relationship between law and medicine, elsewhere in mainland Europe. Irnerus, a significant early legal academic, was teaching Langobardic (a German tribe) as well as Roman law during the last part of the 11th century in the college that was later, in 1119, to become the University of Bologna. The basic legal ideas of Germanic law were also reflected by an edict of the Norman King Roger II of Sicily of 1154 that provided for the appointment of physicians to help the courts. These edicts in turn had a strong influence on the Italian town charters of the 13th to 16th centuries, which contributed much to the development of a systematically consolidated medico-legal discipline.

Mediaeval and Renaissance Europe

[1.09]

12th Century Norman England was the source of the office that most clearly unites law and medicine in modern Ireland and Britain: the coroners office dates from 1194, during the reign of Richard the Lionheart. Elsewhere in Europe however, other new laws also demonstrated an awareness of the role of clinical skills in the legal process. The *Constitutio Criminalis Carolina* (the *Caroline* or *Carolingian Code*) was enacted in 1532 by the Holy Roman (which effectively meant German) Emperor Charles V. The Code was based on an earlier (1507) law drawn up for the governance of the town of Bamberg.

The *Caroline Code* enshrined the realisation, still accepted today, that certain questions cannot be answered by wholly legalistic methods. The *Code* therefore obliged judges to take the evidence, sworn in advance, of physicians in cases where death had resulted from criminal or accidental violence. It also introduced a practice of obligatory autopsies which, because of the new law's coincidence in time with the Renaissance, could build on the new physiological and anatomical knowledge (and indeed, contribute to it). Contemporary records show that, unlike in China, where examinations were almost solely external, wounds examined under the *Caroline Code* were opened to show their depth and direction, although complete post mortems may not have been performed in every case.

Evolution in the modern era

[1.10]

The medical profession gradually started to organise discussions founded on the new knowledge base created by the Renaissance. Forensic monographs became almost commonplace, and the discipline began to emerge as a subject distinct from the general practice of medicine or law by the 17th century. By the 18th century, professorships were being created in German universities for Legal Medicine, Leipzig being the first in or about 1720. The French followed suit with chairs in Forensic Medicine in Paris, Strasbourg and Montpelier by the end of the 18th century and there was a professorship in Legal Medicine in Vienna by 1804. In Great Britain, Edinburgh became, in the opening decade of the 19th century, the first to establish a chair in Forensic Medicine, while Glasgow University had a chair in the subject by 1839 and London appointed its first professor of Medical Jurisprudence in 1834.

Many of the scientific developments associated with the borderline between law and medicine lie more properly within the camp of forensic medicine, which is not the principal area covered by this book. Forensic developments are primarily those scientific discoveries that have made it easier to use medicine and science to help solve crime or resolve legal disputes.

Figure 1.2 – Some milestones in the evolution of forensic

Year/Era	Event
1813	Orfila, a Spanish professor at the University of Paris, published his *Treatise on Toxicology*. Orfila is also credited as one of the first to attempt the use of a microscope in the assessment of blood and semen stains.
1823	Jan Evangelista Purkinje,[20] Professor of Anatomy at the University of Breslau in Czechoslovakia, published the first paper on the nature of fingerprints and suggested a classification system based on nine major types. He did not recognise their potential for identification or crime detection.
1836	James Marsh, Scottish chemist and inventor of the Marsh test for the presence of arsenic, was the first to present toxicological proof of poisoning (with arsenic) in a trial.[21]
1863	The use of hydrogen peroxide as a test for the presence of blood was discovered.
1880	Henry Faulds, a Scottish physician, published a paper suggesting that fingerprints at the scene of a crime could identify the offender. He used fingerprints to eliminate an innocent suspect and indicate the perpetrator of a Tokyo burglary.
1896	Edward Richard Henry developed the modern fingerprint classification and identification system, based on nine points of identification on the fingerprint.
1900	Landsteiner discovered human blood groups (for which he received the Nobel Prize in 1930).
c.1910	Victor Balthazard used photographic enlargements of bullets and cartridge cases and recognised the possibility of connecting a fired bullet to a particular weapon. Balthazard, a professor at the Sorbonne, also studied the forensic uses of human hair.

Year/Era	Event
1910s	Lattes, a professor at the Institute of Forensic Medicine in Turin, developed the first antibody test for ABO blood groups.
1930s	Holzer, working at Innsbruck University, developed the absorbtion-inhibition ABO typing technique that forms the basis of the test that continues to be used in present-day laboratories.
1940s	Lundquist, in the University of Copenhagen, developed the acid phosphatase test for semen.
1960s	Culliford, working in the Metropolitan Police laboratory in London, initiated gel-based methods to test for isoenzymes in dried bloodstains and was instrumental in the development and dissemination of methods for detecting proteins and isoenzymes in blood and other body fluids.
1984	Alec Jeffreys developed the first DNA profiling test, publishing his findings in 1985.
1988	The first use of DNA to solve a crime (involving the rape and murder of two girls)[22] and in the process, to exonerate an innocent suspect.

Also of interest, quite aside from the way medical advances have affected the detection of crime, is the way in which the law has evolved in order to exert an influence on medicine in areas unconnected with investigative techniques. The gradual recognition of the existence and worth of human rights has, as a corollary, changed the way in which law has come to reflect upon the therapeutic encounter. The law of consent has been born out of the legal recognition that each person should have the right, in so far as possible, to exercise control over his own body. The law of negligence has similarly evolved from a situation where historically the consequences of an accident lay where they fell (in other words, the victim of another's negligence could expect no help from the courts). Only in the 20th century was it recognised that everyone owes a duty not to do others avoidable harm through negligent acts or omissions.

The trend therefore (and it is a trend that can be seen throughout this text) has been towards dismantling clinical paternalism – the 'doctor knows best' philosophy – and according rights to individual patients. The Irish Constitution is one document that identifies many of the rights that all, clinicians and patients alike, can expect to have recognised by the courts and the State, while the European Convention of Human Rights identifies similar and often identical rights. As we will see, both have a bearing on clinical practice in Ireland. Law is also increasingly being forced to respond to medical advances and to the ethical questions raised by problems in those areas that might be called the 'margins' of human life, including extreme old age, euthanasia, abortion and advances in genetics and cloning.

Endnotes

1 (5th edn, 1998), although submissions for a new edition are being sought at the time of writing (September 2002).

2 Mant 'A survey of forensic pathology in England since 1945' J Forensic Sci Soc 1973;13:17; Mant, 'The decline in the teaching of legal medicine' BMJ 1986;293:1390.

3 The standard of certification of the medical cause of death has frequently been found to be sub–standard: see James DS, Bull AD. 'Information on death certificates: cause for concern?' Journal of Clinical Pathology 1996; 49(3):213–6; Doyle YG, Harrison M, O'Malley F. 'A study of selected death certificates from three Dublin teaching hospitals'. Journal of Public Health Medicine 1990; 12(2): 118–23. Both studies showed fundamental problems with the information contained on death certificates while the latter study in particular showed wild and frequent discrepancies between the cause of death recorded on certificates and the cause of death found at autopsy. See also section **[16.02]**.

4 Milroy, Rutty, 'If a wound is "neatly incised" it is not a laceration' BMJ 1997;315:1312.

5 Simpson CK 'Postgraduate training in forensic pathology'. Proc Royal Soc Med 1971;64:146–7; Mant, 'The decline in the teaching of legal medicine' BMJ 1986;293:1390.

6 A Miller *The Crucible* (title of epilogue to the play).

7 Much later, c 664BC–525BC. The preceding years had seen him gradually elevated through the pantheon until he was finally accorded the status of a 'full' god. Very early Christians are also reputed to have venerated Imhotep alongside Jesus.

8 During the period known as 'The Warring Kingdoms'. See 'A Brief History of Forensic Medicine in China', Jia Jing Tao, J M Cameron and Wang Xu, *The Criminologist* (1988) Vol 12, p 67.

9 The name 'China' drives from the name of this dynasty.

10 Described in Yi Yu Ji 'A Collection of Criminal Cases dating from the Wu Dynasty in the Three Kingdoms' (264–277 AD). Medical evidence similar to this has been used in modern cases.

11 Thomas Bewick, a 19th century English naturalist, used engravings of his own fingerprints to identify books he had published that only the latter years of the 19th century. It was ushered in the formal classification of fingerprints as a means of identification and detection (see Figure 1.2).

12 See ch 14, *Forensic Medicine and the terminology of Injuries.*

13 Provision 218. Doctors fare comparatively well in the Code of Hammurabi: a builder who built a faulty structure could be put to death, together with his children, if the structure collapsed and killed its inhabitants (provisions 229–230). In all cases the penalties for killing a slave were less onerous that those for killing a free man: the doctor whose negligence killed a slave need not forfeit his hands but instead could merely replace the slave.

14 This question of the 'animation' of the foetus played an important role in the approach of early courts (which were frequently religious courts) to the question of abortion.

15 Otherwise known as the 'Twelve Tables', they were based on an earlier Greek equivalent but were nonetheless the first great exercise in Roman Law.

16 Suetonius *Lives of the Twelve Caesars* Oxford Classics, 2000.

17 See ch 10, The Practitioner and the Lawyer.

18 Barbarians' Laws, of which there were many. Each set of laws bore the name of the invading tribe whose writ controlled Rome at the time, eg *Lex Visigothorum* in the second half of the 5th century or *Leges Langobardorum* during the 7th century, and eventually during the 8th century the laws of the Bavarians, Saxonians, Franks, and Frisians, among many others.

19 Or 'blood-price'. It was paid to the victim or his family (in the case of murder) by the criminal. The amount depended on the type of injury and the status of the victim. If the wound exposed

brain or bowel, the fee was higher than if only blood was shed and the greater the status of the victim, the higher the Wergeld.

20 The same Purkinje as gave his name to the fibres in the conduction system of the heart.

21 Arsenic had cropped up in a murder trial before, although a test for its presence in the body's organs did not then exist. In 1752, a 31 year-old spinster Mary Blandy murdered her father with arsenic in a dispute over her proposed marriage. The witness, Dr Addington, did not possess the knowledge to prove absolutely that the powder Mary used was arsenic, but he convinced the court beyond reasonable doubt of the fact. Blandy had mixed white arsenic in gruel and gave it to her father, who fell ill and died. Some of the leftover gruel was eaten by a charwoman and a maid, who also became unwell. The pan used to prepare the gruel was examined and a white sediment recovered from the bottom. The sediment had exactly the same physical characteristics as arsenic and behaved the same way in chemical reactions. Blandy was convicted and sentenced to death. In the first French case to apply a test for arsenic it was Mathieu Orfila, author of the *Treatise on Toxicology* (see Figure 1.2), who was called upon by the court in 1840 to apply the Marsh test to the exhumed body of a suspected murder victim.

22 *R v Pitchfork*. See (1988) The Guardian, 23 January. Using his DNA technique, Jeffreys compared semen samples from both murders against a blood sample from a suspect and conclusively proved that both girls were killed by the same man, but *not* by the suspect. The police consequently undertook the world's first DNA mass screening, covering all adult males in three villages, a total of 5000 men, who were asked to volunteer and provide blood or saliva samples. Blood grouping was performed and DNA profiling then carried out on the 10% of men who had the same blood type as the killer. Initially the testing proved fruitless but it later came to light that Colin Pitchfork had asked a friend to submit a sample in place of him. A sample was taken from Pitchfork and he proved to be the killer. For more on DNA testing, see ch 14, *Forensic Medicine and the terminology of Injuries*.

Chapter 2

The Healthcare Professions and the Healthcare System

INTRODUCTION

[2.01]

This chapter looks at what constitutes a profession, before making the distinction between statutory and non-statutory professions. We examine the question of professional misconduct and the question of the free movement of health professionals in Europe. The chapter finishes with a brief summary of the structure of the Irish healthcare system.

REGULATING THE PROFESSIONS

What is a profession?

[2.02]

It is hard to fasten on a terse and precise definition of a 'profession'. Historically the term would have applied only to the pursuits of medicine, law and divinity, but the term has become less selective: teaching, nursing and banking among others might all be described as professions in the modern world. One set of elements that might help towards defining a 'profession' is the following:

- the acquisition of learning as a precursor to entry into the profession;
- the presumption of continued learning within the practice of the profession;
- a degree of self-direction and control over the pace and scheduling of work;
- a possibility of advancement to higher levels within the profession.[1]

In general, as well as having the four characteristics listed above, a profession will also generate its own sense of separate identity, which outside observers have come to accept. Most professions will have an ethical code of conduct. In general, a professional ethic may be regarded in a benign light: it sets down rules of conduct through which the profession ensures that those it cares for always receive the best possible care. But a more cynical view can be taken of professional ethics, namely that they are not necessarily essential for the patient or client, but for the safeguarding of the profession itself. An ethic that states that the patient must always come first has benefits for the patient but also for the profession: it encourages practitioners to work longer hours and undertake difficult tasks. It also encourages the junior practitioner to adopt a subservient role in the hierarchy in 'the interests of the patient', but also in the interests of the profession, which enshrines its pecking order and protects the traditional career structure. The ethic against advertising also helps to protect professional hierarchies by helping to maintain the traditional career structure: practitioners remain within the established system to acquire the skills the system itself deems necessary for the professional to reach the pinnacle of her discipline.

Statutory and non-statutory professions

[2.03]

While recognising that there are many different health care professions and that not all will fit as easily or as uniformly into the 'definition' of the profession set out above, there is one neat way of dividing the health care professions. Each discipline is either statutory or non-statutory in nature.

'Statutory' means that the profession is backed up by law. Generally the law creates a regulatory body for the profession and imbues that body with supervisory and disciplinary powers: the profession is therefore self-regulating with the backing of the laws of the state.[2] In essence, the state delegates responsibility to the profession to manage itself within laws made by the legislature. Non-statutory professions lack this backing and exist in a more loosely affiliated way. They may have an overarching body representing the profession but that body is without powers to regulate the profession by setting rules or to discipline practitioners who transgress those rules.

Figure 2.1 – Examples of statutory and non-statutory professions

Statutory (regulating statute in brackets)	***Non-statutory***
Doctors (Medical Practitioners Act 1978)	Physiotherapists
Dentists (Dentists Act 1985)	Radiographers
Nurses (Nurses Act 1985)	Occupational Therapists
Pharmacists (Pharmacy Act (Ireland) 1875, Pharmacy Act 1962)	Speech Therapists
Opticians (Opticians Act 1956)	Social Worker
	Dieticians
	Chiropodists

In this chapter, we look principally at the structures and powers of the regulatory bodies of the statutory professions, including their disciplinary powers. However, it should be pointed out that there is likely at some point to be a move towards placing the regulation of other health care professions such as physiotherapy, occupational therapy and social work on a statutory footing equivalent to that of professions such as medicine and nursing.[3] This is the approach that has been adopted in the United Kingdom for both paramedical[4] and some complementary disciplines.[5]

The advantages of placing a profession on a state-sponsored self-regulatory footing are obvious: it becomes possible for the profession to set nation-wide standards of training, conduct and competence that are binding on all practitioners of that particular profession and to make individual practitioners accountable to the regulatory body. The profession itself can then, through the regulatory body, maintain the standards of the profession by taking steps to deal with those whose continued practice presents an unacceptable risk to the public or otherwise renders them unfit to be registered members of the profession.[6] The over-riding aim of the regulatory bodies is to protect the public and the public interest and to this end, it has frequently been suggested that more representatives of the general public should sit on the governing councils of the statutory professions.

Statutory professions

[2.04]

We look now at the Irish statutory health care professions, concentrating on their structures and roles. Many features are common to the regulation of all of the statutory professions and below we look at the Medical Council in detail before examining the similarities and differences displayed by the analogous bodies overseeing other professions.

Quick Reference Guide 2.1

Features of statutory regulatory bodies for the health professions

- ❖ Created by a specific law which, in addition to bringing the body into being, also gives the regulatory body powers to oversee and regulate certain aspects of the profession, such as registration and disciplinary matters.
- ❖ Responsible for laying down ethical guidelines for the profession.
- ❖ Responsible for disciplinary and other fitness to practise issues within the profession.
- ❖ Responsible for maintaining a register of practitioners entitled to belong to that profession. Punishment for professional misconduct or unfitness to practise may involve erasure or suspension from that register.
- ❖ In general, disciplinary powers involving suspension or erasure from the register or the attachment of conditions to continued practice must be exercised under the supervision of the High Court.
- ❖ Non-statutory bodies lack both a foundation in an Act of the Oireachtas and the disciplinary and regulatory powers granted to the statutory bodies. Plans have been suggested to bring all Irish health care professions within the state-sponsored self-regulatory model.

Medicine

[2.05]

The medical profession in Ireland is regulated by the Medical Practitioners Act 1978[7] and the regulatory body is the Medical Council, which comprises 25 members.[8]

— 5 representatives of the Irish medical schools (one from each) and appointed by them.

- 6 representatives of the subdivisions of the profession.
- 2 appointed by the Royal College of Surgeons: one each to represent surgery and anaesthetics/radiology.
- 2 appointed by the Royal College of Physicians in Ireland: one to represent medicine and pathology and one to represent obstetrics and gynaecology.
- 1 appointed by the Minister after consultation with the representative body of psychiatry in Ireland (to represent psychiatrists).

- 1 appointed by the Minister after consultation with the representative body of general medical practice in Ireland (to represent general practitioners).
- 10 medical practitioners elected by the profession, of whom at least two must be hospital consultants (but not psychiatrists); one must be a consultant psychiatrist; one must work in public health; one must be a non-consultant hospital doctor; two must be general practitioners.
- 4 appointees of the Minister, at least 3 of whom must not be medical practitioners and should represent the interests of the general public.

The Medical Council maintains the register of medical practitioners,[9] controls education and training standards for medical students and doctors and determines cases of professional misconduct and fitness to practise. The Council also has a role in advising the Minister for Health and Children on all matters relating to its functions. Every five years, elections are held for new members of the Council and the Council then elects a president from among its number. Under the Medical Practitioners Act 1978, there is currently scope for a maximum of four lay appointees to the Council, although in practice the Minister typically fills the four vacancies with only three lay members and one medical practitioner." In other countries there has been a move towards changing what is sometimes perceived as an inappropriate imbalance.[10]

At the time of writing, a new Medical Practitioners Bill is in preparation, but its nature and contents have not yet been made public. It is expected to include provisions to encourage and promote the operation of the Medical Council's Competence Assurance scheme (see section **[2.08]**).

Registration

[2.06]

Registration with the Medical Council can be full, provisional or temporary. In all cases, registration is dependent on the payment of the appropriate retention fee. Full registration is available to any doctor who has a recognised medical qualification together with recognised and verifiable experience, either prescribed by law or acceptable to the Medical Council, as a medical practitioner.[11] Doctors from Ireland and other EU member states who hold recognised qualifications and certificates of experience are entitled to full registration, although the Council has the right to refuse to register any person on the grounds that the person is unfit to engage in the practice of medicine.[12] The Medical Council may also temporarily register a person with the necessary experience or satisfactory qualifications to practice in the state for a period of up to five years.[13]

A doctor's name appears on the register together with the degrees she was conferred with on graduation, but she may also add further degrees to her entry on the register, where appropriate.[14] A doctor, if she wishes and for whatever reason, may apply to have her name removed from the register. She may then later apply to have it reinstated.[15] It is a criminal offence for someone to claim to be a registered medical practitioner who is not registered.[16]

Provisional registration refers to the registration, typically of one year's duration, of a medical graduate who does not yet possess the requisite experience to be fully registered. Provisional registration in effect permits the practitioner to engage in the practice of medicine for the time necessary to obtain experience during the 'intern year'.[17]

There is both a general register of medical practitioners and a Register of Medical Specialists,[18] onto which all doctors are expected to enrol themselves once they have obtained the training necessary to be regarded as a specialist in that particular field. It is the Medical Council that decides what fields shall be regarded as specialities and what requirements must be met for a doctor to call herself a specialist in that particular field. It is likely that participation in the Competence Assurance process will be a necessary precursor for a doctor remaining on the Register of Medical Specialists and that, in turn, all doctors will have to be on the relevant specialist register as a necessary element of the Competence Assurance process (see section **[2.08]**).

The Medical Council register is a public document and may be inspected by any member of the public at the headquarters of the Medical Council and the main office of any health board,[19] while at the time of writing there are proposals to include the register on the website of the Medical Council.[20]

Education and training

[2.07]

The Council also has an obligation to assess training and education provided by any body recognised for medical instruction in the state, including the curricula of the universities and the experience necessary for awarding of a certificate of experience on the completion of the intern year.[21] The Medical Practitioners Act 1978 created, in addition to the Medical Council, the Postgraduate Medical and Dental Board with specific responsibility for overseeing postgraduate medical and dental training.[22]

Discipline and professional standards

[2.08]

The Council's most significant responsibility in some respects is the setting, fostering and policing of satisfactory professional standards. This necessitates a tripartite approach by the Council, two elements of which are proactive while the remaining element is reactive or punitive. The proactive elements are the publication of guidelines for doctors and the relatively new process of Competence Assurance, which is currently being prepared for pilot introduction in 2003. Standards are set in the first place by the regular publication of a guide as to what constitutes professional conduct.[23] This guide is the benchmark for medical practice and doctors are expected to follow its precepts and will have to accept the consequences if they fail to do so.

Competence Assurance[24] is a relatively new departure for Irish medicine, first proposed in 1998 and rapidly approaching realisation. It is aimed at the ongoing confirmation of the clinical standards (as opposed to ethical standards, with which the *Guide to Ethical Conduct and Behaviour* is predominantly concerned) of doctors who are no longer operating within formalised ongoing training, including hospital consultants and general practitioners. The process of competence assurance will involve continuing medical education and clinical audit and/or peer review of the doctor's skills over a five-year period. It is likely that for the majority of doctors, participation in continuing medical education (also sometimes called continuing professional development) will be sufficient to meet the requirements of the Competence Assurance process.

The reactive or punitive powers of the Medical Council for misconduct or unfitness to practise for other reasons come in four forms:

- censure or admonishment;
- attachment of conditions to continuing practice;
- suspension from the register;
- erasure from the register.[25]

A person may also be erased from the register for failure to pay the appropriate retention fee. A specific Fitness to Practise Committee of the Medical Council considers matters of unfitness to practice and a person may be found unfit to practise either because of professional misconduct or because of physical or mental disability. Unfitness to practise may result from wholly clinical or ethical matters, but a person may also be 'struck off' or suspended from the register for committing criminal offence unrelated to her practice of medicine.[26]

Any disciplinary decision to suspend or erase a doctor's name from the register or to attach conditions to her continuing practice must be approved by the High Court before it can have effect. Where the Medical Council thinks it necessary in the public interest to do so, it may apply to the High Court for an immediate order suspending a doctor from practice.[27] This might occur where there are extremely serious allegations against a doctor, such that it would be unsafe for her to be permitted to continue in practice while the Medical Council's investigation of matters is conducted.

Nursing

[2.09]

The nursing profession, which including midwives, is regulated by An Bord Altranais, which was created by the Nurses Act 1985.[28] The Board consists of 29 members who are elected or appointed for a term of five years: 17 are elected by their fellow nurses and 12 are ministerial appointees:

- 5 nurses resident in the Republic of Ireland, who are engaged in nurse training (one each from general nursing, paediatric nursing, psychiatric nursing, mental handicap nursing and midwifery).
- 5 nurses resident in the Republic of Ireland who are engaged in nursing administration (one each from the disciplines previously listed).
- 7 nurses resident in the Republic of Ireland who are engaged in clinical nursing practice (two each from general and psychiatric nursing; one each from the remainder).
- 12 persons appointed by the Minister after consultation with relevant bodies, but who must include -
    - a registered medical practitioner from each of three hospitals where (a) general nurses, (b) psychiatric nurses and (c) midwives respectively are trained;
    - a representative of health board management;

- a representative of hospitals other than those under health board management;
- two representatives of the Department of Health;
- a person experienced in the field of education;
- a representative of a third level institution in which nurses are trained;
- a nurse;
- two representatives of the interests of the general public.

As with the Medical Council, An Bord Altranais has responsibility for compiling and maintaining the register of nurses and can refuse to register a person it deems unfit to be registered.[29] The nursing register takes account of the particular division of nursing (paediatric, psychiatric, general or midwifery) in which each nurse is trained to practise. The Board also oversees education and training of the profession, including setting requirements for any courses and examinations, appointing examiners and approving training institutions.[30] The Board in addition publishes ethical guidelines for nurses.[31]

An Bord Altranais has a Fitness to Practise Committee to look into allegations of misconduct or unfitness to practise due to physical or mental disability. Its powers include the recommendation of erasure or suspension from the register or the attachment of conditions to the continuation of practice, with any such decision subject to scrutiny and ratification by the High Court. As with doctors, the Board may admonish or censure a nurse rather than opting for a sanction that impacts on her continued practice. A nurse's name may be erased or suspended from the register if she is convicted of a serious offence. Any decision concerning the erasure, suspension or restoration of a nurse's name to or from the register must be notified to the Minister and, where known or appropriate, the nurse's employer.[32]

As with the medical profession it is an offence for anyone to hold herself out as being a nurse who is not on the register or for anyone to practice in a speciality in which she is not registered or to misuse or falsely obtain registration documents.[33]

The Act makes a number of specific provisions for midwifery. A midwife who is not employed by a health board or a hospital and who is practising midwifery in a specific area must notify the health board responsible for that area and the health board in turn must exercise 'supervision and control' over that midwife.[34] No one may attend on a woman in childbirth, except in an emergency, unless she is:

— a midwife;

— a registered medical practitioner;

— a person who is undergoing training to become a midwife or registered medical practitioner or training in the area of obstetrics as part of a course of wider training.[35]

Dentistry

[2.10]

The dental profession, like nursing, came under new legislative control in 1985[36] when the Dental Council was established (replacing the Dental Board). The Dental Council consists of 19 members who sit on the Council for a five-year term.[37]

- 4 persons appointed by University College Cork and the University of Dublin (2 each).
- 1 person appointed by the Royal College of Surgeons in Ireland.
- 7 dentists elected by registered dentists.
- 2 persons appointed by the Medical Council.
- 1 person appointed by the Minister for Education.
- 4 persons appointed by the Minister for Health at least two of whom must not be dentists and must reflect the interests of the general public as consumers of dental services.

The Dentists Act 1985 was created from a similar template to the Nurses Act of the same year and the powers and responsibilities of the Dental Council are very similar to those of the Medical Council and An Bord Altranais. The Dental Council maintains a register of practitioners,[38] including a register of specialists. While there is scope for temporary registration (as with the Medical Council) there is no equivalent of 'provisional' or 'intern year' registration. The Dental Council has responsibility for overseeing training and education of dentists in the state, including both primary and postgraduate training[39] and has responsibility for curbing the practice of those dentists who are unfit due to misconduct or because of physical or mental disability.[40] The Council publishes ethical guidelines[41] and sanctions similar to those available to the other regulatory bodies are available to the Council as those available to the other regulatory bodies, namely censure, attachment of conditions to practice, suspension from the register and erasure from the register. It is an offence to claim to be or to imply that one is a registered dentist or to practice dentistry if one is not on the register.[42]

The Dental Council also oversees the designation, training and roles of auxiliary dental workers (such as dental hygienists) including the determination of what work auxiliary staff may undertake, the registration of auxiliary dental workers and the titles such workers may claim.[43]

Opticians

[2.11]

Dispensing and ophthalmic opticians are regulated by Bord na Radharcmhastóirí, the Opticians Board, which was founded under the Opticians Act 1956. It is an eleven-member board:[44]

- 4 ministerial appointees who must be registered medical practitioners.
- 1 other ministerial appointee, who may or may not be a registered medical practitioner.
- 6 members elected by the body of registered opticians. One must be a registered dispensing optician and five must be registered ophthalmic opticians.

The Board maintains two separate registers, one for dispensing opticians and the other for ophthalmic opticians[45] and the Board has the power to recognise qualifications based on acquired experience or satisfactory qualifications obtained outside the state. One area in which the powers of the board differ significantly from those of the Medical and Dental Councils and An Bord Altranais is if a person is removed from either Register of

Opticians: there is no automatic High Court scrutiny of the decision, although the affected party has a right of appeal to the High Court. This approach, as will be examined under the question of fair procedure in disciplinary proceedings (in section **[2.16]**), would probably not stand up to scrutiny by the courts. In all cases where a regulatory body exercises powers that adversely affect a person's career or livelihood, its decision should be subject to automatic review by the High Court.

The Opticians Board has responsibility for overseeing the training and examination of opticians and for approving institutions that are suitable for training. Only a person who is a registered optician or medical practitioner may prescribe or dispense spectacles and a person who does so without being an optician or medical practitioner or who claims to be an optician and is not registered is guilty of an offence.[46]

Pharmacists

[2.12]

The Pharmaceutical Society of Ireland is the professional regulatory body of pharmacy in Ireland. It was originally founded under legislation in 1875,[47] but its statutory footing was most recently updated by the Pharmacy Act 1962. All practising pharmacists in Ireland must be registered with the Pharmaceutical Society and the Society is headed by a Council of 21, elected by registered pharmacists. To be eligible to register as a pharmacist, a candidate must generally have completed a recognised degree in pharmacy and have undergone a year's pre-registration training in pharmaceutical practice (which is supervised by the Society). The Society is responsible for assessing and accrediting degree courses in Pharmacy provided by Irish institutions and runs programmes for continuing pharmaceutical education.

The Society publishes a code of ethics and the Society also has the power to punish those whose standards suggest they are unfit to practise, although the powers are not as extensive as those granted to the other statutory bodies. The Pharmaceutical Society is responsible for enforcing the law on retail sale and supply of medicines. Inspectors appointed by the Society can visit premises where medicines are sold or supplied to ensure that legal and professional requirements are met.

Non-statutory professions

[2.13]

The non-statutory professions generally have professional representative bodies, such as the Association of Occupational Therapists of Ireland, the Irish Institute of Radiography and the Irish Society of Chartered Physiotherapists. But these bodies are not creatures of statute: they were not created by law and do not have legal powers (such as regulating the profession or dealing with practitioners who are unfit to practise). They are more in the nature of organisations that represent the profession and its interests. As we have mentioned, plans have been mooted to put the non-statutory professions onto a statutory footing. Many of the non-statutory professions publish ethical guidelines[48] and while a practitioner could be expelled from her non-statutory professional body for misconduct, unfitness to practise or a breach of the ethical code, the expulsion would not prevent her from continuing to practise.

Because these bodies have no statutory origin and no formal or explicit legal powers conferred on them, we do not consider them in further detail here.

Disciplinary proceedings in the statutory professions[49]

[2.14]

From the point of view of the practitioner, one of the most daunting aspects of the statutory regulatory bodies is their power to attach conditions to a practitioner's continued practice or to suspend or erase her name from the register. We examine here the way in which fitness to practise proceedings operate and the procedures that must be followed to ensure that the process is fair. The procedures described here relate to An Bord Altranais, the Dental Council and the Medical Council.[50] Anyone, including the Board or Council itself, may bring an allegation of unfitness to practise against a practitioner. In the Medical Council, fitness to practise on health grounds is dealt with by a separate Health Committee.

A practitioner's name may be suspended or erased from the register for something as simple as failing to her pay her retention fee, but her name may also be erased or suspended, or conditions may be attached to her retention on the register, for unfitness to practise. A finding of unfitness to practise can arise in two ways:

- the practitioner is guilty of professional misconduct, or
- the practitioner is unfit to practise because of some physical or mental condition.

The process of dealing with an allegation of fitness to practise is divisible into three stages. Firstly, the allegation is referred to the Fitness to Practise Committee of the relevant body and the Committee will decide at the initial stage whether there is any substance to the allegation. If there is not, then the decision of the Committee is referred to the full Council or Board and, if the Council or Board is satisfied with the decision, matters proceed no further.[51]

If there is substance to the allegation or the Council or Board disagrees with the Committee's decision and feels that matters should be taken further, then the second stage of the process is activated. The Committee of its own volition or on the instructions of the Board or Council will hold an inquiry into the alleged unfitness to practise. When the inquiry concludes the Committee can find either that there is no case for the practitioner to answer or that the practitioner is unfit to practise, either because of a physical or mental disability or because of professional misconduct. The Medical and Dental Councils and An Bord Altranais also have the power under their respective legislation to apply to the High Court in the public interest to have a clinician immediately suspended from practising pending a hearing of the disciplinary matter.[52] This application will only be granted where there is a strong (*prima facie*) case against the clinician in question.

Fitness to practise inquiries are akin to court hearings and the Committee can call witnesses, examine them under oath and compel the production of relevant documents, including confidential clinical records. The powers and privileges of the members of the Committee are similar, but not identical,[53] to those of a High Court judge. The practitioner is entitled to legal representation and to examine and cross-examine any witnesses. The decision whether to hold an inquiry in public or in private (*in camera*) appears to lie with the relevant Council or Board.[54] While generally Fitness to Practise Committees choose to hold hearings in private, a court may also specifically order them to do so where especially confidential matters are at issue.[55]

At the end of the inquiry, the Committee makes a decision that the practitioner either is, or is not, fit to practise due to disability or professional misconduct. If the Committee exonerates the practitioner, the matter will generally end there.[56] If the finding is that the practitioner is unfit to practise her profession, the Council or Board will consider the appropriate course of action in the circumstances. The regulatory body may choose simply to censure or caution the clinician, in which case matters will proceed no further.

However, it may decide instead that the misconduct or disability is so severe that the only options open to it are either to attach conditions to the continued registration of the practitioner or to suspend, or erase, her name from the register. If that occurs, then matters move onto the next stage. It also appears to be the case that in certain situations, even where a clinician is found not to have met the criteria for professional misconduct, the Board or Council may still attach conditions to her continued registration.[57]

The potential consequences of a decision that a practitioner is guilty of professional misconduct or otherwise unfit to practise are immense. She may be merely cautioned or censured, but she may also have her livelihood constrained by conditions or even taken away from her, either for a period of suspension or permanently. Because of the enormity of such a decision, the courts have reasoned that the final say on any disciplinary decisions taken by a statutory body that significantly affect the livelihood of a professional must be subject to review by the courts before they can be legally binding.[58] Accordingly, once the Medical Council, Dental Council or An Bord Altranais takes a decision to attach conditions to practice or to suspend a clinician's name from the register, they must apply to the High Court to make that decision final. When a practitioner, against whom a finding of unfitness to practise has been made, is notified of the decision, she has 21 days to apply to the High Court to have that decision overturned. If she does not do so, then the Council or Board can apply to the Court to have its decision made final.

The High Court hearing does not rehear the whole Fitness to Practise Committee inquiry. Instead, it satisfies itself that legal formalities have been complied with and that the evidence upon which the decision was taken could reasonably provide the basis for that decision. The court may occasionally wish to hear from an expert as to whether the conduct complained of in the original allegation constituted professional misconduct in the opinion of the expert, but the role of the court is essentially supervisory.[59] The High Court process oversees all decisions to erase or suspend a practitioner's name for unfitness to practice or for conviction of a criminal offence and all decisions to attach conditions to a clinician's continued practice. Where, as with the Medical Council, there is a power of temporary registration, there is no obligation on the court to review a decision not to renew temporary registration if that decision is not the direct result of a decision taken by the Fitness to Practise Committee.[60]

The High Court will either uphold or overturn the Fitness to Practise Committee's decision to suspend or erase the clinician's name. Where the decision was to impose conditions upon the practitioner's continued registration, the High Court may overturn the decision, accept the conditions imposed or attach different conditions as it sees fit.[61]

Quick Reference Guide 2.2

Fitness to practise inquiries

- Any interested party, whether a member of the public or the regulatory Council or Board itself, may make an allegation against a practitioner.
- The complaint is subjected to preliminary scrutiny and may be rejected at this stage with the consent of the relevant Board or Council.
- If necessary, further investigation will be carried out by the Fitness to Practise Committee and the Committee has extensive powers to conduct that investigation. Fitness to Practise inquiries are generally heard in private although there is a discretion granted to the Committee to hold public hearings.
- The Committee may exonerate the clinician or may merely warn or censure her. However, it may also suspend or erase her name from the register or attach conditions to her future practice.
- The subject of the complaint has 21 days to appeal to the High Court to overturn the decision of the Fitness to Practise Committee. If she does not do so, then the Council or Board must apply to the High Court for confirmation of any decision to suspend or erase the practitioner's name or to attach conditions to her name remaining on the register.

What is 'professional misconduct'?

[2.15]

The Medical Council adopts the following definition of professional misconduct:

> '…conduct which doctors of experience, competence and good repute, upholding the fundamental aims of the profession, consider disgraceful or dishonourable.'[62]

Professional misconduct must obviously relate to the clinician's professional activity and must have an element of moral failure (such as dishonesty) or persistent recklessness or negligence to it.[63] Usually negligence or recklessness will have to occur on more than a single occasion for it to be regarded as professional misconduct[64] and typically the misconduct should arise in the course of the practitioner's clinical duties, although that need not always be the case.[65]

Fair procedure and disciplinary matters

[2.16]

We mentioned above the potentially serious consequences of a finding that a doctor, dentist, optician or nurse has been guilty of professional misconduct: she may lose her livelihood temporarily or permanently or find that her sole way of earning a living has been severely curtailed by the attachment of conditions to her continuing in practice. The Irish Constitution says that the administration of justice should be the sole province of judges. In recommending that a practitioner be 'struck off' the register, a regulatory body is effectively administering justice by delivering a verdict with such far-reaching consequences. That in turn is the reason for the insistence on a High Court judge reviewing matters relating to statutory disciplinary proceedings against health professionals: to ensure that the final decision on the matter – the verdict, as it were – is given by a judge. Only a court should have the ultimate decision-making authority over such a profound determination with such substantial consequences for the practitioner.[66]

There are certain things the High Court will be especially concerned about when examining the decision made by a Fitness to Practise Committee. It will want to know that the decision reached by the Board or Council was reasonable, although it will not generally examine the minutiae of the decision. It will be more interested in ascertaining whether fair procedures were followed in making the decision. Any decision made by a body such as the Medical Council and indeed most disciplinary decisions whatever the setting, that affect a person's livelihood or career[67] must observe the rules of fundamental justice. There are many facets to the principle of fair procedures, but we will look at the most important.

Delay

Any allegation against a practitioner must be made and investigated, where possible, without undue delay. Delay can adversely affect a person's ability to defend herself. The need for prompt action cuts both ways: a person who delays in challenging disciplinary proceedings may similarly find that her right to challenge the proceedings evaporates due to the delay.[68]

Notice

A person charged with wrongdoing must have notice of the charges against her, the evidence[69] against her, and of any hearing where matters are to be decided.[70] Without notice of what is going on, a person cannot defend herself against allegations. To ensure fair procedure, when an allegation of misconduct is received against a practitioner, the protocol is to notify the practitioner concerned and invite her comments on the matter.[71] The practitioner must then be given notice of any hearing and then further notice of any decision taken on foot of the hearing.

Hearing

The more serious the consequences of any disciplinary action or the greater the uncertainty concerning the facts at the centre of the issue, the greater the need for an oral hearing of the matter and the greater need for formality and legal representation at that hearing.[72] In general at a disciplinary hearing, the case against the practitioner is presented by barristers on behalf of the Council or Board, while the practitioner's legal team mounts her defence. The Fitness to Practise Committee will also generally cross-examine witnesses. The right to be represented at a hearing includes the right to legal representation and the right to call witnesses, but it does not include the right to have one's witnesses present throughout the whole of a private (*in camera*) hearing.[73] A person who is not given the opportunity to present her side of the case in a disciplinary scenario will generally be able to ask a court to overturn the decision.[74]

If a person has the opportunity to challenge evidence, at a hearing for example, and passes up the opportunity to do so, it is difficult for her to subsequently challenge the evidence, so the opportunity presented by a hearing of the case should be taken very seriously.[75]

Reasons

In the same way that a person must be given the evidence against her, she must also be given the reasons for any decision that is taken concerning her. Without reasons, it would be impossible for her to decide whether an appeal was possible or what part of the decision she should appeal against. The reasons need not be exhaustive, merely sufficient for a person to understand how and why the decision was made.

Prejudice and bias

A disciplinary procedure or hearing is not fair if there is someone involved who has already made up his mind on the matter or who has already heard the evidence and reached an opinion upon it. Therefore, the person who initially screens a complaint against a practitioner, decides that she has a case to answer and refers the matter to the Fitness to Practise Committee, cannot also sit on the Committee hearing the case: she has prejudged the matter and it would not be fair.[76]

Bias is a slightly different and subtler matter: there does not have to be actual prejudice, but a likelihood that a person involved in the decision-making process could have been biased for some reason. Bias can come in many forms, such as a personal relationship, a financial interest in the matter, or a political or personal position that makes it likely that a decision-maker could be hostile or partial towards a person appearing before the decision-making committee.[77]

Proportionate punishment

The punishment should fit the crime. Where a sanction imposed on a practitioner is disproportionate to the decision reached by the disciplinary committee, the court may refuse to uphold it or where it concerns attaching conditions to the clinician's practice, the court may alter those conditions.[78]

Movement of health care professionals throughout Europe

[2.17]

While the application of a non-European Union (EU) clinician to practise in an EU country may be met with resistance, the case of EU citizens who wish to practise in other EU countries is very different. The EU system enshrines what are sometimes called the 'four freedoms':

- free movement of goods;
- free movement of capital;
- free movement of workers;
- freedom to establish oneself in business and to provide or obtain services.

What these 'freedoms' mean in essence is that the presence of national borders within the EU should not be an obstacle to the free market. A product that can be sold in Germany should be capable of being sold just as easily in Greece and Ireland. A company with a shop in Belmullet should be free to open other outlets in Copenhagen and Lille. A clinician qualified in an EU country should also be free to work in other EU countries. Health professionals, depending on whether they are employees or self-employed, have rights thanks to the free movement of workers or the freedom of establishment respectively.

There are some obvious stumbling blocks to free movement of health professionals, among them the fact that qualifications obtained in different countries may not be equivalent and questions of linguistic proficiency. There is an obvious allure in deciding to exclude from practice a clinician whose qualifications do not on paper match the host country's equivalent and who does not speak the language of the host country. In order to overcome the difficulties, the European Union introduced a series of Directives to regulate how the free movement of health and other professionals should work. Some directives are profession-specific,[79] but there are also broader guidelines[80] that bring the bulk of clinical disciplines within their remit.

Whether a profession comes within profession-specific or general rules for free movement, the rules for the mutual recognition of qualifications remain essentially the same. A person who wishes to take up a regulated (and 'regulated' is defined loosely in the general directive, to include all those professions carried on under a professional body, whether statutory or not) profession in another EU country must satisfy minimum criteria:

— she must have pursued within the EU, the equivalent of a three-year higher education course in the profession in question, and

— she must have completed the necessary professional training in an EU Member State.

Once these conditions are met, an EU country cannot refuse someone permission to practise on the basis of her lacking qualifications. However, if the course or training is markedly different from that provided in the host state, then the host state can offer the clinician the choice between an aptitude test[81] and a period of adaptation in the host country. An EU country that refuses an EU citizen with an EU professional qualification from practising within its borders must give reasons for doing so and allow the applicant a legal right of appeal against the decision.

IRISH HEALTHCARE SYSTEM

[2.18]

The Irish healthcare system is an unusual mix of private and public (state) funding.[82] Three quarters of the system is funded by the government, mainly out of tax revenues, while the remaining quarter is funded by payment made from health insurance premiums paid by individuals or by employers on behalf of individuals. Between one-fifth and one-quarter of all government spending goes on healthcare per annum.[83] Over 40% of the population are eligible for free medical care through the General Medical Services scheme and a similar proportion are covered by voluntary health insurance. Everyone is entitled to free public inpatient and outpatient care in public hospitals, should they wish to avail of them.

Administration and delivery of services

[2.19]

The power to decide what health services there will be and how they will be administered does not reside in any one person or institution. Instead there is a mixture of the hierarchical (with the Dáil at the top) and the interdisciplinary, where multiple agencies work together to develop and maintain health care services. Decisions are made within a matrix of governmental and other agencies.

The legislature

[2.20]

The Dáil and Seanad (together the Oireachtas) lay down the laws by which the health services are governed and every person or body affected by those laws must act within their parameters. Many Acts, for example the Health Act 1970 that underpins the modern Irish system, simply lay out the broad details of how something is to be done and will leave to the relevant Minister or government department the making of the specific regulations necessary to make the Act work.[84] However, any regulations must be within the scope of the original law made by the Oireachtas: a Minister or government department cannot introduce regulations that have the effect of changing the law.[85]

The minister

[2.21]

The Minister for Health and Children is a cabinet minister appointed by the government of the day to head the department of the same name. The Minister oversees the strategic development and overall operation of health services and is the conduit through which government policy on the health services is implemented. The Minister also has the power to make regulations based on pre-existing legislation as well as the power to make certain appointments.[86] The role of the Minister is undergoing a certain amount of change, with the aim of making him responsible for overarching policy and strategy rather than for day-to-day management concerns.[87] There is also at least one Minister of State, a junior minister with responsibility for one or more subsections of the department's powers (recently the arrangement has involved two Ministers of State with specific responsibility for food safety, children and older people).

The department of health and children

[2.22]

The Department of Health has been in existence as a separate department since 1947.[88] The person in permanent charge of the Department of Health and Children is the Secretary-General, a civil servant who outlasts the comings and goings of government ministers. The Secretary-General works with a Management Advisory Committee (of senior department officials) in formulating policy proposals.

The role of the Department is to aid the Minister and was laid out in the Department's 1997 *Statement of Strategy*:

- to support the Minister in formulating, developing and evaluating health policy and in his other roles;

— planning strategic development of health services through partnership and consultation with the relevant bodies;
— promoting effectiveness, efficiency, equity, quality and value for money in the health delivery system;
— ensuring accountability and a 'customer service ethos' at all levels;
— optimising staff performance, training and development;
— representing the Irish interest in health affairs at international level.

There are seven divisions in the Department, each of which reflects a specific area of health policy:

i. Blood policy, mental health and services for older people
ii. Children and disability
iii. Personnel management and development
iv. Secondary care
v. Strategic policy development
vi. Primary healthcare
vii. Finance, planning and international

In the same way that the Minister's role has been changing, and as part of the same process, the Department's function is becoming increasingly strategic in nature, devolving day-to-day matters such as the running of certain hospitals[89] to the health boards and creating new agencies to take on other areas of responsibility.

The Department also contains the Office of the Registrar-General for Births, Deaths and Marriages and the Hospital Planning Office. The former has an important statistical function while the latter is concerned with the design and building of health care facilities. The Department, in common with other government departments, also creates Expert Groups consisting of Department officials and external experts to prepare reports[90] and the department similarly commissions external reports from consultants on areas requiring specific expertise.

The health boards and regional health authorities

[2.23]

The Health Act 1970 transferred the planning of the health services from a county-based system to a regional one, creating eight health boards..[91] The Midland Health Board area has the smallest population and the former Eastern Health Board (now the Eastern Regional Health Authority) the largest. Health Board membership is generally drawn from three groups:

— public representatives (County Councillors),
— representatives of the health care professions in the area, elected by their peers, and
— nominees of the Minister for Health

In general the Board meets once a month and each health board's day-to-day running is managed by a Chief Executive Officer (CEO). Health board services are divided into a number of programme areas: the two broadest are Community Care Services and

Hospital Services, which in turn are often subdivided into General and Special Hospital Services.[92] Each programme area functions under the leadership of a programme manager. The Health (Amendment) Act 1996, which aimed to make health boards more financially accountable, also clarified the functions of the Health Boards, which include:[93]

- allocating resources for the maximum and most efficient benefit;[94]
- cooperation with voluntary bodies, other health boards, local authorities and other bodies involved with health care;
- implementing government policy;
- service planning: each health board must give an annual report to the Minister including 'a statement of the services to be provided by the health board and estimates of the income and expenditure of the board for the period to which the plan relates'.

The Eastern Health Board, the largest of the eight,[95] was reconstituted in 1999 as the Eastern Regional Health Authority (ERHA) and sub-divided into three constituent health boards: the Northern Area, the South Western Area and East Coast Area. This reformation aims to give the ERHA overall authority for the coordination, funding and planning of services in the area and to give the Area Health Boards responsibility for delivering the services.

Other bodies

[2.24]

There are a number of other bodies that exist outside the legislative, departmental and health care delivery areas that also fulfil important functions in the Irish health care service. These other bodies are often required where provision of a particular service is better organised at a national rather than at a health board level. Some of the most important are listed below, together with a brief description of their functions.

Irish Medicines Board: Established in 1995, it is responsible for the licensing of new medications for use in medical and veterinary practice and it advises the Minister on the safety and regulation of medicines.

Postgraduate Medical and Dental Board: Established under the Medical Practitioners Act 1978, it coordinates, oversees and advises on medical and dental training in the years following graduation.

Comhairle na nOispidéal: Established under the Health Act 1970, it regulates consultant and other senior medical and surgical appointments to hospitals. It is a 27-member body, half of whom are hospital consultants, while the remainder represent the Department of Health and Children, hospitals and health boards.

Food Safety Authority: Established under the Food Safety Authority of Ireland (Establishment) Order 1997, it advises on food safety issues, including matters relating to the processing and sale of food.

Health Research Board: Established in 1986,[96] it promotes, commissions and conducts health services research and liaises with other research bodies in Ireland and elsewhere to achieve this end.

Blood Transfusion Service Board: Organises and administers the system for making available blood and blood products where needed. The Board is headed by a Chief Medical Consultant and a Chief Executive Officer.

General Medical Services (GMS) scheme

[2.25]

The scheme came into being in 1972 and covers all of the health board areas. The scheme is based on means testing and allows eligible persons to attend the doctor and pharmacist of their choice for medical and dispensing services respectively. Doctors in primary care treating patients under the GMS scheme are paid on the basis of a capitation approach: the doctor receives a fixed annual fee per patient, calculated on the basis of the age of the patient and the distance he lives from the doctor's centre of practice. The fee remains the same irrespective of how often or seldom the patient attends the doctor. Further payments are attracted when the doctor performs certain services not covered by the capitation scheme, such as the removal of sutures or providing nebulised medications for asthmatics.

The Scheme was initially administered on a pure means-tested approach (with some discretion available to those on the margins of eligibility), but since July 2000 the scheme has been extended to cover all those over the age of 70 years.

Endnotes

1 Scruton *A dictionary of political thought* (1984) Pan Books.

2 It may also be called 'state-sanctioned self-regulation': see Moran & Wood States, *Regulation and the Medical Profession* (1993) Open University Press. The authors also identify independent self-regulation and direct state regulation of the professions as alternatives.

3 See O'Dwyer 'Reflections on Future Structures in the Health Services' in *The Irish Health System in the 21st Century*, Austin Leahy and Miriam Wiley (eds), (1998) Oaktree Press p 49.

4 Professions Supplementary to Medicine Act 1960.

5 Osteopaths Act 1993 and Chiropractors Act 1994.

6 Of course, such mechanisms can fail, as demonstrated by the Harold Shipman and Bristol Royal Infirmary cases in the United Kingdom where there was a marked inability to detect aberrant practitioners.

7 The predecessor to the Medical Council was the Medical Registration Council, established in 1927 and which had close links with the UK General Medical Council: there was Irish representation on the UK Council until 1979.

8 Medical Practitioners Act 1978, s 9.

9 Medical Practitioners Act 1978, ss 26-34.

10 The UK House of Commons Health Committee (in *Procedures Related to Adverse Clinical Incidents and Outcomes in Medical Care*, HC 549-I, session 1999-2000) recommended that the lay membership of the UK Medical and Nursing Councils be increased to a majority.

11 At the time of writing (September 2002), the Medical Practitioners (Amendment) Act 2002 has been passed by the Oireachtas, but has not yet been put into action by the Minister. This Act changes, amongst other matters, the conditions for full registration with the Medical Council with the intention of easing problems recruiting and retaining non-EU doctors. Any doctor who has been temporarily registered for a total of not less than 24 months and who has undergone prescribed training or obtained prescribed experience and who (where appropriate) has passed

the requisite examinations will be entitled to full registration (s 5, amending Medical Practitioners Act 1978, s 27(2)(d)).

12 Medical Practitioners Act 1978, s 27(3). A person who is refused registration must have his application considered under the rules applicable at the time of his application and any rules used to preclude registration must be fair and reasonable, otherwise the refusal will be void: *Phillips v Medical Council* [1991] 2 IR 115.

13 Medical Practitioners Act 1978, s 28. The rules for temporary registration have been somewhat modified by the Medical Practitioners (Amendment) Act 2002, but see note 11 above regarding the fact that the Act remains to be implemented. The modifications include an increase in the maximum length of temporary registration from five years to seven years (s 7, amending s 29(2) of the 1978 Act).

14 Medical Practitioners Act 1978, s 32.

15 Medical Practitioners Act 1978, s 33. However, this method cannot be used to circumvent an inquiry by the Medical Council into whether a person should have her name erased from the register. If the Council is aware that an inquiry is in progress against a practitioner or that she has been convicted on an offence in the State, then it can decline to remove her name from the register until it considers whether the name should be erased from the register instead.

16 Medical Practitioners Act 1978, s 61.

17 Medical Practitioners Act 1978, s 28. The term 'provisional registration' is amended to 'internship registration' by the Medical Practitioners (Amendment) Act 2002, s 2(b), but see endnote 11 above.

18 Medical Practitioners Act 1978.

19 Medical Practitioners Act 1978, s 57.

20 http://www.medicalcouncil.ie.

21 In 2000, the Medical Council introduced 'log books' for interns so that they could specifically record the experience they were gaining during their training year and it has also changed the permitted disciplines that can be included in the intern year. Traditionally, the intern year consisted of six months of medical practice and six months of surgical practice. While exposure to general medical and surgical experience remains mandatory for the intern year, in 2002 the Council changed the permissible structure of the year to allow for combinations of the following: medicine (minimum three months / maximum six months); surgery (minimum three months /maximum six months); obstetrics & gynaecology (minimum two months / maximum three months); emergency medicine (minimum two months / maximum three months); paediatrics (minimum two months / maximum three months); psychiatry (minimum two months / maximum three months). See the Medical Council guidelines for the intern year: published by the Medical Council in 2000 or available at http://www.medicalcouncil.ie/guidelinesintern2000.htm.

22 Medical Practitioners Act 1978, ss 39-44.

23 Currently the *Guide to Ethical Conduct and Behaviour* (5th edn, 1998). There are plans at the time of writing (September 2002) to commence work on a new edition.

24 See Medical Council *Competence Assurance Structures – An Agenda for Implementation* (March 2002) Dublin.

25 Medical Practitioners Act 1978, s 46 (erasure or suspension from the register); s 47 (attachment of conditions to practice of medicine); s 48 (admonishment and censure).

26 In the United Kingdom, in addition to 'striking off' doctors whose health or conduct warrants such a step, the General Medical Council has the power to take disciplinary action specifically against those whose clinical performance is seriously deficient.

27 Medical Practitioners Act 1978, s 51. Note that the automatic requirement to involve the High Court in disciplinary decisions does not exist in the United Kingdom. A practitioner in the UK

will still be free to appeal to the High Court, but the court is not required to approve each decision of the Medical Council (and similar bodies) before it is implemented.

28 The Act replaces the Nurses Act 1950.

29 Nurses Act 1985, ss 27-30 (Part III of the Act).

30 Nurses Act 1985, ss 31-37 (Part IV of the Act).

31 An Bord Altranais *The Code of Professional Conduct for each Nurse and Midwife* (April 2000). This is an altogether shorter document than the medical or dental equivalents, but it is based upon the same ethical and legal principles.

32 Nurses Act 1985, ss 38-47 (Part V of the Act).

33 Nurses Act 1985, s 49.

34 Nurses Act 1985, s 57.

35 Nurses Act 1985, s 58.

36 Dentists Act 1985. Among the reasons for this legislation (and the equivalent Act for nursing) was the realisation that the old legislation did not provide the necessary safeguard of High Court review of any decision that was taken to suspend or erase or make conditional the retention of the name of a practitioner.

37 Dentists Act 1985, s 9. The Minister can vary the composition of the Council by ministerial order (s 9(1)),

38 Dentists Act 1985, ss 26-33 (Part III of Act).

39 Dentists Act 1985, ss 34-37 (Part IV of Act). Note also the existence of the Postgraduate Medical and Dental Board established by the Medical Practitioners Act 1978.

40 Dentists Act 1985, ss 38-48 (Part V of Act).

41 Dental Council *Professional Behaviour and Dental Ethics* (1998), Dublin. This guide stresses the 'general principle' of ethical dental practice as 'the three-fold aim of safeguarding the health of patients, promoting the welfare of the community and maintaining the honour and integrity of the dental profession.'

42 Dentists Act 1985, ss 50-51.

43 Dentists Act 1985, ss 53-55.

44 Opticians Act 1956, ss 7-10. The Minister for Health and Children also appoints the President of the Board. Note that there is no guaranteed lay representation on this board at all.

45 Opticians Act 1956, Part III is concerned with the Register of Ophthalmic Opticians and Part IV with the Register of Dispensing Opticians, although the broad rules are the same for both.

46 Opticians Act 1956, ss 47-51 (Part VI of Act).

47 Pharmacy Act (Ireland) 1875.

48 *Code of Ethics and Professional Conduct for Occupational Therapists*; *Rules of Professional Conduct* of the Irish Society of Chartered Physiotherapists; Irish Institute of Radiography *Code of Professional Conduct.*

49 See de Prez 'Self-Regulation and Paragons of Virtue: The Case of "Fitness to Practise"' (2002) 10 Med LR 28.

50 The Pharmaceutical Society does not have such extensive powers and the Opticians Board's processes do not include the automatic High Court review that is an inherent part of the disciplinary procedures of the medical, nursing and dental professions.

51 In the United Kingdom, the General Medical Council appoints a 'screener' to conduct the initial review. If she concludes there is no case to answer, then that decision is referred to a lay member of the Council to ensure that she agrees with the screener's decision. If the screener or lay reviewer feels matters should be investigated further, the case goes first to a Preliminary Proceedings Committee and if necessary to the appropriate decision-making committee.

52 See the summary of events contained in *An Bord Altranais v Ann Ní Cheallaigh* (17 December 1997 ex temp) HC. In that case the order prohibiting a midwife from continuing to practise

pending a fitness to practice hearing was suspended only insofar as it concerned five couples who wished to continue to avail of the midwife's services. The court ordered that they be given the opportunity of knowing the allegations made against the midwife and then choosing whether they still wished to retain her for delivering their babies.

53 The Fitness to Practise Committee cannot punish someone for contempt (eg for refusing to appear) or take a final decision to suspend or erase a practitioner's name or attach conditions to her practice. These steps can only be taken by a High Court judge herself.

54 *Barry v Medical Council And Fitness To Practise Committee Of The Medical Council* (11 February 1997, unreported) HC.

55 *Eastern Health Board v Fitness to Practise Committee of the Medical Council and Others* (3 April 1998, unreported) HC.

56 Although it is possible for a disaffected party to ask the Courts to review any decision taken by bodies such as the Medical Council, a process called 'judicial review'. A judicial review does not involve rehearing the whole case. Instead the judges will only wish to satisfy themselves that the decision was reasonable and that the procedure which led to the decision was fair (see section **[2.16]**).

57 *Casey v The Medical Council* (4 June 1999, unreported) HC. One problem with this judgment, which allows conditions to be attached to the practice of clinicians who have *not* been found guilty of misconduct is that if they fail to meet those conditions, what can the Council do? If the practitioner was not guilty of misconduct then how can she be 'struck off' or suspended if she does not stick to the conditions (or will she become guilty of misconduct for failing to comply?). This case suggests that the Medical Council has the power to attach conditions to practitioners' practice for performance-related rather than conduct-related shortcomings. Future revisions of the Medical Practitioners' Act (and similar Acts) should consider introducing a performance-related complaints process to explicitly enable the Councils and Board to attach conditions in the interests of improving practitioners' clinical skills in situations that do not amount to misconduct. It is expected that the new Medical Practitioners Bill, when published, will contain such elements.

58 *Re Solicitors Act 1954* [1960] IR 239. The process now followed by the Medical Council, Dental Council and An Bord Altranais was challenged in the courts, but it was upheld as fair: *Re M* [1984] IR 479; *M v Medical Council* [1984] IR 485.

59 *CK v An Bord Altranais* [1990] 2 IR 396.

60 *Anachebe v The Medical Council* (12 July 2000, unreported) HC. The plaintiff had been found guilty of professional misconduct and was censured (which does not require the supervision of the Court). When subsequently he applied for renewal of his temporary registration, the Medical Council declined to renew it, citing the previous finding of misconduct. Because the refusal was not part of the misconduct proceedings, the decision of the Council did not require the court's approval. This decision seems discriminatory against those who are temporarily registered: a fully registered doctor who was merely censured would not find herself effectively 'struck off' the register.

61 *Cahill v Dental Council* (15 June 2001, unreported) HC. Following problems that arose during Dr Cahill's attempts to sedate a child patient prior to surgery, the Dental Council imposed a number of conditions on his practice of dentistry. These conditions included that he be prohibited from performing dentistry involving the use of anaesthesia or sedation, that he should complete a course in paediatric dentistry approved by the Council and that he should display a notice in his premises drawing attention to the conditions attached to his practice. The court lifted the requirement to display a notice and limited the restriction on the use of anaesthesia or sedation to only those patients under the age of 16 years. The requirement to complete a course in paediatric dentistry was upheld.

62 *Guide to Ethical Conduct and Behaviour* (5th edn, 1998) para 1.5. The guidelines also specify certain forms of conduct, such as sexual advances to a patient with whom there is a professional relationship, as misconduct.

63 In *O'Laoire v Medical Council* (27 January, 1995, unreported) HC at p 109, Keane J identified the following elements of professional misconduct:

(i) conduct which is 'infamous' or 'disgraceful' in a professional respect is 'professional misconduct';

(ii) conduct that would not be 'infamous' or 'disgraceful' in any other person, if done by a medical practitioner in relation to his profession, that is, with regard either to his patients or to his colleagues, may be considered as 'infamous' or 'disgraceful' conduct in a professional respect;

(iii) 'infamous' or 'disgraceful' conduct in turn is conduct involving some degree of moral turpitude, fraud or dishonesty;

(iv) conduct which could not properly be characterised as 'infamous' or 'disgraceful' and which does not involve any degree of moral turpitude, fraud or dishonesty may still constitute 'professional misconduct' if it is conduct connected with his profession in which the medical practitioner concerned has seriously fallen short, by omission or commission, of the standards of conduct expected among medical practitioners.

64 *McCandless v General Medical Council* (1995) 30 BMLR 53.

65 In *Roylance v General Medical Council* [1999] Lloyds L Rep (Med) 139, a doctor who was the head of a National Health Service Hospital Trust which knowingly permitted substandard paediatric cardiac surgery to take place was found guilty of professional misconduct.

66 *Re Solicitors Act 1954* [1960] IR 239.

67 *Gunn v National College of Art and Design* [1990] 2 IR 168. See section **[5.12]**, where the need for fair procedures in disciplinary proceedings in the workplace is discussed.

68 *O'Flynn v Mid-Western Health Board* [1989] IR 429 (HC); [1991] 2 IR 223 (SC. The Medical Practitioners Act 1978, the Dentists Act 1985 and the Nurse Act 1985 all give the clinician 21 days from when she hears of a decision against her to bring a case to the High Court to have the decision quashed.

69 A disciplinary body does not need to share *every* piece of information available to it with the person facing disciplinary proceedings, but only that material which has a bearing on ensuring the procedure is fair: *Georgopulous v Beaumont Hospital Board* (4 June 1997, unreported) SC. There may be no need to hand over all details to the person complained of if the investigating body is still at the stage of deciding whether a complaint should or should not be entertained: *O'Flynn v Mid-Western Health Board* [1991] 2 IR 223 (SC).

70 *O'Laoire v Medical Council* (27 January 27 1995, unreported) HC. According to the court, a person must have 'adequate notice of the allegations made against him so as to enable him to conduct his defence and to meet [the allegations] with whatever legal assistance was appropriate and with the production of whatever evidence was necessary'.

71 At this point, the practitioner should generally involve her legal advisers before replying.

72 In *Flanagan v University College Dublin* [1988] IR 724 a student was subjected to a formal college hearing concerning alleged plagiarism without being offered the opportunity of legal representation (her only representation was from the Students' Union) – the court did not approve in the circumstances. The potential consequences were so great (being sent down from the university) that representation was necessary.

73 *Ann O'Ceallaigh v The Fitness To Practise Committee Of An Bord Altranais and An Bord Altranais* (22 May 1998, unreported) HC.

[74] In *Aziz v Midland Health Board* (29 October 1999, unreported) SC, a doctor was dismissed for refusing to obey lawful instructions. The Court was satisfied that it was reasonable to dismiss him but criticised the fact that he was not allowed to present his side of the story.

[75] *State (Boyle) v General Medical Services Board* [1981] ILRM 14.

[76] In *O'Neill v Beaumont Hospital Board* [1990] ILRM 419, a court refused to allow three members of the hospital board to sit on a disciplinary panel considering a surgeon's conduct because they had already committed themselves to positions that suggested they had prejudged the matter.

[77] See *O'Donoghue v Veterinary Council* [1975] IR 398, where the person in whose name the complaint was made was also sitting on the panel that decided the fate of the vet in question. The decision of the panel was therefore void.

[78] *Cahill v Dental Council* (15 June 2001, unreported) HC.

[79] The Directive applying to the various professions and to professionals generally are as follows: for the medical profession: Directive No 75/362/EEC; Directive No 75/363/EEC; Directive No 86/457/EEC and Directive No 93/16/EEC. For the dental profession: Directive No 78/686/EEC and Directive No 78/687/EEC. For the nursing profession: Directive No 77/452/EEC and Directive No 77/453/EEC (general nursing) and Directive No 80/154/EEC and Directive No 80/155/EEC (midwifery). For pharmacy: Directive No 85/432/EEC and Directive No 90/658/EEC. All of these Directives passed into law by being made Ministerial Regulations. See also European Communities (European Economic Area) (Recognition of Qualifications in Pharmacy) Regulations 1994, which give free movement rights to pharmacists from the European Economic Area as well as those from the EU.

[80] See Directive No 89/48/EEC, which laid out the basic ground rules for mutual recognition of third-level professional qualifications. See also Directive No 92/51/EEC, which allows for mutual recognition of shorter diploma courses and of other educational certificates.

[81] Which can be in the language of the host country, thereby testing the applicant's linguistic competence.

[82] See also O'Hara, 'Current Structure of the Irish Health Care System' in *The Irish Health System in the 21st Century*, Austin Leahy and Miriam Wiley (eds) (1998) Oaktree Press.

[83] See Wiley 'Health Expenditure Trends in Ireland' in *The Irish Health System in the 21st Century*, Austin Leahy and Miriam Wiley (eds) (1998) Oaktree Press. The OECD has stated that the 'Irish health system is based on a mixture of public and private care which has resulted in good provision of health care at relatively low cost to the taxpayer': see OECD Economic Survey 1996-1997: Ireland (1997) Paris.

[84] Examples of regulations made under the Misuse of Drugs Act 1977 are referred to in ch 6.

[85] In *Cooke v Walsh* [1984] IR 710, the Supreme Court felt that regulations made by the Minister for Health under the Health Act 1970, s 72 limiting the provision of free hospital care in certain circumstances were impermissible because they had the effect of changing the law, a role which is the sole preserve of the legislature.

[86] The Medical Council, the Dental Council and An Bord Altranais all feature ministerial appointees among their membership. The Minister also appoints three nominees to each health board.

[87] See Department of Health and Children Statement of Strategy (1997). The document includes the following 'mission statement' for the Department:

> 'In a partnership with the providers of health care, and in cooperation with other government departments, statutory and non-statutory bodies, to protect, promote and restore the well-being of the people by ensuring that health and personal social services are planned, managed and delivered to achieve measurable health and social gain and provide the optimum return on resources invested.'

[88] Ministers and Secretaries (Amendment) Act 1946. The Department became the Department of Health and Children (and the Minister similarly changed his name) in July 1997: see SI 1997/308, s 1.

[89] The Department formerly had responsibility for 'Voluntary Hospitals' but these have now been moved to come under the auspices of the Health Boards.

[90] For example, Department of Health and Children *Report of the National Task Force on Suicide* (1998).

[91] Health Act 1970, s 4(1).

[92] The Eastern Regional Health Authority has a greater number of programme areas, including (a) Community Services, (b) Acute Hospital Services and the Elderly, (c) Health Promotion, Mental Health, Addiction and Social Development, (d) Services for persons with disabilities, (e) Children and Families Programmes.

[93] Health (Amendment) Act 1996, ss 2 and 6.

[94] Note that unlike in the UK, which has the National Institute for Clinical Excellence there is no national Irish body that takes overall health rationing decisions. Any decision to ration treatment in a given area would be taken by the health boards (and could be challenged in the courts, see section **[3.09]**)

[95] See O'Shea 'A Particular Problem in the East...' in *The Irish Health System in the 21st Century*, Austin Leahy and Miriam Wiley (eds) (1998) Oaktree Press.

[96] Under the Health (Corporate Bodies) Act 1961, which allows the Minister to set up certain agencies without the need for a specific Act of Parliament.

Chapter 3

The Practitioner-Patient Relationship, Ethics and Confidentiality

INTRODUCTION

[3.01]

This chapter looks at the basis of the practitioner-patient relationship in different settings, including some of the legal differences between the private and public environment. There are many other facets to the broad remit of the 'doctor-patient relationship', including the philosophy, sociology and dynamics of the relationship. Such considerations lie largely outside the scope of this text, although this chapter does contain a very brief account of the foremost ethical principles that underpin interactions in the healthcare encounter.

The chapter concludes by examining the question of confidentiality, one of the pathognomic features of clinical care. The relationship between clinician and patient is founded upon a trinity of confidence, professional skill and the duty to provide competent care. Of these three elements, it is trust that is often pivotal to the therapeutic relationship, a confidence not merely in the skill of the clinician, but also in her professional ethics and dispassionate professionalism. A healthcare practitioner is expected to remain silent on what takes place behind the veil of the therapeutic setting. However, there are exceptions to the obligation of confidentiality and in this chapter we examine when those exceptions operate.

THE LEGAL BASIS OF THE PRACTITIONER-PATIENT RELATIONSHIP

[3.02]

In the last chapter, we looked at the questions of 'who is a clinician?' and 'how are the professions controlled?' but the question still remains 'who is the patient?' One irritant when considering this matter is the concurrent existence of two 'tiers' of health care in Ireland – some patients receive entirely free health care funded from the public coffers, others have only a limited entitlement to free health care, while still others opt for paying for their health care, usually through insurance.

Financial considerations

[3.03]

More than 45% of Irish people are entitled to the benefits conferred by the General Medical Services (GMS) scheme, while the rest of Irish population must either make provision for its own health care through private health insurance, or accept such free hospital care as is available while paying for all primary care.

The GMS was designed originally to provide free, or at any rate state-funded, medical care to those sections of the community most in need of such care as a result of financial disadvantage, severe or chronic illness or a combination of both. A patient with GMS eligibility, more colloquially called the 'medical card', is entitled to free primary and hospital care, as well as free prescription medications and medical appliances and has an entitlement to free dental, aural (for example hearing tests and hearing aids) and optical services.

GMS entitlement is determined on the basis of a means test. The factors taken into account when considering the income threshold for a individual or family seeking a medical card include age, household size, marital status and financial expenditure on accommodation (mortgage or rent). There is some discretion in marginal cases where income fractionally exceeds the threshold laid down by law. The exercise of discretion is generally based on the existence of circumstances, such as chronic illness or other dependency on the health services, that mitigate a failure to meet the pure income criteria. Recent changes to GMS eligibility indicate a move away from the traditional means-tested approach and towards a 'category-based' approach. From 1 July 2000, the GMS scheme was extended to include all those over the age of 70, irrespective of income. The policy and politics of health funding fall largely outside the scope of this book.[1]

Since 1991, the provision of state-funded medical care has been extended to the entire population in certain circumstances. From that date everyone became entitled to free inpatient services in public hospitals, free out-patient clinic care and maternity and infant services. This entitlement is irrespective of income. A small charge is levied for hospital care but there is a ceiling of ten days' care billable per annum. Similarly a charge (€40) is levied for attendance at accident and emergency departments, but this fee is waived if a patient attends with a note from his general practitioner. Medical cardholders are exempt from all such hospital charges.

One other important method by which the state seeks to soften the blow for patients who pay for their health care is the Drug Refund Scheme, under which all families are liable only for a prescribed amount of monthly expenditure on prescription medications. Any sum over this amount is paid by the state. At the time of writing, the limit at which the drug refund system is activated is €65 per month.

Who is the patient?

[3.04]

Have we answered the question 'who is the patient?' Probably not. We have certainly identified categories of patient, private and public, but no more than that. The question of being a patient is not answered simply by reference to whether or not someone is paying for healthcare.

In the United Kingdom National Health Service, the majority of people are registered with a particular general practitioner. In such a case it is relatively easy to say that a person registered with a particular practice is a patient of the professionals working in that practice, who may include doctors, nurses, physiotherapists and so on. In Ireland, it is far from being so simple. True, some people are – through the GMS scheme – registered by having a medical card with a particular medical practitioner, but many more people are not attached in this way to a particular practice or any particular health carer and even if attached to a general practitioner, also attend other health outlets, such as hospitals.

A patient may attend one doctor for one minor ailment in one particular year and another doctor for the same or some other problem five years later. Can that person be said to be a 'patient' of either doctor in the period between the two consultations? Once he has attended the second doctor, does he immediately become a patient of that second doctor or does he remain a patient of both? In an emergency, which doctor, if any, has a duty to attend him? These are complex questions. It is suggested that as an element of the concept of patient autonomy, addressed later in this chapter and which is also the keystone of patient consent,[2] it is the patient who chooses the clinician, not the other way around. It might be a more accurate reflection, especially in the sphere of private medical care, to talk about the 'patient and his clinician' rather that the 'clinician and her patient.'

A patient might then possibly be described from an autonomy-orientated perspective as a person who seeks, or is found to require as a matter of emergency or necessity, health care. In other words, it is a question of patient-centred circumstances, either by choice or by necessity, creating the practitioner-patient relationship. Similarly, the patient may terminate the relationship, as in the example of the patient who chooses to attend a different doctor or to seek a second opinion. The patient in such circumstances owes nothing to the doctor other, perhaps, than what courtesy may dictate. The doctor however, continues to have an obligation to preserve the notes of her consultations with her erstwhile patient and may still be the object of legal action concerning the care documented in those notes or may receive a request to send on the notes to a patient's new practitioner.[3]

Of course, such a patient-orientated definition of the patient is not true in all cases: a patient will not always choose his practitioner. A person may choose a particular doctor or hospital, but other health care providers will come effectively 'packaged' with that choice. A patient who chooses to attend a particular hospital will implicitly be compelled to accept that a particular nurse, physiotherapist, radiologist, occupational therapist and other staff, over whom the patient has less control than he had over his initial choice, will be part of the package. It is difficult therefore to say that patient choice always informs the practitioner-patient relationship: it may sometimes be the result of circumstances beyond the patient's control. However, the idea of patient choice as the initiating factor in the practitioner-patient relationship is a valid and an important one.

The practitioner-patient relationship in legal terms

[3.05]

As we have seen, the state pays for the health care of some people, while others pay for their own medical care. This can have an impact on the precise legal relationship between clinician and patient although *not* on the duty the clinican owes to take care of the patient. When a person avails himself of free medical care, there is no direct financial link, or contract, between doctor and patient, rather the contract is between the doctor and the institution that pays her. Of course, any practitioner's employment contract will contain an implied term that she will care for the patients for whom she is responsible and this in turn creates an *indirect* contract between clinician and patient. Conversely, a person who pays his clinician, either out of his own pocket or through an insurance policy, establishes a *direct* financial link between himself and the clinician, a direct link absent in the 'free' public healthcare environment.

The legal basis of the therapeutic relationship is ultimately a contractual one,[4] but the difference being stressed here is that legally any *direct* contract is between the practitioner and the entity which is paying her, which may be the patient or the state. However, it is important to emphasise that this difference in legal relationship does not impact on the standard of care expected of the health carer. Simply because one is paying for healthcare does not mean that one is entitled to, or will necessarily receive, higher quality care. Any real legal difference will only arise where something goes wrong. Because some patients have a direct contractual link with their doctor they will generally take a legal action against that doctor directly should something go wrong. The action might be for negligence but might also be for breach of contract between doctor and patient.

In a case where a practitioner is employed directly by a health board or any other institution, legal action can be taken against not only against the practitioner, but also – and often more importantly – against the institution that employs her. The legal scenario where an employer is legally liable for the acts of its employees and may be sued for them is called 'vicarious liability' (see section **[7.25]**). Furthermore in the public setting the clinician cannot be sued for breach of contract by the patient, because there is no direct contract between them.

The formal legal relationship between the clinician and the patient depends therefore on the nature of the transaction that brings them into contact. In the case of the private patient, the situation is one of a legal contract between doctor and patient *as well as* the duty a professional owes to her client or patient to take care of him competently. The patient pays the practitioner for her professional skill and she in turn is obliged to provide that care diligently and competently in fulfilling the terms of contract. One reason why a direct contract may be important is that any contract may have specific terms that the practitioner will be compelled to satisfy over and above the regular professional relationship or terms that reduce the patient's right to sue the doctor.

In the case of the public clinician, such as the hospital Senior House Officer or hospital physiotherapist, there is no legal contract between patient and doctor. Instead the contract is between the practitioner and her employing authority, whether hospital or health board. The link between the patient and the healthcare professional in such a situation is instead the professional's general obligation to provide competent medical care and to do no harm to the patient through negligent acts or omissions, also called the 'duty of care'.[5]

A therapeutic relationship may also arise in an emergency situation and not due to the express wish of either party. Nonetheless, the duty of the doctor towards the patient to diligently discharge her duties remains once she undertakes the care of the patient.

Finally, the legal relationship between the doctor and patient is also sometimes described as a 'fiduciary' one. This means that the doctor has a duty to protect the patient's welfare in every respect: the patient entrusts her with confidential information and with his health and the doctor must jealously guard that trust. Some judges take this fiduciary approach[6] in interpreting the duties owed by doctors to patients, but it is by no means universally accepted.

Quick Reference Guide 3.1

The practitioner-patient relationship in legal terms

- ❖ Whether a patient is paying for care or not makes absolutely no difference to the care he is due from the clinician.
- ❖ In principle, the relationship between clinician and patient is contractual. However, there is only a *direct* contract if the patient is paying the doctor.
- ❖ A practitioner who breaches her duty to the patient may be guilty of negligence but, if there is a direct contractual link between him and the practitioner, the patient may sue the practitioner for both negligence and breach of contract.
- ❖ The additional direct contractual right of the paying patient is in general of little practical significance. It may be of significance if there is some element of the written contract that explicitly changes the usual terms of the practitioner-patient relationship.

HEALTHCARE ETHICS

[3.06]

What are the rules of engagement between practitioner and patient? Medical ethics are as old as the Hippocratic oath, perhaps older, and most of the clinical professions are moderated by some manner of an ethical code of conduct, either internationally recognised or published by the governing body of the profession in a given country. As far as medicine is concerned, the need for a modern expression of the ethics governing and motivating medical practitioners was recognised in the wake of the Second World War, especially when the horrors of Nazi medical experimentation came to light in the Nuremberg doctors' trial. While there have been many such codes, the building materials remain the same. Ethics are not the same as law: instead they are values that people agree to share, but which are typically not enforceable in the same way as law.[7] While ethical codes and ethical declarations such as oaths are not legally binding, it is often argued that they serve a purpose by emphasising the element of vocation inherent to that particular profession and by formalising the profession's ethical ideal.[8] Ethical codes in particular can also provide a guide for best practice.

One of the clearest articulations of clinical ethical principles is the Declaration of Geneva:[9]

> At the time of being admitted as a Member of my Profession:
>
> — I solemnly pledge myself to consecrate my life to the service of humanity;
>
> — I will give to my teachers the respect and gratitude which is their due;

- I will practice my profession with conscience and dignity;
- The health of those in my care will be my first consideration;
- I will respect the secrets that are confided in me, even after the patient has died;
- I will maintain by all the means in my power, the honour and the noble traditions of my profession;
- My colleagues will be my sisters and brothers;
- I will not permit considerations of age, disease or disability, creed, ethnic origin, gender, nationality, political affiliation, race, sexual orientation, or social standing to intervene between my duty and my patient;
- I will maintain the utmost respect for human life from its beginning, even under threat, and I will not use my specialist knowledge contrary to the laws of humanity;
- I make these promises solemnly, freely, and upon my honour.[10]

The Declaration of Geneva is obviously a medical rather than paramedical testament but nonetheless it enshrines many of the principles common to all healthcare professions. The declaration, like professional ethical guidelines in all fields of healthcare, is ultimately reducible to certain elements. The key facets of practitioner-patient ethics are most frequently (if somewhat simplistically) distilled to four headings: beneficence, non-maleficence, autonomy and justice. It is important to stress that medical ethics are not static. They are as dynamic as any other areas of medicine because they must respond to changes in clinical research and treatment: for example, medical science's increased ability to keep patients alive, but on the cusp of death, or to experiment on embryos in the interest of pursuing new treatment options, raises questions of ethics with which ethics itself must learn to grapple.[11]

Beneficence

[3.07]

This is – put simply – 'doing good' or placing benefit to the patient at the forefront of clinical practice. The flip-side of beneficence – and the second element of clinical ethics – is *non-maleficence*, the imperative that one should not harm one's patients (often enshrined in the traditional axiom, *primum non nocere* – 'above all, do no harm').

Autonomy

[3.08]

This involves respecting the freedom of one's patients to make health care choices. It is the cornerstone of issues such as consent, or the withholding of consent, to treatment. A patient of adult years and sound mind is free to accept or reject any treatment option. The word 'autonomy' derives from the Greek *auto + nomos*, meaning self-law or self-control.

Justice

[3.09]

This is generally taken to mean justice in any of its forms, both individualised and generalised. In the literal sense, it means respect for the law and respecting an individual's rights (such as the right of autonomy), but in a more generalised context it also extends to the way in which medicine interacts with society. This latter conception of justice can be illustrated by considering questions of distribution: a health care budget is limited and must be spent wisely. There are questions of justice implicit in the decision-making process involved in determining how, for example, to spend the last €1m of a budgetary allocation. Is it best spent providing last-chance surgery for severely-ill cardiac patients, providing hearing screening tests for toddlers, or sending health board members on a fact-finding trip that could reshape health policy for years to come? Complex questions of distributive justice are everywhere and often involve economic and demographic modelling in order to help resolve them.[12]

The problems of priority-setting, or rationing, become more complicated as treatments become radical and expensive, with benefits that are sometimes marginal, especially if one considers the cost involved. It is often argued that, while considerations of distributive justice are obviously important in healthcare, rationing decisions should only be taken or enforced when certain criteria are met.[13] These criteria include:

- transparency: the obligation to make rationing decisions public, together with the reasons for the decision;
- reasonableness and justice of any rationing decision (easier to determine if there has been transparency);
- consistency;
- the possibility of appeal against decisions.

Balancing rights

[3.10]

No one principle or right is absolute in its scope and there is an obvious degree of overlap between the four principles listed above. Hence, there are instances where to give fullest expression to one principle of clinical ethics will mean, as a matter of necessity, doing severe injury to another principle.

> **Example 1**
>
> An adult patient of sound mind refuses a blood transfusion on the grounds that his religion forbids it. Without the transfusion, he will die. Ethically, rather than legally[14] what issues does this raise? Absolute adherence to the principle of beneficence (or non-maleficence) would mean that the doctor should not stand idly by and that, ethically speaking, treatment *must* be given to save the patient's life. But to give the transfusion will mean impinging on the patient's autonomy and his right to make his own decisions concerning his healthcare. Conversely, giving full vent to the patient's autonomy will mean the patient dying and the doctor sacrificing beneficence on the altar of autonomy.

Whole textbooks are devoted to altogether more subtle tests of one's ethical mettle than the one outlined above and it is not proposed to exhaustively review them here. Instead, this chapter will go on to focus on one element common to every declaration on the ethics of health care and a core philosophy of clinical practice that may have far-reaching legal ramifications: the issue of confidentiality.

Quick Reference Guide 3.2

The fundamental principles of medical ethics

- Ethics are not laws. They are simply shared moral beliefs that are generally not enforceable in the same way as laws.
- Statements of ethics include the Hippocratic oath and the Declaration of Geneva.
- The fundamental building blocks of ethics are fourfold: the duty to do good (beneficence), the duty not to do harm (non-maleficence), justice and a respect for a patient's autonomy.
- Justice involves basic principles of fairness but also more complex considerations of the justice involved in the distribution of limited health care resources.
- The requirements of any given ethical precept are not absolute and clinical situations may necessitate one ethical principle trumping another.

CONFIDENTIALITY

History

[3.11]

From Hippocrates in Ancient Greece:

> 'Whatsoever things I see or hear concerning the life of men, in my attendance on the sick or even apart therefrom, which ought not to be noised abroad, I will keep silence thereon, counting such things to be as sacred secrets.'

to the Declaration of Geneva:

> 'I will respect the secrets that are confided in me, even after the patient has died.'

confidentiality is crucial to the practice of medicine and its allied professions. We will see below that the exhaustive approach of Hippocrates, mandating that even secrets gleaned outside of the profession should be kept secret, is probably no longer the case in modern law, but nonetheless the requirement to maintain confidentiality is onerous. Its importance is evident: the therapeutic relationship floats upon trust and confidence. A patient who is completely open with his doctor about his past or his concerns can in turn expect her to furnish him with better medical care. In turn, the assurance of confidentiality held out by the doctor permits greater disclosure by the patient. The Irish Medical Council *Guide to Ethical Conduct and Behaviour* states the following about confidentiality:

> 'Confidentiality is a time-honoured principle of medical ethics. It extends after death and is fundamental to the doctor/patient relationship.'[15]

We need first to see how the law defines and regards confidentiality. In *Hunter v Mann*[16] an English court offered this summary of the duty of confidentiality together with an indication of the limits to that duty:

> '[I]n common with other professional men (*sic*) … the doctor is under a duty not to disclose [voluntarily], without the consent of his patient, information which he, the doctor, has gained in his professional capacity.'

In that case, police sought information from a doctor as part of an investigation into a road traffic accident. As well as outlining the general duty of confidence above, the court reasoned that in such circumstances, where it could aid in the detection of a crime, a doctor could breach confidence. The case formalised the principle that there are circumstances in which a doctor may decide or be compelled to disclose confidential information and further that the patient may consent to the doctor disclosing information that would otherwise constitute a confidence.[17] The circumstances in which confidentiality wanes or evaporates will be dealt with in due course, but first we must establish when a matter becomes confidential in the first place.

What makes something confidential?

[3.12]

Not every interaction between a doctor and patient will be deemed 'confidential'. While it might be prudent to err on the side of discretion, it is nonetheless the case that a cross-table conversation in a crowded pub between a doctor and her friend on the subject of that friend's health would probably not necessitate the same regard for confidentiality as a situation where the same friend consulted the same physician in her surgery. One judge offered the opinion – admittedly in the context of commercial secrets rather than medical confidentiality but the principle still holds true – that in order to be confidential the subject matter of any interaction must have

> '[T]he necessary quality of confidence about it, namely, it must not be something which is public property and public knowledge.'[18]

And furthermore, according to another case in the commercial field, the test of whether something is confidential is whether

> '[A] reasonable man in the shoes of the recipient of the information would have realised that … the information was being given to him in confidence.'[19]

The combination of these two excerpts yields a good working definition of what matters are confidential:

1. It must be information that is by its very nature confidential and
2. The information must be imparted in circumstances that imply confidentiality.[20]

The duty of confidentiality extends to information concerning the patient that the practitioner learns from sources other than the patient while acting in her capacity of caring for the patient.[21]

Anonymous information

Information that is not capable of identifying someone is not normally confidential. The test is not whether the information is *said* to be anonymous but whether in fact and in effect it actually *is* anonymous. Hence, anonymous data that is not capable of identifying any patient or patients may be released, processed or even sold without being a breach of confidentiality, so long as all necessary steps are taken to maximise the individual's right to privacy.[22]

However, information that is, in theory at least anonymous may still have strictures placed on its disclosure in certain circumstances. For example, to disclose information that a medical condition affects a member of a very small community (such as an inhabitant of a small village or a dentist working in a particular hospital), even without specifically identifying the individual could be tantamount to breaching confidentiality because of the ease with that individual may be identified within the restricted community.

Example 2

In one case the courts gave protection to two HIV-infected doctors when their right to privacy was threatened by newspapers.[23] The papers planned to identify the doctors or, failing that, to identify the hospitals in which they had worked as well the dates of their employment. However, the courts refused to permit this: to detail the hospitals in which the doctors had worked and when they worked there could effectively lead to their identification.

These principles apply to any clinical information obtained in confidence when an 'anonymous' form of those records might, due to the nature of the information the anonymous presentation contains, lead to the identification of patients. Information remains confidential only insofar as it has the potential to identify the patient to whom it relates

Who is bound by the duty of confidentiality?

[3.13]

Confidentiality is the patient's prerogative. A patient may, after a consultation with a doctor, go straight to the pub and discuss every detail of the consultation and nothing will result, but a doctor who did the same thing would be guilty of a breach of confidence. A practitioner cannot argue that confidentiality is bilateral, binding both her and her patient. An analogy could be made with legal or sacerdotal[24] 'privilege', the legal term to describe the fact that a consultation or confession with a lawyer or priest is exempt (or 'privileged') from being used as evidence in a courtroom. Privilege, like the confidentiality of the therapeutic relationship that binds only the doctor, does not bind the client or penitent. In the case of a 'privileged' relationship the client or the parishioner may not be compelled to testify about consulting with his lawyer or priest but if he decides to do so, there is nothing the lawyer or priest can do to muzzle him. Similarly, the cloak of confidence that covers the doctor and patient in consultation is the patient's to set aside as he wishes, in spite of the protestations of the other party that the obligation of confidentiality should cover both parties to the consultation.[25]

Note, however, that there is only an *analogy* between 'privilege' and the therapeutic relationship. The clinical encounter is not 'privileged' from being used in evidence, it is merely confidential: a court can – and usually will if it thinks it necessary – order a doctor to disclose material arising in the therapeutic context that would otherwise ordinarily be confidential if that information is relevant to court room proceedings.[26]

Where does the legal basis for confidentiality come from?

[3.14]

Confidentiality is not only rooted in ethics. The courts have confirmed – as we have seen (sections **[3.11]-[3.12]**) – that in certain circumstances there is a legally binding requirement for confidentiality and respect for privacy and that the therapeutic setting is one such circumstance. The rule has been arrived at by the courts realising that without confidentiality the practice of many aspects of commercial and professional life would be impossible, including medical care.[27] However, the requirement of confidentiality is not only based on the decisions of the courts; it has other origins too, including the Irish Constitution and Human Rights law.

The Constitution

Irish courts have recognised that a citizen has a right to privacy derived from Article 40 of the Constitution.[28] The right is not absolute. In one case[29] it was accepted that a married couple had a right to privacy within marriage, including the question of whether they used contraception, at that time illegal in the State, while in another case[30] the Courts were more willing to stray into the bedroom in the context of a homosexual relationship, also at the time illegal in the State. Nonetheless, the right to privacy and, by extension, to confidentiality is recognised by the Irish courts. In a later case that was to have political ramifications, two journalists succeeded in a legal action against the State when it emerged that the Government had bugged their telephones, thus infringing their right to privacy.[31]

Human rights law

The European Convention on Human Rights, of which Ireland is a signatory, also provides a legal grounding for privacy and confidentiality by guaranteeing a 'right to respect for … family and private life.'[32] By inference, the requirement therefore is that as a matter of human rights the practitioner should keep confidential those matters that ought to be so guarded. The convention permits failure to respect privacy where the failure is 'in accordance with the law and necessary in a democratic society'.[33]

More generally, courts have also recognised that there is a 'public interest' in trying to maximise confidence in the practitioner-patient relationship in order to maximise the benefits accruing to the therapeutic alliance between health care professionals and their clients. It is only where there is a conflicting and more pressing 'public interest' in the disclosure of medical information that over-rides the interest in confidentiality that the breach of confidence will be permitted. The concept of 'public interest' is more thoroughly examined below (in section **[3.16]**), in the context of circumstances in which confidence may be breached.

Confidentiality after death

[3.15]

It is stated, in the Irish Medical Council *Guide to Ethical Conduct and Behaviour* amongst other places,[34] that the obligation of the practitioner to maintain confidentiality extends even after the death of the patient. This is likely to be correct, but it could also be argued that the requirement for confidentiality is personal and peculiar to the individual relationship between the practitioner and the patient in question and that therefore the imperative for confidentiality dies with the patient. In the same way that only a person who is libelled may sue for libel, it may be the case that only the individual who is affected by the breach of his right to confidentiality may insist upon confidentiality or sue for any failure to preserve confidences. Therefore, after the death of the patient, there may be no one who can sue the practitioner for breaching her duty of confidence to the now deceased patient.

However, the reality is that whether the obligation on the clinician is legal or merely moral, it seems likely that a practitioner has some form of obligation to preserve confidential information about her patients after death. This is especially true where disclosure may cause foreseeable damage or distress to identifiable individuals who in turn may be the ones to take legal action to prevent or punish the breach of confidence.[35] Furthermore and even if no law is broken, it may be that the practitioner's professional body might, if it has the power to do so, take action against the practitioner for the breach of its code of professional conduct.

Quick Reference Guide 3.3

The obligation of confidentiality

- Confidentiality is enshrined in the ethics of clinical practice but it is also a legal obligation.
- A matter is confidential when it concerns information that is, by its very nature, confidential and is transmitted in circumstances that suggest a desire for confidentiality.
- Confidentiality extends not only to what the patient tells the practitioner but also to information the practitioner receives from other sources when acting as the patient's health carer.
- Confidentiality in Ireland is based on the decisions of the courts, the Irish Constitution and Human Rights law.
- The legal recognition of confidentiality in the therapeutic relationship binds only the practitioner, not the patient.
- The requirement to maintain confidentiality towards the patient extends, in theory at least, even after the death of the patient.

Breaching confidentiality

Consent

[3.16]

The most important caveat to the overarching requirement of confidentiality is that if a patient consents to the release of confidential information then the clinician may legitimately disclose the relevant information without breaching confidentiality. Consent removes the obligation of confidence.

Two important things should be borne in mind:

1. It should be clearly understood between the practitioner and patient precisely what information is to be released.
2. The consent of the patient should be documented in writing wherever possible and signed by the patient. This confirms the facts and extent of the consent should any subsequent disagreement arise.

Oral consent to the disclosure of information is just as binding on the patient as written consent, but should the patient later deny the fact or extent of the consent it may be difficult to prove that the patient did in fact consent to the release of the confidential information. Written consent is always preferable.[36]

There is often a presumption that consent to disclosure between health professionals is automatic when a patient is under the care of more than one clinician, as is the case with multidisciplinary care. However, there is also an argument that – even within such a team arrangement – the patient's consent should be sought for any disclosure of confidential information. The question of inter-professional communication concerning a patient whose care is being shared by more than one clinician is not explicitly dealt with in the various codes of conduct of the Irish health professions. It could be assumed that inter-disciplinary communications are exempt from the normal rules on confidentiality because they are deemed to be in 'the interest of the patient', but it is interesting to note that the UK General Medical Council is more circumspect on this subject than its Irish counterparts:

> '[Doctors] must make sure that patients are informed whenever information about them is likely to be disclosed to others involved in their health care, and that they have the opportunity to withhold permission.'[37]

Breaching confidentiality without consent

[3.17]

The circumstances where a practitioner may disclose confidential information in the absence of consent from the patient are conveniently set out in the Irish Medical Council *Guide to Ethical Conduct and Behaviour*:[38]

> 'There are four circumstances where exception may be made in the absence of permission from the patient:
>
> 1. When ordered by a judge in a Court of Law, or by a Tribunal established by an Act of the Oireachtas.
> 2. When necessary to protect the interest of the patient.
> 3. When necessary to protect the welfare of Society.
> 4. When necessary to safeguard the welfare of another individual or patient.'

Questions of disclosure of confidential information in the absence of patient consent involve considerations of 'public interest'. It is in the 'public interest' that practitioner-patient confidentiality exists, but it is also in the public interest that there are times when that confidentiality should be overridden. Public interest considerations frequently involve a balancing act: there is a strong public interest in maintaining the integrity of the practitioner-patient relationship, but there are also legitimate, strong and ultimately competing imperatives. The rule of law, the preservation of life and limb or the integrity of the fabric of society may be of such great public interest as to require the disclosure of information that would otherwise be confidential. We examine below the individual circumstances in which this public interest modification to the obligation of confidentiality arises.

The area is complicated by the absence of a precise legal definition of 'public interest'. English courts have, by way of some definition, pointed out that 'there is a wide difference between what is interesting to the public and what it is in the public interest to make known'.[39] The fact that a tabloid newspaper's readers would be interested in reading about the health records of a Hollywood star does not generally amount to sufficient public interest to justify disclosure of otherwise confidential information, no matter what the editors of such periodicals might argue.[40]

It is worth looking in turn at each of the exceptions to confidentiality as enumerated in the Medical Council *Guide*. It also worth pointing out that, even where a patient articulates an express prohibition against the disclosure of any information, the exceptions below, sensibly and cautiously applied, would still operate to override that express prohibition. Because the starting point of the law is that confidentiality is to be maintained wherever possible, it is argued that an express prohibition against disclosure by a patient really adds very little to the status quo.

Exception one - the operation of law

[3.18]

Once a legal action is in progress, a doctor can be compelled to testify or to release information, notwithstanding the fact that the information is confidential. Even prior to any action being taken, it may be necessary for solicitors to have access to notes in order to ascertain whether there is a potentially successful case, so as not to pursue a fruitless action. Once a case is initiated, solicitors may then seek wider access to notes and records including records belonging to health care practitioners who are not directly involved in the legal action. The name for the legal process of securing documents is "discovery". Also during the investigation of a crime, it is likely that the need to identify the perpetrators may also undermine a clinician's assertions of confidentiality. That was certainly the opinion of the court in *Hunter v Mann,4*[1] where the police sought the doctor's records as an aid in the detection of the culprit in a road traffic offence. The conclusion of the court was that the balance of the competing public interests lay in favour of disclosure to achieve the ends of the legal system.

Another example of disclosure compelled by law can be found in the Infectious Diseases Regulations, that place a duty on doctors to relay information to the public health authorities upon diagnosing certain 'notifiable' diseases. This notification will usually include the identity of the patient, but is not a breach of confidence because it is obligated by law.[42]

Exception two - protecting the interests of the patient

[3.19]

Precisely where the 'interests of the patient' lie is not always clear. If a patient does not want information about him disclosed, even in his own interest, then that refusal should generally be respected. One example where confidentiality might be breached in such circumstances might be where a person – child or adult – is being abused and the person, if capable of consenting,[43] may be so far under a spell of fear or duress that they will not consent to disclose of the abuse. In such cases, especially concerning children,[44] disclosure of the confidential information would be justified. Of course, if would also be possible to justify such disclosure in the interest of society (there is a strong public interest in stopping domestic or sexual abuse).

Exception three - when necessary to protect the interests of society

[3.20]

Again the elements of the balancing act are present. Picture the physician who becomes aware that an airline pilot patient is suffering from alcoholism or epilepsy and is continuing to work. What should the doctor do? The fact of the risk to passengers could justify the doctor relaying his concerns to the airline's occupational physician[45] who could then take appropriate action.

In the English case *W v Egdell,*[46] a psychiatrist was asked to review a patient regarding an application for early release. The psychiatrist found that the patient, who was in gaol for murdering five people and wounding two others, could not in the psychiatrist's opinion be safely released, not least because of his ongoing enthusiasm for explosives and firearms. The prisoner's solicitors prudently decided in the light of the damning report not to proceed with the application for early release. Concerned that his report was not to be utilised and that the psychiatric history that he had elicited (some of which had not been previously noted) could be effectively buried, he communicated his concerns to the prison doctor and asked that the report be passed onto the Home Secretary (who in the United Kingdom has ultimate authority regarding early releases).

The patient in *Egdell* sued the doctor for a breach of the confidentiality he claimed was owed to him by the psychiatrist. The judges took a society-centred view of 'public interest' and summed up the balancing act that must take place before disclosure of confidential information can be countenanced:

> 'Although the basis of the law's protection of confidence is that there is a public interest that confidences should be preserved and protected by the law, nevertheless that public interest may be outweighed by some other countervailing public interest which favours disclosure.'

Accordingly in this case, the court felt that the real threat posed to society by the potential release of the prisoner and the fact that the identified threat was not communicated by the prisoner's solicitors, justified Dr Egdell's decision to release the information to the appropriate responsible bodies.

There was one other key element justifying disclosure in *Egdell*, namely the fact that the release of the information was restricted in scope and sent only to the relevant authorities. If confidentiality is to be breached, the doctor should be cautious about how widely the confidential information is circulated: it should only be disseminated to those who 'need to know'. In one case[47] a New Zealand doctor was concerned about the fitness of a bus driver to drive. He not only requested of the relevant authorities that the man's licence be withdrawn, but also took the drastic step of warning the man's passengers of the risk they were running in travelling with his patient. The court found that this was too radical a breach of confidentiality:

> '[A] doctor who has decided to communicate [confidential information] should discriminate and ensure the recipient is a responsible authority.'[48]

Exception four - safeguarding the welfare of another individual

[3.21]

The Irish Medical Council Guidelines address one specific area in which the necessity of protecting other individuals may warrant the disclosure of confidential information: where a patient has a communicable disease and there is an risk to another identifiable person.

> 'If a spouse or partner is thought to be at risk, the doctor should strongly seek the patient's permission for disclosure. If this is refused, depending on the circumstances of the illness, the doctor is justified in informing the spouse or partner.'[49]

Accordingly, a patient with HIV who is sexually active with an identifiable partner and who has not informed his partner of the risk should be counselled by the doctor regarding his illness and its potential consequences. If the patient will not tell his partner or consent to disclosure (for upon consent to disclosure, the potential for breach of confidentiality evaporates and the doctor may tell the partner), then the doctor may be justified in liaising with the patient's partner to appraise him or her of the situation.[50]

The Data Protection Act 1988 and the Data Protection Directive 1995 also have built-in provisions to permit the disclosure of otherwise confidential personal information 'where required urgently to prevent injury or other damage to the health of a person'.[51] This hints at a wider legal approval for the kind of disclosure suggested by the Medical Council Guide.

There has been no Irish decision on this subject, but in the United States, the situation of disclosure of confidential information to prevent a risk of harm to an individual has been litigated in *Tarasoff v Regents of the University of California.*[52] A student in Berkeley University had confessed to a College-appointed psychologist that he harboured feelings of hatred and violence towards a student named Tarasoff. The psychologist did not take any steps to intervene by attempting to communicate with the female student herself. The patient subsequently shot and killed the girl. Her family sued the psychologist and the University and the court found in favour of the family, saying:

> 'If the exercise of reasonable care to protect the threatened victim requires the therapist to warn the endangered party or those who can be reasonably expected to notify him, we see no sufficient societal interest that would protect and justify concealment. The containment of such risks lies in the public interest.'

The key elements of warning a person at risk are twofold: the person who is at risk should be identifiable and the risk itself should be one of grave physical harm. Does a decision such as that in the *Tarasoff* case amount to a "duty" on the health professional to disclose confidential information in circumstances where she is aware of a risk posed by her patient? The issue has not been legally decided, but it may be that a practitioner who became aware that her patient A, was intending to kill B and did not breach confidentiality in order to prevent that death, could be guilty of negligence. It is hard to be certain however. The question of whether a doctor owes a duty to breach confidentiality in the interests of a third party other than her patient probably depends in part on whether or not any action of the doctor contributes to, causes or increases the risk to the third party[53] as well as whether the person likely to affected by the actions of a patient is identifiable.[54]

Quick Reference Guide 3.4

Breaching confidentiality

- If a patient consents to the release of information, that automatically relieves the practitioner of her obligation to maintain confidentiality in respect of that information. However, she may only reveal the information that the patient permits to be disclosed and only to the entity to which the patient wishes it released.
- If a patient does consent to the release of otherwise confidential information, that consent should be recorded in writing.
- Best practice suggests that the consent of the patient should be obtained for the sharing of information between professionals who co-operate in the care of a patient. Although such consent may be implied, it may be preferable to explain to a patient that his care may involve the sharing of information and to offer him the opportunity to withhold his consent to the sharing of that information.
- If a patient does not consent to the disclosure of confidential information then the practitioner may in certain circumstances disclose the information *without consent*. The test for justifying disclosure is whether the public interest inherent in the integrity of the therapeutic relationship is outweighed by a public interest compelling disclosure.
- In general there are four recognised situations where disclosure of confidential information is readily defensible:
  - (i) Where a law or a court demands the disclosure
  - (ii) Where the disclosure protects the interests of the patient himself
  - (iii) Where a disclosure protects the welfare of Society
  - (iv) Where necessary to safeguard the welfare of another individual or patient
- A risk to society or to another individual posed by a patient must be grave and realistic if it is to provide grounds for the breach of confidentiality.
- If a serious risk is posed to an individual by a patient, and the identity of the person at risk is known, the doctor may be under a *duty* to the person at risk to breach her obligation of confidentiality. In any event she will be justified in doing so on the basis of the risk posed to society and the individual.
- If disclosure of confidential information is made, it should be made to as few people as are necessary to achieve the aims of the disclosure. Oral consent to disclosure is also valid, but written consent is preferable.

Legal remedies for breach of confidence

[3.22]

It has been suggested that a doctor who breaches her duty of confidentiality may be guilty of negligence. In a New Zealand case, *Furniss v Fitchet,*[55] the court reasoned that a doctor's duty to a patient 'must extend also to the exercise of care in deciding whether [confidential information] should be put in circulation in such a way that it is likely to cause to harm to another.' If a doctor's duty of care to his patient is interpreted in that way, then perhaps the clinician who breaches confidence *could* be sued for negligence, but this is rare. It is certainly possible that an act of a doctor, for example leaving files in a public place where they may be seen by others, could be negligence. Quite aside from questions of negligence, the practitioner owes a broad-based equitable duty[56] to the patient not to disclose confidential information and it is on this equitable ground that the patient would generally seek redress.

A person likely to be affected by a breach of confidentiality may seek an 'injunction', a legal remedy that prevents the defendant (if the person bringing the action is successful) from continuing with an ongoing or proposed course of action. In *X v Y*,[57] newspapers proposing to identify HIV positive doctors were prevented from doing so by an injunction forbidding publication. Of course, if the practitioner has already breached confidentiality, the damage may already be done and an injunction is of little practical use. If the action is not imminent or has already taken place, the individual may also ask the court for a 'declaration' that the action would be, or was, an unlawful course of action. If the breach has not taken place, such a declaration, like an injunction, would prevent it from occurring. If it has taken place, the declaration would prevent repetition and may allow for the award of damages subsequently.

The damages available to the victim of a breach of confidence may be limited, but there would be grounds for the patient to seek financial compensation for the distress or injured feelings caused by the breach of confidentiality. Certainly any financial loss, for example, loss of business, could be compensated, but the precise degree to which embarrassment or distress may be recognised by the court for breach of confidence will always variable. In Ireland, there is no legislation specifically catering for embarrassment occasioned by a breach of confidence: such compensation could be awarded, but it is impossible to be certain of the amount. In England the Law Commission report on Breach of Confidence[58] recommended that damages for mental stress caused specifically by a betrayal of confidence should be available, but there has been no formal law introduced.

The effect of legislation on confidentiality

[3.23]

There are many legislative instruments that impinge on medical records, including the Data Protection Act 1988 and the Data Protection Directive 1995 and the Freedom of Information Act 1997. In general, while these laws are often dealt with under the heading of confidentiality, in reality their effect on confidentiality is minimal because they are generally explicit and careful in enshrining confidentiality. They will be dealt with in the chapter on prescription writing and clinical records.[59]

Endnotes

1 See *The Irish Health System in the 21st Century*, Leahy and Wiley (eds.) (1998).

2 See ch 4, *Consent*.

3 How long notes should be preserved is not clear. As will be seen in ch 7, *Clinical Negligence*, there is a limit to how long a patient may wait before bringing a legal action. In general, keeping notes for seven to ten years after the patient was last seen would probably be acceptable, but there are certain cases (for example, surgeons, where the consequences of surgery may not become apparent to the patient for many years) where notes may need to be maintained for longer.

4 Even if the parties to the contract do not draw up a formal document. The patient pays directly or indirectly (through taxes) and the doctor undertakes to care for the patient: see *Sidaway v Governors of Royal Bethlem Royal Hospital* [1985] AC 871 at 904.

5 Examined in greater detail in ch 7, *Professional Negligence*.

6 Especially in Canada – see *McInerney v McDonald* (1992) 93 DLR (4th) 415.

7 Although bodies such as the Medical and Dental Councils and Bord Altranais can police the ethical lapses through their Fitness to Practise Committees, the power to do so does not come from the ethics they are upholding, but from the laws that created the Councils and Board. See ch. 2 The healthcare professions and the healthcare system.

8 Sritharan K et al 'Medical oaths and declarations', editorial article BMJ 2001;323:1440-1441.

9 While swearing an oath or making a formal declaration is rarely a part of Irish graduation ceremonies, in the United States 98% of medical schools swear some form of oath: see Cranshaw 'The Hippocratic oath' BMJ 1994; 309:952. The oath taken or declaration made is most commonly a modified Hippocratic oath, but the Declaration of Geneva is also common.

10 World Medical Association. Declaration of Geneva. London: WMA, 1995.

11 See Singer 'Recent advances in Medical ethics' BMJ 2000; 321:282-285.

12 See *R v Cambridge Health Authority, ex p B* [1995] 2 All ER 129. In this case, a child was refused a course of chemotherapy by the Health Authority on the grounds that the benefit that would be obtained, bearing in mind both the likely clinical outcome and the cost of the treatment, would be minimal and would be in contravention of rationing guidelines. The family appealed the decision of the Health Authority to the court, which pointed out:

> 'I have no doubt that in a perfect world any treatment which a patient, or a patient's family, sought would be provided if doctor were willing to give it, no matter how much it cost, particularly when a life was potentially at stake. It would however, in my view, be shutting one's eyes to the real world if the court were to proceed on the basis that we do live in such a world. It is common knowledge that health authorities of all kinds are constantly pressed to make ends meet.'

13 Daniels 'The ethics of accountability in managed care reform' Sabin Health Aff 1998; 17, 50-64; Syrett 'Nice Work? Rationing, Review and the "Legitimacy Problem" in the New NHS' (2002) 10 Med LR 1.

14 As will be seen in ch 4, an adult patient of sound mind who finds himself in this position would generally be free to refuse treatment, notwithstanding the fact that he would die.

15 *Guide to Ethical Conduct and Behaviour* (5th edn, 1998) para 18.1. The ethical guidelines of dentistry, nursing, physiotherapy, occupational therapy and radiography enshrine a similar approach.

16 *Hunter v Mann* [1974] QB 767.

17 In Northern Ireland there is a legal obligation on doctors to disclose information where they believe that a patient they have treated may have been involved in criminal – and particularly terrorist – activity: Criminal Law Act (NI) 1967, s 5(1); Prevention of Terrorism (Temporary Provisions) Act 1976.

18 *Saltman Engineering Co v Campbell Engineering Co* (1948) 65 RPC 203 at 251.

19 *Coco v AN Clark (Engineering) Ltd* [1969] RPC 41.

20 This tallies with English case law: see *AG v Guardian Newspapers* [1988] 3 All ER 545, per Lord Goff.

> '[A] duty of confidence arises when confidential information comes to the knowledge of a person (the confidant) in circumstances where he has notice, or is held to have agreed, that the information is confidential, with the effect that it would be just in all the circumstances that he should be precluded from disclosing the information to others' [italics added].

21 Gurry, *Breach of Confidence* (1984) pp 148-149.

22 *R v Department of Health, ex p Source Informatics Ltd* [2000] 1 All ER 786.

23 *X v Y* [1988] 2 All ER 648. English courts have recently reiterated this approach to 'confidential' information: *H (A Healthcare Worker) v Associated Newspaters Limited and N (A Health Authority)* [2002] EWCA Civ 195, judgment of 27 February 2002.

24 'Sacerdotal' means related to the priesthood.

25 *Johnson v Church of Scientology* (30 April 1999, unreported), HC (Geoghegan J).

26 It is interesting to note that the Eleventh Report from the UK Criminal Law Revision Committee (1972) considered recommending that the doctor-patient relationship should be made legally privileged, however the idea was rejected and the Committee stated that:

> 'For example it would be a scandal if a criminal who had been injured when blowing a safe or committing a robbery could prevent the doctor who had attended him from revealing what the criminal told him about how he came by his injury.'.

They did contemplate extending privilege to psychiatrists alone, but in the end the idea was shelved.

27 *W v Egdell* [1990] 1 All ER 835.

28 Article 40 of the Constitution refers to the 'personal rights' of the citizens, without saying precisely what those rights are. The Courts have decided that, amongst other things, 'personal rights' include a right to privacy.

29 *McGee v Attorney General* [1974] IR 284.

30 *Norris v Attorney General* [1984] IR 36 .

31 *Kennedy v Ireland* [1987] IR 587.

32 ECHR, art 8(1).

33 ECHR, art 8(2): see *Z v Finland* (1997) 45 BMLR 107.

34 *Guide to Ethical Conduct and Behaviour* (5th edn 1998) para 18.1; the requirement is also in the Declaration of Geneva. The UK General Medical Council takes a similar approach: see *Confidentiality: Protecting and Providing Information* (2000), paras 40-42. There are obvious situations that involve breaching confidentiality after death, such as notifying a coroner or registering a death.

35 See Kennedy & Grubb *Medical Law* (3rd edn, 2000), pp 1081-3 for a discussion of this area. There is also the question of whether the clinician – or more properly the clinician's successors (her children or a person taking possession of the building that housed her consulting rooms) – owes a duty to maintain confidentiality after the *clinician's* death. The answer appears to be that anyone who comes into possession of clinical notes and knows or ought to know that there is a duty of confidentiality owed in respect of those notes will be under some measure of duty to preserve that confidentiality. The situation will be simple when a practitioner takes over the practice of a deceased colleague, but may be more complex if the contents of the practice fall into the hands of a non-clinician. Very often the insurer of the deceased (which will probably be the entity liable for any claims made against the deceased) should be contacted.

36 See ch 4, *Consent*.

37 *Confidentiality: Protecting and Providing Information* (2000) paras 8-9.

38 (5th edn, 1998) para 18.3.

39 *British Steel Corporation v Granada Television Ltd* [1981] 1 All ER 417 at 455 per Lord Wilberforce.

40 A fact recently confirmed by an English High Court case: *Naomi Campbell v Vanessa Frisbee* [2002] EWHC 328, judgement delivered 14th March 2002.

41 *Hunter v Mann* [1974] QB 767 (see para **[3.11]**).

42 Made pursuant to Health Act 1947, s 29.

43 See ch 4, *Consent* for a discussion of the ability of minors to consent to medical interventions (which would include the release of confidential information).

44 *Re C (A minor) (Evidence: Confidential Information)* (1991) 7 BMLR 138.

45 For an account of the sometimes awkward role of occupational physician when it comes to confidentiality, see ch 9, *The Practitioner in the Workplace*.

46 *W v Egdell* [1990] 1 All ER 835.

47 *Duncan v Medical Practitioners' Disciplinary Committee* [1986] 1 NZLR 513.

48 See also ch 17, *The Practitioner and the Driver* which covers the question of how a doctor should deal with a patient whom she realises is driving in defiance of medical advice.

49 *Medical Council Guide to Ethical Conduct and Behaviour* (5th edn, 1998) para 18.14.

50 A similar situation may arise where a doctor becomes aware, in a professional and therefore confidential setting, that a colleague is suffering from a condition or addiction that might impinge on her ability to practice medicine. In such cases, the doctor who became aware of that information would probably be justified in communicating the facts to the Fitness to Practice Committee of the Medical Council, assuming that attempts to get the affected doctor to seek help or to modify her practice had failed.

51 Data Protection Act 1988, s 8. See ch 6, *Clinical Records and Prescribing* for more detail on data protection legislation and freedom of information laws.

52 *Tarasoff v Regents of the University of California* (1976) 131 Cal Rptr 14.

53 In *Reisner v Regents of the University of California* (1995) 31 Cal App 4th 1110, a doctor discovered that blood he had given his patient Jennifer was HIV positive. He did not tell her. She went on to be involved in a sexual relationship with Daniel Reisner. Two years later the doctor told her she had AIDS. She died and her boyfriend subsequently discovered that he was HIV positive. He successfully sued the doctor for his negligence in not having protected him by telling him or Jennifer that she was HIV positive so that they could minimise any risk of transmission.

54 An English Court felt that it would not be possible to hold a doctor liable for an attack carried out on someone by a patient unless the potential victim is identifiable: *Palmer v Tees Health Authority* [1999] Lloyd's L Rep (Med) 351 (CA). One might conclude that, in English law, the doctor is similarly not under a duty to disclose confidential information regarding the potential risk unless the victim is identifiable. The situation is probably the same in Irish law.

55 *Furniss v Fitchett* [1958] NZLR 396.

56 A term used to describe a legal obligation that will be upheld by the court in the interests of fairness (or 'equity').

57 *X v Y* [1988] 2 All ER 648, see example 2, section **[3.12]**.

58 LRC, Breach of Confidence (LRC no 110).

59 See ch 6, *Clinical Records and Prescribing*.

Chapter 4

Consent

Introduction

[4.01]

Consent is one of the most important issues in clinical practice. If a clinician examines, treats or operates upon a person without that person's consent in a situation where consent could and should have been obtained, then the doctor is committing an unlawful act. The law starts from the fundamental premise that almost all touching of another person is unlawful and that consent is required to make that contact, which may be anything from a surgical operation to a football tackle, lawful. Consent to a football tackle will generally be inferred from the fact that the individual chooses to take part in a game of football, but it is the more precise and legally consequential world of consent to medical and surgical procedures, together with its flip-side of the refusal of treatment, that forms the subject matter of this chapter.

Consent can come in different guises: it may be 'express', which is to say positively affirmed orally or in writing, or it may be 'implied' by the conduct or silence of the person whose consent is required. There may be times when obtaining consent is not possible and therefore less necessary, such as in emergency scenarios where a patient is *in extremis* or unconscious. There may also be times when consent, although actually given by the patient, was based on incomplete or inaccurate information, thereby raising the question, of whether consent in such circumstances is really consent at all?

The three ingredients of consent, all of which will be dealt with in greater detail below, are that:

1. It must be given (or withheld) voluntarily;[1]
2. It must be given (or withheld) by an individual who has the legal capacity, in terms of age and mental competence, to do so;
3. Any decision relating to the giving or withholding of consent should be based on sufficient relevant information.

This last ingredient – 'sufficient relevant information' – is an especially vexed issue and one woven into the fabric of the rather abstract concept of 'informed consent'. As we will see when we look at informed consent below, the question of precisely what is 'sufficient' and what is 'relevant' and who sets the standard for the quality of information to be imparted to a patient is not always easy to resolve.

Why is consent necessary?

[4.02]

One of the most celebrated US judges summed up the need to obtain a patient's consent to treatment when he said:

> 'Every human being of adult years and sound mind has a right to determine what shall be done with his own body; and a surgeon who performs an operation without the patient's consent commits an assault.'[2]

Although the case was heard back in 1914, this statement remains good law and is regularly mentioned with approval by modern judges when determining questions of consent. In essence, giving a person medical treatment without his consent is unlawful. The precise scale of the offence will depend on the nature of what is done, but it is easy to see how, for example, sticking a needle or scalpel into someone without his consent could be viewed in a very dim light indeed.

The argument for consent as an indispensable precursor to treatment is born out of the concept of patient autonomy, which in turn is based upon the rights of individual self-determination and of bodily integrity.[3] Once we accept that a person has a right to autonomy then the opportunity for others, including clinicians acting in discharge of their clinical duties, to interfere with that right is curtailed. It is consent that makes it legal for a person to encroach upon another person's bodily integrity. It would obviously be unlawful for a person, whether or not she was a clinician, to walk down the road and, without permission, to jab a needle into everyone she encountered, even if the needle contained a beneficial vaccine. But when a patient attends his doctor seeking vaccinations and gives consent to the administration of the relevant injections, the act of sticking a needle into that person is no longer unlawful.

Rights, however, are not absolute. The right of liberty, for example, is curtailed by laws that say one person is not free to deprive another of his possessions or to kill him and that, if one does so, one may be subject to punishment, even to imprisonment (itself an obvious constraint upon liberty). Similarly, autonomy is not an absolute right. Much of the law regarding consent is a balancing act between the rights of the patient to decide and the need of the medical profession to try to serve the best interests of its patients. Where there is a clash, for example when a child requires an operation and the parents withhold consent, then the law may step in.

The consequences of acting without consent

[4.03]

If touching a person without his permission is unlawful, it follows that the doctor who touches a patient without consent is breaching the law. But what law is being breached? If consent is not obtained from a patient, then the patient has one of two legal actions open to him: battery or negligence, although it is the latter that has come to predominate in the law courts of Ireland and other countries with similar legal systems.[4]

Battery

Battery is a 'tort' and a tort is in turn a legal wrong or disagreement that typically arises between private individuals or between companies.[5] Battery occurs when there is an *intentional harmful or offensive contact with the person of another individual without consent or other lawful justification.* A crucial element in the definition is that the offensive contact is sufficient: no harm need result. If a surgeon operates on an individual with perfect skill and a textbook outcome, her dexterity and success are to no avail if no valid consent was obtained prior to commencing the operation. A battery has been committed and the surgeon may be liable for damages.

Negligence

The second and more common, legal possibility is that the practitioner who proceeds without valid consent to an intervention can be sued for negligence which is also a tort. As with battery, the actual conduct of the operation or treatment need not be negligent in any way: simply failing to obtain the required consent is enough to amount to negligence.

Why negligence rather than battery?

In theory then, any failure to obtain consent could result in a charge of battery, but in reality, courts in Ireland[6.] have taken a policy decision that failure to obtain consent is negligence rather than battery.[7] The reasons for preferring a negligence-based approach to a battery-based approach are many, but they include the fact that finding a doctor guilty of battery may appear to criminalise her when in fact no truly criminal act has taken place. Accusations of battery are reserved)if hey are levied at all) for situations where there has been an extreme failure to obtain consent from the patient or where the doctor deliberately and/or fundamentally misled the patient as to the nature or purpose of the intervention in question.[8]

WITHHOLDING CONSENT

[4.04]

A patient does not have to consent if he does not want to. Flowing from the principles of autonomy and self-determination is the intuitive corollary that a patient 'of sound mind and adult years' capable of giving consent to a given treatment is similarly free to refuse his consent to the same treatment. This is true even if the decision appears irrational to the onlooker. One Canadian judge memorably summed up the potentially far-reaching consequences of such a right: '*The patient has a right to be wrong*[9].' [italics in original]

In the English case of *Re T (adult: refusal of treatment)* the court had to consider the decision of a woman who, for reasons ostensibly rooted in her childhood faith as a Jehovah's Witness, declined a blood transfusion. The court reasoned that the patient's

> '...right of choice is not limited to decisions which others might regard as sensible. It exists notwithstanding that the reasons for making the choice are rational, irrational, unknown or even non-existent.'[10]

Although in that case the court found that the woman had come under undue influence from her mother, which meant that her refusal was not valid, the message was reiterated in starker form by another judge in that same case:

> 'Competent adults... are generally at liberty to refuse medical treatment *even at the risk of death*.'[11][italics added]

Withholding consent in Ireland

[4.05]

In Ireland, the right to refuse medical treatment is enshrined in the 'unenumerated' rights protected by the State under the Constitution[12] and which have been held to include a right to bodily integrity[13]. The approach to consent in Ireland is similar to that adopted by English and Canadian law, and has been most clearly stated as follows:

> 'The consent which is given by an adult of full capacity is a matter of choice. It is not necessarily a decision based on medical considerations. Thus, medical treatment may be refused for other than medical reasons or reasons most citizens would not regard as rational, but the person of full age and capacity may make the decision for their own reasons.'[14]

In essence then, voluntary refusal of medical treatment by an adult of sound mind and in possession of all the relevant information is generally final. As will be seen below, different concerns can come into play in the case of the withholding of consent by minors and those who are not 'of sound mind'. The right to withhold consent also generally includes the right to change one's mind and to withdraw consent previously given: "consent should be considered as a process, not an event, and it is important that there is continuing discussion to reflect the evolving nature of treatment".[15]

GIVING CONSENT

[4.06]

Consent can be given in such a way that it is 'implied' or 'express'. There is no difference in their legal value: implied consent is just as valid as express consent, in the same way that oral consent is just as valid as consent obtained in writing. The difference, as with the difference between written and oral consent, is a matter of proof. It can sometimes be hard to be certain that someone is, in fact, giving implied consent to a course of action. Wherever possible, consent should be both express and in writing.

Implied consent

[4.07]

If a patient attends his doctor with an ailment and undergoes an examination, it would generally be *implied* that he was consenting to be examined and, if appropriate, to be treated or in other words that 'actions speak louder than words'. A clinician does not generally have to get the patient to sign a consent form for a routine examination or investigation (such as the taking of a temperature) because the consent of the patient will be implied by his actions.

> **Example 1**
>
> A good illustration of implied consent is found in the case *O'Brien v Cunard SS Co.*[16] Emigrants to the United States underwent vaccination against smallpox before disembarkation and one woman who had been inoculated during a voyage subsequently sued for damages resulting from alleged battery. The court found that in queuing up to be vaccinated and holding out her arm to be examined and inoculated, she had given her implied consent and therefore could not claim to have suffered battery.

Consent can also be implied in situations where treatment is a matter of extreme urgency. If a person is unconscious and bleeding heavily, there may not be time to enquire whether for any reasons, such as religious conviction, he is implacably opposed to blood transfusions and in such cases consent to intervention can typically be implied.

Similarly, during an operation, it may become clear that an unanticipated problem has arisen[17] that necessitates immediate treatment. In such circumstances, courts are prepared to accept that there was *implied* consent to the additional procedure. The Canadian case of *Mohr v Williams*[18] discussed in broad overview the issue of when consent may be implied in the unconscious patient.

> 'If a person should be injured to the extent of rendering him unconscious, and his injuries were of such a nature as to require prompt surgical attention, a physician called to attend him would be justified in applying such medical or surgical treatment as might be reasonably necessary for the preservation of his life or limb, and consent on the part of the injured person would be implied. And again, if in the course of an operation to which the patient consented, the physician should discover conditions not anticipated before the operation was commenced and which, if not removed, would endanger the life or health of the patient, he would, though no express consent was obtained or given, be justified in extending the operation to remove and overcome them.'

Limits to implied consent – necessity versus convenience

[4.08]

Mohr v Williams is instructive as to the limitations of implied consent. The patient went into hospital for surgery to her right ear, but at the beginning of the operation an examination disclosed that her right ear was in fact normal and no operation was necessary. However, her left ear turned out to be diseased and the surgeon proceeded to operate upon it without waking the patient to inform her of the change of plan. She sued him for battery[20] and succeeded. The court drew a crucial distinction that is important and of lasting validity: there is a vital difference between a 'necessary' intervention and a 'convenient' one.

A court will be quicker to accept that a patient gave his implied consent to a procedure performed while he was unconscious if the intervention was *necessary* rather than merely *convenient*. Compare two contrasting cases: in the first example, a surgeon performing a routine operation noted that the patient had a gangrenous testicle and, without waking the patient, proceeded to remove it.[21] In another case, a surgeon performing Caesarean section also performed a tubal ligation, permanently sterilising her.[22] In the first case, the surgeon could successfully argue – and the court agreed – that the intervention was necessary. In the second case, the sterilisation was merely convenient: there was no necessity for the surgeon to proceed. The woman could have undergone the operation another time, when her consent could have been properly obtained. Consent can only be implied in the unconscious patient for *necessary* interventions

Express consent

[4.09]

Express consent is explicit agreement on the part of the patient with the course of action that is being proposed. It can be given orally, but the preferable method of securing express consent is in writing and often through the medium of the 'consent form'. Different consent forms have different wording depending on the specific context in which they are used, but there are certain common features:

- the name and other personal details of the patient;
- the nature of the intervention to be performed;
- a confirmation that the nature of the intervention has been explained and that any of the patient's questions concerning the procedure have been answered;
- in the case of operations performed in public (and occasionally in private) hospitals there is sometimes a caveat that the operation may not be performed by any particular surgeon;
- a statement that the patient consents to such additional procedures as may be thought necessary during the main intervention;
- space for both the patient and doctor to sign.

Signing a consent form is not the end of the matter. Simply having a patient sign a form which states that 'the effect and nature of the operation have been explained to me' may be worthless if the effect and nature of the procedure have not in fact been properly explained to the patient. The English courts have properly warned against scenarios where the consent is 'expressed in form only and not in reality'.[23] The explanation must be adequate and the patient must understand the explanation. The question of how thorough any explanation must be is dealt with below in the context of informed consent (section **[4.20]** *ff.*)

Limits to express consent

[4.10]

If express consent is given, then what are its limits? If a patient signs a consent form that includes a clause to the effect that he agrees to 'such further or alternative measures as may be found necessary', is the patient signing away all his rights and giving open-ended consent to the clinician to do whatever she wishes? The answer very much depends on the scale and nature of any collateral act carried out under the umbrella of the original consent.

In one Canadian case,[24] the court felt that consenting to a muscle biopsy and 'such further or alternative measures as may be found necessary' gave the surgeon enough latitude also to take a small bone biopsy after noticing a small area of diseased bone adjacent to the area of the muscle biopsy. In another Canadian case, the court found that consent to a laparoscopy[25] also included consent to the snipping of adhesions.[26] However, if a problem differing substantially from the original procedure to which consent was given and not requiring urgent intervention were identified, then the surgeon would be required 'to consult further with the patient and obtain further consent to the major operation.'[27]

Express consent given orally is just as valid as written consent. The problem with oral consent, however, is that it is much more difficult to prove in retrospect that the consent was ever given, so that if, for example, a patient denies having given consent or has died and is therefore not able to testify to having consented, difficulties may arise. The practical approach therefore should be to seek to obtain consent in writing wherever possible. If that is not possible, then there should be witnesses to the oral consent and those witnesses should attest in writing to the fact that oral consent was given.

Quick Reference Guide 4.1

The basics of consent

- There are three elements to consent and they must all be present for any consent to be valid. The consent must be:
  (i) voluntary,
  (ii) given by someone with the capacity (in terms of age and mental competence) to give it, and
  (iii) based on sufficient information.
- If a practitioner touches a patient without consent she may be, in theory, guilty of battery and, in practice, guilty of negligence.
- A person who is capable of giving consent is also capable of withholding consent. A decision by a competent patient to refuse treatment is binding on those who wish to treat the patient even if the decision is one they do not agree with or is made for irrational reasons. *The patient has a right to be wrong.*
- Consent can be 'express' (generally in writing) or implied (generally by conduct or when a patient is unconscious). Both forms of consent are equally binding, but it is easier to prove whether a patient consented when the decision is recorded in writing.
- Merely signing a consent form does not necessarily amount to valid consent: the patient must understand the subject matter of the consent form if the consent is to be both voluntary and informed.
- Consent to a given procedure, for example an operation, can be exceeded when it is *necessary* to do so, but not where it is merely *convenient* to do so, unless the additional procedure is relatively minor.

CAPACITY TO CONSENT

[4.11]

This chapter started with the declaration that 'every human being of adult years and sound mind has a right to determine what shall be done with his own body.' Irish law recognises that one becomes an adult for the purposes of consent to medical and surgical treatment at the age of 16.[28] But does this in turn mean that only an adult and, what is more, only an adult who is of sound mind can ever consent to any medical procedure? Where does it leave those below the age of majority or the 'mentally incompetent'? May such a person consent at all to surgical, medical or dental treatment on his own behalf and if not, then who may consent on his behalf?

Status *versus* individual capacity

[4.12]

How do (or should) practitioners decide whether an individual who is not of adult years or full mental competence is capable of giving consent to medical intervention? Traditionally, the approach to this question was one of *status*. Certain categories of person were automatically designated incapable of making treatment decisions by virtue of their status as a minor or 'mental incompetent'.

Common sense dictates however that a status approach is not necessarily a satisfactory one. There is a wide spectrum of mental disability for, example the schizophrenic who has little or no insight into his psychiatric condition may nonetheless be capable of understanding that he has appendicitis and consenting to an operation. Similarly, a precocious child or mature teenager may be just as competent a decision-maker regarding health issues as his parents.

Courts have gradually recognised that a status approach to an individual's decision-making capacity is unwieldy and not universally applicable and they have therefore begun to take a more discriminating and eclectic approach to the question of consent given or withheld by minors or the mentally incompetent. This approach is based not on the class of person to which the patient belongs, but rather on the individual's own personal capacity to consent, so that in effect the decision-making powers of any young or mentally incompetent person will not be pre-judged but judged on their merits.

The extent of the patient's decision-making power will hinge on both the capacity of the individual and the gravity of the decision. We can examine some of those considerations in the context of decision making by those categorised – according to the status approach – as the mentally incompetent.

Consent and the mentally 'incompetent'

[4.13]

The United States President's Commission for the Study of Ethical Problems in Medicine and Biomedical and Behavioural Research published a report in 1983 entitled *Making Health Care Decisions* and in that report they listed the elements they considered essential to decision making capacity.

1. Possession of a set of values and goals;
2. The ability to communicate and understand information;
3. The ability to reason and to deliberate about one's choices.

Merely because someone is suffering from a particular mental infirmity such as depression, anxiety, schizophrenia or even dementia, it does not preclude him from meeting the criteria above and therefore being capable of consenting to any particular procedure. The test is taken according to an approximate measure of the level of the decision-maker's infirmity and the nature of the proposed intervention. As the President's Commission Report goes on to state:

> 'When the consequences for well-being are substantial, there is a greater need to be certain that the patient possesses the necessary level of capacity. When little turns on the decision, the level of decision-making capacity required may be appropriately reduced (even though the constituent elements remain the same) and less scrutiny may be required about whether the patient possesses even the reduced level of capacity. Thus a particular patient may be capable of deciding about a relatively inconsequential medication, but not about the amputation of a gangrenous limb.'[29]

In other words, the test should be individualised, tailored to each patient whose consent is being sought, rather than to the class to which the patient belongs. The question therefore for people with disordered mental processes is essentially this: does the person have sufficient understanding of the procedure that is proposed?

Example 2

A patient suffers from schizophrenia, including florid delusions that people are trying to kill him and that the radio is sending him personal messages. He develops appendicitis. What should be done?

Applying the *status* approach, the patient is incapable of consenting so that the decision on consent would seem to rest with the doctors or with the courts.[30] However, if one applies the *capacity* approach, then that merely entails talking to the patient. Does the patient understand what is meant by appendicitis, notwithstanding his delusions? Does the patient consent to having his appendix removed? If so, is there any reason why he should not be permitted to consent?

The capacity test is surely preferable to simply assuming that all those with a mental infirmity cannot consent and that decisions must be taken for them. There is no Irish legal decision on the subject, but this approach seems valid, especially when the Irish Constitution guarantees to protect, or to *vindicate* in the language of the Constitution, the rights of all citizens. This would seem to imply that each citizen, irrespective of any mental infirmity, has a right of autonomy as a matter of course, which he should be permitted to exercise whenever it is both necessary and possible for him to do so.

One problem with mental 'incompetence' and consent

The precise nature of the mental infirmity may prove a stumbling block to allowing such a person to make healthcare decisions for himself. A person may fully understand the 'nature of a procedure', but yet have such a misperception of the reality that surrounds him as to fatally undermine his capacity to give or refuse consent.

Example 3

In one American case,[31] a woman required amputation of her feet due to progressive gangrene. However, the woman in question refused to accept that such an operation was necessary, even when faced with the 'obvious facts that the flesh was dead, black, shrivelled, rotting and stinking.' Her chance of survival following amputation was estimated at 50% while the prospect of death in the short term was close to 95% in the absence of surgery.

The court took the decision that woman's refusal of treatment was not valid in the circumstances because she failed to understand the very basic facts involved in taking the decision so the court permitted the surgery to take place.

On the other side of the coin, are situations where the degree of mental incompetence does not affect the decision the patient is making. In another US case, *Lane v Candura*,[32] a woman who suffered from intermittent periods of confusion and forgetfulness was found to be competent to refuse to consent to an amputation, because her senile symptoms could not be shown to impinge at all upon her decision to withhold consent.[33]

Wards of court and power of attorney

[4.14]

What is the current situation in Irish law regarding the adult who is not mentally competent to take his own treatment decisions? If an adult, because of profound depression, chooses to forego life saving surgery or because he is in a comatose state cannot consent to treatment what options are open to the clinician, the family or the court? In such cases, the patient will often be made a Ward of Court[34] and the court can then make the appropriate decisions on that person's behalf. Less commonly, a person may be made a ward of court because he is a minor.

The purpose of wardship is essentially protection of the interests of the ward. An application for wardship is often made by a family member, but it can be made by any interested party including a hospital in which the prospective ward is a patient. The application is made to the Registrar of Wards of Court, usually by a solicitor instructed by the person making the application. The President of the High Court decides whether the order for wardship should be made.

Once the decision is made, then a 'committee', which, perhaps surprisingly, normally consists of only one person, is appointed by the court and this committee takes all routine decisions relating to the ward's finances, property and welfare. Contentious decisions will be referred to the courts and will be taken by the High Court, although any decision may be appealed to the Supreme Court in the event of disagreement on the part of anyone with an interest in the ward's welfare.[35]

Ward of court proceedings are slow and costly, but they are the only real option in circumstances where a person is already mentally incompetent or is for other reasons unable to take decisions. In cases where a person is expected to become mentally incompetent over time, as happens in dementia, the preferable approach is for the patient to confer 'power of attorney' on a person who can then make decisions on the paptient's behalf. It is important to note that the person must be mentally competent at the time he confers power of attorney. The question of power of attorney is dealt with in more detail in section **[13.10]**.

Consent and minors

[4.15]

An ongoing issue regarding minors is whether *all* treatment of minors must be conducted through the medium of the child's parents or whether a minor may give his own consent to a medical examination, investigation or procedure.

Some Irish authors have argued that because of the special position of the family recognised in Article 41 of the Irish Constitution, minors are not entitled to the same recognition of autonomy that is often granted to them in other countries.[36] However, this author believes that the fact that the family is exalted in the Irish Constitution[37] does not alter the fact that, within the family itself, the child has his own rights and that the minor's rights evolve with the passage of time. In one case the situation was memorably phrased as follows:

> '[T]he legal right of a parent to the custody of a child ends at the eighteenth birthday [as was the case when these words were written]; and even up till then, it is a dwindling right which the courts will hesitate to enforce against the wishes of the child, the older he is. It starts with a right of control and ends with little more than advice.'[38]

The crucial English case in the area of recognising the autonomy of children is *Gillick v West Norfolk and Wisbech AHA*[39] decided by the House of Lords. It concerned a mother's attempts to stop her children, who were younger than 16, from being prescribed the oral contraceptive pill without her knowledge or consent. The court decided that children did have a right to consent to medical treatment and one judge stated:

> '[T]he parental right to determine whether or not their minor child below the age of 16 will have medical treatment terminates if and when the child achieves a sufficient understanding and intelligence to enable him or her to understand fully what is proposed.'[40]

This is the seed of what has become known as '*Gillick* Competence', which is the idea that a minor may give consent to his own treatment when he is capable of understanding what is involved. Since the *Gillick* decision, the idea has been approved in Canada when a minor sought the right to undergo a termination of pregnancy against the wishes of her parents, who had refused to give their consent.[41]

Gillick *and Ireland*

[4.16]

It is the opinion of the author that '*Gillick* Competence' would find approval from the Irish Courts in certain circumstances, although the matter has not yet been authoritatively decided.

In a recent case, *North Western Health Board v W (H)*,[42] the court found that, in most circumstances and in keeping with the family's rights under the Constitution, the welfare of a child is best served by deferring healthcare decisions to a child's parents. However. one judge[43] recognised the existence of the particular individual and personal rights of the child within the family and all of the judges recognised that there were circumstances where a treatment decision could be made by parties other than the parents. The court did not define these rights clearly nor did they stipulate the circumstances in which the child's rights would take precedence over the parents' rights as decision-makers. However, it appears that, in some ill-defined form, children's rights to consent to treatment do exist.

It seems logical, and in the opinion of the author preferable, that in Irish law, the minor has limited healthcare decision-making power, albeit ill-defined and that the power should be greater as the child grows older. This assertion is based not only on court decisions, but also on the legislation under which childcare decisions are generally taken in the absence of satisfactory parental care. Legislation refers explicitly to the need to take account of the wishes of the child[44] and it is argued that this further strengthens the argument that there are circumstances in which the under-16 year-old could and should be entitled to take his own health care decisions.

In general, the younger a child is, the more likely the parent is to be the decision-maker. However, this is not always the case and there are exceptional situations where the court will intervene. The test that the courts use is generally that any decision should be, as far as possible, consistent with the child's best interests, but the presumption is usually that the child's best interests are served by respecting the independence of the family,[45]a situation where a child's best interests are not served by a parent's decision, the court may intervene and substitute its consent for the parents' refusal, but only where the parental decision is obviously and significantly aberrant. In hospitals, doctors have given blood transfusions to children whose parents refused them on religious grounds.[46] The rationale for taking such decisions against the wishes of parent was summarised thus:[47]

> 'Parents may be free to become martyrs themselves, but it does not follow that they are free in identical circumstances to make martyrs of their children before they have reached the age of full and legal discretion when they can make choices for themselves.'

Limits to Gillick

[4.17]

It is interesting to note, by way of balance, that while the courts in many countries recognise the '*Gillick* competent' minor's right to seek and to consent to treatment, they are markedly more reluctant to give full rein to a minor's decision to *refuse* treatment. In such circumstances they will more readily uphold the right of the parents or courts to be the final arbiters of whether the minor's refusal is valid. This was explored in one English case[48] that concerned a minor's decision to refuse psychiatric medication. The girl's decision was over-ruled by the court, which decided that treatment should be given notwithstanding the child's refusal. The impression is that courts are happy to permit a minor to take decisions consistent with improving his health, but not decisions that would be dangerous to his health or life.

Consent and pregnancy

[4.18]

The question of the pregnant woman who refuses treatment is not one that can be categorically answered in the present state of Irish law. A woman who refuses treatment and whose refusal will inevitably result in the death of her foetus places a court in a difficult position – should they uphold the right of the foetus to life and therefore compel the woman to undergo treatment?[49] The courts in both England[50] and the United States[51] have reasoned that it is the mother's right to choose or to refuse treatment, even if such a decision is at the expense of the foetus she is carrying. In Ireland, the Attorney General has issued an opinion that it would be permissible to turn off the life support machine of a pregnant woman but the matter has not formally come before the Irish courts.[52] Issues regarding the unborn child in Irish law are dealt with in greater detail in chapter 12.

STATUTE LAW AND CONSENT

[4.19]

Many laws impact on consent: some abridge autonomy, while others enshrine it. Patients suffering from a psychiatric condition may be detained and treated without their consent. New checks and balances to counter the lack of consent in the psychiatric setting, including the independent review of all involuntary and treatment, have been introduced by the Mental Health Act 2001 and these are examined in detail in ch 11. Similarily, to facilitate treatment, the right of the patients suffering certain infectious diseases to give or withhold consent may also be overridden.[53]

Quick Reference Guide 4.2

Consent in special cases

- ❖ The general rule is that only an adult of sound mind may give or withhold consent to clinical intervention.
- ❖ The law has moved away from automatically classifying individuals according to their *status* and towards examining the individual's *capacity* to consent.
- ❖ For the 'mentally incompetent' the question of consent turns not on an individual's diagnosis but on his ability to form an understanding, based in reality, of the matter for which consent is being sought. A person with a psychiatric diagnosis may be perfectly capable of understanding the implications of appendicitis and an appendectomy.
- ❖ A person who is permanently or temporarily mentally incapacitated (or, more rarely, a minor) and therefore unable to give or withhold consent may be made a Ward of Court, allowing the court to take contentious decisions on his behalf. A person who is likely to become mentally incompetent in the future can confer a Power of Attorney on another person that is activated when the incompetence takes hold.
- ❖ In Irish law, a person becomes an adult for the purposes of medical and surgical treatment at the age of 16 years.
- ❖ In Ireland, a child under the age of 16 years has no definite right to consent to clinical treatment. However in England, the *Gillick* decision mean that minors capable of taking mature decisions are in general capable of consenting to treatment. A potential obstacle to Irish courts agreeing with *Gillick* is that the Irish Constitution is often interpreted as guaranteeing certain rights to parents, but nonetheless it is argued that mature minors in Ireland do have some *Gillick* rights.
- ❖ The younger or more immature a child, the more likely the parents are to be the decision-makers on the child's behalf.
- ❖ Courts are less keen to give minors the right to *refuse* treatment than they are to give them the right to *consent* to treatment, especially where refusal may lead to significant harm to the minor.
- ❖ It is unclear in Irish law whether a person can refuse or consent to a clinical intervention where that refusal or consent will adversely affect *in utero* life. It appears that the refusal or withdrawal of such treatment is permissible: for the principle of 'double effect' see section **[12.03]**.

There are specific rules on consent for those participating in clinical trials: the Control of Clinical Trials Act 1987 and the Control of Clinical Trials and Drugs Act 1990 (which was introduced to tackle some of the problems created by the earlier Act). Section 9 of the 1987 Act concerns consent. Rather than leaving it to the medical profession to decide what constitutes valid consent in the case of clinical trials, the Act states precisely what will amount to sufficient consent for participation:

- — A person shall not be a participant in a clinical trial unless consent to participation has been given.
- — Consent to participation in a clinical trial shall not be valid unless given in writing and signed by the person who is to be the participant in the trial.

- The person consenting must be capable of comprehending the nature, significance and scope of his consent.
- Consent must be obtained by or on behalf of the person conducting the clinical trial.
- Every person must, before giving his consent, be made aware of
  - The objectives of the trial,
  - The manner in which the substance or preparation being tested in the trial is to be administered,
  - The risks and the possible side-effects and any discomfort involved in the trial,
  - Whether or not a pharmacologically inactive substance or preparation (placebo) is to be administered to some people in the trial.
- Consent may be withdrawn at any time by a person who has previously consented and any decision to withdraw from the trial must not affect the quality of the patient's care.
- In certain circumstances consent may be given orally[54] or by another person[55] on behalf of the prospective trial subject.

Failure to obtain consent from a participant in a clinical trial is an offence. When we look at the question of informed consent below we will see that the practitioner has a 'therapeutic privilege': the power to withhold information from a patient if she feels that the disclosure of that information would have an adverse effect on the patient. Implicit in the 1987 Act is the philosophy that there is no role for the therapeutic privilege: when it comes to obtaining consent for clinical trials, all relevant information must be disclosed.[56]

INFORMED CONSENT

Introduction

[4.20]

In an ideal world, the section of a textbook purporting to deal with the issue of informed consent would start off with a terse, helpful and authoritative definition of precisely what is meant by the words 'informed consent'. The trouble is that no such neat definition exists. Informed consent is something of a will-o-the-wisp, its meaning elusive and its reach in Irish law uncertain. Some believe that the 'oft-used and somewhat amorphous phrase informed consent'[57] should not be used at all and prefer to see the crux of the matter as the practitioner simply having a general duty to her patient to disclose information. So, the phrase 'duty of disclosure' can be seen as another way of expressing 'informed consent'.

As we have seen, informed consent is only one element of valid consent: consent must also be voluntary and be given (or withheld) by someone who has the capacity to do so.

The problem with informed consent or duty of disclosure is not so much working out what to call it, but working out what it means. It is one thing to say that consent must be informed, but how 'informed' does it have to be? It is a simple matter to say that a doctor has a duty to disclose matters to her patients, but how extensive is that duty? In other words, how much does a patient have to be told before his consent is valid? That the basic nature and purpose of a procedure should be conveyed to the patient is true beyond doubt.[58] But setting aside black-and-white questions such as the nature of the procedure, what about the greyer ancillary areas, such as outlining side effects, complications or the possibility of pain? More importantly, who decides when the patient is sufficiently informed, the practitioner or the patient?

In the section that follows, we look at three matters:

1. The history of informed consent and the question of who decides when a patient is 'informed'?
2. The question of whether a lack of informed consent really made a difference to the patient. Remember that a failure to obtain consent is negligence. One of the elements of proving negligence is proving that the negligent act caused harm to the patient(see section **[7.107]**. A patient has to prove that the lack of information 'caused' him to have, for example, the operation and that if the information had been sufficient he would not have done so.
3. Is there a rule of informed consent in Ireland?

Origins and ingredients of informed consent

[4.21]

When looking at the history of informed consent, one matter becomes clear. There has never been any dispute but that a patient should be informed about any proposed clinical intervention, but battle lines have been drawn over the question of what characterises fully informed consent. One school of thought is that a patient is fully informed when he has been told as much as a *reasonable doctor* would tell a patient in the circumstances (a 'practitioner-centred approach'). In the 'practitioner-centred test' the courts will look at how the conduct of the practitioner in question measures up to what reasonable practitioners would do in the circumstances. The competing opinion is that a patient is fully informed when he has been told as much as the *reasonable patient* would wish to know in the circumstances.

At first sight, these two approaches seem irreconcilable, but in reality, each approach has exceptions built into it that mean that – practically speaking and aside from questions of whether it is politically more correct to have a 'patient-centred test' – there is not as much difference between them as there might seem. The 'doctor-centred test' has two built in *caveats*:

— Even if the amount of information given by the clinician compares favourably with what other clinicians would do in the circumstances, the court reserves the right to ignore the professional standard if it is obviously deficient and find nonethelss that the practitioner has failed to obtain informed consent.[59]

— In Ireland, as we will see [section **[4.27]** below], there are certain possibilities that must always be disclosed to patients, especially the risk of any long-term pain as a consequence of clinical intervention.

Similarily, into the patient-centred test is built the exception known as the 'therapeutic privilege', which is the right of the practitioner to withhold information when she feels it is clinically justified to do so (see **[4.24]**).

These exceptions bring the tests much closer together than they appear initially. In reality, setting aside the question of different tests, there is a simple obligation on the practitioner to share important information with the patient, an obligation that varies with both the individual circumstances and the individual patient. We deal now in greater detail with the elements of informed consent.

The 'reasonable practitioner'...

[4.22]

The United States[60] was the source of both informed consent and the practitioner-centred test for measuring whether consent is informed. The first major US case to consider the matter said that a patient had given informed consent to a procedure once he consented on the basis of the information that a 'reasonable physician' would give in the circumstances. English courts also take a doctor-centred approach to informed consent. In one of the most important cases on informed consent, an English judge summed up the situation as follows:

> '[A] doctor, bearing in mind the best interests of the patient and bearing in mind the patient's right [to] information which will enable the patient to make a balanced judgement must decide what information should be given to the patient and in what terms the information should be couched.'[61]

The stepwise logic involved in the adoption of the doctor-centred approach by the Irish Supreme Court is set out at **[4.27]** below.

... or the 'reasonable patient'?

[4.23]

Two other significant cases on the practitioner's duty to disclose explored the idea that it should be the patient – rather than the clinician – who decided when he had enough information upon which to base his consent.[62] In *Canterbury* – the earlier of the two cases – the court reasoned that:

> '[R]espect for the patient's right of self-determination... demands a standard set *by* law *for* physicians rather than one which physicians may or may not impose upon themselves.' [italics added]

The court was not happy that doctors should be the sole arbiters of what constituted informed consent. Rather the law would attempt to impose a standard upon physicians based on what it expected the reasonable patient would want to know. The later Canadian case of *Reibl* also concluded that it should not be up to the practitioner to decide when the patient is informed.

> 'To allow expert medical evidence to determine what risks are material and, hence, [what risks] should be disclosed and, correlatively, what risks are not material is to hand over to the medical profession the entire question of the scope of the duty of disclosure, including the question whether there has been a breach of that duty.'

The Australian High Court[63] has followed the Canadian approach and reasoned that it is 'illogical' that a patient should be expected to decide on a procedure based only on the information that the doctor is prepared to share. The Australian court dwelt not on the phrase 'informed consent', but on the doctor's *duty* to disclose 'material facts' and said that:

'[A] risk is material if, in the circumstances of the particular case, a reasonable person in the patient's position, if warned of the risk, would be likely to attach significance to it or if the medical practitioner is or should reasonably be aware that the particular patient, if warned of the risk, would be likely to attach significance to it. This duty is subject to the therapeutic privilege.'[64]

In the earlier American *Canterbury* decision the court also felt that the obligation was to disclose 'material risks', which it defined as follows:

'A risk is material when a reasonable person in… the patient's position would be likely to attach significance to the risk or cluster of risks in deciding whether or not to forego the proposed therapy.'[65]

While these cases suggest that the patient is to be the sole arbiter of the information flow necessary for informed case, that is not so. In the same way that courts will step in to question whether the 'reasonable doctor' standard is sufficient, they also set a limit to the right of the patient to know information: the 'therapeutic privilege'.

'Therapeutic privilege'

[4.24]

The therapeutic privilege means that a doctor can withhold information if she feels that it would be psychologically damaging to the patient to disclose it. If a physician were conscious that an anxious man might refuse important surgery if told of every single possible adverse outcome, the doctor might – according to his therapeutic privilege – be justified in withholding certain facts.

Telling the truth

However, the therapeutic privilege does not extend to giving practitioners a right to lie to their patients: clinicians generally have an ethical duty to share information with their patients. As far as doctors are concerned (and the same would appear to extend, by analogy, to the other caring professions), the Medical Council's *Guide to Ethical Conduct and Behaviour* stipulates that:

'A request for information by a patient always requires a positive response. In general doctors should ensure that a patient and, provided the patient agrees, family members, are as fully informed as possible about matters relating to an illness.'[66]

Does this ethical duty mean that the practitioner has to answer absolutely all of her patient's questions and is there an onus on her always to tell the truth and even to answer questions that the patient has not asked? And even if there is an ethical duty, is there a legal duty? The situation is probably best described by the following extract:

'There is… no doubt that, when a medical practitioner is directly questioned by his patient concerning the risk associated with the proposed therapy, he must give a direct and full answer to the patient's questions unless he can rely upon a *compelling* therapeutic privilege; and the scope of the operation of such a privilege is necessarily strictly limited in the face of a direct request for information by the patient.'[67]

In effect, general questions may be answered generally while specific questions warrant more minute attention. What is beyond doubt is that answers must be truthful. While the therapeutic privilege still applies when it comes to answering questions it will only be in *exceptional* individual patient circumstances that the doctor's answers may be economical or circumspect with the truth. A relatively recent Irish case[68] dealt with the issue of the 'inquisitive patient' without really clarifying matters, although it appeared to endorse the argument that the clinician should always attempt to answer direct questions about treatment truthfully and as fully as possible.

Choosing between patient-centred and doctor-centred tests

[4.25]

There is an obvious problem with the simple practitioner-centred approach even though it admits that patients have a right to be informed. If consent is about a patient's autonomy and self-determination then it should be for the autonomous and self-determining patient to decide where his own 'best interests' lie, including when he has enough information to consent, rather than it being for the *practitioner* to determine when the patient has enough information. But there is also a problem with a purely patient-centred test: the practitioner is generally in possession of the specialist knowledge necessary to filter information, including the question of what information is important, having regard to the seriousness and the likelihood of any risk and to the nature of the patient. She is the person in charge of all aspects of her patient's care: could this not include being in charge of the information flow?

The law, in effect recognises both the shortcomings and allure of each approach and it is for this reason that each test – patient-centred and doctor-centred – is leavened with elements of the other. The patient-centred approach is balanced by the existence of the therapeutic privilege that accords a degree of authority and control over the information flow to the practitioner. The doctor-centred approach is curtailed by the court's insistence that it will intervene where the standards a profession sets for itself are too low and that – in Ireland, at any rate – there are certain risks that must always be disclosed.

Some countries, such as Canada and Australia, adopt the view that the patient is informed once he has as much information about what he views as 'material risks'. In other countries including Ireland and England,[69] the patient is informed when he has as much information as 'reputable medical opinion' is prepared to give him. However – as with negligence[70] generally and as we have already mentioned – in both Ireland[71] and England[72] the courts will be prepared to ignore the standard set by the profession if it is obvious that the standard is obviously too low.

The safeguards inserted into each approach to informed consent serve to eliminate certain of the differences between the two and in reality, the differences – such as they are – tend to be subtle. A mechanism to bring to bear on the individual consultation that aims to ensure consent is informed is outlined below (**[4.30]**).

Would more information have made a difference?

[4.26]

If failure to obtain consent is negligence, then the person alleging a lack of informed consent must prove that the lack of information (the breach of duty of care) *caused* the clinical procedure (the harm or damage) to take place. In order to do this the patient has to prove that but for the inadequate information he would not have undergone the procedure.

Example 4

A patient suffers from a chronic ear infection. He consults an Ear, Nose and Throat surgeon. She tells the patient that the operation has an 80% chance of success. She tells him that there is also a chance that the operation could make no difference or even make him worse. She mentions also that he could be left deaf by the operation, but omits to mention the tiny possibility that the operation may leave him with lifelong pain. In the event, the operation leaves the patient with permanent severe pain. He sues the doctor for negligence, alleging that she failed to tell him that pain was a possible complication. What does he need to prove to succeed?

There are two steps in proving this allegation of negligence due to a lack of consent. In the first place, the patient has to show that the failure of the consultant to warn him about the pain was negligent. According to the current state of law in Ireland, the ENT surgeon will be compared to the standard of responsible medical practice in her field of ENT surgery (the practitioner-centred approach). If there is no reputable body of medical opinion that supports her decision not to give the warning about pain, then the consent was not informed (or, put another way, she failed in her duty to disclose information to the patient). Although, as will be seen below (section **[4.28]**) Irish law places a heavy burden on the doctor to disclose at a minimum the possibility of any longlasting pain as a consequence of treatment.

But the patient has to cross one more hurdle if he is to win his case: he has to prove that if the surgeon *had* told him about the pain that he would *not* have submitted to the operation. The law of negligence requires that the negligence must have caused the damage of which the person is complaining. So, the failure to give an adequate warning must have *caused* the patient to have the operation when he otherwise would not have done *or* when he might otherwise have taken more time to think about it, including the possibility that he would have had the operation done by someone else.

There is a problem with this second step that should be evident here and it is one rooted not in law, but in human nature. The patient – disgruntled and bringing a legal action – will tend to claim that he would not have had the operation or might have sought another surgeon if he had received the warning. Should the court accept this claim at face value, laced with hindsight as it is (a *subjective* approach),[73] should it look at the question *objectively*, asking what a 'reasonable man' in the position of the patient would have done or should there be a 'mixed' approach?[74] In Ireland the only case to consider the question appeared to lean towards a mixed approach – asking what the plaintiff in question would have done, but also considering the standard of the reasonable man.[75]

This question of whether the patient would have undergone the operation if he had been given more information is a consideration even if the person would in any event have been obliged to have the operation at some point in the future.[76] In other words, it appears to be no defence for the practitioner to say that she withheld information on the basis that there was no point in full disclosure because the patient needed the procedure done in any event.

Quick Reference Guide 4.3

Informed consent

- ❖ Informed consent is a somewhat vague concept. It can be defined – from a patient's point of view – as whether the patient has received what the *reasonable patient* would regard as sufficient information to make an informed decision or – from the doctor's point of view – as whether the clinician has fulfilled the duty of the *reasonable practitioner* to sufficiently inform the patient.
- ❖ Different countries take different approaches to defining when a patient is informed. Some (eg Canada and Australia) say consent is informed when a patient has been told what the *reasonable patient* would wish to know about any 'material risks'. Other countries (eg England and Ireland) say that consent is informed when the practitioner has given the information that a reasonable body of professional opinion would give in the circumstances.
- ❖ A 'material' risk is one that a reasonable patient in the position of the person undergoing the procedure in question would regard as significant. Patients should generally be informed of material risks where foreseeable and certainly if they directly question the clinician about a specific risk.
- ❖ There is less difference between the two approaches than there might appear at first sight. Each has limitations built into it: the practitioner-centred test has safeguards that help to protect the patient; the patient-centred test has safeguards that give some control to the practitioner, including the 'therapeutic privilege'.
- ❖ A clinician has a 'therapeutic privilege' to withhold information where she feels that the information would be harmful to the patient. This therapeutic privilege does not amount to a licence to lie in response to a direct question.

Ireland and informed consent

Introduction

[4.27]

There is some uncertainty about the Irish Courts' approach to informed consent, which is unfortunate: even in those countries such as Australia where the courts are unambiguous about their approach to informed consent, doctors remain unclear about matters.[77] How much worse is the problem likely to be for practitioners in a jurisdiction where the courts are confused about terms of reference for informed consent? The last time they considered the matter, the Irish Supreme Court[78] followed their English counterparts[79] in adopting the practitioner-centred approach and the logic underpinning their decision is as follows:

- — Failure to obtain valid consent is negligence.
- — The question of valid consent, including the question of whether consent is informed, should be judged by the standard test of negligence.

— This means comparing the conduct of the clinician to a reasonable body of medical opinion held by practitioners of similar ilk to the doctor whose conduct is being questioned

— In general, if the practitioner's conduct in giving information to the patient is consistent with that of a reasonable body of opinion held by comparable medical professionals, then he will not be negligent.

— *However*, if the court is not happy with the standard adopted by the profession, it can set a higher standard.

In essence then the Irish test is a clinician-centred test, where the standard of information provision is that set by the profession. But the test is modified by the preparedness of the courts to intervene if the standards of the profession are too low. This may seem simple, but it is not. In the first place, one Irish High Court decision recently hinted at the adoption of a patient-centred test:[80] although it does it does not supplant the Supreme Court decision in *Bolton*,[81] it may indicate the direction in which Irish judicial thinking is moving. The second issue is that the Irish courts have complicated matters by defining different standards of information for elective and non-elective procedures. Finally, in an attempt to bring some clarity the courts have set out some categories of potential side effect that *must* be disclosed. We look at these issues in the context of the evolution of informed consent – or the practitioner's duty to disclose information to her patient – in Ireland.

Evolution and sources of confusion

Elective versus non-elective

[4.28]

Informed consent first emerged in Ireland (as anything other than an embryonic concept recognisable only to the legal scholar[82]) in *Walsh v Irish Family Planning Services Ltd*,[82] which concerned one of the archetypal informed consent situations: pre-operative discussion of post-operative risks. A man underwent a vasectomy and was left with severe testicular pain as a complication. The case revolved around whether he had been told in advance of this risk and – if he had been – whether he would have undergone the operation.

In the end, the decision was that the doctor had not been negligent in the information he had given, but the reasons given by the court were very confused. One judge took a doctor-centred approach, in accordance with the principles of medical negligence (see **[4.27]**).[84] Two of the judges suggested a patient-centred approach, but they were satisfied that the patient had been told as much as the reasonable patient would wish to know. There was one issue upon which the judges did agree: there should be a distinction drawn between what a patient should be told before an *elective* operation and what he should be told before a *non-elective* operation. This was summed up by one judge:[85]

> '[W]here there is a question of elective surgery which is not essential to health or bodily well-being, if there is a risk – however exceptional or remote – of grave consequences involving severe pain stretching for an appreciable time into the future and involving the possibility of further operative procedures, the exercise of the duty of care owed by [a clinician] requires that such possible consequences should be explained to the plaintiff.'

The judgments in the *Walsh* case indicated that the judges were not at all sure what precisely constituted an elective procedure and the problem of elective *vs.* non-elective was exacerbated in the most recent Irish Supreme Court case on informed consent.[86] The court felt that before performing 'elective surgery' the surgeon had a duty to 'inform the [patient] of *any* possible harmful consequence arising from the operation' (emphasis added). As far as the 'elective' nature of the procedure was concerned,[87] the judge, delivering a single judgment on behalf of the unanimous court[88] said that the lung surgery was

> '[U]ndoubtedly elective surgery in the sense that it was a matter for the [patient] to decide whether or not she would undergo such an operation and to give or withhold her consent thereto.'

There is an obvious problem with this: a person can 'decide' whether or not to undergo *any* operation or procedure unless he is unconscious or otherwise mentally incompetent: therefore, according to the *Bolton* judgment, almost all interventions are 'elective. The courts have come up with a definition of 'elective' very different from that which the practitioner would recognise, namely that an operation is 'elective' whenever it is a matter for a patient to decide whether or not to consent to it. Conversely, a clinician would see an elective procedure – in keeping with the language of the *Walsh* case – as one operation 'which is not essential to health or bodily well-being', such as plastic surgery or the removal of an ingrown toenail.

The situation then in Irish law at present is that all operations where the patient has a choice whether or not to undergo the procedure are deemed, in theory at least, elective.

Patient-centred or clinician centred?

[4.29]

The *Bolton* case did resolve for the time being the question of whether Ireland's approach to informed consent was to be patient-centred or doctor-centred by opting for the latter. In doing so, they clarified the contradictory judgments given in the *Walsh* case, which had sowed confusion in the lower courts.[89] The Court's logic has already been set out in summary form in section **[4.27]**: the key is that the court will apply the rules of negligence.

Some confusion still appears to exist however: the most recent High Court case on informed consent contradicted the *Bolton* decision: in *Geoghegan v Harris*,[90] the judge said that, 'the application of the reasonable patient test seems more logical in respect of disclosure.' However, it is still the case that the law in Ireland on informed consent is better represented by the Supreme Court's statement of the law in the *Bolton* judgment, although it is possible that the next Supreme Court consideration of the matter may endorse the approach taken in *Geoghegan*.[91] However, as we have stated (see section **[4.25]**), the difference between the two approaches is not as great as it may appear.

The balance of the Irish decisions appears to suggest that a practitioner-centred approach will be taken: the practitioner must disclose the information that would be disclosed by a reputable body of comparable medical opinion in the circumstances. Furthermore, there is a scenario that increases the extent of the practitioner's duty to inform her patient. Where, as a result of an elective procedure, there is a risk of an adverse outcome, in particular the risk of longlasting pain, the patient must be warned of that risk. Note however, that according to Irish law, 'elective' means *any procedure where the patient has the opportunity to exercise a choice whether or not to undergo the procedure*.

Quick Reference Guide 4.4

The Irish approach to informed consent

- There is no firm and formal principle called the 'informed consent rule' in Irish law. The courts do however recognise that doctors have a duty to disclose information to patients.
- The Irish practitioner, when informing her patient prior to a procedure, operation or treatment has to pay particular attention to detailing any potential complications that may involve long-lasting or severe pain.
- This is especially true in elective procedures, but it is important to note that the Irish Supreme Court has given an extremely wide-ranging definition of 'elective'.
- Irish law appears for the time being to adopt a doctor-centred approach, applying the same test of the clinician's conduct used in negligence cases: was the practitioner's level of disclosure in accordance with the practice of a responsible body of opinion of comparable practitioners within the practitioner's discipline? One Irish case has flirted with the patient-centred approach but the negligence-based practitioner-centred approach remains the law in Ireland. See Ch 7 for more details of clinical negligence.
- If the patient asks questions, the clinician should answer them as truthfully as possible although there is the possibility that the practitioner can withhold information in the patient's 'best interests', so long as to do so is in accordance with a responsible body of opinion within the practitioner's profession.
- There has been only one Irish decision on the question of whether the lack of informed consent *caused* the damage, or in other words, whether the patient would not have had the operation if consent had been informed. That case suggests that Irish courts judge the matter by reference to what the patient bringing the case would – in the opinion of the court – have done, while also bearing in mind the likely approach of the 'reasonable patient'.

A possible guideline for obtaining informed consent and disclosing material facts

[4.30]

A useful summary of the issues that bear upon disclosure and informed consent was provided by the Australian Law Reform Commission.[92] The Commission suggested that when it comes to disclosing 'material facts' in the context of obtaining consent from a patient, it was possible to compile a checklist that goes some way towards covering all bases.

Figure 4.1 –Australian Law Reform Commission checklist for obtaining informed consent

Matters to be considered when seeking the informed consent of a patient to clinical intervention include the following:

- The personality and temperament of the patient and the patient's attitude;
- Whether the patient wants information;
- Whether the patient asks questions;
- The patient's level of understanding;
- The nature of the proposed treatment;
- The magnitude of any possible harm;
- The likelihood of the risk of any possible harm occurring;
- The general surrounding circumstances.

It is suggested that a checklist of this nature applied to each situation where consent is being sought could help to provide the doctor with the best protection for ensuring that he or she has obtained a patient-centred consent, rather than always relying on the "doctor-centred" approach. While the courts may continue to take a doctor-centred approach at the end of costly, lengthy and stressful litigation, there are to considerations to bear in mind. The first is that the Supreme Court in Ireland (in keeping with the decision in cases such as *Geoghegan v Harris*) may choose to move towards the more patient-centred approach. The second is that the practitioner who takes the patient-centred approach to informing patient from the outset of her clinical career may minimise the chance of ever needing the court's help in the first place.

Endnotes

1 In *Re T (adult: refusal of treatment)* [1992] 4 All ER 649 a woman who refused a blood transfusion was found to have done so because, amongst other reasons, she was placed under undue pressure by her mother, who was a Jehovah's Witness. It is also worth remembering that in institutional settings such as prisons or psychiatric hospitals (or indeed in general hospitals, where the institutional aura surrounding the clinician can be very great), a person's 'voluntary' consent may be more apparent than real. The English case of *Freeman v Home Office (No 2)* [1984] QB 524 related to inmates in a prison 'consenting' to medical interventions and the court noted that the institutional context in which consent is given is important. Similar questions arise in psychiatric hospitals. Other situations where consent may not be voluntary include those people who are not mentally competent or very young children, eg the child struggling against vaccination.

2 *Schloendorff v Society of New York Hospital* (1914) 211 NY 125 at 126 per Cardozo J.

3 See sections **[3.06]** – **[3.10]** for a brief outline of ethical principles.

4 So-called 'Common Law' countries: see the appendix for more detail (section **[A.03]**).

5 Or indeed between an individual and company. Allegations of negligence, defamation, trespass and nuisance are all torts. Because of its very nature, the tort of battery is most likely to arise between two individuals. *Tort* is an old French word for 'wrong'.

6 And in other countries with similar legal systems to ours, such as England, Canada and Australia. *Bolton v Blackrock Clinic* (23 January 1997, unreported), Supreme Court

7 *Chatterton v Gerson* [1981] 1 All ER 257.

8 An example might be the case of *R v Williams* [1923] 1 KB 340 where a man convinced a woman that the act of sexual intercourse was a procedure necessary to improve her singing

voice. In that case, the woman consented but the consent was meaningless because she was so intrinsically misled as to the nature and purpose of the event to which she was consenting. Battery might also arise where the perpetrator misled the victim as to her professional qualifications or some other fundamental matter.

9 *Hopp v Lepp* (1979) 98 DLR 3d 464.

10 *Re T (adult: refusal of treatment)* [1992] 4 All ER 649, *per* Lord Donaldson.

11 *Re T (adult: refusal of treatment)* [1992] 4 All ER 649, *per* Butler-Sloss J.

12 Article 40.3.1° of the Constitution. The rights are 'unenumerated' because they are not specifically listed in Article 40.3 of the Constitution: instead judges have declared that they exist.

13 *Ryan v Attorney General* [1965] IR 294, per Kenny J.

14 *Re A Ward of Court (withholding medical treatment) (No 2)* [1996] 2 IR 79 at 156 *per* Denham J. This approach to withholding consent was upheld in the recent case of *North Western Health Board v W (H)* [2001] IESC 70.

15 *Consent Tool Kit*, British Medical Association, London, 2001.

16 *O'Brien v Cunard SS Co* (1891) 28 NE 266.

17 *Marshall v Curry* (1933) 3 DLR 260.

18 *Mohr v Williams* (1905) 104 NW 12.

20 As we have observed, the trend has been away from actions for battery and towards actions for negligence. If this case were to be decided today instead of 1905, the patient would sue the surgeon for negligence rather than battery.

21 *Marshall v Curry* (1933) 3 DLR 260

22 *Murray v McMurphy* (1949) 2 DLR 442.

23 *Chatterton v Gerson* [1981] 1 All ER 257 at 265 *per* Bristow J. This was also an early case in which it was affirmed that failure to obtain consent should generally be considered as negligence rather than battery.

24 *Bruschett v Cowan* [1991] 2 Med LR 271.

25 Using a camera inserted through the abdominal wall to examine the abdominal and pelvic organs.

26 *Pridham v Nash* (1986) 33 DLR 4th 304. Adhesions are small string-like connections that sometimes arise between organs or between organs and the abdominal wall. The court felt that snipping the adhesions permitted a more effective laparoscopy to be executed.

27 *Pridham v Nash* (1986) 33 DLR 4th 304, *per* Holland J.

28 A position formally expressed in Non-Fatal Offences Against the Person Act 1997, s 23

> (1) The consent of a minor who has attained the age of 16 years to any surgical, medical or dental treatment which, in the absence of consent, would constitute a trespass to his or her person, shall be as effective as it would be if he or she were of full age; and where a minor has by virtue of this section given an effective consent to any treatment it shall not be necessary to obtain any consent for it from his or her parent or guardian.
>
> (2) In this section 'surgical, medical or dental treatment' includes any procedure undertaken for the purposes of diagnosis, and this section applies to any procedure (including, in particular, the administration of an anaesthetic) which is ancillary to any treatment as it applies to that treatment.

29 President's Commission for the Study of Ethical Problems in Medicine and Biomedical and Behavioural Research: *Making Health Care Decisions*, cited in Kennedy & Grubb, *Medical Law*, 3rd edn (2000), pp 618-620.

30 See *In the Matter of a Ward of Court* [1996] 2 IR 73; [1995] 2 ILRM 401. In this case there was a dispute over whether treatment could be withdrawn from a patient in a near-PVS (persistent

vegetative state). The person was a ward of court and obviously incapable of giving consent and so the Supreme Court was asked to make the decision on behalf of the ward. See ch.13

31 *State of Tennessee v Northern* (1978) 563 SW 2d 197.

32 *Lane v Candura* (1978) 376 NE 2d.

33 The Commission Report (No 231), *Mental Incapacity* reasoned that a person locks mental capacity "if at the material time:

a) He is unable by reason of mental disability to make a decision for himself on the matter in question, or

b) He is unable to communicate his decision on that matter because he is unconscious of for some other reason."

For the application of mental capacity to wills see **[11.24]-[11.29]**. For the application of mental capacity to 'end of life' decisions, see ch 13.

34 What follows is only a brief summary. For more information, see Department of Justice, Equality & Law Reform *Wards of Court – An Information Booklet*, (1998). Available at www.justice.ie ('publications' section).

35 This is what happened in the case entitled *In the Matter of a Ward of Court* [1996] 2 IR 73. The question of whether the ward in question should have life-sustaining treatment withdrawn could not be decided by the committee and was decided ultimately by the Supreme Court. This is dealt with in more detail in ch 13.

36 See, for example, Tomkin & Hanafin *Irish Medical Law* (1995) pp 37-44.

37 Article 41.1 of the Constitution:

> The State recognises the Family as the natural primary and fundamental unit group of Society, and as a moral institution possessing inalienable and imprescriptible rights, antecedent and superior to all positive law.

The position of the family and further questions of dealing with it in a health care setting are considered in ch 8, *The Practitioner and the Family.*

38 *Hewer v Bryant* [1969] 3 All ER 578 at 582 *per* Lord Denning MR.

39 *Gillick v West Norfolk and Wisbech AHA* (1985) 2 BMLR 11.

40 *Per* Lord Scarman.

41 *C v Wren* (1987) 35 DLR (4th) 419. In Scotland, legislation has formalised the *Gillick* approach: the Age of Legal Capacity (Scotland) Act 1991 states in s 2(4) that children under the age of 16 have legal capacity to consent to any surgical, medical or dental treatment or procedure so long as that child is capable of understanding the nature and consequences of the proposed treatment or procedure.

42 *North Western Health Board v W (H)* [2001] IESC 70. This case did not concern the rights of an older child, but the rights of the child within the family were discussed as part of the judgment. See Mills, '*PKU:* Please Keep Unclear?' [2002] 23 DULJ 180.

43 See the judgment of Keane CJ.

44 Child Care Act 1991, s 3(2)(b)(ii) refers to the fact that in questions of care of the child, the Courts should 'in so far as is practicable, give due consideration, *having regard to his age and understanding*, to the wishes of the child.' [italics added]. While this law refers only to care proceedings, the deference it gives to the decision-making possibilities of the minor is significant. The Child Care Act 1991 is reviewed in ch 8 (section **[8.24]**). Also, in the Criminal Justice (Forensic Evidence) Act 1990, consent must be given to the Gardaí when they are seeking to obtain body samples from people suspected of crimes. In the case of those aged between 14 and 17, consent must come from parents/guardians *and* the minor himself, again suggestive of the law's intuitive recognition of the autonomy of the minor.

45 *The North Western Health Board v W (H)* [2001] IESC 70. The case concerned a decision by parents to refuse to submit their child, for no clear reason, to a PKU screening test (a 'heel

prick' test performed on a small drop of blood obtained from the heel of the child shortly after birth. The test verifies the presence or absence of a number of metabolic conditions, of which the most serious and common is phenylketonuria (PKU)). The case involved a simple diagnostic test and the evidence was that the child was extremely unlikely to suffer from the conditions the sample was intended to detect. In such circumstances, even though one of the judges said that he was 'impatient with the attitude' of the parents, the court was still reluctant to interfere with the parental decision: an example of the strength of the family's position in Irish law. See Mills '*PKU:* Please Keep Unclear?' [2002] 23 DULJ 180.

46 (2000) *Irish Times*, 3 March. The court was not involved in this instance, but it is probably an example of the 'exceptional circumstances', envisaged by the court in *North Western Health Board v W (H)* - where the court will override the will of the parents .

47 *Prince v Massachusetts* (1944) 321 US 158 at 170 *per* Rutledge J.

48 *Re R (a minor) (wardship: medical treatment)* [1991] 4 All ER 177.

49 Note, however, that abortion is not formally or explicitly permitted under Irish law. (see ch 12).

50 *Re F (in utero)* [1988] 2 All ER 193. This approach was affirmed in *St George's Healthcare NHS Trust v S* [1998] 3 All ER 673.

51 *Re AC* (1990) 573 A 2d 1253.

52 'Brain-dead woman kept alive due to pregnancy' (2001) *Irish Times*, June 15. Note that an Irish court has ordered a woman to give birth in hospital so that her child could receive treatment against HIV transmission: see 'Order on HIV mother to affect religious groups' (2002) *Irish Times*, July 20.

53 Infectious Diseases Regulations: reg 13 allows the public health authorities to isolate infectious persons, to carry out 'cleansing, disinfection or disinfestation of persons' and to require people to present for medical examination. In none of these cases is the absence of consent envisaged as being a stumbling block.

54 If a person were physically unable to sign a consent form.

55 If a person was mentally incompetent or a minor.

56 Courts have decided the same thing: see the Canadian case of *Halushka v University of Saskatchewan* (1965) 53 DLR (2d) 436.

57 *Rogers v Whittaker* (1992) 67 AJLR 47 at 55.

58 In the case of *R v Williams* [1925] 1 KB 340, an aspiring actress – who to modern eyes might seem a little naïve – was told by a man that she would have to undergo a procedure to help her singing voice. Under the guise of performing that procedure, the man instead had sexual intercourse with her. The issue arose at the trial whether the woman had consented to the intercourse (in which case he could not be guilty of rape). Unsurprisingly, she was found to have been so fundamentally misled as to the nature of the act to which she consented as to render meaningless any consent she may have given.

59 See chapter 7 for more details on this aspect of clinical negligence.

60 *Salgo v Leland Stanford, J., University Board of Trustees* (1957) 154 Cal App 2d 560.

61 *Sidaway v Board of Governors of the Royal Bethlem Hospital* [1985] AC 871.

62 *Canterbury v Spence* (1972) 464F 2d 772; *Reibl v Hughes* (1980) 114 DLR (3d) 1.

63 *Rogers v Whittaker* (1992) 67 AJLR 47.

64 In the *Rogers* case a patient developed a rare complication of an operation that left her totally blind. The risk of the complication occurring was roughly one in 14,000. Nonetheless, its severity meant that from the patient's perspective it was a material risk, especially given that – going in to the operation – the patient had only one functioning eye.

65 So, in the *Reibl v Hughes* case, the patient was not told of the 10% risk of a stroke that was attendant upon the procedure. This too was held to be a 'material risk' of which the patient should have been told.

66 Paragraph 3.3. (5th edn, 1998). This is not the most patient-centred ethical provision. A critical reader of it might comment that it only refers to keeping a patient informed about "matters relating to an *illness*." In theory this means that the doctor owes no ethical duty to a patient who is well but undergoing tests or to a patient undergoing a minor cosmetic procedure. It would be preferable in the interests of clarity and certainty to replace this with an injunction to inform patients on "all matters relating to their health care."

67 White, *Medical Negligence Actions*, p 158. See also the Canadian case of *Hopp v Lepp* (1980) 112 DLR (3d) 67:

> '[Specific] questions must be answered, although they invite answers to merely possible risks. If no specific questions are put to possible risks, the surgeon is under no obligation (although he may do so) to tell the patient that there are possible risks since there are such risks in any operation. It becomes a question of fact how specific are any questions that are put.'

In *Sidaway v Governors of Royal Bethlem Hospital* ([1985] AC 871, the plaintiff lost her case in part because she did not ask more questions. One of the judges (Lord Bridge) said that a doctor is obliged to answer questions "truthfully and as fully as the questioner requires."

68 *Geoghegan v Harris* [2000] 3 IR 536 at 561-564.

69 *Sidaway v Board of Governors of the Royal Bethlem Hospital* [1985] AC 871. This case – easily the most important English case on the subject – rejected the idea that there was any such formal concept as 'informed consent' in English law. There *was* on the other hand a *duty* on the doctor to disclose information, measured by the usual standards of negligence (see chapter 7), which is by comparison to the practice and opinion of other comparable professionals. In other words, the English court adopted a 'reasonable practitioner' test.

70 See ch. 7.

71 *Dunne v National Maternity Hospital* [1989] IR 91. See the later text on informed consent in Ireland and chapter 7 for a more thorough explanation of professional negligence.

72 In the *Sidaway* case ([1985] AC 871) one of the judges did accept that – as with Irish law – if the standard set by the medical profession for itself is too low, the courts will intervene and substitute their judgement for that of the profession.

73 In the English case, *Chatterton v Gerson* [1981] 1 All ER 257, the court reasoned that the lady in question *would* have undergone the operation in question had she been properly informed because she was "a lady desperate for pain relief." In another more recent English case, the court was very careful to warn of the risks of accepting a patient's retrospective claims of what he would have done if the information he received had been different: *Smith v Barking Health Authority* [1994] 5 Med LR 285 at 289, *per* Hutchison J. See also *Chester v Afshar* [2002] EWCA Civ 724, a decision of the English Court of Appeal, 27 May 2002. In this last case, the court decided that the woman in question would have sought a second opinion had she been told of the risks of spinal cord compression. In Australia there is also a tendency to ask what the patient bringing the action would have done: *Chappel v Hart* [1998] 72 ALJR 1344; [1999] Lloyd's Law Rep (Med) 223.

74 In *Reibl v Hughes*, the court took a 'mixed' approach assessing the likely response of the 'reasonable patient', but also bearing in mind the subjective concerns of the plaintiff in question where there is credible evidence to support those concerns. Relevant concerns may include age, symptoms, diagnosis, family and financial circumstances, together with attitude towards surgery.

75 *Geoghegan v Harris* [2000] 3 IR 536.

76 *Chappel v Hart* [1998] 72 ALJR 1344; [1999] Lloyd's Law Rep (Med) 223.

77 'Informed consent: lessons from Australia.' Skene, Smallwood 2002 BMJ; 324:39-41.

78 *Bolton v Blackrock Clinic* (23 January 1997, unreported), Supreme Court.

[79] *Sidaway v Board of Governors of the Royal Bethlem Hospital* [1985] AC 871.

[81] *Geoghegan v Harris* [2000] 3 IR 536.

[81] A decision of the Supreme Court is – in theory and generally in practice – binding on all lower courts (which include the High Court) unless there is something about the case before the lower court that is sufficiently different to allow it to take a different approach from that prescribed by the more senior court.

[82] For example, *Daniels v Heskin* [1954] IR 73.

[83] *Walsh v Irish Family Planning Services Ltd* [1992] 1 IR 496.

[84] See also chapter 7.

[85] *Walsh v Irish Family Planning Limited* [1992] 1 IR 496 at 535, *per* O'Flaherty J.

[86] *Bolton v Blackrock Clinic* (23 January 1997, unreported), Supreme Court.

[87] In this case it was major lung surgery necessary to avert the removal of the entire lung.

[88] The Supreme Court typically has three or five judges sitting. On occasions when they all agree, one judgement may be given, with the other judges simply recording their agreement. In more contentious cases all of the judges may issue separate – and frequently contradictory, either by design or by accident – judgments.

[89] Prior to this case being decided, two different judges had heard High Court cases in which one had taken the doctor-centred approach (O'Hanlon J in *Farrell v Varian* (19 September 1994, unreported), High Court) and the other had taken the patient-centred approach (Geoghegan J in the High Court hearing of the *Bolton* case). As the High Court is bound to follow the Supreme Court, some clarity was needed, otherwise judges in the High Court were free to follow the approach of whichever judge they agreed with in the *Walsh* case with unpredictable and potentially contradictory results.

[90] *Geoghegan v Harris* [2000] 3 IR 536.

[91] While the patient-centred test was given great prominence in *Geoghegan*, there are nonetheless inconsistencies in the judgment and in the judge's application and description of the patient-centred test (although the details of this criticism lie outside the present text). In that case, a patient had an operation performed on his jaw and developed severe neuropathic pain. He sued his surgeon for negligence, alleging that the surgeon had not told him of the risk of pain. Expert witnesses indicated that the adverse outcome was an almost unheard of, but nonetheless foreseeable, consequence of an operation conducted close to the course of a nerve (as this one was). The judge, while endorsing the *Walsh* approach – that all possible risks involving pain following an elective procedure should be told to the patient – nonetheless, and somewhat confusingly, found that the doctor was not negligent *even though* he had not told the patient of this risk. The judge felt in part that because the patient did not ask of the risk, the doctor did not have to disclose it. This is an odd interpretation of the *obligation* to disclose even the remotest risk of pain, but perhaps it indicates a welcome pragmatism in the complex area of informed consent.

[92] *Informed Decisions about Medical Procedures*, Australian Law Reform Commission (1989).

Chapter 5

The Practitioner as Employer or Employee

INTRODUCTION

[5.01]

All practitioners should have some knowledge of employment law, as they may find themselves on either side of the employment law fence. Early in their careers they are likely to be working for others, either as employees or as independent contractors, so they therefore need to know the difference between the two and the rights that accompany being an employee. Later in their professional lives, practitioners may find themselves in the position of employer or manager and in both cases, knowing the law governing the employer-employee relationship can be similarly crucial.

This chapter looks at elements of employment law that apply to the practitioner, including the question of when she is, or is not, an 'employee' and the legal rights that go with that status. We look too at the employment contract, including the terms it must contain and what terms are implied into contracts regardless of whether or not they are explicitly included in the contract. In the second section of the chapter, we look at the increasingly important area of discrimination and harassment in the workplace. We conclude by looking at attempts to limit the working week in the interests of health and safety and examine how they have a limited reach to date in the health care sector.

EMPLOYMENT AND EMPLOYMENT CONTRACTS

[5.02]

Broadly speaking, contracts between an employer and the person who works for him[1] can be divided into two groups: contracts *of* service (employees) and contracts *for* service (independent contractors). The former is the conventional employment contract: only a person who has a contract *of* service is an employee and attracts the benefits the law extends to employees. Independent contractors must rely on the terms of the specific contract between employer and contractor as well as certain other legal rules. In this chapter we are concerned predominantly with the employee and her rights.

Defining 'employees'

[5.03]

What are the elements of a contract *of* service? The test is not always a simple one: a contract might appear to have elements of both employee and independent contractor about it, or there may be no contract at all and an inference must be drawn from the nature of the relationship between employer and worker. There are tests that can be applied to the employer-worker relationship to help the courts decide hard cases, but it must be stressed that none of them provides a hard and fast rule and the courts often apply an holistic approach to the question of employment.

Tests for the existence of an employer-employee relationship

'Control test'	Whether an employer actually exercises control – or can exercise control if he wishes – over the person working for him. Can he control her activities and tell her what to do? If so, then the worker is more likely to be an employee.[2] The control test has fallen from favour as the sole test for determining whether a person is an employee.
'Integration test'	Whether the worker is an 'integral' part of the business: if she is, then she is more likely to be an employee. Accordingly a person who works an occasional session in a busy physiotherapy practice might not be an employee, whereas a person who does a regular two sessions a week, even without signing a contract, may well be an employee because she is an integral to the running of the practice.
'Mixed control/ integration test'	Where the judge looks at all the features of the employer- worker relationship in order to get at the reality of the relationship. Among the important elements are the arrangement for paying tax (a person who pays her own tax is less likely to be an employee than someone whose tax is deducted at source by the employer) and ownership of the equipment used to do the job.
'Enterprise test'	The question here is whether the person is in effect working for herself, including deciding on working hours, taking the financial benefits of profit (and risks of loss) and making decisions on hiring and firing staff. Independence and the presence of the profit motive can combine to create the impression of someone who is not an employee.[4] But this test too is not always conclusive and may be counterbalanced by the presence of sufficient employer control over the worker's activity.[5]

Determining whether someone is an employee is a sometimes complex balancing act, but certain elements make it more likely that a person is an employee rather than an independent contractor and the bulk of cases will be extremely clear-cut. The existence of a formal or informal partnership agreement between two parties will typically militate against either of them claiming an employer-employee relationship exists.[6]

Quick Reference Guide 5.1

Some characteristics of the 'employee'

- The employer exercises control over some or all activities of the worker.
- The worker is an integral part of the business in question.
- The employer handles most or all of the tax affairs of the worker.
- There is a contract of employment specifying that the worker is an employee.
- The worker has little or no power to hire or fire staff without reference to the employer.
- There is no direct profit or loss incentive for the worker.
- There is no other relationship between the parties inconsistent with an employer-employee relationship, such as a partnership.

Applying the tests to the health care sector

[5.04]

According to any of the tests set out above, nearly all individuals working as practitioners in the public health care sector will be employees. They are under the control of their employers and pay PAYE (pay as you earn) and PRSI (pay-related social insurance) deducted at source. Rarely will they have the opportunity to hire and fire staff without reference either to their employers or to disciplinary structures provided for by the employer (effectively a form of control).

On the other hand, in the private health care sector matters may not be so clear: clinicians may often be self-employed or working in a partnership and moreover may be in the position of employer rather than employee. Practitioners who work as *locum tenens* will often be independent contractors, unless they satisfy the integration test by working in the same practice on a regular and dependable basis or pass some other test of employee status.

Employee status is important, as we have already mentioned, because many legal protections, including rules on unfair dismissal and payment of wages, given to those in the workplace only extend to employees. Furthermore and as we will see, certain protection is only attracted once the employee has completed a certain period of service in the job. For those who are not employees, their legal rights come down solely to the terms of the specific contract between the worker and the person employing her and those rights are far less extensively backed up by legislation. Some clinicians straddle uncomfortably the worlds of employee and non-employee and we look at one example below.

The case of the GMS general practitioner[7]

[5.05]

The General Medical Services (GMS) general practitioner (GP) bears, at one and the same time, the hallmarks of both an employee and an independent contractor. GMS doctors contract with health boards to provide primary care services to those patients on a GMS 'list' that is assigned to the doctor. The contract itself is described as a contract *for* the provision of services,[8] suggesting the possibility of independent contractor status, but the contract is also characterised by certain countervailing elements:

- Payments are made to the doctor are net of tax[9] and pension contributions
- Control is exercised by the health board over the general practitioner:
    - She agrees not to change her 'place of attendance or the days or hours of attendance so as to materially affect the convenience of...patients in the area' in which she is practising. Changes in hours of availability must be agreed with the health board.
    - The doctor may be required to give reasons to the health board for refusing to accept a patient onto her list. The health board can also assign patients to a doctor's list.
    - The health board may limit the number of patients on a doctor's list.
    - The health board may send a medical officer to inspect the doctor's practice arrangements.
- The general practitioner is subject to disciplinary proceedings under the Health Services Regulations.[10]
- The contract is terminated by the board when the doctor reaches retirement age.

Elements of control are in place along with deduction of taxation and pension at source, but set against this is that the doctor will typically be responsible for her own premises and for staff decisions and payment. Furthermore, if she keeps overheads low and prudently maximises turnover of patients and procedures, the doctor will increase her 'take-home' salary from the health board, suggesting that the 'enterprise test' would be passed. The balancing act is obvious, however it appears that when the courts have considered the matter, they seem satisfied that the relationship between the two is an employer-employee relationship rather than the general practitioner being an independent contractor,[11] but some recent cases have suggested that the courts might look differently at the GP's status if confronted with it again.[12]

The employment contract

[5.06]

A person in employment will usually have a contract containing the terms, conditions, duties and mutual obligations of the job. An employer is under a legal obligation to provide a written contract if one is requested[13] and he cannot avoid liability to the employee by relying on the fact that there is no written contract. The law will, if satisfied the worker is an employee, proceed as if a written contract exists. Contractual terms can be express (written into the contract) or implied, either by statute law or by court decisions.

Express terms

[5.07]

The following generally must be among the express terms in any contract:

- the names of parties to the contract, including the registered address of any company;

— job title and description, often including a 'mobility clause' stipulating that the post includes 'such other duties as may be assigned from time to time';
— working hours and overtime;
— commencement date and, where applicable, termination date of the contract;
— rate of pay and frequency of payment, including whether payment is subject to any deductions (such as PAYE at the applicable rate or pension contributions);
— any notice periods for the termination of employment;
— sick pay, leave entitlement and any other benefits-in-kind;
— references to any agreements to which the contract may be subject, such as negotiations between professional bodies and the Department of Health and Children or health boards.

Other terms often included in employment contracts are the duration of any probation period, expenses arrangements, rules on health and safety[14] and trade union membership, retirement age and disciplinary procedures. More modern additions to the employment contract include clauses limiting or regulating the use or scope of internet access on the employer's computers and network and acceptance of company equality and anti-harassment principles. Where a job involves dealing with confidential information, an express confidentiality clause may also be included (especially where the employee is not a health care professional and therefore not bound by the ethical precepts of a healthcare profession).[15] Some companies, particularly those working with valuable or sensitive products may also insist on a clause giving the employer the power to search employees' belongings.

'Restraint of trade' clauses are rare features of clinician's contacts but they do occur, prohibiting the employee, should she leave the business, from working in a way that damages her former employer by, for example, setting up in opposition in the locality or working for a rival company or disclosing secrets.[16] The key to the legality of such a clause is that it must be reasonable in terms of the area and the period of time covered by the clause. A clause prohibiting a doctor on leaving a job from ever working in Ireland again would be excessive. Conversely, a clause restraining her from working within three miles of the practice for a period of three years with the aim of preventing her from 'poaching' patients could pose fewer problems.[17]

Implied terms

[5.08]

Terms can be implied into a contract either because of the provisions of certain laws (statutory implied terms) or because of decisions courts have made in the past (common law implied terms). Terms may also be implied by collective agreements between employers and representative bodies, so that a salary increase or new disciplinary procedure negotiated between employer and trade union could form part of an employee's contract. Implied terms may not be implied into a contract if there is already an express term in the contract providing for something better.

Common law implied terms

- An employee must be paid for work done.
- An employer will take care for the safety of employees.[18]
- An employee will obey all reasonable orders and requests from her employer.[19]
- An employer will act fairly towards employees, while an employee is likewise bound to show fidelity to his employer and is not permitted to harm the employer's interests (this obligation may extend to spare time activities of the employee incompatible with the employer's interests).
- The right to sick pay – if it is not already provided for in the contract – may also be implied into a contract, but only in certain circumstances.[20]
- Fair procedures must be followed in any disciplinary investigations or decisions.

It is worth noting that there is no implied term compelling an employer to provide a reference for an employee who is leaving. A reference must be provided if there is an express term in the contract providing for it or may be produced by agreement between employer and employee, but there is no obligation to write one.[21] There is also no implied term forcing the employer to find 'light work' for an employee who is not fit to do her original job, although there is an obligation on the employer to try to find appropriate work in such circumstances.

Statutory implied terms

The Payment of Wages Act 1991 implies into every employment contract a term that wages due to the employee will be paid. If wages are not paid, or if they are not paid in the manner that the Act requires, the employee has a right to pursue a legal action for any loss she suffers (or to resign and claim constructive dismissal, see section **[5.13]**). The Act applies to all employees, no matter how short the duration of their employment and no matter how few hours they work per week.

An employee must get a confidential written statement of her gross pay, together with the amount and nature of any deductions, which will only be permitted if they are provided for by law, by the employment contract or by some other agreement with the employee. If the deduction is for any form of penalty, the employee must get written notice.[22]

The Employment Equality Act 1998 also implies a term into every employment contract that all employees, regardless of gender or other grounds for discriminations, will receive equal pay for equal work.[23]

Ending Employment

[5.09]

There are two elements to ending a period of employment that we consider here. The first is the notice that either the employee or employer must give the other of an intention to end employment and the second is the ending of employment itself – what constitutes a legal termination of employment and when is dismissal unfair or wrongful?

Quick Reference Guide 5.2

Employment contracts

- Every employee working on more than a temporary or casual basis is entitled to a written employment contract.
- The terms of a contract can be express (written in the contract) or implied (inserted into the contract by the law).
- Common express terms in an employment contract include details of the job, including working hours and overtime, the commencement (and termination) date of the contract; payment and taxation details; notice periods; holiday entitlements; sick pay and probation periods.
- Some terms are implied by the courts (common law terms), others by laws (statutory implied terms). The former include the right to be paid for one's work; an obligation on the employer to take care for the safety of employees; a mutual obligation of fairness and fidelity; an obligation on the employer to follow fair procedures in any disciplinary process against the employee. All employees – according to the Employment Equality Act 1998 – must receive equal pay for equal work.

Notice periods

[5.10]

The notice period is the length of time between the date when an employer or employee informs or gives 'notice' to the other of an intention to terminate employment and the date when that notice takes effect. One month's notice is the norm, but other periods are by no means uncommon: the contract between GPs and health boards stipulates a three-month notice period.[24] The Minimum Notice and Terms of Employment Act 1973 sets out the minimum notice an employee must be given, protecting employees, especially long-serving employees, against peremptory dismissal without sufficient notice. A clause in a job contract stipulating a notice period shorter that the period to which an employee is entitled under the Act is void,[25] although notice periods in the contract longer than the minimum in the Act are usually binding. The obligation contained in the Act is one way only: while the employer must give the statutory period of notice, the employee need only ever give one week's notice, unless a longer period is provided for in the contract.[26] The notice period to which the employee is entitled increases in proportion to the length of time the employee has been with the business.

Figure 5.2 – Minimum notice periods under the Minimum Notice and Terms of Employment Act 1973

Length of employment	*Minimum notice period*
13 weeks – 2 years	1 week
2 – 5 years	2 weeks
More than 5 years – 10 years	4 weeks
More than 10 years – 15 years	6 weeks
Over 15 years	8 weeks

During the period of notice, the employee retains all her usual rights, including holidays and sick pay entitlement. If the employer wants the employee to leave before the end of the notice period then he must pay the employee for the duration of the notice period as if she were working. There is no need for the employer to give notice, and no right for the employee to be given notice, where an employee is dismissed for serious misconduct (see section **[5.16]**).

Any case against a breach of the minimum notice period is brought to the Employment Appeals Tribunal (EAT), which can order compensation to be paid.

Dismissal

[5.11]

Dismissal from employment is defined as one of three things:

— Termination by the employer of the working relationship, with or without notice to the employee.

— Constructive dismissal. This is termination by the employee, with or without notice to the employer, in circumstances in which, because of the employer's conduct, the employee was entitled to, or it was reasonable for her to, terminate the contract of employment without giving notice of the termination to the employer.

— Expiration of contract of employment for a fixed term or a fixed purpose without it being renewed.[27]

Dismissal by an employer can lawfully occur for several reasons: the employee may be guilty of misconduct or may be incompetent or the company may need to make redundancies for economic reasons. But in other circumstances there may be no satisfactory grounds for the termination of employment and the employee may have a legal case for compensation. There are two main forms of legal action against dismissal:

— 'unfair dismissal', in which the former employee relies on the provisions of the Unfair Dismissals Acts 1977-2001 and brings her case to the Employment Appeals Tribunal or

— 'wrongful dismissal', in which the dismissed employee brings her case to court for a judge's appraisal of the situation and apportionment of blame.

There are advantages and disadvantages to pursuing either form of claim (a person bringing a legal action against his dismissal must choose between unfair or wrongful dismissal proceedings) but they lie outside the scope of this text. A person who has been dismissed may also ask a court in certain circumstances for an interlocutory injunction, a court order prohibiting the employer from terminating her employment until all other outstanding legal issues are resolved.

Unfair dismissal

[5.12]

A claim for unfair dismissal is heard before the Employment Appeals Tribunal (EAT), a three person panel consisting of a lawyer (who also acts as chairman), a union appointee and a nominee of employers' representative bodies. The process of claiming unfair dismissal before the EAT is less formal that pursuing a wrongful dismissal claim before the courts.[28] Witnesses can be called and questioned and the production of documents can be ordered. Evidence is usually taken on oath, although the rules on what amounts to admissible evidence are more relaxed than they would be in court.

To bring a claim for unfair dismissal a person must be an employee and have not less that one year's continuous service with the employer in question, working not less than an average of eight hours each week. This 'service requirement' is slightly elastic and can be ignored completely if the claim is for unfair dismissal as a result of reason of pregnancy, maternity or adoptive leave or trade union activities.[29] A person cannot bring an unfair dismissal case where:

— she reaches normal retirement age or the retirement age specified in her contract;

— she is employed by a family member, or employed in the family home or on a farm where both the employer and employee normally reside;

— she is a member of the Garda Síochána, the army, civil service, a local government or health board officer, a FÁS trainee, an apprentice, or a person in a fixed term or fixed purpose contract where that contract has expired.[30]

Once a claim for unfair dismissal is brought, the EAT generally starts from a pro-employee point of view: it is up to the employer to justify the dismissal by reference to one of the grounds listed in the act and dealt with below.[31] The only exceptions are 'constructive dismissal' (see section **[5.13]**) and when certain other grounds for dismissal are alleged.[32] In such cases, it is up to the employee to prove either that the necessary circumstances for constructive dismissal existed or that the alleged grounds were genuinely the motive for her dismissal.

Defending an allegation of unfair dismissal

An employer can defeat a claim for unfair dismissal by pointing out that the dismissal was based on one of the grounds provided for in the Unfair Dismissals Acts:

— capability, competence or qualifications;

— misconduct on the part of the employee;

— redundancy of the employee (subject to certain rules relating to unfair selection).

Once the employer proves that the employee was not competent or qualified to do the job, was guilty of misconduct or is redundant, then dismissal will not be unfair.[33]

Capability, competence and qualifications

An employee is obliged to be fully fit to perform all the functions required under the contract and, if she becomes unfit to carry out her functions, the employer has grounds to dismiss her. There is no legal obligation on the employer to re-deploy the employee who is unfit or unable to do her job although it is probably preferable for him to do so, or at least to attempt to do so. If medical unfitness is the substantial reason for dismissal, then there must be strong medical evidence to that effect, as well as evidence that the employee received fair notice that he might be dismissed for incapacity and was afforded the opportunity of being heard.

An employee will rarely be dismissed for lack of qualifications where she has not been given the opportunity to obtain those qualifications. Wilful refusal to acquire the skills or qualifications required for the position could however be grounds for dismissal.

Dismissal for incompetence should be predicated on clear previous warnings where faults and routes to improvement (including the contribution expected from the employee in achieving that improvement) are identified and an opportunity is given to the employee to come up to speed. There are no set rules concerning how many warnings should be given or whether warnings must be for the same shortcoming or whether shortcomings in different areas can be aggregated to demonstrate incompetence. In general, if any stage of a disciplinary process may result in dismissal or a permanent note on the employee's employment record, fair procedures should be carefully followed[34] and the employee offered the option of representation (legal or trade union) at any meeting or hearing.

Misconduct

If misconduct is the reason for dismissal, the question becomes whether fair procedures were followed in the decisions leading to dismissal and whether dismissal was a reasonable response to the conduct in question.[35] Any hearing by the EAT of an unfair dismissal claim where the employer alleges misconduct on the part of the employee is only concerned with the reasonableness of the decision and the procedures followed – it is not specifically concerned with whether the employee was actually guilty of the alleged misconduct. In deciding whether misconduct was an acceptable ground for dismissal, the EAT will consider the question of whether fair procedure and the rules of natural justice were followed in investigating and acting upon misconduct.[36]

Figure 5.3 –Fair procedure and misconduct: questions to be asked

- Was the matter fully investigated without undue delay?
- Was the employee made aware of the allegations, complaints and evidence against her?
- Was the employee given an adequate opportunity to challenge the allegations and evidence and to give her side of the story prior to a decision to dismiss being taken?
- Was there any bias in the hearing? For example, was there a person sitting on the disciplinary panel who had an interest in seeing the employee dismissed?
- Is there anything to suggest that the matter had been prejudged before any hearing?
- Was there any requirement for an oral hearing and if so was there a hearing and did the employee have the right to be represented (legally or by a trade union representative), to call or cross-examine witnesses and to make submissions? The more disputed issues of fact there are, the more likely it is that an oral hearing will be necessary to resolve uncertainties before taking a decision.
- Was the employer's belief that the employee was guilty of misconduct based on reasonable grounds?
- In essence the question is whether the employer had reasonable grounds for believing the employee guilty of misconduct and whether dismissal was a proportionate penalty given the circumstances.

The process of investigating misconduct in the work place does not have to adhere to the same high standards as a court, but the important thing to recall is that the need for observation of fair procedures varies proportionately to the potential consequences of the disciplinary process. A complaint that will result only in an informal warning requires less care, while any decision leading to a consequence such as dismissal, that will gravely effect a person's livelihood must carefully observe the basic rules of natural justice.[37]

Misconduct outside the workplace may be a valid ground for dismissal where the conduct has an impact in the work place, for example, a teacher in a religious school could be lawfully dismissed for becoming pregnant due an extra-marital liaison that was contrary to the ethos of the school[38] and a lecturer may be lawfully dismissed for having an affair with a student.[39] Similarly, criminal convictions may be grounds for dismissal, but it will depend on the nature of the conviction and of the employment. An employee will generally not be dismissed for a conviction for a single minor misdemeanour but may be dismissed if her conduct amounts to something more serious or if her job is such that the conviction is incompatible with it. There may also be a term in the contract that provides for dismissal in the event of any criminal conviction or that compels the employee to report any criminal conviction, in which case a breach of those terms may amount to grounds for dismissal. Obviously being in jail could limit the employee's ability to attend work in any case.

Constructive dismissal

[5.13]

Constructive dismissal arises, as we have mentioned above, in circumstances where the employee leaves employment, but she was *in effect* dismissed because the conduct of her employer made her working conditions intolerable. The matter is generally raised in the context of unfair or wrongful dismissal proceedings where, on the face of things, it appears as if the employee left rather than being dismissed. 'Constructive dismissal' means that the court, or more commonly the EAT, 'construes' that the employee was effectively dismissed because she had no choice but to leave the situation in which she found herself. The situation must be one where either the employee is legally entitled to leave[40] or it was otherwise reasonable for her to do so.

> **Example 1**
>
> In one case, a secretary worked for a manager who was dismissed by the company. The secretary was told that her job was safe, but over time her filing cabinet was removed, her break times altered, she was given little or no work to do, and her office telephone was disconnected. The Employment Appeals Tribunal found that her continuous isolation without knowledge of what was going on made it reasonable that her confidence in her employer should be undermined so much that she could tolerate it no longer. She left, but the circumstances meant that in effect she was dismissed.

Redundancy

[5.14]

An employee cannot claim unfair dismissal when the company can show the worker was redundant, or in other words that economic circumstances meant that she had to be dismissed to ensure the viability of the company. The frequency with which redundancy is used to trim the size of a workforce, or 'downsize', depends broadly on the health of the economy and if a person is made redundant in accordance with the rules for redundancy, she cannot claim she was unfairly or wrongfully dismissed.[41] In general, a claim of redundancy must be backed up by credible economic or accounting data that justify the decision and it must be shown that it is the redundancy that is the reason for dismissal. If an employee is made 'redundant' but is replaced days or weeks later, it makes an argument of redundancy look tenuous.

Wrongful dismissal

[5.15]

The difference between wrongful dismissal and unfair dismissal has already been mentioned: the former involves taking one's case to the court for its opinion based on what it thinks just; the latter involves taking the case to the Employment Appeals Tribunal to be decided in accordance with the Unfair Dismissals Acts. The employee has to decide which approach she will take. If one avenue is taken without success, then the employee cannot subsequently pursue her claim by the other method.

Because it is a court-based procedure, a case of wrongful dismissal is more formal and procedurally precise than a claim for unfair dismissal. The essence of wrongful dismissal is that there has been some breach of the employment contract or a breach of fair procedures by the employer resulting in the wrongful dismissal. If the employment contract provided for a certain disciplinary procedure or notice period or duties expected of the employee or employer and those contractual provisions were breached, then that might be sufficient grounds to successfully argue a case of wrongful dismissal.[42]

If a case for wrongful dismissal succeeds in court, the court can award damages and may also issue injunctions against dismissal or the suspension of pay (including sick pay) especially where the employee may suffer serious financial hardship, pending its final decision on the matter. Damages will generally be for loss of earnings but may also be for suffering or emotional distress or to punish an employer who acts in a particularly egregious way.

Summary dismissal

[5.16]

A notice period, whether contained in a contract or provided for by the Minimum Notice and Terms of Employment Act 1973 need not be complied with where the plaintiff is guilty of gross misconduct. Many contracts will contain a list, or a reference to a document or documents (such as an anti-harassment policy – see section **[5.22]**) that contain activities deemed to be gross misconduct.[43]

Equality, harassment and discrimination at work

[5.17]

Equality in the work place is largely governed by the Employment Equality Act 1998 and the Equal Status Act 2000, which apply to almost all employees[44] and cover conditions of employment and access to employment. The impetus for the implementation of equality legislation has come predominantly from the European Union and decisions of the European Court of Justice.

Quick Reference Guide 5.3

Dismissal from Work

- Dismissal occurs when the employer terminates the working relationship, where the employee leaves because of some conduct on the part of the employer ('constructive dismissal') or where a contract for a fixed time or fixed purpose reaches its conclusion.
- Unfair dismissal and wrongful dismissal are simply two different legal avenues for seeking a remedy for dismissal. A person bringing an action must choose between them. Unfair dismissal relies on the Unfair Dismissal Acts 1977-2001 and the case goes to the Employment Appeals Tribunal. Wrongful dismissal relies on broader legal principles and the case goes to the courts.
- A dismissal will not be unfair where the employer can show that the employee lacked the capability, qualifications or competence to do the job, that she was guilty of misconduct or that she was made redundant. Any investigation and punishment of misconduct must follow fair procedures (see figure 5.2).
- Constructive dismissal occurs when the conduct of the employer towards the employee was so bad that she was justified in leaving her employment.
- A person guilty of severe misconduct may on occasion be summarily dismissed from work.

Defining discrimination

[5.18]

Discrimination is defined as treating a person in a less favourable way than another person is being treated, has been treated or would be treated where that less favourable treatment is based on any one of the grounds for discrimination prohibited by the Acts. The Acts lay out nine characteristics against which it is unlawful to discriminate.

Figure 5.4 – Grounds on which unlawful discrimination can occur

Gender	A person cannot be discriminated against on the basis of gender.
Marital status	A person cannot be discriminated against for reasons relating specifically to the fact that she is she is single, married, divorced, separated or widowed.
Family status	A person cannot be discriminated for reasons relating to her responsibility either as a parent or as a person *in loco parentis* for someone below 18 years of age, or as a parent or resident primary carer for someone 18 years or over with a disability who requires a high degree of support and attention.
Age	People in employment between the ages of 18 and 65, or people in vocational training between the ages of 15 and 65, cannot be discriminated against because of their age.

Disability	Defined in the legislation as including total or partial absence of bodily or mental faculties, chronic disease, (whether manifest or not), learning and personality disorders. It includes a condition, illness or disease which affects a person's thought processes, perception of reality, emotions or judgement or which results in disturbed behaviour and includes a disability which exists at present, or which previously existed but no longer exists or which may exist in the future or which is imputed to a person. It is not discrimination if a person is not employed when her disability means that she simply could not do the job.
Race	Includes race, colour, nationality, ethnic or national origin.
Sexual orientation	Heterosexuality, homosexuality and bisexuality can all be raised as grounds for discrimination.
Religious belief	Includes religious background or outlook.
Membership of the Traveller Community	A person cannot be discriminated against for being a traveller.

Forms of discrimination

[5.19]

Discrimination can manifest itself in many ways, but the arenas in which questions of discrimination are most frequently played out are:

— equal pay provision;

— access to employment, including terms and conditions of employment, promotion, advertising, and job interviews;

— sexual harassment and harassment on other grounds.

Discrimination in the work place is generally broken down into two categories: direct and indirect. 'Direct discrimination' is that which is specifically and explicitly based on a characteristic that should not be discriminated against under the Act. Claims for direct discrimination involve a direct comparison between the way in which the claimant has been treated and treatment of a member of a group that does not possess the claimant's characteristic: a man will be compared to a woman, a homosexual person to a heterosexual and so on.

Example 2

If an interviewer tells a female applicant for that she is an excellent candidate for a job but that he is looking for a man because the man will work harder and will not be taking time off to have babies all the time, that would be direct discrimination.

'Indirect discrimination' is much more complex (and need not concern us unduly here) but it does not *explicitly* discriminate against members of a particular class. Instead, it can arise when, once the matter in question is scrutinised, the *implicit* effect is to discriminate against a particular group.

Example 3

If a job has, as one criterion for applying, membership of a particular trade union then that is not *directly* discriminatory. However, if the union in question is one that has long been traditionally male-dominated, then that might be an example of *indirect* sexual discrimination, because more women than men will be effectively precluded from applying for the job.[45]

The employer can defend any allegation of discrimination by showing that a decision taken against an applicant was unrelated to the applicant's gender, disability or other characteristic or that there are specific circumstances[46] that justify the discrimination. While, for many types of discrimination it may be possible for the employer to defend himself, any discrimination relating to gender is very difficult to justify.

Equal pay

[5.20]

There should be no discrimination in terms of pay between different categories of people doing 'like work'. Therefore a disabled person doing precisely the same job as a non-disabled person should be paid at the same rate.[47] 'Like work' means not only identical work, but can also mean work that is very similar or, more nebulously, work that is regarded as being of equal value:[48] thus two different administrative tasks although not identical could be regarded as 'like work'. Special qualifications or skills that a person has, or her ability to do jobs other than the one she is doing, may be taken into account to justify a difference in pay between two people doing ostensibly similar jobs.[49]

Comparison must be made within the same company or associated group of companies. If a claim (generally taken to the Equality Authority – see section **[5.23]**) is successful, the employee will be awarded equal pay from the date of the settlement and can be awarded arrears for up to three years previously. If the reason for the pay disparity is gender rather than any of the potential grounds for discrimination, then the complainant may go straight to the Circuit Court where there is no limit to the damages that may be awarded.[50]

Access to employment

[5.21]

This can include job advertisements, the interview process and job offer[51] and subsequently the promotion system within the company.

Job interviews

At a job interview, questions may only be asked of candidates that are asked of candidates of either gender (or of both traveller or non-traveller candidates and so on). It would therefore not be appropriate, for example, to ask a woman about her plans for pregnancy or a disabled person about whether any periods of hospitalisation are on the horizon. Where an interview board is being constituted attempts should be made to achieve a gender balance. Good practice demands that notes should be made and retained of questions, answers and any written comments on those answers.[52]

Advertisements

Job advertisements that indicate that person of a specific gender or a 'young' person is sought may be discriminatory. In theory, this could extend to describing any characteristics for the job (such as 'cheerful' – does that discriminate against those who are disabled by depression or misanthropy?), but the question of what constitutes a discriminatory advertisement is an evolving area.

Harassment

[5.22]

Harassment can be sexual or based on other grounds. Sexual harassment is defined[53] as unwanted physical intimacy, requests for sexual favours, spoken words and gestures or the display or circulation of written words, pictures or other materials in the workplace, if the act request or conduct is unwelcome and could reasonably be regarded as offensive, humiliating or intimidating.

Harassment can often be difficult for the employer to confirm because it may be covert in nature. However, an allegation that seems to be well-founded should be taken seriously, because an employer can be held liable for harassment by one of his staff members, even if the employer himself is not directly responsible for it and, odd as it may seem, even if he is not aware of it. Harassment or bullying not based on one of the grounds for discrimination contained in the Employment Equality Act is not covered by the Act, but may be grounds for constructive dismissal or for a case against the employer for failing in his duty to care for the safety and welfare of his employee.[54]

If an employer is aware that harassment is or may be taking place within the firm, he is under a duty to deal with the problem or face liability. Even if the employer does not know about the problem, he can still be held liable and that liability extends to all harassment, especially sexual harassment, in the workplace even if those responsible for the harassment are not employees, but clients, customers or other business contacts. Any harassment that takes place in the course of employment or even outside the workplace (if it has repercussions in the workplace) is covered by the legislation. Harassment is not judged by the intent of the harasser, but by the effect it has on the employee being harassed.

Employers are required to both prevent and to remedy harassment. An employer who takes prompt action concerning harassment outside the workplace, such as transferring the harasser on hearing of an allegation, can discharge his liability under the Act. If the harassment occurs in the workplace, the employer will have to show that he took reasonable steps to remedy the problem that has arisen and to prevent the harassment in the first place. The minimum steps an employer must take include the adoption of a sexual harassment policy,[55] together with swift investigation and reaction to an allegation of harassment, following the rules laid down in the anti-harassment policy. Investigation and punishment should be in accordance with the rules of fair procedure and natural justice.[56] The employer has a defence to harassment if he can show that he took all reasonable steps to prevent harassment generally and to remedy the consequences of the particular act alleged.[57] Another possible defence is for the company to argue that the conduct complained of could not in fact be reasonably regarded as 'offensive, humiliating or intimidating'.

An anti-harassment code should contain at a minimum a definition of harassment and the reporting and complaint process[58] open to employees who believe they are victims of sexual or non-sexual harassment, together with allocation of responsibilities for making the policy work. The policy should be put into action and not simply be put in writing: a policy against harassment is worthless and will not be a defence against an allegation of harassment is made if the policy is not implemented or its effectiveness is not monitored.

Claiming discrimination

[5.23]

Initially a complaint will, or should, be raised with the employer, providing an opportunity for resolution of matters within the firm. If a company takes prompt and appropriate action to investigate and deal with any discrimination (whether in terms of pay, promotion, harassment or some other ground), that should be the end of the matter. If the problem is not alleviated, an employee may further her search for satisfaction by contacting the Equality Authority, her trade union, or a solicitor (a person who has been discriminated against on gender grounds can go to court rather than to the Equality Authority). The Equality Authority may choose to investigate matters further and remedy problems, first through informal efforts[59] and then if necessary through a more formal process (although there is no need for legal representation at the early stages). The Equality Authority can refer the matter to the Director of Equality Investigations[60] who can determine the matter and make a finding that is binding on employer and employee. Any decision can be appealed by either party to the Labour Court. Any employee who brings a discrimination case under the Employment Equality Act is prevented by law from being victimised by her employer for having done so.

In cases other than equal pay (see section **[5.20]**), up to two years' pay may be awarded to an employee or up to £10,000 where the person discriminated against was not an employee.[61] In a case where the discrimination resulted in the dismissal of the employee, the case will be heard in the Labour Court or Employment Appeals Tribunal, rather than the Equality Authority. The Labour Court can order compensation to a maximum of two years' salary or re-employment. As mentioned in the context of equal pay, in any case where the basis for discrimination is gender (and only in such cases), the aggrieved person can go straight to the Circuit Court, which can award damages as it sees fit with no upper limit. Any discrimination case must be brought within six months of the most recent act of the alleged discrimination.

Exceptions to equality legislation[62]

[5.24]

The legislation providing for equality is not a total stranger to the realities of the workplace. An employer is not required to recruit, promote, or retain an employee who is not able, willing or competent to perform her duties. Discrimination on the basis of gender is also permissible where gender is an occupational qualification or where a job involves services of a personal nature. Physical prerequisites such as height, good eyesight or a lack of disability are permissible where reasonable (for example, the Garda Síochána or airline pilots).

Obviously, it is permissible to discriminate on the basis of educational attainment. Religious institutions are also permitted to discriminate in a manner that is in keeping with their own peculiar ethos. Discrimination based on age cannot apply to those over the age of 65 years or under the age of 18 years (15 if in vocational training). Discrimination based on the length of time a person has spent in a job may be indirect discrimination (if, for example, women were only employed to that job in the recent past, they are less likely to have the requisite service and experience). Discrimination can be based on age where there are sound economic reasons for doing so, such as where by the time the training of a particular person is completed she will be at or near retirement age.

Quick Reference Guide 5.4

Equality and harassment

- Equality in the workplace is governed by the Employment Equality Act 1998 and Equal Status Act 2000. There are nine possible grounds on which unlawful discrimination may occur (see figure 5.3).
- Discrimination can be direct or – more complexly – indirect. It most frequently relates to equal pay issues, access to employment and harassment.
- All those doing like work should receive like pay, assuming that the only difference in pay is due to discrimination. Therefore, a woman should receive the same as a man, a disabled person the same as an able bodied person. 'Like work' can mean identical work, similar work or work having the 'same value'. Special qualifications that one person has over another may justify discrimination. This does not stop employers paying better workers more money (for example, bonuses), so long as the reason for the differential is not any form of discrimination.
- Job interviews should ask only questions that can be asked of all candidates, whether or not they fit into a group that is covered by the equality legislation. So, a man should be asked the same questions as a woman, a traveller the same questions as a non-traveller. An interview board should attempt to achieve a gender balance in its composition.
- The employer can be held legally responsible for harassment in the workplace, even if he is not personally the perpetrator.
- There are certain exceptions to equality legislation: there is no obligation to recruit, promote or retain an employee who cannot or will not do her job. Physical requirements may be introduced for certain jobs where they are justifiable.

MATERNITY AND OTHER FORMS OF LEAVE

[5.25]

No employee can be penalised for taking any form of leave to which she is entitled under the law although there are often conditions attached.

Maternity leave

[5.26]

The rights of the pregnant woman or recently delivered mother are covered by the Maternity Protection Act 1994[63]. The rights the Act confers are essentially simple:

- the right not to be dismissed because of pregnancy;[64]
- the right to leave employment on health or safety grounds during pregnancy;
- the right to not less than 18 weeks maternity leave and an optional additional 8 weeks;

- the right to be reinstated to the same job or to a position no less favourable on return from leave;
- the right to maternity benefit and benefit paid if leaving work for health or safety reasons (there is no obligation on the employer to pay this, unless it is express or implied in the employment contact – the State generally pays[65] if the employer does not);
- the right to paid time off for antenatal care;
- a limited right to paternity leave equivalent in terms to maternity leave, if the mother of the child dies in childbirth.

The employee is required to give four weeks' notice in writing of her intention to leave, together with medical certification of the pregnancy; similar formalities accompany the return to work and if they are not complied with, the pregnant woman may lose her rights. The leave may be postponed in certain circumstances and may be terminated if an employer becomes aware that the maternity leave is not being used for the purpose it was granted.

The right to return to the same or equivalent job is not absolute. The employee must fulfil the formalities of notifying the employer of her intention to return in writing[66] and the employer has the option of offering the employee suitable alternative employment that is no less rewarding and with conditions that are as favourable as the position held before maternity leave.[67] The employer is also obliged to carry out a risk assessment of the workplace with respect to any hazards posed to the pregnant woman.[68] If as a result of some risk, the employer is required to move the employee away from her present position but it is either not feasible to move her or there is no other work to which she can be moved, then the woman is entitled to take leave.[69]

Complaints about violation of the entitlement to maternity leave are generally brought to the Rights Commissioner, but if the violations result in dismissal (constructive or otherwise) the employee may go to the Employment Appeals Tribunal (unfair dismissal) or the courts (wrongful dismissal).

Parental leave

[5.27]

There is also a right under the Parental Leave Act 1998 for either parent to take unpaid leave for a period to care for children. The employer is under no obligation to pay for such leave and nor is there any Social Welfare payment for it.

Crisis leave

[5.28]

Parents can take paid crisis leave due to urgent reasons relating to the illness of a family member (typically, but not limited to, a child or spouse) and where the presence of the employee is necessary to care for the family member.[70] The urgency of the crisis should generally be judged from the employee's point of view, so that if, for example, a child appears to be seriously ill, the fact that he turns out not to be seriously ill does not undermine the need to take the leave.[71]

Carers' leave

[5.29]

Carers' leave is governed by the Carers' Leave Act 2001 and open to all employees with 12 months continuous services with their employer who require leave to provide full time care for another person. The employee needs a ruling from the Department of Social and Family Affairs that the person in question requires a full-time carer. The employer does not have to pay for the leave and the Department of Social Family Affairs pays a carer's allowance. The employer can refuse to grant the leave in certain circumstances, including where the leave is sought for a short period only (less than 13 weeks). Notification must be given in writing of the intention to leave and to return.

THE WORKING WEEK

[5.30]

The laws regulating the working week consist largely of exceptions to the basic legislation. On the one hand the law lays down strict rules on the maximum hours a person may work each week and the breaks that must be taken from work but on the other hand, it has created a patchwork of exemptions such that the law applies to few people. The law is the Organisation of Working Time Act 1997, which according to its terms, applies to all employees, except Gardaí and members of the defence forces and certain others, including doctors in training.[72] However, a European Directive has instructed member states to reduce the working week of non-consultant hospital doctors to 48 hours by 2010.[73]

The Act sets down, for those covered by the Act, rules on breaks from work (both breaks in the working day and breaks in the working week), the length of the working week and night work.[74] The Act also covers holiday entitlements and Sunday working.

According to the Organisation of Working Time Act 1997, only a maximum of 48 hours can be worked in a seven day period, including overtime. This working week can be calculated by averaging over a period of 4 to 12 months (which can have the value of offsetting overtime during busy times with the shorter week in quieter periods). Night is defined as between 12 pm and 7am and a night worker is someone who works at least three hours at night or who works 50% of his total yearly working hours between those times. The Act limits the amount of night work that may be done by any employee and in particular, workers dealing with hazardous substances are not permitted to work in excess of eight hours per night on any night. Other workers are not permitted to work in excess of an average of eight hours per night over a period of two months or in excess of any other period that has been decided by collective agreement.

The Act is regularly ignored, may be varied by agreement, and in many professions, including medical practice, it is practically impossible to observe its requirements. The government has introduced regulations to exempt a number of jobs, including transport workers and civil protection services,[75] from the provisions of the Act relating to rest periods, length of the working week and night work. Similarly, other general exemptions do not specify particular employees, but rather cover all those whose jobs are not amenable to the rules in the Act, exempting among others those in posts where continuity of provision of service is vital and specifically including the health care sector.[76]

In theory, the Act is designed to protect workers from overwork. In practice the combination of exemptions and the fact that workers can agree with their employer to vary the terms of the Act (coupled with the fact that many workers prefer to work some overtime with the financial benefits it brings) mean that the Act has yet to acquire any real bite in the workplace. The most important area will be the attempt, before 2010, to achieve the target of a 48-hour working week for doctors in training.

Endnotes

1 In this chapter the he/she problem is resolved by referring to the employee as 'she' and the employer as 'he'.

2 *Roche v Kelly & Co Ltd* [1969] IR 100 is an example. Note too a medical example that shows the demise of the 'control test': *O'Donovan v Cork Co Council* [1967] IR 173, a consultant surgeon was found to be an employee in spite of the fact that the hospital did not exercise any direct control over his clinical activities. See also section **[7.25]**, 'Vicarious liability'.

4 *O'Coindeabhlan v Mooney* [1990] 1 IR 422.

5 In *Henry Denny and Co (Ire) Ltd v Minister for Social Welfare* [1998] 1 IR 34, a woman worked as an in-store demonstrator of products and was described in her contract as an 'independent contractor'. There was no obligation on the company to provide her with work and she was similarly free to refuse engagements. She was given a few days' notice of each job and when in-store she had to wear a uniform and was subject to the control of the shop in which she was working. Her salary was paid gross (no tax deductions). The Supreme Court decided she was an employee. On the other hand in a case which shows the balancing elements involved in deciding on employee status, a sub-post master who could only make staffing decision with the approval of An Post (suggesting control by An Post) was not an employee thanks to the presence of other factors: *Tierney v An Post* [1999] ELR 293.

6 *Doherty v Kincasslagh Trawlers* [1999] ELR 251: 'share fishermen' working on a trawler were partners rather than employees. The same would apply to any enterprise where those working in the company were splitting the profits (eg physiotherapists or doctors in a group practice: see *O'Friel v St Michael's Hospital* [1982] ILRM 260, which concerned payments to doctors in practice in a private hospital).

7 And others who provide services to the health board alongside private work.

8 Or more fully, 'Form of Agreement with Registered Medical Practitioner for Provision of Services under section 58 of the Health Act 1970'.

9 Although the tax deducted is not PAYE tax, as it would generally be in the case of employees: it is a 'withholding tax', a deduction that is applied at source to all payments by the State or State bodies to individuals for 'professional services'. A method of structuring withholding tax so that it amounted to a form of double taxation was successfully challenged by a GP: *Michael Daly v Revenue Commissioners, Ireland and the Attorney General* [1995] 3 IR 1; [1996] 1 ILRM 122.

10 The Health Act 1970, s 72(1) allows the Minister for Health to lay down the regulations for schemes such as the General Medical Services: see Health Service Regulations 1972 (SI 1972/88).

11 *Grehan v North Eastern Health Board, The Minister for Health and the Attorney General* [1989] IR 422.

12 *O'Coindeabhlan v Mooney* [1990] 1 IR 422.

13 Terms of Employment (Information) Act 1994. The written contract should be given to the employee within two months of commencing employment, but does not have to be given to those who work fewer than eight hours each week or those whose contract duration is less than a month.

14 See ch 9 (section **[9.10]** *ff.*

15 A confidentiality clause in a non-practitioner's contract relating to confidential material encountered in the practice is probably no longer binding once the employee has left unless the secrets are confidential business information that would be useful to a competitor: *Faccenda Chickens Ltd v Fowler* [1985] ICR 589.

16 See *Esso Petroleum Co Ltd v Harper's Garage (Stourport) Ltd* [1968] AC 269.

17 General practice trainees who spend time in general practice prior to taking their postgraduate examinations are frequently required to sign contracts that contain such clauses. The terms generally prohibit the trainee from setting up within a certain radius of the practice for certain length of time (generally three years).

18 See ch 9 (section **[9.10]** *ff*).

19 What is reasonable may vary with the circumstances. It will obviously be more reasonable for a hospital to require a doctor to remain at work to operate through the night than it will for the hospital to require its secretarial staff to type all night to catch up on an administrative backlog. In *Aziz v Midland Health Board* [1995] ELR 48, a medical registrar was dismissed for disobeying a consultant's instructions. The decision was later overturned by the Supreme Court on a point of fair procedure (the doctor was not given the opportunity to present his side of the case), but the court upheld the right of the hospital to dismiss staff in such circumstances, so long as fair procedures are followed. See *Aziz v Midland Health Board* (29 October 1999, unreported), SC.

20 *Charlton v HH The Aga Khan's Studs* [2000] IEHC 20.

21 We discuss the potential for the practitioner to be liable for a negligently prepared reference in ch 7 (section **[7.17]**). See *Spring v Guardian Insurance* [1995] 2 AC 296.

22 Written notice does not apply to deductions for tax, for payments to third parties (eg a pension or insurance scheme) where the employee has consented to the payments or deductions for over-payment of wages. Wages include fees, bonuses and commission payments together with holiday, sick and maternity pay.

23 Employment Equality Act 1998, s 19.

24 'Form of Agreement with registered Medical Practitioner for Provision of Services under section 58 of the Health Act 1970', para 36. The contract also obliges the medical practitioner to give three months' notice unless a shorter period is accepted by the health board. Termination is immediate if the doctor is erased from the register of medical practitioners (see ch 2).

25 Minimum Notice and Terms of Employment Act 1973, s 4.

26 Minimum Notice and Terms of Employment Act 1973, s 6. Employees who have worked for no fewer that 13 weeks for their employer and for no fewer than an average of 8 hours per week are covered by the Act, although certain employees are excluded by the Act including Gardaí, soldiers and civil servants.

27 Non-consultant hospital doctors are 'dismissed' in this way at the end of their contracts.

28 Preliminary pleadings are reduced to a bare minimum: legal action is commenced by a simple form (Form T1/A) accompanied by the details of the claim and the damages sought. The employer responds in similar fashion (Form T2). See ch 10 for an account of the more complex pleadings involved in a civil court case (section **[10.11]**).

29 If someone alleges that this is the reason for her dismissal, they must prove this allegation to the satisfaction of the EAT before it will be prepared to overlook the service requirement.

30 In order for a fixed term or fixed purpose contract not to be covered (at the expiry of the contract) by unfair dismissal legislation, the original, signed employment contract must include the following term: 'The Unfair Dismissal Acts shall not apply to a dismissal consisting only of the expiry of the fixed term [or, as the case may be, the cesser of the specified purpose] of this contract.' If a person is dismissed for a reason other than the expiry of the contract, then she may still be entitled to bring an action for unfair dismissal. A series of contracts, even with short breaks between them, may be regarded as continuous employment if the EAT thinks the contracts are being used to evade liability under the Unfair Dismissal Acts.

31 Unfair Dismissals Act 1977, s 6.

32 These grounds are: trade union membership or activity; political or religious beliefs of the employee; participation by the employee in legal proceedings against the employer (whether actual or threatened and irrespective of whether the employee is a witness or a plaintiff in the proceedings); race, colour, sexual orientation, age, traveller, nationality, disability, marital or family status; maternity or pregnancy leave or leave following the adoption of a child.

33 There is also the possibility of an employer justifying dismissal on 'other substantial grounds'.

34 See figure 5.3 and section **[2.16]**.

35 *Hennessy v Read and Write Shop* (UD 192/28).

36 Unfair Dismissal Acts 1977-2001, s 7(2) allows the EAT to look at whether fair procedure was followed by the employer in determining to dismiss the employee. In *McNamara v South Western Area Health Board* (16 February 2001, unreported), a consultant orthodontist obtained an order from the court, restraining the health board from suspending her. The health board had received an allegation of misconduct against her and suspended her without giving her a chance to respond to the allegations: a breach of fair procedure.

37 *Gunn v National College of Art and Design* [1990] 2 IR 168.

38 *Flynn v Power* [1985] IR 648. A similar situation could arise with the clinician who had a relationship with a patient under her care, where that relationship was contrary to the ethics of the employer or the contract of employment.

39 *Orr v University of Tasmania* [1956] Tas SR 155.

40 For example, an employee who left employment because she was not being paid would be legally entitled to do so (Payment of Wages Act 1991 – see section **[5.08]**) and could claim for constructive dismissal.

41 The definitions, rules and payments for redundancy are contained in the Redundancy Payments Act 1967.

42 *Mooney v An Post* [1998] 4 IR 288. In *McNamara v South Western Health Board*, a consultant orthodontist employed under the provisions of the Health Act 1970 and the disciplinary procedures set out in the Health (Renewal of Officers and Servants) Regulations 1971 (SI 1971/110) was accused of misconduct. A decision was taken to suspend her without pay on the basis of that accusation, but she was given no opportunity to make representations before the suspension was imposed (see the discussion of fair procedure and misconduct at figure 5.3 and section **[2.16]**) and so an injunction was granted by a court lifting the suspension as part of its consideration of wrongful dismissal.

43 See the 'Form of Agreement with registered Medical Practitioner for Provision of Services under section 58 of the Health Act 1970' which allows for immediate termination of the contract if the doctor is erased from the register of medical practitioners (para 35).

44 Gardaí and members of the armed forces are among those excluded.

45 *Nathan v Baily Gibson* [1998] 2 IR 162.

46 Such as strong economic arguments or negotiated agreements with the employees' representative body.

47 Employment Equality Act 1998. Section 19 of the Act deals with gender-based equal pay claims and s 29 deals with claims based on other grounds, such as sexual orientation or disability.

48 Employment Equality Act 1998, s 7. Whether work is of 'equal value' will be decided by the court and often amounts to a balancing act.

49 In one case a psychotherapist argued that she was being discriminated against on gender grounds by being paid less than a medically-qualified colleague who was also practising psychotherapy. However, the doctor's greater qualifications meant that the two jobs were not interchangeable and the pay differential was permissible.

50 In general, the Circuit Court is limited in the damages it can award (see Appendix, section **[A.10]**), but an exception is made to encourage the employer to settle gender-based discrimination claims immediately rather than facing the prospect of a huge award against him in the Circuit Court.

51 So when a woman was offered a job and the job offer was subsequently withdrawn when she became pregnant, that was considered direct discrimination against the woman in question: see *Dekker* [1990] ECR I-3941.

52 *Mitchell v Southern Health Board* [2001] ELR 201; *Gleeson v Rotunda Hospital* [2000] ELR 206. A candidate applying for a job with a 'public body' such as a health board hospital or a government department would probably have a right to see interview notes under the Freedom of Information Act 1997. For more details on what constitutes a 'public body' and the parameters of Freedom of Information legislation, see ch 6.

53 Employment Equality Act 1998, s 23(3).

54 See ch 9, section **[9.10]** *ff.*

55 See Equality Authority *Code of Practice on Sexual harassment and Harassment at Work* 2002. The code has been given legal effect (in other words, the law recognises it as best practice and thus the employer should adopt it as a matter of course) by the Employment Equality Act 1998 (Code of Practice) (Harassment) Order 2002 (SI 2002/78). The report is available for download from the Equality Authority: www.equality.ie (last accessed September 2002). Also of interest is the Health and Safety Authority (Code of Practice on the Prevention of Workplace Bullying) (SI 2002/17).

56 See figure 5.3 and section **[2.16]**.

57 See Labour Court Case 4/93 *A Worker v A Bank*. A full investigation was undertaken following an allegation of sexual harassment, involving interviewing all relevant personnel and consideration of written statements from parties directly involved and their supervisors. Investigation carried out properly and thoroughly. The harasser was reprimanded and required to apologise in writing and the incident was recorded on his personnel file. The Labour Court described this as an exemplary response.

58 The *Code of Practice on Sexual Harassment and Harassment at Work* (see endnote 55 above) suggests that there should be both informal and formal avenues available to the employee. The latter would be used if informal attempts to solve the problem fail, if the harassment were of a serious nature or if the employee wishes to make a formal complaint.

59 There is an Equality Mediation Officer who may attempt to build bridges and suggest solutions to the problem of harassment in the particular workplace.

60 A post created by the Employment Equality Act 1998, s 75.

61 For example someone who alleges that she was discriminated against in an advertisement or a job interview.

62 Largely covered in Employment Equality Act 1998, s 16.

63 Which brought into force the EU Maternity Protection Directive (92/85/EEC). There is similar legislation in place to allow mothers (and in certain circumstances fathers) to take adoptive

leave: Adoptive Leave Act 1995. Leave periods are, for obvious reasons, shorter for adoptive mothers than they are for mothers who have been pregnant and given birth.

64 The employer has to prove that the dismissal was for reasons unrelated to pregnancy. Dismissal can take the form of not permitting the employee to start back at work on her expected day of return: Maternity Protection Act 1994, s 40(4).

65 Benefit is based on PRSI contributions so it will not always be forthcoming.

66 Maternity Protection Act 1994, s 28.

67 Maternity Protection Act 1994, s 27.

68 Safety, Health and Welfare at Work (Pregnant Employees) Regulations 2000 (SI 2000/218).

69 Maternity Protection Act 1994, s 18. *Coffey v Byrne* [1997] ELR 230 concerned a hairdresser's failure to carry out a risk assessment: the employee's right to leave, when it was recommended by her doctor that she should be allowed to do so on medical grounds, was upheld.

70 Parental Leave Act 1998, s 13. Maximum leave is 3 days in any 12 month period or 5 days in any 36 months.

71 *Carey v Penn Racquets Sports Limited* [2000] ELR 27.

72 Organisation of Working Time Act 1997, s 3 (s 3(2)(a)(iii) specifically exempts 'doctors in training').

73 Council Directive 93/104/EC – the 'Working Time Directive' – covers groups originally excluded from the Organisation of Working Time Act 1997, including junior hospital doctors. The aim is to reach an average working week of 58 hours by 2004 and 48 hours by 2010.

74 Organisation of Working Time Act 1997, ss 11, 13, 15 & 16 respectively.

75 Organisation of Working Time Act (Exemption of Transport Activities) Regulations 1998 (SI 1998/120); Organisation of Working Time Act (Exemption of Civil Protection Services) Regulations 1998 (SI 1998/52).

76 Organisation of Working Time Act (General Exemptions) Regulations 1998 (SI 1998/12).

Chapter 6

Clinical Records and Prescribing

INTRODUCTION

[6.01]

Notes of consultations or prescriptions given to patients and transmitted subsequently to pharmacists may constitute the only permanent record of what has taken place between the clinician and the patient. Allegations of wrongdoing or negligence may sometimes stand or fall almost entirely on the representation of events depicted in the written record.

A clinical record that contains a detailed account of an examination conducted and the findings of any such examination leaves fewer opportunities for contradiction or misinterpretation than a terse few words comprising personalised, non-standardised and often equivocal abbreviations. Similarly a prescription that is clear and unambiguous can save the doctor (and the pharmacist) a great deal of trouble.

This chapter is concerned not merely with the quality of clinical records but just as importantly looks at the records themselves. Who owns them? Who may have access to them? Do different rules apply to records held on computer as distinct from paper records? The chapter concludes by providing an overview of the rules on prescribing and the potential consequences for both clinician and pharmacist if a prescription is inadequate.

THE IMPORTANCE OF THE WRITTEN RECORD

[6.02]

Whether one looks at this question from a medical or a legal perspective, the message is simple and intuitive: clear and accurate records are essential to good patient care.[1] Looked at from the health care professional's point of view, good notes allow for better continuity of care between clinicians who share the same practice or between those in a multi-disciplinary team who jointly share responsibility for the care of the same patient.

Similarly, good notes stand the test of time, an important consideration when any given set of notes may be handled, referred to and added to by a succession of different people, such as junior doctors consecutively rotating through a consultant's 'team' in a hospital. Clear documentation of what has been done also minimises the possibility of the repetition of redundant and potentially dangerous tests.[2]

From the legal perspective, good clinical records are also essential: bear in mind the legal maxim 'no notes, no defence'. If a patient brings a doctor to court alleging negligence and the doctor has no records, it becomes very difficult for her to defend herself. The more deficient the records, the more difficult it will be to make out a plausible defence and the more compelling may be the inference that the doctor was in fact negligent. This is especially significant if one considers for a moment the snail's pace at which the legal process may sometimes move. It can be very many years between the occasion that gives rise to the reason for legal action and the legal action itself. Take the following example:

Example 1

Dr Chekhov works in an exceptionally busy general practice. Amongst her duties is the vaccination of children. In an average week she will vaccinate at least fifty children. In order to maximise throughput she took to recording only the fact of the vaccination and its generic type (for example 'whooping cough') without recording the brand name or identification number of the vaccination or anything about the health of the child.

A child she vaccinated in 1990 began shortly afterwards to experience convulsions. Within two years, he was manifesting definite signs of developmental delay. By 1994, there was a firm diagnosis of mental handicap. In 1996, six years after the initial vaccination, the parents initiated legal action against Dr Chekhov, alleging that she failed to check for or to act upon any contraindications to the vaccination. The parents claim that the child had a fever on the day of the vaccination and an allergy to one of the components of the vaccine.

However, there have also been simultaneous allegations that Unichem, the makers of one particular brand of the vaccine in question, knowingly released a faulty batch of vaccines and they too are facing massive claims for damages, which they have agreed to settle. If the doctor could prove that she had given one of these vaccines, then perhaps the family would think it wiser to pursue the company for damages.

Dr Chekhov's notes cannot confirm that a Unichem vaccine was given and so much time has elapsed that she cannot remember the vaccine used. Similarly, her notes do not record any clinical findings on the child or whether she checked for contraindications. Again, so much time has passed that she has no recollection of the consultation with which to bolster her inadequate notes.

There are two reasons why the notes could help the doctor here. In the first place, she might be able to demonstrate that she had in fact recorded the child as having a normal temperature and that furthermore she had enquired about any allergies and had documented the parents' replies. In the second place, she might be able to demonstrate that she gave a Unichem vaccine and that it was this particular vaccine, rather than any act or omission on her part, that gave rise to the brain damage. Neither avenue is open to her because of the shortcomings of the notes.

A clinician's records may be the only link to the past and more importantly the only written narrative of the encounter that is untainted by any hidden agenda or bias. Once legal action is commenced a patient will naturally wish to right what he perceives as a wrong. Such desires can begin to play tricks with the memory: both clinician and patient may begin to put a slant on what they claim happened, a difference of emphasis that may serve only to polarise the legal dispute and cloud the facts of what actually took place between the two at the time of the original encounter. Therefore, if the clinical notes of the encounter are extant, thorough and unambiguous, they can be crucial. Firstly, because they were written long before any legal action was contemplated, they are not influenced by any subsequent turn of events and may generally be assumed to be an honest account of what took place. Secondly, notes are typically made contemporaneously with or only shortly after the original consultation and so may be less fallible than human memory.

Making good notes

[6.03]

If a practitioner were to sit down and plan an approach to note-taking, where could she look for guidance? The Irish Medical Council's *Guide to Ethical Conduct and Behaviour*[3] provides something of a starting point, saying this on the subject of medical records:

> 'It is in the interest of both doctors and patients that *accurate* records are always kept. These should be retained for an adequate period[4] and eventual disposal may be subject to advice from legal and insurance bodies. There is no objection to patients being supplied with a report of their own medical history.'[5] [emphasis added]

The *Rules of Professional Conduct* produced by the Irish Society of Chartered Physiotherapists state that:

> 'The Chartered Physiotherapist shall maintain *adequate* records of the patient's conditions, treatments and progress.'[7]

It is the case for all health professionals that notes should be made of clinical decisions that have an impact on patient care. Those notes should be, combining the cardinal elements of the medical and physiotherapy guidelines above, *accurate and adequate*. In Ireland, the legal requirement to keep proper records was confirmed by the Irish courts in *Toal v Duignan.*[9]

We have seen that the Irish Medical Council *Guide* and the Physiotherapy *Rules* both offer a benchmark, but they are not very instructive: what after all are 'accurate' records and when can one be sure that they are 'adequate'? Both phrases lack certainty and context, although the word 'adequate' is undoubtedly the more helpful.

Example 2

Compare these clinical notes for two identical medical consultations for two identical complaints, in which precisely the same examination was conducted and precisely the same findings were elicited:

The notes of Dr Keats

20/2

Headache. Flu-like? Reassure.

The notes of Dr Gogarty

20/2/99

Frontal headache. Complaining of occasional flu-like symptoms.

On examination:	Temperature normal. Blood pressure 120/80. No photophobia. Pupils equal, reactive to light. Fundoscopy normal. Alert. No vomiting. No rash.
Impression:	Possible viral infection. No evidence of hypertension, meningitis or intracranial lesion. To return if symptoms persist.

Strictly speaking both sets of notes are accurate but can they both be considered adequate? The first note accurately documents the day of the consultation (but not the year) and the likely diagnosis, but leaves out very many relevant findings including any basis for the doctor's conclusion that she should merely reassure the patient. Nonetheless, there is nothing in the note that is *inaccurate*. Is this enough to satisfy the requirement in the Medical Council *Guide* that clinical notes be 'accurate'? Possibly, but there is more than mere accuracy to be considered.

Suppose that the patient in the above example were to succumb to meningitis three days after the consultation without ever having returned to the doctor who originally examined him. Which set of 'accurate' notes will make the doctor's life easier should it come to defending herself against allegation that she missed the signs of meningitis? There is nothing in the first set of notes to suggest that a full examination was carried out (even if it was) or that the findings of that clinical examination were normal (even if they were) or that the patient was invited to return (even if he was). One cannot even be certain of the year in which the consultation took place. In fact, all the first note shows is that the patient saw the doctor on an unspecified day in February with a headache and that the doctor told him he was fine. It would be very difficult for the doctor, given the death of the patient three days later, to defend herself against an allegation that the signs of meningitis were present at the time of the consultation.

'Accurate' notes are far from being the same as 'adequate' notes. The UK General Medical Council in its booklet *Good Medical Practice*[10] turns the thumbnail sketch of Irish guidelines into an altogether more finished portrait:

> '[Doctors should] keep clear, accurate and contemporaneous patient records which report the relevant clinical findings, the decisions made, information given to patients and any drugs or other treatment prescribed...'

In other words, context is a critical element of a patient's notes and mere *accuracy* becomes a subset or element of the need for a more holistic *adequacy*. If a clinician takes a decision, then there should be enough additional information in the notes to explain or to rationalise that decision. This context will make any subsequent course of events easier to link to, or divorce from, what took place in the clinical encounter. The more information a set of notes contains, the less room there is for doubt if ever the notes are scrutinised.

Abbreviations in clinical notes

[6.04]

Practitioners often work in high-pressure situations where their time is better spent doing things other than writing. As a result, the medical and paramedical professions have gradually compiled a lexicon of abbreviations[11] and shorthand not immediately accessible to the non-clinician. Abbreviations are not necessarily a problem but they should be used sparingly, with the writer mindful 'of the possibilities the future holds for that information to be read by many other people than herself.'[12]

The ideal is that abbreviations, if they are used, should be standardised and conform to the meanings traditionally given to that cluster of letters, although it is recognised that this may not always be possible.[13] If there is the possibility that an abbreviation is ambiguous, then it is preferable that the words are written out in full. In any event the use of a particular abbreviation should always be consistent and the same abbreviation should not be used to mean two different things. Writing a word out in full also has the advantage that one dwells on the word a little longer with the possibility of more time for identifying an error in what one has written. The clearer notes are, the easier it will be to prove the intention and level of care behind what was written.

Quick Reference Guide 6.1

Good written records

- ❖ Clinical notes are generally the only permanent contemporaneous record of what took place at a consultation. They are not tainted with hindsight and are not subject to the vagaries of the human memory.
- ❖ Clarity in clinical records is insurance against the passage of time and against misunderstandings on the part of those reading the notes.
- ❖ If a practitioner keeps no notes of a consultation it will be difficult for her to defend herself against allegations of malpractice, even if those allegations are dubious or unfounded.
- ❖ Clinical records should be both accurate and adequate, they should include not only conclusions reached and decisions taken but the context of any decision or conclusion.
- ❖ If abbreviations are to be used in clinical notes they should be as far as possible standard abbreviations. Whether standard or not, the use of any given abbreviation should be consistent in its meaning.

OWNERSHIP OF CLINICAL RECORDS AND THEIR CONTENTS

[6.05]

There is no suggestion any longer, in these days of patient enlightenment and empowerment, that the doctor is the sole arbiter of what a patient is permitted to see or to know. The days of access to clinical records depending on whether or not doctors, or other clinical practitioners, object to that access are essentially over.[15] The UK National Health Service has long embraced a more patient-centred approach, stating that 'as a matter of principle, patients should be allowed to see what has been written about them'.[16] If we accept that it is a 'matter of principle' that patients should be permitted to see their notes, where does that principle come from, how extensive is it and does an Irish patient have a right of access to his notes?

The idea that a patient could have a right of access to his notes was first affirmed by the courts. More recently laws have further enshrined and formalised that right. The question of the right of access is dealt with below. First however, we need to consider the question of who 'owns' the notes in the first place. If a patient wants access to notes, it can be important for him to know whom he needs to ask.

Who 'owns' clinical records?

[6.06]

As with many legal conundrums, the issue often may only be resolved by reference to the particular facts of an individual case. The answer to this question of ownership of the notes themselves is not absolutely clear, but there are some strong candidate answers:

A clinician

If a doctor or physiotherapist or dentist is in wholly private practice then she will typically own the materials involved in the day-to-day practice of her profession, including computers or paper files on which the details of consultations are recorded. In this situation it is the clinician who 'owns' the records, inasmuch as the paper or disk space on which the information is recorded is hers and the law recognises that documents prepared by a professional person for a lay client are the property of the professional.[17] A patient who made off with a computer disk, or the computer itself, could not justify that it was his because it contained his health care information.[18]

An institution

In a public hospital or clinic, practitioners generally make notes in charts and on forms provided by the institution. Although the notes are made by the clinician, the documents or computer space belong to the institution and it would therefore 'own' the notes.[19]

Both clinician and clinic

In Ireland, care of an individual patient can quite easily elide from public to private in nature and back again. Take the example of a patient who has always attended his general practitioner privately but who, at the age of 70, becomes eligible for a medical card and, staying with the same doctor, becomes her public patient. The doctor continues to use the same file as she has always done but is now paid for the patient's care by the Health Board. Who owns the notes in this instance: the doctor or the Health Board?

The answer is that the ownership, or 'proprietary interest', is probably shared between the two. It is unlikely that, once the patient becomes a GMS Medical Card patient, the Health Board immediately comes to 'own' the chart in which the patient's notes continue to be recorded. But at the same time, it is unlikely that the doctor has quite the same ownership herself from the time that the Health Board is, in effect, contributing towards the costs of the stationery or software being used. It is an anomaly of the two-tiered Irish system and one that is not reducible to a simple answer.

The patient?

Ordinarily the patient will not own his notes but there is nothing to stop him from being given the notes in certain circumstances. A patient who is leaving the country, or changing doctor, may request his notes in order to present them to a new doctor. In such cases it is hard to resist a temptation to say that the patient would, especially if he is given the original notes, commence owning the notes until such time as he chose to present himself to a new practitioner. This is a rare scenario. Indeed it could be argued that in such circumstances, the patient only has temporary custody of the notes rather than ownership. A patient may also have a right of ownership if he has a contract with his practitioner or clinic that includes a term stating that the practitioner or clinic relinquishes ownership of the notes in favour of the patient. This would also be unusual, but certainly possible.

While the patient may not 'own' the notes, we see below that this does not affect his right of access to the notes. In any event, if notes are to be relinquished to another practitioner or institution the originator of the notes should either forward a copy and retain the original notes, or vice versa. Handing over the notes does not mean forfeiting responsibility for the incidents contained in the notes.

Quick Reference Guide 6.2

Who owns the records?

- In general, clinical records belong to whoever owns the medium on which the records are recorded.
- In a private practice setting the practitioner will generally own records; in an institutional setting it will generally be the hospital or clinic.
- There may be circumstances where ownership of the records is effectively 'shared' between practitioner and institution and rarely circumstances in which the patient may have an ownership interest in the records.

PATIENTS' RIGHTS OF ACCESS TO CLINICAL RECORDS

[6.07]

In general then, records will belong to the owner of the material on which the information is recorded or to the person who 'created' the record. The modern right of patients to access their clinical records derives from two principal sources. In the first instance, the courts established ground rules for those patients who wanted access to their records but who were being denied that access. Secondly, and more recently, statutes have been enacted that make it possible for patients, without resorting to court applications, to discover whether other people or institutions maintain files, records or other information about them and to see (and correct or delete, where appropriate) those files. These laws are applicable to almost all forms of stored records and they certainly catch medical records within their very wide net. We look now at the two strands of law that create the patient's right of access – the courts and the written law, especially data protection legislation.

Courts and the right of access

[6.08]

Canadian courts have been extremely proactive in advancing the rights of the individual and, as in Ireland, they do so against the backdrop of a Constitution, so there is much to be learned from their approach. The Canadian Supreme Court has stated that:[20]

> '[A] patient is entitled, upon request, to inspect and copy all information in the patient's medical file which the physician considered in administering advice or treatment… The onus is on the physician to justify a denial of access.'

In *McInerney*, the doctor had received reports from five other specialists concerning the plaintiff that he refused to divulge, suggesting instead that she contact each of the physicians individually for the information contained in each of their reports. The court found that patients have an 'interest' (a legal term for a form of ownership) in information concerning them. This interest persists when the information is conveyed to another doctor, and the doctor who receives that information in turn becomes subject to the duty to afford the patient access to that information. Rather than the patient having to justify why he should be allowed to see his records, it is the doctor who has to justify any refusal.

In England[21] and Australia,[22] the courts took a more cautious approach. English courts have conceded that patients do have a limited right of access to their clinical records, but that right can be curtailed if a doctor thinks it is in the patient's 'best interests' not to see the notes. In Australia, the court was unhappy to accept that the patient had *any* right of access, because that right would automatically clash with the doctor's right to decide on the patient's best interests.[23]

An Irish Court has never been asked to decide this particular question, but if an Irish Court were to make a decision on rights of access to clinical records, they would probably permit some form of access, possibly along the English lines. As we will see, the advent of legislation has to a great degree strengthened the patient's hand when he seeks access to the information in his medical records and has rendered the opinions of the courts less important and relevant in this area.

From an ethical point of view, if trust is to be a cornerstone of the practitioner-patient relationship, then sharing medical records with the patient may help to foster that mutual relationship of trust, confidence and respect. So it is not surprising that, on the whole, the balance of legal opinion on the matter of access to records is that any patient whose records are maintained by a physician should have some right of access to the contents of those records without having to resort to legal action. The extent of the right depends on the circumstances.

The right of access to notes permitted by the courts certainly includes a right to give instructions to the practitioner to divulge information to a third party. In situations where the patient requests that information be disclosed and consents to that disclosure, concerns about confidentiality evaporate: consent modifies the clinician's obligation to maintain confidentiality regarding the matters covered by the terms of the patient's consent to disclosure.[24] This release of information to a third party can occur when a patient needs information released to an insurance company, to a prospective employer or to a solicitor and the clinician should generally respect such a request.[25]

Getting access to records in order to pursue legal action

[6.09]

One common scenario in which a patient may wish his notes disclosed to a third party is when he is pursuing legal action and requires his solicitor to see information about him. If a patient is claiming against a driver who injured him in a road traffic accident he will need the details of his injuries to quantify his claim. If a doctor or institution has committed an act that may have been negligent, a solicitor acting for the injured party will seek the notes that relate to the allegedly negligent procedure or treatment. That the patient should be able to see the notes is obviously in the interests of justice. If the injured party does not have access to the notes, how can his legal advisers ascertain whether or not the legal action has any foundation? If the clinician does not disclose her notes to anyone, how can she clear her name?

If a doctor receives a request from a patient to disclose notes in order to ground a legal action against her, she should contact her medical insurance company or her employers before doing anything else. The insurers will engage legal advice.[26] Generally, relevant notes must be disclosed and a court will order disclosure if the practitioner or her legal advisers drag their feet. The rule, simply put, is that information sought with a view to forming the basis for legal action should generally be disclosed unless there is no justification for the request. If there is no justification for the request, then it may be fought in court. If the disclosure of information might be harmful to the person seeking the information or, more importantly, to the confidentiality of another party then a court may also be asked to decide what information, if any, should be disclosed.

Before legal action commences, a patient may generally only seek information from someone likely to be a party to the legal proceedings, but once the legal action has formally commenced, he may also seek information from other parties who are not directly involved in the case, but who have pertinent information.

STATUTE LAW AND THE RIGHT OF ACCESS

Background

[6.10]

The need for a patient to resort to court action to obtain access to his notes has now been rendered largely obsolete by the introduction of legislation facilitating the right of the individual to access information, including health records, held about him. A court may of course still be required to adjudicate complex cases or to deal with ambiguities in the legislation.

It was increasingly recognised that laws were required to enable a person to see what information was held concerning him, and to rectify or delete that information if incorrect. The main laws in Ireland[27] that seek to achieve this aim are the Data Protection legislation and the Freedom of Information Act 1997.

Data Protection Legislation

[6.11]

Data protection law is contained in two pieces of legislation. The Data Protection Act 1988 is part of Irish law, while the Data Protection Directive 1995 is part of European law, but nonetheless applicable in Ireland.[28] Data protection legislation seeks to protect personal information about individuals that is stored by institutions or other individuals. The fundamental aims of data protection are outlined in the Data Protection Principles,[29] which explain the reasoning and purpose of the laws on personal data. 'Personal data' is very widely defined as any data that can be related to a living individual who can be identified by that data.[30] Under the most recent legislation, it includes any expression of opinions about the individual.

Figure 6.1 Data Protection Principles

1. Personal Data shall be processed[31] fairly and lawfully and in particular, shall not be processed at all unless certain conditions (see below) are met.
2. Personal data shall be obtained only for one or more specified and lawful purposes, and shall not be further processed in any manner incompatible with that purpose or those purposes.[32]
3. Personal data shall be adequate, relevant and not excessive in relation to the purpose or purposes for which they are processed.
4. Personal data shall be accurate and, where necessary, kept up to date.
5. Personal data processed for any purpose or purposes shall not be kept for longer than is necessary for that purpose or those purposes.
6. Personal data shall be processed in accordance with the rights of data subjects (the rights are explained in the data protection legislation, see section **[6.13]**).
7. Appropriate technical and organisational measures shall be taken against unauthorised or unlawful processing of personal data and against accidental loss or destruction of, or damage to, personal data.[33]
8. Personal data shall not be transferred to a country or territory outside the European Economic Area unless that country or territory ensures an adequate level of protection for the rights and freedoms of data subjects in relation to the processing of personal data.

The first principle listed above mentions the fact that certain conditions must be met before anything can be done to personal data, including storing it in the first place. These conditions are not especially burdensome, otherwise no personal data could ever be stored, analysed or processed at all. From the health care perspective, some of the more important conditions that can be satisfied in order for data to be legally processed include the following:[34]

— when the patient consents;

— when the processing is necessary for the discharge of a legal obligation;[35]

— when the processing is necessary in order to protect the vital interests of the data subject;[36]

— when the processing is necessary for the legitimate interests pursued by the data controller or by a third party to whom the data is disclosed;[37]

— when the information is being processed by a health professional for 'medical purposes' (a very widely defined term).

Consent to the processing of data may be implied[38] by the patient's attendance at a clinic or doctor's surgery and the giving of information to the doctor, but it has also been argued that as an additional precaution a notice should be displayed in waiting rooms or consulting rooms to formally make patients aware that records compiled during the consultation may be 'processed' for management, teaching or research purposes.[39]

The Data Protection Act 1988

[6.12]

The Data Protection Act 1988 (hereafter the 1988 Act) is the earlier piece of legislation applying to personal data. Its principal constraint is that it applies only to information that is *electronically* stored, whether on hard disk, floppy disk or any other electronic retrieval device. Paper records, or any other non-electronic storage mechanisms, are excluded.

The *raison d'être* of the 1988 Act is that a person who believes or knows that another person holds information about him in electronic form has the right to know whether information is in fact held and a legal right of access to that information.[40] He also has the right to change or delete inaccurate aspects of that information. The Act creates a Data Protection Commissioner whose job it is to police and enforce the Act and ensure that those in possession of data are discharging their responsibilities.[41]

Rights and obligations under the 1988 Act

[6.13]

The 'data controller' in charge of electronically–hoarded information has a number of obligations that essentially reflect the Data Protection Principles set out above,[42] while the 'data subject' has a number of rights when it comes to accessing and assessing that information:[43]

- The data subject can make a request, which must be in writing, about information held in electronic form by the data controller, who has 21 days to reply to the request.
- If the reply confirms that data is held concerning the applicant, the data controller must also disclose, in comprehensible form, the nature of the stored information.[44]
- If the information is wrong in any way, then it must be corrected or deleted, depending on which is the most appropriate in the circumstances.[45]

If a data controller does not comply with the requirements of the 1988 Act, she can be reported to the Data Commissioner or be taken to court by the data subject who is affected by her refusal to comply. The court can order compliance and also compel the data controller to pay damages and the costs of the legal proceedings.

Personal information must not generally, in accordance with the Data Protection Principles, be disclosed or used for purposes other than those for which it was given. However, information held about an individual that would otherwise be confidential may be disclosed in the interests of preventing crime or protecting the security of the state.[46] It may also be disclosed when required urgently to prevent injury or other damage to the health of a person or serious loss of, or damage to, property or where requested by a court of law or by the data subject himself.[47]

Registration with the Commissioner

[6.14]

People, institutions and other groups that keep personal data on computer must register with the Data Protection Commissioner[48] and this requirement extends to all healthcare practitioners who keep data on any form of electronic system. The 1988 Act specifically refers to those who maintain electronic databases concerning:

> '...physical or mental health (other than any such data reasonably kept by them in relation to the physical or mental health of their employees in the ordinary course of personnel administration and not used or disclosed for any other purpose).'[49]

Application to be included on the register must detail the purpose or purposes for which the data are to be kept.[50] The public can access this register through the Office of the Data Protection Commissioner and obtain copies of it. A data controller who should be on the register, but who has not registered, is precluded from keeping personal data. Any breach of the Act may result in a fine.

Application of data protection in the healthcare environment

[6.15]

What about the confidential nature of medical records and the question of whether a patient should have the right to access his notes in their entirety? To address this issue, regulations were introduced to accommodate the special problems associated with the handling and release of health data.[51] The purpose of the regulations is to:

> '[P]rohibit the supply of health data to a patient in response to a request for access if that would cause serious harm to his or her physical or mental health. They provide also that such data is to be communicated only by, or after consultation with, an appropriate 'health professional' – normally the patient's own doctor.'[52]

In other words, when access to health data is sought, the opinion of a practitioner may be sought as to whether the information is potentially harmful to a patient's health, in which case the information may be withheld. This does not mean that the data controller can simply refuse access to *all* information sought. Instead, she must release any portion of the information sought that is not 'likely to cause serious harm to the physical or mental health of the data subject.'[53]

The 1988 Act contains exemptions that have significance for clinical practice, including the provision that the Act does not apply to data

> 'kept *only* for the purpose of preparing statistics or carrying out research if the data are not used or disclosed...for any other purpose and the resulting statistics or the results of the research are not made available in a form that identifies any of the data subjects.'[54] [italics added]

The key element is that the data must be kept anonymous.[55] If they are not, then the Act will apply. If information is collected as a by-product of the practitioner's work with patients, then that clinical work will require registration with the Data Protection Commissioner for the clinical work and probably also for the subsequent use of the information in the research work.

Limitations of the Data Protection Act 1988

[6.16]

The 1988 Act only applies to information held on computer. If two individuals or institutions hold precisely the same information about two similar patients, but one uses the latest computing technology while the other uses an archaic system of filing cabinets and index cards, only the former is affected by the Act. This is not entirely satisfactory. It means that data subjects' rights are not universal, but depend on the actions of those who maintain the information about them. It is the data controller who decides how he wishes to store information and this decision – which is outside the control of the person whose data are stored – will affect the individual's rights. It seems sensible that all, no matter how their data are stored, should have the same rights of access. It was with this in mind that the European Union introduced in 1995 a directive entitled 'The Protection of Individuals with Regard to the Processing of Personal Data'[56] (called the Data Protection Directive 1995 hereafter).

The Data Protection Directive 1995

[6.17]

The law in Ireland covering data protection is probably more accurately stated by the Data Protection Directive 1995 than it is by the Data Protection Act 1988. When a directive is introduced by the European Union, it is binding on member states, even if they do not implement it into their domestic law.[58]

This is important because the Data Protection Directive effectively supplants the Data Protection Act 1988. The Directive, which will become the new Data Protection Act when introduced, *covers all records contained in a structured filing system, whether in electronic format or any other permanent form.*

The rules, exceptions and structures of the Directive are essentially the same as those that have already been explored under the heading of the 1988 Act,[59] the crucial difference being that all forms of data storage are covered. The practical implication of this is that patients now have a right of access to *all* of their notes, even from those practices or institutions that have no computerised or other electronic storage system. Similarly, all those practitioners or institutions who hold information in permanent but non-electronic format should be seeking to register their status as data controllers with the Data Protection Commissioner.

Freedom of Information Act 1997

[6.18]

The Freedom of Information Act 1997 (hereafter the 1997 Act) is distinct from and complementary to data protection legislation. It is not merely concerned with the individual's right of access to information that concerns the individual himself. Instead it seeks to promote transparency within public bodies. Two key differences from data protection legislation should be made clear. Data Protection legislation is directed at everyone who stores personal data whether in electronic (1988 Act) or any other form (1995 Directive). Also, a person can only exercise his rights under the Act in respect of his own personal data. The Freedom of Information Act on the other hand applies only to information that is held by *public bodies.* If the information holder is not a public body or working within a public body, the Act does not apply. Also, a person seeking information under the 1997 Act may seek *any* information held by that body and not merely that which concerns the individual himself. The Act applies to any information held in any permanent form and on any subject.

What is a 'public body'?

[6.19]

Nailing down a precise definition of a public body is not always easy.[60] The Act permits the Minister to declare entities as public bodies: the health boards and most of the universities were named as public bodies in this way after the passage of the Act. A simple rule of thumb is to ask whether the institution or body in question is either a direct representative of the State, an agency of the Government or was created by a piece of legislation. If the answer is yes, then the body is likely to be a 'public body' for the purposes of the Freedom of Information Act 1997. Government departments and local authorities are therefore obviously public bodies, as are agencies set up under the auspices of Government departments, such as the Irish Medicines Board. Many bodies specifically established by legislation are also public bodies, such as health boards[61] and most universities.[62] All public hospitals are deemed to be public bodies.[63]

What the Act does

[6.20]

The Freedom of Information Act 1997 enables, in the words of its preamble:

> '[M]embers of the public to obtain access, to the greatest extent possible consistent with the public interest and the right to privacy, to information in the possession of public bodies and to enable persons to have personal information relating to them in the possession of such bodies corrected…'

This right of access is not absolute. The right to privacy of other individuals who might be affected by the disclosure of information is respected, so is information covered by the Official Secrets Act 1963, or otherwise important to the security or stability of the State.[64]

The 1997 Act applies to all records held by public bodies in every conceivable format. Every person is given a right under the Act to make a request for access to any records held by a public body.[65] The request is generally made in writing to the head of the public body concerned including any with the request any information necessary to enable the public body to find the information requested and reply to the application.

As with Data Protection legislation the applicant must receive a reply to his request for information. The public body may grant or refuse the request for information in full or in part.[66] If the decision is taken to refuse to release the information then the refusal must be based on one of the grounds set out in the Freedom of Information Act 1997,[67] which include:

- the record does not exist, cannot be found or the request was incorrectly made;[68]
- access is not being refused, but deferred;[69]
- to disclose the record would prejudice the privacy of another person;
- the record requested was created solely to aid Government deliberations or the drawing up of legislation;
- the record would disclose deliberations of a public body that it would not be in the public interest to disclose;[70]

— release of the record would affect tests or investigations conducted by the body in question or otherwise adversely affect its functioning;[71]

— release of the record would undermine the operation of parliament, the courts, the prison service, State security or the legal system.

If access is granted, the applicant is entitled to have the documents released in a form that he can understand and, as with the Data Protection legislation, only part of the record may be released where that is the appropriate course of action.[72] If a request is made for personal information in the possession of a public body and that information is inaccurate or incomplete the applicant has a right to correct or delete the erroneous details.[73]

The decision regarding access is, nominally at least, taken by the head of the organisation, department or institution that holds the records. In the case of a health board that would be the Chief Executive Officer, but in reality such decisions are - or should be - taken in liaison with the staff involved.

Freedom of information in the clinical setting

[6.21]

A clinician working in a public body in whatever capacity should be aware that any records she makes may subsequently be the subject of a request under the Freedom of Information Act 1997. As we have already noted, there are many ways to access information in the possession of another individual or institution, but the Freedom of Information Act is a potent weapon because it permits the requester to seek information about matters other than his own personal data. He can seek any information that is held by a public body, whether or not it relates to him personally, subject of course to the many exceptions listed above. In particular the risk of infringing the confidentiality of medical records relating to an individual other than the person making the request is one of the grounds for refusal of disclosure.[74]

Example 3

If A requests information that would involve disclosing otherwise confidential details about B, the request may be refused if there is no reasonable way of excising the information concerning B and allowing the release of that portion that does not infringe on B's right to confidentiality. The information may be released if B consents to the release of the information, or if there is an imminent danger to life or limb that may be averted by the disclosure, or if there is nothing inherently confidential in the information.

Similarly, in a manner analogous to the data protection legislation, if the release of a medical record might be prejudicial to the physical or mental health of the person making the request, then access may be denied. In those circumstances, however, the refusal of access must be accompanied by an indication that, if the requester so wishes, the information will be made available for inspection by a health professional nominated by the requester.[75]

This confidentiality provision within the Act means that clinical practitioners are less likely to be affected by requests for information under the 1997 Act than may be the case for comparable employees in other parts of the public sector. It is certainly true that patients may request their own records under the Act, and will generally be granted access to them, but they could just as easily, perhaps more easily because there is no need to worry whether the data holder is a public body, seek that information through the data protection legislation.

Freedom of information and confidentiality in action

[6.22]

If a body takes a decision not to grant access to records, citing one of the grounds for refusal contained in the Act, that is not necessarily the end of the matter. The head of the public body can be asked by the requester or by the Information Commissioner at the behest of the requester to review the decision. The applicant may also appeal a refusal of access by a public body to the Information Commissioner, an office created by theFreedom of Information Act 1997 with responsibility for overseeing the operation of the Act. If any party is unhappy with the decision of the Information Commissioner, then an appeal against that decision may be taken to the High Court.[76]

In *ACF and the North Eastern Health Board*,[77] a girl who had spent many of her early years in the care of the heath board sought certain records pertaining to her care. The health board refused, arguing that many of the records also contained confidential information about the applicant's family members. The woman was not happy with this decision and appealed to the Information Commissioner. The decision of the Commissioner was that the confidentiality of individuals who may be affected by another person's request for information must be protected. In addition, it would be more difficult for health boards to liaise with the families of children in care if there was a fear that discussions between health board and family members might subsequently be released. The Commissioner ordered the release of the notes pertaining only to meetings at which the requester was present on the grounds that, given her presence at those meeting, there were minimal confidentiality issues to be considered. The release of all other records was refused.

PRESCRIPTION WRITING

[6.23]

A prescription, together with notes taken during a consultation, is the other element of the indelible record of the practitioner-patient interaction. It testifies to the therapeutic option chosen by the clinician and, as such, may prove invaluable as legal proof in any dispute that arises subsequently. A prescription is also interesting in that it involves a third party in the transaction between clinician and patient, namely the pharmacist, whose job it is to decipher the prescription and dispense the medication indicated. This section looks at the requirements the law places upon the prescriber and dispenser of medications, both in terms of prescribing rules and of what may happen if a prescription is not properly written.

Why are prescriptions necessary?

[6.24]

There are some medications that, while beneficial, need to be used with care. Accordingly, the relevant body, which in Ireland is the Irish Medicines Board, designates medicines as being either prescription-only (POM) or available for over the counter sale

(OTC). In addition there are certain categories of medicines that the Minister for Health can denote as 'controlled medicines', and these are subject to further constraints over and above normal prescription rules.

Quick Reference Guide 6.3

A patient's rights of access to clinical records

- A patient's right of access to his records was previously dependent on either the consent of the doctor or a decision of the courts to allow access.
- In most countries, courts held that patients had at least a limited right to access their notes. In countries such as Canada, that right was very extensive. In England, the right exists but is subject to the doctor's right to refuse access in the 'patient's best interests'.
- A court will more readily find that a person has a right of access to his notes when he needs them for the purposes of exploring or initiating some form of legal action. A patient who authorises or requests the release of his notes for such a purpose should have his wish respected.
- More recently, the introduction of legislation has removed the patient's need to rely on the goodwill of the doctor or the court. Patients now increasingly have a *statutory* right of access to healthcare information held about them.
- The Data Protection Act 1988 and the Data Protection Directive 1995 give rights to those whose personal data are held on file by others, including by clinicians and institutions. The legislation also places obligations on those who hold the data.
- The rights of the individual under data protection laws include the individual's right to know whether information is held about him, to know what that information is and to alter or delete that information if appropriate.
- The Data Protection Act 1988 applies only to electronically stored data; the Data Protection Directive 1995 applies to *all* forms of organised data storage and it is the Directive that most accurately states the legal position in Ireland with respect to stored personal data.
- Any person or institution holding personal data about an individual is required to register with the Data Protection Commissioner. This requirement extends to those who hold healthcare information.
- The Freedom of Information Act 1997 extends to all forms of record and all forms of information (not merely personal data) held by 'public bodies'.
- In the case of both data protection and freedom of information legislation, there are a number of exemptions which can be relied on to decline full (or any) disclosure of information. These include questions of confidentiality or where harm may be done by disclosure.
- On the other hand, there are also situations in which disclosure of personal data to third parties without consent (normally prohibited by the data protection legislation) will be permitted. These include concerns regarding the safety of the indvidual or other persons.

Who may write a prescription?

[6.25]

There are three categories of practitioner in whom is vested the power to write prescriptions: registered medical practitioners, registered dentists, registered veterinary surgeons. Only registered medical practitioners and registered dentists are permitted to prescribe medicines for human consumption. There are also some differences between the nature of dental and medical prescribing[78] but the similarities in the manner in which medical and dental prescriptions are regulated outweigh the differences. A doctor or dentist who is convicted of an offence under the Misuse of Drugs Act 1977 may have her right to prescribe or to work with controlled substances removed or limited in the wake of that conviction.[79]

In America and more recently in Ireland, new categories of health care provider such as Nurse Practitioners and Physician Assistants have begun to emerge, who have limited prescribing powers for certain categories of medication. However, that power is generally only to be exercised under the close supervision and with the authorisation of a physician who in turn may be held liable[80] for any mistakes that are made.

Prescribing – the legal requirements

General requirements

[6.26]

The Medical Preparations (Control of Sale) Regulations 1987 lay down the basic regulations for the prescription and sale of medicines. They include an exhaustive list of the preparations that must only be dispensed in accordance with a prescription as well as providing for the fact that all newly introduced medications must also be prescription-only.[81] They also stipulate that some medicines, which would ordinarily be available only on prescription, may be sold over the counter by virtue of containing a lower dose of the active ingredient or by virtue of the particular form of the active ingredient in the medication.

A prescription must conform to the following criteria:

- It must be in ink and signed and dated by the person issuing it with her usual signature;
- It must specify the address of the person issuing it [unless issued in a hospital, in which case the institution's address will suffice];
- It must clearly indicate the name of the person issuing it and state whether she is a registered medical practitioner or a registered dentist;
- It must specify the name and address and, if under 12, the age of the person for whom it is issued[82]

To this should be added as clearly and unambiguously as possible the name (proprietary, generic or both), the preparation, the dose, the frequency and the duration of the medication being prescribed.

In general a prescription that does not indicate otherwise will be dispensed once only. The majority of medications can be written on a 'repeat' prescription where the doctor indicates that she wishes the medication to be dispensed repeatedly for a period of up to six months. General Medical Services (GMS) prescriptions can be written for one or three months only. Controlled medications may not be repeated: each prescription for a controlled medication may be dispensed only once. It is an offence for a person who is not a practitioner to write or alter a prescription.[83]

A prescription should be accurate, appropriate and unambiguous. If a prescription is not clear and, as a result, the wrong medication is dispensed, a doctor may be held to have been negligent, although she may not be negligent on her own. The blame may be shared with the pharmacist who fails to spot an error or to clarify any ambiguity that may exist on the prescription.

Example 4

In one case[84] a GP wrote a prescription for a patient who was suffering from an acute respiratory tract infection. The prescription was for salbutamol, phyllocontin and amoxycillin[85] 250 milligrammes three times daily for seven days. The pharmacist misread the scrawled prescription and, instead of amoxycillin, dispensed 250mg of daonil, a sugar-lowering medication used by diabetics. The patient was not a diabetic and in any event the dose of daonil dispensed by the pharmacist was many times the recommended dose. The patient suffered a prolonged and catastrophic fall in his blood sugar levels (hypoglycaemia) and irreversible brain damage.

In this case the pharmacist was held liable, but so was the doctor for having written a scarcely intelligible prescription that could easily be misunderstood. The court decided that the doctor was 25% liable for writing the prescription, while the pharmacist was 75% liable for having negligently dispensed the prescription when circumstances (the dose of the medication, the duration and the other drugs prescribed) should have suggested that daonil was not the drug intended by the prescriber.

A doctor therefore has to exercise due care in writing a prescription in order to be certain that it is legible by the pharmacist. If the prescription is not clear and the pharmacist makes a mistake wholly or in part predicated on the ambiguity of the doctor's prescription, then the doctor may be held liable. Similarly the pharmacist is under a duty to question an ambiguous prescription and to take into account elements in the prescription that call the intention of the prescriber into doubt.[86]

Another possibility that may arise with the indecipherable or ambiguously written prescription is that the pharmacist may justifiably refuse to dispense the drugs listed for fear of making an error. If that were to happen and if the pharmacist's fears were reasonable and any harm then occured to the patient because the medicine was not dispensed, the doctor might also be liable for having written a prescription in such a manner that it could not be dispensed.[87]

The 1987 Regulations do, however, allow a pharmacist to dispense medication in an emergency when the doctor is not able to provide a prescription, as long as the doctor undertakes to provide one within 72 hours.[88] The Medical Council *Guide*[89] points out that:

> 'should the need arise to prescribe a drug over the telephone, the doctor should record the call and forward the appropriate prescription to the pharmacist in a reasonable time.'

The problem of an illegible or troublesome prescription may arise between doctors as well as between doctors and pharmacists. Frequently, patients will be discharged from hospital or sent home from an Accident and Emergency Department with a prescription or discharge note listing medications. The general practitioner, in transcribing a hospital prescription to a GMS prescription or from a discharge note to any prescription, is under a similar duty to the pharmacist who receives a prescription. If she transcribes incorrectly, or transcribes correctly from an initially inaccurate prescription, she may be liable in negligence. Similarly, if she transcribes a medicine that she knows, or ought to know, that her patient should not have been prescribed by the initial prescribing doctor (eg a prescription for penicillin when the patient is allergic to penicillin), she may also be liable.

Giving advice with a prescription

[6.27]

As many medications have side effects, the doctor has a duty to warn her patient, as part of her overall duty of care, about any side effects of the medication and any precautions he may need to take. As mentioned when dealing with the topic of consent[90] a patient should be informed before taking any medication of foreseeable risks, with special focus on any potentially serious ones. If the correct advice is given (and is documented as having been given) and the patient ignores the advice, it will be difficult for the patient to argue that the doctor was negligent.

> **Example 5**
>
> In the case of *Buckle v Delaunay*,[91] the doctor prescribed an antidepressant for a patient and advised him about the great danger inherent in eating certain foods while taking this particular tablet. The patient underestimated the gravity of the doctor's warning and did not modify his diet. There was a severe reaction between the food (cheese) and the drug. The patient died. The doctor was able to point to the fact that he had advised the patient and that the patient had chosen to ignore that advice. Accordingly, the doctor was not negligent.

Similarly, if a risk occurs that is unforeseeable, the practitioner will not be liable for failing to warn of it.[92] This is in keeping with the general principles of negligence that apply to informing patients: the clinician can be obliged only to give a warning of foreseeable risks. The precise definition of 'common' or 'serious' risks may be complex and will vary with the precise circumstances of the patient and the medication. The duty to warn of side-effects is greatest with common or serious side-effects or where the patient asks specific questions about certain side-effects.

Controlled drugs

[6.28]

The Misuse of Drugs Acts (MDA) 1977[94] (the 1977 Act) created a category of medicine known as 'controlled drugs', including most of the well-known illicit drugs, but also certain therapeutic medications.

Quick Reference Guide 6.4

Legal requirements for prescribing generally

- Traditionally doctors and dentists are the only practitioners permitted to prescribe for human consumption. New categories of health professional are emerging who have limited prescribing powers.
- Misusing the power of prescription, especially when it comes to drugs of abuse, may lead to the power to prescribe being curtailed or suspended.
- A prescription must be in ink and identify the drug, the prescriber and the patient clearly. A prescription should be accurate, appropriate and unambiguous.
- It is a criminal offence for anyone to alter a prescription who is not a practitioner with the power to prescribe. Similarly, forgery of a prescription is an offence.
- A badly written prescription may amount to negligence either because of errors on the prescription or because of its indecipherability. In cases where a pharmacist dispenses a negligently written prescription, legal blame may be shared between prescriber and dispenser.
- If a doubt arises over the accuracy or contents of a prescription, matters should be clarified before acting on the prescription as written.
- The prescriber has a duty to warn of significant side effects and to give relevant advice necessary for the safe use of the medication.

The 1977 Act fulfils three purposes. In the first place it makes illegal the possession of certain substances and lays down penalties for the possession, trafficking or dealing of those substances. Secondly, it lays down the rules within which certain controlled drugs may be used and classes of person who *may* possess or supply controlled substances. Finally, the Act allows the Minister with responsibility for the Misuse of Drugs legislation (The Minister for Health) to make wide-ranging regulations to clarify the Act or to amend the list of controlled drugs. Attached to the end of the 1977 Act is a series of appendices, called 'schedules', each of which contains a list of drugs, which have tended to be described after the schedule in which they which they appear: LSD for example might sometimes be called a 'Schedule 1 drug'. The most recent apportionment of drugs to the various schedules was contained in the Misuse of Drugs Regulations 1988, but as mentioned, the list may be amended by the Minister. [95]

Figure 6.2 – The controlled drugs schedules

Schedule 1 (sometimes also called CD 1)

Many of the common illicit substances, distinguished not only by their adverse effects but also by the fact that they are held to have no medicinal effects. Such drugs cannot be used except with a special licence. The group includes LSD, cannabis and raw coca leaf (from which cocaine is derived). [96] They may not generally be prescribed.

Schedule 2

Includes most of the opiate analgesics whose use is characterised by the care required to achieve a balance between their definite clinical benefits and their potential for abuse and addiction. Opiate analgesics are frequently used in severe pain, while cocaine is used as a nasal anaesthetic for certain procedures, so both (and the majority of related compounds, including heroin) are included in schedule 2.

Schedule 3

Some sedatives, such as midazolam and temazepam,[97] strong pain-killers, barbiturates.

Schedule 4

Most other sedatives belonging to the benzodiazepine group. Other drugs with a reduced content of barbiturates.

Schedule 5

Any of the drugs contained in the previous schedules but which are in a preparation, form or concentration sufficiently different or dilute that the potential for abuse is minimal.

The classes of people who may have in their possession controlled drugs (from schedules 2-5) are largely obvious: they include doctors, dentists, pharmacists, vets, midwives working in the community[98] and nursing matrons or sisters-in-charge. Exemptions are also given to those whose job is to test, investigate, inspect or work with controlled substances. Any ship or offshore installation (such as an oil-rig) may maintain a store of controlled drugs under the authority of the person in charge of the vessel or installation, so long as there is not a medical practitioner in the crew. Gardaí and others who come into contact with controlled substances in 'the course of their duty' will not be guilty of possessing those substances in the criminal sense.

Prescribing controlled drugs

[6.29]

It is drugs in Schs 1 to 3 above that are truly 'controlled' drugs for the purposes of prescribing. The prescribing of such drugs is subject to importantly different rules from those that apply to ordinary prescribing, dealt with at section **[6.26]**. The reason for the increased stringency is to minimise the possibility that patients or others will alter a prescription.[99] The most recent applicable rules are contained in the Misuse of Drugs Regulations 1988 and they contain the following stipulations *in addition* to the standard rules for prescribing contained in the 1987 Regulations:[100]

— All of the information contained on the prescription relating to the dose and amount of the medication must be in the prescriber's own handwriting. A computer or typewritten prescription for a controlled drug is therefore not valid.

— The strength and quantity of the medication must be prescribed in words and figures. So, if the prescription were for morphine slow release tablets, the prescription would state (in handwriting): 'morphine slow release tablets 10mg (ten milligrammes); *mitte*[101] 60 (sixty).'

— It is also not possible for the prescriber to write a 'repeat' prescription for a controlled drug. If a drug is to be dispensed in instalments, then no instalment may be dispensed more than two months after the date on the prescription. In any event, a prescription for a controlled drug may only be first dispensed within 14 days of the date on the prescription.

The pharmacist cannot dispense the prescription unless she is satisfied that the prescription conforms to the terms above and she recognises, or has taken steps to verify, the name and signature on the prescription.

If a doctor, dentist or pharmacist keeps controlled drugs on their premises, they must be kept in a locked compartment. She must also keep a register of the use of those drugs, which must take the form of a bound book and record the use, purchase, or destruction of any controlled drugs on the premises. The storage arrangements and register may be inspected or requested for inspection by a government inspector.

A practitioner who abuses her power to prescribe either by supplying controlled drugs to others or by prescribing them for her own illicit use may be reported to the appropriate disciplinary body. To take the Medical Council as an example, the disciplinary body may impose a range of sanctions: it may suspend the doctor from practice, strike her off the register of practitioners or attach conditions to her continued practice, such as prohibiting her from prescribing controlled drugs. The Minister for Health may also, in extreme circumstances, prohibit a practitioner from prescribing controlled substances as well as notifying her misconduct to the Medical Council or other relevant body.

Quick Reference Guide 6.5

Legal requirements for prescribing controlled drugs

- ❖ The Misuse of Drugs Act 1977 creates 5 'schedules' of controlled drugs. These schedules may be altered by Ministerial regulations.
- ❖ In general, possession or supply of a controlled drug is illegal, but certain categories of person, including clinical practitioners, are permitted to work with them.
- ❖ Constraints apply to the storage and prescription of controlled drugs, particularly those in schedules 1 to 3.
- ❖ For controlled drugs, the prescription cannot be a computer printout. It must be in the prescriber's own handwriting and detail the dose and amount of medicine to be prescribed in both words and figures.
- ❖ There are also restrictions on dispensing controlled medicines.
- ❖ Controlled drugs stored on premises must be kept in a locked container and a register maintained of the use of the drugs.

Endnotes

1 'Written' in this context refers to all permanent records of the consultation, including those on computer.

2 Eg multiple x-rays of the same area of the body that add nothing to the clinical picture but rather may introduce the risk of cumulative radiation damage.

3 Medical Council *Guide to Ethical Conduct and Behaviour* (5th edn, 1998).

4 It is hard to be certain how long an 'adequate period' is for the purposes of the notes. A sensible approach is to store notes for at least seven to ten years after the last time the clinician sees the patient. As will be seen in ch 7, *Clinical Negligence*, a patient generally only has a limited time-frame within which to bring any legal action, although there are exceptions where the period may be prolonged.

5 Medical Council *Guide to Ethical Conduct and Behaviour* (5th edn, 1998), para 4.7.

6 *Rules of Professional Conduct*, para 2.5.

[7] *Toal v Duignan* [1991] ILRM 135. The case concerned a man who was discovered to be infertile at the age of 22, allegedly due to a negligent failure to diagnose an undescended testicle shortly after birth. Although his case failed because of the time lapse between the alleged failure of the doctors and the patient bringing his action, the court made it clear that good clinical notes are vital to good clinical care. There have been many criticisms of this decision because the young man could not have discovered his infertility any earlier than the time he brought the action, so that the delay was not his fault. This area of law is covered in ch 7.

[8] General Medical Council (1995).

[9] Sometimes referred to as TLA: three letter abbreviations.

[10] Charles J Lewis Clinical *Negligence, A Practical Guide* (2001), p 81.

[11] One dictionary of medical acronyms and abbreviations lists all of the following possible meanings for the common abbreviation CHD: Chediak-Higashi disease; childhood disease; chronic hemodialysis; congenital or congestive heart disease; congenital hip dislocation; constitutional hepatic dysfunction; coronary heart disease and cyanotic heart disease.

[12] The Medical Council *Guide to Ethical Conduct and Behviour* (5th edn, 1998) explicity states – para 4.7 – that there 'is no objection to patients being supplied with a report of their own medical history'..

[13] *DHSS Code on Openness in the NHS*, London, HMSO (1995).

[14] See *Breen v Williams* (1996) 70 AJLR 772; *Leicestershire County Council v Michael Faraday & Partners Ltd* [1941] 2 KB 205.

[15] Some legal commentators have queried what would happen if the clinician made her notes on paper belonging to the patient (for example, a doctor doing a house-call who, having forgotten the patient's file, borrows paper from the patient to record her findings). The answer appears to be that the notes, having been 'created' by the doctor would still belong to her:

[16] In the United Kingdom, patients under the National Health System are registered with a particular doctor. However the notes of that patient remain the property of the local Health Authority. If the patient dies, leaves the country or is in the process of changing general practitioners, his notes are always returned to the Health Authority, rather than remaining with the GP.

[17] *McInerney v McDonald* [1991] 2 Med LR 267.

[18] *R v Mid Glamorgan FHSA, ex parte Martin* [1995] 1 WLR 110.

[19] *Breen v Williams* (1996) 70 AJLR 772.

[20] The court concluded that if there were to be a right of access to medical records, then it would have to come from the Australian Government introducing such a law. In essence, this is what has happened in Ireland with the advent of data protection and freedom of information legislation.

[21] See ch 3, *The Practitioner-Patient Relationship, Ethics and Confidentiality* (section **[3.16]** ff.).

[22] *C v C* [1946] 1 All ER 562.

[23] The step-wise progress of a legal action is detailed in ch 10, *The Practitioner and the Lawyer.*

[24] In the United Kingdom, data protection legislation was first introduced four years earlier than in Ireland. As the Data Protection Act 1984 (UK) covered (like its 1988 Irish equivalent) only electronic data, legislation was introduced to address the particular problems of manually compiled health records. These were the Access to Health Records Act 1990, which governs access to medical records compiled after 1 November 1991, and the Access to Medical Reports Act 1988. In Ireland there was no equivalent legislation to either of the foregoing. Both have been largely supplanted in any event by the European Data Protection Directive 1995 which became the Data Protection Act 1998 (UK).

25 This is a principle called 'direct effect'. Legislation introduced by Europe is binding on member states and can be relied on in the courts, even if it has not yet been formally introduced into the law of that member state. A few elements of the Data Protection Directive 1995 have been formally incorporated into Irish law: see endnote 59 below.

26 The Principles are set out as appendices to the Data Protection Act 1988 and to the Data Protection Directive 1995.

27 Including personal details such as date or birth or address, as well as information on racial origin, political opinions or religious or other beliefs, and personal data concerning health or sexual life.

28 When the Principles refer to 'processing' they mean almost any use of the data, including storing information in the first place, altering it, transmitting it to others and deleting it.

29 In other words, information obtained for one purpose (for example, opening a bank account) cannot be used for another purpose (for example, 'junk' mail) without consent to the information being used for that purpose.

30 In other words, adequate security measures should be in place.

31 This is not an exhaustive list of the conditions that permit the processing of data, but it gives a flavour of the important conditions.

32 Such as the notification of a disease about which a doctor is obliged by law to tell the relevant authorities.

33 For example a GP who tells a hospital doctor what medications her patient is taking.

34 For example, research, audit, or financial management by a health institution.

35 For implied consent, see ch 4, *Consent* (sections **[4.07]-[4.08]**).

36 See *Principles of Medical Law* Kennedy & Grubb (eds) (1999).

37 A person who holds information about another is called a 'data controller'. A person about whom the information is held is called a 'data subject'. Note that the Irish Dental Council's ethical code specifically reminds dentists of their duty to register with the Data Protection Commissioner, where appropriate (para 3.15).

38 Data Protection Act 1988 s 8 *et seq*. The Commissioners' web presence is at www.dataprivacy.ie.

39 Data Protection Act 1988, s 2.

40 Data Protection Act 1988 ss 3 and 4.

41 If the information communicated to the applicant is of a technical nature that is not likely to be readily understood (eg medical records), an explanation should be appended. The data controller may charge a small fee for the release of information. The fee is refundable if information about the data subject turns out to have been inaccurate, incomplete or out of date.

42 Data Protection Act 1988, s 6.

43 Data Protection Act 1988, s 8.

44 These are similar to the general conditions in which practitioner-patient confidentiality may be breached, see ch 3, *The Practitioner-Patient Relationship, Ethics and Confidentiality* section **[3.16]***ff*.

45 Data Protection Act 1988, s 19.

46 Data Protection Act 1988, s 16(1)(c)(iii). Others who must register include the public sector; financial institutions; insurance companies; those involved in direct marketing, providing credit references and debt collecting; and anyone keeping personal information about race, political opinions, religion, sexual life or criminal convictions. The Irish Dental Council's guide to *Professional Behaviour and Ethics* contain an explicit reminder (in para 3.15) to dentists to register with the Data Protection Commissioner.

47 Data Protection Act 1988, s 17.

48 Data Protection (Access Modification) (Health) Regulations 1989 (SI 1989/ 82). A similar set of procedures and safeguards were introduced for the handling of Social Welfare data.

49 Data Protection (Access Modification) (Health) Regulations 1989, Explanatory Note.

50 This is similar to the conclusion reached by the English court in *R v Mid Glamorgan FHSA, ex p Martin* [1995] 1 WLR 110, which held that while a patient had a right of access to information, the doctor could refuse information in the patient's 'best interests' (where 'best interests' are defined by the doctor). Note that the data controller may not necessarily herself be a medical professional – she may, for example, be an employee in a government department. In such a case she would defer the decision to a medical practitioner (the regulations suggest that the practitioner should be the doctor of the person making the application for information).

51 Data Protection Act 1988, s 5(1)(h).

52 This is similar to the opinion that confidentiality of medical information is not an issue where data is wholly anonymous: *R v Department of Health, ex p Source Informatics Ltd* [2000] 1 All ER 786.

53 95/46/EC ([1995] OJ L281).

54 *Van Gend en Loos* [1963] ECR 1; *Francovich v Italian Republic* [1991] ECR I-5357 (see Appendix, section **[A.13]**).

55 Certain aspects of the 1995 Directive were formally incorporated into Irish law from April 2002: see European Communities (Data Protection) Regulations, 2001 (SI 2001/626). This ministerial regulation added some new elements to the Data Protection Act 1988. Personal data may not be exported outside the European Economic Area (the 15 EU countries plus Iceland, Liechtenstein and Norway) unless the destination country provides the same legal guarantees for the protection of data as the exporting country. Furthermore the Regulations place a legal onus on data controllers to ensure that anyone who processes data on their behalf takes care to protect those data. In the UK where the 1995 Directive has become law, the government has made regulations, similar to the Irish Data Protection (Access Modification) (Health) Regulations 1989 (section **[6.15]**), for the new Act that recognise the special demands of healthcare data. It is likely that the Irish Government will update the 1989 Regulations whenever the Data Protection Directive 1995 becomes law in Ireland.

56 See Costello, 33 IJ for examples of how widely it is possible to interpret the meaning of the word 'public' in the context of law.

57 Established by the Health Act 1970.

58 Established by the Universities Act 1908.

59 And private hospitals are not. Information they hold will be covered by Data Protection legislation but not by Freedom of Information legislation. The situation regarding an institution that cares for private and public patient on the same campus and with the same staff is not clear.

60 It would not be possible for example to request the plans to Mountjoy Prison, even though such a document would theoretically be covered by the Freedom of Information Act.

61 Freedom of Information Act 1997, s 6.

62 Freedom of Information Act 1997, s 8.

63 For an Act supposedly directed at the Freedom of Information, there are a great many grounds for refusing access to information.

64 Freedom of Information Act 1997, s 10.

65 Eg until the Government or Oireachtas has finished deliberations concerning the record sought.

66 Eg someone might receive advance notification of planning decisions that might permit him to engage in land speculation.

67 If a student were to approach a University and ask it to make available any summer examination papers in its possession the college would in theory, under the Freedom of Information Act, be obliged to allow the students access to them were it not for this provision.

68 Freedom of Information Act 1997, s 12.

69 Freedom of Information Act 1997, s 17.

70 Freedom of Information Act 1997, s 28.

71 Freedom of Information Act 1997, s 26(4).

72 See *ABK and the Eastern Health Board* [1999] IEIC 20. The decision of the Information Commissioner was upheld by the High Court in April 2001.

73 *ACF and the North Eastern Health Board* [2001] IEIC 4.

74 Dentists, for example, may not generally write repeat prescriptions.

75 Limitations may be imposed by the professional regulatory body after disciplinary proceedings or, where there is an element of urgency, by the Minister. See Misuse of Drugs Act 1977, ss 6-10.

76 Anyone who is liable for the errors of another is said to be 'vicariously liable': see ch 7, *Clinical Negligence*. See also Gore 'Liability for Physician Mistakes' J Legal Med 21(1) 1.

77 Medical Preparations (Control of Sale) Regulations 1987, reg 5.

78 Medical Preparations (Control of Sale) Regulations 1987, reg 6.

79 Misuse of Drugs Act 1977, s 18.

80 *Prendergast v Sam & Dee Ltd* [1989] 1 Med LR.

81 These medications are an inhaler to open the airways, a tablet to improve respiratory function and an antibiotic respectively.

82 See also *Dwyer v Roderick* [1983] 80 LS Gaz 3003, a case in which a doctor prescribed the wrong frequency of the medication. Again liability was split between the two practitioners.

83 *Pharmaceutical Society of Great Britain v Storkwain Ltd* [1985] 3 All ER 4.

84 Medical Preparations (Control of Sale) Regulations 1987, reg 7.

85 Medical Council, *Guide to Ethical Conduct and Behaviour* (5th edn, 1998), para 11.3.

86 See ch 4, *Consent*.

87 *Buckle v Delaunay* [1970].

88 *Hothi v Greenwich Health Authority* [1982].

89 The Act has been updated by the Misuse of Drugs Act 1984 and the Misuse of Drugs Regulations 1988 (SI 1988/328).

90 Eg the Misuse of Drugs (Amendment) Regulations 1993 moved the hypnotic (sleeping tablet) temazepam from schedule 4 to schedule 3 on the basis of evidence that it had become a drug of abuse.

91 Note the ongoing debate about merits of cannabis in the clinical setting that is in stark contrast to the drug's Schedule 1 status. Contrast the following studies:

> Tramèr *et al* 'Cannabinoids for control of chemotherapy-induced nausea and vomiting: quantitative systematic review' BMJ 2001; 3232: 16.
>
> Campbell *et al* 'Are cannabinoids an effective and safe treatment option in the management of pain? A qualitative systematic review' BMJ [2001]; 323: BMJ 13.

92 Both of these drugs were moved into schedule 3 from schedule 4 by the Misuse of Drugs (Amendment) Regulations 1993.

93 But midwives are only exempted for the possession of pentazocine and pethidine (Misuse of Drugs Regulations 1988, reg 10).

94 An offence under of the Misuse of Drugs Act 1977 s 18.

95 Misuse of Drugs Regulations 1988, reg 13.

96 Medical term for 'dispense'.

Chapter 7

Clinical Negligence

INTRODUCTION

[7.01]

Negligence is probably the area of clinical practice and the law that most exercises the minds of practitioners. Certainly it is true that litigation against health professionals, doctors and hospitals in particular, is on the increase and that the cost of insurance is rising correspondingly[1] but the reasons for the increase in medical litigation are not at all clear. Some blame solicitors, others blame the so-called 'compensation culture' and there is no doubt that the increasing empowerment and enlightenment of patients has gone some way towards ensuring that the traditional deference formerly accorded, rightly or wrongly, to the medical profession has been eroded. However, the reasons for increasing litigation lie outside the scope of this text.

The ground rules for negligence, both for negligence in general and for 'professional negligence', are relatively simple. Indeed, negligence has already been mentioned in this book when we dealt with consent.[2] Failure to obtain valid consent[3] to treatment from a patient amounts to negligence. It was mentioned then that a clinician who fails to obtain valid consent will generally be judged by the standards of professional negligence, meaning that her conduct will be judged by comparison with the practice of her peers. But there is more to negligence than this thumbnail sketch.

In this chapter, we look in more detail at the components of negligence and the difference between negligence in general and 'professional' negligence in particular. Through examples, we will scrutinise negligence in action while also answering specific questions about whether certain categories of conduct amount to negligence. Finally, this chapter will deal with the way in which the clinician can defend an allegation of negligence and how strategies can be put in place to minimise the occurrence and consequences of clinical negligence.

WHAT IS NEGLIGENCE?

Definition

[7.02]

One definition of negligence is:

> '[T]he omission to do something which a reasonable person, guided upon those considerations which ordinarily regulate the conduct of human affairs, would do, or doing something which a prudent and reasonable person would not do.'[4]

The desire to stop people from negligently doing (or failing to do) something in such a way that they may cause other people harm is of ancient lineage,[5] but it was only in 1932 that the law began to assume its modern form. In one of the most celebrated of all legal cases,[6] a woman discovered the decomposed remains of a snail in a bottle of ginger ale from which she was about to drink. She brought a case against the manufacturer of the drink for his negligence in having permitted the mollusc to find its way into her drink. Before this case, a person could be found negligent towards another only if both parties were bound together by a contract. However, in a groundbreaking judgment Lord Atkin laid out the 'neighbour principle', the foundation stone of negligence. Lord Atkin expressed himself, defining in the process who is a 'neighbour', as follows:

> 'You must take reasonable care to avoid acts or omissions which you can reasonably foresee would be liable to injure your neighbour. Who then, in law, is my neighbour? The answer seems to be persons who are so closely and directly affected by my act that I ought reasonably to have them in contemplation as being so affected when I am directing my mind to the acts or omissions which are called into question.'

In other words, a 'neighbour' is a person whom you can foresee being affected if you do something negligent. A person who drives a car at excessive speed can foresee that she may strike a pedestrian; a doctor who operates on a patient can foresee that her patient will be harmed if she conducts herself negligently. Similarly, the judge in *Donoghue* felt that a person who makes a soft drink should reasonably foresee that a person is going to consume that drink and might therefore be affected by any negligent omission of the manufacturer, such as failing to check for snails. The 'neighbour principle' is in turn the basis for the fact that one person can owe another a 'duty of care' or, put another way, can be under a duty not to act in a negligent fashion. Because of the 'neighbour principle', a driver owes other road users a duty to take care when driving and a doctor owes her patients a duty of care while treating them. The situations in which negligence can arise are almost limitless, but this chapter confines itself to negligence arising in the clinical setting. We begin, however, by examining the four links in the chain of events that are common to all forms of negligence.

The four elements of negligence

[7.03]

Unless the four formal elements of negligence have occurred, a court will generally not find that the tort[7] of negligence has occurred. The four elements that must occur in order for an allegation of negligence to succeed are:

1. the existence of a 'duty of care' (or of the duty to take care);
2. a failure to attain the standard required by that duty of care;
3. loss or damage occurring to the person affected by the failure to take care;
4. the loss or damage must have been caused by the failure to conform to the required standard.

If any of these elements is missing, it is difficult to sustain an allegation of negligence.[8]

> **Example 1**
>
> Dr Watson is a surgeon. She admits a patient for removal of a cancerous right kidney. The surgeon discusses the operation with the patient, explaining that the right kidney is to be removed. The patient signs a form consenting to the operation. However, during the operation the surgeon removes the left kidney and the patient dies. The family wish to know if they could bring a case against the surgeon for negligence.

Using the above example, can we isolate the presence or absence of the four elements of negligence?

1. **Was there a duty to take care?** If we apply the neighbour principle, the patient falls unquestionably into that category of person whom the surgeon can foresee will be affected by her acts or omissions, therefore yes there was.
2. **Was there a failure to conform to the standard required?** The surgeon was supposed to remove the right kidney, whereas in fact she took out the one on the opposite side, so again broadly speaking the answer is 'yes'. The exact test for the 'professional' standard of care is dealt with at para **[7.15]** below.
3. **Was any damage caused?** The patient is dead, so yes.
4. **Did the act or omission cause the damage?** Yes.

There are many elements of the example that could be altered, each potentially changing the outcome. Suppose that Dr Watson performed the operation, but another doctor, Dr Urbino, explained the operation to the patient and obtained consent to the excision of the wrong kidney. It was on the basis of this incorrect consent form that the wrong operation was performed. Does this change the picture?[9] Or assume that Dr Watson realised Dr Urbino's mistake just in time and did not remove the healthy kidney. Instead she proceeded to the other side to remove the cancerous kidney, doing no damage to the healthy kidney but resulting in a far longer operation.[10] Add to this latter scenario the fact that three days after the operation the patient succumbs to a heart attack.[11] It is easy to see that many factors may affect the question of negligence. In the sections that follow we look at some of the complexities involved in the definition and application of each element of negligence.

Quick Reference Guide 7.1

Negligence and its elements

- Negligence is doing, or failing to do, something in such a way that that your act or omission falls below the standard of care you owe to your 'neighbour', causing him harm. Legally speaking, your neighbour is any person whom you can reasonably foresee as being affected by your acts or omissions.
- There are four elements to proving negligence. If any one is absent, there will generally have been no negligence:
  - (i) The existence of a *duty of care* (or a duty to take care)
  - (ii) A *failure to live up to that duty* to take care
  - (iii) *Damage* caused to the victim of that failure
  - (iv) The damage must be *caused by the failure*

NEGLIGENCE IN THE CONTEXT OF HEALTHCARE

Duty to take care

[7.04]

Ultimately the question of whether a 'duty of care'[12] exists in any given relationship is a question to be decided by the courts. However, in a therapeutic relationship there is no real legal doubt that a duty of care is present. A duty of care arises between the clinician and her patient when she undertakes to care for the patient, whether on foot of a request for care from the patient himself or following a referral from a colleague. Note, however, that there is no definite general obligation on a practitioner to provide care to a person in a 'good Samaritan' situation or to a person who is not ordinarily her patient, but if she does so, then she will be under a duty of care.[13]

In most areas of social and commercial interaction, a duty of care arises precisely where you would expect and clinical practice is no exception. The duty of care is closely allied to the 'neighbour principle' mentioned previously and occurs where person A can foresee that person B will be affected by any act or omission on the part of person A and where there is 'proximity' between persons A and B. In this legal sense, proximity does not necessarily mean closeness in space or time. A manufacturer of a drug that causes birth defects has no proximity in terms of time or geography to a child who may be deformed after his mother takes the drug during pregnancy, but nonetheless there may be *legal* proximity. Similarly, a driver does not have to know the identity of the individual who may be harmed by his reckless driving: it is enough that it is foreseeable that people generally may potentially be harmed. Sharing the road brings with it the necessary proximity.

In Irish law, a duty of care, together with potential liability for a breach of that duty, arises in the following situation:

- there is proximity [in the legal sense] between the parties;[14]
- any damage caused by one party to the other is foreseeable;
- there is no strong public policy that would create an exception.[15]

So a road user obviously has a duty of care not to injure other road users. A doctor or other clinician has a duty to help a patient to get better and not to cause any harm to him by negligent acts or omissions.

The standard of care

[7.05]

The standard of care expected of the person who is under a duty to take care is not absolute: it can vary with changing circumstances. What is of particular concern to the clinician should be the fact that there is a distinction between the standard of care expected from the 'ordinary' person and that expected from a 'professional'. We consider below (section **[7.08]**) the question of who, for the purposes of negligence, falls into the 'professional' category.

The standard of care of the 'reasonably careful man'

[7.06]

In negligence generally, the standard of care – or how careful someone has to be in a situation where he is under a duty of care – is the care 'expected from a reasonably careful man in the circumstances.'[16] In other words, a person (or institution) will be compared to what a reasonable person (or institution)[17] would have done (or not done) in the circumstances and it is the judge[18] who decides whether or not this standard has been met. The 'reasonable person' test is not without problems. Obviously there are times when the test cannot be applied unstintingly: if someone is blind or missing a limb, he cannot be expected to have precisely the same faculties and powers as the 'ordinary man' and this may have to be taken into account.[19]

The standard of care expected of the ordinary person (and of the professional) can be varied up or down according to the circumstances:

- The standard expected may be higher if there is a higher probability of an accident in the circumstances[20] or if any accident that occurs is likely to have particularly serious consequences, even if the likelihood of the accident occurring is small.
- A lower standard may be applied if the defendant's conduct fulfils some important social function, such as the saving of a life or if it would be practically impossible in terms of the cost or manpower involved to completely eliminate the risk in question.

The standard of care of the 'professional'

[7.07]

The standard of care expected from the professional is different. It is not a test by comparison with the reasonably careful man, where the judge decides what is 'reasonable care'. Rather, the key words in summarising the approach of the courts to the professional's standard of care are 'qualified deference'. Courts accept that in the rarefied world of a professional, the profession itself may set its own standards and the courts will generally not interfere with those standards, once the standards appear (to the court) not to be obviously unsatisfactory.

Accordingly the professional is compared in the first instance, not to what the courts think the reasonably careful man would have done in the circumstance, but to the practice and standards of the professional's peers. Furthermore, the courts also bear in mind when it comes to the professional that there may be differences in opinion as to what constitutes best practice. This means in effect that a professional may take any one of a number of courses of action without falling below the requisite standard of care, so long as the course of action she takes is supported by some responsible body of opinion within the profession. The professional standard of care has been distilled as follows:

> '[The standard of care is] that of the ordinary skilled person exercising and professing to have that special skill, and a doctor… [is] not to be held negligent if he acts in accordance with the practice accepted at that time as proper by a responsible body of medical opinion, notwithstanding that other doctors adopt different practices.'[21]

We will return to the practical meaning of this quotation when we look at the Irish test for professional negligence and apply that test in the clinical context (section **[7.14]** *ff*).

Who is a 'professional' in the healthcare setting?

[7.08]

We have drawn a distinction between negligence generally and professional negligence. The question then arises whether all health care practitioners are professionals for the purposes of negligence – do nurses, radiographers, doctors, dentists and pharmacists and the rest all qualify as professionals? The reason the question arises is because the courts have occasionally drawn distinctions between different categories within the health care sector and in one case, concluded that nurses were not professionals for the purposes of negligence.[22]

There appear to be two elements involved in deciding whether a health carer is a 'professional' and will accordingly be judged by the more deferential standard of professional negligence. The first is the possession of a special skill or competence, a skill usually conferred by specialist qualifications. The second is the fact of setting out one's stall as possessing that skill and offering to use it to help people achieve a specific end. A practising doctor or dentist is therefore clearly a 'professional': she possesses the special skills conferred by a medical or dental degree and, in practising medicine or dentistry, claims to be able to use those skills to effect an improvement in health for those who consult her.

Simply claiming to possess a skill is not enough to be termed a professional. A jeweller who pierces ears will not, even though she is performing a surgical procedure, albeit a minor one, be expected to demonstrate the abilities of a surgeon, merely the capabilities the court expects of the average jeweller.[23] In one Irish case, a 'bone-setter' claimed to be able to cure TB.[24] The court decided that he was not expected to have the skill of a physician, for he had never said that he was one, but he was expected to discharge the skill he claimed to have, namely that of being able to cure tuberculosis. The patient had died and the defendant had been negligent but he was judged by the ordinary standard of negligence.

As we have mentioned, at least one Irish case has decided that nurses are not, for the purposes of negligence, 'professionals'. Does this still apply and does it mean that some paramedical staff are not to be regarded, legally speaking, as professionals?

One possibility is that the decision that held that nurses were not professionals was an anomaly, a decision rooted in an old-fashioned mindset or predicated on the non-university-based education that previously characterised nursing training. It seems, on balance, that a course of study conferring a formal qualification in a particular skill that, firstly, the public regards as a 'special' skill not possessed by the majority of persons and that, secondly, is used to achieve specific outcomes (such as health gain) would make an individual a 'professional'. Accordingly on this analysis, a physiotherapist or occupational therapist, to take two non-medical examples, both of whom can work independently and take independent decisions on specific treatment plans directed at producing a specific health outcome, would be regarded as a 'professional' for the purposes of negligence. On the other hand, it could be argued that nursing and radiography, which have less therapeutic independence and a role less focussed on achieving a certain or specific treatment outcome, may be less likely to be regarded as professions when it comes to questions of negligence.[25] Only those disciplines of clinical practice that are 'professional' will be judged by the standard of care of professional negligence, while others will be adjudged by a court using the 'reasonable person' standard.

Damage

[7.09]

Damage can take any number of forms. If may be physical, psychological, psychiatric or financial. A patient left with depression and loss of income after a procedure has suffered 'damage' – in the legal sense – in the same way as has the patient who still experiences pain two years after precisely the same procedure. The damage must have been caused by the act of which the patient complains.

Cause

Factual Causation

[7.10]

> **Example 2**
>
> A car driven by Moriarty accidentally strikes Holmes while the latter is standing on the edge of a high cliff admiring a waterfall, pushing him off the edge. There can be little doubt that the blow from the car is the 'factual cause' of Holmes's fall. Similarly, if a doctor amputates a leg, the amputation is the *factual cause* of the consequent limp.

The test for factual cause is sometimes called the 'but for' test: whether everything would have been alright *but for* the negligent act. Holmes would still be drinking in the view but for the fact that Moriarty pushed him.[26] A medical example is provided by the following:[27]

> **Example 3**
>
> Three workmen became ill after drinking tea. They attended the casualty department of a hospital, but were turned away. The reason they were turned away was that the doctor who should have seen them was himself sick. It transpired that the tea was poisoned with arsenic and one of the workmen died. His wife sued the hospital and lost. The arsenic poisoning would have killed her husband anyway and there was nothing the hospital could have done, even if they had seen the patient. It could not be said that the man would still have been alive *but for* the actions of the hospital. It was the arsenic, not the hospital, that caused the death.[28]

Factual causation and res ipsa loquitur

[7.11]

In order to succeed in negligence action, the plaintiff generally has to prove, on the balance of probabilities, that the alleged act or omission caused the alleged damage as well as proving that the act itself was negligent. Sometimes, however, the patient will not have to prove that the act caused the damage, a scenario that is called *res ipsa loquitur* or 'the facts speak for themselves'.

> **Example 4**
>
> A patient undergoes an operation for the removal of a tumour in the armpit area. The operation is a success but after the operation it becomes clear that damage has been done to the brachial plexus,[30] leaving the patient with profound weakness and loss of sensation in his arm. The patient alleges negligence.

In this case, the facts certainly speak for themselves: the likelihood is that the operation did cause the damage. However, the patient still has to prove that the operation was negligent, while the surgeon may try to prove that there was some other cause for the nerve damage. However, because of the extreme complexity of the human body and the fact that precise outcomes will not always be predictable, *res ipsa loquitur* is rare in medical cases.

Legal causation

[7.12]

As well as factual causation, there is also 'legal' causation, which concerns whether a court will attach legal consequences (such as compensation) to the fact that a certain act caused a certain result. Even though one thing factually causes another, the law may say that the cause is not legally significant either because:

1. The damage is too distantly removed from the original factual cause.
2. Some new event has occurred that has broken the chain of causation.[31]

Example 5 (continued from example 2 above)

When Moriarty's car nudges Holmes off the cliff-edge, the driver is surely responsible for the damage suffered by Holmes. The collision is the *legal cause* of the damage to Holmes as well as the *factual* cause. But is Moriarty also legally responsible for injuries suffered by someone who, seeing what is going on, is so distracted that she drives her car into another car, which in turn strikes a grazing horse that was due to run at Cheltenham the following week? Is Moriarty responsible for the injuries suffered by the person in the second car? Is he responsible to the owner of the horse and to the rider deprived of a mount at Cheltenham? And so on… At some point the court will hold that, even if the *factual* chain of causation is not broken, the *legal* chain must be or else matters will never be resolved.

We see in the above example the limits that the law may need to place on legal causation. Moriarty may be responsible for Holmes's injuries but there is an argument to say that he could not foresee the lack of concentration of the first driver. Furthermore the collision with the second car is arguably a new intervening act that sets off a whole new chain of liability. Yes, Moriarty's conduct is the originating factor – the factual cause – for all the episodes that ensue, but he cannot be said to hold all the legal liability. This is in keeping with the principle that the damage for which a negligent party is held legally liable should be foreseeable.

Combining factual and legal causation

[7.13]

In order for an act to be negligent it, therefore, must cause the damage both factually and legally. The former without the latter is no use at all, which in turn can cause difficulties for a person alleging negligence. Let us look at a medical example.

Example 6

A patient is very ill following a severe heart attack: even if correctly treated, he has less than a 50% chance of survival. A doctor makes a wrong decision regarding a dose of medication. The patient dies.

The negligent decision was *a* factual cause of death, but not *the* factual cause because there is the heart attack to be taken into consideration – was the heart attack rather than the medication the factual cause of death? And was the negligent decision in any event the legal cause of death? The patient was more likely than not to die, whatever happened.

The courts' original approach was uniformly to refuse compensation in such cases,[32] but in the United States a recently emerging trend hints at compensating the victims of such negligent acts or omissions, while also factoring in the degree to which other factors minimise the effects of any negligence. No such case has been decided in Ireland, but in England the courts have continued to set their faces against compensating patients in these situations.[33]

Quick Reference Guide 7.2

Exploring the elements of negligence

1. Duty of care

- There is a duty of care when a professional relationship ('proximity') arises between clinician and patient. A breach of duty of care generally only amounts to negligence where the damage caused by the breach is foreseeable.
- There is no 'good Samaritan' duty to provide medical care, but if care is provided the clinician is under a duty to do her best in the circumstances.

2. Standard of care

- The standard of care takes two forms: one for negligence generally and another for professional negligence. Falling below the appropriate standard of care is one of the indispensable elements of negligence
- In cases of general negligence, the standard is that expected from the 'reasonable man' in the circumstances. The judge decides on what is the standard to be expected of the reasonable man.
- In cases of professional negligence, the standard is that of the profession itself. A professional accused of negligence will be judged by reference to the conduct espoused by comparable members of the profession. A professional does not have to do what *every* other comparable professional would do, merely that which is approved of by a *reputable body of opinion* within the profession.
- A professional is someone who has a special skills (such as clinical skills conferred by education) and who represents herself to the public as capable of practising those skills.
- Most clinicians probably fall within the category of 'professional' for the purposes of negligence.

3. Damage

- The damage caused by negligence can take any form including physical, financial and psychological harm.

4. Cause

- Simply because something was the *factual* cause of an outcome does not mean that it was the *legal* cause.
- It will not be necessary to prove that one thing caused another where the facts speak for themselves.

Applying the Principles of Clinical Negligence

[7.14]

In the preceding sections, we have looked at the principles of negligence, namely the existence of a duty of care, a breach of that duty, resultant damage and a causal link between the act or omission and the damage. Now it is important to see how negligence works in action, especially in the area of professional clinical negligence.[34]

The *Dunne* judgment

[7.15]

The most important case governing clinical negligence in Ireland is *Dunne v National Maternity Hospital,*[35] a case arising out of birth injuries suffered by a child born in the defendant hospital. The court detailed the test for negligence in the medical profession (and by extension comparable clinical professions). The test is reproduced here in full, then explained below and finally applied to a clinical example so that we can examine its workings:

1. The true test for establishing negligence in diagnosis or treatment on the part of a medical practitioner is whether he has been proved to be guilty of such failure as no medical practitioner of equal specialist or general status and skill would be guilty, of if acting with ordinary care.
2. If the allegation of negligence against a medical practitioner is based on proof that he deviated from a general and approved practice, that will not establish negligence unless it is also proved that the course he did take was one which no medical practitioner of like specialisation and skill would have followed had he been taking the ordinary care required from a person of his qualification.
3. If a medical practitioner charged with negligence defends his conduct by establishing that he followed a practice which was general, and which was approved of by his colleagues of similar specialisation and skill, he cannot escape liability if in reply the plaintiff establishes that such practice has inherent defects which ought to be obvious to any person giving the matter due consideration.
4. An honest difference of opinion between doctors as to which is the better of two ways of treating a patient does not provide any ground for leaving a question … as to whether a person who has followed one course rather than the other has been negligent.
5. It is not for a [judge] to decide which of two alternative course of treatment is in [her] opinion preferable, but [her] function is merely to decide whether the course of treatment followed, on the evidence, complied with the careful conduct of a medical practitioner of like specialisation and skill to that professed by the defendant.

The judge also went on to say that:

> "General and approved practice' [mentioned in parts 2 and 3 of the test] need not be universal but must be approved of and adhered to by a *substantial number of reputable practitioners* holding the relevant specialist or general qualification.' [emphasis added]

Translating and applying Dunne

[7.16]

What does this all mean? It is important to understand how the court defines clinical negligence, so we should translate the paragraphs above into less legalistic prose (retaining the same numbering) in order to show how the courts think when it comes to considering whether a practitioner has been guilty of professional negligence:

1. The question of whether a doctor is negligent will be decided by whether his actions or omissions were such of which no comparable doctor would have been guilty. A doctor will be compared to someone of 'equal specialisation'. In other words a general practitioner will not have her knowledge of surgery compared with a consultant surgeon, but with another GP. In all cases the comparison is with the normal, competent comparable professional. A vascular surgeon will not be compared with the most gifted professor of vascular surgery, but with another ordinarily skilled vascular surgeon.[36]
2. Simply deviating from accepted treatment is not enough to constitute negligence. The deviation has to be one that no other comparable doctor would have taken. So, there is no suggestion that there is only one way of doing everything.

It is worth noting in the two sections above that when the court talks about 'no medical practitioner', it means no medical practitioner acting with reasonable care. It would not be enough for a defendant to produce a few doctors who approved of or who routinely adopted the practice of the defendant if it were obvious that the conduct of the defendant was inconsistent with reasonable care.

3. Simply following a standard course of action is not enough to prevent an allegation of negligence. That course of action might have inherent and obvious flaws and if it does, the court may find a practitioner negligent for having followed it.[37] For example, if a hospital's process for monitoring babies during labour has flaws detectable by anyone giving the system any thought, then a gynaecologist could not rely for her defence on the fact that she followed that protocol.
4. An honest difference of opinion between two medical practitioners does not mean that one of them must be guilty of negligence.

The court recognises here that there may be two ways of doing something or, in other words, that there may be more that one 'general and approved practice'. Any difference of opinion between doctors who adopt different general and approved practices must be both honest and reasonable.

5. A jury or judge is not there to decide whether one course of action is preferable to another, but whether the action complained of was negligent or not (by reference to the other elements of the *Dunne* test). The question to be decided is simply whether the conduct was negligent, not whether it was less expedient, less convenient or more painful than another approach might have been.

Essentially, *Dunne* gives latitude and deference to professionals in clinical practice. Doctors are allowed to follow an accepted standard within the profession and, more importantly, to differ from a given accepted practice without the court finding them negligent. A doctor pursuing any course of action must be able to show that her action was consistent with a body, although not necessarily the majority body or even an especially substantial body, of responsible opinion within the profession. However, the deference and latitude are not absolute, but are limited by the court, which will refuse to accept the doctor's behaviour, even if she followed a general and accepted practice, if that practice itself is obviously flawed.

There are reasons why this latitude is afforded to the professions and to the medical profession in particular. Among the most important is that medicine, if it is to advance, needs to be allowed to develop and to explore new avenues of treatment, without a doctor working under the constant fear of being sued every time she pursues an unorthodox, new or not yet wholly proven practice.

Example 7

A patient attends for assessment of a blocked carotid artery. The treating consultant vascular surgeon, Dr Jekyll, is aware that some academic papers have suggested that patients with a blockage of less than 50% may be better treated without surgery. The patient has a 45% blockage in his artery. The decision is taken to manage the patient conservatively with blood-thinning tablets. Dr Jekyll is the only one of the three vascular surgeons in the hospital who is taking this new approach. A month later, the patient suffers a stroke and dies. His wife initiates an action for negligence. She claims that the doctor should have performed the operation. Using the *Dunne* test, is Dr Jekyll likely to have been negligent?

There is obviously a duty of care here, but did the surgeon fall below the expected standard of care? We apply the principles of *Dunne* in the order that they were set out in the case itself:

1. Dr Jekyll will be compared to the practices of other vascular surgeons exercising responsible care. Had she been a general practitioner taking the decision to initiate conservative treatment rather that referring the patient for surgery, then she would be compared to the standards of other GPs and so on.
2. She has deviated from orthodox treatment and chosen to follow a new regimen suggested by academic papers. Is her deviation negligent? Only if no other practitioner of equal skill would follow this course. Dr Jekyll's approach is based on academic research. It is therefore likely that there would be little problem in showing that her approach was consistent with a responsible, if novel, body of therapeutic opinion.
3. Dr Jekyll did not follow any inherently flawed protocol. Were it the case that she drew her therapeutic inspiration from a single journal and, what is more, a journal known to have a poor reputation for accuracy, then the facts might change. Let us assume, however, that the alternative treatment had been thoroughly researched and reported in the most reputable journals. The court is unlikely to criticise the practice taken by Dr Jekyll as having obvious shortcomings.[38]
4. In following this course of action therefore, Dr Jekyll did differ from her colleagues, but it was an honest and responsible difference of opinion.

5. The question to be decided is not whether surgery would have been the preferable option. It may well have been, but the question is whether, taking the facts of the case and the *Dunne* decision into account, the choice of conservative treatment was negligent.

The likelihood therefore is that, even though the patient died, the surgeon was not negligent.

Quick Reference Guide 7.3

Negligence in the professional clinical setting

❖ The test for clinical negligence in Ireland was set out in the *Dunne* case. There are five components:

(i) A doctor is negligent if she does something or omits to do something which no reasonable practitioner of *comparable experience and standing* would have done or omitted to do. The practitioner will be compared to someone of like specialisation.

(ii) One can deviate from standard practice if it is reasonable to do so: there is no absolutely right way of doing everything.

(iii) On the other hand, simply following accepted procedure is not sufficient to prevent an allegation of negligence if the accepted procedure is obviously flawed. In other words, a court will intervene in professional standard-setting where the standard set by the profession is too low.

(iv) A difference of opinion about how to do something does not automatically mean that one of the bodies of opinion must be negligent. There can be two, three or more bodies of professional opinion on any given aspect of medical care. As long as the practitioner whose conduct is impugned can point to a significant and responsible body of her profession that holds the view that her conduct was reasonable, she is unlikely to have been negligent.

(v) The court is not there to decide whether one course of action is preferable to another, simply whether the act or omission complained of was negligent.

Specific areas where negligence may arise

[7.17]

Lack of experience

Is a less experienced practitioner under the same duty as a more experienced one? The court may take into account inexperience, but it will expect nonetheless a qualified clinician to be competent and to be as reasonably skilled in her vocation as another inexperienced practitioner. As one judge memorably phrased it (in the context of learner drivers):

> '[He] may be doing his best, but his incompetent best is not enough.'[39]

Does a practitioner have to be right every time?

No. There is no onus on the practitioner to be right all the time. If a clinician makes a decision, then all the law asks is that the decision be a reasonable one in the circumstances.

The decision must be based on all the available information and the practitioner has a duty to have regard to all available sources of information. In one case,[40] the Supreme Court pointed out that, as well as taking the patient's history and a description of his symptoms into account, a GP also had to include relevant information from other sources, such as, in this case, the patient's wife. In that case, the patient minimised his symptoms while his wife drew attention to the fact that he had a very severe headache and that 'he must be very bad', because he was someone who normally avoided doctors. The doctor had a duty to sift and weigh such information as carefully as he would details gleaned from the patient. In not doing so, he was negligent.

There are certain circumstances in which the practitioner will find it difficult to be right. One example is where she is attempting diagnosis of a particularly unusual or rare condition:[41] in such a case, the onus is to reach a reasonable (by the standards of a comparable professional) diagnosis in the circumstances.

Keeping up to date

It is clear that any 21st century practitioner must be practising 21st century skills. As for how assiduous the clinician must be in staying informed about the latest developments, one judge said the following:

> '[I]t would…be putting too high a burden on a medical [practitioner] to say that he has to read every article appearing in the current medical press; and it would be wrong to suggest that a medical man is negligent because he does not at once put into operation the suggestions which some contributor or other might make in a medical journal. The time may come in a particular case when a new recommendation may be so well proved and so well known and so well accepted that it should be adopted …'[42]

In other words, to miss one reference to a new line of treatment may be unfortunate, to miss dozens would look like carelessness. Referring back to **example 7** above of the surgeon who opted for conservative treatment of a carotid artery blockage, we can build a little upon it. The surgeon was adopting a new treatment, not used by her colleagues in the hospital, but in the circumstances described she was not negligent because her approach was supported by a substantial body of responsible medical opinion, the substance and respectability of that opinion being demonstrated by the academic articles.

> **Example 8**
>
> Ten years after the scenario outlined in **example 7**, a patient attends Dr Love, another vascular surgeon practising in the same hospital as Dr Jekyll. The patient has a 40% blockage of his carotid artery and, notwithstanding the fact that evidence has been steadily accumulating in the intervening ten years to show that conservative management is definitely better in such cases, the surgeon performs an operation. The patient suffers a stroke during the operation and is left disabled. The patient sues.

The surgeon in her defence points to other surgeons who continue to operate on such patients and relies on this body of medical opinion to support her contention that she was not negligent.[43] This, however, is an example *both* of a failure to keep up-to-date *and* of the type of situation in which the court might exercise its right to disregard the opinion of a body of medical practice if that practice is manifestly flawed. The court could conclude that for a doctor to have failed to absorb the lessons of more than ten years of research and discovery, may amount to negligence, no matter that some other surgeons are continuing to treat patients in the same way. In other words, the practice of ignoring the research is negligent, irrespective of the fact that a body of medical opinion continues to do so.

Responding when 'on call'

Most clinicians will be on call at some time, from radiographers to dentists. In most cases, the fact of being on call implies a duty to attend. The specialist doctor on call to casualty will generally have to respond if an emergency within her discipline occurs in the accident and emergency department. A general practitioner will typically be expected to respond to a call from a patient to visit him in his house.

While in certain cases, however, it may be a condition of employment that health care personnel respond to a call to attend to a patient, there are other circumstances where the clinician has greater latitude. A general practitioner may, on hearing a patient recount his symptoms over the phone, feel that a house call is not indicated. Regardless of the doctor's feelings, is she under an obligation to attend? The answer appears to be in the negative. In one case that concerned a general practitioner's failure to make a house call, the court said:[44]

> 'That is not to say that an obligation can arise in every case where a request is made to a general practitioner to visit the patient at home, to comply with such a request. *That would be wholly unreasonable. Every case must be judged on its circumstances.*' [emphasis added]

What is certainly true is that a clinician who holds herself out as being available to provide an out-of-hours service should be available to deal with requests from patients, or should ensure that alternative coverage is available, or that patients seeking her help can be directed elsewhere.

Obtaining consent

This area is dealt with in chapter 4. Suffice it to say that a medical practitioner, or any other clinician, who conducts a procedure without the consent, expressed or implied, of a patient will, unless there is some mitigating factor, be guilty of negligence.

Writing references and reports

A practitioner who writes a report[45] or a reference[46] about a patient or employee has to be careful that its contents are carefully compiled. In the first place, an inaccurate written description of a patient or employee may be libel. The practitioner may also be guilty of 'negligent misstatement' if what she writes is carelessly wrong and results in damage. This may occur, for example, when writing a reference for an employee. If a reference inaccurately describes a former employee in such a way as to make him seem less attractive to potential employees, he may be able to sue for negligent misstatement. Another situation in which this may occur is when a doctor is compiling a medical report for a patient, perhaps regarding an insurance policy or a mortgage.

Example 8

Dr Svengali is asked to complete a medical report for her patient A, who is seeking life insurance and who has always been in perfect health. She confuses the patient with patient B, who has a similar name but an altogether more chequered medical history. In error, she sends the report of patient B's ailments to the insurance company, which declines patient A's application for life insurance on the basis of his supposed ill health. Two months later, and before A has had the chance to discover why he was turned down, he dies in a car crash. His widow discovers the error. Had the error not been made her husband would have been insured and she would not now be penniless.

In such a situation, the widow could conceivably be in a position to bring an allegation of negligent misstatement against the doctor. The test for negligent misstatement is probably the simpler test for general negligence rather that the test for professional negligence, even if the author of the report is a professional. The court therefore simply asks itself whether the letter or report was reasonable in the circumstances.[47]

Quick Reference Guide 7.4

Troubleshooting aspects of negligence

- ❖ A clinician 'doing her best' is not enough – she must meet the minimum standard acceptable for the profession.
- ❖ A practitioner does not always have to be right, but she has to reach a reasonable diagnosis or decision in the circumstances of the case.
- ❖ Failing to keep up to date may be negligent if the gaps in knowledge are such that no reasonable and comparable professional would have allowed those gaps to accumulate.
- ❖ A practitioner is not under an open-ended responsibility to attend on those patients who call upon her. The responsibility varies with the circumstances.
- ❖ Failure to obtain valid consent may be negligence. Valid consent must be voluntary and given by someone with the legal capacity – in terms of mental competence and age – to do so. Furthermore the practitioner is under a duty to keep the patient informed of the potential risks of treatment (so-called 'informed' consent).
- ❖ A report regarding a patient or a reference regarding an employee may give rise to an allegation of negligence if it is not carefully written.

DEFENDING AN ALLEGATION OF NEGLIGENCE

The obvious defence

[7.18]

The first avenue open to the practitioner is to argue that a particular act or omission was not negligent at all because:

- — no duty of care existed, or
- — the conduct complained of did not fall below the required standard of care, or
- — there was no damage, or

— if there was damage, it was not caused by the act or omission complained of, or
— any combination of the above reasons.

Contributory negligence

[7.19]

Sometimes, even if a practitioner is negligent, it may not be entirely her fault. The patient may do something to contribute to the adverse outcome: this is called 'contributory negligence'. There was a time when, if the victim of negligence contributed *at all* to his mishap, the wrongdoer was entirely absolved of her responsibility. The modern approach is that a person's contributory negligence will simply erode the wrongdoer's responsibility in proportion to how substantial the contributory negligence was. A court may decide to award damages to a plaintiff but then to reduce them according to how they view the plaintiff's contributory negligence. If a plaintiff is 50% responsible for his own misfortune, then his damages can be reduced by that amount.

> **Example 9**
>
> A patient attends an accident and emergency department with a broken leg. He is seen by a doctor, who diagnoses the fracture correctly, but applies a cast badly to the patient's leg. She advises the patient that for the next few weeks he must avoid putting weight on the leg and, to that end, she issues him with a pair of crutches. The patient ignores her advice and puts weight on the leg. The badly- applied cast cracks and the leg fracture is made worse, requiring a subsequent operation. The patient sues the doctor for negligence.

The doctor may have been negligent in this case in applying the cast as she did. However, the patient was told not to put any weight on the limb. The doctor could argue that the patient's conduct amounted to contributory negligence.

Contributory negligence will not always succeed as a defence. In one case[48] a hospital was found to have inadequately assessed a psychiatric patient. The patient then jumped from a height. While the hospital was negligent, it contended that the patient's conduct amounted to contributory negligence. However, because the patient was not fully in control of her mental faculties at the time, jumping out of a window did not constitute contributory negligence.

Similar to contributory negligence is 'failure to mitigate damage', which is the question of whether the victim of the alleged negligence took reasonable steps to minimise or to correct any damage caused by the alleged negligence. If a person refuses to do so, perhaps by refusing to go for treatment of a condition caused by the alleged negligence,[49] he is failing to mitigate his damage and the court may take this into account when apportioning liability and consequent damages.

The voluntary assumption of risk

[7.20]

This occurs when a person is made aware of a risk that something may go wrong but nonetheless agrees to go ahead. In broad terms a person can escape liability for negligence if she can show either:

— that there is a contract that includes a term freeing her from any liability for negligence, or

— that there is some other evidence that shows that the injured person agreed to waive his legal rights.[50]

In theory, this could mean that a doctor who explains to a patient that the procedure the patient is requesting is one that the doctor is not very good at and that may consequently go wrong and the patient nonetheless agrees, the patient is voluntarily assuming the risk of the doctor's negligence. The decision by the patient to forego his legal rights to sue for negligence would have to be formally expressed and agreed. It is a rare prospect in the clinical situation but nonetheless legally possible.

Practitioners may also be affected by voluntarily assuming risk as rescuers. A doctor who works as part of an emergency response team might be held to take upon herself any risks inherent in responding to emergency situations, consequently making it difficult for her to sue anyone should negligence result in her injury. In reality however, Irish law has tended to conclude that a rescuer can sue someone whose negligence puts her in danger by creating the situation that leads to the attempted rescue.[51]

The case is brought outside the time limit

[7.21]

In the interests of justice, a person cannot sue another person so long after the act complained of that it would no longer be possible for the defendant to defend herself properly. If a physiotherapist made an error of treatment in her early twenties, it would seem unreasonable if the first she hears of legal action is fifty years later, long after she has sold on her practice or destroyed the notes of the initial consultation. Accordingly there is legislation[52] that sets down the limits within which legal actions must be commenced. In general, no legal action may be commenced after the window of opportunity provided by the Statute of Limitations Act 1957-1991 has closed. In the case of negligence and personal injuries the time limit is three years. The three year period starts to run from whichever is the *later* of two dates:

— the date of the original negligent act or omission, or

— the date when the person becomes aware of the negligent act, otherwise called the 'date of knowledge'.

This second provision, the date of knowledge or date of discoverability, is often important in clinical negligence.

> **Example 10**
>
> A surgeon performs an operation on a young boy of seven to remove a testicle. During the operation she negligently damages the spermatic cord of the other testicle. The boy grows to manhood and wishes to start a family, but finds himself unable to do so. During investigations conducted to identify the cause of infertility, it becomes clear that the man is infertile due to damage to the spermatic cord.[53]

If it were the case that the man could only sue the surgeon in the three years after the date of the injury, he is at an obvious disadvantage – he could not reasonably have discovered the damage until he had at least reached sexual maturity. The law therefore allows people who do not discover that they were victims of a negligent act or omission until many years after the event to commence legal proceedings for that act, as long as they do so within three years of the 'date of knowledge'. The date of knowledge is the date the patient 'could have become aware[54] of the existence of the damage itself', which is not necessarily the date when he becomes aware that the damage was caused by the negligent act.[55] Therefore, if the operation occurred in 1980, the man discovered that he was infertile in 1995 and then discovered in 1997 that the cord was damaged, then the date of knowledge would be 1995 and the action must be commenced within three years to the day of that discovery.

Courts may exercise discretion in some cases. However, where the court feels there has been too long a delay in starting a case, even when the delay was caused only by how long it took the patient to discover the fact of his injuries, the court may stop the case from proceeding.[56] The theory behind this approach is that an excessive lapse of time makes it impossible for the defendants fairly to defend themselves and the interests of justice are best served by striking out the case. Unfairly, even where a patient complies with the time-frames laid down by rule of 'date of discoverability', he may still find the courts unwilling to consider his case for reasons entirely beyond his control.

Quick Reference Guide 7.5

Defending an allegation of negligence: the arguments

- ❖ That the act or omission was not negligence.
- ❖ That some negligent act or omission on the part of the patient contributed to the damage that resulted. Similar to *contributory negligence* is a *failure to mitigate damage,* which is the victim acting in such a way as to fail to minimise damage that he knows exists or is likely to exist.
- ❖ That the victim of the alleged negligence voluntarily accepted the risks of the act or omission and exempted the practitioner from any liability for negligence.
- ❖ That the victim of the alleged negligence has waited too long to bring his legal action.

DOES A PRACTITIONER OWE A DUTY OF CARE TO ANYONE OTHER THAN HER PATIENT?

[7.22]

In certain circumstances: yes. A practitioner can be liable for negligence to a person other than the person to whom she owes the *direct* duty of care (generally the patient). There are two main scenarios.

Occupational health

[7.23]

When a practitioner is involved in occupational health, she has a duty not only to her patient, but also to an employer. This may create some conflicts in terms of how to reconcile the duty owed to the employee with the duty owed by the doctor who employs her.[57] A doctor or nurse may be employed by a company as an occupational health practitioner to care for the employees. In practical terms the practitioner owes a duty of care to both, but it is generally accepted that her duty to the patient predominates in the event of conflict.[58]

By the same logic, a doctor performing a medical examination on an applicant for a job *before* the applicant is employed by the company for whom the doctor is acting, might be thought to owe a duty both to the patient *and* to the company to ensure that the assessment is conducted without negligence.[59] However, the law appears to be in some confusion. In England, the most recent case held that the doctor retained by a company to examine a person owes a duty of care only to the company.[60] However, in the United States, a court reasoned that a doctor who gives advice to a patient during a medical assessment of the patient on behalf of a company does owe a duty to the patient.[61] The law in Ireland is not clear on this point.

The risks posed by a dangerous or infectious patient

[7.24]

A second and more important scenario occurs when a practitioner is negligent and someone other than the patient who was the victim of that negligence is harmed as a result of that negligence. Is the clinician responsible to anyone other than her patient for the consequences of her negligence? The answer to this question harks back to the question of 'foreseeability' that underpins negligence. Harm must be foreseeable if the law is to find that it was caused by negligence. Whether a doctor will be liable to persons other than her patient depends on whether the harm to that other person is foreseeable.

In ch 3, under the heading of confidentiality (see section **[3.21]**), the case of *Tarasoff*[62] was mentioned. In that case a patient confided to a university psychologist that he intended killing Ms Tarasoff. The psychologist did not warn the young lady, but did tell the campus police who detained the young man but released him when he appeared rational. He subsequently killed the girl. The court reasoned that, when a practitioner becomes aware of an identifiable person who is at risk, she owes a duty to warn that person or to inform those who can warn that person. The key element is foreseeability. In English law, if the identity of a potential victim of a dangerous psychiatric patient negligently discharged from hospital or of a negligently performed vasectomy cannot be foreseen, then the doctor does not owe a duty to that victim.[63] It is not enough that the *risk* is foreseen; it must also be possible to foresee the *identity of the person* whom the risk is likely to affect.

In the United States, the legal response to similar situations is more victim-friendly. American courts have decided that where a doctor has negligently failed to advise HIV-positive patients of their diagnosis, the doctor owes a duty not only to the patient, but also to those whom the patient infects.[64] It is hard to predict what approach the Irish

Courts would take. It certainly seems reasonable that a practitioner should be responsible for the consequences of her actions when those consequences affect those other than her patient, but it would also be preferable that there is a limit to the size of the group to which the practitioner might be liable. It would seem harsh that if two doctors make the same error, for example, each failing to inform a different HIV-positive patient of his diagnosis, that the extent of each doctor's liability should depend on how promiscuous the patient is and therefore how many people he might infect. One preferable approach in Irish law might be that a doctor who is negligent to one of his patients should also be liable for negligence to those third parties whom a reasonable practitioner might foresee as being affected.

VICARIOUS LIABILITY

[7.25]

Vicarious liability is an important concept in clinical negligence. It describes the fact that in some circumstances the law will hold one person partly responsible for the negligence of another. Originally vicarious liability was confined to the liability of a master for the acts of his servants, but it has now developed to encompass employer-employee relationships.[65] If an employee commits a negligent act during the course of her employment, then the employer may also be held responsible for that negligence *even if the employer was not responsible for the negligence.*

The original test of whether an employer was liable for the acts of its employees was whether the employer exercised 'control' over the activities of the employee. Problems arose with this test when it was applied to clinical situations: hospitals would claim that they had no control over a practitioner's exercise of her clinical skills and courts seemed prepared to accept this claim.[66] Thus it was the case for many years that if a doctor was negligent, her employers could not be vicariously negligent because they did not control her clinical activities. This stricture was gradually relaxed: initially, hospitals could be held responsible if they failed to ensure that staff members were competent when employed and that hospital equipment was fit for its purpose. However, it remained the case that once a clinician was fit for employment the employer continued to have no responsibility for the actual exercise of her clinical skill.[67]

Eventually, a hospital was held accountable for the clinical conduct of one of its radiographers[68] and in the same case the court also stated that a hospital would be responsible for the conduct of its nurses. A hospital was finally held accountable for the misdeeds of a surgeon in the 1950s[69] and the judge stated that:

> '[W]hen hospital authorities undertake to treat a patient and themselves select and appoint and employ the professional men and women who are to give the treatment, they are responsible for the negligence of those persons in failing to give proper treatment, no matter whether they are doctors, surgeons, nurses or anyone else.'

The same principles apply in Ireland:[70] the employer will be responsible for the negligence of clinical employees. Note that it is not only a situation of hospital responsibility for the actions of clinicians: clinicians themselves who employ staff may be vicariously liable for the actions of her staff, eg, a negligent act by a practice nurse or the disclosure of confidential information by a staff member.

The two elements of vicarious liability therefore are that:

1. The negligent person must be an employee *and*
2. The negligence must have occurred in the course of the employee's employment.[71]

Who is an 'employee'?

[7.26]

This is a vital question. If someone alleges that a hospital is vicariously liable for the conduct of a physiotherapist or other person working in the hospital, the institution may be able to avoid liability if it can prove that the person is not an employee. This might occur in a private institution, where a consultant rents rooms and has the use of beds but is not actually 'employed' by the institution: she is in what is often called 'private practice'. The institutions will often directly employ some staff, such as nurses and radiographers, but the surgeons or physicians may not be so employed. Is the institution then vicariously liable for the negligence of the surgeon or physician? Or what if the person who commits the negligence is an independent practitioner, working for the hospital without any formal contract of employment? The test is not whether or not there is a contract of employment, but, as we have seen above, whether the employer exercises any degree of *control* over the employee.[72]

It appears that in the case of a private institution, there is no question of the institution being vicariously liable for the work of private practitioners caring for their private patients.[73] It is possible, although the question has not been dealt with in the Irish courts, that a doctor or surgeon treating private patients in an institution where she is *also* employed to treat public patients may give rise to a situation where the employer could be vicariously liable for the acts of the physician or surgeon.[74]

Distinguishing vicarious liability from primary liability

[7.27]

The important thing to understand about vicarious liability is that it arises where the servant has been negligent and there is a relationship of servant and master present. It is not necessary that the employer be negligent: the relationship is enough. However, an employer may also be himself liable without any need for recourse to vicarious liability. A hospital that employs incompetent staff or uses outmoded machinery or operates deficient protocols may be itself primarily liable for negligence, quite aside from any negligence on the part of its staff members.[75] An example of such a situation might be where an institution has defective systems in place, such as a faulty system for reporting the results of blood tests. The staff who act on an incorrect report may not be liable for negligence (although they may be if the report is obviously at variance with the clinical findings) while the hospital could be negligent for having such a system in place.

Quick Reference Guide 7.6

Vicarious liability

- Vicarious liability in the modern sense describes the liability of an employer for the negligent acts or omissions of his employee.
- The key elements are that the negligent party must be an employee and must have been acting in the course of her employment when she committed the negligent act.
- An important test of an 'employee' is whether the employer exercises control over her actions.
- An institution may be vicariously liable for negligence but it may also be found negligent in its own right, so-called *primary liability*.

DEFECTIVE PRODUCTS

[7.28]

If someone manufactures a product, then she has a duty of care towards the user of that product. *Donoghue v Stevenson* – the case which introduced the modern concept of negligence – arose from a defective product, namely the drink containing a snail. Historically, a person who sought compensation for damage caused by a defective product had to prove that the manufacturer or producer of the product was negligent by satisfying all the tests for negligence that have been discussed previously. However, this area has evolved greatly in recent years with the Liability for Defective Products Act 1991[76] which introduces a concept called 'strict liability'.

Strict liability is a legal rule whereby a court will not concern itself with the question of whether a person fulfils the strict legal tests necessary to be found guilty of the allegation in question. Instead, when it comes to product liability, the court will simply satisfy itself that the product at issue was in fact defective and proceed to automatically hold the manufacturer or producer liable for that defective product. In other words, a company will automatically be considered legally negligent if a product it produces transpires to be defective and causes death or personal injury to a person or damage to any property (other than the defective product itself). Defective products could include medical equipment, blood products and pharmaceuticals.

ALTERNATIVE WAYS OF COMBATTING NEGLIGENCE

[7.29]

Negligence is a huge drain on the resources of institutions faced with enormous bills for compensation and for the insurance of their staff. Similarly, practitioners find themselves faced with ever-spiralling personal indemnity costs. Any action brought by a patient may also involve enormous legal costs, often exacerbated by the fact that the losing side will generally also have to pay the costs of the winning side.[77] A further problem is the concern that the increased threat of negligence action results in 'defensive practice', the tendency to do every conceivable test or to furnish every conceivable treatment so that all bases are covered, although there are those who argue that defensive practice is less common than generally supposed.[78]

Doctors and other practitioners are insured against negligence in a number of ways. Some are insured (or 'indemnified') by their employers. Others arrange their own medical indemnity insurance. The insurance premium paid each year means that the insurance company will bear the cost of fighting any negligence action and the cost of any award of damages made against the clinician. As medical negligence claims in particular have increased in number, the payments expected by insurers have correspondingly increased, especially in the supposedly high-risk disciplines.

Figure 7.1 Obstetricians' Indemnity Fees by year (€ equivalent):[79]

1991	1992	1993	1994	1995	1996	1997	1998	1999	2000
11811	20955	24130	25711	30988	38074	43484	43484	45656	54610

Ways of dealing with the problems posed by negligence actions fall into two camps divided by where in the natural history of negligence they attempt to intervene. There are measures that try to stop the negligence from occurring in the first place and others that seek a way to minimise the consequences and costs of negligence actions.

Preventing negligence actions

Healthcare risk management[80]

[7.30]

Risk management involves putting into place mechanisms for identifying, prospectively or retrospectively, risks to patients and employees in the health care environment. If risk management can identify and eradicate risks, then legal actions arising from those risks may thereby be prevented from arising in the first place or from recurring. One study has shown that approximately 4% of hospital admissions include at least one adverse event and that, in 1% of admissions, the adverse event is due to negligence.[81]

Typically a risk management system will involve a system of reporting mishaps and accidents, including 'near misses'.[82] Such mishaps might include unexpected deaths, complicated in-patient stays (eg the need for follow-up operations or admission to intensive care) or problems with medication. Once such risks are identified, a mechanism can be put in place to tackle problems that have been isolated.

Healthcare risk management, however, is not merely an expression of common sense but also an expression of the modern ethical approach to medical errors that has been described in the 'Tavistock Principles'. The principles were generated by the Tavistock Group[83] in the wake of a US Institute of Medicine paper on creating a safer health system.[84] The most important principles from a clinical perspective include the following:

- Co-operation with each other and with those served by the health system is the priority for those working within the healthcare system.
- All individuals and groups involved in health care, whether providing access or services have continuing responsibility to help improve its quality.

— In developing a culture of safety, clinicians will need to act as role models for their students by applying these principles themselves the next time they encounter a medical error. Practitioners need to 'declare error reduction to be an explicit organisational goal and [devote] a significant proportion of the board and management agenda... to achieving this goal.'[85]

Competence assurance for the clinical professions

[7.31]

The medical profession has taken the lead in this regard, primarily because it is within their ranks that the most damaging allegations of negligence and incompetence tend to arise. The Medical Council has undertaken to introduce a process of Competence Assurance that will assist doctors to continue to update their skills and help those doctors who are shown to have fallen significantly below the norm. The programmes for keeping practitioners' skills up-to-date include schemes for continuing medical education (CME) and continuing professional development (CPD).

At present, this scheme is not at an advanced stage although many of the plans for it have been carefully drafted.[86] It will depend for its operation on the introduction of a new Medical Practitioners Act. Unfortunately this legislative initiative remains in the drafting stage, so it is impossible to be certain what form it will take. There are many legal obstacles to be met before competence assurance can be made to operate satisfactorily, including those relating to the confidentiality of proceedings and the sanctions to be imposed on incompetent practitioners, but similar systems operate well in other countries such as Australia and the United States.[87]

Minimising the consequences of negligence

No-fault schemes

[7.32]

A 'no fault' scheme is one where a person injured by a clinical incident does not have to prove that anyone was at fault for the accident. There are also some schemes in which the patient does not even have to identify the person responsible for the injury. The two best-known schemes are those in Sweden and New Zealand: both of these schemes do oblige the patient to identify the person responsible for the harm he has suffered.

The first obvious saving is in legal costs. The person alleging that he is injured has only to prove that he has an injury and that his injury resulted from the allegedly negligent treatment by the institution or practitioner in question. There is therefore less likelihood of having to fight a lengthy legal battle. 'No-fault' schemes can also in theory help to improve standards within the healthcare professions. When incidents are identified they can be used by the institution that fielded the claim to provide feedback to clinical staff in that and other institutions, in order to improve standards and avert further incidents.

By setting out a standard list of compensation amounts that will be payable to patients who suffer certain categories of injury, the introduction of 'no-fault' may also counter the element of lottery involved in court awards of damages. How much a plaintiff receives for an injury in the ordinary run of legal action may depend on the performance of his legal team on their day in court and the particular judge he faces. A 'no-fault' scheme would clarify the injuries for which compensation may be obtained and the extent of that compensation. However, one problem with 'no-fault' compensation is that it has proved to be very expensive. The New Zealand scheme has been compelled, in order to avoid insolvency, to undergo a huge number of alterations, diluting the no-fault component in order to ensure that the scheme could continue at all.

Other 'no fault' schemes that have been proposed include the introduction of specific'no fault' compensation for children born with cerebral palsy.[88]

Enterprise liability (Clinical indemnity scheme)

[7.33]

From July 1 2002 a new system came into operation in the Irish public health service, known as Enterprise Liability or the Clinical Indemnity Scheme (CIS). At the time of writing the scheme extends to all non-consultant health care staff, but it is expected that the scheme will encompass consultants working in the public sector in due course.[89] Under enterprise liability, responsibility for defending malpractice claims is placed on the institutions that provide care – the 'enterprises' – instead of burdening the individual practitioner. The aggrieved patient therefore does not need to sue the individual medical practitioner, the hospital and the health board (as is often the case), each represented by separate legal teams who often delay the process (and increase costs) by trying to shift blame or to fight the case on different grounds. Instead, a claim under enterprise liability is managed by a single entity representing the 'enterprise' – in effect, the Government.

Clinical indemnity covers all aspects of public practice including the provision of care to private patients in public facilities and those whose care forms part of a clinical trial or other approved research. The 'public sector' includes staff working in all exchequer-funded health agencies and universities, as well as researchers with the Health Research Board and public health doctors and dentists working with the health boards.

The scheme excludes general practitioners, those working in a private capacity and all 'good samaritan' acts carried out by those who would otherwise be covered by the scheme. The potential benefits of enterprise liability are intended to be threefold:

- It removes from the individual clinician some of the stigma of being sued.
- It should reduce administrative costs by eliminating multiple insurers and requiring only a single legal team to represent the enterprise.
- It should create greater incentives and opportunities for health care institutions to introduce risk management (see section **[7.30]**) schemes.

The plan involves the creation of a State Claims Agency (SCA) to manage and co-ordinate the scheme and the establishment of a State Indemnity Pool (SIP) as the basis for financing future settlements in respect of clinical negligence claims in the public hospital system. The SCA will also oversee the necessary protocol for incident reporting and the risk management programmes intended to accompany enterprise liability.

Tort reform

[7.34]

Negligence is a tort and some countries have introduced reforms to the law of torts in order to make it more difficult to bring a negligence action. These reforms have most commonly occurred in the United States and have generally taken the form of:

— Making it more difficult to sue hospitals or doctors by changing the procedural rules, eg shortening the limitation period within which the action can be brought, and the way in which the law defines the standard of care or informed consent.

— Placing a cap on the damages that can be awarded and the fees that can be paid to lawyers.

— Compelling potential plaintiffs to go to arbitration.[90]

— Reducing payments to take account of any monies received from other sources, such as insurance pay-outs from the patient's own insurance.

California introduced its Medical Injury Compensation Reform Act in 1975, containing many of these new measures. Before the introduction of this legislation, California accounted for almost 30% of all US payments for medical negligence. By 1994 this had fallen to 10%.

Endnotes

1 See Lancet 'Defence union suggests new approach to handling litigation costs in Ireland' 13 November 1999; Lancet 'Ireland discusses how to handle projected increase in medical litigation' 3 March 2001. At the time of the latter article, the Medical Protection Society stated that the frequency of claims against consultants was projected to increase from 200 to 210 per 1000 consultants (compared with 25 claims per 1000 GPs). The Irish Government's bill for state-employed doctors' medical insurance tripled in the 10 years to 2000 while claims against doctors and hospitals in the period 1989-1998 rose by 450%. See also Fenn, 'Counting the cost of medical negligence BMJ 2002;325: 233-234.

2 In ch 4, *Consent.*

3 By way of reminder, valid consent must be 1. voluntary, 2. based on sufficient information and 3. be given (or withheld) by a person with the capacity (mental or age) to do so.

4 *Blyth v Birmingham Waterworks Co* (1856) 11 Ex Ch 781, 784.

5 The Code of Hammurabi, one of the world's oldest legal texts, was probably in existence before 1750 BC. It recognised negligence as a punishable offence, although the punishments were harsher than those imposed today, eg, if an architect negligently constructed a house that collapsed, he and his family could be put to death. See ch. 1.

6 *Donoghue v Stevenson* [1932] AC 562.

7 A tort is a 'wrong' committed by one person (or company or institution) against another and which gives rise to a legal duty on the part of the wrongdoer to make amends to the person affected.

8 We will see below (see section **[7.11]** *ff*)that there are certain times when it is not necessary to prove that the act or omission in question caused the damage. This occurs when there could be no other possible cause for the damage that occurred other than the act or omission in question. This is known as *res ipsa loquitur* or 'the facts speaking for themselves'.

9 In such a case, it is probable that both doctors would be negligent, one for the inaccurate consent, the other for failing to make certain she knew the full facts before proceeding with surgery.

10 Assuming the patient makes a full recovery, it could be argued that no damage resulted and therefore there was no legal negligence even though there was a mistake on the consent form.

11 The family might allege that the heart attack was due to the physical strain of the longer operation and the question then might be whether on the balance of probabilities (the legal standard of proof for all such cases) the operation had caused the subsequent cardiac event. See section **[7.13]** below.

12 A 'duty of care' and a 'duty to take care' are used synonymously.

13 *Lowns v Woods* (1996) A Tort Reps 81. A doctor was requested to visit a child who was not his patient, but who was experiencing seizures. He declined to do so, the child suffered brain damage and the doctor was found guilty of negligence. However, the judgement points out that, although a doctor may feel under a moral obligation to attend someone who is not her patient, this does not necessarily translate in to a legal obligation. In this case, Dr Lowns was found guilty because he had no satisfactory excuse for not attending, he knew the child to be nearby and most importantly, had received a direct request to do so. Many commentators argue that 'professional rescuers' such as the medically qualified should not be exempted from helping in an emergency scenario and that circumstances of a particular situation may suggest that the clinician, as in *Lowns v Wood*, could and should have done something. See Kennedy & Grubb *Medical Law* (3rd edn, 2000) p 298. In Australia, the State of Queensland has a law exempting medical and nursing personnel from liability for negligence when providing emergency care at the scene of an accident or during transport from the accident scene to hospital: Voluntary Aid in Emergency Act 1973 (Qld), s 3.

14 We return to the question of proximity below when we look at the duty of care owed by the practitioner to people other than her patient, including those whom the negligently-treated patient may infect or physically harm.

15 *Ward v McMaster* [1988] IR 337 (SC). 'Public policy' means the creation of a blanket rule or policy that helps to protect the interests of the public at large. For example, in *Ward v McMaster*, the court held that there was a strong public interest in having a rule against the police being found guilty of negligence when they were investigating crimes. Such a public policy means that the police can divert more energy to the detection of criminal activity and less towards 'defensive policing' to minimise the risk of being sued for negligence.

16 *McComiskey v McDermott* [1974] IR 75. The circumstances are important. In the *McComiskey* case, the plaintiff was being driven in a car by his friend who was a rally driver, the driver was expected in the circumstances to show the care when driving that would be expected of a competent rally driver.

17 English courts used frequently to refer to what the hypothetical 'man on the Clapham omnibus' would have done in the circumstances.

18 Or the jury, if there is one. Juries are not used in modern negligence cases.

19 See McMahon & Binchy *Law of Torts* (3rd edn, 2000) ch 7. A blind person will fall below the reasonable person's standard of care if he gets into a car and tries to drive because it is such an obviously negligent thing to do by any standards but will probably not do so if he leaves the house unaided and, in attempting to make his way about, occasionally impedes traffic.

20 There are two contrasting clinical examples: in *Plunkett v St Laurence's Hospital* (1952) 86 ILTR 157 (HC), a woman 'hardly able to move' fell off an x-ray couch. This was so unlikely to have occurred that there was no negligence. In *Kelly v St Laurence's Hospital* [1989] ILRM 437, a patient fell from a window when going to a toilet unaccompanied shortly after all of his

medications had been discontinued. The likelihood of an accident was greater in this latter case and the hospital was found liable for negligence.

21 *Salmond and Heuston on the Law of Torts* (21st edn, 1996) p 232.

22 *Kelly v St Laurence's Hospital* [1989] ILRM 437 (SC).

23 *Philips v Whiteley (William) Ltd* [1938] 1 All ER 566.

24 *Brogan v Bennett* [1955] IR 119. Mr Bennett had produced a pamphlet headed 'TB CONQUERED' and charged £100 for a rich person and £20 for the poor. Mr Brogan, who occupied the latter category, fell for it, just as many people still fall for utterly implausible treatments today. He left hospital and attended Mr Bennett who (according the court's judgment):

> 'produced a bullet on the end of string and said he was going to x-ray the patient. He then caused the pendulum to oscillate and pronounced the case a fairly bad one. He purported to diagnose the exact percentage of impairment of all the main organs of the patient and claimed that by means of his pendulum he could diagnose the ailments of a person at the other end of the world.'

25 None of this is to say that any health care discipline is less of a profession that another. The point that is being made is that as far as the courts are concerned in negligence cases some disciplines will be regarded as professions and others will not. Where the line is drawn or will be drawn is not always easy to say.

26 Some people prefer a test for factual causation that asks whether the act was 'a material element and a substantial factor' in the damage.

27 *Barnett v Chelsea and Kensington Hospital Management Committee* [1969] 1 QB 428. This case also accepted the proposition that every doctor is not under a legal obligation to provide health care to everyone who requires it (see para **[7.04]** and *Lowns v Wood* (1996) A Tort Reps 81).

28 There are some subtleties involved in the 'but for' test, such as the situation in which two separate but connected acts combine to cause the final injury. For example, a driver hits a pedestrian, putting the pedestrian in hospital with relatively minor injuries, where he receives negligent treatment that kills him. This area of joint liability lies outside the scope of this book. See McMahon & Binchy *Law of Torts* (3rd edn, 2000) ch 2.

29 Another scenario in which a similar presumption might arise is after the death of a patient under anaesthetic.

30 The network of nerves in the area of the armpit.

31 Eg *Conole v Redbank Oyster Co* [1976] IR 191, a child was drowned when an unseaworthy boat capsized. The original action was against the boat's owners and manufacturers. The court felt that the manufacturers could not be held to blame. The captain's decision to go to sea, in spite of warnings not to, constituted a whole new act, that meant that liability for negligence lay with the captain, not on the manufacturers.

32 *Kuhn v Banker* (1938) 133 Ohio St 304.

33 *Wilsher v Essex Area Health Authority* [1988] AC 1074.

34 Bear in mind that the 'standard of care' for professional negligence is different from that in 'general' negligence. Also, see the discussion in the section on 'standard of care' at section **[7.08]** concerning who precisely may be regarded as a 'professional' for the purposes of negligence.

35 *Dunne v National Maternity Hospital* [1989] IR 91. The test that is set out in the text is from the judgment of Finlay CJ. The classical statement of medical negligence in the United Kingdom is the *Bolam* test (from *Bolam v Friern Hospital Management Committee* [1957] 2 All ER 118):

'[A] doctor is not guilty of negligence if he has acted in accordance with a practice accepted as proper by a responsible body of medical men skilled in that particular art.'

36 *O'Donovan v Cork County Council* [1967] IR 173.

37 See *Roche v Peilow* [1985] IR 232. In this case, a solicitor sought to avoid liability for negligence that arose out of his failure to conduct a routine search for certain documents by arguing that it was the accepted practice in the profession not to seek these documents. However, the court felt that the shortcomings of this approach were so obvious as not to provide a defence to negligence, even if it *was* what comparable professionals did.

38 English law, like Irish law, includes the proviso that the court will not automatically accept medical evidence of 'accepted practice' where accepted practice has obvious and inherent problems: *Bolitho v City and Hackney Health Authority* [1997] 4 All ER 771.

39 *Nettleship v Weston* [1971] 2 QB 691 .

40 *Collins v Mid-Western Health Board* [1999] IESC 73; [2000] 2 IR 154.

41 *Wolfe v St James's Hospital* (22 November 2000, unreported) HC; [2002] IESC 7 (20 February 2002) SC.

42 Lord Denning in *Crawford v Board of Governors of Charing Cross Hospital* (8 December 1953) CA).

43 Remember that a professional will generally not be negligent if a substantial body of comparable professionals would have done things the way she did, assuming, also that the body of comparable opinion is itself not obviously flawed.

44 *O'Doherty v Whelan* (18 January 1993, unreported) HC.

45 *Hedley Byrne & Co Ltd v Heller & Partners Ltd* [1964] AC 465.

46 *Spring v Guardian Assurance plc* [1995] 2 AC.

47 It may be that the test for professional negligence will apply if the report in question is a wholly clinical one involving the exercise of the practitioner's clinical discretion.

48 *Armstrong v Eastern Health Board* (5 October 1990, unreported) HC.

49 In *Bohan v Finn* DPIJ Trinity and Michaelmas Terms 1994, p 61 (HC). The plaintiff in this case refused to go into psychiatric hospital for treatment of a psychosomatic complaint arising out of an accident, even though there was more than an 80% chance of recovery. The judge took this refusal into account.

50 This is the interpretation given by McMahon & Binchy *Law of Torts* (3rd edn, 2000) ch 17 to the Civil Liability Act 1961, s 34(1)(b).

51 *Philips v Durgan* [1991] ILRM 321. In the United States, there is a so-called 'Fire Fighters' Rule' which states that a fire fighter injured in the course of his duty cannot sue the person whose negligence caused the fire, except in special circumstances: *Butler v Union Pacific Railroad Co* (1995) 68 F 2D 378

52 The Statue of Limitations 1957, amended by the Statute of Limitations (Amendment) Act 1991.

53 A factual example is *Maitland v Swan and Sligo County Council* (6 April 1992, unreported) HC. A surgeon removed a woman's ovary without consent in 1969, she learned of the removal in 1971. In 1983, she learned that her left ovary was abnormal and that she was infertile. In that case the judge decided that the 'harm' arose when the woman discovered that her remaining ovary was abnormal, not when she discovered that the original ovary was removed.

54 The measure of whether a patient could have known of the damage is based on knowledge the patient could be expected to have or facts that he could have discovered by reference to reasonable expert help. So, our hypothetical infertile patient who knew he was having difficulty conceiving could have known that there was a problem from the time the doctor confirmed that he had problems with his sperm count and before he ever knew there was damage to the spermatic cord.

[55] *Hegarty v O'Loughran* [1990] 1 IR 148. This case concerned damage to the plaintiff's nose allegedly caused by the defendant's treatment. The plaintiff had argued that the time should have started to run, for the purposes of the Statute of Limitations, not when he became aware of the damage, but also when he discovered that the act of negligence had caused that damage.

[56] *Toal v Duignan* [1991] ILRM 135.

[57] This area and the conflicts inherent in it are more thoroughly canvassed in ch. 9 *The Practitioner and the Workplace.*

[58] See 'International Code of Ethics for Occupational Health Professionals' *Encyclopaedia of Occupational Health and Safety* (4th edn, 1998) vol 1, pp 19.1-19.31. See also section **[9.04]**, ch. 9.

[59] Including for example, following up with all test results or communicating clinically significant findings to the patient's own medical adviser.

[60] *Kapfunde v Abbey National plc and Dr Daniel* (1998) 46 BMLR.

[61] *Webb v TD* (1997) 95 P 2d 1008 (Montana Superior Court).

[62] *Tarasoff v Regents of the University of California* (1976) 131 Cal Rptr 14.

[63] *Palmer v Tees Health Authority* [1999] Lloyd's L Rep (Med) 351. Similarly in the United Kingdom, a doctor who failed to advise a patient that his vasectomy might reverse itself in future was found not to owe a duty to every single one of his patient's future sexual partners. While it was foreseeable that the patient would have sexual intercourse after his operation, it was impossible to identify with whom he would have intercourse: *Goodwill v British Pregnancy Advisory Service* [1996] 2 All ER 161.

[64] *DiMarco v Lynch Homes – Chester County Inc* (1989) 525 Pa 558; *Reisner v Regents of the University of California* (1995) 31 Cal App 4th 1110. In this second case the doctor did not tell the patient she was HIV-positive and was sued by the boyfriend of the patient, who contracted HIV from the patient.

[65] It may also occur when a firm is held liable for the actions of a partner in that firm. Vicarious liability may go all the way up a chain. So, in theory a hospital may be responsible for the actions of a nurse, the health board for the hospital and the Minister for Health for the Hospital. In theory, all may be sued for their vicarious liability.

[66] *Evans v Liverpool Corporation* [1906] 1 KB 160.

[67] *Hillyer v St Bartholomew's Hospital* [1909] 2 KB 820.

[68] *Gold v Essex County Council* [1942] 2 KB 293.

[69] *Cassidy v Minister of Health* [1951] 1 All ER 574 per Denning LJ.

[70] *Lindsay v Mid-Western Health Board* [1993] 2 IR 147 (in particular p 167).

[71] See *Health Board v BC* (19 January 1994, unreported), HC.

[72] *Moynihan v Moynihan* [1975] IR 192.

[73] *Bolton v Blackrock Clinic Ltd* (20 December 1994 HC, 23 January 1997 SC).

[74] See the dissenting judgment of Kirby P in *Ellis v Wallsend District Hospital* (1989) 17 NSWLR 553. The judge felt that, in such a situation, the institution *would* be vicariously liable.

[75] The question was discussed in *Bolton v Blackrock Clinic Ltd* (20 December 1994 HC, 23 January 1997 SC).

[76] This Act, like the Data Protection Act 1988 (see ch 3, *The Practitioner-Patient Relationship, Ethics and Confidentiality*), was born out of a European Union Directive of the same name.

[77] See endnote 1.

[78] Ham, Dingwall, Fenn and Harris, *Medical Negligence: Compensation and Accountability*, (1988) London/Oxford, King's Fund Institute/Centre for Socio-Legal Studies. They cite as one example the rise in caesarean sections (CS) performed on women in childbirth. The prevailing opinion, then as now, was that the rise in CS rates was an expression of worries about complications in labour leading to a negligence action. However, they demonstrated that rates

were rising in all countries irrespective of the pattern of medico-legal actions in those countries.

79 From Medical Protection Society, cited in Department of Health *Medical Indemnity – Proposals for Change*, (2001) Dublin. Excluding obstetricians, 'low risk' (as defined in terms of their risk to the insurers) consultants in 2000 were paying €8,000, while 'high-risk' specialists were paying approximately €30,000 per annum in indemnity fees.

80 See Cusack, 'Risk Management as a Strategy for Quality' in *The Irish Health System in the 21st Century* Leahy and Wiley (eds) (1998).

81 Hiatt *et al* 'A Study of Medical Injury and Medical Malpractice: An Overview' NEJM 1997;321:7, 480.

82 Although 'near miss' is a nonsensical term: to nearly miss something is actually to hit it.

83 See Smith et al 'Shared ethical principles for everybody in health care: a working draft from the Tavistock Group' BMJ 1999;318:248.

84 '*To Err is Human. Building a safer health system*' Kohn, Corrigan, Donaldson (eds) (1999) Washington DC: National Academy Press.

85 J L Reinersten 'Let's talk about error' BMJ 2000;320:720.

86 Irish Medical Council *Competence Assurance Structures – An Agenda for Implementation* (March 2002). The projected timeframe is as follows (para 4.2):

> 'A structure for CAS [Competence Assurance Structures] will be developed during 2002. In late 2002, half of the doctors on the Register of Medical Specialists or who are eligible for such registration will be notified of their need to enroll (*sic*) in a formal CME/CPD program from 2003 onwards. This is likely to involve some 2000 doctors. These doctors will submit their first CME/CPD returns at the end of 2003 and annually thereafter. This cohort will complete their first five-year cycle of accreditation at the end of 2007. The remaining 2000 doctors will be notified of their enrollment (*sic*) in a CME/CPD program in 2003 and will submit their first return at the end of 2004 and annually thereafter. This cohort will complete their first five-year cycle in 2008.'

87 For a brief summary of the problems and some suggested solutions, see Mills & Cusack 'Legislating for Competence Assurance – Cool Water on a Hot Topic?' MLJI 2000; 7 :1.

88 This suggested approach is partly based on the fact that there is some medical uncertainty concerning whether there is any human component, negligent or otherwise, in the causation of all cases of cerebral palsy: see 'A template for defining a causal relation between acute interpartum events and cerebral palsy: international consensus statement.' BMJ 1999;319:1054.

89 *Medical Indemnity – Proposals for Change*, Department of Health, Dublin 2001. The management of personal injury (and property damage) claims against the State was transferred to the National Treasury Management Agency (NTMA) by the National Treasury Management Agency (Amendment) Act 2000. When discharging its functions under the Act, the NTMA is known as the State Claims Agency (see http://www.stateclaims.ie – last accessed 16 September 2002). At the time of writing, the date of the implementation of this scheme for consultants – initially intended for July 2002 – has been deferred until January 2003. See also 'Changing the face of hospital medicine', Donal Duffy, *Irish Medical Times*, 24 May 2002. The UK has a similar scheme run by the NHS Litigation Authority.

90 Arbitration is a system where both parties to a dispute agree to let an independent third party make a 'final and binding' decision on the settlement of the dispute. Typically it is quicker and less expensive than going to court. It is very common in the settlement of disputes between insurance companies and policyholders. See Forsythe M. Arbitration and the internal market; Quarrie J 'Arbitration in Medico-legal disputes' BMJ 1994;308:792. The Australian Government has also announced its intention to reform the way in which negligence cases

operate, including shortening the time period within which the case must be brought. The plans also include replacement of the expert witness system with peer review. See 'Australia proposes peer review of alleged negligence cases' BMJ 2002;325:565.

Chapter 8

The Practitioner and the Family

Introduction

[8.01]

The family is accorded a very special position in Irish society by the Constitution.[1] Although the Constitution does not define what a 'family' is, the courts have on any number of occasions reiterated the principle that the family exists within a sphere of autonomy into which the law will rarely intrude. The Constitutional rights of the family do not extend in Ireland to the non-married family,[2] although a non-married family will attract Constitutional protection once the formalities of marriage are completed and the children of a non-married couple will be recognised as equal to those of a married couple.[3] For many years, the Constitution contained a prohibition against divorce[4] and to this day contains a provision that many critics feel enshrines the woman's place as being in the home.[5]

Constitutional deference to the family has had a number of consequences. For a long time, the most noticeable effect was the bar on divorce, which meant in turn that civil annulment, the ending of a marriage by the courts, took on especial significance as the only way in which a couple could end their marriage and still be permitted later to remarry. Secondly, the Constitutional deference towards the family has tended to mean that the parents will rarely be displaced as the primary carers or decision-makers for a child.

We look in this chapter at the question of marriage, or more particularly the ending of marriage and in particular the use of nullity to terminate a marriage. We look also at the issue of domestic abuse and how spouses can be protected against it with the help of the courts. Finally we look too at issues affecting children and the newborn: child abuse, child protection and Sudden Infant Death Syndrome (SIDS).

Marriage

[8.02]

There are three ways of ending a marriage in Ireland: divorce, civil annulment (a declaration by the courts that a marriage is invalid because of some fundamental flaw) and judicial separation. Until the introduction of divorce, annulment was the only legal option for those who wished both to quit a dysfunctional marriage and to have the opportunity of remarrying. While nullity, since the introduction of divorce, is no longer the only way of ending a marriage, applications for annulment nonetheless continue unabated. Medical, psychiatric and psychological factors can often provide grounds for nullity. Divorce is a more pragmatic process in which medical considerations rarely arise, while there is also the process of 'judicial separation',[6] which does not end a marriage but rather regulates the agreement of a married couple to live apart, including the division of assets and maintenance payments. A judicially separated couple remain married and must divorce or seek an annulment before either partner can legally marry again. Judicial separation is not dealt with further in this text.

Divorce

[8.03]

The 15th Amendment to the Constitution introduced a new Article to the Constitution allowing for the introduction of legislation to permit divorce[7] and the Family Law (Divorce) Act 1996 now regulates divorce in Ireland. There is no need for either partner to have been at fault for the ending of the marriage: the fact of having lived apart for the requisite aggregate five-year period will suffice. 'Living apart' is an elastic term and has in family law cases been held to include estranged couples who do continue to live under the same roof but who have ceased to have anything to do with each other. The main concern of the courts is to ensure that adequate financial arrangements are put in place to ensure the welfare of the children and of either spouse if he or she was previously financially dependent on the other. There is little in the law of divorce of relevance to clinical practice.

Nullity

[8.04]

It had been thought that the introduction of divorce into the Irish statute books would lead to a reduction in the demand for annulment of marriage, but this has not happened.[8] An application for the annulment of marriage remains the avenue of choice for spouses who seek a totally 'clean break' and annulment is an area in which clinical evidence may often have a role to play. Civil annulment by the courts evolved over the years in an attempt to help couples who wished to end their marriage but who were constrained from doing so by the ban on divorce and an annulment is a declaration by the courts that a marriage is invalid because of some fundamental failing and should be regarded as never having existed in the first place.[9] The effect of a decree of nullity is that the couple were never married and neither partner owes any obligation – financial or otherwise – to the other.

The simplest starting point for understanding nullity is by regarding a marriage as a straightforward contract.[10] In any contract there are certain fundamental conditions that must be met for the contract to be valid and if those conditions are unfulfilled, the contract can be set aside. The terms of the contract must be certain and furthermore, a person entering into the contract must do so voluntarily, must be mentally competent to do so and must not be misled as to the nature of the contract he is entering into. Finally, a contract that binds parties to do something they are not legally permitted to do is also void. All of these strictures apply to the marriage contract and the reason why they can be relevant to the health professional (and to the doctor in particular) is that medical or psychiatric evidence can be important in determining whether the necessary factors exist for a marriage to be annulled.

The ways in which a marriage may be set aside as void are generally divided into four categories, of which the last two below, invalid consent and incapacity, are the most important:[11]

— lack of capacity to enter into the marriage contract itself;
— non-observance of the formalities of marriage;
— absence of valid consent due to insanity or lack of mental capacity or due to being misled as to the nature of the marriage or due to duress;
— incapacity to enter into or sustain a normal marital relationship;

The law generally presumes that all marriages are valid until the opposite is proven, just as the law presumes that persons are sane until the contrary is shown.[12] Accordingly, it is up to the person who alleges that a marriage should be annulled (the petitioner)[13] to prove it and the court will rarely be satisfied with anything less than compelling proof.[14]

Lack of capacity

[8.05]

A lack of capacity to enter into the marriage contract can arise in one of four ways:

— one or both partners may be too young to marry;[15]
— one or both of the married parties may already be married to another person;
— the partners may be too closely related;
— the partners may be of the same biological sex.[16]

The clinician may be obviously involved in cases where the gender of the spouses is at issue. She may be called upon to certify the nature of an operation, may be involved in a determination of what constitutes 'gender' or may be required to give an opinion as to which gender the parties in question belong. Lack of capacity to enter the marriage contract is different to an inability to enter into and sustain a normal marital relationship (see section **[8.08]**).

Lack of formalities

[8.06]

The absence of the required formalities can have little relevance to clinical practice.[17] Formalities include the specific period of notice that must be given before a couple can marry and a requirement that a couple marry in the place stipulated in the instrument that is used to give notice of an intention to marry.

Lack of consent

[8.07]

Just like consent to a medical or surgical procedure valid consent to marriage has three ingredients: it must be given by someone with the mental capacity to do so; it must be voluntary and it must be informed.[18] If any of these elements is missing the marriage can be annulled.

Mental capacity and marriage

A person does not need much in the way of mental capacity to be able to get married: it has been said that 'the contract of marriage is, in its essence, one of simplicity and one which it does not require a high degree of intelligence to comprehend'.[19] In one case, the court held that a particular person lacked sufficient mental capacity to make a will, yet on the same day had his wits about him sufficiently to get married.[20] Unlike when it comes to writing a will, it does not appear to be the case that a person who suffers from an ongoing mental infirmity can consent to marry during a lucid period when not afflicted by his illness.[21]

If a party to a marriage alleges that the marriage should be set aside because one of the parties was suffering from 'insanity' at the time of the marriage, then the person making the allegation must prove it. This proof may often involve expert medical or psychiatric opinion because what must be proved is that:

> '…the respondent [the person named by the petitioner in the nullity proceedings] was suffering from psychiatric disorder *at the time of the marriage* of such a character that it prevented him from giving a full, free and informed consent.'[22] (italics added)

It is not enough for the petitioner to prove that the respondent had suffered from mental illness before the marriage or to prove that mental illness arose after the marriage. The defect must have been present *at the time of the marriage* (a brief period of recovery or improvement at the time of the marriage will not mean that the illness was not present). If it is proved that a mental incapacity caused by psychiatric illness[23] existed at the time of the marriage, then the marriage can be annulled. Note also that a person intoxicated by drugs or alcohol at the time of his marriage cannot be said to have validly consented and it would be open to a court to annul the marriage.[24]

Informed consent to marriage

Historically, it was rare to find a petition for nullity granted on the basis of a lack of informed consent but in the absence of divorce, courts became more flexible in deciding what amounted to a lack of consent. Traditionally, a mistake or misrepresentation had to be of a most fundamental nature if it was to be grounds for a decree of nullity: it had to concern the very identity of the person whom one was proposing to marry. If A thought she was marrying B, was told she was marrying B, but somehow ended up marrying C, then that could be grounds for nullity. A mistake or misrepresentation about the nature, character or wealth of one's prospective spouse or any other matter that did not concern the identity of the parties was not originally sufficient to allow for annulment.[25]

With the passage of time and certainly by the mid-1980s,[26] there was a discernible move away from this hard line approach and towards pragmatism. With this shift came an acceptance that a mistake as to the character or the nature of a life partner could deal just as great a blow to the validity of consent as could a mistake as to identity. Therefore, when a husband concealed from his wife prior to their wedding the fact that he was homosexual, his lack of candour invalidated her consent and an annulment was granted.[27] There is no need for the mistake or misrepresentation to have been deliberate, simply for it to have occurred, even by accident, may be enough to allow the grant of a decree of nullity.

Duress

Just as consent to any form of clinical treatment must be voluntary, so must consent to marriage be voluntary: a marriage born out of fear, threats, intimidation or any other form of duress can be annulled. Traditionally some measure of coercion was permissible,[28] but the courts have again moved towards a pragmatic intolerance of involuntary consent. Any pressure that overrides the free will of the person who is 'consenting' to the marriage can be considered duress, including emotional bullying,[29] pressure due to factors external to the relationship[30] (which might include fear of deportation) or duress from the parents of one or both spouses.[31]

Inability to enter into or sustain a normal marital relationship

[8.08]

This ground for nullity can be divided into two broad areas: (a) physical incapacity and (b) emotional or psychological incapacity. In both cases, the input of a clinician may be required.

Physical inability - 'impotence'

This generally refers to impotence, or whether it is possible for the couple to have sexual intercourse. Intercourse must be 'ordinary and complete'[32] and possible without resorting to extraordinary measures. Ejaculation or pregnancy need not occur and barrier contraception does not prevent consummation from having taken place. Either partner's difficulties can be the reason for non-consummation of the marriage and furthermore obstacles to consummation may be psychological[33] as well as physical, so that erectile dysfunction and vaginismus[34] may both equally amount to physical incapacity or impotence. The impotence does not have to be universal, affecting all of that partner's sexual relations: it is sufficient simply for a spouse to be incapable of sexual intercourse with the person to whom he or she is married.[35]

Any impotence must be 'incurable', but this is a term to which the law gives an unusual and woolly definition. Impotence is, legally speaking, incurable in the following circumstances:

— when it is in fact medically, surgically or psychologically incurable;

— when the only cure is an operation with potentially dangerous consequences;

— when a relatively safe surgical treatment *is* an option, but the spouse requiring the operation refuses to consent to it;[36]

— in psychological conditions, where there is a danger, even if the condition is treatable or has actually been treated, of the condition recurring.

Proving non-consummation can be difficult and a court may require a great deal of convincing before it is prepared to annul a marriage on the grounds of impotence.

Medical inspection

Court rules provide that where a petitioner seeks a decree of nullity on the basis of impotence, the parties must be requested to undergo a medical inspection.[37] Medical inspectors may be appointed by the court or can be agreed between the two parties to the legal case. Where a specialist has already been responsible for the care of the party in question, it will often be she who is requested to prepare a report for the courts. The experts' reports are exchanged between the parties if both sides retain separate experts and as with all medico-legal reports, the authors can be called upon to testify and to be cross-examined in court.

Any such report is intended to help the court, but it is not obligatory for either party to undergo medical inspection (although the parties must be requested to undergo the examination) and the court may nonetheless annul the marriage if it is satisfied that non-consummation is proven.

Psychological or mental inability

The longest stride forward in terms of broadening the parameters of nullity in pre-divorce Ireland came when the courts decided that a person could lack the mental capacity to enter into or sustain a proper or normal marital relationship. Essentially, if evidence suggests that because of 'some inherent quality or characteristic of an individual's nature or personality which could not be said to be voluntary or self-induced'[38] a person lacks the capacity to remain married, then an annulment may be granted.

This 'inherent quality' does not have to reach the threshold of being a definite psychiatric or mental illness, although that may be the case: in one significant nullity case, one of the spouses suffered from schizophrenia. The court appeared not to be concerned with whether he was 'insane' at the time of the marriage and therefore unable to enter into the contract of marriage but instead dwelt on the fact that his illness meant he could not sustain the loving and caring relationship essential to marriage.[39] The 'inherent quality' must exist at the time the marriage was entered into, although it may not be necessary that symptoms of the problem were present at the time. Other, non-psychiatric, grounds for the courts finding that a person lacked the necessary quality to enter into or sustain a normal marital relationship include the sexual orientation of one of the spouses, emotional immaturity and incompatibility.

Medical evidence may be important in all such cases, especially those argued on psychiatric grounds, because it is necessary to prove that the problem existed, even if only latently, at the time of the marriage. The question is whether the person was suffering from an illness that prevented him from entering into and sustaining a normal marital relationship at the time of the marriage and subsequent recovery from that ailment is not necessarily a bar to a decree of nullity. The court can order the parties to attend for a psychiatric review, but, as with investigations and treatment of impotence, they are not obliged to attend. The courts have stated that there are times when they will prefer to hear the opinion of experts in the field of psychiatry, rather than that of general practitioners. Where there is a dispute between the evidence offered by both sides, the judge will decide between them on the basis of any reports, testimony and cross-examination.

Quick Reference Guide 8.1

Grounds for annulment and scope for clinician involvement in the process

- ❖ A decree of nullity, if granted, has the effect of allowing a marriage to be considered as never having existed. A person who brings a legal case in family law is called the petitioner, the other party is the respondent.
- ❖ In general annulment will be granted where there is a fundamental flaw in the marriage contract or in one party's ability to enter into the contract or the marital relationship.
- ❖ Specific grounds for annulment can include:
  - (i) A lack of ability to enter into the marriage contract because of youth, because the spouses are too closely related or are of the same sex, or because one of the spouses is already married
  - (ii) A failure to fulfil the requisite formalities
  - (iii) (The absence of valid consent due to a lack of mental capacity on the part of one of the parties consenting, the absence of sufficient information on which to base consent, or the existence of duress that compelled consent
  - (iv) (Inability to enter into or sustain a marital relationship for physical, psychological or psychiatric reasons
- ❖ A clinician may be involved in assessing and reporting on the presence or absence of any physical or psychiatric infirmity that is alleged in nullity proceedings. A spouse will be ordered to undergo examination when nullity is alleged on the grounds of 'physical incapacity' (impotence). In cases where psychiatric infirmity is alleged, the concern is whether the illness was present *at the time of entering into the marriage.*

DOMESTIC VIOLENCE

[8.09]

Domestic violence is common in Ireland[40] and elsewhere.[41] While there are appreciable numbers of men who are the subject of violence at the hands of female spouses, it is predominantly women who are the victims of domestic violence. Legislation exists in the form of the Domestic Violence Act 1996 to help protect spouses (as well as cohabiting partners[42] and former spouses) and children from domestic violence. An order can also be granted to protect parents from violent children over the age of 18 years. There are three types of order, *barring* orders, *safety* orders and *interim* orders, and they may be applied for by a person at risk or by a health board on behalf of that person. An application for a safety or barring order is made to the District Court or the Circuit Court and a person who breaches an order of this nature can be arrested and prosecuted by the Gardaí. An *applicant* is a person who requests a barring or safety order; a *respondent* is the person to whom the order applies. It is important to remember that orders for protection against domestic violence can be made to help married partners, cohabiting partners, children and the parents of adult children when a member any of those groups is threatened by domestic violence.

A woman who is the victim of domestic violence can go directly to the District Court, usually with the assistance of the police and sometimes with supporting clinical evidence from her doctor, to apply for an interim order (see section **[8.12]**), pending a final court decision. Protection orders can be an important weapon in the armoury of the abused partner. US studies have shown that women who obtain longer-term orders are at an appreciably reduced risk of physical violence.[43]

Barring orders[44]

[8.10]

Where the safety or welfare of any applicant or the welfare of the applicant's dependent children requires it, a court can make a barring order which has two effects. Firstly the respondent can be directed to leave the place where the applicant lives. Secondly, whether the respondent is living with the applicant or not, he can be directed to stay away from the place where the applicant lives until the court directs otherwise. The court can also order the respondent not to use violent or threatening behaviour towards the applicant or her children and to stay away from the vicinity, as well as the home, of the applicant. The place the respondent can be directed to stay away from need not be the family home, it can be any location where the applicant is resident.

If the applicant and her children were forced by the conduct of the respondent to leave the home they shared with him, a barring order can have the effect of forcing the respondent to quit the home, allowing the applicant and children to return. The court decides on the duration of a barring order and a person who breaches it may be arrested and imprisoned.

Safety orders[44]

[8.11]

A safety order differs from a barring order in that it does not compel the violent partner to leave the family home, merely to refrain from threatening violence against the applicant or 'putting the applicant in fear'. If the respondent is already living away from the residence of the applicant then he can be directed not to trespass into her vicinity. Bizarrely, a safety order does not prevent the respondent from returning to the family home and if he does so with the permission of the applicant, he has committed no crime. The theory behind the safety order is that it will restrain less serious threatening behaviour, falling short of violence for example, while allowing the couple to continue to live together if they wish to do so, perhaps in an attempt at reconciliation. However, there is nothing to prevent the applicant who has been granted a safety order returning to court to seek a barring order. Again, a person who breaches the terms of a safety order can be arrested and imprisoned.

Interim orders

[8.12]

Interim orders are a short-term solution, operating to provide immediate protection to an abused partner in the time between when an application for a safety or barring order is made and when the matter is decided by the courts. An interim safety order[45] (which restrains the respondent from violent or threatening conduct) or an interim barring order[46] (which will have the effect of excluding the respondent from the home) can be sought. Often, the application for an interim order is made at the time of seeking the longer term order. An interim barring order will generally only be granted where there is an immediate risk of harm to the applicant or her children if the order were not made and if an interim safety order would not be sufficient. In October 2002, the Supreme Court found that interim barring orders were unconstitutional because no time limit was attached to them; it is expected that the Domestic Violence Act will be amended to plug this gap.

A role for the health boards

[8.13]

Health boards can act on behalf of 'aggrieved' individuals and seek safety or barring orders for them.[47] In cases where a woman is the victim of domestic abuse and her doctor advises her to seek the assistance of the court, but she will not do so due to intimidation or fear, then the doctor may be justified in liaising with health board social workers. A health board application can happen when:

- the health board becomes aware of an incident or a series of incidents that in the opinion of the health board put a person at risk;
- the board has cause to believe that the aggrieved person has been subjected to molestation, violence or threatened violence or has otherwise been put in fear of her safety or welfare;
- threats to the aggrieved person are preventing her from making an application for a barring order or safety order herself;
- taking into account the wishes of the aggrieved person, an application for a barring order or safety order is the appropriate way to proceed.

Such applications are most likely to be made by health boards when the person at risk is a dependent child and where the child's safety from physical or sexual abuse can be best assured by barring the abuser from the home. This is an alternative to taking the child into care under the Child Care Act 1991 (see section **[8.24]**). However, there is no reason why the mechanism cannot also be used to protect abused spouses when those spouses are prevented by fear or threats from taking action to exclude their abuser from the home.

Quick Reference Guide 8.2

Domestic violence

- A woman, whether married or not, can take legal action to protect her or her children from anyone who is perpetrating domestic violence against her. The clinician faced with such a woman can advise her to involve the police or social workers in seeking an order from the District Court. This can normally be done at the next available sitting of the court. Parents can also obtain orders against violent adult children in the home.
- A *barring* order compels the violent partner to leave a specified place, such as the family home, and to stay clear of that place and of the person in whose favour the order is made.
- A *safety* order does not compel the violent partner to leave anywhere, merely to desist from threatening or violent behaviour against the applicant for the order.
- *Interim* orders are orders (which can be safety or barring orders) made in the short term to protect the woman until the full facts of the case can be heard. It is an interim order that the victim or person at risk will ordinarily be granted on her first visit to court.
- A health board can bring an application for a safety or barring order on behalf of a person (partner or child) who cannot, due to fear or threats, bring the application to court herself.

CHILDREN

[8.14]

Certain areas of the relationship between the practitioner and the child have been covered elsewhere in the text, in particular the question of consent.[48] At that time, we mentioned that the child is in an unusual position: the Irish Constitution not only recognises the rights of the family, it also recognises the rights of the individual. In general, Irish law is caught between two stools in its attempts to define where the rights of the child fit into the Constitution. There are judges who believe that, in accordance with the Constitution, the family is paramount and that the child's individual rights are best served by being subsumed into those of the family. However, there are other judges who believe that a child's rights should be considered in isolation from the family, with the child regarded first as an individual and only secondly as a member of the Constitutional family. It is a complex question that we do not consider in depth here, but it bedevils considerations of a child's right to consent to medical treatment against the wishes of his parents[49] or the question of whether a child at risk should be taken from his family and placed in care.

Children at risk – the principles

[8.15]

Approximately 3000 Irish children each year spend some time in care as a result of neglect or of actual or threatened abuse.[50] The legislation that is predominantly used to take children[51] into care is the Child Care Act 1991, but we have noted already that barring orders and safety orders could also be used to ensure the protection of children at risk.

A Government document entitled *Children First: National Guidelines for the Protection and Welfare of Children*[52] was introduced to assist professionals and the relevant bodies in identifying and reporting child abuse and providing services for children and families. The essential principle of legislation governing children at risk is that parents or other legitimate carers such as guardians or stepparents have the primary responsibility for the care and protection of their children. When they do not or cannot fulfil this responsibility, then it may be necessary for state services, generally in the form of the health boards, to intervene. As an aid to assessing when intervention is necessary, the *Children First* guidelines set out a number of 'principles for best practice in child protection'.

Figure 8.1 Principles for best practice in child protection

i. The welfare of children is of paramount importance

ii. A proper balance must be struck between protecting children and respecting the rights and needs of parents/carers and families; but where there is conflict, the child's welfare must come first.

iii. Children have a right to be heard and taken seriously. Taking account of their age and level of understanding, they should be consulted and involved in relation to all matters and decisions that affect their lives.

iv. Parents/carers have a right to respect and should be consulted and involved in matters which concern their family.

v. Actions taken to protect a child, including assessment, should not in themselves be abusive or cause the child unnecessary distress. Every action and procedure should consider the overall needs of the child.

vi. Intervention should not deal with the child in isolation; the child must be seen in a family setting.

vii. The criminal dimension of any action cannot be ignored.

viii. Children should only be separated from parents/carers when all alternative means of protecting them have been exhausted. Reunion should always be considered.

ix. Effective prevention, detection and treatment of child abuse require a coordinated multi-disciplinary approach.

x. In practice, effective child protection requires compulsory training and clarity of responsibility for personnel involved in organisations working with children.

xi. Early intervention and support should be available to promote the welfare of children and families, particularly where they are vulnerable or at risk of not receiving adequate care or protection.

Definition, recognition and reporting of child abuse

[8.16]

Child abuse has been recognised as a medico-legal phenomenon for more than a century.[53] Diagnosis can be difficult, but there are some indicators that should bring the possibility to mind, the most significant of which is a disclosure or allegation by a child of alleged abuse. Such disclosures should always be taken seriously. One of the most formidable obstacles to the detection of child abuse is a failure to accept that it is a possibility. The abuse of children falls into four broad categories: neglect, emotional abuse, physical abuse and sexual abuse.

Definitions

Neglect

[8.17]

Neglect is probably best described as harm arising as a result of omissions by – rather than acts of – the parent. Whereas physical or sexual abuse may be predicated on a single incident, harm caused by neglect will generally only accrue over time. Failing to feed or clean a child or to send him to school may all be examples of neglect and the signs of neglect can include emotional disturbance, low weight or height for age or obvious indicators such as lack of hygiene or dirty, ill-fitting clothes.

Emotional abuse

[8.18]

Emotional abuse arises from the conduct of the relationship between child and parent, with the defining feature commonly a failure on the part of the parent to provide for the child's emotional needs, including the child's desire for affection, approval and consistency. Emotional abuse can be manifested by the child in a spectrum of ways, ranging from clingy behaviour to total avoidance of the parent in question. Other signs can include inhibited emotional and physical development. The *Children First* document lists some of the following as examples of emotional abuse:

- persistent criticism, hostility or blame-casting; harsh disciplinary regimes;
- conditional parenting (making love and care conditional on certain behaviour);
- emotional unavailability or inconsistency;
- premature imposition of responsibility on a child; unrealistic expectations of a child's capabilities or capacity to understand;
- lack of interest and failure to provide opportunities for emotional and cognitive development.[54]

Physical abuse

[8.19]

Physical abuse is sometimes also termed non-accidental injury and can demonstrate itself in a number of ways. Some signs, bruises or burns for example, are obvious, while others, haemorrhages due to shaking, are less so and some, such as Munchausen syndrome by proxy,[55] are insidious and rare in the extreme.

There are some factors in the examination or history of a child that may bring to mind non-accidental injury. There may be a lack of correlation between the history related by the parent and the injuries sustained by the child and perhaps a marked reluctance on the part of the parent to permit a full examination of the child (for fear that other marks or injuries may be noticed). There can also sometimes be an inexplicable delay before the parents opt to seek medical help. Socio-economic class is not directly linked to physical abuse of children, but it may be slightly more common in lower socio-economic groups. Common injuries will be external (bruising, abrasions, bites and burns), but internal damage such as head injuries, eye damage or fractures are not uncommon. X-ray may show numerous old fractures, periosteum (the layer surrounding the bone) damage or fractures at various stages of healing.

Figure 8.2 Injuries that may arouse suspicion of physical abuse

- Bruising especially if:
  - (i) on a baby less than nine months old (the less mobile a child, the less likely he is to sustain accidental injuries);
  - (ii) on the cheek or head;
  - (iii) unusual in shape: consider bites; clusters of disk-shaped bruises may be a sign of tight gripping of the child; there may be the imprint of something that was used to strike the child (eg a belt buckle);
  - (iv) multiple bruises of different ages;
  - (v) black eyes;
- retinal haemorrhage;
- fractures or other bony damage, especially if -
  - (i) in children less than one year old;
  - (ii) rib fractures, particularly when multiple (so-called 'string of beads' appearance on x-ray);
  - (iii) multiple fractures at diffuse locations, whether old or healing;
  - (iv) epiphyseal displacement;
  - (v) periosteal damage or cortical thickening on x-ray.
- Burns and scalds: small circular burns may be caused by cigarettes; look for old scars. There may sometimes be extensive scalding of the extremities (typically lower) with a linear demarcation proximally suggestive of immersion in extremely hot liquid.
- Bruising or laceration in or around the mouth.[56]

Parents or guardians who physically abuse children may demonstrate some of the following characteristics:

— a male abuser may not be the biological father of the child;

— a female abuser may have had several children in quick succession and may lack coping skills or a support network; straitened financial circumstances may also contribute;

— younger parents pose a greater risk;
— there may be a history of personality or psychiatric disorder or a criminal record;
— the parent or parents may themselves have been victims of physical or sexual abuse as children.

Sexual abuse

[8.20]

Sexual abuse is the use of a child for the sexual arousal or gratification of another person or – more fully – the involvement of children or adolescents in sexual activities they do not fully comprehend and to which they are unable to give informed consent. The forms which child sexual abuse (CSA) can take are numerous and can include:

— sexual activity, including exposure of the sexual organs, in the presence of a child;
— touching a child or soliciting the touch of a child for sexual gratification or arousal;
— masturbation in the presence of, or with the assistance of, a child;
— sexual penetration (vaginal, anal or oral) of a child by any part of the abuser or using a foreign implement;
— consensual sexual activity with a child less than 17 years of age.[57]

Indicators of abuse can include disclosure by the child, failure to thrive, signs of neglect, emotional or behavioural disturbance (particularly sexualised behaviour at a young age) and clear physical signs of abuse, including damage to the ano-genital region. Any symptoms suggestive of sexually transmitted disease in the pre-pubertal child should be considered indicative of CSA until proven otherwise. Where CSA is suspected, specialist care should be involved. The more highly trained the person dealing with a child who has experienced CSA, the less traumatic it will be for the child and any evidence or details from the child may be more accurate. Anatomically correct dolls are often used to help and encourage children to describe what they have experienced. Physical examination should only be conducted by someone expert in the field and even then diagnoses that are at best controversial and at worst incorrect can occur.

Recognising abuse

[8.21]

There are three widely accepted steps to the recognition of abuse. The first, and perhaps the most important, is simply to consider the possibility that abuse has occurred when faced with the child who has unexplained injuries, emotional disturbance or behavioural abnormality. The second step is to dwell on whether the possibility may be more than fanciful. Looking through a child's clinical records or the details of previous Accident and Emergency Department visits may disclose patterns consistent with something more than a tentative diagnosis of child abuse. Knowledge of the broader family history may also be useful in isolating cases of abuse[58] and the clinician should be prepared at an early stage to seek a second opinion, ideally from someone with expertise in the area. The final element is to record information that will be useful in facilitating further investigation if it appears to be warranted. Acting on the suspicion or confirmation of abuse is dealt with at section **[8.23]**.

Reporting abuse

[8.22]

There is no legal obligation on anyone to report child abuse. It has been suggested that it should become compulsory to report suspicions of child abuse,[59] but such recommendations were not carried through and never became law.[60] The approach adopted in Ireland is that while reporting of child abuse remains voluntary, a person who does report abuse is given the promise of legal protection so long as she makes her report in good faith. The Protections for Persons Reporting Child Abuse Act 1998[61] shields any person from legal action who reports, in good faith, her suspicions that:

(a) a child has been, or is being, assaulted, ill-treated, neglected or sexually abused, or

(b) a child's health, development or welfare has been or is being avoidably impaired or neglected.

In other words, there is no *obligation* on a practitioner to report child abuse, but she will not be answerable to her patient or to the alleged perpetrator if she makes a disclosure to the appropriate authorities, defined as a member of the Garda Síochána or a designated officer of a health board.[62] The patient will not be able to bring a legal action for breach of confidentiality,[63] nor will the alleged perpetrator be able to bring a legal action against the clinician for defamation if the allegation turns out to be unfounded. On the other hand, a person who 'deliberately and knowingly' makes a false allegation of child abuse against another may not only be sued for defamation by the person she names but she may also face criminal proceedings under the Protections for Persons Reporting Child Abuse Act 1998.[64] The key therefore is that any allegation of child abuse should be made in good faith.

Any duty or responsibility to report is therefore a moral or ethical one, rather than a legal obligation. Indeed, it is arguable that a practitioner who knew of abuse that was taking place and did not report it could be guilty of professional misconduct and subject to disciplinary action by her professional regulatory body. The *Children First* document lists the following as grounds for concerns that could activate the responsibility to report:

- a specific indication from the child that she was abused (which should always be taken seriously);
- a statement from a person who witnessed abuse;
- illness, injury or behaviour consistent with abuse;
- a symptom which may not itself prove abuse, but which is supported by corroborative evidence of deliberate harm or negligence.
- consistent signs of neglect over a period of time.

Quick Reference Guide 8.3

The principles and diagnosis of child abuse

- There are four generally accepted categories of child abuse: neglect, emotional abuse, physical abuse and child sexual abuse (CSA).
- Children who are suffering abuse can demonstrate a range of signs, including obvious signs of neglect, poor school attendance, unusual or extreme emotional behaviour, the physical stigmata of abuse and premature sexualised behaviour.
- Physical abuse – or 'non-accidental injury' – can range from the extremely overt to the covert and hard to detect. There are some traits that appear to be more common in parents who perpetrate physical abuse, including not being the child's natural parent, comparative youth, poor financial resources and a lack of coping skills and support networks. Parents who abuse were often themselves victims of abuse in childhood.
- A key to the detection of abuse is being prepared to recognise it as a possibility.
- There is no legal obligation on a person to report suspicions of any form of abuse, but a person who does so will be protected by the Protections for Persons Reporting Child Abuse Act 1998 which shields a person reporting suspicions of abuse from any legal consequences once the allegation is made in good faith. There is a strong moral and ethical imperative for health care professionals to report any suspicions of abuse to those who are in a position to help the child.

Children at risk – the practice

[8.23]

Dealing with a child at risk, whether it is a risk posed by neglect or by physical, emotional or sexual abuse, is a multidisciplinary matter. The practitioner who suspects or knows that child abuse is taking place should involve those best placed to provide assistance. These will most commonly include health board social workers and paediatricians. A child at risk may require to be taken into care and thus away from the source of the abuse (or as we have noted already, the abuser may be removed from the environment of the child using a protection order) or may require admission or assessment under the care of an experienced paediatrician.

The technicalities of reporting abuse will vary with the environment in which the practitioner finds herself: the community-based clinician will need to contact a health board social worker together with the local paediatric unit, where appropriate. The hospital-based practitioner will usually contact someone within the hospital. In situations where the picture is unclear, a case conference involving all available staff who have knowledge of the family and child in question may be appropriate: it permits the pooling of information and expertise and can allow a clearer picture to develop.

We have noted that the Irish Constitution gives a special place to the family, which is applicable even in situations where members of the family are suspected of abuse. The family should be kept informed of decisions that are being taken with respect to the child at risk, unless to do so would put the child (or, it is argued, other children within the family) at greater risk.

In extreme situations where a child is faced with an extreme risk, the Garda Síochána may be the first port of call. A child should not be left in what appears to the practitioner to be a dangerous situation and both health board staff (typically social workers) and Gardaí are conferred with powers by the Child Care Act 1991 to allow them to intervene when children are at risk. The Gardaí in particular have the power to seize a child without a court order and take him to a place of safety before handing the child over to the care of the health board. It is important to stress that multidisciplinary teams that combine their skills and knowledge bases provide the best care for a child at risk.

Care orders

[8.24]

When a child is shown or believed to be at risk it may be necessary to remove the child from the scene of the abuse and take him into care. The procedures involved in care orders are laid down in the Child Care Act 1991, but all decisions regarding children's custody must be taken in accordance with the so-called welfare principle, which may be expressed as follows:[65]

> Where in any proceedings before any court the custody, guardianship or upbringing of an infant...is in question the court in deciding that question, shall regard the welfare of the infant as the first and paramount consideration.

'Welfare' is in turn defined as 'religious and moral, intellectual, physical and social welfare'.[66] What the welfare principle means in practice is that when considering custody issues, the court will always put at the forefront of its mind the question of what is best for the child. Into the mix of this complex question is also thrown the ingredient of the Constitution and its recognition of the role of the family. Accordingly, the decision is often taken that the child's welfare is best served by being kept with or being returned to the family.

It will almost always be the health board that applies to the courts for a care order to be made regarding a child and the Child Care Act 1991 describes the following responsibility of health boards as well as recognising the complexity of any custody decision:

> 3 (1) It shall be a function of every health board to promote the welfare of children in its area who are not receiving adequate care and protection.
>
> (2) In the performance of this function, a health board shall—
>
> (a) take such steps as it considers requisite to identify children who are not receiving adequate care and protection and co-ordinate information from all relevant sources relating to children in its area;
>
> (b) having regard to the rights and duties of parents, whether under the Constitution or otherwise—
>
> (i) regard the welfare of the child as the first and paramount consideration, and

(ii) in so far as is practicable, give due consideration, having regard to his age and understanding, to the wishes of the child; and

(c) have regard to the principle that it is generally in the best interests of a child to be brought up in his own family.

Accordingly, while it is the health board's responsibility to apply for care orders, the courts will only grant an order removing a child from his family when there are compelling circumstances that override the parents' Constitutional rights and which mean that the child's welfare is best served outside the family.[67] When a court is making a decision therefore, it must hold the welfare principle paramount but must also have regard to the Constitutional rights of the parents and may also as far as practicable give due consideration to the wishes of the child having regard to his age and understanding.[68]

Voluntary care

Parents can consent to a child being taken into care and if this occurs, the child will be kept in care for as long as it appears necessary to the health board.[69] If the parents withdraw their consent, it may be necessary to apply for a care order from the courts (generally the District Court).

Removal of a child to a place of safety by Gardaí without a court order

If there is an immediate and serious risk to the health or welfare of a child and there is no time to wait for the making of any other order (such as an emergency care order, see below), then Gardaí may enter any place without a warrant and remove the child to safety.[70] They may be accompanied by such other persons as may be necessary, such as a doctor or social workers. Once the child is removed, he must be handed over as soon as possible to the local health board, which must then apply for an emergency care order.

Emergency care order

When 'there is an immediate and serious risk to the health or welfare of a child' that either necessitates him being taken into health board care or remaining there, having been seized by Gardaí or detained in hospital, the District Court can make an emergency care order at short notice in response to an application by a health board.[71] If the child is not already in the care of the health board, the judge can direct the Gardaí to go and bring the child into the custody of the health board. The judge may withhold information from the parent concerning the whereabouts of the child if there are extremely strong reasons for doing so[72] and she may also restrict access to the child. The judge may furthermore give consent on the child's behalf to any 'medical or psychiatric examination, treatment or assessment of the child'. Once a child is in care (and assuming that they were not already aware of the proceedings) the child's parents must be notified of the care order as soon as possible.

Interim care order

Once the short-term crisis, necessitating the Gardaí taking a child to a place of safety or the making of an emergency care order, has abated, a child may still need to remain in care pending the court making a decision as to what to do next. In that case, a court can make an interim care order[73] allowing the child to remain lawfully in health board custody until those decisions can be made. For the judge to make an interim care order she has to be happy that an application for a long-term care order has been made or is about to be made and that the circumstances that would justify agreeing to a final decision on a long-term care order exist (see below).

Unlike an emergency care order, which can be made without the knowledge of the parents (although they must be told of it as soon as possible afterwards), the parents *must* be notified in advance of an intention to apply for an interim care order. The judge can also make any other orders she sees fit along with the interim order, including directing medical or other assessments.

Longer-term care order

For a care order to be made the judge must be satisfied that:

(a) the child has been or is being assaulted, ill-treated, neglected or sexually abused, or

(b) the child's health, development or welfare has been, or is being, avoidably impaired or neglected, or

(c) the child's health, development or welfare is likely to be avoidably impaired or neglected

and that the health board can provide the necessary care.[74] The order can be made for as long as the child remains a child[75] or for any shorter period. Orders shorter than the duration of childhood can be subsequently extended. If the child is not already in care the judge can order the Gardaí to go and get him.

The care order has the effect of putting the health board in the place of the parents and it then has the power to decide on all matters affecting the child including medical care and consenting to the issuing of a passport to the child. The 'care' can take the form of foster parents,[76] a residential home, adoption or any 'other suitable arrangements', which can include placement with a relative.

Supervision order

Supervision orders are an alternative to care orders where the court is happy that the child can remain within the home but that nonetheless some measure of observation is warranted.[77] Any disputes between parents and health board about the operation of the supervision order will be officiated by the court if a compromise cannot be reached. Supervision orders have a life span of twelve months but can be extended by the court. The court can also punish anyone who obstructs the health boards in its attempts to carry out the supervision order and the health board may, if carrying out the supervision order proves impossible, apply for a care order instead.

Quick Reference Guide 8.4

Practical aspects of protecting children

- ❖ Dealing with allegations of abuse is a multidisciplinary matter involving police, social workers and medical and nursing specialists. A case conference may be an important forum in which to pool all available knowledge of a particular child's circumstances.
- ❖ In all considerations of child custody, the welfare of the child is of the paramount importance. However, the courts also give great weight to the role of the family and the rights of the parents, based on the Irish Constitution's recognition of the family as the fundamental building block of Irish society.
- ❖ A child can be taken by the Garda Síochána to a 'place of safety' without any form of court order where there is an immediate threat to the child's welfare or safety.
- ❖ A parent can consent to a child being taken into voluntary care by the local health board.
- ❖ Where there is no consent to a child being taken into care or a child has been taken to a place of safety without a court order, the health board must apply to the courts for a care order. In general, the first order made will be an emergency care order, followed by interim or longer-term care orders as appropriate.
- ❖ As an alternative to a care order, a court can put a supervision order in place, allowing the child to remain in the home but also empowering the health board to supervise the ongoing development of the child.
- ❖ With the exception of emergency care orders, the family must be kept informed of all stages of the care order process and, unless there are exceptional circumstances, be told of the whereabouts of the child.
- ❖ As part of a care order, the court can make any other orders as it sees fit for treatment or assessment or the child. Once the health board is awarded a care order for a child, it assumes the role of the child's parent.

Sudden Infant Death Syndrome

[8.25]

Sudden Infant Death Syndrome (Cot Death, SIDS) is the sudden death of an infant, usually less than one year of age, which remains unexplained after a complete post-mortem investigation, including autopsy, examination of the death scene and review of the case history. Its cause remains unknown although there are racial (more common in African-Americans in the USA, for example) and familial (if one sibling in family succumbs to SIDS there is a greater risk for remaining siblings) tendencies, and an association with birth order.[78] The majority of deaths occur between October and March and there is a slightly increased frequency in male children. Children who live in cigarette smoke-filled environments seem to be at greater risk and many victims will have had some form of respiratory tract infection in the weeks leading up to death. There is an association between sleeping position and SIDS and between lower income and the condition. Death generally occurs when the child is laid down to sleep and there appear to be no sounds or signs of distress.

SIDS remains a leading cause of death in babies aged 4 weeks to 1 year but it can affect babies older than 12 months (although the peak is between 2 and 6 months). Irish Central Statistics Office (CSO) infant mortality figures for 1994 suggest that over a third (37%) of all deaths in the 4 to 12 months age group were due to SIDS and overall, SIDS is the third most common cause of death in children younger than 14 years. The number of deaths due to SIDS in Ireland appears to oscillate from year to year, but in recent years the figure has generally been between the mid-30s to 40s.

Figure 8.3 Deaths per year from SIDS in Ireland

Year	*Number of deaths*
1995	33
1996	45
1997	69
1998	42
1999	38

There are a number of medico-legal elements to a diagnosis of SIDS. Firstly, the death must be reported to the coroner. Even if the general practitioner or hospital doctor believes that a death was due to SIDS, the case must nonetheless be referred to the coroner. Similarly, as part of the notification process the Gardaí must attend the scene of death and oversee the formal identification of the baby's body. Investigation is necessary to rule out the small possibility that the death was due to unnatural causes. Both processes, notification of the coroner and involvement of the Gardaí, can be distressing to the family, but they are an inevitable part of the aftermath of SIDS. Because of the coroner notification, there is no need for the doctor to complete a Medical Certificate of the Cause of Death. Elsewhere in this text we dwell on the importance of recording the details of the scene of a sudden or unexpected death.[79] SIDS provides an example of this, because it was the recording of infant sleeping positions that in part led to the identification of sleeping position as a risk factor in SIDS.[80]

Clinical findings

Findings at post-mortem may include some or all of the following:

- normal levels of hydration and nutrition;
- small amounts of frothy fluid in or about the mouth and nose and occasionally there may be vomit present;
- post-mortem lividity, rigor mortis and distortion of the contours of the face due to the infant dying while on his stomach or while pressed up against or lying on something in the cot;
- unusual positions due to muscle spasms can cause blood pooling and/or pressure marks;

— internal examination may show pulmonary congestion and oedema and there are intrathoracic petechiae in about 90% of SIDS infants. There may also be stomach contents and/or microscopic inflammation in the trachea.

The post-mortem can be important in disclosing a cause of death other than SIDS, for example, congenital heart disease or rarely pneumonia.

Handling SIDS

The sudden death of a child can be devastating for a family and support from those involved in a clinical capacity in the immediate aftermath of the death can help the bereaved parents and siblings to come to terms with what has happened. If the practitioner is present at the scene of death, she should observe the location and position of the infant upon arrival and verify whether that was the position in which he was found. She should also observe for presence of objects in the original area where the infant was found that could have contributed to death (for example, medicine bottles following the death of older infants) and the temperature of the room or any odours, such as domestic gas.

Figure 8.4 Considerations in the wake of SIDS

Clinical elements

- In a hospital, if resuscitation is ongoing ensure the parents are kept informed. If unsuccessful, the news should be broken to the parents in a private environment by someone experienced in doing so.
- If in a position to do so, be prepared to offer a tentative diagnosis of SIDS.
- Obtain a history from the family of events leading up to the death (if possible in the circumstances).
- Explain that the coroner and the Gardaí will necessarily be involved and that a post-mortem must be performed, but explain that this does not mean that blame or suspicion is being cast on the parents. Stress that the death is not the fault of the parents.
- Consider practical advice on the suppression of lactation for breast feeding mothers or the use of an anxiolytic medication, but remember too that simply making time to listen can be more important than dispensing advice or medication.
- Liaise with some or all of the following as appropriate: the hospital to which the body will be brought; the family doctor; social services; any hospitals that may be sending out appointments for the child (for example the maternity hospital in which he was born).
- Consider whether monitoring will be needed for siblings.
- Follow up with the coroner and pathology departments to ensure that any post-mortem documentation can be processed speedily.

Emotional and psychological elements

- Allow and expect the venting of feelings by the parents; do not feel embarrassed about sharing those feelings or grieving with the parents. Offer to contact anyone the parents wish to have with them.
- When talking about the child, use his name.
- Allow the parents to spend time with their dead child if they wish to do so; make a quiet private room available for them where they can be undisturbed for a time.
- Be conscious of the needs of siblings as well as parents: in the immediate aftermath, simple explanations may suffice, but siblings will often need to grieve along with the parents.
- People in shock have difficulty retaining information in large chunks. Consider leaving information with parents in the form of a leaflet or the contact number of a local help line.
- Be aware that the family will need support for months to come as they go through the grieving process.[81]

Endnotes

1 Article 41.1 of the Constitution states:

1° The State recognises the Family as the natural primary and fundamental unit group of Society, and as a moral institution possessing inalienable and imprescriptible rights, antecedent and superior to all positive law.

2° The State, therefore, guarantees to protect the Family in its constitution and authority, as the necessary basis of social order and as indispensable to the welfare of the Nation and State.

2 *The State (Nicolau) v An Bord Uchtála* [1966] IR 567; *WO'R v EH & An Bord Uchtála* (July 1996, unreported) SC.

3 *KC & AC v An Bord Uchtála & Others* [1985] 5 ILRM 302.

4 Removed by the referendum on the 15th Amendment to the Constitution which resulted in the Family Law (Divorce) Act 1996.

5 Article 41.2 of the Constitution states:

> 1° In particular, the State recognises that by her life within the home, woman gives to the State a support without which the common good cannot be achieved.
>
> 2° The State shall, therefore, endeavour to ensure that mothers shall not be obliged by economic necessity to engage in labour to the neglect of their duties in the home.

6 Judicial Separation and Family Law Reform Act 1989. Judicial separation is most frequently granted on grounds of adultery, unreasonable behaviour by either party (effectively a breakdown in the relationship) or desertion.

7 Article 41.3.2º:

> Where, and only where such court established under this Constitution as may be prescribed by law is satisfied that –
>
> i. a marriage has failed.
>
> ii. the failure has continued for a period of, or periods amounting to, at least five years.
>
> iii. that there is no reasonable possibility of reconciliation between the parties to the marriage, and

iv. any other condition prescribed by law has been complied with,

the court may in accordance with law grant a dissolution of the marriage provided that the court is satisfied that adequate and proper provision having regard to the circumstances will be made for a dependent spouse and for any child who is dependent on either spouse.

The referendum was passed by a majority of only 9,114, that is to say, that 50.28% of those who voted supported the referendum, although less than two-thirds of those entitled to vote did so.

8 See 'Changes to law on annulment of marriage sought' (2001) *Irish Times*, 4 October. This report cites Irish Law Society figures (derived from a report of the Law Society on nullity submitted to the Department of Equality, Justice and Law Reform) that show that applications for nullity continue to rise in spite of the introduction of divorce.

9 There are a number of practical problems inherent in declaring a marriage never to have existed, but they lie outside the scope of this text.

10 *Griffith v Griffith* [1944] IR 35.

11 Technically, nullity takes two forms: in some cases the marriage is declared 'void', meaning automatically that the marriage is at an end and never existed; in other cases a marriage will be declared 'voidable'. A declaration that a marriage is 'voidable' does not automatically end the marriage but gives either party to the marriage the right to end it. The distinction need not concern us here and the term 'void' will be used throughout.

12 See ch 11, *Psychiatry and Practice* (section **[11.17]**).

13 The person named as the opposite party in nullity or divorce proceedings is called the 'respondent'.

14 *B (O'R) v B* [1991] 1 IR 289 (SC); *S v K* [1993] 1 Fam LJ 18.

15 A person may marry once he is older than 16 years of age, but the permission of the courts must be obtained for those younger than 18 years: Family Law Act 1995, s 31.

16 In Ireland, one's biological sex is the sex of one's birth. A sex-change operation does not change the legal sex of the person who underwent the operation: see the report of the case of Lydia Foy in 'Woman in sex change loses birth certificate challenge' (2002) *Irish Times*, 10 July. However, a decision of the European Court of Human Rights, taken two days after the *Foy* decision, suggests that this position may be open to challenge in the future: see *Christine Goodwin v The United Kingdom (Application No 28957/95)*, which said that failing to allow a person to modify identification documentation after a sex change operation was a violation of the right to privacy guaranteed by the European Convention on Human Rights, art 8.

17 Note however, that some nationalities resident in Ireland (including Romanians) who wish to undergo the marriage ceremony of their native country (typically conducted in an embassy or consulate) may sometimes be required to complete certain medical formalities.

18 See ch 4, *Consent*.

19 See Shatter *Family Law* (4th edn, 1997), para 5.20. Also 'Mental Capacity and Marriage' (1964) 98 ILT & SJ, pp 159-61.

20 *Park v Park* [1953] 2 All ER1411.

21 *Turner v Meyers* (1808) 161 ER 600. See ch 11 for a review of the question of wills made during lucid periods.(section **[11.28]**)

22 *ME v AE* [1987] (HC) IR 147 at 151 per O'Hanlon J.

23 *Legeyt v O'Brien* (1834) Milw Rep 325. In this case, the husband was alleged to have been of unsound mind at the time of the marriage. However, he was suffering from *delirium tremens* rather than acute intoxication and accordingly the court found that he *was* fit to marry.

24 In *Moss v Moss* [1897] P 263 a woman concealed from her husband the fact that she was pregnant by another man. This was not a ground for nullity.

25 In particular *N v K* [1985] IR 733.

[26] *F v F* [1991] 1 IR 348. Similarly a husband who alleged that his wife, during their chaste courtship, had concealed from him the fact that her torso and limbs were disfigured as a result of childhood burns was granted a degree of nullity on the grounds that he had been misled as to the physical character of the woman he was marrying.

[27] *Griffith v Griffith* [1944] IR 35. In this case, the moral pressure brought to bear by the parents of a girl who became pregnant outside wedlock was not enough on its own to be considered duress. The mother of a pregnant girl (who falsely accused the petitioner of being the father) threatened the man with commencing criminal proceedings for unlawful carnal knowledge (she was less than 17 years) if he did not marry her daughter. This additional threat of legal action did amount to duress and the marriage was annulled. See Haugh J at p 52: '...duress must be a question of degree and may begin from a gentle form of pressure to physical violence accompanied by threats of death.'

[28] *B v D* (10 June 1973, unreported) HC.

[29] *Szechter v Szechter* [1970] 3 All ER 905.

[30] *MK v FMC* [1982] ILRM 277 2 ILRM 277; *B v O'R* [1991] 1 IR 289 (SC).

[31] *D-e v Ag* [1845] 173 ER 1039.

[32] Historically (as recently as the 1940s) many difficulties that we would now recognise as psychosexual were categorised as 'wilful refusal to consummate' rather than impotence. Courts of the time refused decrees of annulment and came close to advocating that husbands in such circumstances should overcome their wives' reluctance by force. Now, wilful refusal by either partner to consummate the marriage appears to be grounds for annulment even if it does not constitute impotence, once the refusing partner entered into the marriage with the intention of refusing to consummate the marriage: see *S v S* (3 July 1976, unreported) SC.

[33] *EC v KM* [1991] 2 IR 192.

[34] *R v W* (10 February 1980, unreported) HC.

[35] A spouse suffering from impotence cannot, in accordance with the general principle of patient autonomy, be compelled to undergo treatment to correct a cause of impotence if he or she does not wish to consent to it.

[36] Rules of the Superior Courts, Ord 70, r 32.

[37] *UF v JC* [1981] 2 IR 330 at 356 *per* Finlay CJ.

[38] *RSJ v JSJ* [1982] 2 ILRM 263. Similarly, bipolar affective disorder (or manic depression) has been held to be grounds for annulment (*D v C* [1984] 4 ILRM 173), as has personality disorder (*W(C) v C* [1989] IR 696.

[39] Bradley, Smith, Long and O'Dowd 'Reported frequency of domestic violence: cross sectional survey of women attending general practice' BMJ 2002;324:1–6. This study showed that 40% of women who had ever been in a sexual relationship admitted in a questionnaire to having been a victim of violent behaviour in that relationship. Of that 40%, half had been injured as a result of the violent behaviour they had experienced. The study also demonstrated that doctors in primary care appear only rarely to ask about domestic violence.

[40] Community surveys in the UK have indicated that up to one in four women have experienced domestic violence. Studies in the United States and Australia report that between 5% and 20% of the women attending general practice have experienced domestic violence in the preceding year. See Mooney 'The hidden figure: domestic violence in North London — the findings of a survey conducted on domestic violence in the north London Borough of Islington London' (1993) London Centre for Criminology, Middlesex University; H Johnson and V F Sacco 'Researching violence against women' Can J Criminol [1995] 37:281-304; Hamberger, Saunders and Hovery 'Prevalence of domestic violence in community practice and rate of physician inquiry' Fam Med 1992; 24:283-7; Marais, Villiers et al 'Domestic violence in patients visiting general practitioners—prevalence, phenomenology and association with

psychopathology' S AfrMed J 1999; 89:635-40; Mazza, Dennerstein, Ryan 'Physical, sexual and emotional violence against women: a general practice-based prevalence study' Med J Aust 1996; 161:14-7; McCauley, Kern, et al 'The "battering syndrome": prevalence and clinical characteristic of domestic violence in primary care internal medicine practices' Ann Intern Med 1995; 123:737-46.

41 A cohabiting partner is defined differently depending on whether a safety order or a barring order is sought. For a safety order a cohabiting partner is a person 'who has lived with the respondent as husband and wife for a period of at least six months in aggregate during the period of twelve months immediately prior to the application' (Domestic Violence Act 1996, s 2(1)(a)(ii)). For a barring order, two conditions apply. Firstly the applicant must have lived with the respondent 'as husband and wife for a period of six months in aggregate during the period of nine months immediately prior to the application' (Domestic Violence Act 1996, s 3(b)). Secondly, the respondent cannot be the subject of a barring order when he has a financial interest in the residence the couple shares that is greater than the applicant's financial interest (Domestic Violence Act 1996, s 3(4)). So, if an unmarried couple have been sharing a home for ten years and the man is beating the woman, she cannot seek a barring order if he owns more than 50% of the property even if she is at the risk of serious violence. She can seek a protection order, however. A similar ownership rule applies to parents seeking a barring order against their children.

42 Holt L, M *et al.* 'Civil Protection Orders and Risk of Subsequent Police-Reported Violence,' JAMA (2002) 288;589-594. This study notes however that the risk of 'psychological violence' is not reduced by protection orders.

43 Domestic Violence Act 1996, s 3(2).

44 Domestic Violence Act 1996, s 2(2).

45 Domestic Violence Act 1996, s 5.

46 Domestic Violence Act 1996, s 4(1).

47 Domestic Violence Act 1996, s 6.

48 See ch 4, *Consent* (section **[4.15]**).

49 See Mills '*PKU:* Please Keep Unclear?' [2002] 23 DULJ 180.

50 Department of Foreign Affairs *United Nations Convention on the Rights of the Child: First National Report of Ireland* (1996).

51 Irish law defines children, in terms of abuse or the risk thereof, as unmarried people aged less than 18 years.

52 Department of Health and Children (1999). The report (or a summary) may be downloaded from www.doh.ie/pdfdocs/Children_First.pdf (whole report) or www.doh.ie/pdfdocs/Children_Sum.pdf (summary).

53 A Tardieu 'Etude médico-legal sur les sérvices et mauvais traitments exercés sur des enfants' Annales d'hygiene publique et de medicine legal, 1860; 13: 361-398.

54 *Putting Children First – Summary Document* (1999) p 10.

55 A condition in which parents give false accounts of symptoms in their children and may even fake the signs of their children's supposed illness in order to attract attention to themselves. They seek repeated medical investigations and unwarranted treatment. According to one study, the most commonly reported symptoms are neurological, rashes and bleeding. There is some evidence of collusion by children. It has been suggested that children who have been victims of Munchausen syndrome by proxy will progress to have Munchausen syndrome themselves in adulthood. An early description is contained in R Meadows 'Management of Munchausen, syndrome by proxy' Archives of Diseases of Childhood, 1985:60;385-93. There are those who suggest that there is tendency to over-estimate its frequency: see R Meadows, Journal of Clinical Forensic Medicine 1994:1;121-127. Some attempts have been made to video children

in hospital to detect such abuse: D M Foreman and C Farsides 'Ethical use of covert videoing techniques in detecting Munchausen syndrome by proxy' BMJ 1993;307:611-3.

[56] One common injury, described by Knight in *Legal Aspects of Medical Practice* (5th edn, 1992) is the 'side-swipe' injury, a laceration of the mucosa inside the upper lip around the midline and which may include tearing of the frenum. A similar injury can be caused by forcing a bottle into the child's mouth.

[57] The legal definitions of crimes such as sexual assault and incest are dealt with in ch 15 (see **[15.02]**).

[58] Southall, Plunkett, et al 'Covert video recordings of life-threatening child abuse: lessons for child protection' Pediatrics 1997; 100: 735-760. This study suggested that the abused children were more likely to present with bleeding from the nose or mouth, and more likely to have a family history of sudden and unexpected death or abuse in siblings. In addition, a significant number of the abusive parents were diagnosed as having personality disorders.

[59] The issue was raised in the Law Reform Commission Report, *Report on Child Sexual Abuse* (LRC 32-1990) and the Report of the Kilkenny Incest Investigation Team (1993). The Law Reform Commission recommended the introduction of mandatory reporting of CSA; the Kilkenny Incest Investigation Team called for the introduction of mandatory reporting for all forms of child abuse. The arguments were summarised in Department of Health *Putting Children First – A Discussion Document on Mandatory Reporting of Child Abuse* (1996).

[60] This accords with the position in the United Kingdom where proposals to introduce mandatory reporting were rejected: *Review of Child Care Law: Report to Ministers of an Interdepartmental Working Party* (HMSO, 1985). France, Italy, Norway Sweden and Finland are European countries with mandatory reporting in place.

[61] Protections for Persons Reporting Child Abuse Act 1998, s 3.

[62] Designated officers are those members of health board staff who fall into one of the following categories: social workers; childcare workers; public health nurses; hospital consultants; psychiatrists; non-consultant hospital doctors; all other health boards medical and dental personnel; community welfare officers; speech and language therapists; all health board nursing personnel; psychologists; radiographers; physiotherapists; occupational therapists; health education officers; substance abuse counsellors and care assistants.

[63] As we have seen elsewhere in the text, a clinician's decision to breach confidentiality can be justified if the intention is to protect her patient, another individual or society as a whole (as it would be if the breach of confidentiality protected further abuse) or if compelled to do so by the law (see section **[3.16]** *ff*). If mandatory reporting were introduced then the practitioner would be protected from legal actions for breach of confidence because she would be compelled by law to disclose the confidential information.

[64] Protections for Persons Reporting Child Abuse Act 1998, s 5.

[65] Guardianship of Infants Act 1964, s 3.

[66] Guardianship of Infants Act 1964, s 2, as substituted by the Status of Children Act 1987, s 9.

[67] *Re JH, an infant* [1985] IR 375.

[68] Child Care Act 1991, s 24.

[69] Child Care Act 1991, s 4.

[70] Child Care Act 1991, s 12.

[71] Child Care Act 1991, s 13.

[72] *MF v Superintendent of Ballymun Garda Station* [1991] 1 IR 189 (SC). O'Flaherty J said (at p 206) that parents of a child in care should be kept informed of their child's whereabouts unless 'very exceptional circumstances can be established to justify a different course'.

[73] Child Care Act 1991, s 17.

[74] Child Care Act 1991, s 18.

75 Remember that the legislation defines a child as anyone under the age of 18 years who is not or has not been married.

76 The rules for foster parents are contained in the Child Care (Placement of Children in Foster Care) Regulations 1995 (SI 1995/260), but they do not concern us here.

77 Child Care Act 1991, s 19.

78 50% are second born children, 25% first born and the remaining 25% third born or later.

79 See ch 14.

80 Bass, R E Kravath and L Glass 'Death-scene investigation in sudden infant death' NEJM 1986; 315:100-5.

81 Typically, bereavement proceeds through a number of stages lasting approximately six to nine months in total:

(i) Shock, numbness, blunted emotions and incomprehension for the first two weeks or so.

(ii) Physical and emotional distress, withdrawal and grief; often a preoccupation with memories of the deceased, a feeling that he has not truly 'gone' and a process of idealisation.

(iii) Gradual resolution, the return of realism and the lifting of depression.

Longer bereavement periods are often associated with especially sudden or traumatic deaths, a close relationship between the deceased and the bereaved, and the personality characteristics and social circumstances of the bereaved.

Chapter 9

The Practitioner in the Workplace

INTRODUCTION

[9.01]

This chapter begins by looking at the role of the occupational health practitioner and by extension at all practitioner-patient interactions in which third parties have an interest, such as medical examinations for insurance policies. We examine how the demands of confidentiality interact with the interest of a third party in the outcome of a consultation or with a request from a third party for information relating to a patient.

The second portion of the chapter looks at the legal mechanics of ensuring safety, health and welfare in the workplace – both the approach taken by the courts and the steps taken by the government to compel employers (and employees) to prioritise safety in the workplace. The area of occupational health is important to clinicians from a number of perspectives: any clinician may be at any time an employee, employer or occupational health professional and in all three capacities, might require an understanding of the principles underpinning the safe workplace.

The chapter finishes with a brief overview of occupational disease, absence from work through illness and medical certification under social welfare legislation.

THE OCCUPATIONAL HEALTH PRACTITIONER

The role

[9.02]

Occupational health practitioners work at the interface between employer and employee with the twin aims of safeguarding the health of workers, individually and often collectively, and promoting safe and healthy working environments. Taking a holistic approach to occupational health, any number of disciplines, clinical and non-clinical, can be involved: an architect must design a safe and user-friendly premises and a foreman must oversee working practices to ensure they are safe. In this chapter, however, we are most concerned with the particular role of the health professional in the working environment.

A clinician's involvement in occupational health will fit in somewhere along a spectrum of commitment. At one extreme is the practitioner employed casually by a firm merely to conduct pre-employment medical examinations on behalf of the company. At the intermediate level is the practitioner who provides a part-time commitment to the workplace, while other professionals are employed in a full-time capacity by companies to cater for all aspects of the health of their workforces. It is obvious that those who have different working arrangements with a company, or any other third party, to look after patients will have different responsibilities. The intermittently retained general practitioner has a relationship with the company only in so far as it concerns the individual patient before her, while the part- or full-time occupational health professional will be responsible not just for the individual patients she sees, but will also have a broader duty to the company and workforce as a whole. Whatever the precise relationship, the triangular relationship between practitioner, patient and employer (or any third party) brings with it potential complexity.

We deal principally with the occupational health environment here, but it is important to bear in mind that the principles encountered here apply in all analogous aspects of practice, such as the request for information from an insurer.[1]

The potential conflict

[9.03]

The duty a practitioner owes to her patient may be modified by external factors, some of which are encountered elsewhere in this book: a patient of sound mind and adult years who refuses treatment overrides the clinician's duty to treat; similarly a doctor may feel it is her duty to help her patient end his life in accordance with his wishes, only to find that the law against euthanasia and assisted suicide restricts that 'duty'. Another striking example is confidentiality. A clinician owes a duty of confidentiality to her patient, but in certain circumstances that duty is lifted or modified, and in situations where an outside party desires or requires access to information gleaned in a consultation, confidentiality can be especially tested.

A practitioner employed by a third party to examine and/or report on a patient has a new ingredient in the already complicated mix of the therapeutic encounter, namely the interests of that third party in the end product. A doctor or nurse providing occupational health services for a company and who learns, in consultation with her patient, of information with ramifications for the patient, for other workers or for the company has a problem. What can she disclose? Does she need the patient's consent? If consent is not forthcoming, can she go ahead anyway?

The clinician clearly owes two duties, one, as always, to the patient, but another to the employer (or other third party) who is paying the clinician for her services and with whom the clinician will have some form of agreement. A nurse or doctor working in an occupational health capacity may have signed a contract of employment and must fulfil the terms of that contract, including an implied duty to show loyalty to the company.[2] The polarising tug of commitments to both patient and third party is significant, particularly when the interests of employer and employee do not converge. The patient may have an illness he wishes to keep from his employer, while the employer may have a strong interest in knowing about any illness or infirmity in order to protect other employees or to ensure that customers and clients are protected.

Resolving the conflict

[9.04]

Example 1

Mr McMurphy, an employee of Combine Inc, attends Nurse Ratched who is an occupational health nurse in full-time employment with the same company. He complains of some deafness. He is concerned that he may lose his job, which involves dealing with the public, or be re-deployed elsewhere, which would affect his overtime. His hearing loss is very mild and he asks the nurse not to disclose details of the consultation to the company.

What should the nurse do? We answer this question in the sections that follow.

The *International Code of Ethics for Occupational Health Professionals* lays down the following basic ethical principles for occupational health practice.

> '*Occupational health practice* must be performed according to the highest professional standards and ethical principles. Occupational health professionals must serve the health and social well-being of workers, individually and collectively. They also contribute to environmental and community health.
>
> *The obligations of occupational health professionals* include protecting the life and the health of the worker, respecting human dignity and promoting the highest ethical principles in occupational health policies and programmes. Integrity in professional conduct, impartiality and the protection of the confidentiality of health data and of the privacy of workers are part of these obligations.
>
> *Occupational health professionals* are experts who must enjoy full professional independence in the execution of their functions. They must acquire and maintain the competence necessary for their duties and require conditions that allow them to carry out their tasks according to good practice and professional ethics.'[3]

These precepts clearly indicate that although a practitioner may take on a duty to a party other than the patient, that duty does not supplant her pre-existing ethical obligations as a health care practitioner. However, because the practitioner also has a duty to the employer and to the workers collectively, this may sternly test the confidentiality owed to the individual worker. If a worker's lung condition, for example, suggests an unsafe working practice (such as exposure to dust), the practitioner may owe a duty, not only to the patient but also to the employer who pays her and to the workforce, whose care is one of the reasons why the employer is retaining the clinician in the first place.

Patient first, then third party

The reasons why the patient comes before the employer, or any other interested party acting in a similar capacity, are essentially threefold. Primarily, clinicians are retained to carry out clinical duties, including adherence to the ethical obligations of their professions because if ethical practice were not the case, they could not discharge their professional duty properly. In the words of the 'Basic Principles' of the *International Code of Ethics for Occupational Health Professionals*, they are 'experts who must enjoy full professional independence in the execution of their functions'. The first duty of a health practitioner retained by a company or by a third party is to her patient and this includes ethical aspects of that duty, such as a duty to maintain confidences. This should be the starting point of the relationship and when it is planned to deviate from this, then the patient must be clearly informed.

Secondly, employers owe a duty of trust and confidence to employees[4] and this would seem to include not tampering with the normal practitioner-patient relationship, unless the patient is aware and has agreed that a particular consultation will be played by different rules, including disclosure of information to a third party. Trust and confidence between employer and employee will be undermined if the employer routinely eavesdrops on therapeutic encounters.

Finally, every Irish citizen has a right to privacy, guaranteed by the Irish Constitution[5] and the European Convention on Human Rights.[6] The right to privacy is not absolute and there are situations in which it may be set aside, but it nonetheless provides another strand of logic that says the ethical duty of the clinician towards her patient survives the practitioner signing a contract with a third party.

Confidentiality in the occupational health setting

[9.05]

The duty owed by the practitioner in the context of third-party interest is therefore first and foremost to the patient and includes the patient's right to expect a veil of confidentiality to be thrown over the consultation. Confidentiality has been covered already in this book and we will not revisit it here in great detail:[7] suffice it to remind the reader that there are five headings under which confidentiality may be breached. The most important is when the patient consents – consent by a patient to the release of confidential information neutralises the doctor's obligation to preserve confidentiality as far as that particular information is concerned. The other exceptions, where a doctor may disclose information *in the absence of consent from a patient* are:

- when required by law, either by a judge or because of a provision in written law;
- when necessary to protect the patient's own interests, health or welfare (although there is an argument that this does not apply in the occupational health setting – see section **[9.09]**);
- when necessary to protect another individual;
- when necessary to protect the welfare of society.[8]

Any breach of confidentiality should be moderated by one further consideration: no more information should be disclosed than is necessary and those details should not be disclosed to any wider a circle of recipients than is required to achieve the aims of the disclosure.[9]

It is easy to see how the criteria for breaching confidentiality in the absence of consent could be satisfied in the workplace. There is a statutory obligation on employers to report accidents that occur at work. If a doctor working for a company becomes aware of an accident, he would be under a duty, imposed in effect by the law, to appraise the company of the fact that the accident occurred. A worker may come to the attention of the doctor as suffering from an illness that, if he continues working, may pose a threat to himself, to other individuals or to society. A machine operative who develops a neuro-degenerative condition may be a threat to himself, a soldier with murderous delusions may be a danger to others and a restaurant employee with severe gastroenteritis could pose a risk to wider society. An airline pilot with epilepsy or alcoholism could obviously fulfil all three criteria with ease.

However, in other cases, there may be no grounds for breaching the confidentiality owed to the patient. A doctor who becomes aware during a consultation with a patient, on an utterly unrelated matter, that bullying is occurring on the factory floor may feel she should communicate that fact to the employer and may safely do so without referring to the specific patient and without breaching confidentiality. But what if the matter that is causing concern also relates to the patient's health? In reality, the role of the occupational health professional often involves a measure of 'qualified confidentiality'.

Example 2

Mr McMurphy's (see Example 1) deafness was not disclosed to the employer, in keeping with the general principle that an occupational health practitioner's first duty is to her patient. However, he continues to suffer from deafness. Nurse Ratched notices on reading his records that before working with customers, McMurphy operated machinery on the factory floor. She recalls that two other patients have consulted her recently regarding hearing loss and examining their records she establishes that they both worked with the same machinery. She wonders if there may be a link and whether the deafness may be noise-related.

McMurphy is still worried that his job may be at risk and refuses to permit disclosure of his health status to the employer. His deafness does not pose a risk to anyone else. What may be done now?

One reason why the occupational health professional is in a difficult position when it comes to disclosure of risks she identifies during a consultation lies in the way in which 'knowledge' is defined legally. When it comes to assessing legal liability for a danger that causes damage to a worker, the employer will be deemed to have 'known' of the risk if one of his 'servants' (employees) or 'agents' (people working on behalf of, but not for, the company) knew of the risk. Therefore, if a nurse working for or on behalf of a company knows of a risk, then the company legally 'knows' about the risk and may be held legally accountable for damage caused by that risk. Furthermore, the occupational health professional has an ethical duty to the wider workforce and to the company to make sure that overall health is maximised. There is a strong legal and ethical imperative therefore that the existence of a risk (such as the noisy machinery in the above example) to the health of the workforce should be relayed to the company.

This is where 'qualified confidentiality' comes into the convoluted practitioner-patient-workforce-employer equation. It is not a breach of confidentiality to disclose information about a patient where that disclosure, even though it involves the disclosure of confidential information, will not have the effect of identifying the patient.[10] If a patient will not consent to disclosure of information, it can be enough, where to do so is feasible, for the clinician to notify the employer of the hazard that was brought to light by the consultation without ever identifying the patient.

A protocol for practitioner-patient encounters in which a third party has an interest

[9.06]

If a consultation is explicitly to obtain clinical details for a third party or the practitioner receives a request for information concerning her patient, the patient should be fully informed about what is happening. The patient must understand why he is there, if he is attending the clinician for examination, and the likely destination of any information he discloses or data that has been requested from his medical history. He should understand that the consultation is not a routine one, in that relevant details are intended for an outside interest. This is important because the patient, as in all matters relating to confidentiality and other aspects of care, is free to withhold his consent. If he refuses to permit disclosure, normal rules of confidentiality apply: the clinician cannot disclose the information without the patient's consent unless one of the exceptions exists – the operation of law or a need to protect the patient, another individual or the welfare of society.

The patient's consent must be informed not only regarding the fact that information will be disclosed but also the nature and extent of that disclosure. The patient must understand that the clinician is under a duty to be impartial and must release all relevant information requested, whether it is injurious or beneficial to the patient, although it may be possible for the doctor to withhold information selectively on the basis that it is not relevant. The fact that a person has had a heart attack may be relevant to an application for life insurance; the fact that he was abused as a child and attended counselling in his early twenties may not be relevant, particularly if the patient has no psychiatric morbidity. The question is often one of clinical judgement. It may be preferable to show the patient the form or questionnaire being completed so that he understands the context of his consent.

The Medical Council offers the following guidance for performing medical examinations that bear the added burden of subsequent reporting to third parties:

> 'The significance, **rather than the precise details**, of the medical findings should be conveyed to any third party and then only with the patient's consent.'[11]

and in the specific circumstances of assessing a patient's fitness to work:

> 'A doctor when assessing the significance of a particular disability, should interpret the medical findings in terms of the likelihood of the patient continuing to work, if requested to do so. **An employer does not have the right to be informed of the clinical details of illness or injury without the consent of the patient**'.[12]

In some instances, a patient will not attend the clinician in person, for example when information has been required by a third party by way of a questionnaire. In the case of applications for insurance, a form will be sent to the practitioner by the insurer to be completed by her from the patient's records.[13] Written consent should accompany a request and the information should not be disclosed until the clinician is positive that her patient has given his consent. Again, consent should also be informed: it may be prudent to communicate to a patient the information to be disclosed, especially if there is anything in the history that may be contentious but is necessary for an accurate and complete report. Patients have a legal right, based on Data Protection legislation, to see any report that is prepared concerning them.[14]

In any case where the release of confidential material is at issue, any decision, including the reason for the decision, should be documented, whether it is disclosure with the patient's consent, refusal by the patient to permit disclosure or a decision to disclose in spite of refusal. The withholding of consent may have ramifications for the patient, such as foregoing a job offer, losing an existing job or failing to be insured, but that is the patient's choice. Even if a practitioner is an occupational health specialist working full-time for a company, the company has no automatic right to access the patient's records unless the patient consents.[15]

Withdrawing consent to disclosure

[9.07]

If a person agrees to undergo an examination by an occupational health practitioner, knowing that the results of that examination are to be disclosed to a third party, and then later withdraws that consent, the clinician will generally be protected from legal action if she discloses the information. The initial consent to disclosure remains valid so long as it was validly given and fully informed. In other words, if a patient knows that a third party has an interest in his consultation with the practitioner and goes ahead with the consultation, then that third party interest is enshrined and will not evaporate simply because the patient has changed his mind.[16] The doctor is not *obliged* to release the information, she may prefer to respect the patient's withdrawal of consent, and it may be the ethically preferable course of action. However, the legal position appears to be that she will not be liable if she discloses on the basis of the original consent. Obviously, if a patient was not fully informed about the purpose of the consultation or what was to be disclosed, it is likely that the patient could subsequently withdraw consent on becoming aware that the parameters of disclosure were different from what he had been led to believe. The clinician would be bound by a change of mind in those circumstances.

Pre-employment disclosure

[9.08]

Sometimes attempts are made to access a prospective employee's full medical history, in the form of his general practitioner's notes, as part of pre-employment screening. While this is not illegal, it is not satisfactory, insofar as the patient may be in effect compelled to consent for fear of losing the job. Seeking such information may be a violation of the Constitutional right to privacy unless it could be justified as necessary for the post in question. The UK Faculty of Occupational Medicine argues in its guide to the ethics of occupational health that pre-employment questionnaires demanding disclosure of the applicant's full general practitioner record should not be entertained.[17]

Disclosure in the employee's interest

[9.09]

It is not clear whether an occupational health professional can breach confidentiality where any risk posed is *only to the employee himself*. It is certainly true that in theory a threat to a patient's own health is grounds for breaching confidentiality, but there are few legal cases that support the contention that the clinician may in practice breach confidentiality in such circumstances.

> **Example 3**
>
> Dr Hibbert, a physician working in the occupational health setting for a nuclear power company, diagnoses Mr Simpson, a company employee, as having a knee injury. The patient's job involves a great deal of climbing ladders, but the injury is not a risk to any other person and the risk posed to the patient is uncertain: it is only a possibility that the requirements of the job will exacerbate the knee problem. Mr. Simpson refuses the doctor permission to discuss the diagnosis with the employers and says that he will struggle on with anti-inflammatory tablets and a beer- and doughnut-free diet aimed at weight loss.

What should the occupational health professional do? Is there a right to disclose in the patient's interests alone?

The reluctance to allow a practitioner to breach confidentiality even when she perceives it to be in a patient's best interests is due to the concept of 'patient autonomy': a person is free to exercise control over himself. It is another example of a conflict between the basic building blocks of clinical ethics.[18] On the one hand, the practitioner's ethical code impels her towards 'doing good' for her patient (beneficence), a principle that could involve telling the patient to take time off work or, in the last analysis, telling the employer so that he can take steps to save the worker from himself. On the other hand is the patient's autonomy: if the patient does not want information disclosed about him, even though he knows that it would be in his best interests to do, then who is the clinician to override that refusal in the absence of compelling circumstances? In theory then, if a patient is a risk to himself and to himself alone and refuses his clinician permission to disclose this fact, there is a strong argument to say that the patient's wish should be respected. If the patient discloses a workplace risk that the clinician can pass on to the employer without identifying the patient then that risk may be identified, but without identifying the patient.

If anything happens to the patient as a result of his refusal, then legal liability is unlikely to attach to the employer: the doctrines of 'voluntary assumption of risk' or of 'contributory negligence would apply'.[19] Accordingly, a patient who knew, but declined to tell his employer, of a problem that made it likely that he would be injured at work would have greater difficulty in winning a legal case against the employer.

One compromise that may be considered, although it is not always easy, let alone possible, is to ask the patient to agree to allow the clinician to recommend changes to work practices without specifying the reason for the required alterations. This is a common approach in circumstances where the need for a change is great but the circumstances underpinning the need for change are sensitive, such as psychiatric illness. This approach may help the patient by minimising the chance of worsening any underlying problem and help the employer by preventing the loss of an employee to long term illness or injury. Furthermore, it preserves the confidentiality, albeit in a qualified form, of the patient in question.

Note that in the United States, the courts have decided that a company can override an employee's autonomy and prevent him from exposing his health to risk at work, even if the risk is merely theoretical and one that the employee is perfectly prepared to run.[20] However, in Ireland, it seems certain that where a patient refuses to give a doctor or nurse permission to breach confidentiality and the only basis for such a breach would be the patient's own interests, then the patient's refusal should probably be respected unless other compelling circumstances override the patient's refusal.

Quick Reference Guide 9.1

Occupational health and confidentiality

- ❖ Any consultation with a patient in which a third party has an interest, or any request for information from a third party concerning a patient, can raise ethical and legal complications.
- ❖ Even if a practitioner is being paid for her services by a third party, her first duty remains to the patient. There are three reasons why the patient comes first: the practitioner's clinical independence and consequent ethical duty, the employer's obligation to be fair to employees and the worker's right to privacy under the Irish Constitution and the European Convention on Human Rights.
- ❖ In an occupational health setting (or any other environment where a third party has an interest in information concerning a patient) the patient retains his right to refuse to allow information to be disclosed.
- ❖ Confidentiality may only be breached if the patient consents or, assuming the patient does not consent, if the law requires it or there is a threat to another individual or to the welfare of society.
- ❖ There is probably no right for a practitioner to override a patient's refusal solely in what she perceives to be the best interests of the patient if the patient withholds consent to disclosure. Compromise may be possible in the sense of requesting changes to the employee's working arrangements without disclosing the reason.
- ❖ The practitioner should consider an approach based on 'qualified confidentiality', where elements of the consultation can be highlighted, such as an identified risk to the other members of the workforce, without naming the patient.
- ❖ A patient who is attending for a consultation, or about whom a request for information is made that will necessitate disclosure of otherwise confidential information to a third party should be fully appraised of the situation. The practitioner can exercise her clinical judgment: she need only disclose relevant information and need only use broad brushstrokes in doing so. The patient should know the extent and nature of any disclosure to which he is being asked to consent.
- ❖ A patient will have, under Data Protection legislation, the right to see any report written about him.

SAFETY, HEALTH AND WELFARE AT WORK

[9.10]

There are two mechanisms for ensuring safety, health and welfare at work and for punishing those who fail to maintain satisfactory standards. Firstly, individuals who are injured as a result of accidents at work can go to court to sue their employers for any damage suffered, assuming that the accident is legally the result of the employer's negligence: this is the *common law* approach. It is essentially retroactive, in that it retrospectively punishes employers for lack of care towards the worker who is bringing the legal action. In addition, the government, through the Safety Health and Welfare at Work Act 1989 and the creation of the Health and Safety Authority, created legal mechanisms to compel safe workplaces and to punish those employers and employees who fall short of the legal standards. This is the *statutory* approach to safety at work and is essentially proactive in nature: setting down transparent standards in advance for companies to meet, encouraging companies to meet those standards and, as a last resort, punishing companies that fail to meet them.

Practitioners working in an occupational health setting obviously need to know, at least in outline, the rules laid down by the courts and by legislation, but they are useful too for any practitioner in the workplace, whether employee or employer. The rules on employers' and employees' legal duties extend to almost all work places, irrespective of scale.

Safety, health and welfare at work – the common law approach

[9.11]

Actions by employees against employers for accidents occurring in the workplace are typically based on an allegation that some act or omission on the part of the employer was negligent and that it caused some damage to the employee. We have seen elsewhere in the text that there are four elements to negligence:

- the existence of a duty of care;
- breach of that duty;
- damage caused to the person alleging negligence (the damage must be foreseeable);
- the damage caused must result from the breach of the duty of care.[21]

Until the beginning of the twentieth century, courts were reluctant to find that employers owed employees any duty of care, but with greater acceptance of workers' rights, so the modern approach evolved: the duty of an employer towards an employee is to take reasonable care for the employee's safety in the circumstances.[22] This duty is not absolute or unlimited: an employer only has to take the steps a 'reasonable and prudent' employer would take in the circumstances. After all, there are some jobs that could not be done if all risk were eliminated: climbing scaffolding will always involve the risk of a fall; working with radioactive substances will always involve the risk of exposure. The onus on the employer is to ensure that he takes steps to minimise risks to the employee as far as possible.

Any accident or incident that occurs must furthermore, and in accordance with the general principles of negligence, be foreseeable. In one case, an employee developed folliculitis[23] as a result of exposure to chemicals in the workplace. The evidence showed that there were no other recorded cases of the condition developing in the same circumstances anywhere else in the world: the condition was unforeseeable so there could be no negligence in failing to prevent it. Damage done to the employee need not be physical. A soldier who suffered post-traumatic stress disorder following a tour of duty in the Lebanon during which his employers (the army) had acted in a manner the courts thought negligent was able to win damages.[24]

It does not have to be the company itself that causes the accident. 'Vicarious' liability can occur, which is the liability of the employer for the acts of one of his employees and for example, if one employee is bullying another or the company permits horseplay on the factory floor, the employer may be vicariously liable for injury that results. An employer may also be liable for any faulty equipment that is installed or purchased for use by employees and that subsequently causes harm to an employee.[25] The duty owed to an employee varies with a number of factors, including inexperience,[26] age, training or any disability of the worker as well as any particular dangers involved in the work itself. An employer may also in certain circumstances owe liability to those on his premises who are not employees.[27]

Sub-dividing employers' liability to employees

[9.12]

There are four components of the working environment that can give rise to a legal claim by an employee. The practitioner working in the occupational health setting needs to be conscious of them so that she can work with the employer to minimise any risks of which she becomes aware. The employer must provide employees with the following and a failure to do so can result in a court finding for an employee who brings a case alleging injury caused by the absence of one of them:

— *A safe workplace:* Risks in the workplace cannot be eliminated entirely. One judge stated that 'to make accidents impossible would make work impossible.'[28] Where an employer has taken all reasonable and prudent steps to provide a safe place of work and has complied with any obligations laid down by law, then it is less likely that he will be found negligent.

— *Safe and proper plant and equipment:* Equipment used in the workplace must be used for the purpose it was intended. Misuse of equipment, failure to maintain equipment or a mismatch between the capacity of plant or equipment and the job it is asked to do may all constitute a failure to provide safe plant and equipment.

— *A safe system of work:* This can include a number of elements. Examples can include the duty to ensure that workers use the safety equipment they are supplied with or that they are trained in the safest methods of discharging their duties.

— *Competent and safety conscious staff:* If alleging that an employer's staff were incompetent it must be shown that the employer knew the staff to be negligent or at least had the opportunity to find out about the absence of safe conduct.

Of course these four areas overlap and in that regard they can be a little unhelpful: the lack of competent staff could result in the absence of a safe system of work. Some argue that all four headings should be subsumed into the single simple question of the employer owing a broad duty of care to the employees.[29]

Example 4

(a) *Safe system of work*

In one case,[30] a ward attendant was lifting a patient when she suffered a back injury. The injury occurred in 1990. The last time she had been shown lifting techniques had been in the 1970s. In the meantime, the recommended technique for lifting had changed and the employer had never updated the attendant's training.

This was a failure to provide a safe system of work and the employee won her case.

(b) *Competent safety conscious staff*

In another case,[31] a practice had grown up among the staff in a repair shop of playing practical jokes on each other, during one of which an employee was injured. Because the mischief was short-lived each time and difficult to detect and the employers could therefore not have been aware of it, they were not guilty of failing to provide competent staff. This can be contrasted with another case[32] where an employee had a known track record of playing practical jokes on staff. When one of his antics resulted in the plaintiff sustaining a broken wrist, the company was found liable for failing to ensure its staff maintained a safe working environment.

Contributory negligence and employee carelessness

[9.13]

A worker who takes no or too little regard or for his own safety and suffers an accident at work as a result of the negligence of his employers may himself be culpable of contributory negligence,[33] which may partially, or even completely, absolve the employer of any blame.

Example 5

An experienced fitter took apart a new machine, presuming its construction to be the same as its predecessors. He had no manual because the company had failed to make them available to staff. During the dismantling process, the man heard a noise suggestive of something breaking inside the machine, but continued to take it apart regardless. A portion of the machine came away and damaged the man's hand.

The court found the company only 75% liable for failing to provide manuals (and thereby failing to provide a safe system of work) because the employee had contributed 25% of the negligence in continuing to work on the machine when he should have known there was something wrong.[34]

Similarly an employee who continues to show disregard for his own safety or that of others may be disciplined or even, as a last resort, dismissed.[35] Under the Safety Health and Welfare at Work Act 1989, an employee who fails to take care of his own safety or that of others may be prosecuted by the Health and Safety Authority.[36]

It is also important, however, to point out that while an employee who is at fault for an accident may be denied a legal remedy against her employer, she is still entitled to applicable state disability benefits if she is injured at work because such benefits are paid on a 'no fault' basis.[37]

Breach of statutory duty

[9.14]

As well as obligations under the law of negligence, employers can also have duties imposed on them by legislation. When an employee sues an employer he can, as well as alleging negligence on the part of the employer, also allege 'breach of statutory duty'. Breach of statutory duty means a failure to live up to the requirements of legislation. This is not the employee accusing the employer of 'breaking the law', but simply a case of asking the court to look at what the legislation says the employer *should* have been doing and to compare it with what in fact the employer *was* doing. The comparison can help the judge to find that the employer has been negligent.[38] We will encounter below at section [9.21] a number of regulations that have been introduced to promote health and safety in the workplace. Any one of them may be cited, if their terms have not been complied with, as evidence that the employer has breached his statutory duty towards the employee. In general, where there has been a breach of statutory duty, a negligence action may be easier to prove and contributory negligence on the part of the employee is less likely to be found.

The employee who is unfit for work

[9.15]

An employer, especially where work is hazardous, is under a duty to ensure that his workforce is fit for the duties they are undertaking.[39] This may take the form of a pre-employment medical or may require ongoing health surveillance and an employee who is found unfit for work or who refuses to undergo health surveillance (and has been made aware of the consequences of such a refusal) may be dismissed from her job. There is no absolute duty on an employer to find his employees 'light work' if recommended by a doctor caring for a patient, although it is certainly prudent that they should attempt to do so. If there is no alternative work and if a person is unfit to do the work for which they were initially engaged, then they can be lawfully dismissed assuming all other legal obligations are fulfilled by the employer.[40]

Quick Reference Guide 9.2

Common law approach to safety, health and welfare at work

- Employers owe their employees a duty to provide a safe workplace, safe and proper equipment and plant, safe systems of work and safe and competent staff. If the employer fails in this duty and an employee suffers physical or psychological damage as a result, she may sue the employer for negligence.
- This duty is not absolute: an employer must take such care for the employee's safety in the circumstances as a reasonable and prudent employer would be expected to take.
- The duty owed to an employee varies with the employee's experience, age, training and any disability. The employee herself may be guilty of contributory negligence if she acts without due regard for her own safety. Contributory negligence on the part of the employee can reduce the liability of the employer. An employee who acts without regard for the safety of others may be dismissed.
- If an employer not only fails in his duty towards the employee but also breaches his statutory duties, he is generally more likely to be found negligent.

Safety, health and welfare at work – the statutory approach

[9.16]

The 1983 Barrington Commission Report[41] looked at the question of safety at work and recommended that legislation should be introduced to compel employers and employees to have regard for the need for safety in the workplace and to punish them if they did not do so. The result was the Safety Health and Welfare at Work Act 1989. The Act incorporated many of the legal duties of the employer and the employee that had already been recognised by the court and which we have dealt with in the preceding section, such as the duty to provide safe systems of work, and made those duties into explicit legal obligations. The process which lead to the introduction of the Act was a long one and lies outside the scope of the present chapter, but certain elements can be stated:

- Early legislation for safety in the workplace was the result of attempts to redress the appalling employment conditions that were a by-product of the Industrial Revolution.[42]
- Legislation prior to the 1989 Act was piecemeal and limited in scope and reach (for example, legislation such as the Factories Act 1955 applied only to factories and not to any other workplaces).
- Litigation by employees against employers for failing in their duty to provide safe workplaces was increasing and so were the amounts in damages being awarded by the courts.
- The need was recognised for a statutory and proactive, rather than court-based and retrospective, approach to safety in the workplace.

Safety, Health and Welfare at Work Act 1989

[9.17]

This Act is the law governing safety in the modern workplace. It places a legal burden on both employer and employee as well as creating the Health and Safety Authority (HSA), which has the power to enforce the Act and to punish those who transgress. The Act also provides the legal basis for the introduction of specific regulations that put flesh on the bones of the Act itself. The Safety, Health and Welfare at Work Act 1989 can be divided into seven broad sections:

- An outline of the general principles of safety, health and welfare in and around all places of work. It is important to note that the Act applies to all workplaces and the term 'workplace' in turn covers almost every conceivable working environment.
- Duties are imposed on certain categories of person to ensure a safe workplace. The categories include employers, the self-employed, employees, manufacturers, suppliers, designers and builders.
- An obligation on employers to produce safety statements for the workplace.
- A legal requirement to identify hazards and assess risks in the workplace.
- The establishment of the Health and Safety Authority (HSA) together with its powers to enforce the Act and to prosecute those who violate it.
- The HSA's power to introduce technical standards or accepted codes of practice (ACoP) for the workplace whichin turn constitute legal 'best practice'.[43]
- The repeal of the vast majority of all previous legislation on workplace safety and its replacement with the new Act.

We look now at the four most significant elements of the Act: the general duties it imposes on all involved in the workplace, the Safety Statement, dealing with those who infringe safety rules and the health and safety regulations that translate the Act to the specifics of the workplace.

General duties under the Act

[9.18]

The Act applies to all workplaces, to all employers and to all employees whether full-time or temporary.[44] It is the duty of every employer to ensure, so far as is reasonably practicable, the safety, health and welfare at work of all his employees.[45] Note that this duty reflects the duty laid down by the courts in that it is not absolute but rather requires the employer to ensure safety only 'so far as is reasonably practicable.'[46] The Act lays out specific areas in which the employer has a duty to take care (so far as is reasonably practicable):

— providing a safe place of work, including structure, ventilation and lighting;
— providing a safe entrance to and exit from work, as well as safe routes through the workplace;
— machinery and equipment should be safe;
— systems of works should be safe;
— information, training and supervision should be provided to ensure safety;
— where a risk cannot be eliminated, then safety equipment or protective clothing is required. However, the first attempt should always be to eliminate or reduce the risk;
— emergency plans must be in place;
— the employer should have concern for the welfare of staff and provide facilities (such as first aid, washrooms and seating) and staff, whether in-house or external, to care for that welfare.

Employers and the self-employed are also required to conduct their business in such a way that it is safe for non-employees so far as is reasonably practicable: a doctor, for example, should make sure her needle disposal system does not present a risk to patients. The employer's duty includes taking care not to present a workplace risk to those visiting the workplace or carrying out work on the premises.[47]

Employees are also under a burden to take reasonable care for their own safety, health and welfare and that of any other person who may be affected by their acts or omissions at work. Employees' duties include cooperating with the employer to ensure safety in the work place and utilising any safety equipment or protective clothing that is provided. The employee is also under an obligation to report any defect in equipment, machinery, the workplace or the system of work without unreasonable delay.[48] The employee is forbidden by the Act from intentionally or recklessly interfering with any article or system intended to cater for safety, health and welfare in the workplace.

The Act also obliges anyone who makes, designs, imports or supplies any article for use at work to ensure that the article is safe for use, that sufficient information is provided to ensure its safe use and that changes in specification or use must be communicated to those using the article. Similar strictures attach to anyone who is designing or constructing a place of work.[49]

Safety statements

[9.19]

Safety statements are a crucial element of the modern workplace and every employer must prepare one for his business.[50] The safety statement has two ingredients: it must be based on an identification of hazards and an assessment of risks[51] in the workplace and it must specify how the employer, in the light of the identification and assessment process, will deal with the identified risks and hazards. The statement must in particular include:

— resources and arrangements for maximising the health, safety and welfare of the workforce;

— details of the co-operation required from employees regarding health, safety and welfare;

— names of the people, or their deputies if the named people are absent, responsible for tasks assigned by the safety statement.

Employees must be consulted as part of the preparation of a safety statement and must be aware of its contents. Employees may appoint a Safety Representative to liaise with the employer or with any inspector sent into the workplace by the HSA. A person acting as Safety Representative must be given the necessary training to fulfil the role (together with the requisite leave to obtain that training) and must not be penalised financially or in terms of career prospects for discharging her duties. The Safety Representative will typically be the conduit for health and safety information going between employees and either the employer or any inspectors representing the HSA. An employer should act on the representations of a Safety Representative where possible.[52]

The role of the safety statement in the workplace has been fleshed out by later regulations, which include a requirement on the employer to integrate the measures outlined in the safety statement into all work activities under the control of the employer and at all levels of responsibility in the company.[53] The employer is also required to designate one or more employees or outside personnel to oversee health, safety and welfare at work, who must be competent, meaning that they have the necessary training, skills and experience to carry out the task they are asked to perform.[54] The whereabouts of first aid facilities, together with an identification of who is trained to provide first aid should also be included in any safety statement.[55] The larger the business, the more extensive health, safety and welfare facilities must be.

A safety statement must be a dynamic document and must change to take account of changing health and safety practices. Those companies that are obliged by law to produce annual reports are also obliged to include in their reports an indication of the extent to which the policies set out in a safety statement have been implemented. An inspector from the Health and Safety Authority can ask to see the Statement, which must be in writing,[56] and if it is deficient she can order it to be remedied within 30 days.

Consequences of breaching the legislation

[9.20]

The HSA was set up under Part III of the 1989 Act and it is given the power, as a last resort, to prosecute those who breach the Act. However, before that stage is reached the HSA has other powers to coerce employers into co-operating with the law. The HSA appoints inspectors who can visit workplaces and exercise powers of inspection and investigation.[57] If an Inspector notes a problem with workplace safety, she can proceed in a number of ways depending on the severity of the breach of an employer's (or employee's – the Act applies to both) liability under the Act. In the last analysis, if attempts at remedial measures fail, the HSA can bring a prosecution against transgressing employers or employees. A court can then fine or in certain limited circumstances jail the guilty party.[58]

Improvement direction

Used for relatively minor breaches of the law: the Inspector indicates areas where improvement is required, to which the employer responds with an Improvement Plan and a timeframe within which the improvement will be effected.[59]

Improvement notice

Here the Inspector tells the employer what he must do in order to comply with the law, together with the time frame within which he must do it. The employer must implement the improvements contained in the notice, although he does have the right to take an appeal against the notice to the District Court.[60]

Prohibition notice

The Inspector may stop the employer from engaging in a particular activity that represents a risk of serious personal injury to employees. Once the notice is issued, the employer must cease that activity, even if it means that he cannot carry on any work.[61] This would generally be used where there was a serious and extremely dangerous breach of safety in the workplace. In certain circumstances, the Inspector will go to the High Court to seek a prohibition order, rather than issuing it himself.

Safety, Health and Welfare at Work Regulations

[9.21]

The Safety, Health and Welfare at Work Act 1989 is not an isolated piece of legislation. It serves simply to lay out the broad parameters and principles that underlie safety in the workplace. The Act is buttressed by a panoply of regulations that govern everything from general interpretation and application of the Act to the specifics of health and safety in certain professions or with regard to certain hazards. It would be impossible in a work of this nature to give detailed attention to every such regulation, but we look below at some that are of most interest to the clinician. Many of these regulations are transpositions into Irish law of equivalent or identical European Directives.[62]

General Application Regulations 1993

The General Application Regulations 1993 are the cornerstone of the practical implementation of the 1989 Act. In particular they cover the following elements of safety and lay down the practices that should be adopted by the employer:

- Workplace safety (Part III of the Regulations)
- Work equipment and machinery (Part IV)
- Personal protective equipment (Part V)
- Manual handling of loads (Part VI)
- Display screens (Part VII)

— Electricity (Part VIII)
— First Aid (Part IX)
— Notification of accidents and dangerous occurrences (Part X)

The specifics of the General Application Regulations are extensive, but there are some elements that should be highlighted.

Training[63]

Training in the workplace should be an ongoing process and must be provided where an employee is recruited for the first time or is transferred between jobs or where new equipment or technology is introduced by the employer. Training must be repeated periodically where that is appropriate, such as where the approved practice for doing a certain task has changed or where the employee is noted not to be following the procedures in which she was originally trained. Training may need to take account of certain factors, such as the physical suitability of the employee to carry out the task in question and the clothing, footwear or personal effects worn by the employee when performing a particular task for which she is being trained.

Health surveillance

Where appropriate, employers must have health surveillance in place. This is particularly the case when employees are working in a hazardous environment or with dangerous substances. The requirement for health surveillance is reiterated in many of those regulations that deal with the handling of specific substances, such the Biological Agents Regulations 1994 and 1998.

First aid[64]

First aid arrangements must be specifically included in any safety statement. There should be appropriate facilities and properly trained staff. First Aid is defined as the treatment of very minor injuries or treatment with the aim of preserving life or minimising the consequences of injury until a medically or paramedically qualified individual can arrive. The number of staff to be trained in first aid depends on workplace size and the nature of the work carried on in that workplace: factories and construction sites have a greater requirement for first aid facilities.[65]

Manual handling of loads

There are three elements to the health and safety considerations of manual handling of loads at work.

— The employer must put in place systems wherever possible that avoid manual handling of loads, for example by providing mechanical assistance.[66]
— Where manual lifting is unavoidable the employer must engage in risk assessment and reduction.
— The employer is under a duty to provide training and information to employees.

Manual handling is defined relatively broadly:

> 'any transporting of a load by one or more employees…including lifting, putting down, pushing, pulling, carrying or moving a load, which by reason of its characteristics or of unfavourable ergonomic conditions involves risk, particularly of back injury, to employees'.[67]

In each case the procedures in place should take account of the characteristics of the load in question, the physical effort required in lifting and moving the load, the frequency with which lifting must be done and the environment in which the lifting is done.

Biological Agents Regulations 1994 and 1998[68]

The Biological Agents Regulations 1994 and 1998 cover workplaces where there is the potential for exposure to biological agents, which include bacteria, viruses, parasites and fungi.

The employer must, as with all regulations of this nature, conduct a full assessment of risks in the workplace and where risks cannot be eliminated, for example in a hospital or research facility, then they must be minimised. All employees must be trained in the necessary procedures to ensure safety and there must be health surveillance available to the employees, should they wish to avail themselves of it. There must be training and information available to employees, together with health surveillance. In these and similar regulations,[69] exposure limits are often specified where appropriate.

Ionising Radiation Order 2000[70]

The Radiological Protection Institute of Ireland (RPII) is the equivalent of the HSA when it comes to radiation and was established by the Radiation Protection Act 1991. The powers of the RPII and the regulations governing the use of and exposure to radiation are of particular significance to those working in radiography and radiology. The RPII is concerned with hazards to health associated with ionising radiation and with radioactive contamination in the environment. It also has an advisory function to both the government and the public and licenses and develops regulations for the use[71] of any device that is a source of ionising radiation, such as x-ray machines. Today, the number of people and institutions holding a licence for ionising radiation devices exceeds 1,250 and includes hospitals, dentists, veterinary surgeons, universities, institutes of technology and industrial users. RPII Inspectors have extensive powers under the Radiological Protection Act 1991 to inspect any premises or devices.

The key principles for the licensing for use of ionising equipment are:

— it must be possible to justify the use of the equipment by showing that the benefits it provides to society outweigh the risks posed by radiation ('justification');
— all exposure to radiation must as low as is reasonably achievable in the circumstances ('optimisation');
— the sum total of all doses must be kept below the specified limits contained in regulations ('limitation').

These principles are expressed in Irish law by the Ionising Radiation Order 2000. The order provides the framework for the Institute's licensing system and details the general radiation protection requirements and dose limits for all users of ionising radiation.[72] The aim of the regulations is to control exposure to ionising radiation risk and to achieve that aim, not only must the radiation principles of justification, optimisation and limitation be respected, a full risk assessment must also be carried out as part of the process of minimising exposure. The risk assessment must be submitted with an application for a licence from the RPII. The Order also regulates the provision of health surveillance to those staff working with ionising radiation. Individual dose monitoring must be carried out for all exposed workers by an approved dosimetry service and, with regard to record keeping, dose records for Category A (those receiving greatest exposure to ionising radiation) workers must be maintained by an approved dosimetry service for a minimum of 50 years from the date on which the worker ceased to do the work involving radiation exposure. In the case of Category B workers, dose records must be maintained by the licensee for a period of at least 5 years from the date of measurement.

Quick Reference Guide 9.3

The Safety, Health and Welfare at Work Act and Regulations

- The Safety, Health and Welfare at Work Act 1989 covers all workplaces and imposes obligations on both employers and employees to maintain safety, health and welfare at work. The Act created the Health and Safety Authority (HSA) and empowered it to enforce the Act.
- The obligations the Act places on employers are very similar to those that had traditionally been placed on employers by the courts, including the duties to provide a safe place of work, safe systems of work, safe equipment and safe staff.
- The fundamental point of all safety, health and welfare at work legislation is that employers are obliged to identify risks and hazards in the workplace ('risk assessment'). Once risks and hazards are identified the employer is under an obligation to eliminate them where possible or where elimination is impossible, to minimise them, for example by the use of training or safety equipment.
- All employers must prepare a Safety Statement for the workplace. A Safety Statement must be based on an identification of hazards and an assessment of risks in the workplace and must specify how the employer, in the light of the assessment process, will deal with the risks and hazards identified.
- Employees should be consulted on safety matters and they have the right to appoint a safety representative who must be consulted on safety matters and whose representations to the employer should be given due weight.
- An employer or employee who breaches the Safety, Health and Welfare at Work Act 1989 may be subject to the attentions of the Health and Safety Authority. The HSA may issue improvement directions, improvement notices and prohibition notices regarding the workplace. In the last analysis the authority may prosecute employers or employees, who may be fined substantial amounts or sentenced to imprisonment.
- The Safety, Health and Welfare at Work Act is fleshed out by a variety of Regulations that apply the principles of the Act to the specifics of general and particular working environments. Important regulations for the healthcare community include the General Applications Regulations 1993, the Biological Agents Regulations 1994 and 1998, the Carcinogen Regulations 1994 and the Chemical Agents Regulations 1994.

Safety, health and welfare at work in the health services

[9.22]

Specific research has been conducted into health and safety issues in the health services.[73] HA 2001 report drew attention to the importance of the health care sector as an employer, with over 100,000 people working for it. The *Report of the Health and Safety Authority Advisory Committee on the Health Service* sought to identify and prioritise the principal safety and health problems in the sector and to work out programmes to tackle the problems identified. The most significant areas of concern that were isolated included the following:

— the need to report and record incidents with potential impact on safety at work;

— the importance of having overarching and well-integrated safety systems in place and in particular valuing the role of the Safety Representative;

— paying attention to the need to avoid where possible and to minimise, where avoidance is not possible, the risks posed by manual handling;

— the need to identify the risks posed by biological (such as needlestick injuries) and chemical hazards;

— the need for good housekeeping in health care facilities to reduce the high frequency of slips, trips and falls;

— improved electrical safety in older premises.

Proposed methods for dealing with shortcomings include the HSA liaising with health service employers, the Department of Health, the health boards and the hospitals to foster a greater regard for safety, health and welfare principles. Specific proposals include encouraging safety committees and multidisciplinary occupational health services and emphasising training and the adoption of 'best practice' protocols.

The Organisation of Working Time Act 1997 is a piece of legislation that was introduced with the aim of limiting the working week in the interests of employees' health and safety. It is dealt with at the end of Chapter 5 (see section **[5.30]**).

ILLNESS AND CERTIFICATION OF ABSENCE FROM WORK

[9.23]

Employees who have paid the requisite PRSI (pay-related social insurance) are entitled to social welfare benefits when absent from work through illness or through injuries sustained in the workplace.[74] In cases where a person is claiming benefit on the grounds of being unfit for work, it will generally fall to the doctor[75] to certify that a person is, in fact, unfit for work. Benefits are payable, once PRSI requirements are met, both to people who are absent from work through non-specific illnesses and to those whose absence is due specifically to injury or illness sustained at work. The most common forms of benefit paid to those who are unable to work through illness or injury include the following:[76]

Disability Benefit - a payment made to those people who are qualified for benefit through PRSI contributions and who are unable to work due to illness or injury, including those injuries or illnesses sustained at work. A person who suffers an occupational injury or disease will generally receive a disability payment called *injury benefit* for the first 26 weeks' duration of the injury or illness.

Disablement Benefit - paid to those who are injured at work or who contract a prescribed occupational disease and whose illness outlasts 26 weeks. People with occupational injuries or illness receive other benefits under the Occupational Injuries Scheme, which can include Medical Care[77] and Death Benefit.[78] Disablement benefit can sometimes be paid as a lump sum rather than a periodic weekly or monthly payment.

Disability Allowance - a weekly allowance paid to people with a disability, typically lasting a year or more, who are aged over 16 years and under the age of 66 years. Payments are dependent on a medical examination and a means test.

Occupational injuries and diseases

[9.24]

Occupational diseases are diseases that develop specifically due to the nature of a person's employment. Occupational injuries are injuries sustained at work, including those suffered on the journey to or from work. Benefit is payable to persons who suffer from one of a range of occupational diseases prescribed by regulations, acquired while engaged in a job provided for by the regulations and due to the nature of the employment.[79] A variety of conditions fall within the remit of occupational diseases – figure 9.1 lists some of the most common and the occupations with which they must be associated for benefit to be payable.

Figure 9.1 – Some occupational diseases recognised for social welfare payments and their associated causes

Disease or Injury[80]	*Occupation*
Bursitis or subcutaneous cellulitis of the hand, elbow or knee	Manual labour involving prolonged pressure or friction to the affected part.
Byssinosis	Exposure to cotton or flax in the weaving industry
Nasal carcinoma	Work in wood manufacture or repair; footwear manufacture or repair
Cramp of hand or forearm	Work involving repetitive movements of fingers, hand or arms
Mesothelioma	Exposure to asbestos through handling or manufacture, or as a result of cleaning, building or maintenance work
Radiation-based illness	Work involving radiation exposure
Hearing loss[81]	Use of or exposure to pneumatic, percussive or grinding tools in metallurgy, mining or shipbuilding; exposure to drop-forging or drop-hammering plant; exposure to weaving machinery; exposure to wood-manufacturing or forestry machinery.

Infections, including TB, anthrax, glanders, leptospirosis, brucellosis, streptococcus suis infection, viral hepatitis.	Exposure to the illness in any occupation in which the infection is an occupational hazard (eg viral hepatitis is an occupational disease for clinical practice).
Certain forms of poisoning or cancer	Exposure to poisonous or carcinogenic chemicals at work.
Asthma	Exposure to any of the following: animals or insects in research or education; cereal dusts; fumes from 'hardening agents' or resins; isocyanates; platinum salts; proteolytic enzymes; red cedar wood dust.
Dermatitis	Exposure in the course of employment to any chemical or other agent capable of causing dermatitis.

Certification of illness

[9.25]

The role of the doctor in certifying absence from work is to examine the patient and complete the requisite forms. The most common forms are:

- Form MC1, which certifies the initial week of any illness and will suffice on its own to cover any illness or injury lasting fewer than eight days.
- Form MC2, which certifies either continuing illness (intermediate certificate) or that a patient is fit to return to work after a period of illness (final certificate).

Certificates are issued to doctors from the Department of Social and Family Affairs.[82] A person is unfit to work when he is under the care of the doctor for an ailment and in the opinion of his doctor either cannot work because of that illness or is advised not to work because of the risk his illness poses to others.[83] Typically the doctor will certify illness by completing the appropriate form with the details of the illness and dates of the period covered by the illness.[84] Payment of the doctor for certification is arranged by the Department of Social and Family Affairs and not by the patient. The Department rules state that all first certificates of illness or injury should be based on a medical examination to confirm the presence of the ailment in question. Subsequent (intermediate or final) certificates should be predicated on an examination unless the doctor is satisfied on good medical grounds that the illness is continuing. Certificates must generally be:

- completed clearly and legibly;
- written by the certifier in ink (preferably in capital letters) and signed by the certifier in her own handwriting;
- issued by the certifier to the patient in person at the time of any examination or as soon as possible afterwards.

Certification is generally weekly, but the Department may permit those suffering from long-term illness to submit certificates at longer intervals, such as six months. Where a person is no longer unfit for work, then the doctor can issue a 'final certificate'. Any person claiming disability benefit may be called for assessment by a medical assessor on behalf of the Department and if he is found fit for work, benefit may be discontinued. The patient has the right to take an appeal against the discontinuation of benefit to the Social Welfare Appeals Office.

Endnotes

1 Other examples of the clinician being in effect the servant of two masters include working in the social welfare services assessing claims for benefits, employment in the prison or armed services and working for insurance companies.

2 See ch 5 (section **[5.05]**).

3 International Commission on Occupational Health 'Basic Principles' (1992) Singapore (italics in original).

4 See ch 5 (section **[5.05]**).

5 *Kennedy v Ireland* [1987] IR 587.

6 Article 8. See Kloss 'A servant of two masters?' *Occupational Health Review* (March/April 2001) p 26.

7 See ch 3 for greater detail.

8 The practical applications of these exceptions are dealt with in greater detail in ch 3 (section **[3.16]** *ff*.).

9 *Duncan v Medical Practitioners' Disciplinary Committee* [1986] 1 NZLR 513 – a doctor was concerned about his patient's heart. The patient was a bus driver and rather than confining his concerns solely to the relevant authority he also told the patient's prospective passengers. Even if this was valid grounds for breaching confidentiality, the information was not as narrowly disseminated as it should have been.

10 See ch 3 (section **[3.12]**).

11 *Guide to Ethical Conduct and Behaviour* (5th edn, 1998) para 18.6(4). Bold type in original.

12 *Guide to Ethical Conduct and Behaviour* (5th edn, 1998) para 18.7. Bold type in original.

13 Similarly the request may come from a solicitor in the context of a legal action.

14 See ch 6 (section **[6.10]**).

15 *Dunn v British Coal Corporation* [1993] ICR 591.

16 *Kapadia v Lambeth London Borough Council* (CA) [2000] IRLR 699; *Hammersmith and Fulham London Borough Council v Farnsworth* [2000] IRLR 691.

17 Faculty of Occupational Medicine of the Royal College of Physicians *Guidance on Ethics for Occupational Physicians* (5th edn, 1999) London.

18 See ch 3 (section **[3.10]**).

19 See ch 7 (section **[7.19]-[7.20]**)for more details. In essence, the doctrine (called *'volenti non fit injuria'* in Latin) means that a person who recognises and accepts the risks involved in a certain course of action cannot blame another if those risks actually occur.

20 In *Echazabal v Chevron USA* 9th Circuit, 23 May 2000, the US Appeals Court reasoned that it was not for an employer to decide what was in the employee's best health interests if the employee's health problems (in this case, asymptomatic hepatitis C) posed no threat to third parties. However, this decision was subsequently overturned by a unanimous US Supreme Court on 10 June 2002. The Court stated that employers had the right to decide, on the basis of medical evidence, that an employee should not be allowed to expose himself to risk even where that risk did not affect third parties and where the risk was not even certain to cause harm to the employee himself. This decision does not appear to override the right of the patient to refuse disclosure of his health history but may encourage American patients to be more circumspect

about what they disclose in the occupational health setting, which is disappointing from the point of view of the clinician.

21 See ch 7.

22 *Dalton v Frendo* (15 December 1977, unreported) SC.

23 An infection or inflammation of the hair follicles.

24 *McHugh v Minister for Defence* (28 January 1999, unreported) HC.

25 *Connolly v Dundalk Urban District Council and McMahon & McPhilips* (HC) [1990] 2 IR 1, affirmed by the Supreme Court on 18 November 1992. The court pointed out that while the employer might be initially liable for damage to the employee, he may subsequently be able to sue the party who sold or installed the machinery or equipment in the first place.

26 For example, an apprentice who is being trained will clearly need greater supervision than an experienced employee and accordingly, the duty of care will be higher: *Murphy v Ross* [1920]; *Campbell v Cox* (15 May 1956, unreported) SC.

27 Called occupiers liability and covered by the Occupiers Liability Act 1995. The Act requires the owner of any premises to which the public have access to take care that the premises do not present a danger to the public or, if danger cannot be wholly eliminated, to alert the public to the fact that the premises may be dangerous.

28 *Christie v Odeon (Ireland) Ltd* (1957) 91 ILTR 25 at 29 *per* Kingsmill Moore J.

29 *Mulcare v Southern Health Board* [1988] ILRM 689 at 692 per Murphy J.

30 *Firth v South Eastern Health Board* (27 July 1994, unreported) HC.

31 *Hough v Irish Base Metal Ltd* (8 December 1967, unreported) SC.

32 *Hudson v Ridge Manufacturing* Co [1957] 2 QB 348.

33 See ch 7 for an exploration of contributory negligence (section **[7.19]**).

34 *Doran v Dublin Plant Hire Ltd* [1990] 1 IR 488.

35 *Kellegher v Power Supermarkets Ltd*, a decision of the Employment Appeals Tribunal, 9 March 1990. The employee had been engaging in horseplay on a fork lift truck.

36 Safety, Health and Welfare at Work Act 1989, s 9.

37 Social Welfare (Consolidation) Act 1993, ss 48 *ff.* See also section **[9.23]**

38 *Dunleavy v Glen Abbey* [1992] ILRM 1.

39 *Heeney v Dublin Corporation* (16 May 1991, unreported) HC.

40 See ch 5 (**[5.09]**-**[5.16]**)for an account of dismissal and unfair dismissal.

41 *Report of the Committee of Enquiry on Safety, Health and Welfare at Work* (1993) Government Publications.

42 For example, an Act for the Preservation of the Health and Morals of Apprentices and Others Employed in Cotton and Other Mills and Cotton and Other Factories 1802. This Act mandated quicklime washings for the factory or mill twice a year, fresh air, suitable accommodation (no more than 2 to a bed!) and a working day limited to 12 hours. Only in the mid-nineteenth century did inspectors gain real powers to enforce the laws on safety in the workplace.

43 An example of an ACoP is the Health and Safety Authority *Code of Practice on the Prevention of Workplace Bullying* (2002). (available for download from the website of the Health and Safety Authority: www.hsa.ie).

44 Safety, Health and Welfare at Work Act 1989, s 2.

45 Safety, Health and Welfare at Work Act 1989, s 6(1). Later rules clarified the Act to ensure that it included those who were working for a company via employment agencies : Safety, Health and Welfare at Work (General Application) Regulations 1993, Part II.

46 The words 'so far as reasonably practicable' seem to imply a balancing act between the safety the employer is obliged to provide and the cost, in money and effort, required to achieve that level of safety. Where it would be prohibitively expensive or extremely difficult to put a particular measure in place, the courts seem happy to accept that such a measure is not

'reasonably practicable'. The greater the risk to life and limb of the employee the greater the steps an employer is expected to take to prevent or minimise that risk: *Daly v Avonmore Creameries Ltd* [1984] IR 131; *Boyle v Marathon Petroleum Ireland Ltd* (1 November 1995, unreported) HC, (12 January 1999) SC. Most, but not all, areas of safety, health and welfare at work legislation are governed by the 'so far as reasonably practicable' caveat.

47 Safety, Health and Welfare at Work Act 1989, ss 7 and 8.

48 Safety, Health and Welfare at Work Act 1989, s 9.

49 Safety, Health and Welfare at Work Act 1989, ss 10 and 11. If an article is manufactured outside the state then legal liability under the Act falls on the importer.

50 Safety, Health and Welfare at Work Act 1989, s 12. See *Health and Safety Authority Guidelines on Safety Statements* (1993).

51 Risk assessment may include all or any of the following: safety audit (usually carried out by external safety experts); safety survey; routine safety inspection; safety tour (typically unscheduled); safety sampling; hazard and operability studies (assessment of the particular risk posed by the engineering elements of machinery) and checklists for processes. Essentially there are two types of measurement of risk: quantitative measurements of risks such as noise and qualitative measurement, such as the assessment of techniques and training for manual lifting.

52 Safety, Health and Welfare at Work Act 1989, s 13.

53 Safety, Health and Welfare at Work (General Application) Regulations 1993, reg 5(a).

54 Safety, Health and Welfare at Work (General Application) Regulations 1993, reg 8.

55 Safety, Health and Welfare at Work (General Application) Regulations 1993, reg 56(3).

56 Safety Health and Welfare at Work (General) Regulations 1993, reg 10.

57 Safety, Health and Welfare at Work Act 1989, s 34.

58 See 'Building firm and director fined for deaths on site' (2001) *Irish Times,* 22 November. A construction company was fined c €250,000 and its director c €50,000 for breaches of health and safety law in digging a trench on a construction site. The trench had collapsed killing two men. An employee, the driver of a digger, was also fined, showing the extent of the Act's powers.

59 Safety, Health and Welfare at Work Act 1989, s 35.

60 Safety, Health and Welfare at Work Act 1989, s 36.

61 Safety, Health and Welfare at Work Act 1989, s 37.

62 See appendix (section **[A.13]**) for a brief discussion of European Law.

63 Safety, Health and Welfare at Work (General Application) Regulations 1993, reg 13.

64 Safety, Health and Welfare at Work (General Application) Regulations 1993, Part IX.

65 In a factory or on a construction site, the following would apply: up to 49 employees - one staff member trained in first aid if safety statement risk assessment shows it is necessary; 50-149 employees - a minimum of one; 150-299 employees - minimum two; over 300 employees - one for every extra 150 employees or part thereof. In other workplaces: up to 99 employees - one staff member trained in first aid if safety statement risk assessment shows it is necessary; 100-399 employees - a minimum of one; 400-699 employees – a minimum of two; more than 700 employees - one for every additional 300 employees or part thereof. Common sense dictates that if a company requires First Aid cover, it should train more employees than necessary to cover times when first aiders are on holidays.

66 Safety, Health and Welfare at Work (General Application) Regulations 1993, reg 28(a). See also Health and Safety Authority *Handle With Care* (1998).

67 Safety, Health and Welfare at Work (General Application) Regulations 1993, reg 27.

68 Safety, Health and Welfare at Work (Biological Agents) Regulations 1994 (SI 1994/14) and 1998 (SI 1998/248).

[69] Similar regulations are in place for exposure to carcinogens (SI 2001/78) and chemical agents (SI 1994/445).

[70] The Radiological Protection Act 1991 (Ionising Radiation) Order 2000 (SI 2000/125).

[71] A licence is also required for custody, production, processing, handling, holding, storage, use, manufacture, importing into and exporting from the European Union, distribution, transportation, recycling, reuse or other disposal of radioactive substances and nuclear devices (Amendment) Act 2002 has made some modifications to the licensing process, but the details are beyond the scope of this book.

[72] There are also regulations governing the exposure of outside workers to radiation: European Communities (Protection of Outside Workers from Ionising Radiation) Regulations 1994 (SI 1994/144).

[73] *Report of the Health and Safety Authority Advisory Committee on the Health Services* Health and Safety Authority (2001).

[74] Social Welfare (Consolidation) Act 1993, ss 48 *ff.*

[75] See Medical Practitioners Act 1978 s 59: any certificate required to be signed by a doctor and one which is not signed by a doctor will not 'be of any validity or effect'.

[76] Details on all forms of benefits and specific current entitlements can be found on the website of the Department of Social and Family Affairs: www.welfare.ie.

[77] A patient may be entitled to payments to help cover medical expenses incurred as a result of an accident at work or a disease contracted at work if he is not otherwise entitled to free medical care and the expenses are reasonable and necessary.

[78] Death Benefits include Widow's Pension, Dependant Widower's Pension, Orphan's Pension, Dependant Parent's Pension, Funeral Grant.

[79] For more details, see Department of Social and Family Affairs *A Guide to Occupational Diseases Prescribed Under the Occupational Injuries Benefits Scheme*, Leaflet SW 33.

[80] This is not a complete list of all occupational diseases, but represents some of those specified in Department of Social and Family Affairs documentation.

[81] Certain conditions attach to the payment of occupational injury benefit for deafness: (i) hearing loss must amount to at least 50db in each ear, (ii) the person must have been in the prescribed occupation for ten years or more, (iii) any claim must be made within five years of leaving that employment.

[82] A doctor who wishes to issue certificates completes a form (MC 8) in which she agrees to abide by the rules for certification. If a doctor changes the address from which she proposes to prescribe or adds an additional address, she will be required to complete another form (MC 8(a)).

[83] For example, infection in a child care or hospital worker.

[84] On forms MC1 and MC2, there is a box marked 'Code D' which the doctor may tick to denote either that including the precise details of the patient's illness on his form could be detrimental to his physical or mental wellbeing or that disclosure of the illness to a third party could cause distress. In either case, a Medical Officer from the Department will contact the certifying doctor for a confidential report.

Chapter 10

The Practitioner and the Lawyer

INTRODUCTION

[10.01]

This chapter looks briefly at the nature of the legal profession,[1] before examining areas of the intersection between work of the clinician and the work of the lawyer. Foremost among these is the role of the clinician as expert witness. However, we will also look at how a typical legal action proceeds from the initiation of a claim to the hearing of the case in court. The chapter will finish with a brief review of what takes place in the courtroom and some simple guidelines to help the practitioner through what can seem like a daunting experience.

In the preponderance of cases, the first point of contact between a clinical practitioner and the law will be through the medium of a solicitor. Solicitors are the public face of the law, dealing with the majority of individuals who have a legal problem or grievance. There are certain situations in which a person may directly access a barrister, but these are rare. Solicitors carry out all initial correspondence relating to a claim: notifying the other party of the potential action, securing the reports necessary to further the claim (such as reports from a doctor on injuries sustained in an accident) and the retention of a barrister.

The barrister offers opinions on whether a case is likely to succeed in court and she will also, if the case proceeds to court, typically be the person responsible for presenting the case, although many solicitors take responsibility for advocacy, especially in the lower courts.[2]

A solicitor's letter will generally be a request for information of some sort. The first obligation on the practitioner is to make sure she understands what is being sought. Lawyers are as guilty as health professionals, especially doctors, of using jargon. It is important to be certain that one understands the legal letter and to seek clarification from the sender if anything in it is incomprehensible, obscure or equivocal. Most commonly, a solicitor's letter to a practitioner will request information regarding a patient whom the practitioner has treated for injuries in an accident and this form of information, 'the medico-legal report' is dealt with at section **[10.02]-[10.04]**. However, a letter may also on occasion be a hostile one, alleging wrongdoing on the part of the clinician or seeking information relevant to alleged wrongdoing on the part of the clinician's employer. In such cases, the matter should be put into the hands of the relevant body: the clinician's insurers or solicitors. We return later to the question of how legal action progresses (see section **[10.10]**).

Reports and expert witnesses

Medico-legal reports

[10.02]

In theory, any health care professional may be called upon to write a professional opinion for use in a legal case. In practice, however, doctors, physiotherapists and occupational therapists write the majority of such reports. This is because reports are most commonly required for assessing personal injuries together with the consequences and treatment of those injuries. Any health professional may also be brought in as a 'non-treating expert witness' to give an expert opinion on the facts of an injury or on the treatment a patient has received. In this chapter, we will look at a hypothetical report on personal injuries allegedly caused by negligence, but the same rules apply generally for any medico-legal opinion that a practitioner is called upon to write.

Example 1

For the purposes of looking at medico-legal reports and expert witnesses, let us assume the following: Mr A was walking past a building site when a hod-load of bricks fell from on high, landing on him: injuries resulted and Mr A attended his doctor. She assessed him, recording his injuries and organising investigations and treatments. Over the ensuing weeks, Mr A continues to make a recovery and is now pursuing legal action against the builder.

Mr A is the *plaintiff*; the company running the building site is the *defendant*.

The doctor (but it could just as easily be any health professional involved in the treatment) receives a request from the solicitor acting for Mr A. She requests a report of the investigation and treatment of the patient's injuries and the doctor's opinion as to the diagnosis and prognosis.

A medico-legal report may be also be generated when a health care professional not originally involved in the patient's care is requested to conduct an examination for the other side in the legal dispute. For example, the legal advisers for the building company may wish to have their own assessment of the plaintiff's injuries and they may ask Mr A to attend a doctor of their choosing. In such a case, the protocol for preparing a report is the same.

There are some questions the health professional will wish to consider at this point as precursors to the actual production of a report.

Can the request for a report be refused?

This is not a hostile request for information so, in theory, there is no reason why the health professional should wish to refuse. Perhaps she might be worried that aspects of her treatment were substandard and that this might be exposed in the court, but even if that were the case, it would not be grounds to refuse. Looked at in its simplest terms, this request effectively comes from the patient through his solicitor asking that his own notes be released to help advance his legal argument for compensation. A doctor, like other healthcare professionals, has a duty to care for her patient and furnishing a legal report based on the patient's notes so that a patient can progress a legal action for compensation for a physical or psychiatric injury is part of that extended duty of care. Certainly, as far as doctors are concerned, the Irish Medical Council *Guide to Ethical Conduct and Behaviour* states that:

> 'Doctors have a responsibility to provide medical reports for solicitors or insurance companies on behalf of patients they have seen or treated professionally or for whom they have been responsible. However such reports should not be given without the patient's permission.'[3]

The courts have agreed with this approach, reasoning that patients who wish to have their notes released for the purpose of legal action should be able to ask the doctor to release them without having to resort to even more legal action to compel the release of the notes.[4] Furthermore, under Data Protection legislation,[5] a patient has a statutory right of access to his records, which can only be absolutely refused in exceptional circumstances.

The reality is that a health professional is not generally in a position to refuse a request to release information that would, if released, facilitate the smooth running of justice and the achievement of its aims. If the doctor were to refuse, the lawyer for the patient would probably seek an order for 'discovery' from the court, compelling her to 'discover' the documents and release them to the legal team. In such a case, it is likely that the health professional would bear the financial costs of the patient having to resort to such a measure. The same is true even if a request for details is a hostile one, although in such situations the question of the release of information should be mediated by the practitioners employers, insurers or legal advisers.

Is consent necessary?

Confidentiality is a prerequisite for a satisfactory relationship between healthcare professional and patient.[6] One of the ways in which the general requirement that the clinician must safeguard the patient's confidences may be overridden is if the patient consents to the disclosure of confidential information. In the case where a letter is received from a solicitor, it is possible to infer that in approaching the solicitor, who in turn has written seeking the information, the patient has given implied consent to the release of the notes.

It may not be that simple. It may be that the patient was not aware that a request has issued from the solicitor to the doctor. A patient may be under the impression that the solicitor will send him to a third party doctor, rather than relying on information from his own physician. There may be relevant elements in the clinical records that the patient would prefer not to have disclosed, to the extent that the patient would rather discontinue the legal action.[7] It is always wiser to elicit express consent from a patient to the disclosure of information to any outside party, even where that consent may be inferred from the patient's conduct (such as, in this case, a solicitor's letter). Obtaining consent allows for a discussion with the patient, in broad terms, of the information that is to be disclosed. Such consent, as in all cases when consent is sought, should be recorded in writing and signed by the patient where possible.

Contents of a medico-legal report

The Preliminaries

[10.03]

Most legal cases 'settle', which means that the two sides agree on a mutually satisfactory arrangement before the matter reaches court. A court case is expensive and in general the losing side will have to pay all the legal costs of both sides. Therefore, if one side believes that it is going to lose the case, then it may be prudent to minimise losses and to agree a settlement that is not compounded by the addition of lawyers' fees.

This is not the universal rule, however. Some cases will go to court or will at least seriously threaten to go to court. If a doctor writes a medico-legal report for a case, she may then be called upon as a witness to testify as to the contents of that report. A health care professional should therefore never write anything in a report that she would not be happy to stand over in court. It is important to stress that a practitioner is not appearing in court or involved in the litigation in order to take one side or the other. It is up to the patient's legal team, not his doctor, to make the case for the patient. The role of the medical expert witness – even if she is preparing a report or testifying on behalf of her own patient – is to be objective, fair and truthful. An appearance of bias in a medico-legal report or in courtroom testimony, such as patently exaggerating the effect of a very minor injury or drawing extravagant conclusions not based on the recorded clinical findings may undermine the report and testimony.[8] Again, the Irish Medical Council has offered guidance for doctors that is useful for other practitioners:

> 'Reports must be factual and true. They are not to be influenced by the fee or by pressure from anyone to omit some details or to embellish others, and strict accuracy must be observed. They should concentrate on the medical problems referred to and omit extraneous details.'[9]

It is important to point out that any information withheld from a medico-legal report may subsequently be obtained by the other side by a court application to 'discover' the original notes (or copies of them). This might be done in an especially contentious or potentially costly case in order to verify that any medical report tallies precisely with the notes taken in the consultations that the medico-legal report claims to represent.

While the practitioner will charge a fee for the report,[10] the payment does not or should not sway her from her duty to report on the clinical facts. Also, while the fee charged by the solicitor to her client may be contingent upon a certain outcome ('no win, no fee'), the practitioner is by no means obliged to operate under the same constraints. Payment in advance for a medico-legal report is the norm but subsequent failure by a doctor to furnish a prompt report is frowned upon by the Medical Council.[11] Excessive delay in producing a report or outright failure to provide a report at all, even though a fee has been received from the patient or his solicitor, is unethical conduct.[12]

Quick Reference Guide 10.1

Preliminary issues in medico-legal reports

- A practitioner may be called upon to write a medico-legal report either regarding a patient whom she has treated or as an independent expert concerning a person she has not treated.
- A request for a medico-legal report cannot generally be refused: a patient has a right to pursue legal action and the clinician will generally not be entitled to stand in the way of the exercise of that right.
- The patient's consent to disclosure of the facts necessary for a medico-legal report should be obtained, preferably in writing. The patient should understand what is to be disclosed.
- A charge may be levied for writing a medico-legal report that may be payable in advance. Once payment is made, it would be unethical for the practitioner to withhold the report.
- A medico-legal document produced by an expert is not supposed to be *for* one side or another. It should be professional and dispassionate, dwelling only on the facts and avoiding any tendency to be economical with information unhelpful to the patient's cause. A practitioner is under no obligation to change a report at the request of a solicitor if to do so would involve compromising her clinical assessment of the patient.

The details

[10.04]

The purpose of a medico-legal report is essentially to provide clarity about the past, current and expected future health status of the patient with particular reference to the incident that is the subject of the legal dispute. In our example, the report is concerned with any injuries resulting from the falling bricks.

All the information might be readily available to the doctor if she was the one to treat the patient, but she may also require further opportunities to examine the patient. This may be necessary to clarify certain matters or to verify that certain problems complained of by the patient have resolved (or are continuing). If a practitioner who has not previously been involved in the treatment of a patient – is required to assess him for medico-legal purposes, then as well as conducting the assessment, she will need access to his original clinical records. This is because much time may have elapsed since the original incident and the doctor will need to know what the starting point was. A doctor who has treated a patient and who receives a request from the 'other side's' doctor for a report should provide it. There has been a tradition among doctors of minimising the information furnished in such circumstances. Such a practice goes against the notion that the practitioner is expected to be fair and unbiased in the medico-legal arena.

A medico-legal report should contain at a minimum the following information, although not necessarily in the order that is set out below:

(a) Name, date of birth and occupation of the patient.

(b) The history of the complaint at issue and brief medical background, where appropriate.

(c) The findings of any examination.

(d) The results of any tests or x-rays.

(e) Diagnosis.

(f) The likely medical cause or origin of the diagnosis.

(g) Any treatment given.

(h) The course of the complaint following treatment.

(i) The future likely course of the complaint including any future needs or treatment.

Fleshing out each of these headings gives a clearer indication of why each is necessary in order to produce a rounded report.

Personal details

This information provides clarity and context, establishing the identity and something of the nature of the patient who is under discussion in the report. The age of a patient may go some way towards explaining why his injuries are different from those that might be expected from the injury in question, eg, Mr A may be more likely to suffer serious injuries from being hit by the bricks if he is older. Similarly, a patient's occupation is crucial background information. An innocuous-seeming back injury may present no problems in terms of returning to work for a computer operator but may be an insurmountable obstacle to a professional athlete or manual worker, necessitating a different course of treatment and a different prognosis.

History

The history of the complaint is one of the most important parts of the whole report. Here it is important to recall the role of the person compiling the report: she is not an advocate for the patient; she is there merely to document the medical facts. The details of the incident that led to the injuries should only be dwelt upon insofar as they are relevant and should not attribute blame. It is not the doctor's role to attribute blame, either to the patient or to any other party: she was not a witness to the incident. So a medical report that records that:

> 'Mr A was walking down the street when he was struck by some debris falling from above'

would be preferable to one that states that:

> 'Mr A was walking down the street when a builder, without looking at what he was doing, threw some bricks on top of him. The scaffolding from which the bricks were thrown was obviously unsafe and there was a strong suspicion that the builder in question was under the influence of alcohol.'

All the matters documented in the second letter may well be true but they are not within the knowledge of the practitioner compiling the medical facts.

Background information should be included where relevant and it may be especially important to secure the patient's consent in this regard. If a person has a pre-existing psychiatric history that has been aggravated by the accident, for example, then that may need to be documented in the medico-legal report by way of context for the complaints the patient has been experiencing. Mr A might, since being struck by the bricks, have experienced a re-emergence of previously dormant anxiety problems, making it impossible for him to go out to work. The patient may need to be informed that the practitioner deems it medically relevant to include such information, so that his consent to the release of that information is valid.

Note also that if there have been any previous reports relating to the same complaint, it will be helpful to indicate as much and to refer to any previous reports.

Findings of examination

The findings of the examination should be recorded as minutely and as clearly as possible in the patient's notes. It may be many months before a request arrives for a medico-legal report of an examination or years before the doctor or therapist has to testify in court concerning her findings at the initial examination. Whatever mechanisms one can use to record signs and symptoms more accurately at the time of an examination likely to have medico-legal ramification, the greater one will appreciate it when it comes to writing or justifying a report.[13]

Results

Results of tests or x-rays may add to the picture. If they do not, then reference to them in the report can be cursory or absent.

Diagnosis

The diagnosis is simply the clinician's opinion as to the underlying problem giving rise to the patient's complaints. It may include the background medical history where that has contributed to the diagnosis, eg, if Mr A's accident has exacerbated his pre-existing anxiety state, then the latter information may need to be included in the diagnosis.

Medical cause

Most legal cases, especially those relating to physical or psychiatric injuries arising from negligence, come down to causation.[14] If the accident in question did not *cause* the injury in question then the person responsible for the accident cannot be responsible for the injury. This is where the professional skill of the person compiling the report is called upon most stringently. It is up to the clinician to express an opinion as to whether the complaint is consistent with the incident alleged. It might not be possible to do so in some cases and, if so, that should be stated.

One important factor to bear in mind is the 'standard of proof'.[15] In a civil case,[16] the person making the allegation (in this case, Mr A alleging that the builders were negligent in allowing something to fall on the person beneath) has to prove 'on the balance of probabilities' that the incident occurred and that the injuries were a result of the incident. The balance of probabilities merely means whether the various elements of the case were more probably related than not.[17] Accordingly, in most legal cases, a medico-legal report will need at the very least to express an opinion as to whether, on the balance of probabilities, the injuries reported were caused by the incident alleged.

In a criminal case, the standard of proof is more onerous – a person alleging a criminal act (generally the prosecutor is the Director of Public Prosecutions) has to prove the allegations against the accused 'beyond reasonable doubt'. In such cases, medical or other evidence will generally also need to be couched in such terms. It may need to be stated that it is beyond reasonable doubt that X met his death by strangulation/stabbing/shooting, as appropriate. Doctors will rarely, and other health care professionals will almost never, be involved in writing reports for criminal cases unless they are specifically employed in a forensic medical role but the higher standard of proof necessary is something that needs to be borne in mind.

In a medico-legal report for a civil case it is best to couch one's opinion in terms such as 'reasonable clinical probability' or 'likely' or 'probably', all of which terms mean simply that it is more that 50% likely that the clinical findings are related to any given potential cause.

It may be desirable to leave diagnosis and cause until the very end of the report, by way of summary, but there is no hard and fast rule prescribed for medico-legal reports.

Treatment

Details of therapeutic interventions will go to show how extensive has been the need for medical or paramedical care. If inter-disciplinary referral has occurred eg from a doctor to an occupational therapist, this should be indicated so that a report can be sought from that other practitioner if appropriate. If the person writing the initial report has enough details from a professional colleague (perhaps in letters from a physiotherapist or hospital specialist) then the nature of that colleague's treatment can be included by reference to the letter. The person compiling the report should not hypothesise on the treatment given by someone else unless she has the necessary information (such as a letter) to make such a claim with authority.

Present and future course of the injury

The overall prognosis gives clarity to the legal proceedings. If a doctor's opinion is that a condition has resolved or stabilised, then the legal action may proceed on the basis that future medical uncertainty has been minimised. However, if the condition has not stabilised, further reports may be necessary. To take the example of Mr A, he may still be undergoing physiotherapy or may be enduring a period of observation before a surgeon decides whether to operate. Such matters should be included so that a temporary halt can be put on proceedings or so that further information may be sought from other practitioners.

The language of a medico-legal report

[10.05]

It is very exciting for both lawyers and health care practitioners to be able to speak in a language that no one else understands, but it is not always helpful to communication between the professions or between the professions and the public. It is more desirable that both camps should use unambiguous language when talking to each other, as free of professional jargon and terminology as possible.

The recipient of a legal letter that is shrouded with complicated legal terms should seek clarification of what is required before acting on a interpretation of its contents that transpires to be incorrect. Similarly a health care practitioner providing a report for a solicitor is effectively doing so in order to make matters clear, to assist the two sides in dispute and, if necessary, to assist the court of law. The aim is not to impress or to confuse with clinical erudition and obscure references. Complex medical terms may need translation or elucidation, perhaps in a glossary attached to the report or by putting a layman's translation of each medical word in brackets after the word when it first occurs in the text of the report. References to anatomy may usefully be aided by an indication as to where in the body that particular muscle, tendon or nerve is to be found. A medico-legal report will predominantly be read by people who are not versed in medical or paramedical training and it should always be written with this fact in mind.

Expert witnesses

[10.06]

Witnesses are not ordinarily supposed to give opinions. Usually their contribution is merely to give the facts of what they saw, heard or did. It is then up the judge or the jury to form an opinion based on the evidence that witnesses give. Experts are an exception to this rule. Judges, lawyers and juries do not know everything and sometimes it is necessary to seek the opinion of someone expert in a particular field. In the case of health care or clinical issues in particular, expert opinions are often necessary. They make take the form of the medico-legal report prepared by the patient's own doctor, physiotherapist or dentist such as that discussed in the previous section. Expert testimony may also involve another expert being brought in to give an objective view of the clinical situation. So in reality, the term 'expert witness' has two meanings.

Treating versus non-treating

Treating experts are the practitioners who have treated the patient and who can report and testify on the patient's injuries, treatment and prognosis. Such a report may be tested in court if the case goes to court and the facts in the report or any other facts surrounding the case are in dispute. The writer may be called to testify about the details of her report. If that happens, the witness is an expert witness, but one who is testifying about matters that are a result of her professional experience and knowledge based on her treatment of the patient. She can be termed a 'Treating Expert Witness' or a 'Witness of Primary Fact'. We looked in detail at the nature of treating expert witness's report at section **[10.03]-[10.04]** above.

The other type of expert witness is one who is called upon to give an expert opinion, *not* having treated the patient. If certain issues are in dispute in a legal case, such as the question of whether the care provided to a particular patient was negligent, the legal teams may not be content to simply leave the matter to be haggled out by the parties to the dispute. Instead one side, or both, may wish to call professional witnesses who were not involved in the initial dispute but who have the qualifications, experience and reputation to be able to comment with authority on what took place. An apt term for such witnesses would be 'Non-treating Expert Witnesses', insofar as they were not active participants in the treatment of the person involved and their role is to offer an outsider's view of the medical facts.

Example 2

Mr A's legal action against the builders proceeds to court. Both forms of expert witness may be involved. In the first place Mr A's doctor testifies on her examination and diagnosis of Mr A. She is a *treating* expert witness. The builders wish to question the truth of Mr A's complaints and they call an orthopaedic surgeon to testify that the pains complained of by Mr A are, in his opinion, not consistent with the injuries that the treating doctor identified in her report. The surgeon is a *non-treating* expert. Mr A's legal team may also call its own non-treating expert in an attempt to support the findings detailed by the treating doctor.

The Non-Treating Expert's Report

[10.07]

As far as principles are concerned, the rules for non-treating professionals who prepare reports are the same as those for treating expert witness. They should be truthful, unbiased, objective and fair. Of course, because they are being retained by one side and because their opinions will not be used if they do not advance the case being brought, expert witnesses may appear to be acting as 'hired guns'. Such a perception is often, but not universally, inaccurate. In many medical cases there is an honest difference of opinion and expert witnesses are retained to explore that difference of opinion. However, the principle that while an expert is called by one side or the other, she is not supposed to actually take that side, is not always observed as scrupulously as it should be. Yet, the principle remains true nonetheless. As we will see when we look below at the recommendations of the *Woolf Report*, some jurisdictions have begun to wrestle with the perception of the medico-legal hired gun.[18]

Expert witnesses are required in many cases, not only medical ones. Their role is essentially to discuss and explain issues that are not ordinarily within the knowledge of the judge or of either legal team. In the case of our man injured by falling bricks, the practitioner who cared from him may be called upon, as an expert witness, to explain her notes and perhaps to be examined by the barrister for the defendants about her findings. However, there may also be a dispute about other issues. Expert witnesses not involved in the care of the patient may be called to offer an opinion on any number of matters, including those unrelated to health care. An expert witness from the scaffolding business may offer evidence on whether, given the type of precautions used by the building company, it was possible for the debris to have fallen from the site at all, and so on.

In order to formulate a non-treating expert opinion, the expert will need to have as many details of the case forwarded to her as possible. In general, when a non-treating expert witness is retained to give an opinion, her report may be accompanied by a *curriculum vitae* indicating her qualifications to offer the opinion she has compiled. This summary may include posts held, recent publications and a record of recent previous cases in which the practitioner in question has acted as an expert witness. While there are no specific rules stipulating precisely what a non-treating expert's report to the Irish courts must contain, some guidelines can be derived from England and Wales, where Court Rules[19] dictate that an expert's report to the court must do the following:

(1) Give details of the expert's qualifications.

(2) Give details of any literature or other material on which the expert has relied in making the report.

(3) Contain a statement setting out the substance of all facts and instructions given to the expert, which are material to the opinions expressed in the report or upon which those opinions are based.

(4) Make clear which of the facts stated in the report are within the expert's own knowledge.

(5) Say who carried out any examination, measurement, test or experiment which the expert has used for the report, give the qualifications of that person, and say whether or not the test or experiment has been carried out under the expert's supervision.

(6) Where there is a range of opinion on the matters dealt with in the report–

(a) summarise the range of opinion, and

(b) give reasons for his own opinion.

(7) Contain a summary of the conclusions reached.

(8) If the expert is not able to give his opinion without qualification, state the qualification.

(9) Contain a statement that the expert understands his duty to the court, and has complied and will continue to comply with that duty.[20]

Two matters are critically important for the non-treating expert witness. The first is that she identifies precisely what aspect of the legal case her expert opinion is being sought, and secondly, she must be sure that she does in fact possess the necessary expertise to give an authoritative opinion on the matter in question. A court is entitled to reject, or dilute the importance of, the evidence of a witness whom it feels is not sufficiently expert in the field she is testifying about.

The Woolf Report – a way forward for the Republic of Ireland?

[10.08]

Changes took place in the United Kingdom during the latter years of the 20th century, based on the *Woolf Report*, which took a panoramic view of the problems facing the administration of the civil justice system in England and Wales. One result of the report was the introduction of a new set of rules[22] that made it explicit that the role of the expert witness should be to help the court and not merely to aid the side by which she is retained. In fact Lord Woolf, one of the English Law Lords, explicitly criticised the degree to which expert witnesses had become paid advocates for one side or the other. The report resulted in four main changes to the way in which non-treating expert testimony is to be used in litigation in England and Wales:

(i) Clinical experts are to be appointed jointly, by agreement between both sides or by order of the court. As a result, reports are submitted to the court itself and not to the legal representatives of the parties involved in the legal dispute.

(ii) The content of clinical reports given to the courts is now standardised (see the sample contents of a 'non-treating' experts report set out at section **[10.07]** above), including the requirement that experts set out not only their own personal opinion but also that of 'any other recognised body of opinion.' In other words the report must offer not merely the doctor's opinion but also any research that backs up or even undermines her opinion.

(iii) Expert evidence will only be required where it is necessary to help resolve the issues before the court and most evidence will be provided in writing. Because the expert is appointed by the court or by agreement, there is less likely to be a requirement for lengthy or combative examination of the witness in court.

(iv) The court has greater latitude to limit the amount of money paid to an expert witness.

There are neutral expert clinical witnesses in other countries, such as Germany and Greece, while Italy and Portugal, together with the Republic of Ireland, continue to permit each party to the case to nominate its own experts.

There is one exception built into the *Woolf Report*, which is that in clinical negligence cases, both sides may use their own experts. The reason for this is because one defence to an allegation of negligence is that one's actions were in accordance with a reasonable body of clinical opinion, albeit not the majority school of thought. A single neutral expert may have trouble accurately representing both sides of a potentially complex argument and accordingly in such circumstances the parties to the case may introduce their own witnesses to make the arguments for different bodies of opinion.[23]

There are strong arguments to say that the costs and time involved in personal injury litigation could be greatly reduced if such a system were introduced in Ireland.

Quick Reference Guide 10.2

The non-treating expert witness

- A non-treating expert witness is one who was not responsible for the care of the patient involved in the legal case, but whose expertise is such that she is in a position to offer an opinion on the facts of the case.
- In principle, although an expert witness is normally retained by one side or another in the legal dispute, she is under a duty to be impartial and not to advocate for one result or another. The allegation is often made, however, that some expert witnesses are prepared to act as hired guns.
- The ideal non-treating witness's report should give not only the qualifications of the expert to offer an opinion and the expert's opinion itself, but should also include details of any schools of thought inconsistent with the expert's opinion.
- In England, the *Woolf Report* has attempted to reduce the adversarial element of expert testimony by introducing a system where there is only a single, court-appointed expert who reviews all sides of the matter in dispute. The only exception to this new rule is in clinical negligence cases. In circumstances where an expert is appointed, evidence must as far as possible be in writing to avoid time consuming oral testimony.

What happens to medico-legal reports after they are prepared and submitted?

[10.09]

Prior to the late 1990s some controversy surrounded the use of expert witness reports, both treating and non-treating. Reports obtained by one side in the legal dispute could formerly be kept secret from the other side until the court hearing, unless the other side obtained a court order ordering disclosure (or 'discovery') of the documents. This added to the delay in the pre-trial phase of the legal dispute. It also meant that one side, if it obtained a report from an expert late in the pre-trial phase, could produce that report unheralded in a form of 'trial by ambush' without the other side having sufficient time to mount a challenge to it.

In order to simplify the use of expert reports of all forms in personal injury cases (which form the vast bulk of cases where expert reports are required), new rules were introduced in 1998 by the courts to govern the use of such reports.[24] The rules only apply in personal injury cases, however those personal injuries were caused, and they apply to the reports or statements of 'accountants, actuaries, architects, dentists, doctors, engineers, occupational therapists, psychologists, psychiatrists, scientists, or any other expert whatsoever.'[25]

The new rules oblige the plaintiff's lawyers to send to the defence a list of all experts whom it intends to call as witnesses in court proceedings. Within seven days, the defendant's legal team must reply with its own proposed list of experts. Within one week of that, both sides must exchange any reports received to date. Any further reports that arise after that time must be exchanged as soon as possible. Once exchanged, the reports provided by one side to the other can be shown to the recipients' own expert who can then assess them and may be able to advise on any shortcomings. If one side feels that the other is not complying with its obligations under the Rules, it may bring an application to the court to force the other side to comply.

There are good things and bad things about the decision to adopt the 1998 Rules. On the positive side, the two sides in a legal dispute can maximise the amount of medical evidence before them in order to reach a prompt decision as to whether or not to proceed with the case, to settle it or to abandon it. This, it is hoped, will speed up litigation and make it less expensive by reducing the number of applications that have to be made to the court to force disclosure of reports that may or may not exist in the filing cabinets of the other side. Similarly, failure to comply with the rules can result in the report that would have been relied on if it had been exchanged in accordance with the rules being rendered inadmissible, or even the whole case being 'struck out' by the judge.

However, one problem with the system is that each side has only to disclose the reports of those witnesses whom it intends to call as witnesses in the trial. The difficulty with this is obvious: assume that a patient is bringing an action against a radiologist for burns sustained during a procedure. The patient is subsequently referred to ten different doctors by his lawyers, and nine of the physicians say that there is no evidence that the alleged injuries were caused by the radiologist's actions, but rather were possibly caused by something else. Only one doctor asserts that the radiologist's actions were to blame. The lawyers decide to call only this last doctor to give oral evidence and in the circumstances they are obliged only to declare her report, while the nine other unfavourable reports may be ignored. It could of course be argued that it is up to the defendant radiologist's lawyers to have the plaintiff examined and to obtain any reports that may favourable to the radiologist's side. But it could also be argued that justice is more satisfactorily served if *all* legal reports obtained for the purpose of legal action in personal injury cases by both sides were subject to disclosure, rather than permitting each side to cherry-pick favourable opinions.

THE COURSE OF LEGAL ACTION

The first steps

[10.10]

In talking about 'legal action' here, we focus on civil cases, such as injuries resulting from road traffic accidents or claims of negligence or family disputes. There are important differences between civil and criminal procedure, but it is the former type of case that is far more likely to impact on a clinician's work, life and livelihood.[26]

Anyone can start a legal action against anyone else. The claim may not succeed: a solicitor may refuse to take the case as being frivolous, a barrister may advise that a case has no chance of succeeding, a court may throw it out, but nonetheless it is the right of any individual or body to institute legal proceedings against any other individual or body. The person who brings the case is the plaintiff and the person denying the allegations made by the plaintiff is the defendant.[27]

The seniority of the court that hears a case is proportionate to the value of the claim.[28] The most senior court in which a case can be initiated is the High Court. In most civil cases there will be no jury.

What happens once an allegation is made?

[10.11]

> **Example 3**
>
> A GP prescribes some antibiotics to a patient. She knew, or would have known had she looked at the patient's chart, that the patient was allergic to penicillin, but nonetheless she prescribed penicillin. The patient suffered a massive allergic reaction and was subsequently found to have suffered from brain damage. The patient's family alleges that the doctor was negligent in prescribing the antibiotics and commences legal proceedings.

What has arisen on the facts of our example is a claim for damages as a result of the consequences of the doctor's allegedly negligent actions. It is a civil case between the patient and the doctor, falling into the categories of personal injury and medical negligence.

The patient or someone acting on his behalf will go to a solicitor. The solicitor will make some inquiries about the facts and commence assembling the necessary material in order to build the case. Among the first things she must do is to notify the doctor of the potential legal case. It is a fundamental rule of justice that a person cannot be expected to defend herself against charges that she knows nothing about, so the solicitor will write to the doctor, notifying her that it is intended to start legal proceedings for negligence.

The doctor will, or at least, should, contact her insurers or solicitor and they will handle her legal interests from there. If the insurers are contacted, they will put their solicitor onto the case, while if the doctor contacts her own solicitor (this would be unusual, as most doctors would have professional indemnity insurance), then the legal teams move onto the next step, which is the 'Exchange of Pleadings'. The doctor's solicitors contact the patient's solicitor with the simple information that they will be 'acting' for the doctor. Until they hear from the patient's solicitors, they will generally say nothing and admit nothing. During this time, the clinician's duty of care to the patient does not abate.

It may be the case that the necessary mutual trust between practitioner and patient will have broken down to the extent that the patient may being going elsewhere for his medical care, nonetheless, any clinical issues that arise will still have to be dealt with or forwarded to the patient's new practitioner.

Summons

Generally a personal injuries claim (and our example above is such a claim) is initiated by a document called a 'summons' and assuming the plaintiff wishes to proceed, the issuing of a summons is the next stage. There are several different types of summons with a variety of different names and the type used depends on the type of legal action that is being brought, the legal remedy being sought and the court in which the case is to be heard. A barrister or possibly the solicitor herself will normally assess the relative strength of the case and the likely damages that could be awarded and take the decision on which court is the preferable forum for the case.[29]

The appropriate summons will then be issued through a court office where it receives the number that will identify the case until it is seen through to its conclusion. The summons requests the other side to respond (called 'entering an appearance') to the central office and also briefly outlines what the case is about. A summons is 'served' on the defendant, usually by bringing it or posting it to her home or place of business.

The defendant 'enters an appearance' when her solicitors contact the central office to indicate in writing that they will be defending the claim. The ball is back in the plaintiff's court and matters then move on to the next stage.

Pleadings

The plaintiff will issue a 'Statement of Claim', setting out what he alleges took place, the damage he suffered, the nature of the redress he is seeking and why he should win the case. Pleadings are written in tortuous legal prose, repetitive to the point of tedium, using well-worn ritual phrases to set out the case. Usually, the Statement of Claim, which is often drawn up (or drafted) by a barrister, will include every possible allegation, every possible damage and the maximum possible redress. It is considerably easier subsequently to drop matters from the Statement of Claim than it is to insert them.

The doctor's solicitors may first seek further information about the claim before responding. However, they will eventually respond in kind, typically denying everything and also pointing out matters that may undermine the plaintiff's case in a document unsurprisingly called the 'defence'. For example, it might be that the doctor alleges that she in fact inquired about penicillin allergy before writing the prescription and that the patient denied that he had ever had any such problem. If this were proven, it might amount to 'contributory negligence' on the part of the patient, which in turn could minimise the doctor's liability.[30] The general practice in a defence is to deny absolutely everything. The more the defendant denies the more the other side has to prove if or when the matter comes to court.

Each set of pleadings might raise new issues for the other side to consider and so the plaintiff may wish to issue a supplementary set of pleadings to address issues raised by the defendants and vice versa. This process may go on for a long time, but once all issues have been teased out in the written pleadings, pleadings close and matters may proceed.

Before the trial

It might be that after the exchange of pleadings, one side or the other realises that it has no arguable case. The doctor's solicitors may realise that the doctor's actions were indefensible or alternatively the patient's legal advisers may discover that some other event (such as the care received in hospital, rather than the doctor's prescription) was responsible for the patient's brain damage. In the first case a settlement may be agreed, while in the second the case may be dropped and the patient may instead pursue an action against the hospital. A settlement of the case can occur at any time, right up to the time of the trial and sometimes even as a result of negotiations conducted between the parties during the trial. For example, a particular witness may give a very different testimony to that expected, resulting in a rapid reappraisal by one side of its chances of success, leading in turn to a decision to settle. The bulk of all legal disputes that get as far as a summons being issued will settle without ever reaching court.[31]

If the case is proceeding, then one side or other may wish to get their hands on certain documents to advance the case they are hoping to make. The patient's solicitors will almost certainly want the doctor's notes of her consultation with the patient. These may be obtained by an application to the court for 'discovery' of the document if the other side will not hand it over in response to a written request. The court will hear an application (in a hearing before and separate from the main trial) by the plaintiff's lawyers and the defendant's legal team will have the opportunity to contest the application if appropriate. Once the court is satisfied that the document can be identified and produced and that justice is best served by its production, it can order discovery of the relevant document.

Once a date is set for a trial, there will normally be an informal understanding between the practitioner (in circumstances where she is acting as an expert) and the relevant legal team that she will make herself available to give evidence in the trial. She will be on 'standby' and will typically charge a fee to compensate her for her time and/or for the loss of her practice for that day or portion of the day. The standby fee is variable: it may depend on the nature of the witness, the amount of time involved, the distance the witness has to travel etc. It is important to recognise that the standby arrangement and fee is a matter of courtesy between solicitor and practitioner. In fact, the solicitor would be entitled to issue a *sub poena*,[32] a court-backed order that a witness attend under penalty of punishment if she fails to attend. It is rare that this latter approach would be used, but in circumstances where the medical witness was refusing to attend or setting such conditions upon attending (such as charging an excessive fee) that were felt to be unacceptable, then a *sub poena* could be used.

Appearing in court

Evidence in a trial is given under oath, which can involve the witness swearing on the appropriate religious text or making a solemn affirmation without reference to any deity that she will tell the truth. Lying under oath is the offence of 'perjury' and can be punished by a jail sentence. In general evidence at a trial is given orally, but it may also be given by means of a sworn written statement, called an 'affidavit'. The preference for oral testimony is because it can be tested in court by cross-examination and the reaction of the witness to questioning may be informative for a judge or jury.

In general, the side making the allegation goes first in a trial: in a criminal trial that will be the prosecution; in a civil trial, the plaintiff. The barrister taking the case (although in some cases there may be more than one barrister on each side or a solicitor may take on the advocacy role of the barrister) makes opening submissions to the court and then takes the court through the evidence of the witnesses. Each witness is called and invited, through questioning by the lawyer, to relate the facts of the case. In general, witnesses who are not expert witnesses are not permitted to express opinions and their testimony will be confined to the facts. This initial process is called 'examination-in-chief'. After examination-in-chief is concluded, the barrister for the other side can question the witness in a process known as 'cross-examination'. The purpose of cross-examination is to attempt to point out problems or inconsistencies in the testimony given by the witness. It can sometimes be hostile and aggressive, depending on the personality of the barrister in question and the evidence given during examination-in-chief. Once the plaintiff or prosecution has called all its witnesses, it is the turn of the defence and the process of examination-in-chief and cross-examination repeats itself for the defence witnesses.

The judge oversees the running of the court and can give guidance and help to the witness if she feels herself overborne or confused. In most civil cases, the judge directs proceedings, resolves disputes arising during the trial and reaches the verdict.

When a practitioner is called as a witness in a trial, it will generally be as an expert.[33] Before the trial commences, there may be a consultation with the solicitor or barrister before the hearing. As an expert, the clinician is entitled and expected to express opinions. These opinions must be defensible and based on the facts of the case. She will be examined first by the side calling her and then cross-examined by the other side. A witness may bring notes into the box with her in order to refresh her memory. The advice often given to clinicians appearing in court is hackneyed but nonetheless useful: *dress up, speak up and shut up*. Answers should be honest, objective, accurate, within the witness's sphere of competence and to the point.

Does a clinician who is not the patient's usual treating clinician owe a duty to the patient to testify?

This question arose in an English case,[34] where a police doctor (not the woman's own doctor) examined a woman on foot of her allegations of sexual assault. The doctor made a written record of her findings, which indicated that the woman showed signs of having been sexually assaulted. When the case was listed for trial, the doctor was notified that she would be required as a witness. Four days into the trial and before she was called as a witness, the doctor went on a pre-arranged holiday and indicated that it would be at least a week before she could return. The judge refused to adjourn the trial and the case collapsed in the absence of the doctor's testimony.

The doctor was found guilty of contempt of court and was fined £3000 sterling. However, the woman who had been sexually assaulted also commenced an action against the doctor, claiming that she had failed in her duty of care by not testifying and was responsible for the psychiatric complications experienced by the woman following the collapse of the trial. The court decided that the doctor did *not* owe the woman any duty of care. In the first place, the police doctor was not the woman's own doctor and was therefore only under a duty of care during the examination not to make the patient any worse.[35] The matter would have been different if the doctor had been a doctor chosen by the woman or had been the woman's regular general practitioner. In the second place, as a matter of policy courts are reluctant to run the risk that professionals will steer clear of being witnesses for fear of being sued by those affected by their testimony (or in this case, lack of testimony).

While the 'passing doctor' is not under a duty to testify, the same could not be said either about the patient's own practitioner or a person who was retained, and paid, as an expert witness: both would be under a duty to attend. The former would be under a duty to attend as part of the patient's care, the latter as a part of the contract she has agreed with the side for whom she is acting as an expert.

Quick Reference Guide 10.3

Summary of what happens in legal action

- The sequence of legal action described is for a High Court civil action. Civil actions in the lower courts (the District Court and Circuit Court) involve a similar process. The level of the court in which a case is heard will depend on the monetary value of the claim in question.
- Anyone can initiate legal proceedings against another person although weak or frivolous cases may be winnowed out very early in proceedings
- A civil case generally commences when a solicitor for the person bringing the case (the plaintiff) notifies the person against whom the case is being brought (the defendant). In general, the defendant will contact her solicitor and they will handle matters from there.
- The plaintiff will issue a summons, to which the defendant's solicitors are expected to respond ('entering an appearance'). The two sides then trade the details of their allegations and defences ('pleadings'). When pleadings are closed, then matters can proceed to court.
- Prior to any appearance in court, there will generally be a meeting between the legal term and those they are representing. The court can also order the handing over of any documents required for either side to assess the strength of its case.
- At any time, up to and including the time when the trial is proceeding, the sides can agree to a mutually satisfactory settlement.
- A practitioner who is appearing in court to testify as a witness may offer her opinion on matters within her professional expertise. A practitioner appearing as a defendant or plaintiff will generally be confined to testifying on the facts of her own personal experience.
- Useful advice for testifying in court is *dress up, speak up and shut up.*

Endnotes

1 This topic is dealt with in some more detail for the non-legal reader in Appendix A (section **[A.12]**).

2 In civil cases (as opposed to criminal: see Appendix A (section **[A.10]**), the hierarchy of the courts is, from bottom up, District Court, Circuit Court, High Court, Supreme Court.

3 Medical Council *Guide to Ethical Conduct and Behaviour* (5th edn, 1998) para 9.1.

4 *C v C* [1946] 1 All ER 562.

5 Data Protection Act 1988 and the European Directive on The Protection of Individuals with Regard to the Processing of Personal Data 95/46/EC [1995] OJ L281. Discussed in ch 6 (section **[6.10]** *ff.*)

6 See ch 3, *The Practitioner-Patient Relationship, Ethics and Confidentiality.*

7 The author is aware of at least one case in which a medico-legal report implicitly but inadvertently disclosed the fact that, unknown to the doctor who reported on the consequences of the accident in all innocence from her clinical records, the patient was involved in an extra-marital liaison!

8 Some communications from solicitors to doctors request the doctor to emphasise certain elements of a report in order to 'improve' their client's chances. Such advances should be resisted unless to do so would be consistent with the clinical facts and the doctor's rationally held opinion based on those facts. It is worth bearing in mind that requests of this nature from a solicitor may simply be an indication that the solicitor is doing her best to advance the claim of her client rather than an attempt to override the practitioner's judgement.

9 *Guide to Ethical Conduct and Behaviour* (5th edn, 1998) para 9.2. Physiotherapy and Occupational Therapy Guidelines do not include formal guidance on this issue. It is suggested that the Medical Council regulations provide a good 'best practice' rule of thumb.

10 The fee will generally be agreed between the Law Society (which is the body that represents solicitors) and the relevant body representing the health professional in question. In cases where a patient is in receipt of Legal Aid in order to help him to pursue his case, the practitioner will be required to fill in a form (LA 5) in order to claim payment from the Legal Aid Board.

11 The Medical Council recommends an approximate time limit of two months, running from the date of the request for the report or the date of the examination, whichever is the later: *Guide to Ethical Conduct and Behaviour* (5th edn, 1998) para 9.3.

12 *Guide to Ethical Conduct and Behaviour* (5th edn, 1998) para 9.5. In some States in the USA, a 'licensed physician' may be charged with a criminal offence if she withholds medical records or overcharges for the release of records necessary to advance a legal claim.

13 Rather than merely describing a complex scar, drawing its extent as well may be a more vivid stimulant to the memory when it comes to reporting upon it or monitoring its recovery subsequently. The quality of the art matters not one bit: all that is important is that it acts as a reasonably accurate reminder and illustration. Photography is a more accurate but more expensive method of achieving the same end.

14 See ch 7, *Clinical Negligence* (section **[7.10]** *ff.*).

15 This is dealt with more thoroughly in Appendix A (section **[A.09]**) on the legal system.

16 A case that takes place between two private individuals or between companies or between an individual and a company or institution.

17 Put more simply, whether the chances were more than 50:50. See *Miller v Minister for Pensions* [1947] 2 All ER 372.

18 See Friston. New rules for expert witnesses –the last shots of the medico-legal hired gun. BMJ 1999; 318:1365-6

19 See the section on the *Woolf Report* at section **[10.08]**.

20 English Civil Procedure Rules Pt 35 Practice Direction 35 (2.2). In the United States, Federal Court Rules lay out the following contents to be included in a non-treating Expert Witness's report:

(a) A complete statement of all opinions reached by the expert, together with the reasons for having reached such opinions,

(b) Any relevant data or other information considered by the witness in forming the opinions,

(c) Any exhibits to be used as a summary of or in support for the opinions,

(d) The qualifications and publications of the expert,

(e) A declaration of any financial compensation to be paid for preparation, examination and testimony,

(f) A list of other cases in which the expert has testified within previous four years.

21 Access to Justice: final report to the Lord Chancellor on the civil justice system in England and Wales, London, HMSO, 1996. In force from April 1999. See also, 'Medics, lawyers and the courts', Lord Woolf [1997] 16 CJQ 302.

22 See ch 7, *Clinical Negligence*. Australia has proposed reform of the clinical negligence system, including the use of impartial peer review, rather than expert witness. See 'Australia proposes peer review of alleged negligence cases' BMJ 2002;325:565.

23 RSC (No 6) Disclosure of Reports and Statements 1998 (SI 1998/391).

24 RSC (No 45(1)(e)).

25 Although there are occasions where a clinician may be subject to criminal actions such as manslaughter or criminal negligence, both instances lie outside the scope of this chapter.

26 In a criminal case, they are generally the prosecution and the defendant (or accused) respectively.

27 The various jurisdictions are as follows: the District Court may award financial damages of up to €20,000, the Circuit Court up to €100,000 and the High Court all sums above this. Accordingly, if it were felt that a particular claim was 'worth' only a maximum of €50,000, then the appropriate forum would be the Circuit Court. For more on the damages awarded by the court, see the appendix (section **[A.10]**). If a case changes its value (perhaps because new damages come to light), agreement can be reached to allow the court to award damages higher than its usual jurisdiction or the case can be sent on for hearing to a higher court.

28 The lower the court, the less exacting the procedural requirements can sometimes be. The procedure that is described in the sections that follow is essentially that which takes place in a High Court action. In the lower courts the procedure is similar but less complex. There are generally fewer pleadings and the case is commenced by a document called a Civil Bill (Circuit Court) or Civil Summons (District Court), rather than a summons.

29 See ch 7, *Clinical Negligence* (section **[7.19]**).

30 In the *IBEC National Survey of Personal Injury Claims 2000*, a survey was conducted of 2,900 claims for personal injuries showing that less than one in ten of the cases that had been finalised had ever gone to a court hearing. In Byrne & McCutcheon, *The Irish Legal System* (4th edn, 2001) the authors suggest that about 85% of personal injury claims never come to court.

31 Pronounced 'supeena'.

32 Although this may not always be true. The practitioner may in this case be the defendant, as in the example of the doctor who inadvertently prescribed penicillin. While other doctors may be called as experts, the doctor herself would be an ordinary witness and would be confined to testifying about the facts of the consultation and its aftermath.

33 *Re N* [1999] Lloyds L Rep (Med) 257.

34 The court drew an analogy with the 'passing doctor' who gives assistance at the scene of a road traffic accident. In such a case the doctor would not be under as heavy a duty to the patient as she would be in the ordinary care of a patient during a non-accidental encounter.

Chapter 11

Psychiatry and Practice

INTRODUCTION

[11.01]

This chapter is concerned with the elements of the human mind and the way in which the law regards those elements, especially when there is any deficiency, aberration or dysfunction of mental processes. Firstly, we consider the question of involuntary detention of the psychiatric patient, an area of the law that has recently undergone the beginnings of a radical change. As well as looking at the modernisation of the law in this area, this chapter also reviews the previous legislation, on the edge of obsolescence at the time of writing.[1]

The chapter also deals with the way in which 'insanity' operates as a defence to criminal charges, noting in particular the differences between the medical and legal definitions of insanity. We consider other 'psychiatric defences' to criminal charges, automatism and diminished responsibility, as well as the question of fitness to plead.

Finally we look at the question of making a will. A person who makes a will must be of 'sound mind', but what is a sound mind and what questions should the clinician, usually a doctor, ask when assessing a patient's fitness to make his last testament?

THE DETENTION OF PSYCHIATRIC PATIENTS

Moving into a new era

[11.02]

In essence, the voluntary admission of the mentally disordered patient is no different from the admission of any other patient and is not dealt with in this chapter except in terms of the situation where a voluntary patient may wish to leave a psychiatric institution but is instead detained involuntarily (see section **[11.11]**). Problems tend to arise not with voluntary admissions, but when patient and doctor differ on whether the patient should be in hospital and, by reason of his mental condition, the patient cannot consent to his admission in the interests of his own welfare or that of others.

Take twin examples: firstly, the patient with schizophrenia and suffering from auditory hallucinations ordering him to kill another person and secondly a severely depressed patient who has recently attempted suicide and indicates his intention to do so again. Let us assume that neither wishes to be admitted to hospital. Wholehearted regard for the patients' autonomy[2] would mean that they would be allowed to remain at large and untreated, a risk to others in the case of the patient with schizophrenia or to the patient himself in the case of the depressed patient. Issues arise in this setting of the clinician's duty to help the patient and the law's duty to protect both society and those members of society who cannot protect themselves and it is these factors that form the basis for the involuntary admission, or 'committal', of psychiatric patients to hospital.

Up to the time of writing, approximately 2500 Irish people annually have been involuntarily detained in psychiatric hospitals. This figure represents one of the highest per capita rates of detention in Europe,[3] for reasons that may be related to the lack of safeguards against involuntary admission and the lack of a review process for such detentions. It is partly in an attempt to reduce this rate that new legislation has been introduced. The essence of the old law is contained in the Mental Treatment Act 1945 while a newer and more satisfactory protocol for involuntary admissions is contained in the Mental Health Act 2001. The latter Act brings the rights of the patient, especially his right to have his detention independently reviewed, to the fore. The new Act is officially in force, but its provisions are only just beginning to be implemented at the time of writing.[4] We will therefore look in turn at the procedures, pitfalls and problems of both pieces of legislation, but with far greater emphasis on the more recent law which, during the lifetime of this text, should become the statute governing all involuntary admissions, detention and treatment of psychiatric patients in Ireland.

Procedures and principles under the Mental Treatment Act 1945

[11.03]

The old form of involuntary detention governed by the Mental Treatment Act 1945 will soon be obsolete.[5] Nonetheless, at the time of writing there are many patients who continue, pending the full implementation of the Mental Health Act 2001, to be detained under the old legislation, having originally been admitted to hospital under its auspices.[6] Under the 1945 Act, a person could be admitted to a psychiatric hospital either as a voluntary patient, a 'temporary' patient or a person of unsound mind. Furthermore, distinctions were drawn in the legislation between private ('eligible') and public ('chargeable') patients. The present tense is used below to describe the categories and procedures under the 1945 Act, but it must be stressed that these procedures are on the cusp of being of historical interest only. We look at the two categories of most importance, those of voluntary and temporary patients, and we omit to deal with 'persons of unsound mind', a category that had fallen into practical disuse long before the introduction of the 2001 legislation.

Voluntary patients

[11.04]

A patient can, on application, be admitted as a voluntary patient to a psychiatric hospital and remain there until he recovers.[7] However, if he wishes to be discharged, he must give at least 72 hours' notice of his intention to leave. After those three days have elapsed the patient may leave the hospital, if in the interim he has not been made a 'temporary' patient, allowing him to be detained involuntarily.

Temporary patients

Before admission

[11.05]

'Temporary' is how the Mental Treatment Act 1945 describes the involuntarily admitted psychiatric patient. An application for temporary admission is made by a spouse or a family member or, in the absence of such a person, by a person in authority (generally a community welfare officer), who must be in any case over the age of 21 years. An application for admission must be accompanied by a medical practitioner's certificate of examination and recommendation for admission. In the case of private patients only, the examination must be conducted by two separate doctors who must concur as to the patient's suitability for temporary admission.

The relevant documentation for application, examination, recommendation and detention is combined in a single form, known in the medical vernacular as the 'pink form'. It should be noted that while the burden placed on the practitioner to 'examine' the patient is not an especially onerous one,[8] the medical examination must nonetheless satisfy the doctor (or doctors in the case of the private or 'chargeable' patient) either:

— that the patient is suffering from mental illness and requires treatment (for not more than six months) and is unsuitable because of his mental illness for admission as a voluntary patient, or

— that the patient is an addict requiring up to six months' curative and preventative treatment.[9]

The institution to which the application is made then takes a decision, based on examination of the patient, whether to 'receive and detain' the patient and any detention order is made on the authority of a consultant psychiatrist. The initial application for temporary admission remains in force for seven days after it is made and during that time the hospital in question can make arrangements for the involuntary admission of the patient. Once the patient is in hospital, the order for detention must be made within 12 hours. A patient who is the subject of an application for temporary admission must be offered the opportunity to request a second medical opinion before being taken to hospital.

Admission and detention

[11.06]

Under the Mental Treatment Act 1945 a patient admitted as a temporary patient can be detained until six months elapse from the date on which the order was made or until the patient's earlier removal, discharge or death. Patients who escape can, if caught within 28 days of absconding, be retaken and re-admitted. A patient may have his detention extended by further periods of up to six months, the aggregate of which cannot exceed 18 months[10] (addicts may only be detained for a maximum of a further six months). The patient has a right of appeal to the Inspector of Mental Hospitals (a post created by the 1945 Act) against any such decision and the Inspector will consider whether any recommendation for continued detention should be respected.

The Mental Health Act 2001

[11.07]

It has to be stressed again that the protocols just described under the heading of the 1945 Act are in the process of becoming obsolete, but they are so recent as to still have relevance. The Mental Health Act 2001 and the approaches and principles it espouses are rapidly replacing the 1945 law. The 2001 Act is in force and the Mental Health

Commission created by the Act will set about implementing its requirements in the coming years. Accordingly, we now give greater attention to the new order than we have done to the old.

The touchstone of the Mental Health Act 2001 is the protection, as far as possible, of patients' personal rights. It goes almost without saying that to deprive an individual of his liberty is a weighty power and one that should not be wielded without due regard for its consequences. A person accused of murder may only be deprived of his liberty after a trial in court of law before a jury of his peers, who must find him guilty beyond all reasonable doubt. Under the Mental Treatment Act 1945, a patient with depression could – albeit in his perceived best interests – be detained in hospital against his will on the word of a couple of doctors, one of whom could have 'examined' the patient from the safe vantage point of a garden gate.[11] While from the paternalistic viewpoint of 'doctor knows best', the old regime may have been a satisfactory way of operating a system of state-sponsored and legitimised incarceration, it was perhaps less idyllic from the patient's point of view. There were no safeguards (such as a second psychiatric opinion) prior to involuntary detention and there was no third party review of the continuation of detention. Legal thinking however was beginning to give increasing recognition to the rights of the individual as an essential ingredient of the government of a pluralist State, especially the right to liberty with the sole exception of where liberty is curtailed in accordance with the law and fair procedures. Something had to change.

The background to change

[11.08]

Ireland is a signatory of the European Convention of Human Rights, an international treaty dating from 1950[12] that lays down the basic rights that should be afforded to citizens of signatory countries. The Convention not only enshrines the rights of the citizen but also provides a forum in which disputes over breaches of an individual's rights can be heard and decided by a court other that one in the country alleged to be in breach of its obligations. The European Court of Human Rights sits in Strasbourg and since the court's inception, the Irish Government has agreed to accept its findings in cases involving Ireland as binding. Accordingly, when the Court has found Ireland to be in breach of the Convention, the State has responded appropriately, if sometimes slowly, to remedy that breach.[13]

Article 5 of the Convention is what concerns us here: it guarantees liberty, a right that may be abridged or taken away only in accordance with the law.[14] There is, as far as the Convention on Human Rights is concerned, no *absolute* protection of liberty: a person may have his liberty taken away, but only in accordance with the legal process of the country in question. However, the Convention calls for one extra element in any legal process that purports to deprive an individual of his liberty, namely the availability of a speedy system for the review of any detention that impinges on the right to liberty. It is this latter element that was most conspicuously lacking from Ireland's post-war mental health legislation.

The Convention's impact on Irish mental health legislation arose out of a case brought by a man who claimed that his involuntary detention under the Mental Treatment Act 1945 was in breach of his rights under the Convention.[15] He had been involuntarily detained in a psychiatric hospital during 1994 and complained that the absence of an independent review of the legality of his detention violated the Convention. The case was not decided by the Court, but instead a 'friendly settlement' was reached between the plaintiff and the Irish State before the Court had the opportunity to hear the case. The settlement contained an agreement to pay compensation to the former patient and an undertaking by the government to pass new mental health legislation that would provide the review procedure previously lacking. The legislation, which at that stage was known as the Mental Health Bill 1999, underwent many changes prior to enactment, but ultimately became the Mental Health Act 2001.

Provisions of the Mental Health Act 2001

[11.09]

The watchwords of the new legislation are 'second opinion' and 'independent review'. Under the Mental Health Act 2001 a patient cannot be involuntarily admitted or be subject to further involuntary detention or treatment without the activation of safeguard mechanisms designed to ensure that the rights of the patient are maximised. However, patients' rights are balanced against recognition of the need to treat those who are a danger to themselves or to others and who will benefit from treatment but who are incapable of consenting to such treatment. The Act is divided into six parts, but only three are of concern here. After laying out some definitional parameters, we will review each of the three most significant parts of the Act in turn: involuntary admission of persons to approved centres (Part 2), independent review of detention (Part 3) and consent to treatment (Part 4).[16]

Definitions important to the Mental Health Act 2001

[11.10]

The new Act lays down some definitions that it would be helpful to review. One somewhat surprising definition is that for the purposes of psychiatric treatment a child is any person under 18 years.[17] This contrasts markedly and inexplicably with the approach taken in medical and surgical treatment, which is that one becomes an adult at the age of 16 years.[18] Why this different approach has been taken is not clear.

The Mental Health Act 2001 also removes any distinction between private and public patients and applies to all those suffering from a 'mental disorder', divided for the purposes of the Act into three categories:[19]

(a) 'mental illness'

A state of mind of a person which affects a person's thinking, perceiving, emotion or judgement and which seriously impairs the mental function of the person to the extent that he or she requires care or medical treatment in his or her own interest or in the interest of other persons.

(b) 'severe dementia'

A deterioration of the brain of a person, which significantly impairs the intellectual function of the person, thereby affecting thought, comprehension and memory and which includes severe psychiatric or behavioural symptoms such as physical aggression.

c) 'significant intellectual disability'

Arrested or incomplete development of the mind of a person, which includes significant impairment of intelligence and social functioning and abnormally aggressive or seriously irresponsible conduct on the part of the person.

For the Act to apply, in addition to the presence of a mental disorder, one of two conditions must be satisfied:

i. the mental disorder must give rise to a serious likelihood of harm to the person suffering from the condition or to a serious likelihood of harm to others, or

ii. a failure to admit would result in a deterioration of the disorder or would prevent the administration of treatment that could only be given by such admission.

Assuming either of the above conditions is satisfied there is one further test to be met, namely that the condition must be one that can benefit from or be alleviated by admission to what the act calls an 'approved institution'.[20] Any decision to involuntarily admit must be made in the patient's best interests but also with 'due regard for his dignity and autonomy'.[21] The concept of involuntarily admitting someone while at the same time respecting his autonomy is an oxymoron, but aims to remind the doctor of her duty to give due weight to a patient's wish not to be admitted and to consider the alternatives (such as outpatient treatment) before a decision is taken to override the patient's preference.

There are three specific diagnoses excluded from the remit of the Act, the first two of which are characterised by the fact that they do not meet the criterion of being likely to benefit from in-patient treatment, while the third exclusion recognises advances made in the clinical understanding of addiction:[22]

— those suffering from a personality disorder;

— those who are 'socially deviant';

— those addicted to drugs or intoxicants.

The 2001 Act is therefore somewhat more restrictive that its 1945 counterpart. Its definition of mental disorder is more taut and specifically precludes addicts from forcible detention in a psychiatric institution as well as those who will not clinically benefit from detention. It is interesting to note, however, that the UK, which has had legislation similar to the Irish 2001 Act in place since 1983, introduced recent draft legislation to address perceived problems in its legislation.[23] The two proposals in the UK Draft Mental Health Bill that may have relevance for the Mental Health Act 2001 include:

— A redrafting of the definition of 'mental disorder' so as to permit involuntary detention of those suffering from personality disorders. This projected change is in spite of the fact that such detention is unlikely to alleviate the condition but rather is in recognition of the fact that public safety, as well as clinical diagnosis, is a factor in psychiatric care.

— A legal right to compel psychiatric treatment in the community and to involuntarily admit a person who fails to comply with a community-based treatment plan.

Whether such changes will become law in the United Kingdom or whether they will later be brought to bear on Irish legislation remains to be seen, for now we will confine ourselves to reviewing the operation of the Irish Mental Health Act 2001 as presently constituted.

Quick Reference Guide 11.1

Principles of the Mental Health Act 2001

- ❖ The Mental Health Act 2001 is born out of a desire to show greater care when depriving a patient of his liberty. Ireland has one of the highest per capita rates of involuntary admission in Europe.
- ❖ The 2001 Act replaces the Mental Treatment Act 1945 and its implementation began with the establishment of the Mental Health Commission in April 2002.
- ❖ For the purposes of the Act, adults are those over 18. In most other areas of healthcare, one becomes an adult at the age of 16.
- ❖ The Mental Health Act 2001 applies only to those who suffer from a 'mental disorder', meaning mental illness, severe dementia or significant intellectual disability. Only those who are suffering from such a condition and who are a danger to themselves or to others or who would deteriorate if not admitted *and* who will benefit from treatment but are incapable of consenting to such treatment can be involuntarily admitted.
- ❖ The Act excludes those with personality disorders, those who are socially deviant and those who are addicts. The UK has introduced draft legislation with the aim of bringing those with personality disorders back within the remit of its equivalent to the Irish 2001 Act in view of the potential threat such individuals are thought to pose to society.

Mental Health Act 2001, Part 2 – involuntary admission

[11.11]

As previously noted, two of the arguments for introducing a new mechanism for involuntary admission and detention are the fact that Ireland has an unusually high level of involuntary psychiatric admission and the fact that there is no independent protector of patients' interests. The process of admission activates the review mechanism and puts in place certain safeguards, such as shorter time limits, that may serve to encourage discharge rather than detention of those incorrectly or too precipitately admitted.

An application for involuntary admission is made to a medical practitioner by the 'applicant', who may be a spouse or relative of the patient, an 'authorised officer' of the health board or a member of the Garda Síochána.[24] Any other person may also be an applicant, but he must be over 18 and must have no financial interest in the detention of the patient. The doctor to whom an application for admission is made must examine[25] the patient within 24 hours of the application and decide whether to make a recommendation for admission, if she does so, the recommendation for admission remains valid for seven days.[26]

Once a recommendation is made for admission, the onus of getting the patient to hospital falls in the first place on the applicant. If the applicant cannot arrange transport, then the doctor who made the recommendation for admission can arrange transport or contact the institution for which the patient is destined and request staff there to arrange transport, with or without the help of the Gardaí, who must comply with that request for assistance.[27]

Once in hospital, the patient must been seen as soon as possible by a consultant psychiatrist and the patient can be detained for up to 24 hours to facilitate that examination on the authority of a consultant or other registered medical practitioner or nurse. The consultant who examines the patient, if satisfied that the patient is suffering from one of the mental disorders listed in the Act and fulfils the other criteria for admission, will make an admission order.[28] A similar method is involved in the process of extending the detention of a patient who is already involuntarily detained in hospital.[29]

Patients may be transferred at their request, or without request, between institutions assuming those in charge of the two institutions agree to the transfer. This includes transfer to a general hospital for medical or surgical treatment. Any proposed transfer to the Central Mental Hospital must be notified to the Mental Health Commission, which will refer the matter to a tribunal.[30]

For children who require admission, the Health Board or District Court will need to be consulted when a parent is not available who can, or will, consent to admission.[31]

A patient who is a voluntary patient but wishes to leave the hospital may be detained for 24 hours to allow consideration of whether he should be involuntarily detained.[32] If so, then the rules for involuntary admission or renewal of detention apply as they would for a patient admitted from the community or already an involuntary patient, except that the order must be made by a consultant psychiatrist other than the one who has been caring for the patient during his voluntary admission.[33]

A patient can be given leave of absence when involuntarily detained and may be discharged at any time if recovery has been effected. Following discharge, any proceedings pending before the Mental Health Tribunal will generally be abandoned unless the patient wishes them to continue.[34]

Mental Health Act 2001, Part 3 – Independent review of detention

[11.12]

It is once a patient becomes an inmate of an institution that the differences in the new legislation become most apparent. Once an order for admission or renewal of detention is made, then a copy of the relevant order goes both to the patient and to the Mental Health Commission. The patient's copy of any order must contain the following information:

- the section of the Act under which he is detained (s 14: admission as an involuntary patient, s 15: renewal of existing involuntary detention);

- that the patient is entitled to legal representation and to communicate with the Inspector of Approved Centres;
- a general description of any proposed treatment;
- that the admission or detention of the patient will be reviewed by a Mental Health Tribunal;
- that he can appeal to the Circuit Court against any decision of the Tribunal to renew his detention (but not against a decision to admit him in the first place unless the patient wishes to argue that he is not suffering from a mental disorder);
- that he can opt to be a voluntary patient if he prefers.[35]

The Mental Health Commission

[11.13]

The Commission has overarching responsibility for mental health treatment in Ireland. It appoints members of the Mental Health Tribunals and the panel of psychiatrists who carry out second opinion reviews under the Mental Health Act 2001, s 18. The Commission also arranges the legal aid scheme for patients, advises the Minister for Health on matters relating to mental health and draws up codes of practice for the mental health services. The Commission additionally has responsibility for approving psychiatric treatment facilities (referred to as 'approved centres' in the Act) and appoints an Inspector of Mental Health Services for that purpose.[36] The Commission comprises 13 members, with a minimum of 4 people from either sex, led by a chairperson. The breakdown of membership is as follows:[37]

- a barrister or solicitor of at least 10 years' standing (ministerial appointee);
- three medical practitioners, at least two of whom are psychiatrists;
- two psychiatric nurses;
- one social worker working in the psychiatric arena;
- one psychologist;
- one representative of the general public (ministerial appointee);
- three representatives of voluntary bodies;
- one representative of the Chief Executive Officers of the health boards.

Mental Health Tribunals

[11.14]

Once the Mental Health Commission receives its copy of an admission or renewal order it will refer the matter to a Tribunal and assign a legal representative to the patient (unless the patient wishes to appoint his own). It will also assign another consultant psychiatrist who will examine the patient, review the patient's notes, interview the admitting psychiatrist, and report back to the Commission within 21 days.[38]

The Tribunal is a three-person board, consisting of a lawyer (a barrister/solicitor of at least seven years' standing), a consultant psychiatrist[39] and a lay member, which considers the medical and legal propriety of admission or renewal and of certain forms of treatment, especially psychosurgery. Put at its simplest, the Tribunal assesses whether procedural requirements were wholly or largely complied with and whether the patient is in fact ill.[40] If any procedural shortcomings are such as to cause an injustice or the Tribunal does not believe the patient is ill, it will overturn the order for admission or extension of detention. In reaching this decision, it will take into account the opinion of the Commission-appointed psychiatrist. The Tribunal has 21 days from the making of the initial order to decide whether the admission or renewal was justified, but that time may be extended in the interests of fairness to allow a fuller exploration of matters. The Tribunal's decision is communicated to the patient, to the Commission and to the psychiatrist who is caring for the patient.

The Tribunal can direct the patient or any other person to appear before it. Sittings are held in private and the rules for witnesses and legal representatives are similar to those observed in a court.

A patient who feels that he should not be admitted because he is not suffering from a mental disorder can bring a case against his initial admission to the Circuit Court on that basis and the case will be heard without identifying the patient. The rationale for anonymity is that if it is found that the patient was not suffering from a mental disorder at the time of his admission, there is no reason why he should be potentially stigmatised by having his legal challenge to his detention publicised. Any renewal of existing detention can be appealed by a patient to the Circuit Court either on grounds that he is not ill or that proper procedures were not followed.

Mental Health Act 2001, Part 4 – consent to treatment

[11.15]

Consent to any treatment in the psychiatric setting must, in keeping with the general principles of consent, be obtained voluntarily as far as possible. The consultant psychiatrist must ensure that her patient understands the proposed treatment and that he has been given sufficient comprehensible information regarding the treatment before consent is recorded as given.[41] Consent is required unless the patient cannot or will not consent because of his condition and the consultant psychiatrist caring for the patient is of the opinion that the treatment is necessary, in which case treatment can be given. However, in certain cases, the consultant cannot automatically proceed to treatment without consent. If psychosurgery is proposed, the consent of the patient *and* a Mental Health Tribunal must be obtained. If electroconvulsive therapy (ECT) is proposed, the consent of the patient *or* of a second consultant psychiatrist must be sought and obtained. Similarly, no course of treatment may proceed for longer than three months unless the patient consents or unless a second psychiatric opinion is sought.

Potential problems with the Mental Health Act 2001

[11.16]

At the time of writing, the Mental Health Commission has only recently come into being[42] and there are a number of problems that have been identified with the introduction of the regime propagated by the Mental Health Act 2001. These predominantly relate to funding and resources but other issues also arise. Problems identified by the Irish Division of the Royal College of Psychiatrists include:[43]

Quick Reference Guide 11.2

Operation of the Mental Health Act 2001

- ❖ When a patient is a candidate for involuntary admission as a psychiatric patient, an application is made to a doctor, usually by a family member, but it may be a Garda, a health board 'authorised officer' or any other person over the age of 18 years who makes an application.
- ❖ Prior to any admission, a patient must be examined and a recommendation made for admission. Historically the law has placed a very low burden on the examining GP to conduct her assessment, but such a relaxed attitude may not be in keeping with the aims of the 2001 Act.
- ❖ Transport to the hospital starts as the responsibility of the applicant for admission, but the hospital to which the patient is being taken and/or the Garda Síochána may become involved and must comply with a call for assistance from the doctor who requests the admission.
- ❖ The patient, once in hospital, may be detained for up to 24 hours to facilitate examination by a consultant psychiatrist. A similar detention period applies when a patient's period of hospitalisation is being extended and may apply when a patient who was originally admitted voluntarily wishes to leave the hospital and it is felt that he may benefit from further involuntary detention.
- ❖ If a patient is admitted or his detention period is extended, he is given written notification of the decision and of his legal rights. The Mental Health Commission is informed of the admission or extension of detention.
- ❖ The Mental Health Commission appoints a consultant psychiatrist to review the clinical appropriateness of each admission or proposed renewal of detention. The consultant reports in turn to the Mental Health Tribunal who must then review the legal *and* medical appropriateness of the detention. Strict time limits are in place for the review process.
- ❖ The Mental Health Tribunal is a three-member panel: a lawyer, a psychiatrist and a lay member.
- ❖ Certain forms of treatment, including electroconvulsive therapy and any course of treatment of longer than three months' duration are subject to review either by a second psychiatrist or by the Mental Health Tribunal, where the patient cannot or does not consent. Psychosurgery may only be performed with the consent of the patient *and* the Tribunal.

— the question of whether all members of the Mental Health Commission should be appointed by a transparent process (eg the Local Appointments Commission);

— the administrative burden placed on psychiatrists when it comes to admissions, renewals and the continuation of treatment beyond three months;

— the fact that tribunal review of detention applies only to the detention of adults;

- the fact that new consultant posts will need to be created to allow the tribunals and the process of second opinions regarding admission, renewal, continuing treatment and proposed ECT to function; treating psychiatrists must also be available for interview by second opinion psychiatrists and the tribunals when necessary, with obvious knock-on effects for their availability in a clinical capacity;
- the shortcomings of the act when it comes to the admission of those between the ages of 16 and 18 years and their rights to consent to treatment.[44]

The reality of an under-resourced Mental Health Act has been brought home by recent litigation in the United Kingdom.[45] A practice had grown up in the UK of delaying Tribunal hearings in the interests of administrative convenience or where a Tribunal panel could not be properly constituted. A group of patients brought a legal action, claiming that their rights to liberty, guaranteed by Article 5 of The European Convention on Human Rights, had been infringed by the absence of a speedy review mechanism. The court reasoned that it was not acceptable, when the liberty of patients is at issue, to play fast and loose with scrutinising the legality of detention. An independent review of detention must be provided and it must be speedy. The court had no hesitation in placing the blame for the delay at the door of those responsible for under-funding the review process. Similar applications can be expected to be brought and to succeed under the Irish legislation unless a commitment is made to adequately provide for the reality behind the rhetoric of human rights implicit in the Mental Health Act 2001.

INSANITY AND THE LEGAL PROCESS

The defence of insanity

[11.17]

If a person is accused of a criminal act, he can offer the defence of insanity, arguing that he was 'insane' at the time the act was committed. If successful in making this argument (or in other words, if the jury – guided by the judge as to what constitutes legal insanity – believes him), the accused is found 'guilty but insane': he committed the act, but is considered to have been acquitted and is not imprisoned for it. Instead of prison, he goes to the Central Mental Hospital until such time as his insanity means that he is, in the opinion of the government, no longer a threat to society.[46] An application for release from detention for 'criminal insanity' is not made to the courts but to the Minister for Justice.[47]

Pleading insanity as a defence is a risky strategy. A person convicted of a crime is sentenced to a pre-determined term imposed by the judge, but a person who is guilty but insane is detained 'at the pleasure of the government', an open-ended sentence that may long exceed the term that would have been handed down by the court. There are many critics of this policy of open-ended detention, with criticism centred mainly on the fact that the terms served in hospital by those found guilty but insane appear to exceed those required for recovery, suggesting perhaps that the detention is directed as much at punishment as it is at treatment.[48] The real significance of the insanity plea lay in the era when the penalty for crimes could include execution: better to endure an open-ended incarceration in a mental institution than be executed. In recent years with the abolition of the death penalty, the significance of the insanity plea has diminished, but the plea is nonetheless still raised on occasion.

Crucial to an understanding of 'legal insanity' is the realisation that the law has a very different view of 'insanity' to that taken by clinicians. The reason for this should not be too hard to divine: while medicine is prepared to accept the shades of grey inherent in the analysis, diagnosis and treatment of the human mind, such a state of affairs is less tolerable to the law. A criminal case seeks to answer a simple binary question: is the accused guilty or not? There are no 'shades' of guilt or innocence, there is only guilty or not guilty. If the accused argues that he was insane when committing his crime, the law needs a categorical legal test by which it can decide whether the accused *was* insane or not and therefore whether he can be found guilty or not. Medicine is happy with 'maybe', the law needs a 'yes or no' answer and to achieve this end, the law adopts a formal legal test for insanity: the so-called 'McNaghten Rules'.

Because the definition used by the courts is a legal one and not a medical one, some people argue that legal insanity is not a diagnosis at all, but an excuse,[49] allowing those who should not be held guilty to escape under the guise of 'insanity'. However, in most cases, clinical evidence will have a role to play in determining whether the criteria for legal insanity are present,[50] although the jury are the ultimate arbiters of whether a person is 'guilty but insane'. Medical evidence generally comes from psychiatrists, but the nature of the medical evidence will depend on the precise nature of the illness constituting the alleged insanity. As we will explore below, a non-psychiatric condition, such as epilepsy or sleepwalking, may sometimes be grounds for a finding of 'legal' insanity and in those cases, evidence may be that of someone experienced in such areas, rather than that of a psychiatrist.

The 'McNaghten Rules' for legal insanity

[11.18]

Until the mid-19th Century, it was an uphill task for an accused person to prove that he was insane and therefore escape incarceration or execution. It was necessary for the accused to prove that he was utterly incapable of distinguishing right from wrong in all circumstances, not merely at the time when the crime was alleged to have been committed. A furore arose over the way in which one judge interpreted the rule on insanity in the trial of a man called McNaghten,[51] and it was decided that a set of rules, which bear McNaghten's name to this day, should be laid down to govern the plea of insanity. In full form they are somewhat tortuous, but the most important elements of the McNaghten Rules may be simply summarised (**Figure 11.1**).

Because the medical and legal definitions of 'insanity' are so different, as we will see at section **[11.10]**, a person with a definite psychiatric disorder may not satisfy the legal criteria for insanity, while a person with no discernible psychiatric problem may be found legally insane.

Figure 11.1 Legal insanity (The 'McNaghten Rules')

1. Every person is presumed to be sane and to possess a sufficient degree of reason to be responsible for his actions until the contrary is proved.
2. It is a defence to a criminal prosecution if it is established that, at the time of committing an offence,
   (a) The accused was labouring under a defect of reason resulting from a disease of the mind, *and*
   (b) As a result, he *either* did not know the nature and quality of his act *or*, if he did know the nature and quality of the act, he did not know the act was wrong.

Applying the insanity defence

[11.19]

The person who claims insanity must prove it. The first limb of the McNaghten Rules is that a person is sane until proved otherwise. If an accused person says he was insane when he committed his act, then at his trial he must prove it to the jury on the balance of probabilities: he must convince the jury that it was more likely than not that he was insane.

The effect of the McNaghten Rules is that if a person has a 'disease of the mind' causing a 'defect of reason', with the result either that he cannot tell his act is wrong or he cannot understand the nature of the act, then the act is not a crime. It is important to note that as far as the rules are concerned the 'defect of reason' – the 'insanity' – must relate directly to the act in question. It is also important to note that the defence of insanity is concerned with the effect the alleged insanity has on the person's beliefs: the focus is on 'insane delusions and insane ignorance'.[52]

Example 1

Mick suffers from schizophrenia, but his only symptom is a delusion that Roy is trying to kill him. On day release from hospital, Mick kills another person, Eamon, and when his case comes to trial he argues that he was insane at the time of the act.

Mick will have a harder time proving insanity, even though he suffers from a schizophrenic disorder, having murdered Eamon than he would if he had killed Roy. Legally, his 'insanity' only affects his mind when it comes to Roy, the villain in his delusions. He has no insane beliefs regarding Eamon. Therefore, had he killed Roy rather than Eamon, albeit labouring under the delusion that he was acting in self-defence in the face of Roy's murderous intent, a claim of insanity would be more likely to succeed. Mick may be medically 'insane' but this example shows how there may be a disparity between the legal and psychiatric definitions. The fact that insanity must relate specifically to the act in question and that the courts are in theory precluded from taking a global view of the condition of the accused is one of many criticisms levelled at the McNaghten Rules as a test of sanity.

It is up to the jury, guided by the judge as to the meaning of the McNaghten Rules, to decide whether they believe the claims of the accused. Even if all the evidence points to legal insanity, the jury must decide whether they believe that evidence. A jury's decision, assuming that the judge has correctly instructed them on the law, will only be overturned if it is not based on the evidence and is thus completely unreasonable.

The elements of the McNaghten Rules examined

[11.20]

The term 'defect of reason' applies to cognitive factors only – the powers of brain functioning, specifically including the ability to reason. A change in emotional or volitional state will not suffice in theory, although the Irish Courts have suggested that they may be prepared to take into account elements such as severe emotional derangement or irresistible impulses.[53]

'Disease of the mind' has conversely been far more widely interpreted and includes *any* condition that affects the mind so as to cause a defect of reason, whether or not there is any physical change to the brain itself. The test seems to be whether the factor affecting the mind is an 'internal' one, arising in the physiology or biochemistry of the person concerned without physical external contributing factors.[54] Psychiatric disorders such as schizophrenia are obvious examples, but the English courts have included less obvious non-psychiatric conditions, including epilepsy,[55] sleepwalking[56] and hyperglycaemia.[57] All such decisions in theory have the bizarre corollary of the psychiatric detention of persons suffering from non-psychiatric medical conditions but the reasoning behind them is that the legal definition of insanity is not concerned with accuracy of diagnosis, but with attempting to balance elements of law and public policy. Courts want to ensure that those who are not responsible for their actions are not explicitly punished for them, while also guaranteeing that those who require treatment in order to prevent a recurrence of the criminal act are compelled to receive treatment.[58]

The final element of the 'McNaghten Rules' is that these factors, that is the presence of a disease of the mind causing a defect of reason, result in the accused not understanding the nature or quality of his action *or* not knowing that they were wrong. Either one or both of these criteria must be met for a defence of insanity to succeed.

Appreciating the nature or the quality of the act generally means understanding the physical, rather than legal or moral, quality of the act even if the person was unable to fully comprehend the consequences. In one case, a patient with bipolar affective disorder[59] and a resident in a psychiatric hospital set fire to a wastepaper basket, which then caused a more serious conflagration to break out.[60] Because he could understand that he was setting fire to a basket, he was held to understand the nature and quality of the act, even though, because of his illness, he could not necessarily apprehend the likely result of that act. Other cases have taken a less restrictive approach to 'understanding' the act and have reasoned that the term could imply a more general consideration of whether the accused truly comprehended what he was doing.[61]

'Knowing the act is wrong' could refer either to knowing that the act is *legally* wrong (as is the case in England[62] and Canada) or knowing that it is *morally* wrong (the case in Australian law[63]). In Ireland, the picture is unclear, but juries in this country are generally told by the judge before they retire to consider their verdict that they should consider whether a person claiming to be insane knew the act was morally wrong.

Quick Reference Guide 11.3

Applying the legal insanity rules

- The law presumes that everyone is sane. It is up to a person making the claim of insanity to prove it. If a person raises insanity as his defence in a criminal trial he must prove it beyond reasonable doubt. It is the jury who decides whether or not the defence of insanity is accepted.
- A person who is found 'guilty but insane' after a trial does not go to jail, but is detained in the Central Mental Hospital 'at the pleasure of the Government'.
- Legal insanity only applies when a person has a 'disease of the mind' that causes a 'defect of reason'. The defect of reason – the 'insanity' – must relate to the act that the person is accused of. The defect of reason must mean *either* that the accused did not understand the 'nature and quality' of his act *or* did not understand that his act was wrong.
- A 'defect of reason' refers to the cognitive functioning of the brain, in particular the ability to reason and to think rationally. A 'disease of the mind' can include any condition – psychiatric or not – that affects the functioning of the mind, but which is not brought about by external factors such as drugs.
- Whether someone who pleads insanity 'understands the nature and quality' of his act can be interpreted in different ways: it may mean simply understanding what he was doing, without inquiring into whether he understood the consequences of his act. Alternatively, it may involve a global assessment of whether the accused understood the general circumstances and consequences of his situation.
- In Irish law, the question of 'knowing the act was wrong' (the alternative element in the insanity defence to not understanding the 'nature and quality' of the act) means knowing that the act in question was *morally*, not legally, wrong.

Unfitness to plead

[11.21]

A person who is mentally impaired, whether his impairment is psychiatric or intellectual in origin, may not be able to stand trial if his state of mind is such that he cannot understand the charges or the evidence against him, cannot instruct or comprehend the advice of a legal team or cannot give evidence. The situation has been summed up as follows:

> 'The issue is not merely that it would be unfair to the defendant to continue with the trial once he has been found unfit to plead, or that it would be unsafe to convict someone who cannot plead … but rather that it is in the nature of a criminal trial that the defendant is capable of playing a rational part in the proceedings.'[64]

The question of 'fitness to plead', effectively fitness to stand trial, is couched in terms of 'sanity' and 'insanity', but as with the McNaghten Rules discussed above, legal insanity can be a different beast to medical insanity:[65] a person may be found unfit to plead for physical, psychiatric or intellectual reasons. Unlike the McNaghten Rules, the question of fitness to plead is nothing to do with whether or not the accused was insane at the time of the act but whether he is sane at the time of trial. A person may have been perfectly well at the time of his alleged crime and subsequently become unfit to plead, perhaps due to intervening psychiatric illness. Conversely, he may have been legally insane at the time of the commission of the offence, but perfectly fit to stand trial.

Fitness to plead is usually decided by a jury in a separate hearing to the trial itself.[66] Each member of the jury takes an oath 'to well and diligently inquire' whether the accused 'be insane or not' and the jury then hears medical evidence; the jury is also entitled to take into account the demeanour and conduct of the accused in court. If the accused is found unfit to plead, he is detained in the Central Mental Hospital at the pleasure of the government but may be brought back to court when he is fit to plead. If the accused is found fit to plead, the trial proceeds, but with a different jury.

A person may also be technically unfit to plead because of a physical handicap or disability such as deafness. In such a case, the court will arrange translation facilities, such as sign language.[67]

Automatism

[11.22]

A person who is not conscious of his actions is in a state of automatism: the actions of the body are done without any control by the mind.[68] Automatism is confined to conduct that arises due to external factors, for example, an insulin injection causing hypoglycaemia[69] or perhaps an extreme emotional stimulus. This is in contrast to legal insanity, which as we have seen, can only be caused by 'internal' diseases of the mind.

Traditionally, the ingestion of alcohol was not permitted as grounds for automatism, but that has been thrown into doubt by a number of recent cases, including some high-profile decisions suggesting that, in very rare circumstances, the imbibing of excessive alcohol can lead to a state of automatism.[70] It must be stressed that the circumstances in which the 'drunk's defence' will arise are rare, in general if a person deliberately and recklessly brings about the situation in which his automatism arises, for example by drinking to excess, he cannot rely on it as a defence. Only if the consequences of his actions are especially unpredictable might the defence be sustainable.

The ups and downs of life, such as the ending of a relationship or dismissal from employment, will not generally be grounds for a defence of automatism, but severe psychological trauma, for example, in the context of ongoing domestic violence or post-traumatic stress, may do so. This will generally only be permitted where the person suffering the trauma takes a 'snap' decision to attack or kill a persecutor.[71] Evidence of planning or of acting in a controlled manner prior to a crime will tend to defeat a claim that automatism was present.[72]

Diminished responsibility

[11.23]

The defence of diminished responsibility does not exist in Ireland.[73] It is on the statute books in the United Kingdom however and its elements are as follows:

— it applies only when a person murders another or is involved in the murder of another;

— the accused must be suffering 'from such abnormality of mind as substantially impaired his mental responsibility for his acts and omissions in doing or being involved in the killing';

— the abnormality of the mind may arise from a condition of arrested or retarded development of the mind or any inherent causes or be induced by disease or injury.[74]

If a person is found to be suffering from diminished responsibility he is guilty of manslaughter (non-intentional killing of another) rather than murder. The defence of diminished responsibility could be said to be a catch-all, covering the 'margins' of the legal definition of insanity: those who are not suffering from the 'defect of reason' that is necessary for the McNaghten Rules to apply, but who are nonetheless not wholly responsible for their actions. Conditions meeting the criteria for diminished responsibility have included personality disorders,[75] depression[76] and epilepsy.[77] The voluntary consumption of alcohol leading to a state of intoxication does not amount to diminished responsibility.

TESTAMENTARY CAPACITY (THE MENTAL CAPACITY TO MAKE A WILL)

[11.24]

A will is a very important document.[78] The law takes the giving away (or 'disposing') of property very seriously and will carefully scrutinise transactions that involve personal property changing hands. There are two indispensable precursors to making a valid will. Even if all other formalities are complied with, no will can be valid unless the following criteria are satisfied:

— the testator (the person making the will) must be either over 18 or married;[79]

— the testator must be of sound mind.

The first issue is generally a simple one to resolve, but the second is more complicated and forms the subject matter of much that follows: what is a 'sound mind' for the purposes of writing a will? When a doctor is asked to certify that a patient has the capacity to make a will, what should she look for? There are two useful starting points. Firstly, it should be remembered that the law presumes that everyone is sane (and therefore capable of making a will) until the opposite is proven. Secondly, the testator needs only to have sufficient mental capacity *at the time he is making the will.*[80] It makes no difference if a patient makes a will, having only just recovered from a period of mental incapacity, or if he succumbs to some form of mental capacity as soon as he has drawn up and signed his will, so long as he possessed a sound mind at the time of making the will. Conversely, if a person is not of sound mind when he makes his will, but then recovers his mental faculties after drawing up the will and does not change the will because he is happy with its contents, then the will is still void.

A patient may be of sound mind at the time when he initially draws up and signs a will, but what happens if, several years later, he wishes to make an addition to his will, called a 'codicil', but has in the meantime developed a form of mental incapacity, such as

Alzheimer's Disease? The principle remains the same and identical rules apply to alterations to the will as govern the making of the original will. The original will (made when the testator was of sound mind) will remain valid, while additions made when the testator is suffering from mental incapacity will not be valid.

When exactly a will or an addition to a will is 'made' is not entirely clear. It is ideally the case that the testator should be of sound mind both when he gives instructions about what the will should contain (usually to a solicitor) and when he signs the will. The law seems happy however to separate making a will into two steps: a person who is competent when he gives instructions to the person drawing up the document will generally be held to have made a valid will even if some event intervenes that affects his capacity before he can sign it.

> **Example 2**
>
> In one case,[81] a man had his will drawn up by a friend, but before he could sign it, he suffered a stroke that left him unable to speak. The will was read out to him in hospital. After each part, the patient agreed by nodding and then signed the will with an 'X'. The court held that this was a valid will, even though the patient could not articulate his wishes prior to signing and despite medical opinion that he was not mentally competent when the will was signed. The crux was that there was evidence from witnesses that the will was wholly in accordance with the deceased's wishes and with the instructions he had given when he possessed the mental capacity to do so.

If a person wishes to challenge a will on the basis that the person making the will was not of sound mind at the time, then it is up to the person making that allegation to prove it.[82] A doctor who is asked to assess a patient's competence to make a will should bear in mind that the will may later be challenged and should therefore carefully document any decision taken and the basis upon which the decision was taken.

What constitutes a 'sound mind'?

[11.25]

A sound mind is in many ways similar to the concept of 'capacity' encountered when we dealt with the topic of consent[83] and is a highly individualised matter. There is no fixed diagnosis or exhaustive list of symptoms that the clinician can refer to in order to decide absolutely whether a patient is of sound mind or not, but there is a degree of common sense involved. Testamentary capacity disappears somewhere along a line between obvious capacity and manifest incapacity but where precisely the transition occurs is uncertain. In the politically incorrect but evocative and memorable language of the time, one judge stated the situation as follows:

> 'There is no difficulty in the case of a raving madman, or a drivelling idiot, in saying that he is not a person capable of disposing of property; but between such an extreme case and that of a man of perfectly vigorous understanding, there is every shade of intellect, every degree of mental incapacity. There is no possibility of mistaking midnight for noon, but at what precise moment twilight becomes darkness is hard to determine.'[84]

In general the mental standard for disposing of one's worldly goods in a will is a relatively high one: in one case, a person was held to have the necessary mental capacity to consent to getting married, but not, on the very same day, to make a will.[85] Judges have tied themselves into knots attempting to define the phrase 'sound mind'. The word 'mind' has caused special problems, with one judge sub-dividing mental functioning into the distinct elements of 'mind, memory, understanding, thought, judgement and reflection'[86] in a misguided attempt to bring some clarity to matters. Courts have recognised that the mind need only be defective in one respect for it to be unsound,[87] but they have also concluded that the defect in question must go the very root of the person's ability to make a reasoned decision about how to dispose of his property. Therefore the presence of delusions, depression, dementia or any other mental impairment is only relevant if it has a bearing on the will.

Ultimately, the approach taken by the courts is like the 'capacity approach' mentioned in the chapter on consent: there is no automatic presumption that a person is automatically unfit to make a will simply because he suffers from mental illness or from some organic deterioration of the brain. Each individual must be considered separately and the courts have tended to look at the precise details of the individual's mental capacity, rather than the general category into which the testator fits. Essentially, the testator must be:

> '...[A]ble to appreciate his position; he must be able to appreciate his property, to form a judgement with respect to the parties whom he chooses to benefit by it after his death...[88]'

Mere perversity in the testator is not enough: sociopathic or personality disorders that cause the testator to behave in a perverse manner, for example by precluding his family from the will do not necessarily amount to unsoundness of mind.[89] Considerations of mental capacity are concerned not with the decisions themselves but with the thought processes that underpin the decisions and a finding of a lack of capacity will generally only arise in the presence of some form of organic or psychiatric disease. The doctor has to decide whether in the circumstances of the illness or cognitive decline exhibited by the patient, he is fit to make a will and the essential questions the clinician has to resolve are threefold:

1. Does the patient understand the general nature and effect of a will?
2. Does the patient know the extent of the assets to be distributed in the will?
3. Is the patient able to bring to mind the people (be they family members or others) who should be considered as beneficiaries of the will?

The test of whether a patient knows the extent of his assets may not be so strictly applied in cases where the estate is exceptionally large and where it would be an extreme feat of memory to recall its exact details.[90] A court, in keeping with the presumption of sanity set out in the 'McNaghten Rules', will generally presume a testator to have been competent to make the will unless there is 'firm medical evidence by a doctor in a position to assess the testator's mental capacity' to the contrary.[91]

Psychiatric conditions and the unsound mind

[11.26]

Psychiatric conditions are not, as we have mentioned, automatically a bar to making a will. The court will ask, and the doctor should ask, one simple question of a patient's psychiatric condition: does it affect the making of a will? If it does, then the will cannot be valid. If a patient suffers from a psychiatric condition but is nonetheless able to appreciate and understand what is meant by making a will and able to make a will unencumbered by his condition, then the will is likely to be valid. In limited circumstances, where only one portion of a will is affected by a psychiatric condition, then that portion may be struck out where it is possible to do so, with the remainder left intact.[92]

Alcoholism is not automatically a bar to a valid will, but acute intoxication or acute alcohol withdrawal at the time of drawing up the will or instructing a solicitor would probably render the will void. Similarly, brain damage caused by chronic alcohol abuse, such as Korsakoff's syndrome, could bring with it a lack of capacity.

Cognitive impairment and the unsound mind

[11.27]

There are many facets to cognitive function and impairment of any one element will not necessarily destroy testamentary capacity, as long as it does not affect the ability to understand the issues involved in making a will. Simple failures of memory, occasioned either by the great size of the property to be disposed of[93] or by a minor slip in recall will not void the will.

Cognitive impairment can generally be assessed either by the clinician's knowledge of the patient or more formally, and preferably, by using a mini-mental state examination.[94] Such tests record the cognitive state of the patient as a numerical result based on the answers to a series of questions relating to the orientation of the patient in place, time and person, his memory, and his ability to comprehend and carry out instructions. If a general practitioner conducts such a test and the result is 'borderline',[95] then repeating the test or referral to a specialist in psychology or in medicine or psychiatry of the elderly may be the appropriate course to take.

Lucid intervals and the unsound mind

[11.28]

Many conditions, psychiatric as well as physical, follow a pattern of remissions and relapses, where the condition improves for a time, followed by a return to the status quo. Alzheimer's Disease is an example of an organic condition that can evidence such fluctuations in mental capacity. A will made during a so-called 'lucid interval' will be valid, but it is necessary, where a patient is known to suffer from a mental disorder, to prove that the lucid interval was in fact present.[96]

In other words a doctor called upon to certify that a patient, known to suffer from some mental infirmity, is fit to make a will during a lucid interval, should record the absence of those symptoms that would otherwise render the will invalid. A patient who normally suffers from delusions should be thoroughly questioned to ensure the absence of any delusions that could relate to the will or to establish the presence of insight into his condition (when a patient has insight into the facts of his condition, the courts can take that insight as evidence of a sufficient recovery).[97] A patient suffering from cognitive impairment should undergo a test of his cognitive function to be sure that his comprehension and reasoning faculties are, on this occasion, sufficient for him to instruct a solicitor and to sign a will.

The doctor's role summarised

[11.29]

When a doctor is called to see a patient with a view to assessing his capacity to make a will, then she must bear in mind the points raised above.[98] It is often wise to assess a patient on more than one occasion if in doubt. The patient should understand the reason for the examination so that consent to it is validly obtained. The process of assessment should ideally involve three steps:

1. defining the diagnosis;
2. quantifying any resultant disability;
3. interpreting how the disability affects the making of a will.

It is also important to consider the importance of bringing background information to bear on the examination. In this respect the patient's own doctor can often be the best person to conduct an examination. She is likely not only to know the patient but also to have an appreciation of the patient's financial and familial circumstances, both of which are potentially important factors in assessing whether the patient appreciates what is involved in making his will. Where the doctor is not the patient's own doctor, she should consider informing herself about such matters, perhaps from more than one source to avoid being misled, as well as familiarising herself with the clinical history before assessing the patient. Information on mental, cognitive or any other aspects of functioning can come from third parties, whether clinical or family, but where information comes from a person with an interest in the outcome of the assessment, it may need to be treated with caution.[99]

Attempts should also be made to maximise the patient's testamentary capacity so that he is not seen in circumstances unrepresentative of his general mental state. Steps that can be taken include the following:

- Treat underlying conditions that may be impairing soundness of mind or decision-making capacity, such as infections or the presence of depression.
- Recognise that a patient's mental powers may fluctuate and that any impairment may be temporary. Delaying or repeating an assessment may be appropriate.
- Consider that apparent deficiencies in mental functioning may in fact be deficiencies in the power of communication, such as dysphasia[100] after a stroke, and attempt to overcome these hurdles.
- Conduct the assessment where possible in the circumstances and surroundings where the patient feels most comfortable. Consider whether the presence of a third party might help or hinder matters.

In circumstances where the doctor is happy that a patient is fit to dispose of his worldly goods, she will be required to confirm the fact not only in her medical notes, but generally also by acting as a witness to the will. If the doctor is of the opinion that a person is not fit to make a will, then she should record as much in her medical notes together with the reasons for reaching that conclusion.[101] In cases of uncertainty it may be appropriate for the non-specialist practitioner to seek a more expert opinion.

Quick Reference Guide 11.4

A suggested checklist for the medical certification of testamentary capacity

- ❖ Not every condition that affects the mind will necessarily mean that a patient cannot make a will, nor will every irrational decision regarding a will indicate an unsound mind or lack of capacity.
- ❖ The key is that any deficit must go to the heart of the ability to make a will: define the diagnosis, quantify resultant disability and interpret how the disability could affect the making of the will.
- ❖ Ask whether the patient suffers from any psychiatric condition, organic brain disease or any other cognitive impairment unrelated to a specific psychiatric or organic disease.
- ❖ If the patient does suffer from any psychiatric or cognitive impairment, does it result in a situation where the patient is unable to appreciate any or all of the following:
  - (i) The general nature and effect of a will (or of a change to a will)?
  - (ii) The approximate extent of the assets covered by the will?
  - (iii) The people (family or others) who should be named as likely beneficiaries of the will?
- ❖ *Both* elements – an unsound mind *and* the operation of that defect on testamentary capacity – must be present for the person to lack testamentary capacity. It may be wise to examine a borderline patient on more than one occasion or to enlist outside specialist help in cases of uncertainty.
- ❖ All the necessary clinical and non-clinical information should be in place to allow the doctor, especially if she is not familiar with the patient, to assess the patient and his circumstances
- ❖ Take steps to maximise the potential of the person being assessed. Such steps may include: treating underlying conditions; deferring or repeating the examination; overcoming communication difficulties and conducting the examination in the most comforting, familiar and secure (for the patient) environment possible.

If a will is later challenged, then the doctor may have a role in testifying as to the patient's testamentary capacity. This may take the form of a sworn statement (an affidavit) concerning the clinical facts or it may involve a court appearance as a witness.[102] In any situation when reporting her deceased patient's testamentary capacity, the doctor owes a duty of impartiality. She should also as far as possible respect the requirement of confidentiality, respect for which, according to the Medical Council *Guide to Ethical Conduct and Behaviour*, is an ethical obligation extending beyond the grave.[103]

Endnotes

1 The question of consent and mental incapacity has been dealt with in ch 4, *Consent* (see section **[4.11]** *ff.*)

2 See ch 3, The Practitioner-Patient Relationship, Ethics and Confidentiality, section **[3.06]**.

3 In Ireland, the rate of involuntary detention each year is 75.3 people per 100,000: compare this with England and Wales (49 per 100,000) and Italy (26 per 100,000). See 'New law to cut psychiatric detentions' (2002) *Irish Times*, 17 April.

4 The Mental Health Commission, the body charged with implementing the Mental Health Act 2001, was formally constituted in April 2002.

5 There are also some important legislative provisions enacted after 1945, but for the purposes of this chapter we will refer to all of the older legislation under the broad heading of the '1945 Act'. For more detail on the minutiae of the old legislation see Casey & Craven *Psychiatry and the Law* (1999) ch 18 or Tomkin & Hanafin *Irish Medical Law* (1995) ch 7.

6 The Mental Health Act 2001 provides that the detention of those detained involuntarily in hospital under the 1945 legislation must be reviewed under the terms of the new Act within six months of the establishment of the Mental Health Tribunals (see section **[11.14]**).

7 Mental Treatment Act 1945, s 190 (public patients) and s 191 (private patients)

8 It was decided in the case of *O'Reilly v Moroney* (16 November 1993, unreported) SC, that the 'examination' could be extremely cursory. In that case, the doctor, who was not the patient's usual general practitioner, merely regarded the patient from a distance and did not physically examine her or put any questions to her. He claimed that he was worried that more detailed examination might exacerbate the situation. The majority of the judges in the Supreme Court felt that he had carried out a sufficient examination, the shortcomings of which were cured in any event by the subsequent examination conducted in hospital. One judge (Blayney J) was extremely – and, it is suggested, rightly – critical of such a cavalier approach. The Department of Health *White Paper on a New Mental Health Act* (1995), which formed the foundation of the Mental Health Act 2001, recommended that the nature of psychiatric examinations should remain a question of 'professional discretion' (para 3.19). This approach has not been explicitly translated into the 2001 Act.

9 Mental Treatment Act 1945, s 184 (public patients) & s 185 (private patients). The Mental Health Act 2001 has abolished the option of involuntary detention for addicts: see para **[11.10]**.

10 Mental Treatment Act 1945, s 189.

11 See endnote 8: *O'Reilly v Moroney* (16 November 1993, unreported) SC.

12 The Convention is due to be formally incorporated into Irish law by the European Convention on Human Rights Bill 2001 but, unlike other European law, it will be subservient to the Irish Constitution because it emanates from the Council of Europe rather than from the European Union (see Appendix A (section **[A.13]-[A.14]**), for more detail on EU law and European human rights law). The Convention was brought into being by the Council of Europe of which more than 40 European Countries are members, it is not an EU institution, although the EU Court, the European Court of Justice, has been influenced by the Convention.

13 *Airey v Ireland* (1979) 2 EHRR 305 led to the introduction of the civil legal aid system; *Norris v Ireland* (1988) 13 EHRR 136, led ultimately to the decriminalisation of homosexuality.

14 The relevant provisions of Article 5 of the European Convention on Human Rights are as follows:

> Everyone has the right to liberty and security of person. No one shall be deprived of his liberty save in the following cases and in accordance with a procedure prescribed by law:
>
> ... e) The lawful detention of... persons of unsound mind.
>
> ...
>
> Everyone who is deprived of his liberty by arrest or detention shall be entitled to take proceedings by which the lawfulness of his detention shall be decided speedily by a court and his release ordered if the detention is not lawful.

[15] *Croke v Ireland* (21 December 2000) ECHR. The case arose out of an earlier decision by the Irish Supreme Court that the absence of an independent review did *not* violate the plaintiff's constitutional rights: *Croke v Smith* [1998] 1 IR 101. See also 'Tribunals needed to hear appeals against detentions.' (2000) *Irish Times*, 28 December.

[16] Mental Health Act 2001, Part 1 of the Act is concerned with definitions; Part 5 concerns the registration of Approved Centres; Part 6 relates to miscellaneous provisions.

[17] Mental Health Act 2001, s 2(1).

[18] Non-Fatal Offences Against the Person Act 1997, s 23.

[19] Mental Health Act 2001, s 3(2).

[20] Meaning a psychiatric facility approved by the Mental Health Commission.

[21] Mental Health Act 2001, s 4.

[22] Mental Health Act 2001, s 8(2).

[23] Draft Mental Health Bill (Cm 5538–I), presented to Parliament by the Secretary of State for the Department of Health, June 2002, HMSO. Note, however, that there has been substantial disquiet at the proposals: see Lancet 2002 360; 9332:553 'Proposed UK Mental Health Law opposed.'

[24] Mental Health Act 2001, ss 9 & 12. An 'authorised officer' is not a term that is satisfactorily defined in the Act: it appears to give the health board wide powers to nominate those who may initiate the process of involuntary detention. The right of the Gardaí to detain a person suffering from a mental disorder includes the right to enter a dwelling to seize that person.

[25] Note again the low standard that has been accepted by the courts for a psychiatric examination in primary care: *O'Reilly v Moroney* (16 November 1993, unreported) SC (see endote 8).

[26] Mental Health Act 2001, s 10. A doctor cannot make a recommendation if she has a financial interest in the centre to which the patient will be admitted, if she is a relative of the patient or if she is also the person making the application for admission. If a doctor refuses a recommendation and the applicant seeks a second opinion, the applicant must tell the subsequent doctor of the previous refusal (s 11).

[27] Mental Health Act 2001, s 13. Again, the Gardaí have the right to enter a dwelling and detain and restrain the patient.

[28] Mental Health Act 2001, s 14. The consultant cannot make an admission order if she is a spouse or relative of the patient or if she is also the applicant.

[29] Mental Health Act 2001, s 15. Initial detention is for a maximum of 21 days (s 15(1)) which can be extended for periods of between 3 months (in the first instance) and 12 months (ss 15(2)–(3)).

[30] Mental Health Act 2001, ss 20–22.

[31] Mental Health Act 2001, s 25 and 26.

[32] Under the Mental Treatment Act 1945, the patient could be effectively detained for 72 hours during which his status as a voluntary patient could be reviewed. One possible criticism of the 24–hour periods stipulated by the 2001 Act is that they take no account of and make no allowance for weekends or other holiday periods.

[33] Mental Health Act 2001, ss 23 and 24.

[34] Mental Health Act 2001, s 28.

[35] Mental Health Act 2001, s 16.

[36] Mental Health Act 2001, ss 50–55.

[37] Mental Health Act 2001, s 35. Elected public representatives cannot serve on the Commission and must resign on election.

[38] Mental Health Act 2001, s 17.

[39] Who may be a consultant psychiatrist who has retired not more than seven years previously.

[40] Mental Health Act 2001, s 18.

41 Mental Health Act 2001, s 56. Essentially 'informed consent' – dealt with in greater detail in ch 4, *Consent* (section **[4.20]** ff.)

42 See 'New law to cut psychiatric detentions' (2002) *Irish Times*, 17 April.

43 See 'Comments on the Mental Health Act 2001' Irish Psychiatry Online, homepage of the Irish Division of the Royal College of Psychiatrists: http://www.irishpsychiatry.com/public.html.

44 It will be remembered that the Act defines a child as one under the age of 18 years. In other words, a 17year-old, who can consent to medical or surgical treatment, cannot consent to psychiatric treatment. The lock of satisfactory facilities for minors suffering from psychiatric problems has been highlighted by cases such as *DG v Eastern Health Board* (16 July 1997) SC. In that case, a disturbed but innocent child was committed to a penal institution in the absence of any appropriate psychiatric institution.

45 *R v The Mental Health Review Tribunal and The Secretary of State for Health ex p KB, MK, JR, GM, LB, PD and TB* [2002] EWHC 639 (23 April 2002).The English legislation (Mental Health Act 1983) has provisions regarding tribunal review of detention equivalent to those in the Irish legislation.

46 Trial of Lunatics Act, s 2. The Central Mental Hospital was created by the Mental Treatment Act 1961, s 39.

47 *John Gallagher v DPP* [1991] ILRM 339. This case concerned a man who was detained following a 'guilty but insane' verdict for the murder of his ex–girlfriend and her mother in Sligo. Following his detention he promptly made an application for release, claiming that he had recovered from his mental affliction. The Minister considered the application by appointing a series of advisory committees to inquire into Gallagher's mental state. The first two committees recommended continuing detention and their findings were challenged by Gallagher (*Gallagher v The Director of the Central Mental Hospital* (16 December 1994, unreported) HC) but upheld by the Courts. A third committee recommended a phased day release programme and that decision was similarly upheld (*Application of Gallagher (No 2)* [1996] 3 IR 10).

48 See McAuley *Insanity, Psychiatry and Criminal Responsibility* (1993); German & Singer 'Punishing the Not Guilty: Hospitalisation of Persons acquitted by Reason of Insanity' (1976) 29 Rutgers LR 1011.

49 McAuley, *Insanity, Psychiatry and Criminal Responsibility* (1993).

50 In England, the Criminal Procedure (Insanity and Unfitness to Plead) Act 1991, s 1(2), demands the evidence of at least two doctors, one of whom must be an experienced psychiatrist.

51 *Daniel McNaghten* [1843] 4 St Tr (ns) 817. McNaghten had killed the Private Secretary to the British Prime Minister, but claimed he was insane. The judge, when directing the jury, told them they need only be concerned about whether the accused could tell the difference between right and wrong *only as far as the offence he was charged with was concerned*. McNaghten was acquitted. It was felt the law on insanity was unclear and hence the Law Lords (the UK's most senior judges) were asked to set out formal ground rules for legal insanity.

52 Charleton, McDermott & Bolger *Criminal Law* (1999) p 1105.

53 *Doyle v Wicklow County Council* [1974] IR 55, in particular the judgment of Griffin J. This case made clear that while the McNaghten rules apply in Ireland, they are not necessarily the only determinant of whether a person is legally insane.

54 See Ashworth *Principles of Criminal Law* (2nd edn, 1995) pp 204–206.

55 *R v Sullivan* [1984] AC 196. Epilepsy has also been considered a form of automatism in Irish law (see *Ellis v DPP* [1990] 2 IR 291) and in England may also amount to diminished responsibility: which defence epilepsy affords seems to depend on the precise clinical manifestation of the condition in the individual concerned.

56 *R v Burgess* [1991] 2 QB 92.

57 *R v Hennessy* (1989) Cr App R10. 'Hyperglycaemia' is an abnormally high blood sugar level, commonly found in untreated or under–treated diabetes. Perhaps perversely at first sight, the courts have held that 'hypoglycaemia' following an insulin injection is not a form of insanity, but rather a form of 'automatism'. The difference between the two cases appears to be the presence of the 'external' element of an injection in the latter (*Quick* [1973] 3 All ER 347). See the discussion of automatism in section **[11.22]**.

58 In the case of *US v Lyons* 731 F 2d 243 (1984), the Court said that 'what definition of "mental disease or defect" is to be implied by courts enforcing the criminal law is, in the final analysis, a question of legal, moral and policy not of medical judgement.'

59 Colloquially called manic depression.

60 *R v Dickie* [1984] 3 All ER 176.

61 In Canada, a woman robbed a bank to get money to buy a crucifix she believed was being blasphemously displayed in a shop nearby. She was, even though she certainly knew she was robbing a bank, held not to understand the nature and quality of her act: *Adamcik* [1977] 3 CCC (2d) 1 (BC CC).

62 *R v Windle* [1952] 2 All ER.

63 *R v Willgloss* [1979] 2 NSWLR 1.

64 McAuley, *Insanity, Psychiatry and Criminal Responsibility* (1993) p 136.

65 In *R v Governor of Stafford Prison, ex p Emery* [1909] 2 KB 81, the accused was deaf, mute and illiterate. He was found unfit to plead due to 'insanity'.

66 This is because the issue usually arises before the trial and there is a desire not to prejudice the trial jury. Sometimes the issue of fitness to plead will only arise for the first time *during* the trial, in which cases, the trial jury will decide the matter. In cases where there is no jury, eg in the District Court, the judge can direct that medical reports be prepared on the accused.

67 A person may also simply *refuse* to say anything in court: in that case, the court will presume a plea of 'not guilty' and proceed accordingly.

68 *Bratty v Attorney General for Northern Ireland* [1963] AC 386.

69 *Quick* [1973] QB 910. As we have noted above (endnote 57), the situation where hyperglycaemia caused by untreated diabetes is 'insanity' (it is a purely internal factor, although it can be caused by the failure to eat or take insulin, both 'external' factors), while hypoglycaemia caused by an insulin injection is 'automatism' is bizarre and counter–intuitive.

70 'Suspended sentence for man who killed baby' (2002) *Irish Times*, 17 May; 'REM man beats air rage charges' (2002) *Irish Times*, 6 April. In each case, the accused argued that he had experienced a severe and unforeseeable reaction to a mixture of substances (poitín, beer and cider in the former case; sleeping tablets and alcohol in the latter). A similar result occurred in the Canadian case of *Vickberg* (1998) 16 CR (5th) 164, where a combination of psychotropic medication and alcohol induced a state of automatism.

71 *R v Falconer* (1989) 46 A Crim R 83.

72 For example, in *The People (DPP) v Courtney* (21 July 1994, unreported) CCA, the accused claimed automatism as a result of his traumatic experiences as a soldier in Lebanon. The fact that he had driven his victim to a secluded spot before killing her tended to suggest that he was not acting in a state of automatism.

73 Although it was recommended as long ago as 1978: 3rd Interim Report of the Inter–Departmental Committee on Mentally Ill and Maladjusted Persons on Treatment and Care of Persons Suffering from Mental Disorder who Appear before the Court on Criminal Charges (1978), Government Publications.

74 Homicide Act 1957, s 2.

75 *R v Turnball* (1977) 65 Cr App R.

76 *Ford* [1972] QWN 5.

77 *R v Price* [1963] 2 QB 1. Epilepsy, as we have seen, has also been held to fulfil the criteria for insanity and for automatism. Which defence will be raised, whether insanity, automatism or diminished responsibility, on the basis of the accused suffering from epilepsy will probably depend on the precise clinical manifestation of epilepsy in the individual.

78 The steps involved in 'executing' a will are relatively simple in principle. The will is drawn up, usually by giving instructions to a solicitor but it may be drafted by anyone. The document identifies the property of the person in question and to whom he wishes it to be given. A will must be in writing. It must be signed, although the signature can take the form of almost any written mark. The signing of the will must be witnessed by at least two witnesses, who must also sign. A will may later be altered or revoked. When a will is made, the property left in the will is known as the 'estate' of the deceased. The person responsible for distributing the estate is a 'personal representative', either an executor (appointed in the will) or an administrator (appointed by the court). The personal representative is appointed once the will is 'proved' or 'admitted to probate' in court – generally a straightforward administrative step in non–contentious wills, but where there is a dispute as to the will there may be a legal challenge to it. Once the will is admitted to probate, the executors pay all the deceased's outstanding debts, before distributing the rest in accordance with the terms of the will.

79 Succession Act 1965, s 77.

80 *Re JR* [1993] ILRM 657.

81 *Re Glynn* [1990] 2 IR 326.

82 *Blackhall v Blackhall* (28 June 1996, unreported) HC. On the other hand, if a person is known to have suffered from an illness affecting mental capacity and a suggestion is made that the will was made during a 'lucid interval' (see section **[11.28]**), then the person claiming the existence of a lucid interval will have to prove the truth of that claim.

83 See ch 4, *Consent.*

84 *Boyse v Rossborough* 6 HLC 1 at 45, *per* Cranworth LJ.

85 *Rė Park* [1953] 2 All ER 1411.

86 *In the Estate of Bellis, Polson v Parrott* 45 TLR 452.

87 *Banks v Goodfellow* [1870] QB 549 at 559, per Cockburn CJ.

88 *Sefton v Hopwood* 1 Fos & F 578.

89 Succession Act 1965, Part IX (s 117) affords the immediate family of the deceased protection from being cut out of wills, whether motivated by malice or by unsound mind. The spouse of the deceased has a claim on the property of the deceased, while children of the deceased have a right to be provided for by the courts out of the deceased's property in circumstances where the deceased has failed in his 'moral duty' to do so in the will.

90 See *In the Estate of Agnes Blackhall, decd* (28 June 1996, unreported) HC, (1 April 1998, unreported), SC.

91 *Re Corboy* [1969] IR 148 at 167, per Budd J.

92 In *Bohrmann* [1938] 1 All ER 271, an English man suffered from a delusion that the local council was persecuting him and for that reason made a codicil (addition) to his will that substituted US charities for the English charities originally specified. Because the man's delusions led him to this conclusion, only the codicil was struck out and the rest of the will was valid. Even though he suffered from schizophrenic delusions, the delusions did not affect the rest of his will, save for that single portion.

93 *In the Estate of Agnes Blackhall, decd* (28 June 1996, unreported) HC, (1 April 1998, unreported) SC.

94 There are many such tests. One such is contained in Folstein (1975) 12 J Psychiatric Research *(*1975) 12:189–198. The lower the score, the more likely the patient is to be demented.

95 A score of 25–27 on the Folstein MMSE.

96 *Cartwright v Cartwright* (1793) 1 Phillim 100. When the testator was known to suffer from a condition that affected his capacity, it is up to the person who claims that a will was made during a period of recovery to prove that allegation.

97 *Re Dyce Sombre* 1 MN&G 116, per Cottenham LJ.

98 See also British Medical Association and the Law Society *Assessment of Mental Capacity – Guidance for Doctors and Lawyers* (1995).

99 A doctor may wish to disqualify herself from conducting such an assessment where she knows she is likely to be a beneficiary in the will of the patient being assessed.

100 The loss or impairment of the power of speech.

101 *Duffy v Duffy* (10 August 1994, unreported) HC; *Kenward v Adams* [1975] CLY 3591; *Re Simpson* (1977) 121 SJ 224.

102 See ch 10, *The Practitioner and the Lawyer.*

103 *Guide to Ethical Conduct and Behaviour* (5th edn, 1998), para 18.1. See ch 3, *The Practitioner-Patient Relationship, Ethics and Confidentiality*, for a discussion of whether confidentiality survives the death of a patient [section **[3.15]**).

Chapter 12

The Extremes of Life I: The Beginning of Life

INTRODUCTION

[12.01]

This chapter and the one that follows are about those at the sharp end of the process called 'life': those in the womb or in infancy, as well as those on the edge of death. We examine in this chapter the medico-legal issues that arise at the start of life, in particular abortion and the law in Ireland. We also look at the question of infanticide, the killing of a young child by his mother in the first year of life.

ABORTION IN IRELAND

Murder, manslaughter and unborn human life

[12.02]

In general, and speaking legally, rather than ethically or morally, abortion and homicide are considered two different things or put another way, *legally* abortion is not the same as murder or manslaughter. Murder is the killing of another person where there is an intent to kill or to cause serious injury to the person killed.[1] Manslaughter is the killing of another where there is no specific intention to kill or cause serious injury, or where the killing is the result of provocation leading to a loss of self-control, or where the accused used force he believed to be necessary in the circumstances (perhaps in self-defence). For a homicide to be committed, the person killed must, at the time of the alleged killing, have been both alive and capable of sustaining independent life: in short, he must have been born. One judge summed up the issue as follows:

> 'A baby is fully and completely born when it is completely delivered from the body of its mother and it has a separate and independent existence in the sense that it does not derive its power of living from its mother. It is not material that the child still be attached to the mother by the umbilical cord.'[2]

Abortion then is the destruction of *in utero* life and the courts, and the written law, regard it in a different light from murder or manslaughter. The Irish Constitution does contain a guarantee to respect the life of the unborn, while having regard to the equal right to life of the mother.[3] In theory then, if (a) the right to life of the mother and unborn is equal and (b) if to kill the mother would be murder, then to kill the unborn could be regarded[4] as murder or manslaughter. As we will see when we deal with the complexities of the interpretation of the Irish Constitutional guarantee of the right to life of the unborn, what the provision says and what it has been found to mean are two very different things. In English law, if injuries are inflicted on a pregnant woman that also affect the foetus and the baby is subsequently born alive, but dies as a result of the injuries, then the attacker can be convicted of the child's manslaughter[5] and the same approach would almost certainly be adopted in Ireland.

'Double effect'

[12.03]

It should be pointed out that there is a difference between abortion and the unavoidable death of *in utero* life that occurs during or as a consequence of an attempt to avert an immediate threat to the life of a mother. This is called 'double effect'.

> **Example 1**
>
> A surgeon is operating on a woman to staunch severe and life-threatening abdominal bleeding following a stabbing. During the operation, she realises that the woman she is operating upon is pregnant, but also that a hysterectomy is necessary to save the woman's life. The weeks-old pregnancy would not be viable outside the womb and without the operation both mother and unborn child will die.

The hysterectomy in such circumstances would not amount to an abortion in law – the life-saving operation would have a 'double effect', namely the necessary hysterectomy together with the unavoidable loss of the foetus. Double effect is concerned with the primary intention of the practitioner: if the primary intention is to treat the mother, then the double effect of loss of *in utero* life will not be unlawful. We return to double effect in the context of treating the extremely ill patient in the next chapter and the same principles apply there. In the above example the threat to life is obvious, immediate and inevitable, but what of the threat of non-fatal or of psychological damage? In such cases, double effect would not apply and it is questions of what constitutes an immediate threat to a mother's life on which much of the controversy and divisiveness surrounding abortion in Ireland has turned.

The evolution of current Irish law on abortion

[12.04]

Abortion in Ireland is covered by an aged piece of legislation that pre-dates the foundation of the state itself, the Offences Against the Person Act 1861. The Act sets out the following crimes relating to abortion and the maximum sentences (in brackets) that may be imposed on those found guilty of such crimes:[6]

- performing or procuring an abortion (life imprisonment);
- providing the equipment or 'poison or other noxious thing' used to perform an abortion (five years);
- concealing the death of a child, whether it died before, during or after birth (two years).

In England,[7] the legal position before laws were passed to regulate abortion was that in order to protect the physical and mental well-being of, for example, a teenage rape victim, a doctor could justify performing an abortion notwithstanding the ban imposed by the Act.[8] In other words, abortion remained illegal, but the doctor would have a defence if she could show that the abortion was necessary to safeguard the life or health, physical or mental, of the mother. No similar interpretation of the 1861 legislation has ever been made in a criminal case in Ireland, although the effect of the *X* case judgment was, as we will see, somewhat similar.

Not only was there no tendency to liberalise the law on abortion in Ireland, but the 8th Amendment to the Constitution, formally adopted in 1983, was believed to copper-fasten the prohibition against abortion. By placing a Constitutional guarantee on the life of the unborn it was anticipated that only by a further countermanding Constitutional amendment could the guarantee ever be threatened in any way.[9] The following provision became part of Article 40 of the Constitution:

> 'The State acknowledges the right to life of the unborn and, with due regard to the equal right to life of the mother, guarantees in its laws to respect, and, as far as practicable, by its laws to defend and vindicate that right.'[10]

However there was a problem: no law was ever introduced to explain precisely what the Amendment meant and, in particular, to clarify exactly what was implied by 'the equal right to life of the mother'. It was simply presumed that the net effect of the 8th Amendment was that abortion was definitively illegal in Ireland. Therefore when it fell to the Supreme Court to consider the prohibition on abortion in Ireland, their response was both eagerly awaited and surprising. In the *X* case,[11] the court was asked to resolve the predicament of a 14 year old girl, pregnant as a result of rape, who wished to travel to the United Kingdom for an abortion, but who was prevented from doing so by the authorities once her plight became known to them. Expert evidence had been presented to the High Court (which heard the original application) that the girl would commit suicide if not permitted to terminate the pregnancy.

The Supreme Court placed great reliance on the fact that the Constitution recognised 'the equal right to the life of the mother'. The Court reasoned that this particular clause clearly envisaged that abortion would sometimes be permissible, for example the scenario of 'double effect' (see section **[12.03]**). Accordingly, the Court was prepared to find that where the right to life of the mother was threatened, as it was in the *X* case by the risk of suicide, then the mother's right to life *could* permit her to have an abortion. As with many legal cases involving personal rights there is a degree of balancing involved between the different rights, but at the core of the *X* case judgment is a certain pragmatism. If the right to life of the child were to be defended to its uttermost limit in the circumstances of the case, one possible outcome could be the suicide of the mother, with the resultant loss of both of the lives that the Constitution was attempting to protect.[12] The conclusion of the Court, in deciding that the girl should be permitted to travel for an abortion is important and was as follows:

> '...[T]he proper test to be applied is that if it is established as a matter of probability that there is a real and substantial risk to the life, as distinct from the health, of the mother, which can only be avoided by the termination of her pregnancy, such termination is permissible, having regard to the true interpretation of Article 40.3.3° of the Constitution.'

In other words, the Constitutional amendment of 1983, far from providing a bulwark against abortion, instead proved a springboard for the Irish courts to hold that abortion is legal in certain circumstances. Those circumstances must pose a 'real and substantial risk' to the life, not merely the health,[13] of the mother and could include a risk to life in the form of threatened suicide. Furthermore, the court's decision meant that an Irish citizen was free to travel outside the jurisdiction for the purpose of procuring a termination of her pregnancy.

Following the *X* case, three further amendments were put forward for approval or rejection by the Irish people. While the electorate voted not to accept a provision that would allow for termination of pregnancy in limited circumstances, including a real and substantial risk to the life of the mother but *excluding* the threat of suicide,[14] two new Constitutional provisions relating to abortion were accepted:[15]

— Nothing in Article 40.3.3° would limit the freedom to travel between Ireland and any other State.[16]

— Nothing in Article 40.3.3° would limit the freedom to make available information relating to services lawfully available in another state.

If it was hoped that these amendments would resolve matters, it was a forlorn hope: while the Constitution and the Offences Against the Person Act 1861 still nominally banned abortion, the Supreme Court had found that the ban was at best, conditional. In addition, new Constitutional provisions now enshrined a right to travel for an abortion and a right to provide information to women regarding the availability of abortion in other countries, but there was no clarity about whether or not abortion was legal, although the *X* case judgment suggested it was in certain circumstances. Only the Offences Against the Person Act 1861 stood between abortion and legality in Ireland and even so, a termination would, according to the *X* case logic, probably be legal where there was a real and substantial risk to the life of the mother, including the threat of suicide.

Providing information

[12.05]

After the passage of the Constitutional amendment allowing for information about abortion the government introduced legislation to govern the provision of that information: the Regulation of Information (Services Outside the State for Termination of Pregnancies) Act 1995. As far as clinicians are concerned, the Act means that it is unlawful to advocate or promote abortion when providing information, although 'advocacy' and 'promotion' are not defined in the Act. If information regarding services for the termination of pregnancy is given, it must be given in the context of 'truthful and objective' information about all options open to the pregnant woman and the information must relate to services that are legal in the state to which the information refers.[17] Information on abortion cannot be provided by a person who has, or whose employer has, a financial interest in the provision of abortion services outside the state, which may include receiving financial benefits, such as donations or commissions, from a body that provides services for the termination of pregnancies.[18]

Bizarrely, even though:

(a) a practitioner may legally give information to a patient relating to a termination of pregnancy outside the State,

(b) the woman may travel outside the state for that termination of pregnancy, and

(c) many commentators[19] feel that a necessary consequence of the decision in the *X* case is that abortion is in certain circumstances legal in Ireland, the 1995 Act insists that the practitioner may not assist in the making an appointment for her patient. She may however, furnish the patient with relevant 'medical, surgical, clinical, social or other like records or notes relating to [the patient].'[20]

The latest chapters

[12.06]

A succession of governments resolutely failed to introduce legislation that would help to clarify the law on abortion in Ireland. After a protracted period of consultation,[21] the government sought to introduce another Constitutional amendment in 2002. The proposed amendment took the step of proposing a change in the Constitution that would make the protection of the 'life of the unborn in the womb' dependent not on a provision in the Constitution itself but on the Protection of Human Life in Pregnancy Act 2002. The Act would have been brought into law only if the amendment had been passed and its key provisions were as follows:[22]

— No person would be permitted to carry out or effect an abortion in the state.

— Abortion was defined as 'the intentional destruction by any means of unborn human life after implantation in the womb of a woman'.

— Abortion did not include the carrying out of a medical procedure by a medical practitioner in the course of which or as a result of which unborn human life is ended, where the procedure is, in the reasonable opinion of the practitioner, necessary to prevent a real and substantial risk of loss of the woman's life other than by self-destruction.

In other words the referendum would have modified the *X* case position. Abortion would be unlawful. It would not, however, be an abortion for a medical practitioner to perform a termination with the aim of averting a real and substantial risk to the life of the mother, but such a risk could not include the threat of suicide. The amendment to the Constitution was narrowly defeated, so the Protection of Human Life in Pregnancy Act 2002 was not introduced and the law remained unchanged. We look below at how this leaves the law on abortion in Ireland.

The medical council element

In mid-2001 and as part of the penumbra of the referendum to amend the Constitution, the Irish Medical Council set about changing the expression of its stance on abortion set out in its *Guide to Ethical Conduct and Behaviour*. After an amount of rancour and a failed legal challenge, a compromise was achieved. The compromise provision reads:[23]

> THE CHILD IN UTERO
>
> The Council recognises that termination of pregnancy can occur when there is a real and substantial risk to the life of the mother and subscribes to the views expressed in Part 2 of the written submission of the Institute of Obstetricians and Gynaecologists to the All-Party Oireachtas Committee on the Constitution...[24]

As can be seen from its text (see endnote 24), the submission of the Institute does not say much although it recognises (in paragraph 2) that:

> '[T]here is a fundamental difference between abortion carried out with the intention of taking the life of the baby, for example for social reasons, and the unavoidable death of the baby resulting from essential treatment to protect the life of the mother'.

The Institute submission, however, does not define 'essential treatment' and is careful to say in part 1 of its submission that its opinion is a 'medical' one, suggesting that the Institute is avoiding, rather than necessarily rejecting, consideration of the psychiatric imperative for termination. Nothing in the *Guide* or in the Institute submission suggests that the latter is an exhaustive opinion and for the Medical Council to say that it 'subscribes' to the views in the submission is very far indeed from saying that it is 'bound' by that submission.

The Medical Council guideline appears to accept that an abortion may be performed by an Irish doctor where there is a real and substantial risk to the life of the mother. It takes support for the fact that such 'real and substantial risks' occur from the submission made by the Institute of Obstetricians and Gynaecologists. However the *Guide*, like the Institute of Obstetricians and Gynaecologists submission makes no determination on the subject of the 'risk of self-destruction'. It is unlikely, although the matter would be for a court to decide, that if a doctor were involved in a termination that was acceptable within the terms of the *X* case, she could be prosecuted, disciplined or struck off for doing so.

When pregnancy begins

[12.07]

There are multiple dimensions to any discussion of when human life begins, but we are concerned here only with the legal position and its effects on clinical practice. It is the teaching of many churches and the belief of many individuals that life begins at the moment of conception, but the legal position is different. One reason why this legal distinction is important is that a legal definition of human life or pregnancy beginning with fertilisation has an impact on methods of contraception such as post-coital contraception (or the 'morning after pill') and intrauterine contraceptive devices (the IUCD or 'coil') that operate as post-fertilisation contraceptives. If the law identifies fertilisation as the starting point of pregnancy, then these contraceptives could legally speaking be regarded as abortion.

Irish law's approach is that life begins at implantation and a number of sources support this contention. One semantic reason was identified by the report on abortion produced by the All-Party Committee on the Constitution:[25]

> 'The Family Planning Act 1979 specifically prohibits the importation, sale and distribution of abortifacients. In as much as the morning after pill [and by logical extension, the IUCD] is available and prescribed the legal presumption must be that it is not regarded as an abortifacient.'

Similarly, when the Protection of Human Life in Pregnancy Bill was drafted with the intention of being enacted were the 2002 amendment passed, the Bill defined abortion as 'the intentional destruction by any means of unborn human life *after implantation in the womb* of a woman.'[26] Modern English legislation[27] and case law[28] uniformly supports the idea that implantation rather than fertilisation is the legal point at which pregnancy starts. It appears therefore that in Irish law there is no question of the 'morning after pill' or coil use (or insertion) being regarded as abortifacient so long as it is either used or inserted before the likely time of implantation, which is anything from five to ten days after intercourse.

The law on abortion as it stands?

[12.08]

Even the most casual reader may have a growing awareness that the legal position on abortion in Ireland is confused. Essentially, the starting point of the law, laid out in the Offences Against the Person Act 1861 is that abortion is illegal in Ireland. What the Supreme Court did in the *X* case was to create an exception to the law: abortion would not be illegal if performed by a medical practitioner to avert a real and substantial risk to the life of the mother, including the risk of suicide.

It remains to be seen whether the Irish Government will opt for a further referendum that seeks to define the parameters of abortion in Ireland or whether it will introduce a law that enshrines either the position set out in the *X* case or some other statutory approach to abortion. In *A & B v Eastern Health Board and* C,[29] the courts continued to apply the logic of the *X* case. The child C was a teenage girl in the care of a health board after she had been raped and consequently became pregnant. The child wished to have an abortion: her parents opposed that course of action, while psychiatric evidence suggested that the child was at a risk of suicide if the abortion were not performed. The court decided that the health board, as part of its responsibility to care for the child, had the right, under the Child Care Act 1991, to make decisions on the child's 'medical treatment', into which category abortion fell.[30] Accordingly, the board was empowered by the court to take the decision that the girl, in accordance with her own wishes, should undergo a termination in England.

The author's opinion is that, irrespective of personal moral considerations, the *X* case brings the only clarity and certainty to this fraught issue and should provide the basis for legislation. Irrespective of the form that legislation ultimately takes, there is a strong philosophical argument to say that abortion, as with other areas of life, should as far possible be 'governed by rules which are fixed, knowable and certain'[31], in preference to the confusion that presently reigns.

Quick Reference Guide 12.1

Abortion and the law in Ireland: the current position?

- Human life in pregnancy – legally speaking – begins at implantation.
- A practitioner may legally give information to a patient relating to termination of pregnancy outside the state. She may not, however, make an appointment for her patient.
- A woman has the freedom to travel outside the state for a termination of a pregnancy that presents a real and substantial risk to her life, and not merely to her health (an important distinction from the equivalent English approach), including the risk of suicide. The termination of which she wishes to avail herself must be one that is legally available in the country to which she is travelling.
- Many feel that a necessary and obvious consequence of the decision in the *X* case is that abortion would, in those circumstances where there is a real and substantial risk to the life of the mother including the risk of suicide, be legal in Ireland.

The law in Great Britain

[12.09]

On the basis that the majority of women in Ireland who opt for termination of pregnancy set out for England,[32] it is sensible to briefly set out the law in Britain[32] when it comes to abortion. As we have noted, information on abortion can only be provided and women may only travel for terminations when those terminations are legal in the destination country, therefore knowledge of what constitutes a legal abortion in Britain may be important for the clinician. As in Ireland, the British law nominally prohibits abortion but the law, in the form of the Abortion Act 1967, also creates exceptions. A termination of pregnancy will not be an offence

> 'when a pregnancy is terminated by a registered medical practitioner, if two registered medical practitioners are of the opinion, formed in good faith
>
> (a) That the pregnancy has not exceeded its 24th week and that the continuance of the pregnancy would involve risk, greater than if the pregnancy were terminated, of injury to the physical or mental health of the pregnant woman or any existing children of her family, or
>
> (b) That the termination is necessary to prevent grave permanent injury to the physical or mental health of the pregnant woman; or
>
> (c) That the continuance of the pregnancy would involve risk to the life of the pregnant woman greater that if the pregnancy were terminated; or
>
> (d) That there is a substantial risk that if the child were born it would suffer from such physical or mental abnormalities as to be seriously handicapped'[34].

It should be noted that there is only a time limit of 24 weeks[35] for the termination of pregnancy where there is a risk of physical or mental injury to the pregnant woman. No time limit applies to any of the other grounds. In any event, there is no question that the risk must be one only to the life of the mother as is the case in Ireland: a threat posed to her health or to any children she already has will suffice. The UK Abortion Act 1967 allows doctors to opt out of a termination if conscientiously opposed to the procedure (and where the procedure is not immediately necessary to save the life of the mother),[36] but the doctor is still obliged to refer her patient to someone who will provide the service.[37] The right to opt out only applies to those who actively participate in the termination and not to those who are ancillary to the process or procedure.[38] Note too that a father has no right under English law, or indeed under the law of most countries, to intervene in a woman's decision to consent to an abortion.[39]

INFANTICIDE

[12.10]

We mentioned at the beginning of this chapter that for a killing to be homicide, the victim must have been born. There is one further qualification that is of interest here. A mother, who kills her child in the first year after its birth as a result of mental imbalance caused by that birth, may be found guilty of infanticide rather than homicide. The elements are that the killing must occur at some time in the child's first year of life, the woman must cause the death by some 'wilful act or omission'[40] and the mind of the killer must be disturbed in some way. If the killing does not fulfil the criteria, it is likely to be murder or manslaughter.[41] Either the prosecuting authorities can bring an accusation of infanticide instead of murder against the mother or the accused herself can raise the question of infanticide at her trial and it is then open to the jury to find her guilty of that rather than homicide if they choose to do so. Infanticide, if it attracts a custodial sentence at all, is often punished more lightly than murder or manslaughter.

Infanticide is a crime that may only be committed by a mother, fathers cannot commit it - a gender-specific element that has come in for criticism.[42] It has also been argued that the leniency afforded to mothers who kill infants of less than one year is disproportionate to the gravity of the crime and the risk faced by infants.[43] The necessary mental imbalance required for a verdict of infanticide is not entirely clear[44] and it may be sufficient (although this point is uncertain) for it to be social and/or psychological in origin, rather than purely medical or psychiatric. The Royal College of Psychiatrists, when submitting evidence to a UK commission considering infanticide, called for the recognition of social and psychological as well as psychiatric factors as mental triggers for infanticide, including 'overwhelming stress' from the social environment or from the addition of a new member to a household already struggling with poverty. They also advocated a failure of bonding between mother and child due to illness or disability as a possible cause. The commission however was reluctant to accept these contentions.[45]

Quick Reference Guide 12.2

Elements of infanticide

- ❖ Only a mother may commit an infanticide and death must occur as the result of a wilful act or omission due to the balance of the mother's mind being disturbed
- ❖ The victim must be a child of the woman in question and less than 12 months old at the time of the killing.
- ❖ The disturbance of the mind leading to the killing will often be a psychiatric derangement, but there is an argument that it may be sufficient for the mother to be suffering a psychological reaction, perhaps due to social pressures such as poverty or domestic abuse.
- ❖ It is for a jury to decide whether an infanticide has been committed. The prosecuting authorities may bring the charge of infanticide when prosecuting a mother for the killing of her child or the mother herself may raise the question of infanticide if charged with murder.

Endnotes

1 Criminal Justice Act 1964, s 4.

2 *R v Hutty* [1953] VLR 338, *per* Barry J.

3 Article 40.3.3° (inserted by the 8th Amendment to the Constitution).

4 This is appears to be the view of the authors of Charleton, McDermott & Bolger *Criminal Law* (2000) para 7.54.

5 *Attorney General's Reference (No 3 of 1994)* [1997] 3 All ER 936.

6 Offences Against the Person Act 1861, ss 58-60.

7 Where the Offences Against the Person Act 1861 was law until the passage of the Abortion Act 1967.

8 *R v Bourne* [1939] 1 QB 687, *per* Naghten J: 'If the doctor is of the opinion on reasonable grounds and with adequate knowledge, that the probable consequence of the continuance of the pregnancy will be to make the woman a physical or mental wreck, the jury are quite entitled to take the view that the doctor who, under those circumstances and in that honest belief, operates, is operating for the purpose of preserving the life of the mother.'

9 If the ban on abortion were only dependent on the Offences Against the Person Act 1861, the Act could have been repealed and replaced by a decision of the Oireachtas, perhaps by an Act permitting abortion. Only the Irish people, by referendum, may change the Constitution.

10 Article 40.3.3º.

11 *Attorney General v X* [1992] IR 1.

12 Similarly, if the threat was a physical or organic one, refusal to countenance saving the mother's life could result in the loss of both lives.

13 This contrasts with the approach of the English courts before legislation was introduced to regulate abortion in Britain. In *R v Bourne* [1939] 1 QB 687, the threat of the woman becoming a 'physical or mental wreck' was sufficient to provide a defence to a doctor accused of performing an abortion.

14 The rejected amendment read:

> 'It shall be unlawful to terminate the life of an unborn unless such termination is necessary to save the life, as distinct from the health, of the mother where there is an illness or disorder of the mother giving rise to a real and substantial risk to her life, not being a risk of self-destruction.'

Two-thirds of those who voted in the 1992 referendum rejected this particular amendment, while just over two-thirds of voters accepted the amendments permitting travel and the provision of information relating to abortion.

15 The 13th and 14th Amendments to the Constitution, formally enacted in December 1992.

16 It is important to note that this is not a *right* to travel but rather a *freedom* to travel in certain circumstances. A woman who wished to travel to have an abortion for reasons other than a real and substantial risk to her health could in theory be legally prevented from doing so. See also *A & B v Eastern Health Board and C* [1988] 1 IR 464 which reiterates this approach.

17 The Regulation of Information (Services Outside the State for Termination of Pregnancies) Act 1995, s 5.

18 The Regulation of Information (Services Outside the State for Termination of Pregnancies) Act 1995, ss 6 and 7.

19 See Shatter, *Family Law* (4th edn, 1997) para 1.103.

20 The Regulation of Information (Services Outside the State for Termination of Pregnancies) Act 1995, s 8.

21 See All-Party Oireachtas Committee on the Constitution *5th Progress Report- Abortion* (2000).

22 Twenty-fifth Amendment of the Constitution (Protection of Human Life in Pregnancy) Bill 2001, Second Schedule

23 *Guide to Ethical Conduct and Behaviour - Amendment No 1 to Fifth Edition 1998* (2001). Inserts para. 26.5 into the 1998 Guidelines.

24 *Fifth Progress Report – Abortion* (2000) p A407. The written submission of the Institute of Obstetricians and Gynaecologists to the All-Party Oireachtas Committee on the Constitution was as follows:

1. The Institute of Obstetricians and Gynaecologists is the professional body representing the speciality of Obstetrics and Gynaecology in Ireland. The Executive Council of the

Institute has examined the Green Paper on Abortion and the members have been consulted. We welcome the Green Paper, which provides a comprehensive, up to date and objective analysis of the issues arising in the care of the pregnant woman. Our expertise is in the medical area and our comments are confined to these aspects.

2. In current obstetrical practice rare complications can arise where therapeutic intervention is required at a stage in pregnancy when there will be little or no prospect for the survival of the baby, due to extreme immaturity. In these exceptional situations failure to intervene may result in the death of both mother and baby. We consider that there is a fundamental difference between abortion carried out with the intention of taking the life of the baby, for example for social reasons, and the unavoidable death of the baby resulting from essential treatment to protect the life of the mother.

3. We recognise our responsibility to provide aftercare for women who decide to leave the State for termination of pregnancy. We recommend that full support and follow up services be made available for all women whose pregnancies have been terminated, whatever the circumstances.

[25] *5th Progress Report – Abortion* (2000) p 102. Material in square brackets added.

[26] Second schedule to the Protection of Human Life in Pregnancy Bill 2001 (italics added).

[27] Human Fertilisation and Embryology Act 1990, s 2(3). See also the New Zealand Crimes Act 1961 (amended 1977), s 182A.

[28] For example *R (Sheaton) v Secretary of State for Health ex parte Society for the Protection of the Unborn Child* [2002] EWHC 610 (18 April 2002), HC. This case specifically concerned the question of whether the 'morning after pill' constituted abortion.

[29] *A & B v Eastern Health Board and C* [1998] 1 IR 464.

[30] See ch 8 for a discussion of care orders made under the Child Care Act 1991 to allow health boards to care for 'at risk' children.

31 Raz, *The Authority of Law*, Oxford, 1979.

[32] Figures from 2001 suggest that 6625 women who underwent abortion in British clinics gave Irish addresses (source: UK National Statistics Office: www.nso.gov.uk). This represented an increase of 244 (3.8%) on the previous year and maintains a continuing upward trend. See also *Women and Crisis Pregnancy* (1998) Stationery Office, Dublin. The figure is likely to be higher: it is believed that many women give false addresses.

[33] The law is governed by the Abortion Act 1967, amended by the Human Fertilisation and Embryology Act 1990: the Act does not extend to Northern Ireland. For more on the law on abortion in the UK, see Kennedy & Grubb *Medical Law* (3rd edn, 2000) ch 11.

[34] Abortion Act 1967, s 1.

[35] See Kennedy & Grubb *Medical Law* (3rd edn, 2000) p 1422 for a discussion of the question of the date from which the 24 weeks should begin to run. In the interests of legal certainty, the conventional medical practice of dating the start of pregnancy from the first day of the last menstrual period should probably be followed: see Francis and Johnston *Medical Treatment Decisions and the Law* (2001) London p 78.

[36] Abortion Act 1967, s 4(2).

[37] Similar provisions exist in the Medical Council *Guide to Ethical Conduct and Behaviour* (5th edn, 1998) para 2.5: Conscientious Objection

> 'If a practitioner has a conscientious objection to a course of action this should be explained [to the patient] and the names of other doctors made available to the patient.'

[38] So a secretary could not refuse to type referral letters and claim conscientious objection: *Janaway v Salford AHA* [1989] AC 537.

[39] *Paton v Trustees of British Pregnancy Advisory Service* [1979] QB 276; *Paton v United Kingdom* (1980) 3 EHRR 408. In the USA, the Supreme Court has said that a woman is not

under any obligation to consult her husband, let alone seek his consent to termination: *Planned Parenthood of SE Pennsylvania v Casey* (1992) 112 S Ct 2791.

40 For example, smothering the child would be an 'act'; failing to feed it would be an 'omission'.

41 Infanticide Act 1949. For more detail on the principles underpinning infanticide, see Oberman 'Mothers Who Kill' 34 Am Crim LR 1 (1997).

42 Wilczynski & Morris 'Parents who Kill their Children' [1993] Crim LR 31.

43 Maier-Katkin & Ogle 'A Rationale for Infanticide Laws' [1993] Crim LR 903.

44 The Infanticide Act 1949 speaks (s 1(3)(a)) of the balance of the mind being disturbed 'by reason of the effect of lactation' – lactation is no longer regarded as a cause of such a disturbance. Postnatal depression would be an obvious example of a psychiatric disorder occurring in the first year of life.

45 Criminal Law Revision Committee, *14th Report* (1980) paras 100-114; draft Criminal Code, (LCR -177) clause 64.

Chapter 13

The Extremes of Life II: the End of Life

Introduction

[13.01]

This chapter addresses the questions of law that arise at the end of life. In particular we examine the question of whether or not there is a 'right to die' in Ireland. We look at the meaning of the term 'right to die' and examine how the system of voluntary euthanasia and assisted suicide operates in Holland. We consider too decision making at the end of life, including 'Do Not Resuscitate' orders, advance statements on medical treatment and power of attorney.

Death and dying

[13.02]

There is no legal definition of 'death' in Ireland. In many other countries, such as England, the definition is taken to be that of brain death and the Irish Medical Council envisages brain death as being diagnostic of death.[1] This chapter however is less concerned with death itself and more concerned with the decisions and decision-making that precede death.

There is certainly no legal question that, as a matter of clinical necessity or inevitability, doctors may take steps to desist from futile treatment. There is no legal or moral stigma attached to calling a halt to a prolonged but fruitless resuscitation attempt on a patient who has suffered a cardiac arrest. There is no problem with turning off the life-support machine of a patient who has suffered brain stem death. However, there are many greyer areas, including patients who are not clinically dead, or for whom death is not imminent, or who request help in securing a peaceful death on their own terms. The Medical Council *Guide to Ethical Conduct and Behaviour* says the following about the dying patient:

> 'Where death is imminent, it is the responsibility of the doctor to take care that the sick person dies with dignity, in comfort and with as little suffering as possible. Deliberately causing the death of a patient is professional misconduct.'[2]

A right to die?

[13.03]

There are those who argue that all life is sacred and that life, insofar as it can be, should be protected at all costs. Questions of the moral value of all human life lie outside the consideration of this book, but it should be pointed out, that as with abortion in the previous chapter, some disagree with the legal position adopted in this country, which is that respect for the sanctity of life does not mean preserving life at all costs. In the words of one judge:

> 'To care for the dying, to love and cherish them, and to free them from suffering rather than simply to postpone death, is to have fundamental respect for the sanctity of life and its end.'[3]

Two broad issues should be considered when discussing the existence of a 'right to die' in Irish law. The first is the question of consent. As we have seen elsewhere in this book,[4] there is an obligation on the practitioner to seek consent to proposed treatment from her patient and the patient has the right to refuse treatment, even if refusal will result in death and even if refusal is for irrational reasons. The Irish position on refusal of treatment has been stated authoritatively by the Irish Supreme Court in the *Ward of Court* case:

> 'The consent which is given by an adult of full capacity is a matter of choice. It is not necessarily a decision based on medical considerations. Thus, medical treatment may be refused for other than medical reasons or reasons most citizens would not regard as rational, but the person of full age and capacity may make the decision for their own reasons.'[5]

In that sense then, there is a 'right to choose to die' but that right, as will be seen when we deal with the question of euthanasia below (see section **[13.06]**), is merely a right to refuse treatment or to opt for a treatment with a poorer prospect of success. It does not extend or amount to a right to involve others in bringing about or hastening death, but allowing for that exclusion there is a 'right' to choose to die in the sense of a competent adult exercising his choice not to continue with a course of treatment.

The Ward of Court Case

[13.04]

The second and more complex consideration, involves the person who cannot make a choice at all about lifesaving or life-sustaining treatment and who therefore cannot refuse or consent to treatment. The above extracts taken from the *Ward of Court* case are significant in this regard not only because of what they say, but also because they arose in a case that determined whether a patient in a Persistent Vegetative State (PVS) had the 'right' to be allowed to die. The questions the court had to answer were many. Should such a right be recognised or should sanctity of life be paramount? If there was such a right, what were its limits? And finally, if a decision were taken to allow a person to die who was incapable of consenting to or refusing life-sustaining treatment, then on what basis and from what perspective should such a decision be taken?

In the *Ward of Court* case, a woman had undergone a minor operation in 1972 at the age of 22 years and during the operation suffered a series of cardiac arrests that resulted in profound brain damage. She remained a patient in a long-stay hospital facility and in 1974 was made a Ward of Court.[6] The woman was in what was known as a near-persistent vegetative state (near PVS[7]). She was almost entirely unresponsive, totally unable to care for herself and was fed artificially by a nasogastric[8] tube until 1992 and thereafter by a gastrostomy[9] tube. Part of the reason for replacement of the former with the latter was the woman's apparent resistance to insertion of the nasogastric tube. Without such feeding and without the intervention of medical care during times of clinical crisis (such as when she suffered infections), she would have died. The mother of the Ward (who was also the 'committee' of the ward[10]) applied to the courts for permission to withdraw further life-sustaining treatment, including artificial feeding.[11] Evidence before the court suggested that if feeding were discontinued the woman would die without distress in the space of approximately two weeks.

The High Court found that the withdrawal of treatment would be legally permissible in the case of a patient who was suffering from PVS and its decision was subsequently endorsed by the Supreme Court. In reaching their decision, the courts laid down a number of markers:

— Treatment decisions on behalf of the incompetent patient should in the first instance be taken by the family of the patient in the light of available medical opinion.

— Feeding of the woman by means of nasogastric tubes and subsequently the gastrostomy tube was inherently artificial and also a form of treatment. One judge saw 'no difference in principle between the artificial provision of air by a ventilator and the artificial provision of nourishment by a tube.'

— Taking decisions of such magnitude involves a balancing of all of the issues involved, but the paramount concern will be the 'best interests' of the patient. The views of the family were important, but could not be the sole decider of the case.

— The court should approach the matter from the standpoint of a 'prudent, good and loving parent' in deciding what course should be adopted.

When it came to the question of a patient's 'best interests', the court favoured the way it had been defined by the English House of Lords in the case of a young man left in a PVS in the aftermath of the Hillsborough football stadium disaster:[12]

> 'It is crucial for the understanding of this question that the question itself should be correctly formulated. The question is not whether the doctor should take a course which will kill his patient, or even take a course which has the effect of accelerating his death. The question is whether the doctor should or should not continue to provide his patient with medical treatment or care which, if continued, will prolong his patient's life ... The question is not whether it is in the best interests of the patient that he should die. The question is whether it is in the best interests of the patient that his life should be prolonged by the continuance of this form of medical treatment or care.'

Outcome of the Ward of Court *case*

The outcome of the case can be viewed in a narrow and a broad sense. In the narrower sense, the courts found that, having balanced the rights of all of those involved including the question of the 'best interests'[13] of the patient and having decided from the 'standpoint of a prudent, good and loving parent', it was legally permissible to withhold artificial life-sustaining treatment from this particular patient in a near-PVS.[14] The right to life includes the right to die peacefully and naturally and not to have life 'artificially maintained by the provision of nourishment by abnormally artificial means which have no curative effect and which are intended merely to prolong life.'[15] It does not, however, give the caring parent discretion to withhold treatment whenever they think that non-intervention is in the patient's best interests. Care must be exercised in withholding care from the incompetent patient, but it can be legally permissible.

In the broader sense, the case enshrined the twin principles of autonomy and consent and the natural corollary of the right of the adult of sound mind to refuse treatment, even at the risk of death. Only in cases where the possibility of obtaining such consent is absent may the court decide the matter and it will do so in what it adjudges to be the best interests of the patient. It is worth noting that the Medical Council is more cautious than the Irish courts when it comes to the question of withdrawing treatment from the patient who cannot communicate his consent. Unlike the courts of Ireland and England, the Medical Council categorises feeding and hydration as 'basic needs' rather than medication or 'abnormally artificial means' of prolonging life:

> 'For the seriously ill patient who is unable to communicate or understand, it is desirable that the doctor discusses management with the next of kin or the legal guardians prior to reaching a decision about the use or non-use of treatments **which will not contribute to recovery from the primary illness.** The Council reiterates its view that access to nutrition and hydration remain (*sic.*) one of the basic needs of human beings and all reasonable and practical efforts should be made to maintain both of them.'[16]

What characterises 'reasonable and practical efforts' is not clear, perhaps deliberately so, in order to allow for the exercise of clinical judgement as each individual situation demands.

The right to die and euthanasia

[13.05]

The *Ward of Court* case is not, however, a manifesto for euthanasia nor does it create an untrammelled right to die. The case certainly upheld the doctrine of the patient's autonomy[17] to consent or to withhold consent to treatment as he sees fit. Furthermore, the court took a stance that artificial life-sustaining treatment could be lawfully withheld when it is a patient's best interests to do so. However, the decision on withdrawing treatment applied only to effectively insensate patients with no prospect of recovery and who were being kept alive by 'artificial' means. The Chief Justice was explicit:

> '[The issues in the case] are not about euthanasia and are not about putting down the old and the infirm, the mentally defective or the physically infirm but are about the question whether, under our law and Constitution, artificial feeding and antibiotic drugs may be withheld from the [woman in the *Ward of Court* case].'[18]

There is no legal provision for euthanasia in Ireland. While it may be possible to omit to do something, such as the continuation of artificial life-sustaining treatment, it is not permissible to take an explicit step with the principal aim of shortening the patient's life.[19] A practitioner, whatever her clinical discipline, who administers medication to a patient for the purpose of ending his life would be guilty of murder. This is true even if the patient asks for such treatment to be given. The only exception is the principle of 'double effect', already discussed above in the context of abortion (see section **[12.08]**). A patient, for example a terminally ill patient with cancer, are in such extreme and debilitating pain that high doses of morphine may be necessary for the relief of his symptoms. It may be the case that the dose will hasten the patient's death as well as relieving his symptoms. Such a 'double effect' scenario is not regarded as legally or ethically blameworthy: the primary aim of the clinician in giving the morphine is to relieve pain and suffering, not to cause death (even if she is aware from clinical experience that death may result).[20] Indeed, if the legal position were not so, doctors might be inhibited from relieving their patients' symptoms for fear of being guilty of homicide. The key is that the doctor stops when she has given enough medication to relieve the relevant symptoms; she must not continue beyond that point or her intention may be doubted. Similar scenarios arise with the patient who is manifestly dying: there will not be an obligation on the clinical team, having duly weighed the medical issues, to prolong life through enforced feeding or futile treatment through tubes or drips or by forlorn attempts at resuscitation but there is no licence to quicken the patient's passing.

There is then a great difference between withholding treatment that is of no benefit or giving treatment that may have the unavoidable consequence of hastening a patient demise and taking steps explicitly and deliberately aimed at causing death, even if the motives for doing so are compassionate. In the *Ward of Court* case, one judge said starkly:

> 'Even in the case of the most horrendous disability, any course of action or treatment aimed at terminating life or accelerating death is unlawful.'[21]

In 2002, the English courts were asked to consider a request from a woman with motor neurone disease that her husband not be prosecuted if he aided her in committing suicide. The English House of Lords[22] and the European Court of Human Rights[23] both rejected her application. Of particular significance was that the Court of Human Rights said that any right to life did not bring with it a right to have that life ended nor did the refusal of the right to an assisted treatment amount to 'degrading' treatment of the woman.[24] An Irish court would take the same approach.

Some definitions

[13.06]

There are at least two definitions of euthanasia. The word 'euthanasia' means 'good (or peaceful) death' and is used in two main contexts. The first is the ending of a patient's life in what is determined to be in the patient's interests, a concept which tallies with the terms 'passive' euthanasia and 'selective non-intervention' and which reflects the decision in the *Ward of Court* case. The other category and the one generally recognised by observers as being 'classic' euthanasia involves taking active steps to end a patient's life at the request of the patient, sometimes termed 'voluntary' or 'active' euthanasia or even 'mercy killing'. It is this second category, the taking of active steps to bring about or hasten death, against which the Irish courts were most determined to erect a firewall in the *Ward of Court* case.[25]

In Ireland the law prohibits both voluntary euthanasia and 'assisted suicide' (that is providing a person with the means to take his own life).[26] Very often both are casually regarded as an inseparable entity, but that is not so, the two are obviously different and there is one state in the USA that has legalised assisted suicide while keeping voluntary euthanasia outside the law.[27]

The Dutch experience

[13.07]

In the same way that it seemed prudent to scrutinise briefly the way in which English abortion laws worked, at this point we look at the operation of a law that provides for euthanasia. One of the very few countries to have formally enshrined euthanasia is Holland in the Termination of Life on Request and Assisted Suicide (Review Procedures) Act.[28] The historical process that led to the current state of affairs lies largely outside the scope of this text,[29] but the present position is this: In Holland, euthanasia and assisted suicide are both illegal, although they have both long been categorised differently from (and attracted far lighter punishment than) murder or manslaughter. However, there is an exception: in a case where a doctor is involved in an act of euthanasia or assisted suicide, she will not be prosecuted if she adheres to the requirements of the law. The Dutch Criminal Code in relation to euthanasia reads as follows:

> Any person who terminates another person's life at that other person's express and earnest request shall be liable to a term of imprisonment or a … fine.
>
> The [above] act … shall not be an offence if it is committed by a physician who fulfils the due care criteria set out in section 2 of the Termination of Life on Request and Assisted Suicide (Review Procedures) Act, and if the physician notifies the municipal pathologist of this act …[30]

This exception only applies to doctors, so that in all other circumstances euthanasia and assisted suicide remain illegal. The patient in question must be suffering unbearably, hopelessly and without any prospect of improvement.[31] A doctor is not obliged to perform euthanasia but, as with abortion in England and the broad medical ethical approach adopted in Ireland,[32] she must refer the patient to another practitioner who would in principle be prepared to consider the request. The Dutch Criminal Code requires the doctor to show she has fulfilled the 'due care' criteria laid down in the Termination of Life on Request and Assisted Suicide (Review Procedures) Act.[33] The physician must demonstrate six things to show 'due care' has been taken:

- she was satisfied that the patient made a voluntary and well-considered request for euthanasia;
- she was satisfied that the patient was suffering unbearably and hopelessly and that there was no alternative treatment available;
- the patient was informed about his position and prospects for improvement;
- the doctor's decision about the hopelessness of the patient's position had been reached together with the patient;
- an independent doctor was consulted (and examined the patient);
- the patient's life was terminated with due medical care and attention.

The precise meaning of each of these criteria remains to be fully explored, but it has been established that euthanasia can occur before the patient enters the terminal phase of an illness and that a patient's suffering may be psychological or psychiatric rather than physical. It is not necessary that the request is made to the physician in writing, but it must be voluntary and must be made by someone who is able to reason in an ordered fashion. Minors between the age of 12 and 15 years may request euthanasia and it may be carried out with their parents' consent; those of 16 years and over may take the decision alone, but their parents should be consulted.[34]

It is interesting, although in the longer term perhaps not significant, to note that in the two years to 2002, the number of deaths due to 'mercy killing' reported in Holland fell. This may be due to under-reporting or may be due to advances in training in palliative care,[35] but it may also indicate that so-called 'slippery slope' arguments against voluntary euthanasia or assisted suicide may need to be treated with scepticism.[36]

Quick Reference Guide 13.1

The 'right' to die and euthanasia

- ❖ No legal blame attaches to deaths that result from a decision to allow a dying patient to die peacefully and without further intervention or to abandon futile attempts at treatment or resuscitation. Similarly, 'double effect' deaths that occur as a natural corollary of symptom relief are not unlawful.
- ❖ There is a right to choose to die. A patient of adult years and sound mind may choose to refuse lifesaving or life-prolonging treatment even if the inevitable conclusion is the patient's death. The reasons for refusing treatment do not have to be rational.
- ❖ In certain circumstances, which include patients who are in a PVS (persistent vegetative state) or a near-PVS, it may be legally permissible to withdraw artificial life-prolonging treatment, which the law holds to include artificial feeding methods. This might be termed a 'right to be allowed to die', based on the premise that the right to a peaceful and dignified death, when there is no prospect of recovery, is a part of the right to life.
- ❖ The decision to withhold treatment in cases where there is no prospect of recovery should be taken in the patient's 'best interests', judged from the standpoint of a 'prudent, good and loving parent'. The Medical Council does not agree that nutrition and hydration are artificial treatments, preferring to see them as basic needs.
- ❖ The *Pretty* case suggests that while the right to life may include the right to a peaceful and dignified death due to the withdrawal of treatment, it does not include a right to have one's life ended by euthanasia or assisted suicide.
- ❖ The law in Ireland and England draws a distinction between acts that are intended to end or shorten life and selective non-treatment that may have the effect of permitting a patient to die. The distinction, which is a tenuous one, is aimed at erecting a bulwark against euthanasia.
- ❖ Holland is the only European nation that presently explicitly permits euthanasia and that has formally legislated for its provision.

Difficulties with the 'right to die'

[13.08]

There are tensions created by the distinction between what the law allows and what it forbids – tensions that represent an intersection between law, morality and clinical pragmatism. The distinction between acts and omissions is in particular a tenuous one: is it truly an 'omission' rather than an 'act' to switch off a life-support machine or to stop feeding a patient? Many writers have explored some of the complex issues involved in the fraught relationship between patient autonomy and the presence or absence of a 'right to die'.[37]

If a patient with a debilitating condition wishes to end his life and wants or needs medical assistance to do so, he will not be permitted to obtain it. But if the same patient becomes incompetent as a result of his pre-existing condition or a supervening new complaint and his life is being sustained by artificial means, doctors could, if they believed that further treatment was of no benefit, withdraw life-sustaining treatments, including hydration and nutrition. In these circumstances, doctors may 'omit' to do something even though the foreseeable consequence is death. The doctor may choose to 'omit' treatment of the incompetent patient in his best interests, but the competent patient cannot, in what he perceives as his own best interests, ask the doctor to 'omit' to take from the patient tablets that, if taken, would allow him to commit suicide, or ask the doctor to 'omit' to check the dose of morphine she is about to administer.

The distinction appears to be, in part, how justifiable the clinical outcome is: where the choice is between death and what can scarcely be called life, then withdrawal of treatment is acceptable, as is death by double effect. However, where the choice is a stark one between life and death, the law argues that the clinician should always choose life. But this distinction operates without considering autonomy: if the incompetent patient's life can be ended without his consent but in his 'best interests', where does that leave the patient who is competent but terminally ill and expresses a wish to end his life? He can opt to refuse all treatment, feeding and hydration and can starve to death and the law cannot intervene in any way, as long as the patient is of sound mind.[38] He can hoard some of his medication and administer it to himself. He can wait until he is terminally ill and further treatment may be withdrawn. But he cannot request that he be helped to end his life or that his life be ended sooner than it would otherwise end.

That suggests one 'pro-euthanasia' line of thinking but the converse is the argument that all life is worthwhile and that the clinical professions should not be terminating anyone's life, whether by assisted euthanasia or by withdrawing artificial feeding. Applying such logic, it will generally only be permissible to withdraw treatment where there is no longer any medical benefit to be gained from the treatment, or where treatment is an evident burden on the patient. Those who adopt an 'anti-euthanasia' approach argue that such a consideration should be independent of whether the patient's life is 'worth living' or whether the decision is in the patient's 'best interests'. Furthermore, opponents of life-ending acts or omissions argue that withdrawing treatment for severely incompetent patients must never be done with the intent of causing death even if death is a foreseeable consequence. It can only be done to relieve suffering. To do otherwise, they claim, is tantamount to active euthanasia, and this they see as morally wrong.

The arguments can, and do, go on forever[39] and it would be impossible to review them all here. Much of the logic for drawing the line at 'omissions' is a fear of the slippery slope, a concern that permitting the active ending of life in certain circumstances at the request of a patient could open the floodgates to involuntary euthanasia. The position taken by the law against permitting medical euthanasia or assisted suicide is an example of the balancing of different rights discussed in chapters 3 and 4. The right of autonomy or euthanasia is curtailed in the interests of protecting the old, the infirm and the vulnerable who the law fears, may be unwitting victims of a decision to countenance legalisation of life-shortening interventions.

'Do Not Resuscitate' orders

[13.09]

One occasional feature of hospital care is the annotation of a patient's chart with a 'DNR' (Do Not Resuscitate)[40] order, which indicates that the patient is not for attempted resuscitation in the event of cardiac or respiratory arrest. Often such decisions are non-contentious and perfectly justifiable: patients in a PVS or those who have suffered a massive stroke and are deteriorating rapidly are examples. Yet one must be conscious that entering a DNR instruction in a patient's chart is not a decision that should be taken lightly. A frail and unwell patient may nonetheless be immaculately capable of making his own decision on resuscitation and may well benefit from resuscitation. Alternatively, family members may wish to be consulted or kept informed of any such decision, although it is the patient, if competent, who should be the final arbiter of all decisions concerning his health care. There are many considerations to be weighed in taking a decision to resuscitate, including the fact that CPR (cardiopulmonary resuscitation) is only effective in approximately one-in-five cases and the fact that a patient may be extremely ill,[41] but paramount among the considerations should be patient consent and autonomy.

Lack of transparency can sometimes characterise the use of the DNR order: decisions may be made by the clinical team without proper discussion with the patient or his family.[42] It is true that a patient or family member may, when told of the diagnosis and prognosis and the likelihood of emerging from CPR alive or with the same quality of life, opt to decline resuscitation.[43] But does that likelihood justify failing to consult with a fully informed patient, about the decision that is proposed?[44]

English courts have decided that DNR orders are legal[45] and it is likely they would be upheld in Ireland but there are no systematic guidelines governing the use of DNR orders in Irish hospitals.

DNR guidelines

In the principal case in these islands to formally consider not for resuscitation orders,[46] the court was strongly persuaded by the joint British Medical Association/Royal College of Nursing statement on DNR orders. These guidelines were recently updated[47] and in the absence of an Irish equivalent, they are a useful indicator of how DNR decisions should be made.

Figure 31.1 A framework for DNR decision-making

- Effective, sensitive communication is essential and advance discussion with the patient or his family should be encouraged, but not forced. The information imparted in such discussions should be realistic and outline both the limitations and potential benefits of treatment.
- Decisions must be based on the individual patient's circumstances and should be reviewed regularly.

- Competent patients should be involved in discussions about attempting CPR unless they indicate that they do not want to be involved. Where patients lack the competence to participate, people close to them can be helpful in reflecting their views. Patient autonomy is always an important consideration and there may be a role for the advance directive, or 'living will' (see section **[13.11]**).
- Written information on DNR policies should be available for patients and families.
- In emergency situations, where no advance decision has been made or is known, CPR should generally be attempted unless:
  (a) The patient has refused CPR, or
  (b) The patient is clinically in the terminal phase of illness, or
  (c) The burden of the treatment outweighs the benefit.
- Medical staff should not be compelled to provide treatment where such treatment is clearly inappropriate.

A New York perspective

In New York, a law was passed in 1986 to deal with DNR orders.[48] The law boils down to the requirement that all patients should be resuscitated unless the individual patient consents to the making of a DNR order. Before giving consent to an order that he is not for resuscitation, the patient must be informed of the particulars of his condition including diagnosis and prognosis and the risks and benefits associated with resuscitation in his case, together with the consequences of refusing resuscitation. Consent must be given in writing or orally before two witnesses. Consent can be given by all adults of sound mind, by parents on behalf of children or by a family member or 'designated decision-makers' (see 'Power of attorney' at section **[13.12]** below) on behalf of a person incompetent to give consent. The consent can be revoked at any time by telling any member of staff in the institution. A DNR order may be made without consent where a discussion with the patient intended to explore the issue would cause the patient 'injury', but a second opinion must be obtained before taking such a step.

A DNR order under the New York law must be kept under weekly review in hospital or under two-monthly review in a nursing home. As with many other areas of medicine that are ethically difficult, the doctor can decline to sign a DNR order if she does not agree with it, in which case a mediator, and ultimately the courts, can become involved in the process.

Other decisions at the margins of life

[13.10]

What of those who have made a decision on their future treatment and wish to have that decision respected at a time when they are no longer capable of expressing that decision? Or alternatively, what of those who wish to repose decision-making responsibility in the hands of another person? We have already looked at the question of Wards of Court,[49] but Wards are those who have already lost the power to make their own decisions and hence the courts appoint a 'committee' to take non-contentious decisions on behalf of the Ward, while the courts reserve the right to take more contentious decisions on behalf of the ward. There are two mechanisms open to the person who is presently competent to make decisions but who knows or fears that he will one day lose that competence: advance statements about medical treatment or power of attorney.

Advance statements about medical treatment ('living wills')[50]

[13.11]

Advance statements or 'living wills' (although the former term will be used in this section) contain instructions about how a patient wishes to be treated in the event of a certain set of circumstances arising if, at the time, the patient is unable to consent himself. Not all advance statements are legally binding, as we will see below, but they may furnish a potentially vital piece in the jigsaw of obtaining valid consent to treatment or non-treatment from the incompetent patient. An advance statement allows a patient to participate in decisions about his care after he has lost the power to express his opinion contemporaneously. Advance statements can operate in many scenarios including temporary loss of capacity due to psychiatric illness,[51] but here we are concerned predominantly with advance statements activated near the end of life or with implications for the end of life. There are a variety of forms that such statements can take, including any one or a combination of the following:[52]

— a general statement of a person's aspirations and preferences that does not expressly request a certain form of treatment or non-treatment;

— a statement of beliefs, often in the form of answers to a set of questions about the individual's wishes for the present and desires for the future;

— a statement that names another person who should be consulted in the event of incapacity arising (this overlaps with the 'power of attorney' – see section **[13.12]**);

— a clear instruction refusing some or all medical interventions – sometimes called an 'advance directive' (because it 'directs' a specific course of action) rather than an advance statement;

— a statement that specifies a condition or clinical state which, should it arise, is the limit beyond which no further life-sustaining treatment should be administered.

The forms of anticipatory decisions can be roughly divided into wishes, statements and directives. There is no law governing advance statements in Ireland and the courts here have not considered the matter explicitly, but one can draw upon the experience of other countries and reason that under certain circumstances, an advance statement that refuses certain treatment or refuses treatment in a certain set of circumstances will be binding on clinical staff. English courts have agreed that, if contemporaneous refusal of treatment by a patient whi has the capacity to refuse is binding, then:

> 'The same principle applies where the patient's refusal to give his consent has been expressed at an earlier date, before he became unconscious or otherwise incapable of communicating it.'[53]

Other forms of non-directive statement act as beacons that may guide the care given to a patient and decisions taken regarding treatment, but they do not place any obligations on the clinician other than to consider them with due respect. This is in keeping with the principle that while a patient can refuse a particular treatment option, he cannot compel a practitioner to pursue a specific clinical course of action.[54] The only advance refusal of care that will never be binding – because refusal will affect others beside the patient, including staff, family members and other patients – is refusal of basic care, such as hygiene measures and the relief of pain or distress. Medical Council guidelines, as we have observed, indicate that basic care also includes hydration and nutrition.[55]

An advance statement can be written, sometimes recorded serially through the narrative of a patient's clinical notes, or oral, but a written record is preferable. An oral statement will not constitute an advance directive unless it made repeatedly and consistently and it should be recorded in writing by the practitioner and its truth should be attested by a witness. Advance statements should always be voluntary[56] and they should also be regularly reviewed. A person who has become reconciled to his illness, or whose views have changed over the passage of time, may not realise that he needs to alter a directive and a clinician's opinion that the patient's mind remains unchanged may be wide of the mark: the healthy do not choose in the same way as the sick.[57]

If refusal of treatment, recorded in the form of an advance directive, is to be binding, then it must have been a voluntary[58] and informed decision, made at a time when the patient had the mental capacity to refuse treatment and crucially the refusal must envisage the scenario currently facing the patient. As has been said elsewhere in this book, the more serious a decision, the greater the mental capacity required to make that decision.[59] A decision to refuse treatment – with death as the almost inevitable result – requires greater mental capacity than a refusal of treatment where the consequences are negligible. The refusal can be for irrational reasons or for reasons that most people would strongly disagree with, but that is not the point. Autonomy exercised by a patient with the mental capacity to do so is generally binding and there is no reason in theory that an advance directive should be any different, once the scenario envisaged in the directive has eventuated.

Mental capacity arises at two junctions on the journey between conceiving of an advance statement and death – firstly when the patient makes his statement and secondly when it is sought to rely upon that statement. In the first instance the patient must possess mental capacity, while in the second he must lack it, so that the statement is the only possible way of ascertaining his views. While the law will presume a patient possesses the capacity to make a decision until the contrary is proven, there are matters that need to be considered with the patient who wishes to draft an advance statement refusing treatment:

— Does the patient have a broad understanding of what treatment is at issue and the circumstances in which it may be used, together with a comprehension of the benefits, risks and alternatives to that treatment?
— Does the patient have sufficient powers of memory to be able to retain the information long enough for the decision to be properly informed?
— Does the patient understand the consequences of refusing treatment?
— Is the patient making a free choice?
— Has capacity been maximised through the removal or amelioration of any factors that would tend to undermine it, such as infection, depression, certain medications or a strange environment?

Where the clinical team is aware of the existence of an advance statement by a patient, they should consult that statement before proceeding to treatment. If the advance decision indicates a wish or a broad statement of values then the clinical team may wish to be bound by that statement or may factor it in to the care given to the patient but they are not obliged to do so. If the statement nominates a person who should be consulted about treatment decisions, then that person should be consulted, although his opinion may not be binding unless he has been given a formal legal power to take decisions on the patient's behalf (see 'Power of Attorney'at section **[13.12]**). However, a statement containing an express refusal of treatment in certain circumstances or an express refusal of certain treatment should be considered as binding when it fulfils the following criteria:

— it is clear and unambiguous;
— it was made originally by a person who had the mental capacity to do so;
— it envisages the circumstances that have presently arisen;
— it is a voluntary statement;
— the patient is not capable of giving a contemporaneous consent or refusal.

Quick Reference Guide 13.2

Advance statements ('Living wills')

- ❖ There is no reason why some advance statements – sometimes called 'living wills' – should not be binding in certain situations, in particular those statements that direct the refusal of treatment in a particular foreseen scenario.
- ❖ An advance directive refusing basic care such as cleaning and pain relief can never be binding. Whether, in Irish law, 'basic care' includes feeding and hydration is not clear.
- ❖ Even where an advance statement is not binding, its contents may offer guidance to a clinical team when deliberating on a range of treatment options.
- ❖ As with many expressions of patient opinion, such as consent to treatment or to the disclosure of confidential information, an advance statement should preferably be in writing. The decision to make an advance statement must have been voluntary. It must also have been informed and made at a time when the patient had the mental capacity to express his wish.
- ❖ An advance statement is only 'activated' when the patient loses mental capacity (for example, when he is unconscious).
- ❖ A directive refusing treatment is likely to be binding only if passes the following tests:
  - (i) It is clear and unambiguous
  - (ii) It was made originally by a person who had the mental capacity to do so
  - (iii) It envisages the circumstances that have presently arisen.
  - (iv) It was a voluntary statement
  - (v) The patient is not capable of giving a contemporaneous consent or refusal

POWER OF ATTORNEY

[13.12]

We mentioned above that one form the advance statement may take is naming a designated decision-maker. In Ireland, this form of statement may have legal force when a patient has given 'power of attorney' to the person named in the statement, allowing that person to take legally binding decisions on his behalf. Power of attorney differs from the 'Ward of Court' in that the former allows a person to plan for mental incapacity before that mental incapacity arises, while the Ward of Court procedure is only applicable to a person who has become incompetent without any pre-existing system in place for decision-making.

'Power of attorney' is a legal arrangement whereby one person (the Donor) gives authority to another (the Attorney) to act on his behalf. Prior to 1996, a person could continue to exercise power of attorney for only so long as the person who gave the power to him remained mentally competent. However, the Powers of Attorney Act 1996 changed this position and created the 'Enduring Power of Attorney', a decision-making power that outlives the mental capacity of the donor. Indeed, Enduring Power of Attorney is only *activated* by the onset of mental incapacity: until that event, the donor remains in charge of his own affairs.

There is a specific form for creating an Enduring Power of Attorney and if the form is not used, then the power cannot be exercised. The powers that can be transferred include responsibility for any or all of the following:

— all or part of the donor's property, business or financial affairs;
— personal care decisions affecting the donor;
— making appropriate gifts or donations on behalf of the donor;
— any other specified things.

A power given to an attorney can be subject to any specified conditions or restrictions. There is no obligation on the person giving over power of attorney to yield power over personal care decisions. There is no reason, for example, why a person could not give power over financial decisions to a donor whilst also preparing an advance directive refusing certain forms of medical intervention.

The attorney has a duty to ascertain as far as possible past and present wishes of the patient and factors that will inform his decisions. If possible, the attorney should involve the donor or family and any other person named by the donor or involved in his care, in making decisions.[60] All decisions must be taken in the donor's best interests and personal care decisions include making following:

— where and with whom the donor should live;
— whom the donor should see and not see;
— the donor's training, rehabilitation, diet and dress;
— who may inspect the donor's personal papers.

There is no specific statement in the 1996 Act that the Power of Attorney cannot extend to treatment decisions and there is no reason why this should not be the case. Whom the 'donor should see and not see' could conceivably include medical staff, while 'training, rehabilitation and diet' could include matters such as medical care and artificial feeding. However, the matter has not been decided by an Irish court. If a situation arises which is not covered by the power of attorney, it may be necessary to revert to an application for the person to be made a Ward of Court. An attorney must be over 18 years of age and have no vested financial interest in the donor (for example being the owner of a nursing home in which the donor is resident).

Clinicians may be involved at a number of stages in the process. A doctor may be required to assess the patient at the time of making the Power of Attorney to ensure that he has the necessary mental capacity to give away the power of attorney in the first place. A patient who lacks mental capacity cannot make a power of attorney document. According to one report, a person lacks mental capacity:

> 'If at the material time:
>
> (a) He is unable by reason of mental disability to make a decision for himself on the matter in question, or
>
> (b) He is unable to communicate his decision on that matter because he is unconscious or for any other reason.'[61]

A doctor may also be involved in determining whether a person lacks mental capacity sufficiently so as to activate the power of attorney. Lastly, a doctor or any other member of a team caring for a patient may be affected by a power of attorney vesting health decision-making authority in the attorney. If the power of attorney document reposes decision-making authority in another person then that person may have the necessary power to take decisions on the discontinuation or refusal of life-sustaining treatment. An English discussion document on the topic recommended that 'Continuing Power of Attorney' (as it was called in the document) should extend to treatment decisions.[62] This power was proposed to be limited to situations where the donor is known, or is believed by the attorney, to lack capacity to refuse or consent to treatment. No attorney should be allowed to consent to the refusal of basic care or to consent to treatment where a patient had refused treatment by means of advance directive refusing that treatment. The attorney, it was recommended, should not be allowed to withhold consent to life-sustaining treatment unless expressly authorised to do so. This would appear to be the logical approach for Irish law to take.

Quick Reference Guide 13.3

Power of Attorney

- ❖ A patient who is currently competent can appoint another person to take care of his affairs in the event that the patient later becomes mentally incompetent. The Power of Attorney is only activated in the event that the patient loses his mental capacity to take decisions for himself.
- ❖ The 'donor' of the Power of Attorney can give to the other person (who need not be an attorney or lawyer) as many or as few powers as he wishes.
- ❖ There is no reason why this power should not – if the terms of the Power of Attorney document permit it – extend to treatment decisions, including the withdrawal of life-sustaining treatment. In England, it has been recommended that Power of Attorney should be capable of encompassing treatment decisions.

Endnotes

1 See *Guide to Ethical Conduct and Behaviour* (5th edn, 1998) para 23.3.

2 'The Dying Patient' *Guide to Ethical Conduct and Behaviour* (5th edn, 1998) para 25.1.

3 *Re A Ward of Court (withholding medical treatment) No 2* [1996] 2 IR 79 at 156 per Denham J.

4 See ch 4, (section **[4.04]**).

5 *Re A Ward of Court (withholding medical treatment) No 2* [1996] 2 IR 79 at 156 per Denham J. This approach to withholding consent was upheld in the recent case of *North Western Health Board v W (H)* [2001] IESC 70 (8 November, 2001).

6 See ch 4, section **[4.14]**. See section **[13.11]-[13.12]** for a discussion of powers of attorney and advance treatment decisions.

7 PVS has been described as a 'twilight zone of suspended animation where death commences while life, in some form continues' (*Rasmussen v Fleming* 154 Ariz 207, at 21 (1987)). It is an irreversible condition of 'unawareness of self and environment'. The diagnosis is not frustrated by the presence of movements that are 'non-purposeful and explicable as a reflex response', but according to some guidelines nystagmus, a 'menace response' to threats and the tracking of objects with the eye do militate against the diagnosis: see 'The Permanent Vegetative State, a review by a working group convened by the Royal College of Physicians' [UK], Journal of the Royal College of Physicians, March/April 1996, vol 30, no 2. However, at least one recent English case has found deficiencies in the College of Physicians definition and preferred the International Working Party Report (1996) in Andrews,Brain Injury (1996) p 797, which found that tracking and vague localisation to touch or sound can be consistent with PVS: see *NHS Trust A v H* [2001] FLR. PVS is regarded by some as a burden on the family (who are unable to mourn), on carers and on the state (which must spend its limited resources on the care of long term patients who have no prospect of recovery).

8 A very narrow tube inserted through the nose and down into the stomach, through which food can be introduced.

9 A tube that travels through an opening made in the abdominal wall and therefore directly into the stomach.

10 The person appointed by the Court to take non-contentious decisions on behalf of the ward, see ch 4 (section **[4.14]**).

11 The institution in which the woman was resident had already agreed that it would not use antibiotics in the event of any further infections.

12 *Airedale NHS Trust v Bland* [1993] AC 789 at 868 per Lord Goff.

13 The decision based on 'best interests' is in contrast to that taken in some countries. In the United States for example, the courts attempt to decide matters such as this by 'substituted judgement': the court assesses what the patient in question would have wanted and uses that as the basis for its decision.

14 The question of whether the diagnosis of PVS is always sufficiently certainly made to allow decisions to allow a patient to die in his 'best interests' has also been raised: see Andrews K et al, 'Misdiagnosis of the vegetative state: retrospective study in a rehabilitation unit' [1996] BMJ 313: 13-16. According to this paper, 42% of patients in one unit had been incorrectly diagnosed (one 'PVS' patient was dictating letters to his wife!). A diagnosis of PVS must be made and confirmed by at least two specialists – as well as being kept under review – before the diagnosis can be satisfactorily accepted. See also J T Giacino, et al 'The minimally conscious state: Definition and diagnostic criteria.' (2002) Neurology 58: 349-353.

15 *Re A Ward of Court (withholding medical treatment) No 2* [1996] 2 IR 79, 156 per Hamilton CJ.

16 'Inability to Communicate and Consent' [bold type in original], Guide to Ethical Conduct and Behaviour (5th edn, 1998) para 24.

17 And recognised how autonomy could be impaired by invasive and involuntary feeding of the unresponsive patient: see the judgement of Denham J.

18 *Re A Ward of Court (withholding medical treatment) No 2* [1996] 2 IR 79 at 100, per Hamilton CJ. Later on his judgment was categorical that the court would 'never sanction steps to terminate life.'

19 The point was well made in *Airedale NHS Trust v Bland* [1993] AC 789 at 865, per Lord Goff:

> '[To] act is to cross the Rubicon which runs between on the one hand the care of the living patient and on the other hand euthanasia.'

Of course, there is no reason why it could not, or should not, be argued that withdrawing treatment such as artificial feeding is indeed an act (see section **[13.08]**).

20 In *R v Cox* (1992) 12 BMLR 38, an English doctor gave a patient potassioum chloride. The patient was in chronic severe pain and the potassioum chloride was not intended to relieve pain, but to end the patients life. The patient died and the doctor was convicted of attempted murder (for reasons related to the destruction of evidence through cremation, he could not be accused of murder – see ch 16 section **[16.21]**). See 'When doctors might kill their patients' editorial article [1999] BMJ 318:1431-3

21 Per Finlay CJ.

22 *R v Director of Public Prosecutions and Secretary of State for the Home Department ex p Mrs Dianne Pretty* (29 November 2001), HL.

23 *Case of Pretty v The United Kingdom (Application no 2346/02).* See appendix A (section **[A.14]**) for a brief account of the role of the European Court of Human Rights.

24 The right to life is guaranteed by the European Convention on Human Rights, Art 2; degrading treatment is prohibited by the European Convention on Human Rights, Art 3.

25 The English courts took the same stance in their decision in *Airedale NHS Trust v Bland* [1993] AC 789.

26 Criminal Law (Suicide) Act 1993, s 2(2).

27 State of Oregon Death With Dignity Act (enacted in 1997). Note that there have been attempts by the U.S. Federal Government to overturn this law: see *Federal Register*, November 9, 2001.

28 See de Haan 'The New Dutch Law on Euthanasia'. (2002) Med LR 57. Australian law had a brief flirtation with euthanasia: the Northern Territory Government enacted the Rights of the Terminally Ill Act 1995 (NT), only for it subsequently to be invalidated by a decision of the Australian Federal Government to remove states' powers to introduce euthanasia laws (Euthanasia Laws Act 1995). The State of Oregon in the USA has a Death with Dignity Act (enacted in 1997) which legalises physician-assisted suicide (patients receive, upon written request, the medications, typically barbiturates, necessary to end their lives), but not euthanasia. See A Chin et al 'Legalized Physician Assisted-Suicide in Oregon – The First Year's Experience' (1999) NEJM 340; 577. The text of the Act is available at http://www.ohd.hr.state.or.us/chs/pas/ors.htm (last accessed 14 September 2002). According to the Fourth Annual Report (2001) on Oregon's Death with Dignity Act, 21 people accessed physician-assisted suicide during 2001 (a decrease on the preceding two years).

29 See J Griffiths, A Bood and H Weyers, Euthanasia and Law in the Netherlands (1998) Amsterdam University Press chs 2-4. In 1984, a Dutch court accepted in the *Schoonheim* case (NJ 1985, 106) that euthanasia could be legal in certain circumstances. The GP had in that case performed euthanasia on a 95-year-old woman who had requested it. The rules for reporting deaths were also subsequently changed to allow doctors to voluntarily report to the prosecuting authorities, via Regional Review Committees, details of acts of euthanasia performed. The authorities would generally not prosecute, assuming that the facts indicated that the doctor had complied with rules set down by the government and by the courts in the Schoonheim case.

30 Suicide (Review Procedures) Act, s 293 (1) & (2). There are identical provisions for assisted suicide (s 294 (1) & (2)).

31 The majority of cases of euthanasia are for patients with cancer. In 2000, there were 2123 reported cases of euthanasia of which 1893 (89%) involved patients with cancer: Dutch Regional Review Committees Report 2000, cited in De Haan, 'The New Dutch Law on Euthanasia' (2002) Med LR, p 57.

32 Ethical Guide to Conduct and Behaviour (5th edn, 1998), para 2.5

33 Termination of Life on Request and Assisted Suicide (Review Procedures) Act, s 2(1). The Dutch law also recognises the validity of advanced directives, or 'living wills', that request euthanasia (see section **[13.11]**).

34 Termination of Life on Request and Assisted Suicide (Review Procedures) Act s 2(3) & (4).

35 Many of those involved in palliative care argue that improvements in palliative symptom relief can help to militate against the suffering that leads to euthanasia or assisted suicide requests: see D Jeffrey 'Active euthanasia – time for a decision'[1994] British Journal of General Practice, 44,136-8.

36 Tony Sheldon 'Reported euthanasia cases in Holland fall for second year' [2002] BMJ 324: 1354. Criticism, and a defence, of the Dutch system are contained in the following two articles: Jochemsen H. and Keown, 'Voluntary Euthanasia Under Control? Further Empirical Evidence from the Netherlands' (1999) J of Med Ethics 25:16; Van Delden, 'Slippery Slopes in Flat Countries – A Response' (1999) J of Med Ethics; 25:22.

37 'Why active euthanasia and physician assisted suicide should be legalised' Len Doyal and Lesley Doyal [2001] BMJ 2001; 323 1079-1080; British Medical Association Withholding and withdrawing life-prolonging medical treatment: guidance for decision making (2001) pp 1-14.

38 Courts have opted for the forced feeding of a mentally disturbed individual who has refused food with the intention of causing his death: *R v Dr Collins and Ashworth Hospital Authority, ex p Brady*. However, they will not intervene in the case of a patient of sound mind who is refusing food and English courts have also opted for stating that refusing food and drink is not suicide (because food and drink in the hospital setting can be regarded as medication): *Secretary of State for the Home Department v Robb* [1995] 1 FLR 412.

39 See for example, J Finnis 'A philosophical case against euthanasia' and J Harris 'The philosophical case against the philosophical case against euthanasia'! Both in: Euthanasia Examined J Keown (ed) (1995) Cambridge University Press pps 23-35. See also R Weir 'The Morality of Physician-Assisted Suicide' (1992) 20 Law, Medicine & Health Care 116; Blake 'Physician-Assisted Suicide: A Criminal Offence or a Patient's Right?' (1997) 5 Med LR 294.

40 Other phrases are 'NFR' (not for resuscitation) or 'not for 222' (or whichever number is the hospital's arrest code).

41 R de Vos, R W Koster, et al 'In-hospital cardiopulmonary resuscitation: pre-arrest morbidity and outcome' Arch Intern Med 1999; 159: 845-850.

42 Age Concern England, *Turning your back on us – older people and the NHS London* (2000).

43 Many patients and family members recognise that conversations about death are an important part of their care and it is doctors and nurses, rather than patients, who find such conversations difficult. See H M Krumholz HM et al 'Resuscitation preferences among patients with severe congestive heart failure: results from the SUPPORT project' Circulation 1998; 98: 648-655

44 Some studies suggest that only one-third of patients subject to DNR orders in the USA are involved in making DNR orders (see J R Levin et al 'Life-sustaining treatment decisions for nursing home residents: who discusses, who decides and what is decided?' J Am Geriatr Soc 1999; 47: 82-87). Even if involved, many appear to have a poor grasp of the decision they have taken (see G M Sayers et al 'An analysis of CPR decision-making by elderly patients' J Med Ethics 1997; 23: 207-212). DNR orders are more common for older people and, in the US, for

black people, alcoholics, non-English speakers, and people with HIV. It has been suggested that doctors have stereotypes of who is worth saving and who is not (see B L Thompson *et al.* 'Do patients' ethnic and social factors influence the use of do-not-resuscitate orders?' Ethnicity Dis 1999; 9: 132-139.) Burdens of treatment could include the risk of brain damage (if resuscitation is slow to be implemented) or physical damage as a direct result of the CPR process, such as fractures or internal organ rupture.

45 And also that decisions on DNR may be taken for incompetent patients, in certain circumstances, by doctors even against the wishes of the guardians of the incompetent patient: *Re R (adult: medical treatment)* (1996) 31 BMLR 127 (Fam Div)

46 *Re R (adult: medical treatment)* (1996) 31 BMLR 127 (Fam Div).

47 Decisions Relating to Cardiopulmonary Resuscitation - A Joint Statement from the British Medical Association, the Resuscitation Council (UK) and the Royal College of Nursing (2001).

48 Article 29-B, Consolidated Laws of the State of New York.

49 See ch 4, 'Consent', section **[4.14]**.

50 See Advance Statements About Medical Treatment (1995) BMA Books.

51 Although a psychiatric patient will not be permitted to refuse in advance any treatment authorised under the Mental Health Act, he may do so regarding other medical or surgical treatment.

52 See British Medical Association Advance Statements About Medical Treatment (1995) BMA Books. The first law providing for the legalisation of the 'living will' was the Natural Death Act 1976 in California.

53 *Airedale NHS Trust v Bland* [1993] AC 789, 866 per Lord Goff. See also *Re C (adult: refusal of medical treatment)* [1994] 1 All ER 819.

54 Where a doctor has formed a reasonable and responsible clinical judgement that treatment is not required, the law will not compel her to provide it: *Re J (a minor) (wardship: medical treatment)* [1992] 4 All ER 614 (CA). Obviously if a patient requests treatment that is not futile, the clinician is under a moral and ethical duty to provide that care.

55 See *Guide to Ethical Conduct and Behaviour* (5th edn, 1998) para 24. The English Law Commission, in their report in Mental Incapacity (LRC - 231, para 5.34), found that a refusal of treatment should not be permitted to include a refusal of basic care, defined in the Report as 'care to maintain bodily cleanliness and to alleviate severe pain as well as the provision of direct oral nutrition and hydration'.

56 Situations where a decision may be less that ideally voluntary may include the immediate aftermath of a devastating prognosis or straight after admission to hospital.

57 Report of the House of Lords Select Committee on Medical Ethics (HMSO, 1994) vol 1, p 41.

58 *Re T (adult:refusal of medical treatment)* [1992] 4 All ER. A woman indicated that she did not wish to have a blood transfusion were she to lose consciousness due to blood loss following a road traffic accident. Her refusal was not valid because she had come under strong pressure from her mother, a Jehovah's Witness, to refuse a transfusion. As with consent, a refusal of consent must be voluntary if it is to be valid.

59 See ch 4 and *Re T (Adult: Refusal of Treatment)* [1993] Fam 95, per Lord Donaldson.

60 This provision in the Act seems to disagree with the principle that the donor must have lost mental capacity before the power is activated.

61 English Law Commission Report (LRC - 231, 1995) on Mental Capacity

62 English Law Commission Report (LRC - 231, 1995) on Mental Capacity, para 7.7 *ff*.

Chapter 14

Forensic Medicine and the Terminology of Injuries

INTRODUCTION

[14.01]

This chapter and ch 15, concerned with rape and sexual assault, contain an outline of those elements of legal medicine that are often called 'forensic medicine' and which are the aspects of legal medicine most likely to lend themselves to novels, television and film. Perhaps that occurs with good reason: while most of the rest of this book is concerned with helping the clinician to understand the complexities of the law from the outside, forensic medicine is where the practitioner herself becomes part of the criminal justice system and where her skills can help to isolate clues that could conceivably rule out foul play or find a killer. These two chapters are by no means exhaustive: they serve simply to outline the elements that should be in the mind of the practitioner, generally a doctor, when faced with a suspicious death or any injuries.

For most clinical practitioners, involvement with the dead or injured body will rarely go beyond the administrative or the clinical but there are times where circumstances conspire to demand at least something of the detective from the clinician. This may occur because of her job (such as a pathologist) or because of isolation in rural practice that means that the local doctor may be the only person able to attend the scene of a death in the first hours after a death has occurred or been discovered. However, the need for some measure of forensic skill may also arise in the more commonplace scenario of the consulting room, where any professional may be required to compile a medico-legal report detailing the clinical findings apparent on examination of an injured person. Clarity and certainty in description and conclusions can be vital to the usefulness of the report and knowing the terminology of injuries, together with the degree to which the injuries identified are consistent with events alleged by the patient, can be the foundation upon which plausible and sustainable conclusions are built.

THE DOCTOR AND THE DEAD BODY

[14.02]

Post-mortem clerical issues, including referrals to the coroner, are dealt with in ch. 16, while the question of what constitutes 'death' and the ethical issues involved in life-death decisions have already been touched upon (in ch. 13). In cases where death is sudden or overtly suspicious or where the deceased has not been seen in the month preceding his death, the coroner will need to be informed. It may also be necessary to notify the police. It will be a matter for the coroner and police to involve the State Pathologist if that is deemed necessary. We are more concerned here with the dead body itself: the signs that may lead the clinician to suspect foul play or to identify the cause or time of death.

The scene of death

[14.03]

Many clues can be garnered from the scene of death and may prove useful when death is violent or otherwise sudden and unexpected. The position of the body should be recorded and, if later forensic examination is likely, should as far as possible remain undisturbed. One should also note the presence, the location and the nature of any substances, instruments or other objects that might be linked to the death. If a person is found dead in bed and on a bedside cabinet are several empty bottles of tranquillisers or anti-depressants, this should obviously indicate to the doctor that an overdose is the likely cause of death. Torn or unusually arranged clothing or missing undergarments may suggest an assault, possibly a sexual assault.[1] A bloodstained implement, taken with signs of damage to the body, may also be diagnostically helpful.

If there is any obvious sign or suspicion of foul play, the Gardaí and the coroner should be informed. However, it is important not to neglect to confirm that death *has* actually occurred. While this may involve disturbing potential evidence, it may also afford the opportunity of downgrading the scene from one of a death to one of an assault or attempted overdose and of getting a person to hospital in time to avert death.

The duty of detailed investigation of the dead body in the case of foul play or sudden death will typically fall to the State Pathologist, one of the deputy State Pathologists or, in many cases where the coroner is involved, a pathologist from a local hospital, but it is still useful for the physician to be aware of certain clues that may be present on or around the dead body. It is important also to reiterate that, wherever a death has an air of suspicious circumstances about it, the doctor or any other witness should be extremely cautious about tampering with the scene of death, in order not to inadvertently damage, erase or interfere with potentially crucial evidence.

External examination of the body

[14.04]

The appearance of the body after death can speak volumes as to the cause of death. The skin may go a cherry-pink colour after carbon monoxide poisoning;[2] acute septicaemia or asphyxiation may also leave obvious petechial[3] marks on the skin. Obvious injuries should also be examined. Some common indicators include the following:

- In cases of strangulation or asphyxiation there may be petechial haemorrhages around the eyes and ears or on the face.
- The face bruises quite easily and may demonstrate signs of injury, notably around the neck and under the chin (especially in cases of strangulation or attempted strangulation).
- If there is bleeding, try to establish the source: is it from an obvious wound, or from the mouth, ears or some other orifice? Bear in mind that the hair may conceal a serious head injury.
- Is the body cold and stiff? Within the first 36 hours after death, one very rough and far from accurate rule of thumb is that the greater the 'frigidity and rigidity', the longer it has been since death. We look at this in more detail in the following section.

Time of death

[14.05]

It is always difficult to be absolutely certain of the time of death and the longer the period that elapses after death, the more difficult that task becomes. All measures of the time of death have in-built shortcomings and the best that can ever be offered by the clinician is a 'window' of time within which the death is most likely to have occurred. A doctor who ties herself to too specific a time without good reason may be offering a hostage to fortune – if her estimation of the time of death is shown to be inaccurate, that may in turn cast a pall of doubt over all of her other findings.

Immediately after death

[14.06]

In the first day or so after death the core temperature of the body falls gradually and relatively predictably to the temperature of the surrounding environment. For the first few hours after death occurs, the temperature of the corpse typically remains static (the 'plateau' phase) and then begins to fall over a period of about 24 hours to the ambient temperature. Then as decomposition begins, although the time at which decomposition starts is very variable indeed, the temperature of the cadaver rises a little once more.

Taking a measurement of the core temperature therefore, either *per rectum*[4] or, far less accurately, via the external auditory meatus, can give an approximate indication of time-lapse since death. Temperature curve estimates are susceptible to any number of interfering factors: the person who dies of hypothermia will obviously have a very different temperature drop after death compared to a person who dies of a fever. In the case of hypothermic death, two potentially confounding factors exist: firstly that the starting temperature at the time of death is by definition low and secondly that if the prevailing environment continues to be cold, the fall of the core temperature to that of the ambient environment may be accelerated. In the case of a person dying with a fever, the first confounding factor applies but in reverse: the starting temperature is higher than expected. Similarly the ambient temperature, clothes worn by the deceased and the amount of fat on the body will alter the rate of core body temperature change. In warm weather, the climatic conditions may accelerate the process of decomposition, as well as altering the cooling curve.

An experienced forensic scientist may be able to adjust for any number of variables, but it remains the case that relying on core body temperature alone in the immediate aftermath of death will never afford more than an approximate time of death.

The stiffness of the body in the first day or two after death may also furnish helpful clues but as with body temperature, the presence or absence of stiffness may confound as much as it enlightens. *Rigor mortis* occurs after death when the body's oxygen-starved muscle cells produce high levels of lactic acid due to the breakdown of glycogen, which in turn causes the actin and myosin proteins in muscles to fuse and form a gel. It is this which causes the stiffness that persists until the process of decomposition begins to take hold. *Rigor mortis* can commence at almost any time after death (even instantaneously in very rare circumstances) and one rule of thumb is that '*rigor* commences in six hours, taking six hours to become fully established, remains for 12 hours and then passes off over the next 12.'[5]

An approximate rule of thumb for deaths occurring in temperate countries (such as Ireland) can be derived from a combination of temperature and *rigor mortis*, but it must always be borne in mind that the determination of time of death is rarely if ever a precise science.

Figure 14.1 – Temperature and stiffness as approximate indicators of time since death

Body Temperature	*Body Stiffness*	*Time since death*
Warm	Not stiff	Dead less than three hours
Warm	Stiff	Dead between 3 and 8 hours
Cold	Stiff	Dead between 8 and 36 hours
Cold	Not stiff	Dead more than 36 hours

The medium term after death

[14.07]

Decomposition commences approximately two to three days after death but yet again the ambient surroundings have a part to play. A body in a very cold environment may not decompose until the weather warms up,[6] while a body in a warm and humid environment may move into the decomposition phase very quickly (in a matter of a few hours). The process of decomposition begins in the area of the gut, which is rich in bacteria that rapidly multiply unchecked, so that the abdomen is the first to discolour: gas production, a by-product of bacterial activity, leads to the rupture of the intestines and to the spread of the bacteria. With time the putrefaction spreads, distorting the face and body cavities. The skin breaks down after approximately one to two weeks.

Decomposition is yet again an unreliable indicator of time since death. Different organs do start decomposing at different times after death, so they may have some value in estimating time of death but in reality, the information provided by such decomposition is variable and often equivocal and will again only offer an approximate window of time within which the death is most likely to have occurred.

Figure 14.2 – Stages of decomposition

Stage	*Description*
Initial Decay	The cadaver appears fresh externally but is decomposing internally – starting in the gut – due to the activities of bacteria, protozoa and nematodes already present before death
Putrefaction	The cadaver swells due to gas production, accompanied by the odour of decaying flesh
Black putrefaction	Flesh of creamy consistency with increasing black discoloration. The body begins to collapse as gases escape. Odour of decay very strong
Butyric fermentation	Cadaver drying out. Some flesh generally still remains initially. 'Cheesy' odour develops.
Dry decay	Cadaver almost dry; rate of decay slows

The longer term after death

[14.08]

Once all soft tissue has disappeared, any dogmatically precise assertion of the time of death becomes extremely difficult. A body left in the open air will decompose to a skeleton in approximately a year, depending on the weather, the activity of scavengers and of insects.

Forensic dentistry (or odontology)

This can be useful because teeth are one of the structures of the body most resistant to physical processes such fire or putrefaction. Furthermore, the precise arrangement of the teeth and fillings is virtually unique to each individual and if dental records can be found for comparison they can be as useful as fingerprints. While the dental perspective is not dreadfully useful for isolating the time since death, it may fulfil the more important function of verifying the identity of the deceased.[7] The obvious way of identifying the deceased is by comparison of the dentition of the deceased with dental records of those who are candidates for a match with the deceased. Even if only a few teeth are available and too few for a positive identification, the dentist can still offer an age estimation as well as other clues: smoking habits, the state of the deceased's oral hygiene, and other features that may match ante-mortem records. Where the subject has no teeth, information can nonetheless be obtained from the study of dentures or by X-raying the mouth and skull.

The work of a forensic odontologist also includes:[8]

- identification of bite marks on the victims of attacks, including comparison of bite marks with the teeth of a suspect and presentation of this evidence in court as an expert witness;[9]
- identification of bite marks in other substances such as wood, leather and foodstuffs;
- age estimation of skeletal remains, including the identification of neonatal remains and estimation of age at death.

Forensic entomology

One specialised tool for the determination of time of death is 'forensic entomology': the application of the study of insects and other arthropods to legal issues. The arthropods that are most important in forensic entomology are carrion feeders attracted by the decomposing flesh of the body. The females lay their eggs or deposit larvae on the body, especially around the natural orifices and in any wounds. Many of these insects go through dependable and predictable life-cycle phases. The forensic entomologist can look at insect pupae or larvae obtained from the body and by gauging the species and where they are in their lifecycles can offer a tentative time since death. Again this technique is hamstrung by the unreliability of estimating exactly when decomposition may have started, attracting the insects in the first place.

Different types of insects may yield different clues by virtue of their preference for different parts of the body. Beetles that specialise on bone, for example, have to wait until bone is exposed. Predatory beetles or parasites that feed on maggots have to wait until other beetles have arrived and deposited their eggs. Several insects specialise in living in very decayed dead bodies and their larvae usually appear three to six months after death. If there is a forensic entomologist involved in scene of death inquiries, her role at the scene will generally include the following:

— recording the scene;
— collecting climate data for the scene;
— collection of specimens from the body before body removal and from the surrounding area (up to 6 m from the body) before removal of the remains;
— collection of specimens from directly under and in close proximity to the remains (1 m or less) after the body has been removed.

Identifying the dead body

[14.09]

Deaths frequently occur of those whom it is difficult to identify. A body may be unrecognisable due to the time since death, the nature of the incident or simply because there are no clues as to identity. There are some circumstances that can point to identity, including the location of the body, missing person investigations or documentation found on or near the body. In the absence of such indicators, some of the factors useful for clarifying the identity of the unknown deceased are as follows:

— bodily dimensions (height, weight);
— coloration (hair, skin, eyes);
— sex;
— age (x-rays of epiphyses can be useful in those younger that their 20s, dentition may also be especially helpful as a determinant of age in the young);
— deformities, such as missing limbs or digits;
— scars or other marks, such as tattoos or piercings;
— dentition (see 'forensic odontology' at section **[14.08]**);
— DNA profiling (see para **[14.10]**)

DNA Identification

[14.10]

DNA technology has revolutionised our ability to identify people using their 'genetic fingerprints'. In particular in the criminal setting, the possibility of identifying a perpetrator has been hugely augmented by refinements in DNA techniques that permit the use of ever-smaller samples obtained from victims or crime scenes.

DNA is often collected from crime suspects or from others who have need to submit themselves to DNA testing (perhaps as part of a paternity case) using mouth swabs, but it may be isolated from traces of blood, semen, saliva, hair roots or bones. Trace DNA may even be picked up from objects touched by the suspect, such as the inside of gloves. Following a sexual assault, semen may be deposited on or in the victim or she may have some of the assailant's hair or skin under her fingernails as a result of attempts to fight him off.[10]

Quick Reference Guide 14.1

The dead body

- Many clues about the cause of death may be gleaned from the scene of death. However, it is important to bear in mind that where a death is obviously due to foul play, too much untrained tampering at the scene of death may result in evidence being destroyed.
- A cursory external examination can point to obvious signs as well as affording the opportunity to confirm death.
- Nearly all methods of estimating the time since death are unreliable: the best that can usually be obtained is an approximate time window during which death is most likely to have occurred.
- In the immediate aftermath of death (first 36 hours), the temperature and stiffness of the corpse may afford some guidelines.
- With the passage of time, the presence of decomposition and the stage it has reached may also be an aid to estimating when death occurred; once decomposition is complete, methods for determining time since death are scanty, but they may include the use of forensic dentistry or forensic entomology.
- Other aids to identifying the deceased include bodily dimensions; coloration; sex; age (estimated by x-rays or dentition); deformities; scars, tattoos or body piercing; DNA profiling.

As tests have become more sensitive, they have permitted the testing of samples retained during the investigation of crimes that took place many years before the advent of DNA profiling and that had remained unsolved until DNA linked the crime with great certainty to a particular suspect. Similarly, the increased finesse of DNA profiling techniques has allowed smaller and smaller samples to yield potentially significant results on analysis.

Obtaining and analysing a DNA sample

[14.11]

1. *Extraction:* DNA is extracted from a sample: the extraction method depends on the cells being used as the source for the DNA. The amount required is minimal. The DNA present in a single hair root would suffice.
2. *Digestion and amplification:* The sample is then digested by 'restriction enzymes', each of which recognises a particular known DNA sequence called a restriction site and cuts the DNA there. The result is many fragments of varying sizes. This stage of the process can also involve the use of PCR (polymerase chain reaction) to 'amplify' the available DNA by reproducing it accurately in a series of chemical reactions. PCR mimics DNA's self-replicating properties to make up to millions of copies of the original DNA sample in only a few hours. By adapting PCR to copy particular areas of DNA called short tandem repeats (STR), DNA profiling can work with very small or damaged samples to produce sensitive and discriminating results. In the PCR technique fluorescent tags are sometimes added to each sample to help with profiling in latter steps.

3. *Separation:* The DNA pieces are sorted according to size by electrophoresis. The DNA is poured into a gel, such as agarose, or onto a sheet that has been coated with gel. An electrical charge is applied to the gel, with the positive charge at the bottom and the negative charge at the top. Because DNA has a slightly negative charge, it will be attracted towards the bottom of the gel, but the smaller pieces will be able to move more quickly and thus further towards the bottom than the larger pieces. The DNA strands will therefore be separated by size, with the smaller pieces towards the bottom and the larger pieces towards the top.
4. *Analysis:* The resulting DNA fragments can be read in a number of ways, including the use of lasers to detect fluorescent tags inserted by PCR. The DNA may also be transferred to a sheet of nylon by a process known as Southern blotting, denatured ('unzipped') and read using a radioactive tag. The final product is a pattern of bands not unlike a bar code in appearance.

A final profile requires the investigators to check several areas of DNA looking for matches between the donor of the sample and the DNA sample being investigated. How accurate a match is obtained will depending on the quality and quantity of the sample being investigated and how common are the DNA types that were found. The more DNA there is and the better quality it is, the more areas (loci) of the DNA can be used for analysis. The more loci match, the more certain the identification can be. The results of DNA profiling with current technology cannot give results that claim that a sample could only have come from one particular person, but they can give results that may help to prove matters beyond reasonable doubt, especially when considered with other evidence.[11] One of the important roles of DNA profiling is not only to convict people but also to exonerated them: the very first use of DNA profiling in a criminal case not only found the guilty party but cleared a man who had been wrongly arrested.[12] In a criminal setting, a DNA profile is most commonly used in sexual and homicide cases, but it can also have a role to play in proving or disproving paternity.

DNA, Blood and paternity testing

[14.12]

DNA can also be used to establish the paternity of a child,[13] but it should not necessarily be the first port of call for the person seeking to prove or disprove paternity. Because of the manner in which blood groups are inherited, a comparison of the blood groups of mother, child and putative father can be usefully made.

Blood group genes are passed on from parent to offspring and all possibilities are combinations derived from the letters A, B and O (each of which represents a 'blood group antigen'). Each parent has a blood group determined by two of the letters (including the possibility of a homozygous pair, AA or BB) and each parent donates one of those antigens to the child. Therefore, a blood group antigen cannot be present in the child unless it is also present in at least one parent and if one parent possesses a homozygous allelic pair[14] (AA or BB) then that gene *must* be present in all of his or her progeny. The simplified ramifications are worked out below for convenience.

Figure 14.3 – ABO blood group inheritance

1st Parent	2nd Parent	Potential offspring	Impossible offspring
O	O	O	A, B, AB
O	A (AA, AO)	O, AO	B, AB
O	B (BB, BO)	O, BO	A, AB
A (AA, AO)	A (AA, AO)	O, AA, AO	B, AB
A (AA, AO)	B (BB, BO)	O, AA, AO, BB, BO, AB	No grouping impossible
B (BB, BO)	B (BB, BO)	O, BB, BO	A, AB
O	AB	AO, BO	O, AB
A (AA, AO)	AB	AA, AO, BO, AB	O
B (BB, BO)	AB	BB, BO, AO, AB	O
AB	AB	AA, BB, AB	O

Other blood tests[15] can be done in addition to ABO blood grouping and taken together they give a 93% chance of correctly excluding a father who has been wrongly accused of paternity. A person's blood group remains constant throughout life except for transient disturbances that may occur after a blood transfusion (it is important to bear in mind that no one should undergo a blood test for paternity within 3 months after a blood transfusion). Issues of parentage will generally be decided by the courts 'on the balance of probabilities', so the degree of uncertainty inherent in blood testing will not stop the courts from accepting it as decisive of the matter.

However, if blood test results are inconclusive then there is certainly a role for DNA testing, a role that is increasing as the cost and accessibility of DNA services improve. If a child's paternal DNA does not match the alleged father, then it is 100% certain that he is not the father. On the other hand, if there is a match, the chances are greater than 99.5% that he *is* the father.

DNA as evidence and the 'chain of evidence'

[14.13]

DNA evidence may be used before a court. It may be useful in settling custody disputes between 'parents' by establishing that one of them is or is not the father of the child in question. It can also provide crucial evidence of the involvement of an accused person in an offence in circumstances where there is no other identification evidence. In the English case of *Dennis John Adams (No 2),*[16] an English court confirmed that DNA evidence was acceptable in criminal cases and laid down the rules by which the jury should attempt to judge the worth and weight of that evidence.

The Irish police have powers to obtain bodily samples from a person in custody, with his consent.[17] If a person refuses to give sample then the court may be told of this fact and the judge or jury are permitted draw their own conclusions from the refusal.[18] The logic is that the innocent man would wish to clear his name and would therefore furnish the sample.

The key steps to using DNA evidence are that there must be sufficient material at the crime scene or otherwise available to provide a DNA sample.[19] Secondly the DNA sample must be of sufficient quality. There is also the question of whether the sample represents the genetic code of one or more people. In crimes where there has been more than perpetrator or where evidence has been contaminated, there may be more than one DNA fingerprint at the scene. As with any form of evidence, it is important that a court can be sure that the evidence will not have become tainted in any way: the so-called *chain of evidence.* As we will also see in chapter 17, *The Practitioner and the Driver* (section **[17.22]**), a sample that could be used in evidence must be carefully shepherded through the testing process. This is typically achieved by the completion of a series of forms that make clear the origin of the evidence, who has possession of the evidence at any given time and what has been done to the evidence (and by whom).

Quick Reference Guide 14.2

DNA and blood grouping

- Thanks to the polymerase chain reaction step in DNA sampling, it is possible to extract meaningful amounts of DNA for analysis from small and poor quality samples.
- DNA can be assayed easily from a blood sample, a swab of the inside of the mouth or a sample of hair, skin or sperm.
- With a good sample and reliable testing it is possible to obtain a DNA match between a test sample and a suspect (or other donor) sample that is extremely accurate, certainly sufficiently so for it to be acceptable as evidence in a court case.
- DNA genetic material matches can be used to help secure a criminal conviction. Like all other evidence, DNA must be handled with great care and be transferred scrupulously from person to person during the investigation of a crime in such a way as to rule out the possibility that the evidence has been tampered with.
- The steps involved in obtaining a DNA profile include collection and extraction of the sample, digestion and amplification of the DNA portion (locus) being tested, electrophoresis, reading of the result and comparison with the relevant sample.
- DNA or blood testing can both be used for paternity testing. Blood sampling is cheaper and there is a greater than 90% chance of reaching a correct conclusion. Blood testing is sufficiently accurate for it to be accepted as evidence by the courts in civil cases. DNA testing is more accurate, but also more expensive.

THE FORENSIC SCIENCE LABORATORY

[14.14]

The Forensic Science Laboratory was founded in 1975 and has as its responsibility the provision of scientific analytical services for criminal investigations in the Republic of Ireland. The laboratory is a part of the Department of Justice and works mainly for the Gardaí, although some work is done for the Military Police if they are investigating criminal activity within the army and the laboratory can also carry out work for any other government agency investigating crime.

The laboratory is divided into three analytical sections. The Biology section deals largely with crimes against the person, examining hairs, fibres, blood and other body fluids in cases such as assault, murder and sexual assault.[20] The Chemistry section deals mainly with crimes against property, examining materials such as paint, glass, soil, explosives, hair, fibres and fire debris. In the Drugs section all suspected drugs of abuse seized by the Gardaí are analysed to see if they are indeed controlled substances and similarly, items that might have come into contact with drugs (such as weighing scales or hypodermic syringes used to inject drugs) can also be examined for traces of controlled drugs. The services available in the laboratory include the following:

- Microscopy: light, comparison, scanning electron
- Electrophoresis
- DNA profiling
- Infra-red spectroscopy (including FTIR-microscopy)
- Chromatography: thin layer (TLC), high-pressure liquid (HPLC), capillary column gas (GC),
- Mass spectrometry
- Microspectrophotometry,
- UV spectroscopy
- X-ray fluorescence.

Describing Injuries

[14.15]

The need to document injuries may arise in any number of scenarios. It may form part of the routine admission of a patient to hospital following an accident or assault or it may arise as a necessary part of the compilation of a medico-legal report. Whatever the circumstances, it is useful to be aware of the words that are formally used to describe certain injuries. If healthcare professionals adhere to correct terminology and demonstrate internal consistency in the use of such terms within their notes, then life is easier both for the clinician when it comes to consulting her own notes, possibly after the passage of a considerable time, and for those external parties who have to read her notes. Proper descriptions of injuries at the time of the accident or of the original examination can help in compiling a report that may not be required until months or years after the original incident. This is especially true if, as may happen in a hospital setting, the clinician with responsibility for compiling the report and deciphering the original consultation may not be the same person as the one who originally dealt with the complaint. The usefulness of drawings (or photographs, where such facilities exist) of injuries as an excellent aid to recollection cannot be overstated when it comes to trying to describe injuries in writing at a later date.[21]

As with all medical interventions consent must be taken into account when recording injuries with a medico-legal outcome in mind. In general, the fact that a patient has submitted to examination for this purpose will imply consent, but it is always best to formally record the patient's consent in writing to the subsequent release of information to the relevant recipients.

Injuries common in assaults or accidents

[14.16]

While all of the injuries below are dealt with as if they were separate entities, it is a truism that they often occur together. A person in a road traffic accident who strikes his head on a windscreen could expect to suffer lacerations, abrasions and contusions. However, each has different characteristics and it is as well to be aware and confident of the difference between the various categories of injury so that they can be accurately described either when they co-exist or when found in isolation.

Abrasions

[14.17]

Abrasions are essentially scratches or scrapes: they are superficial wounds to the skin that do not penetrate the full thickness of the skin. Abrasions may be deep enough to bleed. They generally occur when the skin is rubbed against a rough surface. The skin or the rough surface (or both) may be in motion at the time of contact so that a person who is flung headlong along a road surface may sustain abrasions, as may a person who is dealt a glancing blow from an object (such as a weapon). Abrasions may sometimes contain foreign bodies although in general they are too superficial to do so.[22] An abrasion may sometimes also record a relatively faithful impression of the object that caused the injury, such as a rope. Abrasions can often become more livid after death.

Careful examination of abrasions can disclose the direction in which the injury occurred: small skin tags will generally be found at the end of the abrasion where the abrading surface parted contact with the skin.

Contusions

[14.18]

Contusions are essentially bruises: the accumulation beneath the skin's surface of blood released from small (or sometimes larger) blood vessels following a blow. Bruises are variable in size, nature and duration, depending on where the bruising occurs. The extent of a bruise can be variable but intra-dermal bruises (which occur just below the level of the epidermis) may accurately mirror the precise dimensions of the object that caused the physical insult. The soles of boots may sometimes leave such accurate marks that it is possible to identify with some certainty the pattern on the sole.[23]

Whether a bruise occurs depends on how much room there is for blood to collect beneath the skin. The more lax the overlying skin and the less dense the tissue beneath the skin, the more likely bruising is to occur. Similarly where skin is stretched taut over bony prominences, such as the cheek or the jaw, bruising is more common (as are lacerations – see section **[14.19]**). The very old and the very young bruise most easily and even tight gripping of a child's arm may result in contusions: a series of discrete discoid marks relating to each finger or fingertip. Clusters of bruising may be consistent with repeated blows. A belt buckle or a long object may leave a characteristic mark. On children, such marks should raise the concern of child abuse. A bite, if it does not break the skin, may leave mirrored semicircular bruises. As already mentioned at section **[14.08]**, the services of a forensic dentist can help in the documentation and investigation of bite marks.

As bruises age they change colour, which can be a useful adjunct to verifying when an alleged incident took place. The rate of change is variable but the course is generally the same. New bruises are purplish in colour, changing to brownish and then to green-yellow before resolving over the course of a week or two. However, superficial bruises may disappear much more quickly than this.

Lacerations

[14.19]

A wound penetrating the full depth of the skin, but which is caused by a blunt or relatively blunt object rather than by a sharp implement. A blow to an area of skin that is taut over a bony surface (such as the scalp) is particularly likely to result in a laceration. Such a wound may resemble an incision, but what distinguishes a laceration from an incision is the presence of the signs of crushing around the margins of the former. On the scalp for example, hairs will have been forced into the wound. In other areas of the body, foreign bodies may be forced into the wound, which by contrast is an unusual event with an incision. Lacerations also tend (although this is not universal) to bleed less than incisions because the blunt trauma to the blood vessels encourages coagulation of blood.

The fact that a laceration may contain a foreign body should be borne in mind. Such a wound should generally not be closed up without ensuring that any foreign matter has been removed and, if possible, retained, labelled and stored especially if legal action is a possibility.

Incisions

[14.20]

Incisions are penetrating wounds caused by sharp objects and they fall into two categories – the 'stab' wound and the 'slash' wound. The difference between the two is fairly self-evident: the former is deeper than it is long while the latter is longer than it is deep.

As with abrasions (see section **[14.17]**), slash wounds should have their dimensions and direction recorded, using drawings if possible. The sharper the weapon, the smoother the edges of the incision will be. In many cases the deeper end of a slash wound is where the cutting edge first went into the body, but this is not always the case. A stab wound may not reveal much unless it is explored at a post mortem examination, but the two extremities of the usually elliptical wound may indicate whether the weapon had two sharp edges (in which case there will be a neat cut at both ends), one (in which case the skin will often be split rather than neatly cut at the extremity where the blunt edge was) or none (split skin at both extremities).

Again foreign bodies should be in the mind of the clinician examining such a wound: there may be a part of the weapon (such as a piece of glass) contained in the wound that may be invaluable at a later date in linking the injury to a particular implement.

Fractures

[14.21]

The clinically trained reader will not need an account of fractures at this point, but it may be useful to point out certain characteristic fractures that may occur in the medico-legal setting. The driver of a car who braces himself against an impending impact by clutching the steering wheel or forcing his feet down on the pedals will often demonstrate fractures of the wrist, forearm or lower limb. A person who fends off an attcker may also sustain fractures in his attempts at self defence. The non-clinically trained reader should also be made aware that in terms of bones a 'fracture' is synonymous with a 'break'.

Underlying damage

[14.22]

Even if examination suggests minimal damage to the external surface of the skin, it is always worth considering the possibility of moderate or severe underlying harm. Even a small penetrating injury or blunt trauma to the abdomen and flanks can cause kidney, liver or spleen damage and these possibilities should always be considered. A person who has received a kick or other blow to the loins should, as well as undergoing a physical examination, be asked to provide a urine sample to exclude damage to the kidneys. Consider not only the external evidence of injuries or accidents but also the potential visceral consequences.

Head injuries

[14.23]

Without going into the physics that underpin this anatomical irregularity, the practitioner should always be aware regarding head injuries that there are crucial differences in the way skull fractures may manifest themselves, depending on whether the head is stationary or moving at the time of contact. If the stationary head is struck by a moving object, the injury will typically be at the site of the impact. Conversely, if the moving head strikes a stationary object, then injury to bone or brain tissue may also occur at the point diametrically opposite the contact *as well as* at the point of contact. If conducting an examination of a living or deceased patient suspected of having sustained a head injury, it is always important to consider the possibility of such *contre-coup* injuries.

Burns

[14.24]

In clinical practice, only the hospital doctor or nurse is likely to encounter extensive burns or scalds,[24] but the question of classification of burns may nonetheless be relevant for any practitioner who is compiling a medico-legal report following an assault or accident.

The extent of burns may usually be gauged approximately by the so-called 'rule of nines':[25] the whole arm or head each equates to 9% of the body surface; the entire leg and the front or back of the torso equate to 18% each. The palm of the hand and the genital area each comprise around 1% of the body surface. A description of burns should indicate the amount of area affected, the shape of the burn and the degree of the burn. There are three degrees of burn for the purposes of description:

First degree	Superficial redness (erythema) and blistering.
Second degree	Full thickness of skin affected, exposing underlying tissue. Typically painless, because of extensive damage to the nerves which would ordinarily carry pain sensation.

Third degree	Severe damage to underlying tissue exposing bone or muscle. A person who has suffered third degree burns will often have severe muscle contractures and skin tearing due to the shrinkage of the tissues through heat.

A burn can occur at quite low temperatures if the exposure to heat lasts long enough, eg sitting by a fire or the use of electric blankets or hot water bottles may sometimes cause burns, especially in the elderly. Burns are occasionally a feature of severe child abuse (see ch 8, section **[8.19]**). There may be evidence of small circular burns, caused by cigarettes, or of scalding of a limb with a horizontal margin around the proximal end, a sign of a limb having been dipped into hot water.

Burns caused by electricity can come in two forms. The burn caused by firm contact with the electrical source will often result in a blister-type lesion surrounded by a paler area of skin. Lighter contact with an electrical source may leave a small pit, but it is often very hard to find the mark. Especially high currents may cause severe burns.

Bullet wounds

[14.25]

The different types of wound caused by bullets may not be of immediate concern to the doctor or nurse who is attempting to resuscitate a gun shot victim, but again the type of wound can offer clues as to the type of weapon involved, so it should therefore be documented as minutely as the circumstances allow. Similarly, knowledge of the type of weapon involved may give the surgeon an indication of the likely damage she will encounter before she attempts to repair it. The main differences in the type of wound caused by a bullet generally depend on the velocity of the bullet as it enters the body:

Low velocity	The damage essentially results from the bullet slowing down, transferring its kinetic energy in the form of friction and heat damage. A bullet that does not slow down (for example, passing through the body without encountering bone or a major organ) is less likely to cause serious damage.[26]
High velocity	The slowing of the bullet is also important with high velocity missiles, but there are further elements that may complicate the picture and render the injuries far more serious. A high velocity projectile may be travelling faster than the speed of sound and accompanying it is a shock wave causing compression to surrounding tissues. The pressure increase caused by the shock wave can cause severe tissue damage. High velocity bullets can cause cavitation injuries far more extensive than the size of the bullet would suggest.

A gunshot injury should result in an entry wound and an exit wound unless the bullet has struck a bony object or was of such low velocity that it has come to rest in the body.[27] With high velocity bullets the exit wound may be several times larger than the entry wound. Other clues as to exit and entry wounds are that the entry wound will generally have inverted edges and the exit wound everted edges although this is heavily dependent on the range from which the gun was discharged and the points of entry and exit.

Shotgun injuries

The shotgun is among the most common legally-held firearms and it is therefore a weapon that is with depressing frequency used in suicides, but because of their regular use on farms and for hunting, accidents are also common. A shotgun discharges lead pellets[28] from cartridges comprised of a plastic or cardboard cylinder with a brass plate at one end and a 'wad' at the other to hold the pellets in the cylinder. The plate contains a primer which, when struck by the hammer of the shotgun, explodes to propel the shot (and the wad) from the barrel of the gun. As the shot moves away from the end of the barrel, it begins to spread out. A small amount of the explosive propellant will also escape from the barrel and travel a very short distance from the muzzle.

Calculating the distance from the weapon at the time of firing may enlighten the investigation of a shotgun death. A 'contact' wound may suggest a suicide or that someone was able to approach the victim very closely before discharging the weapon. The distance the victim was from the weapon as it discharged may be demonstrated by some or all of a variety of defining characteristics:[29]

Contact discharge	There may be contusions (bruising) caused by the pressure of the barrel against the body. The entry wound may be almost circular, approximating to the size of the barrel (or barrels) of the shotgun but if it is fired over bone[30] the pressure of gases between skin and bone may result in a larger, more ragged wound. There may be burn or other marks caused by escaping flame, soot and gas (from the exploding propellant in the primer) especially with older weapons or cartridges. Any hairs or clothing fibres may be obviously singed. The wad from the cartridge will be in the wound.
Close firing (cm)	There may be singeing around the edges of the wound and soot staining or 'tattooing' caused by escaping unburned propellant. The wound will be circular if the gun was discharged straight at the wound, but elliptical if discharged at an angle. The wound will usually contain the wad from the cartridge.
Discharge within 2m	Once the cartridge was discharged more than (approximately) 30cms away, soot deposition is uncommon, but tattooing with unburned propellant may still occur. The margins of the wound will be more irregular as the pellets begin to spread out. The wad will generally (but less frequently than in the case of closer discharge) be found in the wound.
Discharge beyond 2m	No soot, no tattooing, and the wad is less likely to be in the wound as the distance increases. The neatly circumscribed single wound is likely to be replaced by a series of different wounds inflicted by individual pellets as the distance increases.

In any event, exit wounds are rare if the area of the body the pellets are passing through is dense.[31] The exit wounds may be multiple of they occur, either because of the dispersal of the shot or because of shattering and fragmentation of bone. There will be no signs of discharge, such as burning or tattooing, on an exit wound. If there is a particular weapon known or suspected to have been involved in the death, it can be test fired and its spread pattern can be compared to the injuries on the body and used to estimate the distance at which it was fired.

Other bullet injuries

Most other long-barrelled guns, as well as most handguns, are 'rifled' meaning that the internal aspect of the barrel is grooved in such a way as to impart a spin to the departing bullet.[33] This means the bullet travels faster, further and straighter. As with shotgun injuries there are telltale elements associated with the distance from which the gun is fired.

Contact discharge	Over soft tissue, the wound will typically be round, with abrasions complementing the calibre (diameter) of the barrel. Smoke and tattooing may mark the skin, but they are less likely than with shotgun wounds. More damage to the skin is likely if the gun is fired with the muzzle over bone: in such cases, the entry wound will often be star-shaped (stellate) rather than round and the edges of the wound may be everted rather than inverted.
Discharge within 1m	The entrance wound will generally be inverted. There are two 'rings' around the margin of the wound. Closer to the wound will be grease soiling (the *grease collar*) caused by the bullet effectively wiping itself clean as it passes through the skin.[34] The outer ring will show signs of abrasion or contusion (the *contusion collar*) caused by the bullet forcing itself through the skin, traumatising the skin in the process. There may be damage to the skin caused by the heat and debris from the discharge of the gun.
Discharge beyond 1m	There will rarely be any signs of detonation (tattooing or burns). The entry wound will be similar regardless of the distance. Unlike the shotgun there is no pattern of spreading pellets to gauge the distance. All that can be confirmed is that the weapon was fired from far enough away that it is unlikely to have been a self-inflicted wound.

Exit wounds of rifled bullets are often, but not universally, larger than entry wounds and again the presence of fragmented and expelled bone may result in multiple exit wounds. The higher the velocity of the weapon, the larger the exit wound is likely to be. There will be no signs of discharge, such as burning or tattooing, on an exit wound.

Gunshot suicides

Evidence of a gun discharged against the skin is generally, but not absolutely, indicative of suicide. The trajectory of the bullet can help to corroborate this theory. Common sites for the fatal injury include the head, the chest and rarely the abdomen.[35] Handguns are often used to inflict injuries to the head, in particular the temple, mouth or underside of the chin. Unusual locations for the injury may suggest murder rather than suicide. About one in five suicides will be discovered still clutching the weapon. High velocity bullets may be associated with 'splash-back' of blood onto the hand or hands holding or steadying the weapon.

Strangulation/asphyxia

[14.26]

In many cases, the fact of strangulation or asphyxia may be obvious, for example hanging is a common method of suicide,[36] but in other circumstances the identification of asphyxia may be more difficult. Asphyxiation may occur at three levels: there may be no oxygen available in the atmosphere,[37] there may be a mechanical obstruction (internal or external) to oxygen reaching the lungs,[38] or there may be a problem with the lungs or heart preventing the harnessing of available oxygen. Only the second of these, mechanical obstruction, will generally result in obvious signs of what took place although some forms of gas poisoning (such as carbon monoxide) may result in a recognisable discoloration of the skin.

The supposedly 'cardinal' signs of mechanical asphyxiation are cyanosis,[39] congestion and petechial haemorrhage.[40] All of these signs occur because mechanical obstruction of breathing, whether due to pressure on the neck or on the chest, causes two effects: firstly, pressure increases markedly within the veins that return blood to the heart and secondly, the veins are unable to return sufficient blood to the heart. These signs are most commonly seen on the face, where the pressure change and the accumulation of oxygen-poor blood are most severe. Petechiae are also common on the lung and its lining, the pleura. Even in the absence of external pressure (eg choking on food), cyanosis and petechial haemorrhages may occur, although congestion is less likely.

The signs are not universal and they are often scanty or absent in the very old or very young. Sometimes too, initial asphyxiation can lead to abrupt death due to a reflex cardiac arrest.[41] Sudden death may eschew the build-up of pressure and fall-off in oxygen concentration that lead to the signs of strangulation and asphyxia.

Where strangulation is suspected, there are other signs that may help in diagnosis. As well as cyanosis, congestion and petechiae there may be bleeding from the nose and mouth (and sometimes the ear) and the indicia of strangulation such as disk-shaped bruises consistent with an assailant's fingers or rope marks may be present on the neck. At post-mortem, the hyoid bone and/or the thyroid cartilage may be broken.

Quick Reference Guide 14.3

Describing injuries

- ❖ Accurate recording of the correct terminology and extent of injury at the time of any examination can greatly aid recall should it come to having to report or testify on clinical findings.
- ❖ Drawings and photographs can be included in clinical notes as more accurate reflections of the injuries recorded.
- ❖ Abrasions are scratches or scrapes: superficial wounds to the skin that do not penetrate the full thickness of the skin, although they may be deep enough to bleed. They generally occur when the skin is rubbed against a rough surface.
- ❖ Contusions are essentially bruises, the colour change (purple - brown - green/yellow) as they resolve may give some indication of the time frame within which the bruises were incurred.
- ❖ Lacerations are wounds penetrating the full depth of the skin, but caused by a blunt or relatively blunt object rather than by anything sharp. Lacerations frequently bleed less that incisions and the edges of the wound frequently show crushing.
- ❖ Incisions may be stab wounds (deeper than they are long) or slash wounds (longer than they are deep).
- ❖ Underlying damage should always be considered in conjunction with the external evidence of injury. Head injuries may sometimes be accompanied by damage to areas of the skull and brain diametrically opposed to the site of impact: *contre-coup* injuries.
- ❖ Burns are extremely common injuries and can have a number of causes. A burn caused by a liquid is sometimes termed a scald. Burns in infants may sometimes be an indicator of non-accidental injury. Burns caused by electricity can be variable in nature, but may be extensive when caused by high-current shocks.
- ❖ The key element of bullet damage is that the characteristics of the wound change most significantly in proportion to two factors: the speed of the bullet and the distance of the victim from the muzzle when the gun was discharged.
- ❖ The 'cardinal' signs of mechanical asphyxiation are cyanosis, congestion and petechial haemorrhage.

Endnotes

1 Although as Professor Knight notes in his book *Legal Aspects of Medical Practice* (5th edn, 1992), missing undergarments may merely indicate death occurring suddenly while the deceased was dressing or defecating!

2 Carbon monoxide poisoning may occur by accident or in suicides using car exhaust fumes.

3 Petechial marks or petechiae are tiny areas of bleeding under the skin.

4 Taking rectal temperature may be contraindicated when there is any suspicion of rectal trauma, such as may occur in a sexual assault. If the temperature must, for whatever reason, be taken in the axilla (arm pit) or deep in the pharynx, then 3 or 4°c should be added to the recorded temperature in an attempt to more accurately reflect the core temperature. Methods for adjusting for variations in body cooling include the Henssge homogram: see 'Death time estimation in case work' Forensic Sci Int (1988) 38:206-236. Other methods for estimating

time since death can include the stage of digestion of stomach contents (where the time of the last meal is known) or vitreous potassium concentration.

5 Knight, *Legal Aspects of Medical Practice* (5th edn, 1992) p145.

6 The bodies of the homeless that the spring thaw annually yields up in cities such as Moscow and St Petersburg are a depressing contemporary example.

7 Hitler's doctor, Ludwig Stumpfegger, and right hand man Martin Bormann escaped from the Reich Chancellory bunker in May 1945. Faced with capture by the Russians, they took prussic acid capsules and perished. Their bodies were subsequently unearthed by building work in Berlin in 1972 and could be identified with near certainty from their WWII-era dental records. See Kershaw *Hitler 1936-1945 – Hubris* (2001) p 833, fn 15.

8 One useful resource is http://www.bafo.org.uk/, the address of the British Association of Forensic Odontologists (last accessed September, 2002).

9 Bite marks are quite common in assaults, including sexual assaults and child abuse. As part of the assessment of the victim of a sexual assault, consideration should be given to the involvement of a forensic odontologist if bite marks are present. Any roughly semicircular bruise around 3cm in diameter should be treated as suspicious. A forensic odontologist may be able to arrange the photography of the bite mark, using different light sources to demonstrate the bite to advantage, and may record an impression of the bite, and later take dental impressions of any suspects and present any evidence in court as an expert witness.

10 See the following chapter for more details of the examination of the sexual assault victim (section **[15.11]** *ff.*). Similarly, samples from the victim may be found on the assailant. The Criminal Justice (Forensic Evidence) Act 1990 allows for taking forensic samples from a suspected assailant for analysis and allows a jury or judge to draw the appropriate inference (namely, that he may have something to hide) if the assailant refuses to allow samples to be taken.

11 See Robertson and Vignaux, *Interpreting Evidence: Evaluating Forensic Science in the Courtroom* (1995).

12 See ch 1 *Introduction* figure 1.2.

13 In Ireland a parent can seek a 'declaration of parentage' under the Status of Children Act 1987. This might be done where maintenance payments are being sought (or avoided). The Act only explicitly provides for the use of blood samples, but the courts have held that DNA profiling may be used: see *JPD v MG* [1991] 1 IR 47.

14 Each of the human body's cells contain 23 paired chromosomes, with one of each pair inherited from each parent, and these chromosomes store the body's genetic information. Each little parcel of code is called an allele. If the corresponding alleles on each chromosome (the allelic pairs) are identical, they are called homozygous (allelic) pairs, if not they are heterozygous. When humans reproduce, each parent provides one of each pair of chromosomes and the other parent provides the other. Hence a parent who has the blood group called AB (where A is on one chromosome and B on the other) will donate *either* an 'A' genetic code or a 'B' genetic code to the child. A parent who has and AA code *must* donate an A, and so on.

15 Other red Cell Antigen systems that can be typed include the following factors: Rhesus, Duffy, Kidd, Kell, and Luthran. The serum protein systems that can be typed include haptoglobins, while Red Cell Enzymes systems that can be typed include erythrocyte acid phosphatase, glutamate pyruvate transaminase and phosphoglucomutase.

16 *Dennis John Adams (No 2)* (CA) (Crim Div) 16 October 1997.

17 Any of the following samples may be taken (by a medical or dental practitioner as appropriate) blood; pubic hair; urine; saliva; hair other than pubic hair; a nail; any material found under a nail; a swab from any part of the body including a body orifice or a genital region; a dental

impression; a footprint or similar impression of any part of the person's body other than a part of his hand or mouth: Criminal Justice (Forensic Evidence) Act 1990, s 2.

18 Criminal Justice (Forensic Evidence) Act 1990, s 3. This section does not apply to minors or in circumstances where consent was refused by someone other than the suspect himself (for example, his parents).

19 PCR can be applied to replicate or 'amplify' the amount of genetic material obtained from the victim or crime scene until there is enough to conduct a test (see section **[14.11]**).

20 Dealt with in more detail in ch 15, *The Law and Forensics of Sexual Assaults*.

21 See ch 10, *The Practitioner and the Lawyer*, for more detail on the preparation of medico-legal reports (section **[10.02]**-**[10.05]**).

22 Although after a road traffic accident, tiny fragments of glass will frequently be present in abrasions.

23 In the author's experience, one such bruise (drawn at the time of the initial examination) was important in answering the question of whether an assault was perpetrated by a police officer or not. In the event, the shape of the bruising appeared to be inconsistent with the boots of the alleged assailant and rather more suggestive of a pair of Doctor Martens belonging to a 'friend' of the assault victim.

24 The distinction is rarely clinical significant, but 'scalds' often refer to burns caused by liquids.

25 In children, the proportions are a little different: the head is larger than 9% and the leg less than 18%.

26 Although this is not always true, a bullet may sever a major artery (for example, in 'punishment shootings', where the victim is 'kneecapped').

27 This is common in shotgun injuries.

28 Different types of cartridges can contain pellets of different sizes.

29 This assumes that the wound is inflicted directly onto the skin. Overlying clothing can make a big difference eg 'tattooing' is less likely if clothing intervenes between cartridge and skin - and clothing should always be retained to assist in analysis.

30 Into the skull or the sternum for example.

31 Shotgun wounds to the mouth are common in suicides. In these cases, exit wounds are typical and substantial.

33 The rifling of the barrel also leaves a reproducible mark on the bullet. This means that if a suspect weapon is recovered, it can be test fired and the marks it leaves on a bullet compared with the impressions left on the bullet retrieved from a shooting victim. Because of the history of paramilitary activity on this island, there have long been strict controls on handguns and rifles (long barrelled sporting/military weapons).

34 This may be absent if the bullet passes through clothing.

35 For handgun and shotgun suicides the distribution of wounds are 80% to the head, 15% to the chest and less than 5% to the abdomen. Other long barrel rifled weapons are associated with fewer head injuries and a greater preference for the chest and abdomen.

36 In judicial execution by hanging, the aim is to break or dislocate the neck of the victim (at the level of the first cervical vertebra) causing near-instantaneous death rather than asphyxiation: the length of the rope and the drop through the trapdoor are calculated accordingly, bearing in mind the weight of the person to be killed. In suicide and *ad hoc* hanging in lawless environments, death by asphyxiation is more common, but death may also occur suddenly due to pressure of the rope on the carotid arteries, leading to cardiac arrest. See *Lachman's Case Studies in Anatomy* (4th edn, 1997) ch 9, 'The Anatomy of Hanging'.

37 In environments where poisonous gases have accumulated for example.

38 There are a huge number of potential causes for this: manual strangulation, hanging, choking or plastic bags (children's accidents, suicide and sexual thrill-seeking are all causes of plastic bag

asphyxiation). Pressure to the chest is a common cause of asphyxia in the crushing of panicked or compressed crowds, similar to the deaths that occurred in the Hillsborough disaster in the Sheffield football stadium of the same name on 15 April 1989. Asphyxia due to compression of the chest is sometimes referred to as 'traumatic' asphyxia.

[39] A blue-ish tinge to the skin caused by lack of oxygen.

[40] Small bruise-like areas of bleeding under the skin.

[41] This occurs due to stimulation of the vagal nerve, which reacts by slowing the heart to a standstill (called a vagal response). Indeed, very rarely sudden death can occur in otherwise healthy individuals as the result of a vagal response to a playful blow or touch to the neck.

Chapter 15

The Law and Forensics of Sexual Assaults

INTRODUCTION

[15.01]

There are two aspects to this chapter. In the first place is a discussion of what constitutes rape and sexual assault in Ireland and secondly, we look at the clinical approach to the diagnosis, investigation and recording of the evidence of sexual assault.

In the Republic, heterosexual acts that do not include intercourse are permitted between consenting partners aged 15 years or older; the legal right to consent to heterosexual or homosexual intercourse is conferred on the occasion of a person's 17th birthday. Any sexual conduct is permissible between consenting partners, on condition that it does not cause physical harm[1] or otherwise offend public decency. The frequency of rape and sexual assault cannot be stated with certainty. A recent United Kingdom survey suggested that in a single year as many as one in 200 women were raped and one in 100 had been the victim of some form of sexual victimisation, including rape. One in 20 women surveyed admitted to having been raped since the age of 16. Current partners or acquaintances were the most common perpetrators.[2] Quite aside from these statistics, the reasons why the law intervenes in the conduct of individuals' sexual practices were summarised by the Wolfenden Committee:[3]

> '[T]o preserve public order and decency, to protect the citizen from what is offensive and injurious and to provide sufficient safeguards against exploitation and corruption of others, particularly those who are especially vulnerable because they are young, weak in body or mind, inexperienced or in a state of special physical, official or economic dependence.'

The question of child abuse, aside from issues of the detection of the clinical signs of sexual assault, which will be reviewed at para **[15.11]** *ff*, is dealt with in ch 8, *The Practitioner and the Family*.

THE CATEGORIES OF SEXUAL CRIME

Incest

[15.02]

Incest was criminalised in Ireland in 1908[4] and the law was updated in 1995.[5] The law only covers actual sexual intercourse and only intercourse between those members of a family who are within the 'forbidden degrees of relationship'. If there is no intercourse, even if the act involves those within the relationships covered by incest legislation, the crime that has been committed is one of sexual assault. If a person over the age of 17 years consents to incestuous intercourse, that will not be a defence. In such a case, *both* will be guilty of an offence and the person who perpetrates the sexual act (typically the male, and envisaged as such in the 1908 Act) will be guilty of the more serious offence. A man guilty of incest may be sentenced for up to a maximum of life in prison,[6] while a woman similarly convicted of engaging in incestuous intercourse may receive a sentence of up to 7 years in jail.

The relationships prohibited by the laws against incest are laid out in the 1908 Act, s 1(1), which covers 'any male person who has carnal knowledge of a female person, who is to his knowledge his grand-daughter, daughter, sister or mother.'[7] Incest cannot occur between a father and his stepchildren or adopted children, an anomaly when one considers the frequency with which sexual abuse is perpetrated by a stepfather on his stepchildren.[8] This shortcoming in the legislation has come in for criticism from a number of quarters[9] as has the fact that incest cannot legally occur in the absence of sexual intercourse.

Child Sexual Abuse

[15.03]

This area is dealt with in greater detail under the broad heading of 'Child Abuse' in ch 8, *The Practitioner and the Family* (section **[8.14]** *ff*). For the purposes of a brief elucidation here, let it be said that a person under 17 years cannot legally consent to sexual intercourse and a person under 15 years cannot legally consent to any sexual act. The abuser cannot claim that his (and it is typically a male abuser) victim consented.

It is also important to note that the clinician is not under an obligation to disclose information about child sexual abuse received from the victim if she feels it would be detrimental to the therapeutic relationship. However, she may do so without fear of legal action by her patient or the alleged perpetrator. This area is referred to again below (section **[15.19]**) and dealt with in greater detail in ch 8.

Rape

[15.04]

Rape is a little different from many other crimes in terms of what must be proved if the guilty person is to be convicted. In general, if the prosecution wishes to prove that a person committed a crime, they have to prove two things: firstly that the accused did commit the crime he is accused of and secondly, and just as importantly, that he intended to do the crime he committed.[10] This second element is the so-called 'mental element' or *mens rea* of the offence. In rape cases there is a second 'mental element' added to the mix, the need to prove that the victim did not consent to the act in question. In other words rape, unlike most other crimes, is not merely concerned with the mindset of the perpetrator but also that of the victim.

Rape happens when a man penetrates, or continues sexual intercourse with, a woman who is not consenting to sexual intercourse and where the man, knowing that the woman is not consenting or that she may not be consenting, continues with the sexual act. It is up to the jury to decide whether they accept a contention by the accused that he 'believed' the woman was consenting to sex. A jury can reach a conclusion that the man believed the woman was consenting by reference to what the 'ordinary person' would have believed in the circumstances. If a jury believes that there were 'reasonable grounds' for a man to believe that the woman was consenting, then they are entitled to find him not guilty.

A woman may withdraw her consent to sexual intercourse at any time during the act: consent to penetration is not tantamount to consent to continuation or completion of the sexual act. Nor does silence amount to consent. The law is that 'failure or omission by [a] person to offer resistance to the act does not of itself constitute consent to the act'.[11] One judgment offered examples of evidence capable of indicating that consent was not given, even if refusal was not formally or explicitly expressed:

> 'It may be evidence of threats issued by the defendant. It may be evidence that the complainant [victim] was by reason of drink or drugs incapable of giving consent or incapable of being aware of what was occurring. It may be evidence that by reason of age or lack of understanding due to mental handicap the complainant did not give consent. The jury may accept that the complainant was asleep when sexual intercourse occurred or that she was tricked into giving her consent in the belief that the defendant was her husband or partner. We do not for a moment suggest that these examples exhaust the possible factual situations which may arise.'[12]

Historically, a crucial element of rape was that not only did the prosecution have to prove penetration but also that ejaculation had happened. However, the law now is that once there is penetration of the vagina by the penis then rape has occurred.[13] Until 1990, Irish law did not recognise that it was possible for rape to occur within marriage although it did state that a husband could not use any more than 'gentle violence' to coerce his wife into sexual congress.[14] This obvious gap in the law was corrected by the Criminal Law (Rape) (Amendment) Act 1990.[15]

Consent and rape

The Law Reform Commission suggested the following definition of consent to sexual intercourse:

1. 'Consent' means a consent freely and voluntarily given and...a consent is not freely and voluntarily given if it is obtained by force, threat, intimidation, deception or fraudulent means.[16]
2. A failure to offer physical resistance to a sexual assault does not of itself constitute consent to a sexual assault.

Alleging rape

Historically, there appears to have been a belief that women routinely made false allegations of rape. One of the 17th Century's most celebrated judges described rape as 'an accusation easily to be made and hard to be proved and harder to be defended by the party accused though never so innocent'. Because of the intimate circumstances in which a rape or sexual assault might often occur and the consequent lack of witnesses to confirm or deny the allegation, there was a traditional reluctance on the part of the courts to accept a rape victim's word at face value in order to avoid 'successful' false allegations.[17] This reluctance was at one time so marked that the jury was formally warned that it was dangerous to convict a man of the rape of a woman in the absence of any corroborating evidence.[18] The more enlightened rule now is that it is up to the judge to decide whether she thinks it appropriate, in the circumstances of the case, to warn the jury of the dangers of convicting the accused of rape on the uncorroborated evidence of the alleged victim.[19] This has replaced the obligation to warn in all cases, a requirement that was suggestive of an institutional belief that women could not be trusted when they made allegations of rape. The need for the judge to consider whether a warning about corroboration is needed applies to allegations of both rape and sexual assault.

The fact that a woman tells someone she has been raped is not corroboration as such, but it may be important evidence that tends to show the consistency of a victim's allegation of rape or sexual assault. For example, if a woman describes a rape in some detail to her doctor (or to a family member or friend) soon after it happened and her account tallies closely with the later statement made to Gardaí, this may be suggestive that the allegation is true. This issue of 'previous consistent statements' is dealt with in more detail at section **[15.16]**.

Sexual assault

[15.05]

Sexual assault occurs when a person intentionally assaults another person and the attack has an element of indecency to it. It is up to the jury to decide whether an assault is a sexual assault or not, although in general the sexual element of the attack may be all too clear. Unlike rape, which is by definition perpetrated by a man upon a woman, sexual assault is gender neutral and people of either sex may be convicted of it. There is also an offence entitled 'aggravated sexual assault' which is:

> '[A] sexual assault that involves serious violence or the threat of serious violence or is such as to cause injury, humiliation or degradation of a grave nature to the person assaulted.'[20]

Part of the logic behind the Criminal Law (Rape) (Amendment) Act 1990 (the 1990 Act) was to address the fact that certain acts, analogous to rape, were not properly covered by the criminal law. There was no mechanism, to take two examples, for appropriately prosecuting homosexual rape or acts of forced oral sex. Accordingly, the Act provides for a new offence: 'section 4 rape', so-called because it was introduced in that section of the 1990 Act. Section 4 rape is:

> [S]exual assault that includes:
>
> (a) penetration (however slight) of the anus or mouth by the penis, or
>
> (b) penetration (however slight) of the vagina by any object held or manipulated by another person.[21]

Bestiality

[15.06]

Vaginal or anal intercourse with any animal remains a crime under the Offences against the Person Act 1861.[22]

Homosexuality

[15.07]

Homosexuality is no longer a crime, but it would still be possible for someone to be prosecuted for a homosexual act. The reason for this is that it was not until 1993 that the law changed to permit homosexual acts between consenting males[23] over the age of 17 years. However, laws generally only have force from the time they are passed: if a law is passed tomorrow prohibiting a person from driving at more than 20 mph near schools and a person drove past a school yesterday at 30 mph, she cannot be convicted of an offence for having done so. It is only from tomorrow that the law comes into effect. Precisely the reverse is true in the case of homosexuality in that it only became legal from when the Criminal Law (Sexual Offences) Act 1993 came into force and a person could still, technically, be convicted of a homosexual encounter that occurred before 1993.

In 1990 the Irish Law Reform Commission proposed that the same legal regime should exist for consensual homosexual activity as for heterosexual.[24] Nothing happened until 1993, which is strange when one considers that laws such as the Prohibition of Incitement to Hatred Act 1989 made it illegal to discriminate against people because of their sexual orientation.[25] In other words, it was illegal to discriminate against homosexuals, even though the State itself was discriminating against homosexuals by making certain physical expressions of their sexual orientation illegal.

Intercourse between consenting males is legal if both partners are over 17 years and neither partner is mentally impaired. The same applies to anal intercourse between a man and a consenting woman.

Quick Reference Guide 15.1

The essentials of the sexual crimes

- By law, sexual acts (not including intercourse) are permitted between consenting partners over the age of 15 years. Sexual intercourse is legal from the age of 17 years.
- The basis of laws against sexual crimes is the need to preserve public order and decency and to safeguard the weak, young or inexperienced individual against exploitation or corruption.
- Incest is sexual intercourse between a man and his daughter, grand-daughter, sister or mother. If there is no sexual intercourse or the relationship is not one of those listed, it cannot be incest. Consent is not a defence to incest.
- Child sexual abuse is examined in ch 8 but a person less than 17 years cannot consent to sexual intercourse and a person less than 15 cannot consent to any sexual act.
- Rape is sexual intercourse with a woman without her consent or the continuation of sexual intercourse after she has withdrawn her consent. Whether a woman consented to intercourse is judged by whether the 'reasonable person' in the circumstances would have believed her to be consenting. Silence or acquiescence does not necessarily amount to consent.
- Sexual assault covers most other sexual crimes, including the area of 'aggravated' sexual assault, that is sexual assault with violence or the threat of violence, and 'section 4 rape'.
- Bestiality is vaginal or anal intercourse with an animal and is a criminal offence.

SEXUAL CRIMES AND THE PRACTITIONER[26]

Allegations against the practitioner

[15.08]

A practitioner may on occasion be exposed to the possibility of allegations of sexual assault arising in the wake of an examination or procedure. Two scenarios in particular call for the practitioner to be attuned to the sensitivities of the clinical situation. One is where a patient is under an anaesthetic and the other is where the doctor is conducting an intimate examination of a patient.

Anaesthesia

[15.09]

The patient who is succumbing to, or emerging from, the effects of anaesthesia may be susceptible to vivid sensations that may include imagining an encounter of a sexual nature. Of course, it may also be the case that a sedated patient could be the victim of a sexual assault while disabled by anaesthesia. In any case, the presence of another member of staff who can corroborate what took place while the patient was under anaesthesia will militate against any unfounded allegations being made by the patient.[27]

Intimate examination

[15.10]

The second scenario, when a doctor is conducting an intimate examination on a patient, is more common and there are some practitioners who argue in favour of the presence of (or at least the offer of) a chaperone in all such cases.[28] The reality and diversity of clinical practice is such that in many instances it will not be feasible to provide a chaperone. A doctor in a hospital may have little difficulty in finding a nurse to act as chaperone during the examination, but it may be more difficult for the general practitioner in a practice that lacks a nurse or whose nurse is engaged in her own clinical duties. In any event, not all patients wish to have a chaperone present during examination, while some actively prefer to undergo an examination without a chaperone. The gender of the patient, taken together with the nature of the examination and gender of the clinician or available chaperone, seems to underpin whether a patient will express a preference regarding a chaperone. Research suggests that most women want to be offered a chaperone and that furthermore they feel uncomfortable asking for one if it is not offered. More women prefer having a third party present when the examining clinician is male, fewer if she is female. In general, patients are perfectly happy simply to have one of their family members present as chaperone. Men, particularly teenagers, may find the presence of a female nurse as observer during genital examination unwelcome. However, a substantial proportion of patients in primary care, the arena in which chaperones may be hardest to come by, are unconcerned as to whether a chaperone is present or not, a fact suggestive of the easier familiarity and closer therapeutic relationship often characteristic of primary care.[29]

A legal need for chaperones?

It is hard to know what is the most satisfactory approach to chaperones. The offer of a chaperone should be probably made, together with an explanation that if a chaperone is not available at that time, the patient may need to return when a chaperone is available or with a family member who can act as a chaperone.

It is certainly true that doctors have been accused of unprofessional conduct and sexual assault after non-chaperoned examinations. In one study, 8% of women reported experiences where they felt a doctor had conducted a gynaecological examination in a 'less than professional manner'.[30] It is often suggested that, by way of medico-legal prophylaxis, a third party should always be present during genital examination[31] but this can be difficult to arrange and, what is more, if the patient does not wish a chaperone to be present, should that reluctance be overridden by the clinician in the interests of medico-legal protection? In addition, some clinical set-ups will not lend themselves to the presence of a chaperone unless the patient brings one to the consultation. There is no legal obligation on a practitioner to have a chaperone present for examinations or when a patient is anaesthetised. However, it would be desirable and preferable firstly to make one available if the structure and manpower of the healthcare facility in question permits it and secondly not to object if a patient wishes to be accompanied by a chaperone of his or her own choosing.[32]

Quick Reference Guide 15.2

Chaperones and intimate examinations

- ❖ Patients who are under anaesthesia or recovering from anaesthesia may sometimes experience vivid dream-like memories of an encounter of a sexual nature. It is best clinical practice to be accompanied by at least one person who can act as a witness to what occurred while a patient was under anaesthesia.
- ❖ Some patients prefer to have a chaperone present when undergoing intimate examinations and there are those clinicians who argue that chaperones should be present for all such assessments.
- ❖ Patient preferences and manpower issues both need to be taken into account when considering whether a chaperoned examination is to be the norm for any given health care setting.
- ❖ There is no legal obligation to provide a chaperone.

The examination of the rape or sexual assault victim[33]

[15.11]

A person who alleges that she has been the victim of a sexual assault presents particular problems for the practitioner (typically the doctor, but it may also be the accident and emergency nurse and, later in the process, it may be a psychologist) who must deal with the patient. Any clinical findings may be used in evidence in any subsequent legal action and as a corollary, the examining clinician may not be experienced in noting or understanding the clinical findings. Evidence relating to the assault may be subtle, hard to obtain and easy to destroy.

As we have noted already, corroboration may be important in any allegation of sexual crimes and particularly in cases of rape. The evidence gleaned from a meticulous examination may ultimately prove crucial in confirming the victim's story or in exonerating an innocent accused. A patient undergoing examination after a sexual assault may not have decided whether or not to pursue criminal charges, but the doctor should nonetheless proceed as if criminal proceedings are inevitable and adhere to the highest standards of history-taking and evidence-gathering.

A forensic examination should take place as soon as possible after the incident and prior to the victim bathing or showering. Ideally, the examination should be conducted by a doctor skilled in the steps involved in a careful and thorough assessment in the wake of an alleged sexual assault. There is a strong argument that the doctor should be of the sex preferred by the victim in the circumstances in order to minimise any trauma involved in an examination that by its very nature will be intimate. At the same time, a determination to provide a female rape victim with a female doctor should be tempered by the consideration that an inexperienced doctor may not be able to obtain evidence or put the patient at her ease as well as an experienced examiner, of whatever sex, may do.

Consent to forensic examination

[15.12]

The victim who is being examined, or her guardian if he or she is a minor,[34] should be asked to consent in writing to the examination taking place. The doctor should have the correct tools for the job of properly examining a patient after a sexual assault. This is sometimes referred to as a 'rape kit'. The examination should take place in an environment of appropriate privacy and where facilities are available to maximise the quality of the examination (adequate lighting and an examination couch are two of the minimum requirements). If the victim is still upset or nervous at the prospect of the examination, the presence of a family member or a chaperone may help the patient through the process.

The Association of Police Surgeons in the UK has produced a document[35] that details some of the considerations that may be involved in obtaining consent in certain situations:

Temporary loss of capacity due to intoxication: In such circumstances the forensic assessment should normally be deferred until the patient's capacity to consent has returned. The period of the deferral will depend on the type, time, amount and quantity of the substances that have been consumed. It may be necessary to assess the patient repeatedly within a given period to determine if the patient's capacity has returned.

Serious injury: The family of the patient should be informed and, assuming the patient is unconscious, as much of the examination as is possible should be done. The patient should be informed as soon as possible of what was done. The circumstances that necessitated carrying out the examination without express consent should be documented.

***Mental disorder**:* The individual patient's capacity to consent to (or refuse) the forensic examination should be gauged. If it is not possible for the patient to consent, then the decision should be taken with the patient's family or carers. Similarly, the circumstances of examining without consent should be documented.

***Children**:* The English document is less applicable in this area because there is no Irish equivalent to the *Gillick* case. However, as the author has argued elsewhere in this text,[36] a mature minor's consent to medical treatment, including forensic examination, is almost certainly valid in Irish law. If parents withhold consent in the instance of a young minor (perhaps because the parent are the people responsible for perpetrating or enabling the assault) it may be necessary to consider making the child the subject of a care order.[37]

The examination

[15.13]

In essence, the examining clinician's medico-legal duties following a sexual assault are threefold:

(a) Performing a careful medical assessment to provide corroborative evidence in a claim of sexual assault. Evidence is sought that may demonstrate (as appropriate)

- that a sexual assault has taken place within the period of time claimed,
- that the victim did not consent,
- the identity of the assailant,
- the site or sites on the body where the assault took place.

(b) Keeping detailed and exact records made at the time of the examination.

(c) Providing a subsequent expert opinion on the significance of any findings in relation to allegations of sexual assault to the police and possibly later to the court.

There is also the doctor's medical duty to care for the patient by treating any injuries and arranging for appropriate follow-up care.

History

The doctor needs to get the patient to relate the history of what occurred. The details of the assault can help to inform the examination that follows. As well as the history of the assault, the general medical history of the victim should be canvassed. A victim of a sexual assault may appear to be composed after the assault (a 'dissociative' state), but may also be in such an understandable state of emotional derangement as to make it impossible to establish a coherent history. In such cases, it may be beneficial to return to the details of the assault and the victim's medical history again at the end of the consultation.

A truncated sexual history may be clinically important.[38] If a person has had unprotected intercourse with another partner in the same general time period as that in which the sexual assault occurred, this may have ramifications for the identification of any semen that is obtained as a result of the examination. Semen may be recoverable from the vagina or anus, depending on the assault, up to 72 hours after ejaculation.

Gleaning evidence

The time of the examination and how much time has elapsed since the alleged assault should be recorded. Any information or samples obtained during an examination following sexual assault should be treated with reverence for their potential use as evidence. As has been mentioned elsewhere,[39] drawings can be enormously useful in helping to capture the precise location, extent and shape of injuries. All specimens should be labelled and the labels should detail:

— the nature of the specimen;

— the anatomical source of the specimen;

— the person from whom and by whom the specimen was obtained;

— the time and date obtained.

Procedure and potential findings

The general demeanour of the victim should be noted, including damage to clothing and mental state. Potential evidence is forwarded to the Forensic Science Laboratory. Clothing worn during the attack should be retained for forensic examination,[40] there may be fibres or bodily fluids belonging to the assailant on the victim's clothes. The victim will need to undress, traumatic as this may be, in order to facilitate the examination. The Forensic Science Laboratory *Sexual Offences Examination Form* (a new version of which is in preparation at the time of writing) should be used where available.[41]

Approximately 70% of adult victims of a rape or serious sexual assault will have some external signs of injury. Children are less likely to show signs of physical injury following sexual assault, either because they are less likely to be aware of what is happening or because their struggles are more easily subdued. External examination should be as minute as possible and the following signs in particular should be sought:

— Obvious injuries such as abrasions and contusions, especially those consistent with the victim having been struck or tightly gripped. Teeth marks or petechiae caused by suction by the mouth[42] on the skin may also be present.

— Dirt, mud or grass stains, all of which may be consistent with a struggle on open ground or with clothing having been removed during the attack.

— Semen may be deposited almost anywhere on the body, although common external sites are the torso, thighs or face. The area surrounding the vagina or rectum may also show signs of seminal deposition.[43]

Samples of semen can be obtained either by absorption onto swabs, by being snipped off with any hairs to which it is attached or by being carefully washed with sterile saline into a sample container. Hairs on the body that appear not to belong to the victim should also be retained as they may belong to the assailant. Physical examination should also include the fingernails of the victim under which may have gathered hair or skin of the assailant as the victim attempted to fight him off.

Ano-genital examination should also take notice of any obvious physical injuries, which following penetration are likely to include contusions, abrasions and lacerations. Severe vaginal injuries are rare, but signs of less severe injury are found in about one-third of rape of victims. If there is any bleeding from the vagina it is important to exclude menstruation as the cause of that bleeding. The extent of injuries to the vagina or the anus depends on:

— the degree of force used;
— the type and size if any implement, if used;
— the size, lubrication and elasticity of the orifice;
— the age of the patient.

The pubic or anal hair should be combed to isolate any of the assailant's pubic hairs that may have been shed in that area. A sample of the victim's pubic hair should also be taken. Vaginal swabs (or where appropriate, anal swabs) should be taken. The hymen of a female victim may have been ruptured in the assault. In the pre-pubertal victim, the hymen is thin and inelastic and may be obviously and painfully torn.[44] Attempted masturbation or oro-genital contact with a pre-pubertal girl is unlikely to cause damage to the hymen. In the older victim the hymen may be absent for reasons other than penetration.

A blood sample should also be taken from the victim. This can be compared with any DNA results that show up in forensic analysis, helping to exclude any tissue samples that merely identify the victim.

Other considerations

Psychological

[15.14]

The examining doctor should consider the state of mind of the victim and there are three simple statements that should form a part of the examiner's repertoire during the course of the examination and in the longer term aftermath following a sexual assault or rape. They may all bear repeating on more than one occasion.

— 'You are safe now'
— 'I am sorry this happened to you' or another similar expression of empathy and of your belief in the worth of the patient
— 'This [the attack] is not your fault'

Sympathetic and empathic care can help to reduce the impact of the physical and psychological trauma of the assault, to support existing and emerging coping skills and to set the tone for resumption of normal functioning. Any attack victim should be allowed to tell their story and the listener should acknowledge their trauma and try to recognise that a crime has been committed. Victims often feel guilty for not struggling. Reinforce the fact that this may have been what have helped them survive the assault.

Psychologically, it is impossible to gauge accurately just how traumatic a sexual assault will be on the victim. The impact of the abuse is related to the age of the victim, the extent of the abuse, the duration of the abuse, the number of perpetrators, the use of violence during the abuse, the relationship if any between victim and abuser and the response of others to any disclosure of the abuse[45] or assault. There are usually short- and long-term consequences. The short-term or 'acute-phase' response will arise over the initial weeks and may include:

— fear, shock, disbelief, denial;[46]

- somatic complaints (the expression of psychological disorders through the medium of physical symptoms);
- acute anxiety, nightmares, insomnia and lack of concentration;
- obsessive washing;
- mood swings, fear, guilt, anger, desire for revenge;

In the longer term (which may extend over very many years), different problems may predominate. Measurable long-term psychiatric consequences or *sequelae* are present in 25% of victims of sexual abuse, compared with an incidence of 6% of the same symptoms in the non-abused population.[47] Sometimes, a victim may cope very well until circumstances, such as the trial (or release) of the assailant, conspire to cause a setback. A quarter of women continue to experience serious negative effects a year after the event.[48] Features of long-term adjustment include the following:

- a person may elect to undergo major lifestyle changes, such as moving to a different area or changing jobs;
- phobic behaviour may emerge, triggered by general or specific stimuli;
- somatic symptoms/chronic pain;
- recurrent nightmares;
- sexuality issues;
- substance abuse or other destructive behaviour.

Medical

[15.15]

Any person who has been a victim of sexual assault may be at risk of sexually transmitted diseases and a woman may be at risk of pregnancy. The history taken from a rape victim should include attention to menstrual dates, any pre-existing pregnancy and any contraception that is being used. A series of follow-up visits should be arranged to allow, although only with the consent of the patient, testing for the presence of sexually transmitted infections.

Figure 15.1 – Suggested timetable for testing for infection

At 2-3 weeks	Test for Gonococcus, Chlamydia, Trichomoniasis,[49] and cervical cytology, pregnancy test, where appropriate
At 6 weeks	Syphilis serology and test for hepatitis B/C
At 3 months	HIV test and repeat hepatitis B/C[50]

Active Hepatitis B immunisation should also be offered, where appropriate, with the first dose of vaccine given within 7 days of the attack. Also, where appropriate and with any necessary consent, emergency post-coital contraception[51] may be prescribed. This does not extinguish the need to do a subsequent pregnancy test. The probability of conception from a single, random, unprotected intercourse is estimated to be between 2% and 4%, while the likelihood of conception from a single, unprotected, mid-cycle intercourse[52] is at least 10% and may be as high as 30%[53] if the attack was on the estimated day of ovulation.

Legal

[15.16]

When we looked at the definition and features of rape above, we mentioned that the fact of the complaint to the doctor about the rape or sexual assault might be important should the matter ever come to trial. Quite aside from the evidence gathered by a doctor who conducts an assessment or examination on a victim of sexual assault, there is also the fact of the victim telling someone about the attack.

In general, the fact that someone tells someone else about a crime that was perpetrated against her is not admissible in evidence. The courts take the view that if all of my friends stand up in the witness box to relate the fact that I told them individually that I saw X break into my house and steal my collection of rare hunting mice, that repetition adds nothing to the weight of the evidence. However, an exception is made to this so-called 'rule against previous consistent statements' in the case of sexual assaults. A complaint by a victim about a sexual attack[54] made to any person soon after the attack,[55] voluntarily and at the first reasonable opportunity, can show the consistency of the victim's allegation when compared to any statement made later to the police. This consistency may in turn lend credence to arguments that the allegation of the assault was not fabricated and that consent was absent. The complaint must be made at the first opportunity and must be made without any more than light prompting.[56]

Thus, a doctor may be in a position of having to furnish two forms of evidence. There is firstly the evidence gleaned from examination, which should be minutely detailed and will generally be presented with the doctor acting in the role of Treating Expert Witness.[57] Then there is also the fact that the doctor might have been the audience for the earliest possible complaint of the assault and she may therefore be asked to testify to this fact as well, but this time as a normal witness. It is a further reason why notes of consultations relating to rape and sexual assault should be exceptionally faithfully recorded. In an Accident and Emergency Department environment, a nurse or a casualty officer may be the witness to the earliest complaint, while a more experienced doctor in forensic examination may be the expert witness as to the findings of examination.

DISCLOSURE OF PAST SEXUAL ABUSE OR ASSAULT

[15.17]

The disclosure of past sexual abuse, either in childhood or in earlier adulthood may sometimes be made to a practitioner, particularly to a doctor or nurse and often in the context of a related consultation, such as a discussion relating to a psychiatric problem. In general, such disclosures will only be made when the patient feels he or she is in a safe, sensitive and confidential environment. The news may be delivered spontaneously or it may be mentioned in response to careful and sensitive questioning by the doctor. In the case of questioning, each practitioner will find her own way to word such questions that is appropriate for the situation. Such questioning should be put simply and directly, but prefaced with an opportunity to decline to answer, for example: 'I am going to ask you a question you may not have been asked before and you do not have to answer it if you do not want to. Has anyone ever made you have sex that you did not want and did not agree to?'

Quick Reference Guide 15.3

Examination and follow-up of the sexual assault victim

- The examination and history taken from a sexual assault victim has strong legal as well as medical significance. It is always best if someone trained in such an examination is available to conduct it.
- The sooner a forensic examination can be conducted after the assault, the easier it may be to glean relevant findings/evidence.
- The examination should be conducted only with the consent of the patient and should take place in an environment and a manner that does not exacerbate the traumatic experiences of the victim.
- The purpose of the examination is both medico-legal and medical – to obtain evidence and to diagnose any problems that may need treatment or follow-up. A sexual history is important as it may help to explain the finding of semen inconsistent with sexual assault by the alleged assailant. A history of the attack may be difficult to obtain from a distressed patient in the aftermath of an assault. It may be necessary to return to the history on more than one occasion.
- All evidence collected during examination should be carefully gathered, stored, sealed and labelled.
- External examination is important because signs of injury, staining of clothing or skin and the presence of semen deposited on the body may all provide significant evidence.
- Anal or genital examination may indicate the fact of assault as well as the violence, nature and extent of the assault.
- Examination and follow-up should pay careful attention to the psyche of the victim. Affirmation of the fact that the victim is not to blame for the attack is important. Psychological reactions to sexual assault can be manifold, grave and long lasting.
- Medical considerations include testing, with the patient's consent, for pregnancy and the presence of sexually transmitted disease. Emergency contraception ('the morning after pill') should be offered together with any appropriate active immunisations.
- All records of the history and examination, together with the fact of the complaint itself, may ultimately be admissible as evidence in a future criminal trial.

There is no need to press for full details of the abuse or attempt to deal with all the issues raised in a single consultation, but the clinician who attempts to elicit the details of past sexual assault should bear in mind that a patient who discloses a history of sexual assault will need not only the care of the doctor, but of a trained counsellor too.

Managing the disclosure

[15.18]

It is important to provide an empathic, non-judgemental and affirmative response to allow the patient to answer as fully as she feels comfortable with: the patient's first need is to be heard. A simple statement by the clinician about the widespread incidence of sexual abuse may help the patient feel less isolated.

Check whether the patient is safe now and if other family members or others potentially affected by the abuser are safe. Offer an examination to check physical injuries, scars or medical conditions related to the abuse. Normal findings may address the patient's unspoken concerns and reassure him. When performing a physical examination request permission for even minor procedures, be gentle, take time, give encouragement. Involve the patient, ensure the patient understands that consent to the examination is not final and can be withdrawn at any stage in the procedure.

For most patients a routine enquiry about past abuse does not precipitate a crisis, but it might. Advise the patient that many people find it helpful to talk things over with a trained sexual abuse counsellor and refer if this is their wish. The clinician should know her limits. If she has not had in-depth training in counselling or other 'talking therapies', such as psychotherapy, she should not usually attempt to be a sexual abuse counsellor for her patient, unless the patient declines any referral to another professional. Some patients require increased attention and medical care for a while following disclosure because of the emergence of delayed post traumatic stress symptoms. Patients previously employed and coping may need time off work after a disclosure and in the early stages of recovery. Problems that may preface, accompany or follow a declaration of previous sexual abuse include:

- alcohol problems;
- eating disorders;
- anxiety or sleep disturbances;
- depression or general stress;
- problems with a current relationship or with partners from previous relationships.

Ask the patient how the abuse has affected or still is affecting his life and what he wants to do about this. The patient's decision concerning what action he wishes to take should be respected as far as possible. On some occasions it may be appropriate to talk to the patient about making a complaint to the police and if a patient declines to do so, there may be a question of the clinician being obliged to breach confidentiality in the interests of protecting other potential victims of an identifiable abuser who continues to be a risk to others. The breach of confidentiality may be kept to a minimum by identifying the potential abuser without identifying the source of the information. As we have already seen,[58] one of the exceptions to the general requirement of maintaining confidentiality is when there is an identifiable risk to a specific person or where there is a risk to the welfare of society. It is beyond argument that an ongoing risk of sexual abuse of children or adults would, in all but the most unlikely circumstances, merit such a breach of confidence.

Reporting child abuse – historical or otherwise

[15.19]

The specific question of child abuse is dealt with in ch 8, *The Practitioner and the Family*, but it is worth pointing out at this juncture that the Protections for Persons Reporting Child Abuse Act 1998[59] protects any person from legal action who reports, in good faith, her suspicions that:

(a) a child has been or is being assaulted, ill-treated, neglected or sexually abused, or

(b) a child's health, development or welfare has been or is being avoidably impaired or neglected.

In other words, while, there is no obligation on a practitioner to report child abuse, she will not be answerable to her patient or the perpetrator if she makes such a disclosure to the appropriate authorities. On the other hand, a person who deliberately and knowingly makes a false allegation of child abuse against another may not only be sued for defamation by the person she names but she may also face criminal proceedings under the Protections for Persons Reporting Child Abuse Act 1998.[60] The key therefore is that any allegation of child abuse should be made to the relevant authorities in good faith.

Endnotes

1 See *Brown* [1994] 1 AC 212. The authors of Charleton, McDermott & Bolger *Criminal Law* (1999) argue that sexual conduct that gives rise to mental damage may also be illegal. The charge that would be brought against those involved in such acts, whether causing mental or physical damage, would be one of assault.

2 *Rape and sexual assault of women: findings from the British Crime Survey*, UK Home Office, July 2002. These figures probably underestimate the prevalence of rape and sexual victimisation: the BCS did not cover institutions, the homeless or women under the age of 16, thus excluding some 'high risk' women and the interviews were not always conducted in private possibly inhibiting disclosure. Others put the figure for the percentage of women who have been raped between 14% and 25%: see Goodman *et al.* 'Male violence against women: current researches and future directions' (1993) Am Psychologist 46, 1054-1058.

3 The Wolfenden Committee on Homosexual Offences and Prostitution, Comnd 247, 1957. Also see Richard Card 'Sexual Relations with Minors' [1975] Crim LR 370 at 371.

4 Punishment of Incest Act 1908.

5 Criminal Law (Incest Proceedings) Act 1995. This Act allows for incest trials to be conducted in private, although the press may be present, and for the accused to be afforded confidentiality so that none of the people involved may be identified by the press. The anonymity is for the benefit of the victim (to minimise the trauma of the trial) and the accused (who, were it not for the 1995 Act may be acquitted only to find that his name and alleged offences have been trumpeted in the media with potentially harmful consequences). The details of the case may be published or broadcast, but not the identity of the accused or the victim or any details that would tend to identify them. If a representative of the media breaches the requirement of confidentiality imposed by the law, she may be liable to a jail sentence of up to three years or fine up to €12,700 (s 4).

6 'Life' imprisonment normally means a sentence of seven to ten years.

7 Contrary to popular belief, first cousins are not covered by incest legislation.

8 A point made in the *Irish Law Reform Commission Paper on Child Sexual Abuse* 1989 (see Appendix 1 of the paper).

9 Fifteenth Report from the English Criminal Law Revision Committee (1984) paras 8.25-8.35.

10 Or that he was reckless regarding whether his conduct would result in the criminal act.

11 Criminal Law (Rape)(Amendment) Act 1990, s 9.

12 *R v Malone* [1998] 2 Cr App R 447. Another example of where consent is not truly given is where a woman consents through fear (*R v Olugboja* [1982] QB 320) and a similar situation *may* arise where the person initiating the sexual encounter is in a position of authority over the

woman in question and she acquiesces in recognition of that authority (eg a teacher and a student: *O'Connor* (1998) 123 CCC (3d) 487).

13 See Criminal Law (Rape) Act 1981, s 1(2), '...intercourse is deemed complete on proof of penetration only'. It has been decided in Irish law that 'if the male organ is proved to have entered the opening of the vagina this amounts to penetration even if there is no emission [of semen].' This means that if rape is alleged by a virgin whose hymen is intact after the assault, the fact that the hymen is intact does not automatically preclude penetration having occurred. See also *The People (AG) v Dermody* [1956] IR 307.

14 *McN v McN* [1936] IR 177.

15 Criminal Law (Rape) Act 1990, s 5. The Act also abolished the legal supposition that any male under the age of 14 years was incapable of rape.

16 See *Williams* [1923] 1 KB 340, where a man told the woman that sexual intercourse was a surgical procedure that would improve her singing voice and for that reason alone she consented. The fraud implicit in what the man said was so profound that it rendered the woman's consent meaningless and therefore a rape was committed.

17 Estimates of false allegations are unreliable but some Canadian figures suggest that the figures may be as high as one in twenty. Other authors have suggested a one in 50 chance of a false allegation (see Charleton, McDermott and Bolger *Criminal Law* (1999) para 8.150).

18 'Corroborating evidence' is evidence that tends to support the allegation being made. DNA testing of sperm emitted during the commission of the alleged crime may corroborate the woman's story that the accused was the person who had sexual intercourse with her. Marks of injuries on the woman's body may be inconsistent with the assailant's story that the victim consented and may instead be corroborating evidence for an allegation of rape or assault.

19 Criminal Law (Rape)(Amendment) Act 1990, s 7. The fact that the warning is now optional does not mean that it may always be omitted. There may still be cases in which it is desirable for the judge to warn of the dangers of convicting on the uncorroborated evidence of the alleged victim: *The People (DPP) v Reid* [1993] 2 IR 186. However, the circumstances in which a warning need be given are only where there is a strong doubt hanging over the veracity of the victim's evidence and if a judge does not give a warning, that is very unlikely to be grounds for an appeal.

20 Criminal Law (Rape) (Amendment) Act 1990, s 3(1).

21 Criminal Law (Rape) (Amendment) Act 1990, s 4(1).

22 Offences against the Person Act 1861, s 61.

23 Criminal Law (Sexual Offences) Act 1993. Lesbianism was never outlawed in Britain or Ireland. The reason for this is often apocryphally stated to be that Queen Victoria refused to believe that lesbianism could exist and argued therefore against any need to ban it.

24 *Report on Child Sexual Abuse*, 1990.

25 Prohibition of Incitement to Hatred Act 1989, s 1(1).

26 In this section and the sections that follow the standard convention, used elsewhere in the text, of describing the practitioner as 'she' and the patient as 'he' is abandoned for obvious reasons and gender-related pronouns are used in the manner necessary to make sense of the text.

27 There was, for a long time, a tolerance of permitting medical students to perform 'practice' internal examinations on women while they were anaesthetised. It is hoped that this practice has disappeared with the practitioner's increasing awareness of the need for consent in such situations. Of course, with the patient's consent, it is possible to perform such examinations.

28 Bignell 'Chaperones for genital examination' BMJ 1999; 319:137.

29 See the following: Penn and Bourgnet 'Patients' attitudes regarding chaperones during physician examinations' J Fam Pract 1992; 35: 639-643; Webb and Opdahl 'Breast and pelvic examinations: easing women's discomfort' Can Fam Physician 1996; 42: 54-58; S Phillips *et al*

'Teenagers' preferences regarding the presence of family members, peers and chaperones during examination of genitalia' Pediatrics 1981; 68: 665-669; D P K Ng *et al* 'The practice of rectal examination' Postgrad Med J 1991; 67: 904-906; R Jones 'Patients' attitudes to chaperones' J RCGP 1985; 35: 192-193.

30 Webb and Opdahl 'Breast and pelvic examinations: easing women's discomfort' Can Fam Physician 1996; 42: 54-58. 'Unprofessional' behaviour in this study included overexposure of the woman's body, unusual positioning of the woman for examination and inappropriate comments, gestures or facial expressions.

31 Bignell 'Chaperones for genital examination' BMJ 1999; 319:137.

32 In December 2001, the UK General Medical Council published guidelines on intimate examination (which it defines as examination of the breasts, genitalia or rectum). The full text is at http://www.gmc-uk.org/standards/intimate.htm. (last accessed September 2002). Its recommendations, in addition to those outlined in the text above, include the following:

- Explain why the examination is necessary and what it will involve,
- Avoid unnecessary personal comments,
- Give the patient privacy to dress and undress, including using drapes or curtains where possible. Do not assist the patient in this unless you have clarified that your assistance is required.

33 In the 1996 New Zealand Crime Victimisation Survey of 5000 respondents, with a response rate of 57%, 11.6% of women and 1.5% of men said that someone had forced them or attempted to force them to have sexual intercourse against their will in their lifetime. (W Young *et al NZ National Survey of Crime Victims 1996* The Victimisation Survey Committee). Other studies have shown comparable rates between different countries. See also fn. 2.

34 But note the discussion of consent by minors in ch 4 (section **[4.15]**).

35 *Consent in Relation To Complaints of Sexual Assaults* (24 May 2001), produced for the Education and Research Committee of the Association of Police Surgeons.

36 See ch 4, *Consent* (section **[8.15]**).

37 See ch 8, *The Practitioner and the Family* (section **[8.24]**).

38 Although this part of the history may not be admissible in the courtroom as evidence. The prior sexual history of the victim (whether with the accused or another) cannot be used in evidence merely to cast doubts on the victim's character, but it may be used where it may tend to suggest that the victim consented or that the accused may have been mistaken about whether she consented (see Criminal Law (Rape) Act, s 3).

39 See section **[14.15]**.

40 A family member should be asked to bring in a change of clothing.

41 The form should also be available in paediatric units. See 'Care of the Adolescent Sexual Assault Victim – A Policy Statement' Paediatrics 2001; 107:1476-1479.

42 So-called, and, in these circumstances, misnamed 'love bites'. See ch 14 (section **[14.08]**) for the potential role of the forensic dentist/odontologist with respect to bite marks on assault victims.

43 As an aid to locating semen, it should be noted that it may sometimes fluoresce under Wood's Light.The lack of satisfactory facilities for minors suffering from psychotic problems has been highlighted by cases such as *DG v Eastern Health Board* (16th July 1997) SC. In that case, a disturbed but innocent child was committed to a penal institution in the absence of any appropriate psychiatric institution.

44 Examination of children in cases of suspected child sexual abuse may disclose a notched or scarred hymen as an indicator of previous assault.

45 Finkelhorn and Browne 'The traumatic impact of child sexual abuse: a conceptualisation' Am J Orthopsychiatry 1985; 55:530.

[46] Denial is a common psychological response to traumatic events whereby the person continues to behave as if nothing has happened. People who have told they have a terminal illness or who have lost a loved one often go through a period of denial.

[47] Mullen *et al* 'Childhood sexual abuse and mental health in adult life' Brit J Psychiatry 1993; 163: 721.
Watkins and Bentovim 'The sexual abuse of male children and adolescents: a review of current research' J Child Psychol Psychiat 1992; 33:197.

[48] Rothbaum *et al* 'A prospective examination of post traumatic stress disorder in rape victims' J Traumatic Stress 1992; 5:455.

[49] Because patients may fail to attend for follow-up, so it is sometimes suggested that they should be given a prophylactic antibiotic at the time of the original examination to minimise the possibility of subsequent development of bacterial STDs. The antibiotic chosen will depend on regional bacterial resistance and prevalence patterns.

[50] HIV testing should be accompanied by appropriate counselling, the details of which lie outside the scope of this book.

[51] Ethinyloestradiol 100 microgrammes (typically in combination with a progestogen) preceded by anti-emetic and repeated 12 hours later. Note that a follow-up pregnancy test is still essential. In countries such as New Zealand, it is a legal requirement to offer protection against pregnancy after rape, or to refer the victim to another doctor who will do so: Contraception, Sterilisation and Abortion Act 1977. There is no equivalent legislation in Ireland.

[52] Approximately days 11 to 18 of a 28-day cycle.

[53] J C Barret and J Marshall *Population Studies* (1969) pp 455-61.

[54] Including but not limited to rape.

[55] How soon after the attack is not clear. It appears to vary with the precise circumstances of the case.

[56] See Ní Raifteearaigh 'The Doctrine of Fresh Complaint in Sexual Cases' (1994) ILT 160.

[57] See ch 10, *The Practitioner and the Lawyer* (section **[10.06]**).

[58] Ch 3, *The Practitioner-Patient Relationship, Ethics and Confidentiality* (section **[3.17]**).

[59] Protections for Persons Reporting Child Abuse Act 1998, s 3.

[60] Protections for Persons Reporting Child Abuse Act 1998, s 5.

Chapter 16

Coroners and the Aftermath of Death

INTRODUCTION

[16.01]

Death is one circumstance that regrettably, yet inevitably, must be dealt with by almost all health professionals at some time in their careers. In many cases, the cause of a person's death will be clear and the aftermath for family and professionals left behind is, from a legal perspective, uncomplicated. In such cases, a doctor will be in a position to sign a medical certificate of the cause of death that will allow the family of the deceased or the institution in which the death occurred to register the death.

It is nonetheless one of the more unpleasant and inconvenient facets of mortality that people will sometimes die suddenly and in suspicious or untoward circumstances. Where there is uncertainty about the circumstances of death, or in other situations circumscribed by the law, certain investigations may be necessary and these inquiries are most commonly the remit of the coroner.

This chapter looks at some of the principal consequences for clinicians of patients' deaths. We look predominantly at the history and role of the coroner, the individual typically responsible for the investigation of the circumstances that surround certain categories of death. As we will see the coroner is not responsible for the attribution of blame for that death: investigations into the blame attaching to death are the responsibility of the police and final decisions on individual culpability are generally made by a court of law. Instead, the coroner is concerned only with the factual and relatively immediate causes and scenario of the death. This chapter also considers the question of the certification of the uncomplicated death.

Quite aside from the question of the death itself, other consequences can arise from a patient's demise, such a previously expressed desire for cremation. Also of interest to us here is the 'dying declaration', words spoken by an individual who is at death's door. Such words may express a dying wish regarding a last bequest of property not accounted for in a will, they may identify a murderer or they may be a divesting of one last secret to unburden the soul of a person who knows himself to be dying. We look at the status of such dying declarations and ask whether they can be given as evidence in a court case.[1]

DEATH CERTIFICATES AND THE REGISTRATION OF DEATH

[16.02]

A doctor involved in the care of a patient who has passed away will frequently be asked to complete what is often called a 'death certificate', but is more correctly termed a 'Medical Certificate of the Cause of Death'. This document is necessary for two reasons. Firstly, the family require it in order that they may register the death, which in turn will furnish them with acceptable proof of death for any administrative tasks in which they may need to engage to tidy up the affairs of the dead person, such as activating insurance policies. Secondly, it is compulsory in Irish law to register every death with the Registrar of Births and Deaths.[2] The cause of death stated on the medical certificate is entered *verbatim* onto the register of deaths by the Registrar. This register is then used for epidemiological and statistical analysis, a compelling reason why certificates regarding cause of death should be completed as carefully and accurately as possible by the doctor.[3]

The Medical Certificate of Cause of Death is a statement of the 'disease which was directly responsible for the death'[4] together with any pre-existing conditions that gave rise to the condition directly responsible for death. Only a doctor may certify the cause of death and even then a doctor certifying the cause of death must be one who has been personally in attendance upon the deceased during his last illness. As we will see below, one situation in which the coroner's role is activated is where no doctor has seen the deceased during the month prior to his death. In such case, the coroner may satisfy herself that no further investigation is necessary, and permit the Certificate to be signed. It is important to note however, that in circumstances where the doctor has not seen the deceased in the month before death, she cannot sign a death certificate without first notifying the coroner.

Any term used in defining or describing the medical cause of death should be as precise and accurate as possible. For example the anatomical and clinical precision of 'acute infero-lateral myocardial infarct' would be far preferable to the vagueness of 'heart disease' and a certification of 'post-operative death' should be accompanied by the details of the operation and the condition for which the operation was being performed. A list of undesirable terms, together with guidelines for filling the form and the form itself are set out in Appendix C of this book. An schematic example of a correctly completed death certificate is set out below (figure 16.1).

Figure 16.1 – A schematic example of the completion of the 'Cause of Death' Section of a Medical Certificate of the Cause of Death

I *Disease or condition directly leading to death*	I	*Approximate interval between onset and death*
(This does not mean the mode of dying... It means the disease, injury or complications which caused death)	(a) Acute renal failure *due to (or as a consequence of)*	5 days
Antecedent Causes (morbid conditions if any, giving rise to the above cause, stating the underlying condition last)	(b) AIDS-associated renal disease *due to (or as a consequence of)* (c) AIDS/HIV	9 months 5 years

II	II	
Other significant conditions contributing to the death but not related to the disease or condition causing it.	Hypertension, Mycobacterium avium complex infection	8 months 2 months

If a death occurs in hospital, the hospital will typically register the death with the Registrar of Births, Deaths and Marriages. Deaths that occur at home or at a nursing home must be registered with the local registrar by a 'qualified informant' attending the registrar's office. A qualified informant is defined as:

— a relative of the deceased *or*

— a person present at the death *or*

— an occupier of the house in which the death occurred.

The informant who goes to register the death must bring to the Registrar the completed Medical Certificate of the Cause of Death, which is then used to complete the registration form. There is a plan[5] to introduce a new form for the registration of deaths, combining both the Medical Certificate (part 1) to be completed by the doctor (or coroner where appropriate) and the death registration form (part 2) to be completed by the qualified informant.

Deaths referred to the County or City Coroner are registered when the Registrar receives a certificate of the post-mortem examination or inquest from the coroner. The coroner is involved in circumstances where there is a suggestion of uncertainty, suddenness, wrongdoing or violence (or any combination of the four) attaching to the death or where the deceased has not been seen by a doctor in the month leading up to his passing away.

Quick Reference Guide 16.1

'Death certificates'

- ❖ Death certificates are more properly called Medical Certificates of the Cause of Death
- ❖ All deaths must be registered by law and the death certificate enables that to be done. Only if the death is registered can proof be issued from the Registrar of Births to allow the family to deal with the formalities that can arise in the aftermath of death.
- ❖ The information provided on Medical Certificates of the Cause of Death is also used for statistical and demographic purposes. Information provided on the certificate should be as accurate as possible for this reason.
- ❖ The notification of the death, together with the presentation of the Medical Certificate of the Cause of Death must be done by a 'qualified informant'.
- ❖ There are plans to modernise the process of death certification.

THE CORONER

Introduction[6]

[16.03]

The role of the coroner probably represents the most highly engineered interface between law and medicine in the British Isles. A coroner must be legally qualified or medically qualified or both[7] for she makes legal determinations based on medical facts of the cause of death and her decisions are generally legally binding, although her decision may on occasion be appealed to the courts. The dovetailing of the two disciplines could scarcely be more neatly arranged and the role of the coroner has been described as 'coordinating' the medical and legal aspects of investigation into sudden or unsatisfactorily explained deaths.

The evolution of the modern office has been a slow process unfurling over centuries. The coroner initially acted as little more than a fundraiser-in-chief for the Crown until many of the powers of the office gradually eroded or were whittled away, leaving only the duties we now recognise as lying within the province of the coroner.

The modern coroner presides over a system for investigating and certifying deaths in those settings where there is some question, doubt or lack of clarity concerning the death. In many cases, there is little need for the coroner to do anything other than satisfy herself that no further investigation or formal inquest is required, but, where necessary, she does have broader powers to conduct an investigation or to constitute an inquest. The investigation may be relatively informal, but at the other extreme a coroner's inquest, should one be called, is in effect a court that investigates the circumstances of death without attaching blame for the death. A coroner, like a judge in a conventional court, can swear in witnesses and hear testimony that helps to clarify or indicate the cause of death. The objective of an inquest, and the overarching role of the coroner, is to establish the answers to four basic questions pertinent to the death being scrutinised:

- Who is the deceased?
- How did the deceased meet his end?
- When did the deceased die?
- Where did death occur?

A summation of the coroner's role is contained in a recent review of the coroner service:[8]

> 'The coroner performs a public service by making inquiries into sudden and unexplained deaths, independently of the medical profession, the Gardaí, the State or any parties who might have an interest in the outcome of death investigation… In other words, society is demanding that no death be left uninvestigated unless there is a clear and certifiable reason for that death.'

In the preamble to its review, the Working Group review of the coroner service pointed out that:

> '[I]t is critical to focus on the fact that the coroner service is a service for the living. It serves and reassures society as a whole by public investigation of sudden or unexplained death. It informs and supports the bereaved by establishing the cause of death – a service

often critical to the process of mourning and adaptation especially where the circumstances of death may have been unusual or tragic.'[9]

While that may be the principal role of the modern coroner, the office has nonetheless an ancient lineage that needs some exposition in order to put its current functions in context.

Origins of the coroner's office

[16.04]

The role of the coroner is encrusted with history. Its precise roots are shrouded in antiquity, and some legal historians argue that the office dates back to the time of the Roman Empire, but while that contention may have some merit there is little evidence to support it. Most commentators tend to accept that the history of the coroner's office in Ireland can most accurately be traced back to 12th century Norman-controlled England.[10]

In September 1194, a quarter of a century after the Normans first set foot in Ireland, Richard the Lionheart instituted the office that is undoubtedly the linear predecessor to the modern day coroner. Money was the main motivating factor: Richard had been captured in Austria and imprisoned near the Danube while making his way back from the Third Crusade and in order to secure his release he was obliged to pay an enormous ransom that all but bankrupted the Crown treasury. Richard's plenipotentiary in England[11] decided therefore to institute a new office with responsibility for securing more revenue for the crown. This new office would also simultaneously and – from a political perspective – conveniently undermine the corrupt and rapacious Sheriff system, which was the object of popular loathing as well as costing the Treasury revenue due to systematic embezzlement by the Sheriffs. In the 1194 document was an edict called the 'Articles of Eyre' and it stated simply that:

> '[I]n every county of the King's Realm shall be elected three knights and one clerk to keep the pleas of the crown.' [12]

The edict was originally in Latin and in that language, keeping 'the pleas of the crown' is rendered '*custos placitorum coronae*' and from the Latin word *corona*, meaning crown, came the word coroner (via the word 'crowner', which was current for several centuries). The first mention of the coroner in Ireland is in 1264 and according to some sources, the coroner may first have followed his Norman creators across the Irish Sea as early as 1212.[13]

Duties of the ancient coroner

[16.05]

'Keeping the pleas' meant recording details of legal disputes and cases that arose in the coroner's district and which required a later hearing either in local courts or before the more senior judges who would visit each district regularly to hear cases.[14] As it could be many years between each judicial visit, careful compiling and tending of records was vital, lest cases that should be heard might be forgotten.[15] Coroners were in theory prohibited from hearing the cases themselves, but many did so until the practice was formally countermanded by the *Magna Carta*, an early attempt to rein in autocratic excess and to guarantee basic rights of justice and of fair procedure to the people of Britain.[16]

Of course, it should be pointed out that for many years, the coroner's powers in Ireland only extended as widely as English rule was recognised and in many areas, the Norman law espoused by the coroner existed side by side with ancient Irish Brehon law. The coroner investigated and recorded any offence that might subsequently give rise to a fine and hence crown revenue, the ultimate reason for the institution of the coroner's office, and stored the results of the investigation until the case could be heard. Offences that the coroner investigated included the principal role that survives to this day, namely sudden deaths (especially murders) but also robberies, rapes and assaults. The coroner also had responsibility for determining the ownership of any buried treasure (treasure trove) and other somewhat more unusual duties, which are dealt with below (section **[16.06]**).

The Norman laws concerning death in mediaeval England and Ireland were especially complex and any breach of the duties placed on the individual who discovered a dead body or on the district in which the death occurred could be punished by heavy fines. Hence sudden death, suspicious or not, represented a potentially lucrative source of income for the state coffers. Any deviation on the part of citizens from the Byzantine rules laid down by the law in the case of the discovery of a possible murder would be noted down by the coroner with a view to the subsequent imposition of a fine by the courts.

Coroners were initially obliged to be Knights of the realm and had to satisfy a certain minimum property threshold: the theory being that the wealthier a coroner was, the smaller would be the temptation to skim off illicit commissions or to take bribes. Coroners were elected, but only by a very exclusive electorate that typically enfranchised only the local landed gentry.

It was during the time of King Edward I that the coroner's inquest began to be formalised, although it long remained a more unwieldy affair that the one that exists today: the membership of juries could run into three figures and jurors could also be called as witnesses. The inquest was traditionally held at the site of the death or crime and the coroner[17] was required to conduct an examination of the corpse or victim and record the clinical findings associated with the murder, rape or assault. Not until 1836 was a coroner permitted to hire an outside medical expert to conduct a post mortem.[18]

The coroner would also be present at any trials by ordeal to record the results.[19] The coroner's role at the ordeal was in essence to assess any possibility that the alleged wrongdoer undergoing the ordeal should subsequently (and often posthumously) be required to forfeit his goods to the crown.

One additional duty of the early Irish coroner was the 'presentment of Irishry.' Unless it could be proved otherwise, any murder victim was presumed to be Norman and a consequent fine[20] was levied on the Irish population of the locality in which the body was found. To avoid the fine, the natives had to prove, by way of a 'presentment' typically made by the relatives of the dead man, that the victim was Irish.

Historical curiosities and the coroner

[16.06]

One of the more curious, and long-lasting, of the coroner's historical powers was that of *deodand*, an ancient legal tradition where the object responsible for a person's death was believed to be cleansed by its forfeiture to the Church or to the Crown. The object (a sword, an animal, a mill wheel, even a tree are all examples) could be confiscated by the coroner for the Treasury. Alternatively the object or its estimated cash equivalent might be given over to the victim's family as partial compensation for their loss. In one of those occasional oversights that entertainingly pepper legal history, *deodand* survived into the 19th century, when legal applications for *deodand*-based recompense were made by the families of individuals killed in locomotive accidents. One case in 1838 involved a death caused by an exploding locomotive engine, another in 1839 involved a man and a horse killed by a locomotive at a crossing: a jury at the inquest in the latter case awarded the family £1400, the full value of the locomotive engine. The practice of *deodand* was only abolished in 1846, to the enormous relief of the fledgling railway industry.

A coroner also took charge of felons[21] who chose to 'abjure the realm'. Certain classes of criminal could, after making a full confession and forfeiting all possessions, quit the kingdom in accordance with a formal and tortuous set of rules. The coroner would hear the swearing of an oath and then direct the route and timetable by which the felon should leave the country. Failure to adhere to the rules or to leave the country in time made the abjurer fair game, his head 'forfeit to any man who can lift a sword'. The coroner was also responsible for the confiscation of all of the felon's goods and the subsequent decision as to whether those goods would go to the coffers of the Crown.

Few of the coroner's historical roles survive into the present.[22] The foremost among them is the coroner's role in the investigation of death, but there is another known as 'treasure trove', the archaic description for the process of dealing with the finding ('trove' comes from the French *'trouver'*) of treasure. Depending on the nature of the find, treasure could be forfeit to the crown and it would be the coroner who would investigate and decide. As we will see below (section **[16.19]**), the coroner's jurisdiction over treasure trove has effectively, although not formally, vanished.

Quick Reference Guide 16.2

History of the coroner

- ❖ The coroner's office is of late 12th century origin in England and dates to the early 13th century in Ireland.
- ❖ In essence the historical role of the coroner was as a fundraiser for the crown. He fulfilled this role by investigating and recording the details of matters that would have to be determined later by the courts (called 'keeping the pleas'). The courts would hear the cases and the fines they imposed would be directed to the state coffers.
- ❖ The main areas of concern for the coroner were those involving violent crimes, but the job also involved determining the ownership of buried treasure ('treasure trove') as well as certain other matters including *deodand*, the presentment of Irishry and abjuration of the realm.
- ❖ The coroner's inquest was initially an unruly affair, taking place at the scene of the crime and featuring an enormous jury.
- ❖ The evolution of more orthodox forms of taxation led to the diminution of the coroner's fund-raising role and left the office with its current predominant focus on the investigation of sudden and unexplained deaths.

THE MODERN CORONER

[16.07]

Over the years, many of the powers of the coroner were stripped away. Taxation gradually became a more rational process and thus revenue to the crown increasingly came through more uniform and orthodox channels. By 1500, the Eyre, the wandering Court for which the coroner had to 'keep the pleas', was long gone and Acts of Parliament had been passed to limit or eliminate the authority of the coroner over the confiscation of property and abjuration of the realm, leaving the coroner predominantly concerned with investigations of death and the determination of treasure trove. It is the first of these functions over which the 21st century coroner presides.[23] The law that regulates the modern office of coroner in Ireland is contained in the Coroners Act 1962 (the 1962 Act) and the legislation has in turn been fleshed out by decisions of the Irish courts. The 1962 Act took the various statutes that had previously formed an ill-fitting patchwork cloak of guidance for the coroner and consolidated them, updating and replacing laws that dated back as far the reign of Edward I.[24]

Who can be a coroner?

[16.08]

Echoing the origins of the original coroners who had to be independently wealthy, the Coroners Act (Ireland) 1846 stipulated that the only requirement to be a coroner was that the prospective coroner should satisfy a certain property threshold.[25] The 1881 Act of the same name adopted a more pragmatic and constructive approach, necessitating only that a coroner be a surgeon, physician, solicitor, justice of the peace or barrister. The 1962 Act reflects this:

> 'No person shall be appointed to be a Coroner or deputy Coroner unless he is a practising barrister of at least five years standing, or a practising solicitor of at least five years standing or a registered medical practitioner who has been registered, other than provisionally or temporarily…for at least five years.'[26]

According to a recent survey[27] about half of the coroners working in the Republic of Ireland are medical practitioners while half are legally qualified. One or two have a foot in both camps and all are, by the nature of the post, required to have a familiarity with both law and medicine. Each coroner has a deputy who acts for the coroner if the principal is away or ill. Coroners may work on a full-time or part-time basis, depending on the demands of the area for which they have responsibility. Most coroners are part-time, but there have been recommendations that this should change in future.[28]

The coroner service is administered on a geographical basis, divided largely along county or borough lines and coroners are no longer elected, but are appointed[29] and paid[30] by the relevant Local Authority. There are 48 coroner districts in total in the Republic of Ireland, each of which is served by a coroner and her deputy.[31] Many of the larger counties are divided into several districts, while smaller or sparsely populated counties may have a single coroner. Each of the cities of Dublin, Cork, Waterford and Limerick has its own coroner.[32]

Coroners have responsibility for investigating the sudden, suspicious or unnatural deaths that occur in their geographical area of responsibility. It is the place of death that is generally determinative of which coroner will investigate a death, although an investigation may be moved to the jurisdiction of another coroner by agreement. This might occur when two people who were injured following the same accident were moved to different hospitals under the jurisdiction of two different coroners and subsequently died in those hospitals. Even though the deaths might have occurred in two separate coroner districts, the investigations or inquests into the deaths, after all the result of a single accident, could be heard by the coroner for only one of the districts, perhaps the one in which the accident took place.

Duties of the coroner

[16.09]

The coroner makes inquiries into sudden and unexplained deaths acting independently of outside influences, but how many such deaths are there? According to recent figures,[33] approximately 32,000 deaths occur each year in the Republic of Ireland, of which 7250 (22%)[34] are reported to a coroner. There are certain categories of death that *must* be reported to the coroner in charge of the area in which the death took place:[35]

— where there is reason to believe that the deceased person died, either directly or indirectly, as a result of violence or misadventure or by unfair means;

— where there is reason to believe that the deceased person died, either directly or indirectly, as the result of negligence or misconduct or malpractice on the part of others;

— where there is reason to believe that the deceased person died, either directly or indirectly, from any cause other than natural disease.

Furthermore, even if a death is thought to be a result of natural causes, it must nonetheless be reported to the coroner if the deceased was not seen by a medical practitioner within one month before his death.

There are certain categories of person laid down in the Coroners Act 1962 who are obliged by law to notify the coroner if they become aware of a death that occurs in any of the circumstances outlined above:

> Every medical practitioner, registrar of deaths or funeral undertaker and every occupier of a house or mobile dwelling and every person in charge of any institution or premises, in which a deceased person was residing at the time of his death who has reason to believe that the deceased person died [in any of the circumstances outlined above] …[36]

However, the obligation on any of these persons to inform the coroner is purged once the person, instead of informing the coroner of the death, notifies a Garda of the rank of sergeant or higher.[37] While anyone from householder to undertaker might therefore technically be obliged to report a death to the coroner, in most cases it will be a Garda, an undertaker or a health carer, most often the doctor, responsible for the care of the patient at the time of his death who does so.

If the coroner is satisfied in the circumstances that there was nothing untoward about the death, then she may direct the doctor to issue a death certificate without further investigation and certainly without requiring an inquest.

Example 1

A patient who had not been seen in the month prior to his death but who was known to have a long history of heart disease complained to his GP over the telephone of chest pain and weakness. He died before the doctor could attend. As the patient had not been attended by his doctor in the month prior to death, the GP is required to notify her local coroner's office.

The history and circumstances reported to the coroner in the above example could lead her to the conclusion that a heart attack was to blame and she may be happy in those circumstances to direct the attending physician to issue a death certificate. In other situations, the cause of death may be less clear and the coroner may direct that further investigation, often a post mortem[38] examination, be held to establish the cause of death.

Example 2

Take the example above of the cardiac patient but alter the scenario insofar as there was no witness to the final symptoms of the deceased. Let us say instead that he died in his sleep and was found dead by a relative the next day. Again, he was not seen by his doctor in the previous month.

The inference in this case might be that heart disease was to blame because of the long standing history of heart disease, but the coroner may prefer to confirm that particular hypothesis in this scenario by ordering that a post mortem examination be conducted. The coroner does not conduct the post mortem herself, but instead relies on facilities and personnel provided by local hospitals.[39] The body will therefore be moved to a local hospital so that the examination can be conducted. The post mortem is performed by a single doctor (typically a pathologist) but *cannot* be carried out by:

— a doctor who is not a pathologist and who was involved in the care of a patient in the final month of that patient's life, or

— a doctor, whether a pathologist or not, whose care of the deceased may – in the opinion of the coroner – be called into question at the inquest.[40]

The reason for this is obvious: either of the above doctors conducting the post mortem would raise the uncomfortable spectre of bias or of conflict of interest. If a doctor cares for a patient who dies suddenly, perhaps after an operation or within moments of a visit by her general practitioner, it would evidently be wholly inappropriate for that surgeon or that GP respectively to perform the post mortem.

If the post mortem demonstrates death due to natural causes the coroner can then issue a Coroner's Certificate, which is her equivalent of the Medical Certificate of Cause of Death and which indicates that she is satisfied that a death certificate should issue for the deceased. The Coroners' Certificate is communicated to the Registrar of Births and Death for the district in order that the death can be formally registered.[41]

INQUESTS

[16.10]

If the post mortem does not disclose a natural cause of death, then the coroner may at her discretion proceed to hold an inquest to try to establish the cause of death.[42] However, the coroner's discretion on this matter is by no means universal or unlimited and there are some situations in which the coroner *must* hold an inquest:

[W]here a coroner is informed that the body of a deceased person is lying within his district, it shall be the duty of the coroner to hold an inquest in relation to the death of that person if he is of the opinion that the *death may have occurred in a violent or unnatural manner or suddenly and from unknown causes or in a place or in circumstances which* [because of any provision laid down in other laws] *require that an inquest should be held.*[3] [emphasis added]

Quick Reference Guide 16.3

The role of the coroner outlined

- ❖ The prime residual power of the coroner is the investigation of sudden or unexplained deaths, through the use of informal investigations, post-mortems or inquests.
- ❖ In essence, the coroner has four questions to pose and to answer: *Who* died? *When* did he die? *Where* did he die? *How* did he die?
- ❖ The coroner is forbidden by law – in answering those questions – from apportioning any blame for the death. Blame-casting is the responsibility of the regular courts.
- ❖ To be a coroner, one must be a lawyer or a registered medical practitioner of at least five years' standing. A coroner has responsibility for a particular geographical district and may discharge her duties in a full- or part-time capacity.
- ❖ The coroner investigates sudden, suspicious or unnatural deaths occurring in her area of responsibility.
- ❖ Certain deaths must be reported to the coroner including those involving potential foul play, malpractice or unnatural causes. Any death of a person who has not been seen by a doctor in the month preceding death must be reported to the coroner.
- ❖ There are defined categories of person, including medical practitioners and persons in charge of a premises or institution where a death occurs, who are obliged to inform the coroner if they know of a sudden, suspicious or unnatural death.
- ❖ The coroner has discretion to decide whether or not to investigate any given death. Informal inquiries may be sufficient to satisfy the coroner of the cause of death. If not, she may proceed to order a post-mortem or to hold an inquest.
- ❖ Once the coroner is satisfied as to the identity of the deceased and time, place and cause of death, she may either direct the medical practitioner to issue a Medical Certificate of Cause of Death or issue a Coroner's Certificate, either of which will allow the death to be registered.

In other words sudden, unnatural or violent deaths in suspicious circumstances necessitate an inquest, as do deaths that occur in situations envisaged by other laws as requiring an inquest. An example of a law outside the Coroners Act that mandates the holding of an inquest is found in the Defence Act 1954.[44] It requires that:

Whenever a person under sentence dies in a military prison or detention barrack … the coroner having jurisdiction in the place where such prison or barrack is *shall* [which in legal terms means *must*] hold an inquest on the body of such person.[45] [italics added]

In cases where the cause of death is strongly suggestive of homicide (unlawful killing), the post-mortem will often be conducted by a State Pathologist at the request of the coroner, subject to the approval, which is never withheld, of the Minister for Justice, Equality and Law Reform. In circumstances where a suspicion of violent or unnatural death comes to light after the burial of the deceased and that suspicion is communicated to the coroner by a senior Garda, the coroner for the area may request the Minister to order that the body be exhumed and, if the body is exhumed, the coroner's powers are precisely as if the body had never been interred in the first place.[46]

An inquest may also be ordered by the Attorney General[47] in any situation where the Attorney General thinks that such an inquest is required in the public interest or in the interests of justice, even in circumstances where the body is irrecoverably lost or destroyed. If such an order is made then any coroner, even one who does not have jurisdiction over the area where the death occurred, may be directed to conduct the inquest, irrespective of any previous inquests or inquiries. The Attorney General's power to do so has been confirmed by the Irish Supreme Court[48] but only if the power is not exercised unreasonably or irrationally.[49]

Reasons for deciding to hold an inquest

[16.11]

In the *Farrell* case the Supreme Court listed the broad grounds upon which a coroner should generally exercise her discretion to hold an inquest:[50]

- to determine the medical cause of death;
- to allay rumours or suspicions;
- to draw attention to the existence of circumstances which, if not remedied, might lead to further deaths;[51]
- to advance medical knowledge;
- to preserve the legal interests of the deceased person's family, heirs or other interested parties.[52]

What happens at an inquest

[16.12]

In a traditional court case, there are battle lines drawn between one side and another: one side has made an allegation that it is trying to prove, while the other side is attempting to put the opposite case. In a criminal case for example, the State is trying to prove that the accused committed a crime, while the accused is trying to establish his innocence or, at the very least, raise a reasonable doubt as to his guilt.

There is, or at least, there should be, no such conflict at an inquest: the coroner is simply inquiring as to the facts of death and is expressly forbidden by legislation from attributing any blame for the death.[53] An inquest may involve a jury being called upon to consider and reach a verdict. It may involve witnesses being called and testimony being heard, but it does not involve a finding of guilt against any party and unlike a civil or criminal court case where the various parties involved can call witnesses, at a coroner's court only the coroner herself may call witnesses.[54] The legal framework of the coroner's inquest is usually described as 'inquisitorial', rather than the 'adversarial' system associated in the public mind with criminal and civil courts. The coroner is the questioner seeking to determine the four cardinal facts already referred to:

— the identity of the deceased (who?);
— the time of death (when?);
— the location of death (where?);
— the cause of death (how?).

The coroner's court seeks the facts of the death, rather than seeking to blame or exonerate, an outlook well summed up in one English case:

> '[A]n inquest is a fact finding exercise and not a method of apportioning guilt. The procedure and rules of evidence which are suitable for one are not suitable for the other. In an inquest, it should not be forgotten that there are no parties, there is no indictment,[55] there is no prosecution, there is no defence, there is no trial, simply an attempt to establish the facts. It is an inquisitorial process, quite unlike a trial…' [56]

The same principle was put another way by the UK Committee on Death Certification and Coroners in 1971 (*Broderick Report*), cited in the Department of Justice *Review of the Coroner Service*:

> '[T]he function of an inquest should be simply to seek out and record as many of the facts concerning the death as the public interest requires, without deducing from the facts any determination of blame.'

An inquest is generally held in public.[57] The usual venue is a courtroom in the coroner's geographical area of responsibility, but this is not uniformly so. The body is not often produced at an inquest and the jury, if there is one, does not have to view the body.[58] The coroner has a certain degree of discretion about whether to empanel[59] a jury depending on the circumstances of the case[60] but again her discretion is circumscribed – some inquests *must* take place before a jury if the coroner believes that:

— the death was the result of murder, manslaughter or infanticide (the killing of a newborn within the first year after birth);
— the death occurred in circumstances where an Act other than the Coroners Act 1962 states that an inquest must be held;[61]
— the death occurred in circumstances where, under provisions contained in any Act other than the Coroners Act 1962, a Minister, government department or inspector working on behalf of a Minister or government department must be notified of the death;[62]
— the death was the result of using a vehicle in a public place;
— the death occurred in circumstances that would, were they to continue or to recur, constitute a danger to the health and safety of the public or a section of the public.

The jury may consist of anything from six to twelve people and they are sworn in before the inquest commences. The jury's duty is to reach a verdict and if it cannot do so, the coroner can discharge the jury and hear the case afresh with a new jury. Once a majority of the jury is agreed on a particular verdict, the coroner will accept that verdict.

During the inquest, the coroner can call witnesses if she chooses and those witnesses may be examined under oath. Refusal to attend can be punished by law, although the scope for punishment is extremely limited.

A witness who testifies before a coroner's inquest is treated as if he was a witness before the High Court and is entitled to all of the safeguards and protection that would be afforded to him if he was testifying before that court. These might include the right not to testify about certain material that is legally privileged.[63] The coroner is limited by the 1962 Act to only being able to call two medical witnesses to testify, but there are no other express limits to the power to call witnesses.[64] In general, anyone who wishes to testify may indicate his desire to give evidence before the inquest and will be heard as long as the coroner believes that the evidence is relevant to the inquiry being conducted. Therefore, a person who has a series of grievances that he wishes to air and which have no bearing on the matter under investigation may be prevented from taking the stand or permitted to do so only if their testimony confines itself to relevant matters.

During the inquest, the coroner herself also has judicial 'privilege', meaning that she is immune from legal action for anything she says or does provided always that she is acting within her powers (or *intra vires*[65]). In one case,[66] a pop concert promoter sought to sue a coroner for defamation based on unflattering observations the latter had made during an inquest into the death of a teenager who had drowned while swimming the River Lee in an attempt to gain access to a concert. The court reasoned that:

> '[A] coroner enjoys absolute privilege in respect *of anything that he says while he is performing his duties as a Coroner* in the holding of an inquest in accordance with … the Coroners Act 1962…Once, however, he strays outside of the functions which he is required to perform under the Act which are defined…as being to ascertain the identity of the person in respect of whose death the inquest is being held and how, when and where the death occurred and *once he knows that he is no longer performing one of these functions* he ceases to enjoy this privilege.' [italics added]

In other words, a coroner, like a judge, is free from the inhibiting threat of being sued as long as she acts at all times within the powers that are given to her by the 1962 Act. Thus a coroner who knowingly attributes blame to an individual (hence stepping outside her powers) and in the process defames that individual may be liable to be sued for that defamation.[67]

One corollary of the fact that the inquest is a fact-finding exercise rather than a trial is that the coroner is not obliged to adhere as strictly to the rules of the courts, such as notifying every single party to the inquest of every evidential matter that may be brought up.[68] In many cases, the evidence illuminating the facts surrounding death is simple and clear-cut. Witnesses and post-mortem reports will combine to provide an unambiguous description of the circumstances of the death. However, in some more contentious cases, there may be some dispute as to the facts or the interpretation given to the facts by certain witnesses. Those involved at an inquest are entitled to have legal representation at the inquest to ensure that the coroner follows due procedure in complex situations and remains within her powers and also to verify that the rights of participants in the inquest are not abridged in any way. The coroner will permit, if permission is sought, examination of witnesses by an interested party or by the legal representative of an interested party[69] but will not permit that interested party to call its own witnesses: only the coroner may call witnesses at an inquest.

Interested parties to an inquest can include the following, but the list is not necessarily exhaustive, as the final category in the list below suggests:

- the family or next-of-kin of the deceased;
- representatives of an institution where the deceased was residing at the time of death;
- those factually responsible for the death in some way, such as the driver of a motor vehicle involved in an accident that claimed the life of the deceased;
- representatives of insurance companies;
- where death results from an accident at work: trade union representatives, the employer of the deceased, Health and Safety Authority inspectors;
- others who are considered interested parties at the coroner's discretion.

The conclusion of the inquest

[16.13]

Once all the evidence is heard from witnesses or from reports submitted to the inquest, the coroner or the jury, if a jury has been empanelled, will endeavour to reach a verdict, which may include one of the following common verdicts:

- accidental death or misadventure;
- suicide;
- open verdict;
- natural causes;
- unlawful killing;

Some of the more general duties imposed by the 1962 Act in respect of the inquest provide echoes of the coroners mediaeval role as 'Keeper of the Pleas'. The coroner must record in writing the names and addresses of any witnesses and keep a record of documentation arising at each inquest, namely the details of depositions (written submissions) to inquests, witnesses, post-mortem results and verdicts returned at inquests.[70] On retirement, resignation or dismissal the coroner must return the documentation to the county registrar. All the documentation generated by the coroner is public and the 1962 Act stipulates that a copy of any documentation must be given to anyone who requests it.[71]

Blame and the coroner

[16.14]

It is obvious that verdicts such as 'unlawful killing' may mean that the coroner can walk a fine line when it comes to the rule that her inquests should neither make a finding of guilt nor attribute blame to any person. The fact that the coroner is prohibited from making findings of liability or the attribution of blame is one of the essential things that must be understood about her role, but it is also important to note that there is a difference between attributing blame and finding that there is some measure of blame that may need to be attributed in another setting by an appropriate body such as the criminal courts. A verdict that a person was unlawfully killed is merely an objective finding that *someone* has unlawfully killed the deceased. The inquest's verdict does not find a particular person guilty or point the finger in any particular direction. It is a matter for the criminal justice system to amass the evidence necessary to apprehend, prosecute and convict any wrongdoer.

The avoidance of imposing blame can be a far-reaching doctrine. In the case of *The State (McKeown) v Dr Thomas Scully*,[72] the inquest returned a verdict that included a finding of suicide. At the time suicide was illegal,[73] meaning that according to the coroner's verdict the deceased was guilty of the criminal offence of having killed himself. Because a coroner is forbidden from considering questions of criminal liability or attributing blame, the High Court quashed the verdict reached at the inquest and stated that in any event there was insufficient evidence to have reached a finding of suicide in the first instance.

Postponing an inquest in the interests of justice

[16.15]

In a situation where criminal charges are being considered or pursued against any individual in respect of a death that is being investigated by the coroner, the Gardaí may request the coroner to adjourn the inquest until such time as the criminal matters are concluded. The coroner is obliged to accede to that request,[74] the reason being to ensure that the coroner's inquest would not compromise the criminal proceedings by appearing to prejudge the matter (which could in turn prejudice public opinion, making a fair trial impossible). Of course if the criminal process results in the conviction of an individual for an offence such as murder or criminal negligence, it might then be redundant to bring the inquest to its conclusion (a verdict of unlawful killing would after all add little to the overall picture) and the coroner may decide not to reconvene the inquest. Conversely, if the criminal proceedings fail to materialise or to secure a conviction, it may be that the coroner will wish to resume the inquest in order to reach a verdict in the interest of the grieving family and in the wider public interest.

Coroner's recommendations

[16.16]

As well as reaching a verdict with or without a jury, the coroner may also issue any general recommendations that she may think necessary to minimise the recurrence of similar avoidable tragedies.[75] Examples of such recommendations include a verdict returned by the Dublin City Coroner's Court that called for a dangerous junction, the scene of several previous accidents, to be remedied[76] and a call from a Galway coroner for a national policy to ensure safer building sites after the death of a schoolboy nightwatchman on one site.[77] These recommendations have no legal force, in that the coroner cannot compel action to achieve the ends stipulated in her recommendation, but they do exemplify the coroner's role as a servant of the public interest.

The conclusion of the coroner's role

[16.17]

Once the coroner is satisfied that the cause of death has been established to her satisfaction without the need for further enquiries, she may direct the doctor caring for the patient to sign the death certificate. However, in more complicated cases, where a post-mortem or inquest is conducted, the coroner then assumes responsibility for issuing a Coroner's Certificate to the Registrar of Births and Deaths containing all the necessary details to allow the death to be registered and which takes the place of the Medical Certificate of Cause of Death. If a death certificate had already been issued but the cause of death upon it has subsequently been adjudged incorrect, an amending certificate may be issued, detailing the new cause of death as amended.[78] The coroner does not need to retain the body of the deceased until the utter end of any investigation and if she feels no purpose would be served by retaining the body, it may be released for burial or cremation even before an inquest has taken place.[79]

Limits of the coroner's powers

[16.18]

In reaching a conclusion to each case, the coroner must satisfy herself that one question paramount among the four posed has been answered: how the person died. When it comes to this question of 'how?' there has in recent years been some degree of disagreement about how far the coroner's enquiries should be permitted to go in order to obtain an answer. The Coroners Act 1962, s 30 is one of the most important provisions of the legislation, limiting the degree to which the coroner can raise questions of criminal and civil liability in examining the cause of death. In addition, s 31 prohibits the 'censure or exoneration' of any person. How can one reconcile these limits with the ambition of the coroner to get as close as possible to the source of the cause of death? What in any event is meant by the 'cause' of death? Some coroners have questioned whether ss 30 and 31 of the 1962 Act confine them solely to examining only the immediate medical cause of death or whether they have a wider ranging remit.

The case of *Eastern Health Board v Farrell (Dublin City Coroner)*[80] reflected some of these issues and provided the answer that for the time being constitutes the limit to the coroner's inquisitorial powers in Ireland. The Dublin City Coroner, Dr Brian Farrell, was conducting an inquest into the death from aspiration pneumonia of a young man who had suffered from mental retardation since infancy. However, it was suggested at the inquest that his brain damage was itself a possible consequence of the administration of the pertussis (whooping cough) vaccine in infancy. Dr Farrell wished to call witnesses to examine this claim, while the Eastern Health Board argued that for him to do so would lie outside his powers under the Coroners Act and would in any event be counter-productive.

Both the High Court and subsequently the Supreme Court (after the coroner appealed the initial decision) felt that the vaccination as a 'cause' of death was too indirect to be legitimately investigated by the coroner. The Supreme Court upheld the earlier High Court ruling that the role of the coroner is to investigate the 'proximal medical cause' of death.[81] The High Court judge, Geoghegan J did, however, leave the coroner a little latitude, when he stated that:

> 'I think it would be unwise to set down any hard and fast rules but in each case, the Coroner should be investigating what is the real and actual cause of the death. This death it appears to me, was caused by pneumonia. Any conceivable link with the three-in-one injection [of which the whooping cough vaccine was a part] is too nebulous and indirect to make it appropriate for an investigation by the Coroner.'

In other words, there may be circumstances in which the coroner has some latitude[82] in order to examine the circumstances or cause of death but in this instance the leeway sought was too great. Unless the Government changes the law, the coroner's powers appear to be limited to examining the proximate circumstances and medical cause of death alone, except in exceptional situations.

TREASURE TROVE – AN ANACHRONISM

[16.19]

Treasure trove is a vestigial coroner's power nominally part of her remit[83] but in reality now residing elsewhere. In *Webb v Ireland*,[84] the case that arose in the aftermath of the unearthing of the Derrynaflan chalice and hoard, the then Chief Justice defined treasure trove as:

> '[V]aluable chattels [the legal term for possessions] which it could be established were concealed for the purpose of protecting them and with the intention of subsequently recovering them on the part of the person who hid them and which were made of the precious metals of silver or gold, a combination of them or an alloy containing a substantial ingredient of either or both of them.'

Furthermore, the identity of the person who originally concealed the precious artefacts must be unknown. In historical times, the coroner decided whether a cache fitted the description of treasure trove: if so, it was annexed by the State and the money realised from its sale went to the treasury. The doctrine of treasure trove long ago ceased to be a method of raising finances for the state and its significance today is that it permits the state to secure archaeological treasures from the country's history and pre-history that might otherwise fall into private hands.

After the passage of the National Monuments (Amendment) Act 1994, all duties to do with precious artefacts found in the Republic were transferred to the Director of the National Museum in Dublin, an apportionment of responsibility more in keeping with the purpose of contemporary treasure trove. In any event, treasure trove has no discernible connection with clinical practice, so it is not considered further here.

Quick Reference Guide 16.4

The inquest

- ❖ An inquest may become necessary when further investigations are required to determine the answers to the four key questions for the coroner: Who? When? Where? How?
- ❖ In general an inquest will be held either when required by law or when informal or post-mortem investigations have failed to answer critical questions concerning the death.
- ❖ The coroner has *discretion* to call an inquest in many cases, but when she is of the opinion that the death may have been sudden, violent or unnatural or where a provision in any other law demands an inquest, then one *must* be held.
- ❖ When the coroner is deciding whether or not to hold an inquest, there are five principal grounds on which she will generally decide to do so:
  - (i) to determine the medical cause of death
  - (ii) to allay rumours or suspicions
  - (iii) to draw attention to the existence of circumstances which, if not remedied, might lead to further deaths
  - (iv) to advance medical knowledge
  - (v) to preserve the legal interests of the deceased person's family, heirs or other interested parties
- ❖ At an inquest there is no competition between two sides, simply an attempt to determine the facts leading to the death. The coroner decides which witnesses are to be called, but she is limited by law to a maximum of two medical witnesses. A witness who refuses to attend or testify may be reported to the High Court for contempt of court.
- ❖ An inquest is generally heard in public; there may be a jury, but there are certain circumstances in which there *must* be a jury, including road traffic accidents. The inquest can hear from any interested party at the discretion of the coroner.
- ❖ Persons involved in an inquest may have legal representation and the legal representative may question the witnesses. However, only the coroner may call witnesses and witnesses may only testify on matters relevant to the inquest.
- ❖ A coroner is exempt from legal action against her for anything she says or does while acting in her role as coroner. At the end of the inquest, the jury, if there is one, will return a verdict and the coroner may make recommendations. The verdict or the recommendations must not apportion blame and the investigation must only concern itself with the proximal medical cause of death.

THE FUTURE OF THE CORONER SERVICE

[16.20]

At the time of writing there is no new legislation on the horizon to update the Coroners Act 1962, but updating is certainly needed. As just stated, references to treasure trove in the Act are irrelevant and there are many other aspects of the legislation that need to be renovated. In 2000, the Department of Justice, Equality and Law Reform published its *Review of the Coroner Service*, compiled by a working group appointed by the Department.[85] The Working Group made more than 100 recommendations for reform of the coroner service and they include the following:

Figure 16.2 – Proposals for reform of the coroner service

- The drafting of a new Coroners Act, to include Coroners Rules that would aid in the interpretation of legislation and the establishment of 'best practice' for coroners in the Republic of Ireland.
- An extension of the coroner's powers, in order to permit a more extensive investigation of both the cause of death and the circumstances of death, while recognising that the coroner should still be constrained from apportioning civil and criminal blame. Other increases in her powers would also permit the coroner to take certain decisions unilaterally, such as ordering a post-mortem by the State Pathologist, without reference to the Minister for Justice, Equality and Law Reform.
- Guaranteed provision and funding of pathology, post mortem and mortuary facilities together with structured training for coroners, including formal legal training for medically qualified coroners and medical training for their legally qualified counterparts.
- Fewer but more specialised full-time coroners, supported by dedicated administrative staff and overseen by a new agency with responsibility for the coroner service.
- More information to be made available to the public about the role of the coroner and clear information and documentation should be available to the next-of-kin of the deceased throughout the coroner process.[86]
- The categories of death to be reported to the coroner should be extended to include maternal deaths and more vaguely 'vulnerable people', a group not really defined in the report but which appears to encompass those 'in some category of formal care', itself also a vague description.
- Not only deaths occurring under anaesthetic[87] but all deaths occurring after 'any medical or surgical procedure' should be reported to the coroner.[88]
- Juries should become optional at inquests into road traffic accidents adjudged by the coroner, using her experience of such matters, to be 'routine'. Juries should also comprise only an odd number of members (7,9 or 11) to prevent hung juries.
- A review board should be implemented to consider requests for an inquest to be held or re-held in certain circumstances where either there was no inquest in the first instance or some new matter necessitates the holding of another inquest. The Attorney General would then make a decision about holding a first or subsequent inquest based on the recommendations of the Review Board. Aggrieved parties would still have the option of seeking to challenge the decision of the Review Board or Attorney General in the High Court.

These are all recommendations and even then only a summary of the exhaustive recommendations made by the Working Group. There has been no movement yet by the Department of Justice, Equality and Law Reform on a timetable for the reform of the coroner service, but any new legislation is likely to give prominence to many of the amendments suggested above.

Cremation

[16.21]

Formal rules applying to cremation in Ireland were introduced in 1989.[89] Cremation must be authorised by the medical referee attached to a crematorium, based on certificates completed and furnished by the doctor who attended the deceased. The rules on cremation are obviously somewhat tighter than they might be in case of burial. Cremation by its very nature reduces the body to a form which makes later investigation of an alternative cause of death, such as foul play, practically impossible. Accordingly, it is necessary to be absolutely certain that there is no irregularity in the background to an application for cremation. The Medical Referee, before authorising a cremation, must be satisfied:

- (a) that the attending doctor, who must have been registered for at least three years, has completed and signed a certificate in the prescribed form (form 'C' – see appendix C) stating the cause of death, or
- (b) if the attending doctor is not available or has not been registered for the requisite three years, that form 'C' has been completed and signed by another doctor registered for at least three years, and that the second doctor has viewed the body and made such inquiries as she deems necessary to satisfy herself as to the cause of death before signing the certificate, or
- (c) the death has been reported to the coroner and the Medical Referee is in receipt of a completed certificate in the prescribed form (form 'D' – see appendix C) from that coroner.

Therefore, in the case of a death reported to the coroner where the coroner is satisfied as to the cause of death a coroner's certificate circumvents the need for a form signed by a doctor and the cremation may go ahead. The coroner may, as has already been mentioned, release the body for burial or cremation when she is satisfied that no purpose would be served by retaining the body further, or in other words when any necessary investigations such as a post-mortem examination have been completed and sufficient evidence has thereby been obtained for the investigation and determination of the cause of death (section **[16.17]**).

The form must usually reach the crematorium before mid-afternoon of the day before cremation is scheduled to take place to ensure that there is ample time for the Medical Referee to instigate any necessary investigations or clarifications prior to authorising or refusing the cremation. If the forms are not correctly filled or the Medical Referee is not happy with the information supplied, she can attempt to get further information from the signatories of the form or from anyone else having knowledge of the death. If the Medical Referee is still not satisfied she may perform an examination of the body, extending, with consent of the next of kin, to 'internal dissection' if necessary to rule out any reason why the body should not be cremated. It follows that the Medical Referee has the discretion to refuse to authorise cremation.[90] A Garda, not below the rank of

Superintendent, may also put a stay on cremation where further examination of the body is or may be necessary.[91]

As we have noted in the case of the coroner, where certain doctors are precluded from performing a post-mortem, conflict of interest is a potential concern with cremation. In the same way that a doctor whose conduct may be called into question by a death will not ordinarily be permitted to conduct the post-mortem on the victim of that death (section **[16.09]**), a doctor who is related to the deceased or who has a financial interest in the affairs of the deceased (such as being named in the will) cannot sign the cremation form.[92]

One key aspect of the examination after death of a body intended for cremation is to ensure that there are no prostheses left *in situ*. Of particular concern are cardiac pacemakers or any radioactive devices, neither of which respond especially well to the high temperatures of the crematorium. In particular, mercury batteries in a pacemaker may explode.

Dying declarations

[16.22]

In law there is a rule against 'hearsay' evidence in court. What this means in essence is that a statement cannot normally be admitted in evidence unless the person who made the statement is in a position to testify as to the truth of the contents of that statement. Therefore, if I were to say in a witness box that I heard person X say that he saw person Y kill person Z, my statement would be hearsay and inadmissible as evidence. It would be necessary for person X to get into the witness box to state whether he saw person Y kill person Z. Only then could X be tested on the truth of what he saw.

There are some exceptions to this rule. Sometimes in order for justice to be done, some statements will be admitted in a courtroom even though the person who could testify to the truth of that statement's content is unable to do so. The perfect example is where the person who made the original statement is dead.

> **Example 3**
>
> In a row that takes place before no witnesses, Cain stabs his brother Abel and then runs away, leaving Abel bleeding on the ground. Unknown to Cain, his victim is still alive. He is found and taken to hospital where in spite of every effort by the team in the Accident and Emergency department, he bleeds to death. At almost the last moment, Abel seizes the lapel of the nearest doctor and whispers, loud enough for the doctor to clearly discern the words, 'I know I'm dying, I have to tell you, it was my brother Cain who stabbed me…'

This is a dying declaration. Abel is no longer around to point the accusatory finger at Cain and there were no other witnesses. Does this mean that, because it is hearsay (Abel cannot have his statement tested in court), that it cannot be evidence? The answer is that in extreme situations such as this, the 'dying declaration' of a murder victim is admissible evidence. This exception is naturally subject to certain conditions: the person making the declaration must have been under what is termed a 'settled hopeless expectation of death'. In other words, he must know that he is dying and therefore is unlikely to have much incentive for lying.[93] A dying declaration can only be evidence in a murder charge, not in any other case. For example, if a person involved in a road traffic accident declares before dying that the person in the other vehicle was on the wrong side of the road, that declaration is not valid unless a charge of murder is brought against the other driver.

Accordingly, it may be good practice for a doctor in a situation where she is treating the victim of violence who subsequently dies and where she becomes aware that the patient has said something of potential significance to consider recording that statement, in some permanent form.

Endnotes

1 Questions of the legal definition of 'death' and the 'right' of the individual to choose death over life are dealt with in ch 13, *The Extremes of Life II: the end of life.*

2 Births and Deaths Registration Act (Ireland) 1880, amended by the Vital Statistics and Births Deaths and Marriages Registration Act 1952, the Births, Deaths and Marriages Registration Act 1972 and the Stillbirths Act 1994. Registrars operate under the auspices of the health boards and each county will generally have one registrar.

3 The standard of certification of the medical cause of death has frequently been found to be sub-standard: see James DS, Bull AD 'Information on death certificates: cause for concern?' Journal of Clinical Pathology 1996; 49(3): 213-6; Doyle 4G, Harrison M, O'Malley F 'A study of selected death certificates from three Dublin teaching hospitals Journal of Public Health Medicine 1990; 12(2): 118-23. Both studies showed fundamental problems with the information contain on death certificates while the latter study in particular showed wild and frequent discrepancies between the information on the certificate and the cause of death found at autopsy.

4 From 'Notes and Suggestions Regarding Certification of Causes of Deaths' which accompany each book of Medical Certificates of the Cause of Death.

5 Department of Health & Department of Social Community and Family Affairs *Bringing Civil Registration into the 21st Century* (May 2001) para 3.50 *ff.* There is also a plan to introduce electronic registration of deaths for hospitals and subsequently for coroners' offices while also permitting postal registration of deaths by qualified informants.

6 A more exhaustive account of the coroner's history, role and powers is contained in Farrell *Coroners: Practice and Procedure* (2000).

7 One recommendation made by the Coroner Review Group (see section **[16.20]**) is that specialist coroner training programmes should be introduced to formalise instruction in both medical and legal matters focussing, although not exclusively, on the discipline in which the particular coroner is not already qualified. See Department of Justice, Law Reform and Equality *Review of the Coroner Service – Report of the Working Group* (2000).

8 Department of Justice, Law Reform and Equality *Review of the Coroner Service – Report of the Working Group* (2000), p 25.

9 Not all commentators take such a rosy view of the coroner's role in these islands: see Pounder 'The coroner service – A relic in need of reform' BMJ 1999; 318:1502:

> 'Every coroner's investigation is an enforceable intrusion by the state into what would otherwise be a private family matter – the death of a loved one. Striking the correct balance between the reasonable needs of the state to investigate and the rights of the next of kin to privacy and religious ritual is not easy, and present evidence suggests that it is not done well in England and Wales.'

10 Although the office of coroner enigmatically and tantalisingly features in some documents from as early as the eighth to the tenth centuries, these documents offer no context or explanation for the office to suggest whether it is a still earlier predecessor of the modern post.

11 Richard never learned English and spent as little time there as possible.

12 Article 20. An 'eyre' was a travelling court that stopped in each township to hear major cases that had accumulated since the last visit of the court. Minor cases would be heard in the Sheriffs' Courts.

13 Otway-Ruthven *A History of Mediaeval Ireland* (1968) ch 5 (cited in Farrell *Coroners: Practice and Procedure* (2000)). Dr Farrell plumps for a date in 1215 as being the formal birthday of the office of coroner in Ireland.

14 This travelling court was known as an 'eyre', hence the 'Articles of Eyre'.

15 One writer records a gap of 44 years between visits of the court, so coroners had to be patient as well as meticulous.

16 And also to ensure that the land-holding interests of the wealthier barons faced fewer threats from the crown.

17 He would invariably have been male at that time.

18 One commentator points out that a medical expert would not always have been necessary: given the available implements, mediaeval murders were rarely subtle affairs. In England, the coroner was obliged to view the body of the deceased until 1980. In 1767, a surgeon was appointed to assist the coroners of Dublin (see Farrell *Coroners: Practice and Procedure* (2000) p 19). In Ireland the Coroners Act 1962, s 27(1) places an obligation upon the coroner to view the body prior to an inquest unless a Garda gives evidence that she has viewed the body of the deceased.

19 Trials by ordeal were a primitive method for ascertaining guilt or innocence, most strongly associated in the popular consciousness with the detection of witchcraft, but also the investigation of murders and other serious offences. Ordeals could include being bound and thrown into deep water: floating meant guilt, sinking (and therefore frequently drowning) signified innocence. Other ordeals included bringing the alleged perpetrator before the body of the victim, if the victim's wounds began to bleed again, then guilt was determined.

20 Called the *murdrum.*

21 A legal term for a person guilty of a more serious crime. The less grave counterpart of a felony is a misdemeanour.

22 Easily the most esoteric of the coroner's mediaeval duties was the obligation to investigate certain catches made by fishermen, namely sturgeon and whale. All whales and sturgeon belonged to the crown and failure to yield up the catch or its equivalent in cash to the royal coffers would result in a fine.

23 The plethora of legislation that regularly punctuated and prompted the transition from mediaeval to modern coroners is exhaustively dealt with in Farrell *Coroners: Practice and Procedure* (2000) ch 1.

24 Who ascended the throne of England in 1272.

25 Prior to this and in keeping with the 'democracy' of the age, there were also property requirements for those who elected coroners: Coroners (Ireland) Act 1829.

26 Coroners Act 1962, s 14(1).

27 Report of the Working Group, Department of Justice, Law Reform and Equality *Review of the Coroner Service* (2000), pp 24-25.

28 Report of the Working Group, Department of Justice, Law Reform and Equality *Review of the Coroner Service* (2000).

29 In general the coroner must live within the district for which she is responsible unless she has obtained permission of the Minister for Justice, Equality and Law Reform to do otherwise: Coroners Act 1962, s 8(2). While the Coroner is appointed by the Local Authority, the coroner herself is responsible for the appointment of her deputy. The coroner may also cancel the appointment of any deputy, so long she has appointed a replacement.

30 Coroners Act 1962, s 9(1).

31 Coroners Act 1962, s 12.

32 The boundaries between adjoining areas over which any combination of coroners has jurisdiction may be redrawn by the Minister for Justice, Equality and Law Reform, assuming all the relevant districts affected are under the control of the same Local Authority, Coroners Act 1962, s 6(3). In certain circumstances, coroners' districts may be amalgamated (Coroners Act 1962, ss 6(4) and 7); this might occur with depopulation or if the service in an area were to be taken over by a full-time, rather than part-time, coroner.

33 Report of the Working Group, Department of Justice, Law Reform and Equality *Review of the Coroner Service* (2000).

34 This figure is appreciably lower than in the UK, where 190 000, or one third, of all deaths in England and Wales were reported to the coroner in 1996. In 1970 that number was 130 000, 20%. See Tarling 'Coroner service survey' (1998) Home Office Research and Statistics Directorate.

35 Coroners Act 1962, s 18(4).

36 Coroners Act 1962, s 18(4).

37 Coroners Act 1962, s 18(5).

38 A post mortem may, at the discretion of the coroner, involve only an external examination of the body to rule out signs of violent death: *Hanley v Coroner for County Kildare* [1999] IEHC 6.

39 This reliance on facilities that are often already overburdened and over which the coroner has no prior call can lead to long delays in obtaining the results of post mortems.

40 Similarly, a coroner (or deputy coroner) may not act as coroner in a case where she (as a doctor) treated the patient within a month of his death or (as a solicitor) drafted the will of the deceased. Nor may a coroner who is a solicitor or barrister act in any legal case arising out of any matter that may have come before her while acting as coroner or deputy coroner.

41 As already mentioned in section **[16.02]** on Death Certification, it is planned to introduce electronic communication between coroner and Registrar of Births and Deaths. See Department of Health/ Department of Social Community and Family Affairs *Bringing Civil Registration into the 21st Century* (May 2001) para 3.50 *ff.*

42 Cusack 'The Coroner's Court' MLJI 1995; 1:82.

43 Coroners Act 1962, s 17.

44 Defence Act 1954, s 238.

45 There are similar provisions regarding deaths in prisons. In countries such as Scotland, reforms introduced have included fewer mandatory inquests, limiting them only to deaths in custody and accidents at work: see Pounder 'Law and forensic medicine in Scotland' (1993) 14 Am J Forensic Med Pathol 340.

46 Coroners Act 1962, s 47.

47 Coroners Act 1962, s 24.

48 *Farrell (Dublin City Coroner) v Attorney General* [1998] 1 IR 203.

49 In England, the courts have forced a coroner to hold an inquest when the coroner initially declined to do so on grounds that the court felt were irrational: *R v HM Coroners Court of St Pancras* [2001] Lloyd's L Rep (Med) 67.

50 *Farrell (Dublin City Coroner) v Attorney General* [1998] 1 IR 203. These recommendations were in turn based on the United Kingdom Committee on Death Certification and Coroners (*Broderick Report*, 1971),

51 Eg in a situation where lack of institutional care was responsible, the coroner may hear evidence as regards that lack of care (but without, we must stress, explicitly laying blame for that death at any individual door). See *Northern Area Health Board v Geraghty (Coroner for*

County Dublin) (20 July 2001, unreported) HC. See also *R v HM Coroner for Inner London North (ex parte Touche)* [2001] EWCA Civ 383, where the court held that a coroner's decision not to hold an inquest where there were obvious questions of lack of care was irrational and directed that one be held.

52 In other words there may be legal consequences for the family of the deceased, depending on the cause of death that is established. If a coroner's inquest holds that a person was the victim of an accident rather than having killed himself, such a decision may have ramifications for insurance policies, reputation etc.

53 Coroners Act 1962, s 30.

54 While the coroner's inquest is heard in public, there are certain circumstances in which witnesses may be screened from the public in the interests of their security. In *Morris v Dublin City Coroner* [2000] 3 IR 592(HC); 603(SC); [2000] IESC 24 (SC) the Court agreed that police under a verifiable death threat from a paramilitary organisation could give evidence screened from the public gallery, but not from the coroner, jury, legal representatives or press. The coroner's ability to compel witnesses to attend is more theoretical than real. Fines for refusal to attend are negligible and it has been suggested that for the coroner to report a witness to the High Court for failing to attend would be unconstitutional: *Attorney General v Lynda Lee* (23/10/2000, HC).

55 An 'indictment' is the formal charge that the accused faces in certain types of criminal trial.

56 *R v South London Coroner (ex parte Thompson)* (1982) SJ 625, per Lord Lane.

57 In *Morris v Dublin City Coroner* [2000] 3 IR 592(HC); 603(SC); [2000] IESC 24 (SC). See fn. 54. The presence of the press as reliable reporters of what takes place at the inquest is sufficient to give it the required quality of being held in public.

58 The legislative predecessor to the Coroners Act 1962 was the Coroners (Ireland) Act 1846, which permitted the coroner to order that the body be brought to the nearest convenient tavern until the inquest could be heard. Now the body will have been brought to a mortuary and will usually have been buried by the time an inquest takes place.

59 The technical term in such cases for appointing and swearing in a jury.

60 Coroners Act 1962, s 40.

61 Eg General Prisons (Ireland) Act 1877, s 56, mandates the holding of an inquest 'on the body of every prisoner who may die within the Prison'. Similarly the Defence Act 1954, s 238 which covers deaths in military custody explicitly compels that an inquest be held and that a jury be utilised.

62 This would commonly occur under the Health, Safety and Welfare at Work Act 1989, which states that any accident at work must be notified to an inspector of the Health and Safety Authority.

63 In brief, legal privilege refers to protection from legal action for statements made during the discharge of duties that are privileged, such as a lawyer-client discussions, what a priest hears in confession, a judge's ruling or a speech made in parliament. Privilege may be absolute or qualified, but the distinction need not generally concern the reader of this text. For a more detailed discussion, see Fennell *The Law of Evidence in Ireland* (1995) ch 7.

64 This limit is found in the Coroners Act 1962, s 26(2). This provision formed the core of the contribution made by Hardiman J to the Supreme Court decision in the case of *Eastern Health Board v Farrell,* an important case, see section **[16.18]**. As previously mentioned there are circumstances in which a witness may give evidence screened from the public: *Morris v Dublin City Coroner* [2000] 3 IR 592 (HC); 603 (SC).

65 And by analogy, the legal term for operating outside one's legal powers is *ultra vires.*

66 *Desmond v Riordan (Coroner for City of Cork)* [2002] 1 ILRM 502.

67 Defamation is the legal term for publishing or uttering an untrue statement about a person, which lowers them in the estimation of others.

68 *Northern Area Health Board v Geraghty (Coroner for County Dublin)* (20 July 2001, unreported), HC.

69 Eg *Eastern Health Board v Farrell (Dublin City Coroner)* [2000] 1 ILRM 446 (HC); [2001] IESC 82 (SC), the health board was represented at the original inquest by a Senior Counsel.

70 Coroners Act 1962, s 29.

71 Even if the Act did not expressly provide for this, it would probably be incumbent, with certain exceptions, upon the coroner or county registrar under the Freedom of Information Act 1997, to release documentation relevant to inquests. The recent *Review of the Coroner Service* suggests that a copy of the inquest's finding should be given to the next-of-kin as a matter of course.

72 *The State (McKeown) v Dr Thomas Scully* (29 April 1985, unreported) HC.

73 It remained so until the Criminal Law (Suicide) Act 1993. Similar considerations and conclusions arose in the case of *Greene v McLoughlin (Coroner for Galway West)* (26 January 1995, unreported) SC.

74 Coroners Act 1962, s 25. See also the case of *Costello v Bofin* (21 November 1980, unreported) SC, which confirmed that the coroner is obliged to adjourn the inquest at the request of the Gardaí, but may only do so for a specified period.

75 Coroners Act 1962, s 31.

76 'Cyclist was crushed by Truck' (2002) *Irish Times*, 24 January.

77 'Coroner calls for inspection of building sites' (2002) *Irish Times*, 29 January.

78 Coroners Act 1962, s 51.

79 Coroners Act 1962, s 51. The decision to release the body for cremation will often have to be a more considered one. Cremation will after all destroy any evidence and later exhumation will not be an option.

80 *Eastern Health Board v Farrell (Dublin City Coroner)* [2000] 1 ILRM 446 (HC); [2001] IESC 82 (SC).

81 In the Supreme Court, the ruling of Hardiman J differed from the other judges in that it was predicated on the fact that Dr Farrell had already heard evidence from two medical witnesses. Introducing a third witness to expound on the alleged link between the pertussis vaccine and mental retardation would have violated the Coroners Act 1962, s 26(2), which imposes a ceiling of two medical witnesses.

82 The Chief Justice in the Supreme Court pointed to the absurdity of giving the coroner no leeway at all:

> 'It cannot have been the intention of the Oireachtas that, in the case of a road accident, for example, the verdict should be simply confined to a finding in accordance with the pathologist's report and that the coroner or jury would be precluded from finding that the deceased had met his death while travelling in a motor car which collided with another vehicle.'

See also *Northern Area Health Board v Geraghty (Coroner for County Dublin)* (20 July 2001, unreported), HC. In that case, the court held it was acceptable for a coroner to hear evidence about the nursing care provided in the hospital where the deceased last resided in order to establish whether that may have been an element in the death.

83 Coroners Act 1962, s 49.

84 *Webb v Ireland* [1988] IR 353.

85 Department of Justice, Equality and Law Reform (2000). See also Pounder 'The coroner service - A relic in need of reform' BMJ 1999 318:1502.

86 Both Dublin City Coroner and the Kildare Coroner already have helpful and informative web sites written in a style accessible to the general public.

87 Coroners Act 1962, s 18(4).

88 There is no discussion whatsoever of this question in the *Review of the Coroner Service* or of why this recommendation, which appears out of the blue in the *Review*, is made. It is thought by many, including this author, that some clear definition of 'medical or surgical procedure' would be required before such a potentially radically amendment to the jurisdiction of the coroner could wholeheartedly be endorsed.

89 The Dublin Cemeteries Committee Rules 1989. Professor Knight, in his book *Legal Aspects of Medical Practice* (5th edn, 1992) relates the story of eccentric Welsh GP William Price who attempted to cremate his infant son, named Jesus Christ Price, after the child's death in 1884. At the time cremation was illegal and Dr Price was tried. He conducted his own defence and was acquitted. The British Government felt obliged thereafter to legislate for cremation and introduced the Cremation Act 1902. Dr Price was an extraordinary figure, he became fascinated by the pagan rites of the ancient druids, carried out his own rituals around a supposedly ancient stone on a hill above Pontypridd, dressed frequently in a fantastic costume of green and blue and capped by an animal skin.

90 There are also cremation forms (Form BB, CC and EE) which are used for cremation of body parts separate from the body of the deceased. Typically these will have been organs retained during post mortem examination and released subsequent to the interment or cremation of the rest of the body. The institution that held the body organs certifies that there is no reason why the organs or body parts should be further examined and that they are suitable for cremation. These forms contain no explicit requirement for a doctor to sign: they may be signed by any person acting 'on behalf of' the hospital or institution that held the body parts.

91 Dublin Cemeteries Committee Rules 1989, r 19.9.

92 Dublin Cemeteries Committee Rules 1989, r 19.8.

93 The person making the declaration must also be someone who would have been a 'competent' witness if he had survived. The vast majority of people (including minors) are competent witnesses. For more details see Fennell *The Law of Evidence in Ireland* (1995).

Chapter 17

Doctors and Driving

INTRODUCTION

[17.01]

Health care professionals, doctors in particular but also nursing staff, interact with drivers in a number of ways and this chapter looks at some of the most important. Many of the situations in which the interaction occurs may seem to be purely administrative but as we will see, there are complications that may underpin seemingly simple affairs such as the certification of fitness to drive.

In situations concerning the drunk driver there are also complex legal rules at play, of which the clinician needs to be aware so that she can be sure that she is discharging her legal responsibilities, while at the same time protecting the rights of any patient under her care.

This chapter deals with the question of certification of fitness to drive, and with those patients who are no longer fit to drive. Also important is the question of driving under the influence of drugs and alcohol and this chapter looks at the law regarding driving while intoxicated and the potential role of the doctor or other clinician. The chapter concludes by looking at likely and recommended future directions of legislation affecting the driver.

PRACTITIONERS AND THE DRIVING LICENCE

[17.02]

The general rules for the medical standards that apply to drivers are set out in legal form in the Road Traffic (Licensing of Drivers) Regulations 1999[1] (the 1999 Regulations). However, they are also laid out in an allegedly more user-friendly format in a Department of the Environment booklet intended for medical and paramedical professionals and entitled *Medical Aspects of Driver Licensing* (see para **[17.05]** *ff*).

Categorising licences

[17.03]

While there are 14 categories of motorised vehicle for which a licence may be obtained, ranging from mopeds[2] to substantial heavy goods vehicles, as far as the doctor is concerned there are only two groups of licences for the purpose of medical certification. Group 1 consists of all motorcycles, cars and tractors (with or without trailers). Group 2 comprises in effect vans, trucks and buses.

The essential difference between them as far as the practitioner is concerned is the nature of the examinations that must be carried out and certified before a prospective driver can be declared fit to sit behind the wheel of the relevant vehicle. Group 2 vehicles are heavier, they have lower braking capacity and they are generally regarded as higher risk vehicles.

Accordingly the standard of physical and mental fitness required on the part of the driver is higher and it is the doctor who has the responsibility of assessing that the standard is met.

Figure 17.1. The classes of driver licence (figures in brackets denote the minimum age for holding the licence)

Group 1 Licences	
M	mopeds (age 16)
A1, A	Smaller motorcycles (age 16), motorcycles over 125cc (age 18)
B, EB	Vehicles with passenger accommodation for not more that 8 persons and a design gross vehicle weight not exceeding 3,500kg (age 17)[3]
W	Work vehicles and tractors with or without trailers (age 16)
Group 2 Licences	
C, C1, EC, EC1	Vehicles with a capacity of not more than eight people with (C1) or without (C) an upper limit of 3,500kg (age 18)
D, D1, ED1, ED	Vehicles with a capacity greater than 8 people and with (D1) or without (D) a maximum capacity of 16 people (age 21)

The distinction between the two groups, regarding certification in practical terms, is that a person seeking a Group 1 licence needs merely to undergo an eyesight test, conducted by an optician or physician.[4] A person seeking a Group 2 licence must undergo, in the words of the 1999 regulations, a 'full medical examination' conducted and recorded by a registered medical practitioner.[5] There *are* certain categories of driver who, even if only applying for a Group 1 licence, must undergo a medical examination as well as an eyesight test. Such applicants are those who fall into either or both of the following categories:

— A person over 70 years of age.

— A person who suffers from any of the disabilities listed as requiring a medical report (see para **[17.04]** below).

Older drivers

It should be pointed out that the requirement to subject those over 70 years of age to a mandatory medical examination might not be rooted in reality: drivers in that age bracket are amongst the safest on the roads.[6] In the UK, only 6 per 1000 male drivers in the 65-74 age group were involved in a crash in 1998. The corresponding rate for drivers in the 25-34 age group, at 21 per 1000, was more than three times greater. However, while the crash rate for older drivers is often lower than for younger drivers, fatality rates tell a different story. United States data show that the number of road deaths among motorists aged 65 or more in 1997 was 12.7 per 100,000 people in this age group compared to 10.3 for 25-64 year-olds. Of course, one of the reasons why over-70s are the safest drivers could be because mandatory medical assessment screens out many who would be a risk on the roads. Equivalent individuals are not weeded out from the under-

70s group because there is no routine requirement for that group to be medically examined.

Certification of fitness to drive

[17.04]

The purpose of medical review of drivers 'is to keep the more seriously affected drivers off the roads or to restrict their driving within the limitations of their disability.'[7]

The first port of call for an applicant for a driver's licence may be an optician rather than a medical practitioner. A person who does not suffer from any medical conditions or who does not declare that he suffers from any condition that necessitates a medical examination need only undergo an eye-test, conducted by a doctor or an optician. It may be that if an optician identifies a problem during ophthalmic examination that suggests an illness incompatible with driving, such as diabetes, she should decline to sign the form, indicating that the applicant should seek a medical opinion.

A patient who has received a completed form regarding his eyesight or medical condition from his doctor concerning fitness to drive has one month to file that form with their application. If they fail to do so, the findings on the form lapse and the applicant must resubmit for a further examination.

The doctor has a number of options upon the completion of any assessment of fitness to drive. There will be circumstances where she may refuse to certify fitness to drive in situations where the patient should simply not be on the road. She may indicate that the applicant's fitness to drive does not need further review in the foreseeable future based on the information available to her and the clinical findings at the time of the assessment. Finally, she may certify fitness to drive for a limited period only. The available options for a limited period of certification are one, three and ten years.

There are some automatic restrictions on any period of certification. Mindful of the pace at which the health status of older individuals may change, the regulations permit persons over the age of 70 to be certified for a maximum period of three years only. Similarly, in the case of certain medical conditions, such as insulin-dependent diabetes affecting an applicant for a Group 2 licence, a doctor may only certify fitness to drive for a period of one year at a time.[8]

One problem presents itself to the practitioner who is faced with a decision on whether a medical examination rather than a simple eye test is necessary. The 1999 Regulations refer to 'disabilities that are listed as requiring a report' but as will be seen below, those disabilities are by no means clear. This means that, in theory, the doctor who is unfamiliar with a patient's history will need to take a full medical history and conduct a full examination in order to ascertain the presence or absence of any of the exhaustive, and not always clearly defined list, of illnesses that would preclude or limit certification of fitness to drive. In practice, however, the onus appears to be on the applicant to declare his fitness to drive and in situations where the doctor has no reason to believe the patient is unfit to drive, she may confine herself to administering an eye test.

MEDICAL REQUIREMENTS FOR FITNESS TO DRIVE

Eyesight

[17.05]

The key elements of eyesight are fourfold as far as determination of capacity to drive is concerned: visual acuity, field of vision, night vision and the presence of any progressive eye disease.

A person applying for a Group 1 licence and who has vision in both eyes must have (with corrective lenses if necessary) a visual acuity of not less than 0.5, using both eyes together.[9] He must also have a horizontal field of vision of not less that 150 degrees. A person with one eye is permitted to drive but he must have a visual acuity of not less than 0.6[10] and an unrestricted field of vision in that eye. Furthermore, the monocular vision must have existed for long enough for adaptation to the new state of affairs to are occurred.[11] The eyesight test may only be conducted and certified by either a registered medical practitioner or an ophthalmic optician.

A person making an application for a Group 2 licence must have (again with corrective lenses where necessary) a visual acuity of 0.8[12] in the better eye and 0.5 in the worse eye. However, there are conditions attached to the use of spectacles when it comes to Group 2 applicants that are not imposed on applicants for Group 1 licences. If corrective lenses are used in the case of an applicant for a Group 2 licence then either the unrestricted acuity in each eye must read 0.05 or else the minimum acuity must be achieved either

- by correction by means of glasses with a power not exceeding plus or minus 8 dioptres *or*
- by means of contact lenses.

Anyone with monocular vision or who suffers from diplopia (double vision) cannot under any circumstances be certified as fit to drive vehicles that fall into the Group 2 category. Any deteriorating vision in applicants over the age of 40 for any licence should be investigated before that person is certified as fit to drive.

A gap in the rules?

The Irish provisions on eyesight testing place no obligation on the doctor to test for colour blindness or on the applicant to declare that he suffers from colour blindness. This is at odds with the policy in many other countries. Colour blindness, which is typically genetically inherited, occurs in as many as 8% of men and in about 0.2% of women and the majority of those affected will have difficulty with red, green or both: important colours when it comes to driving. According to some studies, drivers with a severely impaired red colour perception defect (protans) have a reduced visual distance for other vehicles' rear lights and for red traffic signals and consequently they have an increased nose-to-tail collision rate when driving. It is arguable that, irrespective of the current guidelines, doctors should screen for colour blindness as part of the eyesight test for a driving licence. It is certainly the case in countries such as Australia and the United States that colour blindness is one criterion to be taken into consideration when it comes to assessing fitness to drive, although in the United Kingdom colour blindness is not considered to inhibit driving in any way. It could be a sensible inclusion in future medical guidelines that all applicants, particularly men, should undergo testing for severe red perception difficulty. The preferred initial method for screening is the Ishihara Test.

General health issues

[17.06]

Regarding general health issues, matters become confusing. According to the 1999 Regulations, medical examination for a licence is a requirement for Group 2 licences, for the over-70s and for those who suffer from conditions that require a report to be compiled. The examination should take account of the applicant's 'general health insofar as it affects the ability to drive'.

The health parameters that need to be considered are very general indeed and include an assessment of both physical and mental health. The test that the examining doctor is expected to apply when considering an applicant's health status is whether any defect would render the applicant a danger to other road users. Any physical handicap or locomotor defect that affects strength, muscle control or defect needs to be considered.

However, the Irish Regulations fail to offer specific guidelines or a definitive list of the conditions that fall into this category, unlike their UK counterpart, the Driver and Vehicle Licensing Authority (DVLA) whose regulations form an invaluable resource[13] for patching the many gaps left in the Irish regulations. In the consideration of the medical guidelines that follows, the UK regulations will be drawn upon where they add clarity to the Irish situation. It should be remembered that the UK guidelines are not Irish ones and are relied upon because there is little clear Irish guidance. The doctor faced with doubts as to certification could do much worse than adopt the UK guidelines except where they expressly conflict, as they do in the case of epilepsy, with the Irish Regulations.

Hearing

[17.07]

There is a requirement for Group 2 licences only that 'fitness to drive shall not be certified if the applicant's hearing is so deficient that it interferes with the proper discharge of his duties.' However, there is no stipulation in the regulations as to what the appropriate standard for hearing is or as to what constitutes the 'proper discharge' of a driver's responsibilities. Accordingly, the decision may become dependent on the judgement of the individual physician, who is unlikely to be fully conversant with all the nuances of driving a Heavy Goods Vehicle. In the United Kingdom, the DVLA Medical Regulations state the following regarding profound deafness in Group 2 applicants:

> 'Of paramount importance is the proven ability to be able to communicate in the event of an emergency by speech or by using a device eg a MINICOM. If unable to do so the licence is likely to be refused or revoked.'[14]

In other words, the DVLA perceives the difficulty as not being one of simple hearing, but of overall capacity for communication in a crisis situation. This approach goes someway towards helping to identify what may be meant by the Irish 1999 Regulations' reference to an applicant's 'discharge of his duties.'

The requirement of meeting a satisfactory hearing threshold does not extend to moped, motorcycle or car users at all. The doctor is not required to assess hearing in an applicant for a Group 1 licence and furthermore deafness, even if declared by the applicant, is not a bar to certification of fitness to ride a motorcycle or to drive a car. This reflects the situation in most jurisdictions including the United Kingdom.

Heart

[17.08]

The 1999 Regulations state the following in terms of heart conditions to be considered:

> 'Any disease capable of exposing an applicant for a first licence or a driver applying for a renewal of a licence to a sudden failure of the cardiovascular system such that there is a sudden impairment of the cerebral functions constitutes a danger to road safety.'

That covers a plethora of illnesses and the guidelines do not add much in the way of clarification or of categorisation. A serious arrhythmia (with a concomitant risk of loss of consciousness) is expressly mentioned, specifically including patients with implantable cardioverter-defibrillators. Those with heart function at the poorer end of the spectrum ('New York Heart Functional Class III'[15]) shall also not be certified as fit to drive, while those with less impaired function may be passed fit to drive by a consultant cardiologist. Neither a heart pacemaker nor high blood pressure presents an automatic stumbling block to driving as long as the patient is kept under regular medical review. All considerations of cardiovascular health have to be weighed more carefully when it comes to drivers applying for Group 2 licences.

Specific heart disorders

The UK DVLA lists a number of specific conditions and how they should be approached with regard to each of the two groups of applicant. Common cardiac conditions dealt with in the UK are illustrated in Figure 17.2, together with the limitations they impose upon the driver:

Figure 17.2 – Heart conditions and driving restriction (from UK DVLA guidelines)

Condition	*Group 1*	*Group 2*
Angina	May drive if stable when at rest or behind the wheel of the car.	May not drive if symptomatic and unable to perform an exercise stress test.
Angioplasty/ MI/ CABG	May return to driving from one (angioplasty) to four weeks (MI/CABG) after the procedure or event.	Disqualified for at least 6 weeks after the procedure or event and until exercise test requirements are met.
Hypertension	No problem if medication tolerated.	Disqualified if blood pressure over 180mmHg (systolic) or 100 mm Hg (diastolic) until successfully treated.

Diabetes

[17.09]

Diabetes is not an automatic stumbling block to obtaining a Group 1 licence, once the applicant remains under medical supervision.[16] A candidate for a Group 2 licence with non-insulin dependent diabetes may be certified as fit to drive, but insulin dependence is a bar to certification for a Group 2 licence unless:

(i) there are exceptional circumstances, and

(ii) the patient is certified by a consultant endocrinologist with an interest in diabetes, and

(iii) subjected to annual medical review.

'Exceptional circumstances' are another unhelpful ingredient in the Irish guidelines. Must the circumstances be exceptional from the patient's point of view or from the doctor's or from a combination of both? Are the circumstances to be considered purely clinical in nature or may they include social, financial or psychological factors? The guidelines are silent on this question.

Neurological problems, including epilepsy

[17.10]

According to UK DVLA guidelines, epilepsy is the most common cause of loss of consciousness at the wheel. In the case of an applicant in Ireland for a licence to drive a vehicle who suffers or has suffered in the past from epilepsy, fitness to drive may be certified for a limited period in relation to Group 1 licences where the applicant has not suffered any epileptic attack during the twelve month period preceding the date of medical examination. However, an applicant who suffers, or has ever suffered in the past, from epilepsy cannot be certified as capable of holding a Group 2 licence. All episodes of epileptic activity (including auras or seizure warnings in which consciousness is retained) count as seizures. Night and daytime seizures appear to count equally, insofar as no discrimination is made between them in the 1999 Regulations.

It might be argued that these strictures are too oppressive of those who suffer from epilepsy. In the United Kingdom, greater latitude is afforded to those who suffer only from night-time seizures. Also in the UK, applicants for Group 2 licences are not excluded in perpetuity solely because they have suffered from epilepsy at some time in the past. Instead, a person who has been fit-free for ten years or more without medication may subsequently apply for a Group 2 licence.[17] This seems a more sensible approach, but it remains the law in Ireland that anyone who has ever suffered seizures must be refused medical certification for a Group 2 licence.

Patients who have any form of paralysis or other cerebrovascular disease may be certified as fit to drive if surrounding circumstances so permit. They may need a vehicle that has been modified to suit their changed physical circumstances. Any such certification should be for a limited period, in order to allow for regular review. Again, applicants for a Group 2 licence are precluded from holding licences if they have suffered from a cerebrovascular disease or lesion with resultant damage to the spinal cord and paraplegia.

Specific neurological conditions, other than epilepsy, that are envisaged by the Irish regulations include:

(a) encephalitis, multiple sclerosis, myasthenia gravis, hereditary diseases of the nervous system associated with progressive muscular atrophy and congenital myotonic disorders,

(b) diseases of the peripheral nervous system, or

(c) trauma of the peripheral nervous system.

In all such cases, the question of fitness to drive should be judged on the merits of the individual case. Fitness to drive should, if certified, be only for a limited period in order to facilitate regular review of progress or deterioration.

There is no explicit provision that Group 2 applicants should be refused if they suffer from the above conditions. It is likely that, by analogy with the policy on cardiovascular diseases, greater scrutiny and reluctance to certify should be brought to bear upon applicants for licences to drive larger vehicles. This would tally with the DVLA philosophy that neurological conditions other than epilepsy are not a bar to Group 2 licences once there is no evidence of impairment or deterioration. After a stroke or transient ischaemic attack (TIA), UK Group 1 licence holders are not permitted to drive for at least a month after the event; UK Group 2 licence holders or applicants may not drive for 12 months after a stroke or TIA.

Mental disorders

[17.11]

The logic that greater care should be applied before certifying those applying for Group 2 licences is made explicit when the 1999 Regulations concern themselves with mental disorders. Applicants for a Group 2 licence are not explicitly precluded but the medical examination 'shall take due account of the additional risks and dangers involved in the driving of such vehicles'. No psychiatric condition is expressly listed as being a bar to certification of fitness to drive. The categories of mental disorder listed by the regulations are the following and in all cases certification may be for only a limited period when deemed necessary to permit regular review:

(a) severe mental disturbance, whether congenital or due to disease, trauma or neurosurgical operation on the central nervous system;

(b) severe mental retardation;

(c) psychosis, which in particular has caused general paralysis; or

(d) severe behavioural problems due to dementia; psychoneurosis; or personality defects or disorders leading to seriously impaired judgement, behaviour or adaptability.

In the United Kingdom, severe anxiety or depression, a psychotic episode and dementia are all bars to driving until the condition is investigated and treated. UK Drivers with stable anxiety and depression and whose medication does not interfere with their performance behind the wheel may continue to hold both Group 1 and Group 2 licences.

Alcohol

[17.12]

An applicant who has in the past suffered from alcoholism[18] should be considered for limited certification only, in order that his ongoing sobriety can be kept under review. Active current alcoholism is an obvious reason for the refusal of certification.

Drugs - illicit and prescribed

[17.13]

The 1999 Regulations stipulate that anyone who is 'dependent upon psychotropic substances or, if … not dependent upon such substances, regularly abuses them' shall not be certified to drive. However, it appears that a person who is prescribed such medications may be certified as fit to drive, so long as the medication does not hamper his ability to drive. This seems another confused section.

What about a patient who is prescribed 'psychotropic' medication and is dependent upon those medications? For example, a doctor may be prescribing a course of sedatives or heroin substitute intended to wean a patient off an addiction. If that patient is 'dependent' upon prescribed medication, but otherwise unaffected by the medication in terms of fitness to drive, may he be certified as fit to drive? What, in any event, does 'psychotropic' mean?[19] Does it include anti-depressant tablets, short acting sleeping tablets or depot injections of anti-psychotic medication? None of the answers to these questions are contained in the guidelines. According to the UK DVLA medical guidelines:

> 'The prescribed use of [benzodiazepines] at therapeutic doses, without evidence of impairment, does not amount to misuse/dependency for licensing purposes.'

It would probably follow in Ireland that prescribed psychoactive medications at therapeutic doses without any evidence of impairment of concentration or reaction are not 'psychotropic' drugs for the purposes of the regulations. The question of driving under the influence of alcohol and drugs is examined at from section **[17.17]** onward.

Other health considerations

The regulations on certification of fitness to drive also request the physician to take into account diseases of the blood, renal disorders, organ transplants and 'any disorder not mentioned … which gives rise to, or is likely to result in, functional incapacity affecting safety at the wheel'.

Discussion

[17.14]

When it comes to driver licensing, much hinges on the doctor's judgement. There are situations in which the doctor may be at best tentative about the wisdom of allowing a particular patient out on the roads. An example is the patient known to have failing eyesight, but who nonetheless satisfies the legal limit on the day of examination. The solution in such circumstances may be to opt for a review of the situation in one year or it may be to refuse to certify the patient as fit to drive in the knowledge that he will surely be below the prescribed limit for visual acuity before the expiry of even a one-year licence. Such decisions can generally only be made on the facts of each specific case, but in all such borderline cases it will be important for the doctor to document the decision taken and the reason she took that decision.

One problem with the assessment of the prospective driver, however, is the claim in the regulations that what is ordinarily required for certification of an application for a Group 1 licence is an eye-test. The guidelines, however, also impose an exhaustive range of medical, surgical and psychiatric conditions that the doctor must exclude before opting to merely administer an eye test. Although the guidelines themselves make reference to a 'list' of complaints that necessitate a medical examination, nowhere in the current guidelines is a satisfactorily specific list set out.

It is reasoned therefore that the doctor, in order to satisfy the requirements of the regulations for the certification of Group 1 applicants and in order to be certain that only an eyesight test is required, should quiz the patient (or satisfy herself by reference to the patient's notes) regarding the existence of any problems of the systems listed in the regulations:[20]

- Ear conditions (vertigo and labyrinthine conditions),
- General physique and physical disabilities,
- Condition of cardiovascular system,
- Condition of haemopoietic system,
- Condition of endocrine system,
- Condition of respiratory system,
- Condition of gastrointestinal system,
- Condition of genitourinary system
- Condition of nervous system,
- Condition of mental system.

If such a system review demonstrates a problem, then medical examination may be necessary. If not, certification of visual competence is likely to be all that will be necessary. It is hoped that future Irish guidelines will follow the more coherent English approach. In the case of Group 2 applicants, a medical review will be necessary in all cases and the systems review above should be implemented.

Ethical aspects of driver licensing

[17.15]

Chapter 3 looked at the question of confidentiality and it is an important consideration again in the context of certification of fitness to drive. Typically, when a person applies for a licence, it is up to that person to declare any illness that may preclude him from driving or that may limit the life span of his licence. Most patients will do so. But what about the patient who suffers from epilepsy, for example, and withholds that information from the licensing authority and from the doctor or optician who conducts the eyesight test? The fact that an optician's report is all that may be required from an applicant who chooses not to declare an illness or submit himself to medical examination demonstrates the degree to which the whole edifice of driver certification is erected on the principle of full disclosure by the patient.

Quick Reference Guide 17.1

Medical certification of fitness to drive

- For certain categories of licence and where there is a condition (including age) perceived as likely to affect driving, a prospective driver needs to undergo a medical examination as well as an eyesight test.
- For medical examination purposes licences may be divided into two categories: Group 1 and Group 2. The latter places a heavier burden on the driver to be fit to drive. Ordinary car licences are Group 1 licences.
- The need for a medical examination is based either on the risk inherent in the category of vehicle or the risk posed by a driver's age or medical condition.
- A driving licence eye-test may be performed by an optician or doctor; only a doctor may conduct the medical examination.
- Eyesight testing is concerned with visual acuity, field of vision, night vision and the presence of any progressive eye disease. Neither colour-blind people nor those with monocular vision are precluded from driving.
- If there is doubt over an applicant's fitness to drive, certification may be refused or the applicant may be certified for a limited time only. A limited period *must* be chosen where the application is for a Group 2 licence or the applicant is over 70 years of age and/or suffering from a medical condition that is likely to impede driving.
- In general a practitioner should be more careful certifying a person who suffers from illness when that person is applying for a Group 2 licence.
- Deafness is not a bar to a Group 1 licence, but is probably a bar to a Group 2 licence when it affects a person's ability to communicate in an emergency.
- Heart conditions that should lead to care when certifying fitness to drive include arrhythmias and poor heart function. It may be necessary for the primary care physician to involve specialist opinion in certifying fitness to drive in the heart patient. For suggested responses to specific heart conditions, see Figure 17.1.
- In general, but not always, insulin dependent diabetes precludes a person from holding a Group 2 licence.
- Epilepsy is a stumbling block to Group 1 certification for 12 months following any form of attack; any form of seizure activity during the lifetime of the applicant will prevent him from ever holding a Group 2 licence. UK guidelines permit an individual to hold a Group 2 licence once he has been fit-free for 10 years.
- Psychiatric disorders are not an *automatic* bar to holding any form of licence, but limited certification only, if certification is warranted at all in the circumstances, should be given to those with severe psychiatric problems, mental retardation, psychosis, dementia or any condition affecting judgment, behaviour or adaptability.
- A patient's use of psychotropic medications or any addictive substance, prescribed or illicit, should be a factor considered before certifying fitness to drive.

Example 1

A person with uncontrolled epilepsy is seeking a Group 1 licence. He arranges for his eyesight test to be conducted by an optician who is unaware that the applicant suffers from epilepsy and that he has had recent seizure activity. Subsequently, the patient's general practitioner spies her patient, whom she knows to be epileptic, behind the wheel of his car. What should she do?

Medical confidentiality is important, but as we have seen, the requirement to maintain confidentiality is modified in certain circumstances among which is the exception created by a situation where it is necessary to betray confidentiality to protect the welfare of society. The point was made in the case of *W v Egdell,*[21] which concerned disclosure by a psychiatrist of a confidential report to prevent the release of a potentially dangerous prisoner. The doctor who becomes aware that a patient is a danger to others on the road should first approach the patient and counsel them on the appropriate course of action. If this is not successful then the next step would be for the doctor to communicate her concerns to the medical authorities of the relevant licensing authority. The Irish Medical Council *Guidelines* do not deal specifically with this matter, but the United Kingdom General Medical Council (in *Duties of a Doctor,* Appendix 1) suggest the following protocol:

> 'If patients continue to drive when they are not fit to do so, you should make every effort to persuade them to stop. This may include telling their next of kin. If you do not manage to persuade patients to stop driving, or you are given or find evidence that a patient is continuing to drive contrary to advice, you should disclose relevant medical information immediately, in confidence, to the medical adviser at the [local licensing authority].'

The importance of telling only the relevant authorities can be identified by reference to the case of *Duncan v Medical Practitioners' Disciplinary Committee*[22] where a doctor warned the relevant authorities of the fact that a particular driver suffered from a heart condition that made it unsafe for him to drive. However, the doctor also took the trouble to warn all the passengers upon his patient's bus of their prospective driver's infirmity. The court said that:

> '[A] doctor who has decided to communicate [confidential information] should discriminate and ensure the recipient is a responsible authority.'

Legal consequences of certification of fitness to drive

[17.16]

Any disclosure by a clinician of the risk posed by a driver would, based on the above reasoning, be immune from legal action once the breach of confidentiality was grounded upon an appreciable risk and notified only to relevant authorities.

It has also sometimes been suggested that a doctor or other health professional who failed properly to establish a patient's fitness to drive could be liable for negligence to the victims of any injury caused by her patient on the roads as a result of his lack of fitness to drive. This might also be a concern for practitioners in the position of the optician in the example, above, of the clandestine epileptic. As medico-legal matters stand, it is unlikely that any attempt to sue the clinician would succeed. In the United States, attempts to sue the doctor have been rejected[23] and it is probable (but not certain) that any attempt to take such a case against an Irish clinician by those injured as a result of shortcomings in the certification of an applicant's fitness to drive would also fail.

Quick Reference Guide 17.2

Confidentiality, ethics and the unfit driver

- In general, the onus appears to be on the driver to declare the presence of illness that may render him unfit to drive.
- If a doctor is aware that a patient is suffering from an illness that renders him unfit to drive but nonetheless continues to drive, that knowledge may place her in a difficult position.
- A clinician may breach confidentiality when it is in the interests of the welfare of society and when it is in the interests of the patient himself. Keeping an unsafe driver off the road fulfils both of those categories.
- The first step should be to obtain the patient's agreement to cease driving or to the release of the information that he is unfit to drive. In the absence of such consent, the doctor would be justified in disclosing the information in her possession to the relevant authorities.
- If disclosure is made, it should be to the smallest number of recipients consistent with achieving the aim of the breach of confidentiality.
- A practitioner is unlikely, as the law stands, to be successfully sued by a person injured by a driver who was wrongly certified by the practitioner as fit to drive.

DRIVING, ALCOHOL AND DRUGS

[17.17]

Drinking and driving has been illegal in Ireland since 1961, when the first Road Traffic Act was passed. The original Act has been amended on a number of occasions since then, and it is the Road Traffic Acts of 1994 and 1995 that are of most relevance to health practitioners, especially doctors (although there may be repercussions for other health professionals, typically in the accident and emergency environment). The Road Traffic Act 1994 is the statute essentially responsible for the form of contemporary drink-driving legislation in Ireland and among the measures it put in place were fine-tunings of provisions regarding the Medical Bureau of Road Safety, which is dealt with at section **[17.22]**.

Alcohol limits for drivers

[17.18]

The Road Traffic Acts 1961-1995 set down the maximum permissible levels of alcohol in the three types of sample that may be provided by a driver suspected of being intoxicated: blood, urine and breath. Blood and urine samples are generally taken by doctors. Breath samples will generally be provided by the suspect to a member of Garda Síochána. The basic rule against drunk driving and the maximum permissible levels of alcohol are set down as follows in the legislation:

49.-(1)(a) A person shall not drive *or attempt to drive* a mechanically propelled vehicle in a public place while he is under the influence of an intoxicant to such an extent as to be incapable of having proper control of the vehicle [italics added].

(2) A person shall not drive or attempt to drive a mechanically propelled vehicle in a public place while there is present in his body a quantity of alcohol such that, within 3 hours after so driving or attempting to drive, the concentration of alcohol in his blood will exceed a concentration of 80 milligrammes of alcohol per 100 millilitres of blood.

(3) A person shall not drive or attempt to drive a mechanically propelled vehicle in a public place while there is present in his body a quantity of alcohol such that, within 3 hours after so driving or attempting to drive, the concentration of alcohol in his urine will exceed a concentration of 107 milligrammes of alcohol per 100 millilitres of urine.

(4) A person shall not drive or attempt to drive a mechanically propelled vehicle in a public place while there is present in his body a quantity of alcohol such that, within 3 hours after so driving or attempting to drive, the concentration of alcohol in his breath will exceed a concentration of 35 microgrammes of alcohol per 100 millilitres of breath.[24]

Figure 17.3 – Drink-driving limits

Blood	80 milligrammes (mg) alcohol per 100 millilitres (ml) blood
Urine	107 mg alcohol per 100 ml urine
Breath	35 microgrammes (µg or mcg) alcohol per 100 ml exhaled breath

An 'intoxicant' mentioned in s 49(1) includes alcohol, drugs or any combination of drugs or any combination of drugs and alcohol.[25] The Road Traffic Acts 1961-1995 also permit the relevant Minister (Environment and Local Government) to make subsequent orders changing the upper limit of alcohol in blood, breath or urine. There is increasing pressure from Europe to take the decision to vary the limit downward in keeping with the policy of most other European nations. At present, there is no evidence to suggest that such changes will occur.

Dealing with drunk drivers

[17.19]

Members of the Garda Síochána have extensive powers to stop, detain and investigate those whom they suspect of driving under the influence of alcohol. In certain circumstances, those powers may intersect with the role of health professionals. Moving through the drink-driving 'process' one can identify those points at which clinicians may be involved.

A Garda may arrest anyone who, in her opinion, is committing or has committed the offence of driving while intoxicated. A person who is so arrested is obliged to provide a preliminary breath specimen where the facilities exist for taking such a sample (see section **[17.23]**). In circumstances where a device for breath alcohol measurement is available but not immediately to hand, the Garda may detain the suspect for up to an hour until such a device is available. Refusing to provide a specimen is an offence. A person may be arrested on suspicion of being intoxicated or he may be requested to accompany a Garda to a station to provide a blood or urine specimen. If a person refuses to accompany the Garda, he may then be placed under arrest.

Once a person is brought to a Garda Station, then the doctor may be involved. A person can be taken to a Garda Station on foot of a failed preliminary breath test, or where facilities do not exist for a preliminary breath test, or where he is, in the opinion of a member of the Garda Síochána, under the influence of an intoxicant and was driving or attempting to drive. A person brought to a Garda Station under these circumstances is required to:

— permit two specimens of breath to be taken for determining alcohol concentration in the breath, and/or
— permit a designated doctor to take a blood sample, or
— provide for the designated doctor a specimen of urine.

A doctor will be called to the station in order to take the sample. The doctor can express the opinion that on medical grounds the taking of a particular sample would be inadvisable, in which case another form of sample should be taken. Accordingly, if a doctor felt that a blood sample should not be taken, then a urine or breath test would be taken instead. If the person refuses to provide any specimen at all, then that is an offence.

This obligation to provide a sample extends to any person who is admitted to or attends at a hospital as a result of an alleged drunk-driving event.[26] A person who is in hospital or who is otherwise not under arrest, but who rather has voluntarily accompanied a Garda to a police station may be required to undergo a blood or urine test conducted by a designated doctor. Again the doctor may indicate that, on medical grounds, one or other test should not be conducted in which case the person in question will be required to give another form of sample.

In the Road Traffic Acts 1961-1995, the legislation refers to a 'designated' doctor, which means designated by the Garda Síochána and not by the patient. Each Garda Station will typically have a doctor or a roster of doctors upon whom they can call for the purposes of attending to take samples. A fee is payable for attendance by the doctor in a range that depends on the specific day and time of day of the attendance at the Garda Station or hospital. Additional samples taken from other people in custody during a single visit to the Garda Station or hospital are reimbursable at a lower rate. An additional fee is also payable if the Station or hospital visit lasts longer than one hour.

There are strict requirements in place regarding the handling of specimens obtained from a suspected drunken driver. These are to ensure that the samples' integrity as potential evidence in a criminal case will not be challenged. A drink-driving suspect who was able successfully to challenge the probity of the evidence against him could expect to have any prosecution against him overturned for fear that the unsound evidence would result in an unsafe conviction.

Breath samples

Two breath samples are obtained[27] from the suspected drunken driver and, where there is any discrepancy in the results obtained from the two samples, the lower of the two results is the one taken into account for the purposes of evidence. This approach is to ensure that the process errs in favour of the presumption of innocence that characterises criminal law. In fact, for the purposes of any prosecution that results from a sample in excess of the legal limit, not only is the lower figure used, but an additional 17.5% is subtracted from the lower reading to allow for any variability in the analysis and the apparatus used and to ensure that a person is not convicted on the basis of mere statistical error. In essence, the accused is given the benefit of any doubt. If the two results tally exactly then either may be used. A statement of any reading that exceeds the legal limit is produced in duplicate and given to the suspect, who must sign both readings and return one to the Garda. These readings may then be used in evidence.

Blood and urine samples

Of more concern to doctors is the procedure regarding urine and blood samples that are taken under the Road Traffic Acts from suspected drunk drivers.[28] A specimen taken must be divided into two parts and sealed 'forthwith'. The person who furnished the sample is offered in writing the opportunity of retaining one of the two sealed containers holding the relevant sample. The doctor must also complete the form that accompanies the sample. The sample is then forwarded to the Medical Bureau of Road Safety. If the detained person has declined to retain the offered portion of the specimen, both are forwarded to the Bureau. The same process applies to both urine and blood samples. What happens to the sample once it reaches the Medical Bureau of Road Safety is examined at para **[17.22]**.

Drink driving and the practitioner

[17.20]

One new power given to the Gardaí by the Road Traffic Act 1994 is the power to request that a sample for alcohol analysis be provided by a person in hospital and to achieve that end, Gardaí have the power to enter a hospital without warrant for the purposes of securing that sample. Similarly the designated doctor has the right to enter the hospital in order to take the sample. Clinicians should be aware that if they are acting as the designated doctor, they have this power. Similarly, practitioners caring for a patient in hospital who has been involved in a road traffic accident should be aware that the police and the designated doctor have the legal power to require that a specimen of blood or urine be taken for the purposes of analysis of alcohol concentration or the presence of any other intoxicant.

Consequences of failing a drink-driving test

[17.21]

Automatic disqualification from driving applies to all drink driving convictions but the minimum period varies depending on the alcohol level in individual cases. As we saw above there are a number of situations where a person's refusal to adopt a certain course is itself an offence. These would include amongst other offences refusing to provide a sample, without a 'special and substantial reason' for such refusal[29] or refusing to sign the print-out of the results of an analysis of a breath sample. Disqualification orders are made by a court on the basis of amendments introduced by the Road Traffic Act 1995. Details of the disqualification periods if convicted of a particular offence are set out in Figure 17.4.

Figure 17.4 – Disqualification periods

Offence	*Minimum Period*	
	1st Offence	*2nd Offence*
1. Alcohol level/100mls *blood* 81 mg — 100 mg *urine* 107mg — 135mg *breath* 36μg -44μg	3 months	6 months
blood 101 mg — 150 mg breath 135mg-200mg urine 45μg — 66μg	1 year	2 years
blood >150 mg urine >200mg breath >66μg	2 years	4 years
2. Refusal offences	2 years	4 years
3. Drunk Driving	2 years	4 years

Mandatory disqualification periods of one year or more may subsequently be halved by the courts if the person appeals to a higher court. A period of three months or six months may not be reduced. In addition to disqualification, a court can impose a jail sentence or fine on anyone who is convicted of drunk driving. According to the 1994 Act, a person convicted of drunk driving or of having an alcohol level above the legal limit may be liable to a fine 'not exceeding £1000' (c. €1270) or to imprisonment for a term not exceeding six months or to both. Any decision of a lower court (in general driving offences are heard in the Circuit Court) may be appealed to a higher court by either the accused or by the Director of Public Prosecutions (DPP). The latter may occur if the DPP feels that the punishment handed down is too lenient. A person who is disqualified from driving may also be ordered to resit his driving test.

The Medical Bureau of Road Safety (MBRS)

[17.22]

The Medical Bureau of Road Safety (MBRS) was established in 1968 under Road Traffic Act 1968, Part V. Its primary role has been alluded to previously: it takes receipt of samples of urine or blood provided by those suspected of driving under the influence of intoxicants and tests them for the presence of those intoxicants. The Bureau issues certificates in respect of the results of these analyses, which may then be used as evidence in the prosecution of individuals whose samples demonstrate the presence of an intoxicant. The particular duties of the MBRS in respect of specimens received are laid out in the Road Traffic Act 1994.[30]

As soon as practicable after it has received a specimen forwarded to it, the MBRS analyses the specimen and determines the concentration of alcohol or (as may be appropriate) the presence of a drug or drugs in the specimen.

The doctor who takes a urine or blood specimen from a person suspected of driving under the influence of intoxicants is required to split the sample into two portions and seal each portion. One sample of the specimen will be offered to the alleged offender and the other forwarded to the MBRS. If the suspect declines the portion offered to him, then both samples are forwarded to the MBRS, but it is required only to test one of them.[31] The MBRS then returns the results of the analysis to the Garda Station from which the specimen originally emanated as soon as is practicable on a special certificate form designed for this purpose. A copy of the certificate is also forwarded to the person who provided the specimen for testing. The certificate issued by the MBRS must contain the following particulars:[32]

- the name and address of the person from whom the specimen was taken, or who provided the specimen;
- the nature of specimen (whether blood or urine);
- the date and time when the specimen was taken or provided;
- the name and address of the Garda Station or hospital at which specimen was taken or provided;
- the Garda Síochána station from which the specimen analysed was forwarded (in the case of those specimens taken or provided in a hospital);
- the result of the analysis;
- the signature of the person who carried out the analysis.[33]

The MBRS is financed by an annual grant from the Department of the Environment and is currently based in University College Dublin. It is overseen by a five-member Board, headed by a Director and appointed by the Minister for the Environment. Other roles of the MBRS include the provision of equipment for the taking of blood and urine specimens, research on drinking and drugs in relation to driving, including the methods of determining the amount of alcohol or drugs in a person's body. One more recent role has been the approval of apparatus for indicating the presence and the concentration of alcohol in breath (see section **[17.23]**).

Figures released in the MBRS Annual Reports offer a snapshot of the way in which the Bureau operates.[34] It also indicates the way in which the Road Traffic Act 1994 has increased the powers of the Gardaí and their designated doctors by permitting them to secure samples from those in hospital.

Figure 17.5 – Results of MBRS Analysis of blood and urine analysis 1999-2000

	1999	2000
Total samples tested	8,476	10,134
Number of blood/urine samples tested	8,476	6,567
Number of hospital samples (% of total)	217 (2.6%)	255 (3.9%)
Requests for drug analysis (% positive)	50 (N/A)	78 (91%)

According to the 1999 Report, 217 samples (2.5%) came from individuals obliged to provide the sample in hospital, while by 2000 that proportion had risen to 3.9%. The MBRS has also noted the upward trend in the number of individuals who are testing positive for drugs as well as alcohol.[35] The total number of recorded samples has continued to rise, but the number of blood and urine analyses conducted by the MBRS fell in 2000 as a result of the increased implementation of evidential breath testing.

THE FUTURE OF DRINK DRIVING LAW

The spread of breath testing

[17.23]

The Road Traffic Acts 1994 and 1995 make reference to breath testing for alcohol levels, but the reality is that the process of introducing Evidential Breath Testing (EBT) into the Garda Síochána armoury for the detection of drink driving has been quite slow. The MBRS, in conjunction with the Gardaí, was involved in the assessment of satisfactory testing mechanisms, including the appraisal and comparison of machines that could be reliably used for the purpose of the collection and analysis of samples.[36]

In late 1999, infra-red breath analysis machines were introduced into a number of Garda stations in Ireland, with the intention of a nation-wide introduction by the end of 2002. Gardaí were trained and examined in association with the MBRS on their competence to administer EBT and the Bureau also continued to monitor the use and accuracy of the EBT machines. However, the plans to introduce EBT nation-wide were temporarily hamstrung by legal challenges.[37] The failure of these challenges means that the use of evidential breath testing will become the national norm over the next few years.

The legal limit

[17.24]

The alcohol levels tolerated in Irish drivers have come in for criticism and it is true that among EU countries only Ireland, the United Kingdom, Luxembourg and Italy permit a legal limit of 80mg of alcohol per 100ml of blood. In all other European Union member states, the upper limit is 50mg per 100ml and in Sweden, the only exception, the level is even lower at 20mg per 100ml. In 2001,[38] the European Commission adopted a recommendation that blood alcohol limits be harmonised at a maximum of 50mg alcohol per 100ml of blood for drivers generally, with a maximum permitted level of 20mg alcohol per 100ml of blood for commercial drivers, motorcyclists and inexperienced drivers. This position has been reiterated in the EU White Paper *European Transport Policy for 2010: Time to Decide.*[39] It seems likely that the maximum Irish blood-alcohol levels permissible in drivers will eventually be lowered in order to accord with the overall direction of European policy in this matter. This will – and should, as an urgent matter of road safety – entail a lowering of the current Irish limit to a maximum blood alcohol level of 50mg/100ml.[40]

Quick Reference Guide 17.3

Driving, alcohol and drugs

- Driving or attempting to drive, while under the influence of alcohol or intoxicants is a criminal offence, punishable by time in jail, a fine, disqualification or any combination of the three. The punishment varies with the gravity of the offence (see figure 17.3).
- Alcohol concentration can be measured in breath, blood or urine samples. The maximum permitted concentration is different (but equivalent) for each of the three forms of sample.
- A doctor will be involved in the drunk-driving detection process when she is required to obtain a urine or blood sample from a patient. The 'designated doctor' will usually obtain the sample at a Garda Station, but she also has the legal right to enter a hospital and take a sample from a patient there.
- A 'designated doctor' can indicate that any particular sample should not be taken for medical reasons, in which case an alternative form of sample will be sought.
- In order not to inhibit their value as evidence there are safeguards attaching to the manner in which any sample should be taken and handled. In particular, blood and urine samples are divided into two portions and sealed, with one being offered to the suspected drunk driver. The sealed sample that is retained by the doctor is forwarded to the Medical Bureau of Road Safety (MBRS) for analysis.
- The MBRS sends the results of its analysis back to the Garda Station where the sample originated. The certificate accompanying the results must contain certain information to ensure that its evidential value is secure.
- Breath testing is likely to increase in frequency across Ireland.
- There is a realistic probability that in the near future European pressure will lead to a reduction in the Irish maximum blood alcohol level for driving from 80mg per 100ml (the joint highest in Europe) to 50mg per 100ml.

Endnotes

1 Department of the Environment and Local Government *Medical Aspects of Driver Licensing - A Guide for Registered Medical Practitioners* (1999) p 2.

2 For which a special licence was introduced by the 1999 Regulations.

3 The prefix 'E' whenever it occurs in a licence category indicates the relevant class of vehicle with a trailer attached to it, so B indicates a light minibus, while EB signifies the same vehicle towing a trailer.

4 The eyesight test is certified on form D 502.

5 The result of the examination is recorded on form D 501.

6 Organisation for Economic Co-operation and Development *Ageing and Transport: Mobility Needs and Safety Issues* (2001) ch 3.

7 Department of the Environment and Local Government *Medical Aspects of Driver Licensing - A Guide for Registered Medical Practitioners* (1999) p 2.

8 Note that this applies only to insulin dependent patients applying for a Group 2 licence (see para **[17.09]**).

9 This equates to 6/12 using a metric Snellen Chart.

10 Equating to 6/10 using a metric Snellen Chart.

11 Usually adaptation to monocular vision takes a matter of months rather than weeks or years.

12 6/7.5

13 www.dvla.gov.uk

14 Driver Vehicle Licensing Authority *Medical Guidelines* ch 8.

15 The New York Heart Association Classification is a gradation of the severity of symptoms in patients with congestive heart failure that operates approximately as follows:

I Symptoms develop at extreme levels of exertion (Workloads >7 METs)
II Symptoms develop at moderate levels of exertion (Workloads 4-7 METs)
III Symptoms develop at mild levels of exertion (Workloads <4 METs)
IV Symptoms of congestive heart failure are present at rest

One method of measuring units of work is the MET. One MET is the utilisation of 3.5ml Oxygen/kg/min and is the typical amount of oxygen used at rest.

16 The DVLA adds the rider that the applicant must be able to recognise the symptoms of hypoglycaemia. In the UK any insulin dependent diabetic who did not already have his licence by 1991 may not hold a Group 2 for a Heavy Goods Vehicle or a Public Carriage Vehicle.

17 In the United Kingdom, patients are also forbidden from driving while anti-epileptic medication is being withdrawn.

18 Which is not defined in the *Medical Aspects of Driver Licensing*.

19 Could it for example include caffeine?

20 *Medical Aspects of Driver Licensing – A Guide fo Registered Medical Practitioner* (1999), pp 8-9.

21 *W v Egdell* [1990] 1 All ER 835. See also section **[3.17]**.

22 *Duncan v Medical Practitioners' Disciplinary Committee* [1986] 1 NZLR 513.

23 *Crosby v Sultz* (1991) 592 A 2d 1337 . Note, however, that some more recent US cases have suggested that a doctor may sometimes owe a duty to those harmed by her negligent treatment of a patient. See *Reisner v Regents of the University of California* (1995) 31 Cal App 4th 1110. We examine in ch 7 *Negligence*, the principle that a doctor owes a duty to third parties (persons other than her patient who are harmed as a result of negligent treatment of that patient) only when it is possible to foresee *not only* the possibility of damage to a third party *but also the identity* of that third party. See *Palmer v Tees Health Authority* [1999] Lloyd's L Rep (Med) 351.

24 Road Traffic Act 1961, s 49, as amended by the Road Traffic Act 1994.

25 Road Traffic Act 1961, s 50, as amended by the Road Traffic Act 1994.

26 Road Traffic Act 1994, s 15. See section **[17.20]**.

27 Gardaí are the individuals responsible for obtaining breath samples and the procedure they must follow is laid down in Road Traffic Act 1994, s 17.

28 Detailed in the Road Traffic Act 1994, s 18.

29 Road Traffic Act 1994, s 23.

30 Road traffic Act 1994, s 19(1).

31 Testing is conducted using gas chromatography.

32 Road Traffic Act 1994, s 19.

33 SI 1994/351, reg 4 and Sch 2.

34 From the Annual Reports of the MBRS 1999 and 2000.

35 See Moane, Leavy, and Cusack 'Drugs Driving in Ireland – A Preliminary Study of the Prevalence of Driving under the Influence of Drugs on Irish Roads' MLJI 2001; 7:21.

[36] The Bureau evaluated different types of instruments from June 1999 to September1999: the Lion intoxilyzer 6000IRL and the INTOXIMETER EC/IR (see Reynolds, Kearns, Mullany, Leavy, Cusack 'Introduction of Evidential Breath Testing in Ireland.'MLJI 2001; 7:9). The former apparatus operates by measuring infra-red wavelengths, the latter by measuring the current flowing through a fuel cell that absorbs alcohol vapours. Infra-red absorption and current respectively are proportional to the amount of alcohol in the sample. Entertainingly, the infrared measurements of the intoxilyzer are dependent upon the operation of the physics equation, which is appropriately and entertainingly known as Beers Law.

[37] See *Director of Public Prosecutions v Syron* [2001] 2 IR 105; *DPP v Moloney* [2001] IEHC 178 (20 December 2001), HC.

[38] 17 January 2001. A recommendation of the Commission is not binding on member states, but is often indicative of the direction that future legislation will take.

[39] Office for Official Publications of the European Union 2001; COM (2001) 370. See in particular Part 3. The report draws attention to the fact that a proposal first put forward in 1988 to set a legal blood alcohol limit has remained a dead letter since that time. The report also points to the anomaly of a driver crossing the Channel from England to France with a legal amount of alcohol in his blood on one side of the border, becoming illegal when he crosses into France.

[40] See Organisation for Economic Co-operation and Development *Safety on Roads – What's the Vision?* (2002) pp 63-68. This report documents the fact that there was a steady decline in the rate of drink driving noted by most countries surveyed during the 1980s and early 1990s. However, rates of improvement have declined or halted in most nations. They also observe that alcohol consumption by pedestrians is a contributing factor in many accidents. Among the mechanisms reported by the OECD as successful in reducing rates of drunk driving is the use of random breath testing. United States figures included in the report have suggested that the raising of the legal drinking age to 21 also contributed to a reduced rate of drunk driving accidents.

Chapter 18

Law at the Cutting Edge of Science

INTRODUCTION

[18.01]

The material in this chapter is set aside from the other chapters for a simple reason. Much of the law it contains is currently uncertain because few or no court decisions have been taken, or because no legislation has been passed to date in Ireland or because the full potential of the scientific advances themselves have not yet become clear. Where there is law, its applicability to Ireland is uncertain. Irish legislators are only beginning to come to grips with areas such as genetics and assisted reproduction and so we look predominantly in this chapter at the lessons to be learned from other countries.

GENETICS

[18.02]

The use of genetic material in medical research is commonplace and the likelihood looms ever larger that human and other genetic material may yet have an enormous role to play in the future of medical diagnosis and treatment. The issues that gene research and therapy raise are ones that legal and ethical opinion has begun to face only in recent years.

In many ways, the principles of DNA-related law and ethics are uncomplicated: issues of consent and information and patient autonomy remain, or should remain, at the forefront of all considerations and the rules for consent in the fields of genetics or assisted reproduction are no different from the rules in other areas of clinical practice.[1] Where problems most starkly arise are in the execution rather than the principles of DNA research work.

There are two facets to DNA research. The first is the harvesting of genetic material for specific directed research, such as studies of the genetic basis for cardiovascular disease. Secondly, and perhaps more importantly, there is the question of storage and later research on the genetic material that does not tally with the initial immediate purpose for which it was given. Later research, with new techniques and researchers armed with new knowledge, may disclose novel information about genetic disorders or predispositions afflicting the original donor: in such circumstances should the donor be told? The genetic material may subsequently turn out to have commercial value in treatment or further research, should the original donor come in for a cut of any profits? We look at these two questions below.[2]

The process of harvesting, storing and using genetic material will be done in one of several ways:

— 'unlinked' - where there is no longer any identifying link between the donor and the sample;

— 'coded' - where the genetic material is anonymised and no longer directly linked to the original donor but the donor may nonetheless be identified through the code system;

— 'linked' - where the original donor continues to be linked or identified directly to the sample.

Consent issues

[18.03]

Issues of consent in the field of genetics are especially complex when a patient donates his genetic material not merely for immediate research purposes but also for later and often unspecified research use. If consent is given now, but the material may later be used for purposes not yet invented or thought of, then how are those future circumstances to be catered for? The UK Genetics Commission has observed that:

> 'Genetic research is subject to the same standards as any other branch of medical research in that informed consent is required from the donor at the time a sample is obtained.'[3]

The Nuffield Council on Bioethics has made some of the most thorough considerations and recommendations for the use of genetic material in research.[4] The group recognises that genetic material that is analysed for the presence of diseases may disclose the presence either of the particular disease being researched or of other conditions. The question then is whether information gleaned from the sample should be relayed back to the original donor.

> '...To provide an individual with information from a research study about gene mutations which they might or might not carry and which, at the time samples and information were collected, could not have been foreseen, could be to give them information they would choose not to have, and/or information for which they or other members of the family are not prepared or cannot understand in terms of its implications.'

The Working Party of the Nuffield Council therefore makes the following recommendations on donor consent to the taking of genetic material:

— As a general rule, those who consent to take part in research should be told that individual information derived from analysis of their DNA will not be given to them. This is especially true where any information on genetic predisposition suggests a weak susceptibility to illness.[5]

— When consent to research that could yield genetic information which is clinically relevant to a research participant and/or their relatives is given it should be made clear whether or not such information will be made available. If it is to be made available, then before consenting to the research an individual should receive genetic counselling. They should also give written consent to make clear whether they wish a designated medical adviser to receive any relevant information or whether they would prefer to receive such information themselves.

In view of the potentially complex uses of genetic material after initial donation, the US National Bioethics Advisory Committee has identified that consent forms may need to consider offering the donor all or any of the following options:

(a) refusing use of their biological materials in research;

(b) permitting only unidentified or unlinked use of their biological materials in research;

(c) permitting coded or identified use of their biological materials for one particular study only, with no further contact permitted to ask for permission to do further studies;

(d) permitting coded or identified use of their biological materials for one particular study only, with further contact permitted to ask for permission to do further studies;

(e) permitting coded or identified use of their biological materials for any study relating to the condition for which the sample was originally collected, with further contact allowed to seek permission for other types of studies;

(f) an open-ended consent permitting use of their biological materials in any form for any kind of future study.[6]

Essentially then, there are two dimensions to patient consent for the use of genetic information. Firstly, has consent been given for the use of the sample in the research for which it has been taken and secondly for the storage and possible future use of the genetic material?[7] If a person consents only to the first, then the material should subsequently be destroyed. Only if specific consent has been given to storage and future use can that be done. Patients should also have the opportunity to change their minds where necessary.[8] If consent is absent, then the material cannot be used.[9]

Financial considerations

[18.04]

One other difficult area of genetic research is the fact that it is possible to patent (effectively to own) genetic material that has been subject to research and development.[10] Patients and researchers need to be clear about the limits and consequences of ownership of genetic material. The Medical Research Council made the point in its report on genetic research:

> 'Research participants may be particularly sensitive to the idea of a company or an individual making a profit out of the tissue that they have freely donated. It is important that research participants are made aware of the potential benefits of allowing commercial access, and that the role of any one individual's sample in the generation of future profits is likely to be minimal as well as impossible to quantify. Given the possible sensitivities, it is essential that research participants are made aware that their sample or products derived from it may be used by the commercial sector, and that they will not be entitled to a share of any profits that might ensue.'

The reality then is that a patient involved in genetic research should be made aware that legally they will have no right to any share in profits that might emerge, but nonetheless, their consent to the use of their genetic material in the commercial environment should be sought.

Quick Reference Guide 18.1

Issues in genetic material research and storage

- ❖ The issues and rules of consent and confidentiality are precisely the same in this area as they are in any other area of clinical practice.
- ❖ Two main scenarios in which problems arise are (a) the storage and subsequent use of genetic material for purposes other than those for which it was originally given and (b) the commercial exploitation of genetic information.
- ❖ If storage and later research are to happen, they must only occur with the consent of the donor.
- ❖ The current ethical recommendations are that a donor should generally not be told of the outcome of later genetic research performed on a sample originally donated for other purposes unless he has specifically requested that he be told. There may of course be compelling clinical reasons for telling a donor in certain circumstances.
- ❖ A patient being asked to consent to the donation and use of genetic material should have it made clear to him what he is consenting to and the fact – if applicable – that he will not be contacted with further information resulting from later research.
- ❖ A donor of genetic material has no right to a share in subsequent profits made by the commercial exploitation of his genetic material.

Assisted human reproduction issues

[18.05]

In the United Kingdom there is legislation, in the form of the Human Fertilisation and Embryology Act 1990, governing the whole area of assisted reproduction and embryo research. The legislation established the Human Fertilisation and Embryology Authority (HFEA),[11] which has responsibility for:

- — regulating and inspecting standards at all UK treatment clinics offering *in vitro* fertilisation (IVF), donor insemination (DI) or storage of eggs, sperm[12] or embryos, ensuring that they conform to high medical and professional standards and are inspected regularly;
- — licensing and monitoring human embryo research.[13]

There is no equivalent legislation or authority in Ireland but the need for some guidelines on questions of infertility[14] and embryology[15] is clear. In February 2000, the Minister for Health announced the establishment of an Irish Commission on Assisted Human Reproduction:

> '[T]o prepare a report on the possible approaches to the regulation of all aspects of assisted human reproduction and the social, ethical and legal factors to be taken into account in determining public policy in this area.'

The Commission has yet to report (the report is expected in 2003), but it seems likely that its report will include a recommendation for the establishment of an authority with responsibility for the area. Considerations of policy in this field may be coloured by the

Constitutional recognition of the right to life of the unborn, but as we have seen in Chapter 12 that right appears not to be absolute and appears only to commence, legally speaking, from the moment of implantation in the womb (see section **[12.17]**).

Questions that English legislation and case law have considered and attempted to answer include the following and they may provide some guidance for how Irish courts may consider such matters in future. It must be stressed that these examples are how British legislation and English courts have dealt with the matter, but it is to be expected that they will exert some influence upon the deliberations of the Commission on Assisted Human Reproduction.

Who should have treatment?

[18.06]

IVF or Donor Insemination (DI) treatment will not be given to any woman unless the welfare of any child she may give birth to (including the need of that child for a father) and the welfare of any other children who may be affected by the birth of a sibling[16] is considered.

It is acceptable to limit the maximum age of a woman to whom state-funded IVF treatment may be given. The courts have held that, in view of the limited budgets available for IVF and the fact that the effectiveness of IVF diminishes with age, it is permissible to set a maximum age for women who will be given treatment.[17]

Use and storage of sperm (or eggs) taken without consent

[18.07]

The sperm of a deceased husband cannot be used by his surviving spouse for the purposes of donor insemination without him having given his consent when alive - consent is an indispensable precursor to the use of a eggs or sperm for IVF. In one case,[18] a woman's husband had passed into a coma following meningitis, sperm was obtained from him by electro-ejaculation and following her husband's death, the woman sought to undergo donor insemination in the UK or abroad. The HFEA has responsibility for licensing the use or export of sperm. It refused to sanction either avenue in the absence of the husband's explicit consent and the woman challenged the HFEA decision. The HFEA defended its decision by arguing that the law required consent.[19] The court confirmed that in all cases consent must be obtained for the harvesting and use of sperm or eggs and where there is no consent, there could be no legal storage or use.[20] In this particular case the court acknowledged that the sperm had been taken and stored before the law had been clarified and therefore allowed the sperm to be exported so that the woman could undergo treatment. If there is no consent, the current legal position is that there can be no use of sperm or egg.

The right to information of those born as a result of fertility treatment

[18.08]

A person over the age of 18 years, who applies to the UK HFEA has the right to find out whether he was in fact born as the result of fertility treatment. This can include the necessary information to ensure that the applicant is not about to marry someone to whom he is related. The legislation in the UK does not, however, provide for any information at all to be given about the donor.[21] Among the arguments for perpetuating donor anonymity are that donors may be more reluctant to donate sperm if they feel that they can be identified by an unknown number of children an untold number of years later. Many countries, including Sweden[22] and the State of Victoria in Australia,[23] have laws providing that children have the right on attaining adulthood to know the identity of their donor parent.

Certain details are made available to the mother when she undergoes IVF: she may for example wish the donor to have certain characteristics that mirror her husband's, so she could be told information gleaned from the donor's registration form, such as height, eye and hair colour or profession. The mother may pass on that information to the child[24] but she is under no obligation to do so and the HFEA is under no obligation to disclose that information either.

A case in the United Kingdom has suggested that the failure to provide basic non-identifying information[25] on a voluntary basis to a child concerning his donor parent's identity may be a violation of the respect for family life guaranteed under the European Convention on Human Rights.[26] The court did not give a final decision on the matter however, in part because the Westminster government is considering the matter further.[27] In view of the recognition, founded on human rights law, that children born of donor sperm are entitled to some information about their father, it is hoped that Irish legislation on the subject will adopt one of the approaches adopted elsewhere:

- ensuring that non-identifying information can be provided to children and must be provided by donors *or*
- permitting donors to indicate whether they wish identifying information to be provided to children and in any event increasing the amount of non-identifying information made available *or*
- making it a precondition of donation – as in Sweden – that the donor voluntarily agrees to the giving over of identifying information if those data are requested by the child on attaining maturity.

Who are the parents of a child born through assisted reproduction?

[18.09]

In many cases the answer is clear: if a couple go through IVF and provide the sperm and the egg for the treatment, then they will obviously be the mother and the father of the child. But what if a couple cannot conceive because the male partner is sterile and instead they opt for donor insemination. Is the male partner, even though he has no genetic input in the pregnancy, still the child's father? The Human Fertilisation and Embryology Act deals with the issue thus:

- A woman who carries a child, whatever the origin of the sperm and egg, as a result of assisted reproduction treatment is the mother of that child.[28]
- If a woman is married at the time of undergoing assisted reproduction therapy and the sperm with which she is inseminated is not her husband's, then assuming her spouse consented to her undergoing treatment, he will be legally

regarded as the father of the child. A similar (but not identical)[29] approach is brought to bear on unmarried couples who undergo treatment together.

Quick Reference Guide 18.2

Assisted reproduction

- There is no Irish legislation governing this area, although a Commission on Assisted Human Reproduction has been established. In the United Kingdom, the relevant legislation is the Human Fertilisation and Embryology Act 1990.
- The UK legislation creates the Human Fertilisation and Embryology Authority (HFEA), which oversees and licenses assisted reproduction treatments and embryological research.
- The HFEA and the United Kingdom Courts have brought some clarity to how a regulated system of assisted human reproduction might operate in this country. Their decisions and determinations include:
  - (i) It is lawful to introduce an upper age limit for assisted reproduction treatment
  - (ii) The donor's consent is an indispensable precursor to the use of any eggs or sperm in assisted human reproduction
  - (iii) Children born as a result of donor artificial insemination appear to have a legal right to certain information, possibly including identifying information, about their biological father
  - (iv) The woman who carries a child following assisted reproduction treatment is legally the child's mother, even if the egg is not hers
  - (v) The woman's husband (if he has consented to the course of treatment that the woman has undergone) or partner (if 'going through' the treatment with the woman) at the time of the treatment will be legally regarded as the child's father, even if the sperm is not his

Cloning and stem cell research

[18.10]

There are two types of cloning:

- — reproductive cloning, where the aim is to produce a living organism genetically identical to the donor organism, and
- — therapeutic cloning, where the aim is to produce specific cells or tissues for use in medical treatment, but not a cloned living organism.

The distinction is an important one and the world's governments have taken a firm stance against reproductive cloning insofar as it has the potential to produce cloned humans, although neither the UK nor Ireland has legislated explicitly to ban it.[30] Therapeutic cloning, including stem cell research, is a different matter and is one for which governments are beginning to legislate in ways that reflect, in the words of some commentators, 'liberal' and 'conservative' approaches. Other countries, including Ireland, have yet to adopt a formal position but the question of cloning lies within the remit of the Irish Council for Bioethics established under the auspices of the Royal Irish Academy in May 2002.

Therapeutic cloning in general involves the duplication or culturing of a particular cell line for the purposes of repair or treatment of damaged or diseased tissues. In particular cloned stem cells, which have the potential to become any required body cell (pluripotential cells) if stimulated appropriately are a rich source of the required cells. There are three widely recognised categories of stem cell:[31]

- embryonic stem cells, which are found in early human embryos and which can be created by IVF, by cloning techniques or from already existing cell lines;
- embryonic germ cells, which are found in the primitive reproductive organs of the developing foetus and can be obtained from cadaveric foetal tissue;
- adult stem cells, which can be obtained from certain adult tissues, such as the bone marrow, brain, intestine and blood cells.

It is embryonic stem cells that have the greatest potential to be encouraged to develop into other forms of cells and therefore have the greatest potential in the area of treatment. The creation of embryos through therapeutic cloning offers an opportunity to derive embryonic stem cells that are immunologically compatible with a person being treated, thus avoiding problems of rejection. Therapeutic cloning can also enable scientists ultimately to learn about the mechanisms of reprogramming adult cells to behave like embryonic stem cells again. If this line of research were successful, adult cell reprogramming could ultimately make it unnecessary to resort to using embryos to derive stem cells at all.

The question of whether embryonic cells can be produced solely for the purposes of research is the area of cloning that most exercises the minds of the lawyer and the ethicist at the present stage of the cloning debate. The ethical debate involves resolving the fact on the one hand that embryonic life will be created (and ultimately destroyed) for the purposes of research and on the other hand that the resulting research could have huge benefits for humankind. The question of the creation of the embryo is in particular coloured by the debate over whether the embryo constitutes a 'life': if it does, then what are its rights and, if it has any rights, how can they be reconciled with the way in which the embryo is used? At the other extreme is the opinion that an embryo is no more than a clump of cells. In general, those considering the matter from a legislative viewpoint have tended to adopt an 'intermediate position that a human embryo has a special status as a potential human being, but is not of the same status as a living child or adult.'[32] Respect for the special status (the 'rights') of the embryo is weighted against the benefit to be obtained from violating any right to life the embryo possesses.

Stem cell legislation

[18.11]

This intermediate position is being adopted by many countries and is further modified by a determination to avoid creating embryos purely for research purposes and to completely restrict the use of embryos for reproductive cloning. Elements that laws on therapeutic cloning tend to share are:[33]

- an absolute ban on the cloning of humans for reproductive purposes;[34]
- a time limit from fertilisation beyond which embryos cannot be used: 14 days is the limit in the United Kingdom;
- an insistence that there must be strong scientific merit in – and no alternative to – any decision to permit the use of embryonic stem cells for the purpose of research and decisions must be made on a case-by-case basis by an approved statutory body (in the UK, it is the HFEA) to whom those requiring a licence for research must apply;
- embryonic stem cells should only be used where adult and embryonic germ cells[35] are not satisfactory and the first sources of embryonic stem cells, if required, should be -
    i. existing stem cell lines held in laboratories,
    ii. surplus embryos originally created for purposes of medically assisted reproduction but not used for that purpose. It is thought preferable to use such embryos for research rather than simply destroying them;
- only if such routes are not productive will the use of embryos created through therapeutic cloning be considered;
- commercial trade in embryonic material is prohibited, as is the creation of cloned embryonic material for the purposes of producing human life;[36]
- fully informed consent to the provision and use of material for the purpose of stem cell cloning a research must be obtained.

Specific legislation on stem cell cloning

[18.12]

The approaches that have been adopted in countries that have chosen to legislate for embryonic stem cell research require scrutiny, because such approaches may point the way forward for the deliberations of the Irish Council for Bioethics. The European Commission has introduced a proposal for a Directive that will harmonise standards of safety and quality for the "donation, procurement, testing, processing, storage and distribution of human tissues and cells." The directive applies only to the use of human tissue on human subjects and does not make the use of any form of tissue (such as stem cells) mandatory: it will remain for Member States to decide whether they wish to permit the use of any form of tissue for therapeutic purposes.[37]

UK

[18.13]

In 2001 the United Kingdom altered the terms of the 1990 Human Fertilisation and Embryology Act to allow for the introduction of stem cell research.[38] It was not a popular decision in many circles and even the European Parliament called on the Houses of Parliament in London to reconsider its decision.[39] The original United Kingdom position was previously that human embryos up to 14 days old could be used for non-cloning research purposes, but the amendments made by the regulations have widened the scope of research to include therapeutic cloning. All research projects remain subject to the granting of a licence by the HFEA.

Quick Reference Guide 18.3

Cloning and stem cell research

- Cloning can be 'reproductive' (with the aim of producing a living creature) or 'therapeutic' (with the aim of producing treatments or advancing research).
- The three sources of stem cells are embryonic stem cells, embryonic germ cells and adult stem cells. Embryonic stem cells are the richest source of pluripotent cells.
- Ethical questions include whether the embryo is 'alive' and whether it has rights for that reason. In Ireland, the fact that the life of the unborn is not regarded as beginning until implantation means that it is not clear whether embryo research would be prevented by the Irish Constitution's regard for the life of the unborn.
- No country expressly permits reproductive cloning of humans and many have expressly banned it, although in many countries such as the United States, there is only a voluntary code prohibiting it. It is prohibited by the EU Charter of Fundamental Rights.
- Legislation that permits therapeutic cloning of human embryos generally demonstrates the following features:
  (i) A time limit from fertilisation beyond which embryos may not be used
  (ii) Proof to the satisfaction of a regulatory body that there is a need for the proposed research and a need for cloning of embryos as part of that research
  (iii) Cloned embryonic cells to be used only where there is no other source (such as existing stem lines or surplus embryos created for IVF)
  (iv) Prohibition of commercial trade in human embryos
  (v) The need for fully informed consent

The Act permits research on embryos that arise both from IVF and from Cell Nuclear Replacement (CNR – where DNA is injected into a cell to permit cloned cells to develop from a particular DNA donor). Licences will be issued only if the HFEA is satisfied that the creation of an embryo is necessary for the purposes of the project in question and that the project is within the list of specified purposes. Reproductive cloning is not expressly banned by the Act, as the HFEA believes that the current regulation and guidelines offer sufficient protection. In September 2002 the UK Government announced its intention to create the world's first embryonic stem cell bank consisting of embryos surplus to IVF requirements.

United States

[18.14]

In the United States, privately funded research projects are not subject to any restriction, whilst research using Federal public funding is regulated. In 1999, the National Bioethics Advisory Commission produced a report recommending that federal funding be allowed for research involving human embryonic germ cells from cadaveric foetal tissue, but not for research involving human embryonic stem cells from embryos created solely for research purposes using IVF or CNR.[40] The position in the United States supports limited public funding for research on human embryonic stem cells obtained from established human stem cells lines only. The legislation prohibits federally funded projects from using any further embryos for the purpose of research.

Consequently, the National Institute of Health (NIH) established a Human Embryonic Cell Registry to list human embryonic stem cells in the United States meeting the eligibility criteria necessary to obtain funding for such research. Before federal funding is granted, each request for federal funding must cite the human embryonic stem cell line listed on the NIH Registry that is being used for the research, meet existing scientific and technical merit criteria and must be recommended by the National Advisory Council.[41] In contrast, privately funded human stem cell research remains free from such controls. Reproductive cloning is forbidden in all projects subject to federal funding and although there are no legal barriers to privately funded bodies carrying out reproductive cloning, those institutions, at the time of writing, have subscribed to a voluntary moratorium on reproductive cloning. The contrast between the absence of strictures on privately funded research and the imposition of constraints on federally funded work appears to be an American solution to an American problem rather than a coherent and consistent approach to the stem cell cloning issue.

Australia

[18.15]

The Australian Health Ethics Committee (AHEC) produced a report entitled *Scientific, Ethical and Regulatory Considerations Relevant to Cloning of Human Beings*[42] and the Australian House of Representatives Standing Committee on Legal and Constitutional Affairs reviewed it with the aim of drafting recommendations for legislation. The decision on the form legislation will take is expected to be made by the Commonwealth Parliament.

The AHEC was of the view that given the number of surplus embryos available, the specific creation of new embryos for research purposes is unnecessary and should not in general be permitted, unless it could be shown to be absolutely necessary. The Committee called for the creation of a body to oversee research in the area and recommended too that a three-year moratorium could be imposed on the creation of embryos via CNR, as there is currently no therapeutic purpose to be served by the use of the technique and research has not identified any specific opportunities that require the deliberate formation of embryos.

Lessons for Ireland

Because of the Constitutional provision that respects the life of the unborn child, there is an argument that stem cell research could never be countenanced in Ireland. However, as we have noted at section **[12.07]**, Irish law states that pregnancy, and therefore the existence of the unborn child, starts at implantation rather than fertilisation. Therefore, it could be argued that an embryo is not an 'unborn child' and therefore attracts no Constitutional protection. Such matters will be for the Commission on Bioethics to consider.

Endnotes

1 See ch 4 for an exploration of consent.

2 Many of the issues raised by genetics in clinical practice have been identified and summarised by the Health Research Board: Sheikh A. *Genetic Research and Human Biological Samples - The Legal and Ethical Considerations* (2002) Health Research Board. Available for download from the Health Research Board website at www.hrb.ie.

3 UK Human Genetics Commission *Whose Hands on your Genes? - A discussion document on the storage, protection and use of personal genetic information* (2001) p 23. An Irish Council for Bioethics has been established under the auspices of the Royal Irish Academy: see 'Body to examine ethics of stem-cell research' (2002) *Irish Times*, 21 May.

4 Nuffield Council on Bioethics Report on Mental Disorders and Genetics: The Ethical Context (1998). See http://www.nuffieldbioethics.org/home/.

5 And presumably it is less true where the genetic information provides extremely strong evidence of a very serious condition that would benefit from the earliest possible intervention.

6 National Bioethics Advisory Commission (NBAC) *Research Involving Human Biological Materials: Ethical Issues and Policy Guidance* (1999). Recommendation 9.

7 The fact that consent is required for use of a sample beyond the original purpose for which it was taken was identified in *Moore v Regents of the University of California* (1990) 793 P 2d 479 (Cal SC). In this case, a doctor took samples from a patient with a hairy cell leukaemia and entered into an arrangement (without the express consent of the patient) with a pharmaceutical company to clone and patent those cells. This was a breach of the doctor's duty to obtain informed consent.

8 'Consent should be considered as a process, not an event, and it is important that there is continuing discussion to reflect the evolving nature of treatment.' British Medical Association *Consent Tool Kit* (2001) p 9.

9 This would probably include where the patient has died and is incapable of giving consent (see section **[18.07]** below)

10 See the EU Directive on the Legal Protection of Biotechnological Inventions. To comply with the Directive, a person from whose body the material used for an invention is taken must have had the opportunity to express free and informed consent (Recital 26). The directive became law in Ireland with the European Communities (Legal Protection of Biotechnological Inventions) Regulations 2000 (SI 2000/247). See also: Sheikh 'Owning' Life: New Frontiers in Patent Law, Genetics and Biotechnology' MLJI 1999; 1:23. See also *Ethical Aspects of Patenting Inventions involving Human Stem Cells*, Opinion of the European Group on Ethics in Science and New Technologies to the European Commission, No 16, 7 May 2002. The Group re-iterated the principle of "non-commercialisation" of the human body. It rejected the idea that stem cells could be patented but accepted that inventions that allowed for the modification of stem cell lines *could* be patented.

11 The Authority itself is a 21-member panel appointed by the Secretary of State for Health. A majority of the Authority must be drawn from disciplines other than medicine or human embryo research. Website: www.hfea.gov.uk.

12 Including ovarian and testicular tissue from children who are undergoing treatment, such as radiotherapy, that will have the effect of rendering them infertile.

13 In the context of IVF, the research that has been licensed includes pre-implantation genetic diagnosis (PGD) for medical reasons (therefore excluding its use for sex selection). See HFEA *HFEA/Advisory Committee of Genetic Testing Consultation Document – Pre-implantation Genetic Diagnosis* (1999) London. Both PGD and pre-natal diagnosis (eg amniocentesis) involve ethical and legal complications. A prenatal diagnosis of a severe genetic abnormality may lead the couple to seek an abortion. Pre-implantation diagnosis raises the problems of

disposal of fertilised, but not implanted, embryos affected by the genetic condition. PGD is available currently in the UK only to those couples with a family history of severe genetic disorder (see Consultation Document, para 26).

14 Approximately one in six couples are subfertile and many will seek intervention in the form of assisted reproduction: see Cahill and Wardle 'Management of Infertility' BMJ 2002; 325:28-32. Infertility or subfertility are generally recognised when a couple does not conceive after two years of regular unprotected intercourse.

15 See discussion on stem cell research at section **[18.10]** below.

16 Human Fertility and Embryology Act 1990, s 13(5).

17 *R v Sheffield Health Authority, ex p Seale* (1994) 24 BMLR 1. The woman in this case was over 35 years of age and the rules stipulated that in view of the greater failure rate of IVF in older women, the cut-off age for treatment was 35. English law had also upheld rules limiting the number of embryos that may be implanted in a woman during any single course of IVF treatment: *R v Human Fertilisation and Embryology Authority ex parte Assistant Reproduction & Gynaecology Centre and 'H'* [2002] EWCA Civ 20 (31 January 2002), Court of Appeal.

18 *R v Human Fertilisation and Embryology Authority, ex p Blood* [1997] 2 All ER 687. It could be argued in this case that, aside from questions of the storage and use of sperm, taking the sperm from the comatose husband in the first place was illegal, as it was done without consent and in the absence of an emergency situation. It has been suggested that sperm could be removed in a person's 'best interests' when he is unconscious and treatment that would help him to recover consciousness would also render him sterile: see McClean *Review of the Common Law Provisions Relating to the Removal of Gametes and the Consent Provisions in the Human Fertilisation and Embryology Act 1999* (1998) Department of Health, London. See ch 4.

19 Human Fertilisation and Embryology Act 1990, s 4(1).

20 The fact that valid consent is a firm and unalterable precursor to the posthumous use of sperm was affirmed again by the English Court of Appeal in *Mrs U v Centre for Reproductive Medicine* (24 April 2002).

21 The *Report of the Committee of Inquiry into Human Fertilisation and Embryology* (HMSO, 1984) Cm 9317, upon which the 1990 Act was based recommended that 'on reaching the age of 18 the child should have access to the basic information about the donor's ethnic origin and genetic health'. However, the legislation did not include this 'basic information' provision.

22 Insemination Act 1984. Research into the Swedish law has suggested that lifting anonymity does not result in a fall in donors: Daniels *et al* 'The Views of Semen Donors Regarding the Swedish Insemination Act 1984' (1998) 3 Med Law Int 117. Cited in Kennedy & Grubb *Medical Law* (4th edn, 2000), pp 1325-1332.

23 Infertility Treatment Act 1995.

24 One large study of donor insemination families in the UK, Italy, the Netherlands and Spain found that, although just over half of mothers had told a friend or family member about the method of conception, not one of them had informed the child. Only 12% of the mothers planned to tell the child in the future, while 75% had decided not to do so. By the time the children reached 11-12 years old, only 8.6% of parents had told their child about the donor insemination. See Golombok *et al* 'The European Study of Assisted Reproduction Families' *Human Reproduction* (1996) 11(10); 2324-31; Golombok *et al* 'The European Study of Assisted Reproduction Families: The transition to adolescence.' *Human Reproduction* (2002) 17; 830-40

25 Such as those concerning medical history (including diseases that may be inherited), aptitudes, profession and beliefs.

[26] *Rose v Secretary for State for Health and the Human Fertilisation and Embryology Authority* [2002] EWHC 1593; judgment handed down 26 July 2002. See also the European Court of Human Rights judgment (unreported, published on 7 February 2002) in *Mikulic v Croatia* (App No 53176/99) where the court held that the right to family life included the right to identify, where a legal mechanism to do so existed, one's biological father if one was born out of wedlock.

[27] See the consultation document, *Donor information consultation – Providing information about gamete or embryo donors* (2002) Department of Health London.

[28] Human Fertilisation and Embryology Act 1990, s 27.

[29] For reasons that are not clear, the consent of an unmarried partner of the woman is not required.

[30] The HFEA called on the UK Government to explicitly ban reproductive cloning (see HFEA/Human Genetic Advisory Commission *Cloning Issues in Reproduction, Science and Medicine*, (1998) para 3.4/para 9.2) but this has not yet happened. There are some who argue that reproductive cloning could be carefully regulated rather than prohibited: see Harris 'Goodbye Dolly? – The Ethics of Human Cloning' (1997) 23 J of Med Ethics 353. For an extremely thorough analysis of the potential 'harms' of human cloning (and whether in fact they constitute reasons to ban cloning), see Robertson, 'Liberty, Identity and Human Cloning' (1998) 76 Texas LR 1371, cited at length in Kennedy & Grubb *Medical Law* (4th edn, 2000) pp 1251-1265. It may also be the case at the time of writing (August 2002) that unregulated laboratories and clinics are engaged in conduct that will lead ultimately to successful – if illicit – reproductive cloning.

[31] Stem cells are cells that can divide to produce either cells like themselves (self-renewal), or cells of one or several specific differentiated types. Stem cells are not yet fully differentiated and therefore can be used to reconstitute one or several types of tissues. Those that have the potential to form many different types of tissue are 'pluripotent' cells. There remains some dispute about the precise taxonomy of cells.

[32] Ethical, Legal and Social Issues in Human Stem Cell Research, Reproductive and Therapeutic Cloning - A Report from the Bioethics Advisory Committee (2002) Singapore p 24.

[33] See the Opinion of the European Group on Ethics in Science and New Technologies to the European Commission, *Ethical Aspects of Human Stem Cell Research and Use* No 15, 14 November 2000 . This opinion in particular cautions against rushing headlong into the use of embryonic stem cells for research that – regardless of its promise – remains speculative. See para 2.7 of the Opinion. See also fn10.

[34] In December 2000, The EU Charter of Fundamental Rights was proclaimed at the Summit of Nice. Article 3, Chapter 1, on 'Dignity' prohibits the reproductive cloning of human beings. There is also a Council of Europe (the organisation of all European nations that also brought the European Convention and Court of Human Rights into being) Protocol on the Prohibition of Cloning Human Beings, which came into force on 1 March 2001. The 'protocol' is added to the Convention on Human Rights and Biomedicine and bans 'any intervention seeking to create a human being genetically identical to another human being, whether living or dead'. The Protocol leaves it to countries' domestic law to define the scope of the term 'human being'.

[35] See section **[18.10]** above for definitions.

[36] Directive 98/44/EC on the legal protection of biotechnological inventions stipulates that 'processes for cloning human beings' and 'uses of human embryos for industrial or commercial purposes ... shall be considered unpatentable'.

[37] COM (2002) 319 final (published 19 June 2002). The proposed directive includes recognition of the necessary for a central licensing body. It also lays down rules on suitability of donors traceability of samples, staff training and import from non-EU countries.

[38] Human Fertilisation and Embryology (Research Purposes) Regulations 2001.

[39] European Parliament resolution on human cloning B5-0710, 0751, 0753 and 0764/2000.

[40] US National Bioethics Advisory Committee *Ethical Issues in Human Stem Cell Research* (1999) Rockville, Maryland.

[41] US National Institute of Health, NIH Guide: *Notice of criteria for federal funding of research on existing human embryonic stem cells and establishment of NIH Human Embryonic stem cell registry* 7 November 2001. See also 'Bush angers all sides with stem cell compromise' (2001) *Irish Times*, 11 August.

[42] National Health and Medical Research Council, Canberra, December 1998.

Appendix A

Sources of Law

Introduction

[A.01]

The Irish legal system is a blend, in part at least, of everything from the mediaeval to the ultra-modern. Some laws remain in force that were originally enacted in the sixteenth and seventeenth centuries (including fundamental rules that affect the buying and selling of property) while in more modern times, the complexities of social structures, industry, commerce and international relations are such that new laws and other legal rules are enacted on an almost daily basis.

The law of Ireland is susceptible to any number of influences that shape its form and overall direction. Irish law is most fundamentally underpinned by our written Constitution, but law also comes from the Oireachtas, from the decisions of Irish courts and, perhaps most significantly of all in latter years, from Europe. The different types of law can be confusing, even to lawyers, but some generalisations can be made and this appendix attempts to distil some of those generalisations for the non-legal reader. It does not attempt to be an exhaustive guide to Irish law, simply to give a flavour of its overall structure and influences.[1]

Legal Systems

[A.02]

Ireland operates under a Common Law system, which is a legal heritage that comes with our colonial past and one we share with countries such as Australia, Canada and the United States. There are other countries that follow what is often called a Civil Law or Codified System. We look at the two systems below.

The common law system

[A.03]

Common law does not exist in a single book or a single written document. Rather it is a broad descriptive term with two generally accepted meanings, one broad and one more constrained but both of which combine to give us the legal systems that we live in.

The narrower definition of common law refers to the way in which the gradual accumulation of the experience of the courts over the years, documented in the recorded decisions handed down by the courts, has established binding legal rules. Long before there was the amount of legislation that there is today, most areas of legal uncertainty were policed by the courts. With each decision, a little more certainty was created and that decision became a precedent for later decisions. This system of common law precedent continues today: if a case comes before a court, the court can look back to any earlier decisions concerning similar facts and circumstances and it will be guided by those decisions if it is appropriate to do so. These common law rules represent the way in which the courts have viewed society's disputes over the years and their attempts to solve them have become a source of legal inspiration and certainty.

In general, if a decision has previously been made by a higher court, then a lower court must follow the earlier decision, or precedent, of the higher court. Courts can depart from earlier precedent if a decision they are considering is different in an important way from the previous decision or if to follow the previous decision would be unreasonable or unjust.[2] For example, if a District Court is faced with a case very similar to one which the Supreme Court[3] has previously decided, it would be a brave District Justice indeed who ploughed the lonely furrow of disagreeing with the Supreme Court's precedent unless there were exceptional circumstances that justified her doing so.

The common law system, the second and broader definition of the term, refers to the way in which this judge-made, precedent-based law exists alongside written legislation and, with it, forms the overarching system of legal rule called 'common law'. The decisions of courts continue to form a set of legal rules, but only when the decision involves an area of the law not covered by legislation or involves an area of legislation that is unclear and requires clarification by the courts.

Example 1

There are very few statute laws on negligence in Ireland. Accordingly, it has fallen to the courts to decide the common law rules on what constitutes negligence.[4] If the government were to introduce a law that defined negligence, then that new law would replace the decisions of the courts, but the courts would still have a role in interpreting the legislation. An example encountered in this text[5] was the Statute of Limitations, which restricts the time within which a legal action may be brought. While the courts are bound by the Statute of Limitations, in a common law system they also have the responsibility of clearing up ambiguities. We saw the example of the courts being asked to consider precisely when, for the purposes of the Statute of Limitations, a patient had 'discovered' the negligence of a practitioner.[6]

In practical terms a common law system means that the courts and the elected lawmakers operate side by side to administer law – the government makes the law and the courts interpret it in the light of the facts of cases before it. Where there is no government-made law, the courts apply the 'common law' body of decisions made by previous courts. One judge has referred to the common law system as 'common sense under a wig'.

There is one especially useful consequence of the fact that common law systems exist in different countries and it is a benefit that is encountered throughout this text. Common law countries tend to share similar written laws and traditions of legal decisions, and their courts tend to interpret those written laws and earlier decisions in a manner with which a court in Ireland can identify. Many enlightened decisions in various areas of law have been made first in one jurisdiction before spreading, sometimes unchanged, sometimes modified, to some or all other common law countries. If an issue is being tried before an Irish court and no Irish law, government- or judge-made, has ever even considered the matter, the Court may look to similar decisions made in other common law jurisdictions (such as England or Australia) and be informed, persuaded or guided by such decisions. A practical consequence for readers of this book is that they will often find references to cases decided in other countries. These cases are not always indicative of the law in Ireland but they often point to the way that the such cases might be decided in Ireland or to an alternative point of view that an Irish court might or should consider when deciding a particular issue.

The civil law system

[A.04]

A contrasting system used in many of our European neighbours is called 'civil law' (which should not be confused with the more restrictive 'civil law' that simply refers to private legal disputes – see section **[A.09]**). Civil law means, at the risk of gross over-simplification, writing a legal code of rules so compendious that it hopes to deal with every eventuality that may arise in the field of human intercourse. Judges then apply this formal and hopefully exhaustive set of rules to any dispute that comes before them. In essence then, unlike common law, which takes its inspiration both from written legislation or the decisions of the courts or both together, civil law has only one principal source, namely the written code. Previous decisions made by similar courts in similar circumstances are sometimes used in the civil law systems of nations such as France and Germany, but to a far smaller degree than in the common law world.

Quick Reference Guide A.1

The common law system

- Common law legal systems involve a combination of two elements.
  - (i) The first is the 'common law' itself – the body of decisions made by courts and forming precedents on which later courts can base their decisions when faced with similar facts and circumstances
  - (ii) The second element is the existence of a legislature that can introduce statute laws alongside the common law courts. In areas of human life where there are no statute laws, the courts continue to base their decisions on the common law, but where there are statute laws, the courts' role changes to one of application and interpretation of those laws
- Most countries that were hosts to English influence during their history have common law systems, including the USA, Canada and Australia.
- Decisions made in the courts of other common law countries can sometimes be helpful to courts in Ireland when they are considering matters that have not previously come before Irish courts but that have been decided in other common law countries.

THE MECHANISMS OF LAW

[A.05]

The law of any land, whether a common law country like Ireland or a civil law nation such as the Netherlands, has a number of engines that are involved in creating, understanding and applying the law. In Ireland there are a number of layers to this process of law creation and application. Fundamental is the Constitution, the set of rules with which all other laws and all legal conduct must conform. The Constitution is the basic charter of the State and any rule or law that conflicts with it is not valid. Within the constraints of the Constitution, the courts and the legislature then operate side-by-side to make or interpret law as appropriate. Above the national level, European commitments mean that rules can be made for Ireland in Brussels that have the force of law throughout Ireland. Irish law-makers and Irish courts are subservient to and bound by the decisions made by the courts and law-makers of the European Union. We look at each of these elements in turn.

The Constitution

[A.06]

In a manner of speaking the Constitution is a blueprint for the running of the Irish State and a working knowledge of the Constitution goes a long way towards outlining how Ireland operates in the legal sense. The Constitution is the supreme benchmark for Irish law, so that if a law or activity is unconstitutional it is not valid. Only the two highest courts in the land – the High Court and Supreme Court – can take decisions regarding the Constitution including deciding whether a particular activity or law is unconstitutional or determining the meaning of a particular section of the Constitution. No person or is immune from the provisions of the Constitution and that includes the courts and the State itself.

The first Irish Constitution was born when the State became independent in 1922, but in 1937 a newer Constitution of Ireland, Bunreacht na hÉireann, was introduced and it continues in force to this day. The Constitution lays down the manner in which the country is to be run, delineating and delimiting the structures and role of government, the manner in which elections are to be carried out, as well as the roles of judges and the President. There are certain aspects of the Constitution that, as can be seen from this book, directly relate to the application of law to clinical practice. The Constitution also both explicitly and tacitly circumscribes the rights of the individual citizen and by extension therefore, it also limits the degree to which any individual may impinge upon another's rights.

Any law that is enacted by the Oireachtas must be compatible with the Constitution. Before the President signs an Act of Parliament (which is a necessary precursor to it becoming law) she has the option to refer it to the Supreme Court who can assess its constitutionality. Thus, the Regulation of Information (Services Outside the State for termination of Pregnancies) Bill 1995 (see section **[12.05]**) was referred and found to be constitutional by the Supreme Court, while the Matrimonial Home Bill 1993 was found to be repugnant to the Constitution because it violated the right to private property contained in the Constitution. If only one part of a law is unconstitutional then in certain circumstances, only that unconstitutional part may be removed or set aside and the rest of the law permitted, as long as the severance of the offending portion does not make a nonsense of the law.

The right to liberty – an express right

As we have mentioned, the Constitution guarantees to the citizen a number of rights, some expressly, some tacitly. The right to liberty in one example of an expressly guaranteed right: the Constitution adverts to the fact that 'No citizen shall be deprived of his personal liberty save in accordance with the law'.[7] This in turn automatically trammels the right, to take a clinical example, of a doctor to compulsorily detain an individual who has a psychiatric disorder unless she has followed a protocol laid down by law.[8]

Autonomy and the right to life – implied or 'unenumerated' rights

Furthermore, the courts over the years have recognised other rights that although not explicit in the Constitution can be inferred from the guarantee contained therein that the State will 'respect and, as far as practicable, by its laws defend and vindicate the personal rights of the citizen'.[9] Using this guarantee, the courts have 'found' rights in the Constitution that are not expressly listed in it: these are often known as the unenumerated rights.

Unenumerated rights of the citizen that the courts have recognised and which have repercussions for clinical practice include:

- the right to bodily integrity;[10]
- the right to privacy.;[11]
- the rights of the child;[12]
- the right to travel out of the State;[13]
- the idea that the right to life includes a correlative right to die;[14]

None of these constitutional rights is absolute: they exist, to use the words of the Constitution itself, 'as far as is practicable' and where necessary one right may need to be limited in order to protect another more important right. In the case of abortion for example, the right to travel out of the State for an abortion is limited, in the interests of the right to life of the unborn,[15] to those circumstances in which the mother's life is threatened by the pregnancy (including the possibility of suicide) .[16]

Separation of powers

Another aspect of the Constitution that is of particular importance to the practitioner is the separation of powers doctrine, which means that powers are distributed to the various organs of State and only those organs given a power under the Constitution may exercise that power. Accordingly, only the government (meaning the Cabinet) should run the country, only the legislature (meaning the Oireachtas) should make laws and only the courts should administer justice. One consequence of this is that only a judge may determine those legal matters that have far-reaching, rather than purely administrative, consequences for the citizen. This is the principal reason why a decision of the Medical Council (or any similar disciplinary body with such powers) to suspend or strike off a medical practitioner for serious professional misconduct must be ratified by the High Court before it can take effect. To do otherwise would be to make the Medical Council the judge – the Medical Council therefore may hear a fitness to practise case and make a recommendation but only a judge may rule on the validity of any decision they make that affects the individual doctor's career.[17]

Changing and challenging the Constitution

The Constitution is not a testament written in stone. It can be amended and has been on a great number of occasions. Of particular relevance to medical practice is the 14th Amendment, which in 1982 inserted Article 40.3.3° ostensibly, but not actually, as matters transpired,[18] to enshrine the right to life of the unborn child.

No authority but the people of Ireland can amend the Constitution. The government is expressly prohibited by the terms of the Constitution itself from amending the Constitution without a popular vote. Amendments to the Constitution are approved or rejected by referendum in which all Irish citizens over the age of 18 are entitled to vote.[19]

An individual or institution may approach the High Court and ask it to decide whether a particular decision or purported act is unconstitutional. This process is usually called judicial review and will often concern the decision of a public body, which include the Medical Council, governments department and most of the universities[20] (although not the Royal College of Surgeons in Ireland.[21])

Quick Reference GuideA.2

The Constitution

- The Constitution is a blueprint for the operation of the Irish State. The present Constitution dates from 1937.
- Any law or conduct that is incompatible with the Constitution will be struck down by the courts. The President can refer any new Bill (the precursor to an Act of the Oireachtas) to the Supreme Court so that the court can gauge its constitutionality.
- The Constitution guarantees a number of rights to citizens. Some are explicitly expressed in the Constitution, while others have been implied by the courts – the 'unenumerated' rights.
- The Constitution separates powers and gives them to different bodies: only judges may decide the law, only the legislature may make the law and only the government may run the country.
- The Constitution can be changed by referendum and any law or act can be challenged regarding its constitutionality by means of judicial review.

The Legislature

[A.07]

The legislature is the Oireachtas, the collective term for the Dáil and the Seanad combined. It is the Oireachtas that generates the majority of legislation that has the force of law in Ireland.[22] Legislation, or statute law, is essentially written law produced by a law-making body. Article 15 of the Constitution lays down the rule that only the Oireachtas may make laws, which are called Acts of the Oireachtas or 'primary legislation'. Laws that were enacted by the English Parliament for Ireland prior to independence in 1922 remain in force as long as they have not been expressly repealed or supplanted by a more modern law that achieves the same end.

Legislation also includes rules made by Ministers as a result of previous Acts of the Oireachtas. An Act will often bestow a power on a relevant Minister to take further decisions that are in keeping with the original act. The Misuse of Drugs Act 1977 gives the Minister for Health the power to amend the lists of various controlled drugs, a power that has been exercised on a number of occasions.[23] The creation of secondary legislation is the mechanism by which many European Union rules come to be included in Irish laws. These secondary rules are generally called Statutory Instruments (SI).

Legislation essentially tries to reduce rules of conduct to a fixed and written formula, and typically those rules are stated as precisely as possible. A Statute comes into being through a stepwise process involving both houses of the Oireachtas and the President. A Bill is drawn up, containing the legislation that it is intended to enact. In theory, any Senator or TD can introduce such a bill, but in practice for the bulk of new legislation, it tends to be the Minister for the Department that oversees the area for which the legislation is being introduced. The fact of an Act being passed does not automatically mean that the new Act immediately becomes law. Many Acts will contain a provision that the Act is to come into force on a day appointed by the relevant Minister. The Medical Practitioners (Amendment) Act 2002 (see section **[2.06]**) is an example of a law containing such a provision.

A Bill generally goes through five stages, although there are exceptions.

Figure A.1 – The stages by which a Bill becomes an Act

- First Stage: permission is sought from the House to circulate the Bill, drafted in outline form.
- Second Stage: a debate on the generality of the Bill in which its principal provisions are outlined. At this stage the Bill may be voted down but if it is not, matters progress towards the Bill becoming an Act of Parliament.
- Third Stage: also called the 'Committee Stage'. Once a Bill has reached this stage, it can no longer be voted down in its entirety and the debate turns to the individual sections of the Bill. The debate is often conducted, not by the whole house, but by a special committee - consisting of members of both Dáil and Seanad in proportion to their parties' strength in the Oireachtas.
- Fourth Stage: the report of the progress made in the Committee Stage, when amendments recommended by the Committee may be inserted into the legislation.
- Fifth Stage: essentially a formality that results in the final form of the Bill.

Once the Bill is passed by a vote of both Houses,[24] it is signed by the President, at which point it becomes an Act of the Oireachtas. The fact of the President having signed the Bill is published in *Iris Oifigiúil* (the Official Gazette of the Government). Before signing the bill, the President may, as previously mentioned, use one of the few powers she is given under the Constitution[25] and send a Bill for scrutiny by the Supreme Court in order that they can assess whether the new Bill is constitutional.

An Act when published will have short title by which it will tend to be colloquially known, such as 'The Misuse of Drugs Act 1977' but it also has a long title (which, in the case of the Misuse of Drugs Act, ran to total of 98 words). The long title will tend to set out the broad parameters of the Act and draw attention to any other Acts that the new Act is repealing or amending.

The Courts

[A.08]

The courts oversee the administration of Irish Justice and arbitrate nearly all legal disputes in the State, especially those involving civil or criminal matters and the interpretation of legislation or the Constitution. Indeed, according to the Constitution, the courts are the only body empowered to make judicial determinations between parties that have legal differences, although in certain circumstances other bodies may do so. Broadly speaking there are two types of legal case: criminal and civil. In general this book is concerned with civil legal cases, but it is important to understand the difference between the civil and legal systems.

Criminal and civil law

[A.09]

The phrase 'civil law' has a meaning in Ireland other than that imported by an exhaustive code of written law such as characterises the legal systems of countries such as France or Germany (see section **[A.04]**). Instead in Ireland, the phrase is also used as an antithesis to 'criminal law', although the division between the two is not always a clear one.

Criminal law is largely concerned with the rules laid down by society for the good of society as a whole. If these rules are broken then society as a whole, represented in Ireland by the Director of Public Prosecutions, initiates criminal proceedings against the person accused of breaking the law. Murder, theft and drunk-driving would all constitute examples of criminal offences.

Civil law is largely concerned with private disputes, whether between individuals or between companies or between companies and individuals. Claims for accidents in the workplace, legal action against a practitioner for negligence and divorce proceedings are all examples of civil legal actions.

The key distinction between criminal and civil legal proceedings, and the principal reason for the difference between them, lies in the consequences. A civil claim is usually for damages or for an injunction.[26] A successful criminal prosecution will often result in a fine (paid to the State) or, more importantly, a term of imprisonment.

Because the consequence of a criminal conviction can potentially be more serious, the 'burden of proof' – the degree to which the person making the allegation has to prove that allegation – is far greater in a criminal case. In a criminal case, the charge, eg that X murdered Y, must be proved 'beyond all reasonable doubt'. In a civil case the argument, eg that X pulled out in front of Y's car without indicating, must be made out 'on the balance of probabilities'. The phrase 'beyond reasonable doubt' is one that many judges have had difficulty defining, but can be said to mean that the jury[27] must have no substantial worries that its decision to convict an accused person is the wrong one. On the other hand, the 'balance of probabilities' merely means 'more likely than not'. If it were the case that criminal cases were decided only on the balance of probabilities, the legal system would run the risk of jailing many innocent people and therefore, even at the risk of seeing some guilty people, whose guilt cannot be proved beyond reasonable doubt, go free, the higher standard is imposed in all criminal cases.

The fact that the fine or term of imprisonment is 'given' to the State rather than to the person affected by the criminal act is another distinction between criminal and civil matters. If a person wins damages in a civil case, then that person will generally receive the damages.

Example 1

A good example of how the different burdens of proof, and indeed the different consequences of civil and criminal law, operate was provided by the protracted saga of O J Simpson's prosecution for the murder of his ex-wife Nicole Brown Simpson and her friend Ron Goldman. In a criminal court, he was acquitted of murder: the jury found that he had not been proved guilty beyond all reasonable doubt. However, the families of the victims subsequently brought a private civil case against Simpson. Again there was a jury but in this case but because it was a civil case they had only to consider whether the case was proven on the balance of probabilities. Simpson was found guilty of 'willingly and wrongfully' causing the two deaths. Again, because it was a civil case he could not be jailed, but he was ordered to pay $33 million to the families of the victims.

It is worth noting as well that a single wrongdoing can have both criminal and civil consequences. The two elements, criminal and civil, will be the subject of separate trials and each will be governed by the rules applicable to each. This might mean for example that arising out of the same crash, a person might be accused of negligence for having struck another person's car (judged on the balance of probabilities) and of drunk-driving (judged on the basis of beyond reasonable doubt).

The hierarchy of the courts

[A.10]

Irish courts are hierarchical in nature. Aside from the obvious differences in authority that accompany ascension through the hierarchy, there are some practical differences. One key difference is the power, or jurisdiction, of each court in question. On the criminal side, the cases a court can hear are limited by the jurisdiction of the court: the District Court may generally (there are some exceptions) only hear minor, or summary, cases, while other more serious cases must be heard in the Central[28] or Special[29] Criminal Courts.

Figure A.2 – The hierarchy of the Irish courts (highest first)

Civil	*Criminal*
Supreme Court	Supreme Court
High Court	Court of Criminal Appeal
Circuit Court	Central Criminal Court (or Special Criminal Court for certain offences)
District Court	Circuit Court
	District Court

On the civil side, each court has an upper limit to its 'monetary jurisdiction' which means that there is a limit to either the amount of damages the court may award at the end of a case, or the maximum value of any goods or contract that can form the subject matter of the case the court is hearing. In essence, the higher the court, the greater is its monetary jurisdiction.

Figure A.3 – Monetary jurisdiction of the civil courts

District Court	maximum **€20,000**
The Circuit Court	maximum **€100,000**
High Court	minimum of **€100,000** – no upper limit

Accordingly, if a person were to sustain minor cuts and bruises following a trip and fall in a supermarket and chose to pursue legal action, the District Court would be the most likely port-of-call. If on the other hand, catastrophic injuries resulted from a road traffic accident, then the High Court would almost certainly be the forum. There is no upper limit to the amount of damages that the High Court can award.

The Supreme Court does not feature in the Figure concerned with monetary jurisdiction and that is because it exists solely to resolve issues that remain unresolved by the lower courts and to hear appeals from decisions of the High Court. Generally, each court can hear appeals from the court or courts below it. If a case involves the Constitution, it may only be heard in the High Court or the Supreme Court.

Note that any decision of the High Court or of the Supreme Court on almost any matter relating to European law may be appealed to the European Courts of Justice and any decision of the European Court of Justice is binding on the Irish Courts. Cases concerning human rights may also be brought on appeal to the European Court of Human Rights, the decisions of which, while not binding on the Irish government do tend to have some influence in shaping the judicial and legislative response to human rights issues.[30]

On the criminal side, the hierarchy of the courts is slightly different. A criminal case is first heard in the District Court where it is either decided by a judge sitting without a jury or sent forward for hearing to whichever more senior court is appropriate for the crime in question. A person who is accused of a criminal offence may be entitled to bail, allowing him or her to remain free until the trial takes place, but the courts have considerable powers to refuse bail when it is possible that a person might commit further crimes while on bail. An appeal against a criminal verdict from the District Court is taken to the Circuit Court, while an appeal from the decision of any other court may be taken to the Court of Criminal Appeal and may rarely proceed to the Supreme Court.

Separate to the criminal and civil courts, there is one other court although it may not always be intuitively recognised as such. The Coroner's Court has an important role to play in exploring the causes of certain types of death and has many powers similar to a conventional court.[31] There are some other bodies that have powers similar to the courts, including the Fitness to Practise Committee of the Medical Council, which has some powers similar to the High Court. As a logical corollary of the powers of the coroner's court and disciplinary bodies such as the Medical Council, any person appearing before it is entitled to legal representation and to expect that proper and fair legal procedure is followed.[32] Any decision made by the Medical Council to suspend or to strike off a doctor must be ratified by the High Court. Bodies such as the Medical Council and other similar disciplinary or regulatory bodies are sometimes called 'quasi-judicial' tribunals.

Damages – special and general

[A.11]

'Damages' are commonly awarded by the civil courts following a legal action and they do not refer to the harm or damage done, but to the money that is to be paid out, usually by the wrongdoer, in compensation for any harm caused. If a person is hurt in an accident to an extent that he is unable ever to work again, the court may award him damages equal to his projected loss of income over the rest of his working life. Damages may be very extensive, depending on the consequences of the mishap in question.

Damages are payable once the plaintiff has established that a wrong has been committed against him or her. The underlying principle of damages is that the compensation attempts to leave the plaintiff no worse off than if the wrong had not been committed in the first place.[33] But this is not a universally simple demand. In some cases, compensation may be easy: if X destroys Y's unoccupied car, then the damage can be rectified by X replacing Y's car. However, consider an alternative scenario: if a negligently performed operation leaves a patient with lifelong, irremediable pain, how might that be adequately compensated?

Accordingly damages are multifaceted and apportioned to compensate for different forms of loss. There are 'special' damages and 'general' damages. Special damages compensate for concrete losses that can be quantified precisely, such as loss of earnings (past, present and future) and medical expenses. General damages are more flexible and include compensation for pain and suffering, for 'loss of amenities' (eg, the loss of the use of an eye or a limb) and for reduction in life expectancy. Payments tend to be made on a once-off lump sum basis, but may sometimes be payable in instalments. It is often general damages that constitute the bulk of damages awarded by the courts.

Quick Reference Guide A.3

Damages

- Damages awarded by a court as compensation at the end of a legal case can be 'special' or 'general'.
- Special damages are generally for concrete and measurable expenses such as loss of income.
- General damages are an attempt to compensate for pain and suffering.

The legal profession

[A.12]

Judge, solicitors and barristers are the legal personnel of most concern to the clinician. Some commentators in the arena of legal medicine liken the division between barrister and solicitor to that between general practitioner and specialist among the physicians. It is a useful metaphor, but should not be taken too far. In the first instance, general practitioners and consultants regard themselves as belonging to the same profession, that of medicine, and bound by the same regulatory body, the Medical Council. Secondly, at any stage in a doctor's training she may elide from one speciality into another with far greater ease than a barrister may become a solicitor or vice versa.

In the legal profession, unlike medicine, there are two different, if superficially similar, professions with separate regulatory bodies and a measure of inter-professional rivalry and, while those differences can be both underestimated and overstated by turns, they are nonetheless important and jealously guarded.

Solicitors

Solicitors are very often a person's first contact with the law. If a member of the public has a legal query, the first person they must generally approach is a solicitor: a barrister cannot receive legal instructions from a member of the public, only from a solicitor. This is one probable source of the general practitioner/specialist analogy with medicine, but again it is a limited comparison. If a person has a sick child, there is no obstacle to prevent him bringing that child to a paediatric accident and emergency unit, where he or she will often be tended to by a doctor trained or training in that speciality, possibly even a consultant. There is generally no avenue for similarly circumventing the interface between solicitor and general public, although some very few exceptions do exist to allow direct access to barristers.

Some areas of law are to all intents and purposes the sole province of a solicitor, such as the uncomplicated sale of a house (conveyancing) or the drawing up of wills. A solicitor may represent her clients in court, although this is a more common occurrence in more minor offences tried before lower courts. The profession is regulated by a body known as the Law Society of Ireland, which also oversees legal training for student solicitors and which was brought into being by a number of laws.[34] It is in many ways similar to the Medical Council.

After completing a degree or diploma in law, students sit a series of exams, which if successfully negotiated, permit them entry into the professional training course for solicitors at Blackhall Place in Dublin. During their training, aspirant solicitors must also serve an apprenticeship to an established solicitor. Unlike barristers, solicitors are permitted to advertise. Like barristers, solicitors may be in general practice or specialise in certain areas, such as company law.

Barristers

The barristers' professional environment is sometimes collectively known as 'the Bar'. All Barristers are required to be members of the Law Library in the Four Courts in Dublin and have a degree or diploma in Law coupled with two years' study at the Honourable Society of King's Inns in Dublin. After completing the King's Inns degree of Barrister-at-Law, the would-be barrister must also serve an apprentice year (called 'devilling') to a more experienced 'master' after which he or she is free to set up in independent practice.

There is no formal legislation governing the Bar, but a body called the Bar Council, which is elected by and from among the members of the Law Library and has responsibility for regulation of the profession. While most barristers practise in Dublin, some work in other areas of the country ('on circuit'), while others are based in chambers in Cork. A barrister's work generally comes from being 'briefed' by a solicitor to act for a client. This briefing will not always result in a court appearance. The barrister's role may be solely to advise in writing on a legal point or even to caution against proceeding to court action at all. There are two tiers of barristers, junior and senior counsel, the latter also known as the 'inner bar' or 'silks' and denoted by the letters SC after their names. Whether senior or junior counsel, much of a barrister's work may not involve spellbinding oratory or advocacy (pleading a case) and in particular for junior counsel, much of her work may involve drafting pleadings and other paperwork or conducting more routine administrative court proceedings. The Senior Counsel is perhaps the individual more likely to do high-profile courtroom work, especially in more complex cases.

Judges

Judges are chosen from the ranks of solicitors and barristers (although some may come from academia, they will have also qualified as a solicitor or barrister). According to the Constitution, the President appoints judges to the Bench, but elsewhere in the Constitution it is also stated that the President will act 'only on the advice of the Government' (meaning the Cabinet). In reality, appointments to the 'Bench' were for a long time the effective gift of the Cabinet of the day. For many years, there were allegations of political 'grace and favour' associated with judicial appointments. In part to counter this, the Judicial Appointments Advisory Board, comprising a mixture of legal and lay individuals, was established in 1995 with the task of preparing lists of candidates for the Bench and bringing more transparency to the appointment of judges.

Any solicitor or barrister who has been in practice for up to ten years may be appointed a Judge of the District or Circuit Court. In turn, increasing seniority as a judge, coupled with the requisite experience as a solicitor or barrister, qualifies a judge for appointment to the High and Supreme Courts, although some judges are appointed directly to the higher courts without serving in the lower courts. Judges serve in office until they are anything between 65 and 72, the age depending on the date of their appointment and the court in which they serve. Supreme and High Court judges retire when they are 72. A judge may only be removed from office, according to the Constitution, 'for stated misbehaviour or incapacity'[35] in which case, a resolution calling for that removal must be passed by both the Dáil and Seanad.

A judge's job is often described as 'finding' the law. If the application of a particular written piece of legislation is at issue, the judge will interpret the legislation. If the matter concerns a legal dispute, he or she will, in accordance with the principles of common law already outlined, be guided by the weight of decisions taken by previous courts in similar circumstances, by the arguments of barristers and by the evidence of witnesses. If a jury is involved in case, the judge's job is to make sure that the trial is conducted fairly and to use her experience and knowledge of the law to guide the jury before it retires to reach its verdict.

Europe

[A.13]

Since Ireland's accession to the European Economic Community in January 1973, the influence of Europe on Irish law has been immense. The reality is that European Union membership necessitates and imposes a legal order that has its source outside the State: an imposition that is manifestly necessary when one considers the aims of the EU – fostering closer political and economic relationships, while also creating an open economic environment by assuring as far as possible the free movement of goods, workers, capital and services.

In terms of institutions, four principal organs constitute the EU: the Commission, the European Parliament, the Court of Justice and the Council of Ministers.

The European Commission

The Commission has hitherto comprised nominees from each of the member states, but as the European Union enlarges, it seems likely that nations will hold Commissionerships only on a rotating basis. Each Commissioner has a specific policy area of responsibility, operating under the direction of the President of the Commission. The Commission as a whole works to produce a legislative programme for the EU. Traditionally the Commission's power was huge and it was in effect the paramount law-making body in the EU, but more recent treaties (including the Treaty of Amsterdam) have reined in its powers somewhat, compelling it to cooperate and collaborate more with the Parliament and the Council of Ministers. The Commission is sometimes referred to as the 'guardian of the Treaty'. If a member state steps out of line vis-à-vis its Treaty obligations, it is the Commission that will normally institute legal proceedings against the errant State.

The Council of Ministers

The Council represents the governments of the member states. At each meeting a Minister with responsibility for the policy area under discussion and authorised to take decisions on behalf of her government, attends on behalf of each member state. There are different Councils dealing with each area of Community policy: a Council of Health Ministers oversees health discussions, Finance Ministers (ECOFIN) discuss fiscal affairs and so forth. The Council of Ministers takes decisions on the basis of a complex voting system that reflect the population and influence of each member state.

The European Parliament

The Parliament is directly elected by the people of Europe and each country has a number of MEPs (Members of the European Parliament) approximately relative to its population, although this arrangement is somewhat skewed in favour of the smaller nations. Within the parliament, members tend to ally themselves first along national party lines and then along lines of broadly shared political philosophy, so that the Irish Labour Party is aligned with other Leftist parties and Fine Gael with the Christian Democrats. The Parliament has seen an incremental growth in its power in the last generation or so, to the extent where it may now successfully object to legislation without fear of simply being overruled by a vote of the Council or Commission.

The European Court of Justice

The European Court of Justice (ECJ) hears all cases that concern alleged violations of the various European treaties (now consolidated into one document by the Treaty of Amsterdam). If a person or another body, such as the European Commission alleges that country is violating its obligations under the treaty, then he may bring an action at first in the courts of that country or in the ECJ. Any decision made by the ECJ is binding on all member states and on the courts in the member states

The effect of EU membership

EU membership is important to Ireland's laws for a number of reasons. The most significant is that it creates a whole new legal order and limits Irish sovereignty inasmuch as Irish courts and law-makers are bound by the provisions of European law and by the decisions of the European Court of Justice. Ireland cannot enact laws, which are contrary to the provisions of the European treaties, without attempted legal retribution from the European Commission.

We have noted above that the Irish Constitution states that only the Oireachtas may exercise law-making powers,[36] so how is European Union membership compatible with that statement? The short answer is that in order to contemplate membership of the EEC, there needed to be a referendum in 1972 on a Constitutional amendment to bring the demands of the Irish Constitution and the prospective demands of EEC membership into harmony. The section of the Constitution that was originally amended, and has been amended repeatedly to take account of the ever-expanding reach and nature of the European project, is Article 29. The Irish courts have conceded that, in signing up to the European treaties, Ireland was 'signing up to a moving train' and as part of the journey, it has proved necessary to go to the country repeatedly to seek approval of European treaties.

EU law-making

Laws from Europe have a number of forms. Obviously, the various treaties themselves are binding and must be obeyed by signatories to the treaties, but in order to further the aims of the treaties, the institutions of the EU have a number of legislative weapons in their armoury: regulations, directives and decisions:

Figure A.7 – How the EU makes laws

Regulation:	A regulation is a rule made by the EU that is applicable to all member states without any further ado. It becomes binding as soon as it is introduced, without any need for the government of that member state to introduce any new legislation. There are thousands of new regulations introduced each year.[37]
Directive:	A directive is a rule made by the EU that is applicable to all member states, but which leaves to the government of the member states the question of precisely how that directive is implemented, so long as it is done within a certain time-frame. Usually, this will necessitate the introduction of new legislation and/or the amendment of existing legislation to achieve the end sought by the Commission or Council. Failure to enact the directive will result in the Commission taking legal action against the recalcitrant member state.

Decision:	A decision is normally directed at one particular member state or one particular dispute. It is binding on those concerned in the dispute. For example, in 1993 the Irish government sought to provide Aer Lingus with a cash injection. This could only be done after Commission approval was sought in the form of a Decision.

European rules have 'direct effect' on Irish law. What this means is that once a law is made in Europe, it becomes effectively the law of Ireland.[38] While there may be various administrative requirements necessary to formally integrate the EU rules into Irish law, it is nonetheless true that any Irish citizen may generally rely on the new directive or regulation as directly applicable from the moment of its adoption by the EU.

There are few areas of Irish life upon which European law has not impinged. One clear example is the workplace: as an essentially economic entity, the EU is intimately concerned with satisfactorily regulating the means, methods and conduits of economic productivity. Similarly rules on safety in the workplace, rules of labour law, the international recognition of qualifications and the free flow of information are all examples of EU legislative concerns. Some areas of domestic Irish law, relating primarily to property or family, are comparatively only barely touched upon by European Law, but as legislation and philosophy of a increasingly social nature emanates from the European Union and its lawmaking bodies, this is a situation that seems likely to change.

Human rights in Irish law

[A.14]

The Irish Constitution recognises – as we have seen (para **[A.06]**) – a large number of human rights. However, Ireland is also a signatory of the European Convention of Human Rights, a document produced by the Council of Europe, which is a pan-European organisation with the aims of promoting human rights, pluralism and democracy in Europe. The Council of Europe, although distinct from the EU, has had a particular effect on the latter organisation in terms of shaping EU policy on human rights. The European Convention on Human Rights is relevant to Ireland in two ways:

- A corollary of the Convention was the creation of the European Court of Human Rights, by the decisions of which Ireland is bound. A person who feels that his rights (under the Convention) have been curtailed can bring a case before the Court for determination. If the Court finds against Ireland, then the Irish Government is bound to bring its laws or policies into line with the Court's findings.
- The Convention of Human Rights itself is due to be incorporated into Irish Law. The European Convention on Human Rights Bill, when passed into law, will allow the European Convention on Human Rights to be cited as law in Irish courts. The only stricture on the use of the Convention that where the Convention and the Constitution are in conflict, the Constitution will prevail.

The rights guaranteed by the European Convention are extensive and we encounter many of them in this text, including the right to the review of detention in the context of involuntary psychiatric admission (see **[11.08]** and the right to privacy in the context of confidentiality (see **[3.14]**). As with all rights, the rights guaranteed by the Convention are not absolute and any individual right may be constrained by the need to respect other rights or by the need to maintain the security or stability of the state.

THREE IMPORTANT SUBSETS OF LAW

[A.15]

In the course of legal education, students are taught law, not as a generic mass of principles, statutes and rulings but according to certain divisions, most of which are logical, some of which are more time-honoured and traditional. Three main areas of law encountered in this book are worth examining in a little more detail here. All are civil rather than criminal areas of law and are generally decided according to common law principle or in other words, by reference to how courts have decided similar cases in the past.

Tort

Tort is an area of law that recognises the general rights of individuals (or indeed of companies) and helps the individual or company protect those rights as far as possible with appropriate remedies such as damages. If a person is walking down the street, he has the right generally not to be accosted or molested by another individual. If he is, then he can bring a case against that person under the tort (which essentially comes from a French word for 'wrong') of battery or trespass against the person who hits him. Similarly, and of more relevance to this text, a person has, if he undergoes a surgical procedure, the general right to have the operation performed carefully. If the operation is negligently botched then the patient might bring an action against the surgeon for negligence.

Important torts include negligence,[39] defamation (libel and slander), trespass and liability for defective products.

Contract

The law of contract is almost self-explanatory. There are three elements to a valid contract:

— an offer,

— an acceptance,

— consideration.

'Consideration' is the legal term for something that transfers from one party to another to cement the contract, in general that means money, such as a payment of some kind, but it can take other forms.[40] If a nurse is offered a job and she accepts that job and the employer agrees to pay the nurse for taking the job, there is a valid contract of employment.

A contract can be written or oral and can be open-ended or for a fixed period. The employment contracts of most junior doctor would be for a fixed length of time, at the end of which the contract expires and the employment ends. A contract will generally contain 'terms' or conditions that attach to a contract and must be satisfied if the contract is to be valid. A term may be expressed in the contract or it may be implied. There is an implied term in every contract that any salary agreed in the contract will be paid – if they are not, then the contract fails. Some contractual terms can outlive the contract. Some employment contracts contain terms to the effect that after the employee leaves her job, she will not set up in competition within a certain area close to the location of her current employer for a certain length of time.[41] Such 'restrictive covenants' are valid only if the restriction they place on the employee is not too great.

Equity

Equity is a 'supplementary' form of law that is interested in ensuring fairness in the outcome of the legal process. It exists alongside the law of tort and has much in common with contract law, for example equity will often operate to force a person to honour a contract that he is attempting to avoid. Where the law does not formally protect a person's rights and a serious injustice would result from not protecting those rights, equity will typically step into the breach. The key element is fairness: equity tries to promote fairness and prevent unfairness in human legal relations. Common equitable approaches to the law include:

Injunctions:	preventing a person from doing or continuing to do something.
Specific performance:	forcing a person to do something he signed a contract to do and started to do, but is now trying to get out of.
Estoppel:	preventing someone from trying to get out of a promise made to another person where it would be unfair to allow him to escape the promise.
Undue influence:	allowing someone to escape from a contract or promise made because he came under 'undue (or excessive) influence' to enter into the contract or promise.

Endnotes

1 For a more through review, see Byrne and McCutcheon *The Irish Legal System* (4th edn, 2001).

2 In ch 7, we encountered the decision in *Donoghue v Stevenson* [1932] AC 562. The case revolutionised the law of negligence because one of the judges was prepared to depart from the precedents that said that negligence could not exist where there was not a contract.

3 See the discussion on the courts at section **[A.08]**.

4 Those rules are discussed in ch 7.

5 Also in ch 7 (section **[7.21]**). Another example of the relationship between courts and legislation is the right of patients to access their notes (see ch 6). For many years there was no legislation governing this and it was the courts that decided whether patients had such a right. With the introduction of Data Protection legislation, the decision was taken out of the hands of the courts and put on a statutory footing. The role of the courts is now one of interpreting difficult or ambiguous provisions of the legislation or deciding on the Act's applicability in certain situations.

6 See *Maitland v Swan and Sligo County Council* (6 April 1992, unreported) HC. A surgeon removed a woman's ovary in 1969. In 1971, she learned of the removal. In 1983, she learned that her left ovary was abnormal and that she was infertile. There was no question but that the Statute of Limitations applied in this case, but there was a question of when the Statute had begun to operate. In that case the judge decided that the 'harm' arose when the woman discovered that her remaining ovary was abnormal, not when the original ovary was removed. See ch 7, under 'Defending an allegation of negligence'.

7 Article 40.4.1°. Other express rights include the right to a fair trial (Article 38.1), the right to own property (Article 43) and the right to express ones opinion, subject to public order and morality (Article 40.6).

8 The legal safeguards in place for the involuntary detention of those with psychiatric conditions are dealt with in ch 11.

9 Article 40.3.1°.

10 *Ryan v Attorney General* [1965] IR 294; See also ch 4, which deals with consent.

11 *Kennedy v Ireland* [1987] IR 587.

12 See *G v An Bord Uchtála* [1980] IR 32 and *PW v AW* (21 April 1980, unreported) HC for contrasting views of the rights of the child within a family. See also ch 4 (under 'Consent and minors') and ch 8.

13 *The State (M) v Attorney General* [1979] IR 73. See ch 12.

14 *Re A Ward of Court (withholding medical treatment) No 2* [1996] 2 IR 79.

15 Article 40.3.3°.

16 *Attorney General v X* [1992] 1 IR 1.

17 *Re Solicitors Act 1954* [1960] IR 239. In this case the Law Society, the solicitors' equivalent of the Medical Council, struck off two solicitors guilty of misconduct. The two solicitors argued successfully that this was the exercise of a far-reaching judicial power by a non-judicial body. Accordingly, when the Medical Practitioners Act 1978 was passed, it included the stipulation that all decisions of erasure and suspension affecting doctors had to be ratified by the High Court. In *M v Medical Council and Attorney General* [1984] IR 485, this approach was held to be legally satisfactory. The same approach as that contained in the Medical Practitioners Act was subsequently adopted by the nursing and dental professions: Dentists Act 1985, ss 39(3)-(4), and Nurses Act 1985, ss 39(3)-(4) (see section **[2.14]**).

18 See ch 12.

19 Articles 46 and 47.

20 In *Flanagan v University College Dublin* [1988] IR 724 a student was accused by the college of plagiarism She took a Judicial Review action against the college, asking the court among other things to answer the question of whether her constitutional right to fair procedure had been infringed. The court held that it had been and overturned the decision of the College.

21 Which is regarded by the courts as a private body: *Rajah v Royal College of Surgeons in Ireland* [1994] 1 IR 384.

22 Although some European legislation, eg directives can have the force of law without being formally being introduced by the Oireachtas. See the discussion of the Data Protection Directive 1995 in ch 6 (section **[6.11]**).

23 For example, the Misuse of Drugs (Amendment) Regulations 1993 moved the hypnotic (sleeping tablet) temazepam from sch 4 to sch 3 on the basis of evidence that it had become a drug of abuse (see section **[6.28]**).

24 Although there are circumstances in which legislation may be rushed through.

25 Article 26.

26 A declaration that an offending party should cease what he is doing: eg that he should stop extending his house onto my property or claiming to use my name to endorse a product. An injunction might be sought against a clinician if she were breaching, or about to breach, confidentiality owed to a patient: see ch 3, section **[3.21]**.

27 Another difference between civil and criminal cases is that there is generally a jury in all but the most minor (or 'summary') criminal cases, while civil matters are generally decided by a judge, sitting without a jury.

28 Such as rape or murder.

29 Terrorism and organised crime case are generally heard in the Special Criminal Court.

30 See ch 11 and the discussion of matters leading to the introduction of the Mental Health Act 2001 (section **[11.08]**).

31 Its history, role and powers are more fully explored in ch 16.

32 Fair procedure includes the following: the tribunal or person hearing a case should not be biased, whether for financial or personal reasons; both sides of the argument must be heard (the legal term is *audi alteram partem*); a person has to be given notice of charges against her; a person has a right to legal representation; reasons must generally be given for any decision taken by such a body (eg to allow for an appeal). See section **[2.16]**.

33 Also called restitutio in integram

34 The Solicitors Acts 1954 to 1994.

35 Article 35.

36 Article 15.

37 The are common in the area of safety at work: see ch 9.

38 See the discussion of the Data Protection Directive 1995 in ch 6.

39 See ch 7, *Negligence* and ch 4, *Consent.*

40 Such as a promise not to pursue a certain course of action in exchange for the contract being agreed.

41 Such restrictions are common for doctors training in general practice. Typically the stipulation is that the trainee, on leaving a practice where he has been in training, will not set up in medical practice within a certain radius for a period of three years. See ch. 5.

Appendix B

Glossary of Legal Terms and Abbreviations

IMPORTANT ABBREVIATIONS USED IN THE TEXT

This list does not include every abbreviation in this book, but focuses on those that recur most frequently and which are likely to be a source of confusion for the reader not versed in their meaning but also a potential source of further information for those interested in reading outside the confines of this book.

AC	Appeal Cases (England & Wales)
AJLR	Australian Journal of Law Reports
All ER / AER	All England Reports
BMJ	British Medical Journal
BMLR	British Medical Legal Reports (England & Wales)
CCA	Court of Criminal Appeal (Ireland)
C.J.	Chief Justice
Cr App R	Criminal Appeal Reports (England & Wales)
DLR	Dominion Law Reports (Canada)
EWCA	England and Wales Civil Appeals
EHRR	European Human Rights Reports
ELR	Employment Law Reports
FAM LJ	Family Law Journal
HC	High Court
HL	House of Lords (United Kingdom)
HMSO	Her (or His) Majesty's Stationery Office
IESC / HC / IC	Irish Electronic Supreme Court / High Court / Information Commissioner Reports
ILRM	Irish Law Report Monthly
ILT(R)	Irish Law Times (Reports)
IR	Irish Reports
J	Judge/Justice *or* (depending on context) Journal
JAMA	Journal of the American Medical Association
KB	Kings Bench (England & Wales)

LJ	Lord Justice
LS Gaz R	Law Society Gazette Reports (England & Wales)
Med LR	Medical Law Reports (England & Wales)
MLJI	Medico-Legal Journal of Ireland
NEJM	New England Journal of Medicine
NSWLR	New South Wales Law Reports (Australia)
NZLR	New Zealand Law Reports
per	In the words of… (in the context of a quotation from a particular judge)
QB	Queens Bench (England & Wales)
RPC	Reports of Patent Cases (England & Wales)
SI	Statutory Instrument
SC	Supreme Court
unreported	When a judgment is recorded as 'unreported' it means that it has not been included in any one of the books of legal reports, such as the Irish Reports. Unreported judgments will generally be available from behind the issue desk in the law section of academic libraries.
WLR	Weekly Law Reports (England & Wales)

Appendix C

Forms and Certificates

MEDICAL CERTIFICATE OF CAUSE OF DEATH

BIRTHS AND DEATHS REGISTRATION ACT (IRELAND) 1880

REGISTRATION OF DEATHS

MEDICAL CERTIFICATE

of the

CAUSE OF DEATH

To be signed and given by the Medical Attendant to some person by the Act required to give information concerning the Death to the Registrar of the District in which the Death occurred, and to no other person — See back of Form of Certificate.

REVISED 1986

NOTES AND SUGGESTIONS REGARDING CERTIFICATION OF CAUSES OF DEATHS

1. A medical certificate of cause of death is essentially:

(i) a statement of the disease which was directly responsible for the death;

(ii) a statement of any antecedent diseases or causes giving rise to the disease or condition directly leading to death.

Other significant conditions contributing to the death but not related to the disease or condition causing it are frequently of great value for statistical purposes, and should be added to the certificate, but in no case should they be stated to the exclusion of the primary cause.

2. The cause of death as certified is entered by the Registrar in the death register and forms part of that record. The entry in the death register and the certificate of the cause of death itself are utilised as material for statistics of mortality for the weekly, quarterly, and annual reports on vital statistics.

The value of these statistics will be materially enhanced if certifying medical practitioners will read and adopt, as far as possible, the following suggestions.

3. No medical practitioner should give a medical certificate of the cause of death unless he has been personally in attendance upon the deceased during the last illness and no other person or practitioner may sign the certificate on his behalf.

4. A registered medical practitioner who was in attendance upon the deceased during his or her last illness is required to give a medical certificate on the prescribed form in every case.

5. The use of vague and ill-defined terms is to be avoided. Examples of such terms are given on Pages II and III.

The terminal condition or mode of death such as "Heart Failure," "Respiratory Failure," "Syncope," "Asphyxia," "Exhaustion," and the like should never appear in a certificate.

6. In cases where an indefinite term has to be employed because more definite information is lacking, it would be well to indicate this fact in the certificate by the addition of some such word as "idiopathic," indicating that the probable cause of the condition stated is unknown, i.e. "idiopathic peritonitis," "idiopathic anaemia," etc.

7. A certificate merely naming the organ which was diseased but without giving any indication of the nature of the disease of the organ is incomplete and consequently it is not sufficient to certify death as due to "disease of stomach," "disease of heart," "disease of lung," etc.

8. In addition to the foregoing general considerations, the following points as to special causes of death call for attention:

CANCER — If possible, both the nature and the position of the original growth should be stated. In no case should a malignant tumour be described merely as a tumour.

PREGNANCY — Whenever pregnancy has been in any way a contributory cause of death, the nature of the abnormality should be mentioned on the certificate. State whether death occurred during pregnancy or after abortion or after birth.

OPERATIONS — In all deaths following operations, the nature of the disease or injury for which the operation was performed should be stated.

9. ***LEGIBILITY OF CAUSE OF DEATH IN CERTIFICATES*** — The cause of death is copied from the certificate into the register when the death is being registered. It is particularly requested that the names of diseases be written as clearly as possible, preferably in block letters.

10. The attention of certifying doctors is drawn to Section 18 (4) of the Coroners Act, 1962 which states:-

"Every medical practitioner, registrar of deaths or funeral undertaker and every occupier of a house or mobile dwelling, and every person in charge of any institution or premises, in which a deceased person was residing at the time of his death who has reason to believe that the deceased person died, either directly or indirectly, as a result of violence or misadventure or by unfair means, or as a result of negligence or misconduct or malpractice on the part of others, or from any cause other than natural illness or disease for which he had been seen and treated by a registered medical practitioner within one month before his death, or in such circumstances as may require investigation (including death as the result of the administration of an anaesthetic) shall immediately notify the coroner within whose district the body of the deceased person is lying of the facts and circumstances relating to the death."

LIST OF INDEFINITE OR UNDESIRABLE TERMS

Reference No.	**Indefinite or Undesirable Terms** (i.e. when used without further particulars indicated opposite).	**Further Information Required** (if available), and Notes on the use of certain Terms.
1	Abscess	State cause (especially whether tuberculous) and situation.
2	Anaemia	Disease causing this condition. If primary, state variety.
3	Aneurysm	State whether of aorta, other artery, vein or heart.
4	Aorthis, arteritis endarteritis	Was the condition due to syphilis? (If so, see No. 70).
5	Bedsores	Condition confining patient to bed.
6	Bronchitis	State whether acute or chronic.
7	Bright's Disease	State whether acute or chronic. (See No. 44).
8	Caesarean section	State indication for this operation. (See No. 48).
9	Cancer, carcinoma	*(a)* Variety; *(b)* seat of primary occurrence, if known, otherwise of fatal growth; *(c)* part of organ or where it originated in case of uterus, mouth, nose, stomach, intestine.
10	Cardiac asthma	Disease causing this condition.
11	Cardiac debility, failure, weakness	"Cardiac failure" may connote nothing beyond the fact of death.
12	Cardiac dilation	Disease causing this condition.
13	Cerebrospinal meningitis	Cause of this condition. Always certify meningococcal meningitis or cerebrospinal fever if this disease is meant.
14	Congestion of brain, kidney, liver, lung, or other organ	If the disease amounted to an inflammation, use the appropriate term (lobar- or broncho-pneumonia, acute or chronic nephritis, etc.). Merely passive congestion should not be reported as a cause of death when its cause can be stated.
15	Convulsions	Disease causing this condition.
16	Curvature of spine, angular, lateral, etc.	Cause of this condition.
17	Debility, atrophy, or aesthenia	Disease causing this condition.
18	Diarrhoea	Cause of this condition, if known.
19	Dropsy, ascites	Disease causing this condition.
20	Dysentery	State variety.
21	Eclampsia	Disease causing this condition. Was it associated with pregnancy or parturition?
22	Embolism	Site and cause of the embolism. Was it post-abortive or puerperal?
23	Encephalitis	Cause of this condition, if known.
24	Endocarditis	Acute or chronic? Was rheumatic fever present at time of death?
25	Gangrene	Disease causing this condition.
26	Gastritis, gastro intestinal irritation	Avoid using these terms as synonyms for gastro-enteritis.
27	General paralysis, paresis	If general paralysis of the insane is meant add the words "of the insane" and in all other cases indicate the disease causing the condition.
28	Glioma	State whether the glioma was benign or malignant in character, or if not known, add "type unknown."
29	Growth, new growth, tumour	Situation and nature of growth, if known. If not known, add "nature unknown."
30	Haematemesis	Disease causing this condition.
31	Haemoptysis	Disease causing this condition. Was it a case of tuberculosis of lungs?
32	Hemiplegia	Nature and cause of lesion, if known.
33	Hepatitis	Cause of this condition (e.g. epidemic, toxaemia of pregnancy). If transmission by serum or inocculation is the suspected cause state this.
34	Hydrocephalus	Cause of this condition, especially if congenital or tuberculous.
35	Hypertension, high blood pressure	State whether benign or malignant and mention heart and/or kidney affection, if any.
36	Infantile asthenia, atrophy or debility	Disease causing this condition.
37	Jaundice, icterus	Disease causing this condition (and see hepatitis).
38	Jaundice, malignant	Disease causing this condition. Was it cancer?
39	Malignant disease	Taken as equivalent to cancer. The word malignant should never be used in reference to any other disease, when such use may cause confusion with cancer.
40	Marasmus	Disease causing this condition in an adult.
41	Meningitis	Cause of this condition, e.g. sepsis (stating source), tuberculosis, meningococcal infection, etc.
42	Myocarditis	Acute or chronic? State cause if known. Avoid use of the term for degeneration of myocardium.
43	Neoplasm	Situation and nature of neoplasm.
44	Nephritis	Acute, chronic parenchymatous or arteriosclerotic? Did it result from scarlet fever, etc? Was there hypertension?

CAUSE OF DEATH

In part I of the section headed "Cause of Death" in the Certificate should be stated the cause leading directly to death [line (a)] and also the antecedent causes or conditions [lines (b) and (c)] which give rise to the cause shown in line (a), the underlying cause being stated last. No entry is necessary in lines (b) and (c) if the entry in line (a) describes completely the train of events.

In part II should be entered any other significant conditions which unfavourably influenced the course of the morbid process and thus contributed to the fatal outcome but which were not related to the disease or condition directly causing death. (See examples below.)

Examples of Method of Using the Form of Medical Certificate of Cause of Death

EXAMPLE 1	EXAMPLE 2	EXAMPLE 3	EXAMPLE 4	EXAMPLE 5	EXAMPLE 6	EXAMPLE 7
I	I	I	I	I	I	I
(a) Lobar pneumonia	(a) Puerperal eclampsia after premature parturition (7 months' gestation).	(a) Carcinoma of liver	(a) Haematemesis	(a) Acute peritonitis	(a) Diabetes mellitus	(a) Bronco-pneumonia
(b) —	(b) —	**due to** (b) Carcinoma of rectum (excised).	**due to** (b) Chronic gastric ulcer.	**due to** (b) Intestinal perforation.	**due to** (b) —	**due to** (b) Operation
(c) —	(c) —	(c) —	(c) —	**due to** (c) Enteric fever	**due to** (c) —	**due to** (c) Strangulated inguinal hernia.
II	II	II	II	II	II	II
—	—	—	—	—	Chronic gastritis.	Chronic interstitial nephritis.

An tArd-Chlaraitheoir acknowledges with thanks the replies kindly supplied by medical practitioners to his requests for further information relating to causes of death, in order that they might be more accurately classified in the report on vital statistics. This further information has been and will be treated as strictly confidential, being utilised for statistical purposes only.

In view of the importance for many public purposes of the information contained in these certificates, An tArd-Chlaraitheoir hopes that he may rely on the continued co-operation of the medical profession in these matters.

LIST OF INDEFINITE OR UNDESIRABLE TERMS — Continued

Reference No.	**Indefinite or Undesirable Terms** (i.e. when used without further particulars indicated opposite).	**Further Information Required** (if available), and Notes on the use of certain Terms.
45	Obstruction of bowel or other organ	Cause of this condition. Was it due to cancer?
46	Oedenia of lungs	Disease causing this condition.
47	Old age or Senility	Disease causing death.
48	Operation	Always state the condition for which the operation was performed, and any antecedent cause of that condition.
49	Papilloma	State site and whether benigh or malignant.
50	Paralysis	Nature, cause, and situation of lesion.
51	Paralytic ileus	If following an operation, state cause of the operation.
52	Paraplegia	Nature, cause and situation of lesion.
53	Parametritis	
54	Pelvic abscess, cellulitis ...	State the cause of this condition. In the case of females none of these terms should be used alone in certifying deaths due to puerperal or post-abortive infection (see No. 63).
55	Perimetritis, pelvic peritonitis	
56	Peritonitis	
57	Phlebitis	
58	Pemphigus, infantile	Was this condition due to syphilis? If so, see No. 70; if not, indicate this (e.g. non-luetic).
59	Perforation of bowels, stomach, etc.	Cause of this condition.
60	Pneumonia	Was the case one of lobar- or broncho-pneumonia? Did it follow influenza, measles, or other infectious disease?
61	Pneumothorax	Disease causing this condition.
62	Pregnancy	Disease or condition causing death. See para. 9 of "Notes and Suggestions."
63	Puerperal fever	Avoid the use of the indefinite term by stating the form of infection and clearly distinguishing post-abortive conditions, e.g. puerperal pyaemia, puerperal septicaemia, post-abortive septic phlebitis, etc.
64	Pulmonary abscess	Disease causing this condition. Avoid using this term to describe cases of pulmonary tuberculosis.
65	Pyaemia	Cause of this condition. Was it puerperal, post-abortive, etc.?
66	Rheumatism	State whether rheumatic fever, rheumatoid arthritis, osteo-arthritis, etc.
67	Sclerosis of central nervous system	Define as disseminated or multiple, posterior, lateral, etc.
68	Senility	See No. 47.
69	Septicaemia, septic infection, sepsis, etc.	Cause of this condition, and if localised what was the situation? In the case of females see No. 63.
70	Specific disease	The word "specific" will always be understood in the sense of syphilitic.
71	Stricture or stenosis of intestine, larynx, oesophagus, pylorus, rectum, etc. ...	Cause of condition. Was it a case of cancer? Was it a late effect of burn, ulcer, gonorrhoea, etc.?
72	Suppression of urine ...	Cause of this condition.
73	Syncope, cardiac syncope	Cause of this condition.
74	Tabes (unqualified)	Avoid using this term, which may refer to locomotor ataxy or to the wasting conditions of children.
75	Toxaemia	Cause of this condition. The term intestinal toxaemia should not be used.
76	Toxaemia of pregnancy ...	Was there eclampsia, albuminuria or yellow atrophy? Did death occur in the pregnant state or after abortion or childbirth?
77	Tuberculosis	State whether general or local, and if local state the part affected. If the bacillus was typed, state whether bovine or human. Avoid the term miliary unless further defined, e.g. acute generalised miliary tuberculosis.
78	Uraemia	Was it associated with puerperal, post-scarlatinal, or other acute nephritis, chronic nephritis, etc.?
79	Uterine haemorrhage ...	Cause of haemorrhage. If associated with pregnancy was there placenta praevia and did death occur in the pregnant state or after abortion or childbirth?
80	Valvular disease	Form and site of disease. Was acute rheumatism present at the time of death or was there a rheumatic history?
81	Yellow atrophy of liver, acute	In the case of females, was it associated with pregnancy, and had abortion or childbirth occurred? See also hepatitis.

The certificate opposite should be completed and signed by the medical practitioner who personally attended the deceased during the last illness, and by no other person.

COUNTERFOIL

Name of Deceased ....

Age ....

Last seen ....

Died on ....

At ....

Cause of Death

I. (a) ....

(b) ....

(c) ....

II. ....

Signed ....

Date ....

BIRTHS AND DEATHS REGISTRATION ACT (IRELAND), 1880.

S.R.D. ....
District ....
Entry No. ....

MEDICAL CERTIFICATE OF THE CAUSE OF DEATH

Name of deceased: .... Age ....

Place of death: ....

Last seen alive by me on: .... Date of death: ....

Whether seen after death by me (answer "yes" or "no" in all cases): [ ]

If a woman, was the deceased known to have been pregnant at the time of death or within the previous 42 days (answer "yes" or "no" in all cases): [ ]

Former Residence of Deceased

CAUSE OF DEATH (please print clearly)		Approximate interval between onset and death
I *Disease or Condition directly leading to death.* (This does not mean the mode of dying, e.g. heart failure, asthenia etc. It means the disease, injury or complications which caused death.)	(a) .... due to (or as a consequence of)	....
Antecedent Causes. (morbid conditions if any, giving rise to the above cause, stating the underlying condition last)	(b) .... due to (or as a consequence of) (c)	....
II *Other Significant Conditions* contributing to the death but not related to the disease or condition causing it.	II	....

Name of Medical Practitioner (block capitals): ....

Signature: .... Registered Qualification: ....

Residence .... Date: ....

When completed and signed, this certificate should be given to one of the qualified informants listed overleaf, who will bring it to the Registrar of Births and Deaths for the district in which the death occurred, and to no other person.

PERSONS QUALIFIED TO BE INFORMANTS FOR THE REGISTRATION OF THE DEATH

1. The nearest relative of the deceased present at the death, or in attendance during the last illness.
2. Any other relative having the necessary information required to be registered concerning the death.
3. A person present at the death.
4. The occupier or any other resident of the house in which the death occurred.
5. The person responsible for the disposing of the body.

In addition to the cause of death as certified overleaf the informant must be prepared to state to the Registrar:-

(1) The date and place of death.
(2) The full names and surname of deceased.
(3) The marital condition of deceased (single, married, or widowed).
(4) The correct age of deceased.
(5) The rank, profession, or occupation of deceased. (If deceased was a child or young unmarried person without occupation, the full names and rank or profession of the father will be required; if a wife or widow, those of the husband or deceased husband.)

Cremation Certificate

This form is issued by Glasnevin Crematorium Limited Finglas Road, Glasnevin, Dublin 11. Tel: 01 - 8305211 **FORM C**
Web Site. www.glasnevin-cemetery.ie email: cemetery@indigo.ie

These Certificates should be in the hands of the Medical Referee.
NOT LATER THAN 3.00PM ON THE DAY PRIOR TO THE CREMATION.

PURSUANT TO THE BYE LAWS MADE BY GLASNEVIN CREMATORIUM LIMITED

The Doctor signing this form must be fully registered on the Medical Register of Ireland for at least three years. Completion of this form is mandatory. All the questions must be answered to complete the Certificate for the purposes of Cremation.

The doctor Completing the Certificate must see the body before and after death.
The medical Certificate is Strictly Confidential.

PLEASE PRINT IN BLACK PEN ONLY

I Hereby certify that the answers given below are true and accurate to the best of my knowledge and belief.

Name .... (Signature) ....
Date: ....
(please insert name here in block capitals). (Address) ....
Telephone No. ....

Registered Qualification ....
Month .... Year ....
of Full Registration on The Medical Register of Ireland

MUST BE AT LEAST 3 YEARS QUALIFIED

MEDICAL CERTIFICATE

FORM C

I am informed that application is about to be made for the cremation of the remains of:-

(Name of Deceased) ....

(Address) ....

(Occupation or Description) .... (Age) ....

HAVING SEEN AND IDENTIFIED THE *BODY BEFORE AND AFTER DEATH.*

I give the following answers to the questions set out below:-

1. (a) Were you the regular attending doctor of the Deceased) (a) ....
   (b) If so, for how long?) (b) ....

2. (a) Did you attend the Deceased during his or her last illness) (a) ....
   (b) If so, for how long?) (b) ....

3. When did you last see the Deceased alive?) Date ....
   (say how many days or hours before death)) Days or Hours ....

4. (a) How soon after death did you see the body? and) (a) ....
   (b) What examination did you make?) (b) ....

5. On what date and at what hour did he or she die?) Date .... Hour ....

FORM C (CONTINUED)

6. (a) What was the place where the Deceased died?) (a)........................
   Give address and
   (b) Say whether Deceased's own residence, lodging, hotel, hospital, nursing home etc.) (b)........................

7. (a) Are you a relative of the Deceased;) (a)........................
   (b) If so, state relationship) (b)........................

8. Have you, so far as you are aware, any pecuniary interest in the death of the Deceased.) ....

9. Cause of death and duration of last illness: **NO ABBREVIATIONS**		Approximate interval between onset and death
I.	**I.**	
Disease or condition directly leading to death	(a)........................ due to (or as a consequence of)	....
Antecedent causes. Morbid conditions, if any, giving rise to the above cause, stating the underlying condition last	(b)........................ due to (or as a consequence of)	....
	(c)........................	....
II.	**II.**	
Other significant conditions contributing to the death but not related to the disease or condition causing it.	....	....

NOTE: IF DEATH IS NOT DUE TO NATURAL CAUSES, CORONERS CERTIFICATE IS REQUIRED FORM D.

10. (a) State how far the answer to the last question is the result of your own observation.) (a)........................
    (b) If not your own observation, what was the source of your information?) (b)........................

11. (a) Have you or any other doctor made a Post Mortem examination of the body.) (a)........................
    (b) If "YES" state by whom the examination was made.) (b)........................

12. By whom was the Deceased nursed during his or her last illness.) ....
    (Give names and say whether professional nurse, relative etc. If the illness was a long one this question should be answered with reference to the period of four weeks before the death).) ....

Coroner's Certificate for Cremation

FORM D.

CORONER'S CERTIFICATE FOR CREMATION

I Certify that:-

I am satisfied that there are no circumstances likely to call for a further examination of the body.

PARTICULARS OF DECEASED PERSON

Full Names ....

Sex ....

Age ....

Date of Death ....

Place of Death ....

(Please insert name here in block capitals) ....

Signature ....

Coroner for the of

Date ....

(1.) Has the Deceased been fitted with

(a) A Cardiac Pacemaker) (1.) (a) Yes/No ....

(b) A radio-active or other implant) (b) Yes/No ....

(c) Other Prosthesis) (c) Yes/No ....

(2.) If the answer to (a) (b) or (c) above is in the affirmative has this been removed?) (2.) Yes/No ....

NOTE: CREMATION MAY BE REFUSED IF ANY PROSTHESIS IS NOT REMOVED.

NOTE: **This Certificate is issued for the purposes of cremation only and must be delivered to the Medical Referee appointed by Glasnevin Crematorium Limited. The Cremation cannot be proceeded with unless this Certificate is so delivered.**

FORM C. (CONTINUED)

13. Who were the persons present (if any) at the moment of death.) ....

14. In view of your knowledge of the Deceased's habits and constitution, do you feel any doubt whatever as to the character of the disease or the cause of death stated in 9. above?) ....

15. Have you any reason to suspect that the Deceased person died either directly or indirectly as a result of:

(a) Violence or misadventure	(a) Yes/No
(b) Unfair means	(b) Yes/No ....
(c) Negligence or misconduct	(c) Yes/No ....
(d) Malpractice on the part of others	(d) Yes/No ....
(e) Any cause other than natural illness or disease for which he/she had been seen and treated by a registered medical practitioner within one month before his/her death;	(e) Yes/No ....

16. Do you know or have you any reason to suspect that the death occurred under or within 24 hours of an anaesthetic)

17. (a) Have you any reason to suspect that the death of the Deceased should properly be reported to the Coroner?) (a)

(b) If YES state why) (b)..........

18. Have you any reason whatever to suppose a further examination of the body to be desirable?)

19. (a) Did you sign the Medical Certificate of the Cause of Death?) (a)

(b) If not who has?) (b)..........

20. (1.) Has the Deceased been fitted with

(a) A Cardiac Pacemaker	) (1.)	(a) Yes/No
(b) A radio-active or other implant	)	(b) Yes/No..........
(c) Other Prosthesis	)	(c) Yes/No ....

(2.) If the answer to (a) (b) or (c) above is in the affirmative has this been removed?) (2.) Yes/No

NOTE: CREMATION MAY BE REFUSED IF ANY PROSTHESIS IS NOT REMOVED.

N.B. HAVE YOU SIGNED THIS FORM

N.B. THE DOCTOR SIGNING THIS FORM MUST BE FULLY REGISTERED ON THE IRISH MEDICAL REGISTER FOR AT LEAST THREE YEARS.

NOTE: THIS CERTIFICATE MUST BE HANDED TO OR SENT TO THE MEDICAL REFEREE IN A SEALED ENVELOPE TO ARRIVE NOT LATER THAN 3PM ON THE DAY PRIOR TO CREMATION.

Index